D0265824

European Culture in the Great War

It is a commonplace to refer to the First World War as a historical watershed, but the nature of that great cataclysm's impact upon European society and culture remains a hotly debated topic. Many recent works have dealt with the Great War's role in shaping artistic and intellectual modernism and with the social history of the war. Yet the English-language literature remains dominated by a disproportionate emphasis on the western European experience.

This book redresses the balance by giving equal attention to the countries of eastern and central Europe, where the consequences and repercussions of the war were arguably even more drastic than in the West. The volume also distinguishes itself by focusing specifically on cultural change during the course of the war, as distinct from the after-effects and memories of the conflict.

"... an important collection that casts new light on the cultural history of the Great War ... essential reading for anyone who is interested in the complex relationship between progaganda and popular culture". *History Today*

AVIEL ROSHWALD is Associate Professor of History, Georgetown University, Washington DC.

RICHARD STITES is Professor of History, Georgetown University, Washington DC.

Studies in the Social and Cultural History of Modern Warfare

General Editor
Jay Winter *Pembroke College, Cambridge*

Advisory Editors
Paul Kennedy *Yale University*
Antoine Prost *Université de Paris-Sorbonne*
Emmanuel Sivan *The Hebrew University of Jerusalem*

In recent years the field of modern history has been enriched by the exploration of two parallel histories. These are the social and cultural history of armed conflict, and the impact of military events on social and cultural history.

Studies in the Social and Cultural History of Modern Warfare intends to present the fruits of this growing area of research, reflecting both the colonization of military history by cultural historians, and the reciprocal interest of military historians in social and cultural history, to the benefit of both. The series will reflect the latest scholarship in European and non-European events from the 1850s to the present day.

Titles in the series

European culture in the Great War

The arts, entertainment, and propaganda, 1914–1918

Edited by

Aviel Roshwald and Richard Stites

PUBLISHED BY THE PRESS SYNDICATE OF THE UNIVERSITY OF CAMBRIDGE
The Pitt Building, Trumpington Street, Cambridge, United Kingdom

CAMBRIDGE UNIVERSITY PRESS
The Edinburgh Building, Cambridge, CB2 2RU, UK
40 West 20th Street, New York, NY 10011–4211, USA
477 Williamstown Road, Port Melbourne, VIC 3207, Australia
Ruiz de Alarcón 13, 28014 Madrid, Spain
Dock House, The Waterfront, Cape Town 8001, South Africa

http://www.cambridge.org

© Cambridge University Press 1999

This book is in copyright. Subject to statutory exception and to the
provisions of relevant collective licensing agreements, no reproduction
of any part may take place without the written permission of
Cambridge University Press.

First published 1999
First paperback edition 2002

Printed in the United Kingdom at the University Press, Cambridge

Typeset in 10/12 pt Plantin   [GC]

A catalogue record for this book is available from the British Library

Library of Congress cataloguing in publication data

European culture in the Great War: the arts, entertainment, and
propaganda, 1914–1918 / edited by Aviel Roshwald and Richard Stites.
    p.   cm. – (Studies in the social and cultural history of
modern warfare; 6)
ISBN 0 521 57015 8 (hb)
1. World War, 1914–1918 – Social aspects – Europe. 2. World War,
1914–1918 – Influence. 3. Popular culture – Europe. 4. Europe –
Intellectual life – 20th century. I. Roshwald, Aviel. II. Stites,
Richard. III. Series.
D523.E85   1999
940.3′1 – dc21   98–27978   CIP

ISBN 0 521 57015 8 hardback
ISBN 0 521 01324 0 paperback

Contents

Illustrations

Contributors

WALTER L. ADAMSON is Samuel Candler Dobbs Professor of History at Emory University. He is the author of *Avant-garde Florence: From Modernism to Fascism* (Cambridge, MA: Harvard University Press, 1993) and is currently at work on a book on the cultural politics of modernism in Europe in the early twentieth century.

STEVEN BELLER is a historian who lives in Washington, DC. His most recent book is *Francis Joseph* (London and New York: Longman, 1996).

MARIA BUCUR is Associate Professor of History at Indiana University, where she teaches Eastern European and Romanian history, specializing in gender history, and memory and identity. Her latest publication is "Philanthropy, Nationalism, and the Growth of Civil Society in Romania," *Working Papers of the Johns Hopkins Comparative Nonprofit Sector Project*, no. 31, Lester M. Salamon and Helmut K. Anheier eds. (Baltimore: The Johns Hopkins Institute for Policy Studies, 1998).

MARC FERRO is Directeur d'études at the Ecole des Hautes Etudes en Sciences Sociales (EHESS), Paris. He is also President of the Association pour la Recherche at EHESS and Co-Director of the journal, *Annales. Economies, Sociétés, Civilisations*. He is the author of *The Great War, 1914–1918* (London: Routledge and Kegan Paul, 1973; 1995). His most recent books are *Nicholas II: The Last of the Tsars* (London: Penguin, 1991) and *Colonization: A Global History* (London: Routledge, 1997).

JOSEPH HELD is Professor Emeritus, Rutgers University. His interests lie in Eastern European history, focussing on Hungary from the fifteenth to the twentieth centuries.

PETER JELAVICH is Professor of History at The University of Texas at Austin, where he teaches modern European cultural and intellectual history.

EVELINA KELBETCHEVA is a scholar at the Institute of History, Bulgarian Academy of Sciences, Sofia.

CLAIRE NOLTE is Associate Professor of History at Manhattan College, New York.

AVIEL ROSHWALD is Associate Professor of History at Georgetown University, Washington, DC, where he teaches European international history and the politics and history of nationalism.

SOPHIE DE SCHAEPDRIJVER is Visiting Associate Professor of Modern European History at New York University. Her most recent book is *De Groote Oorlog: Het Koninkrijk België in de Eerste Wereldoorlog* (The Great War: The Kingdom of Belgium in the First World War) (Amsterdam: Atlas Publishers, 1997).

HAROLD B. SEGEL is Professor Emeritus of Slavic Languages and Comparative Literature at Columbia University. The most recent of his many major publications is an edited volume entitled *Stranger in Our Midst: Images of the Jew in Polish Literature* (Ithaca and London: Cornell University Press, 1996).

RICHARD STITES is Professor of History at Georgetown University, where he teaches Russian history. His most recent book is *Russian Popular Culture: Entertainment and Society since 1900* (Cambridge: Cambridge University Press, 1992).

ANDREW WACHTEL is Professor of Slavic Languages and Literatures at Northwestern University.

JAY WINTER is Reader in Modern History at the University of Cambridge, and Fellow of Pembroke College Cambridge. Among his many publications is *Sites of Memory, Sites of Mourning: The Great War in European Cultural History* (Cambridge: Cambridge University Press, 1995).

Acknowledgments

The editors wish to thank the contributors to this volume for their hard work and for their patient indulgence of our editorial demands. We are grateful to the Georgetown University Graduate School's Publication Fund and Competitive Grant-in-Aid program for defraying the expenses of editorial assistance and photographic reproduction. We are indebted to Richard Wiggers for his invaluable editorial assistance. We also thank Rebekah Davis and Jim Ludes for their help with this project. Last but not least, we are grateful to William Davies and the editorial staff at Cambridge University Press for their support of this undertaking.

Introduction

Aviel Roshwald and Richard Stites

World War I is widely recognized as a turning point in the political, ideological, economic, and social history of Europe.[1] Yet, while most historians would agree that it marks a watershed, considerable disagreement exists about the nature of its impact. Did the war catalyze and accelerate tendencies that were bound to rise to prominence in any case or did it decisively change the course of historical evolution? Was its cultural impact as clearly discernible as its material consequences? Did the responses of common folk to the experience of war roughly correspond to, or diverge significantly from, those of socio-political and intellectual elites?

In recent years, much of the scholarly debate about the specifically cultural repercussions of the war has focussed on the relationship of the conflict to the development of modernity and modernism. In his seminal study of British literary culture and the war, Paul Fussell argues that the hellish trauma of the Western Front experience defied the expressive power of conventional literary tropes and undermined traditional cultural sensibilities.[2] Long-held notions about sacrifice, duty, honor, respect for one's social betters, and trust in government gave way to an attitude of cynical disillusionment and ironic skepticism that established itself as the quintessential characteristic of the modern worldview.

Modris Eksteins has proposed an alternative conception of modernism and its relation to the war.[3] Focussing primarily on the international artistic avant-garde and on German society and culture during the first decades of the twentieth century, he describes cultural modernism as a backlash against what was seen as the alienating materialism and stultifying rationalism of industrial modernity. The cult of the irrational, the fascination with violence, the notion of self-sacrifice in warfare as the path to "inner freedom" – such neo-romantic and Nietzschean ideas were already widely prevalent in German society before the war. The conflict itself reinforced many of these tendencies and contributed to the divorce of politics from ethical values and to the aestheticization of politics, a process that was to culminate in what he terms "Nazi kitsch."[4]

1

Eksteins also contends that variants of this sort of modernist sensibility became increasingly influential in France and Britain over the course of the war, as traditional notions of order and morality – which had survived in those societies longer than in Germany – were fatally undermined by the cataclysmic conflict.[5]

Jay Winter has been the most noted among a group of historians dissenting altogether from the notion that World War I marked the incontestable triumph of cultural modernism.[6] Winter argues that a study of war memorials, commemoration ceremonies, and other loci and modes of bereavement in post-war France, Britain, and Germany suggests that the war's survivors tended to cling to familiar rituals, symbols, and forms of communal behavior in their attempt to honor the dead and find meaning in their "sacrifice." The design of some war memorials can be seen in retrospect as having protofascist implications[7], and some members of wartime and post-war intellectual elites may have had iconoclastic impulses; on the whole, though, Winter argues that it was not until Auschwitz and Hiroshima that the expressive potential of pre-modernist artistic themes, spiritualist ideas, and religious iconography was surpassed and that true modernism came fully into its own.

Controversies such as these are partly semantic in nature. Fussell's identification of the modern with the ironic, for example, allows him to characterize as modern the many writers and artists who deployed conventional images in a caustic and sardonic manner. In Winter's view, the very fact that such works hark back to earlier frames of reference sets them apart from modernism, which in his definition involves a complete break with the past. But, more substantively, these interpretive disputes reflect disagreement about what type of source material and which social classes are most representative of a given period. Focussing on the writings of highly educated people will lead to conclusions very different from an approach that is founded on the exploration of popular sensibilities.[8] Moreover, much depends on which countries one selects as one's primary case studies. Fussell's literary analysis is explicitly limited to the Anglo-American sphere; Eksteins clearly encounters difficulties when he tries to find a way of incorporating Britain and France into a thesis that is largely informed by the study of German cultural history. More generally, most English-language contributions to the debate have hardly paid any attention whatsoever to the dramatic wartime developments in Eastern Europe.[9]

It is our hope that this book will encourage the development of analytical approaches that explore the nature and origins of modernism in the context of the evolving relationships between "high" and "mass" cultures and within the framework of the wartime political and military history of Europe as a whole. In so far as culture is both a reflection of broader socio-political trends and a dynamic factor in shaping historical development, a comparative analysis of European culture during the Great War can serve as a critical tool in helping to understand the war's impact on European society. Furthermore, a study of cultural developments in the midst of political and military upheaval may serve to focus attention on the intimate connections between cultural and material factors in history. Indeed, a major purpose of this collection is to increase interest in cultural history and its relationship to politics and society for all eras of modern European history. The editors believe it is useful to begin with a volume on the war that is thought to have been the first great transformative experience of the twentieth century.

European Culture in the Great War is a title that invites explanation, if not justification. We have reverted to the earlier term, "Great War," precisely because it shucks off the semantic burden placed on that war by the more familiar "World War I," with its inevitable link to World War II. Not that these wars are not linked; if anything, their connections have been understated in most of the literature. But recovering the language of our parents or grandparents might go some way to promote thinking about the earlier war in its own time and on its own terms. It was called the Great War in those days because nothing like it in scope had been seen since the titanic Napoleonic struggles which had rolled across Europe a century earlier. And of course nothing like it in terms of technological devastation had ever been seen. Contemporaries, for various reasons, wanted to make that point, just as recent generations refer to World War II as "the big one" in order to distinguish it from the lesser hostilities that have followed. We also wish to emphasize that this volume is explicitly and specifically intended to focus on the evolution of European culture *during the course of the war*. The memory of the war and the nature of its legacy are worthy subjects in their own right, which should not be confused or conflated with the topic of this book.

Our globalizing inclinations notwithstanding, we have limited this study to the European continent. As Michael Howard has observed, "in spite of the title, 'The First World War,' bestowed on it after the event, [the conflict] was Eurocentric – far more so, indeed, than the earlier great European wars fought between 1689–1815."[10] The war, of course, did extend to the Middle East and parts of East Asia and Africa; it had an impact on India, North America, and Australasia. The geopolitics of empire pulled in subjects from diverse colonies of the great powers: Indian recruits to the British war effort, Central Asian Muslims conscripted into Russian labor battalions, Senegalese troops and porters and Vietnamese coolies among the French forces on the Western Front, indigenous people forced to fight one another by their German, French, and British imperial overlords in the struggle over German colonies in Africa, and so on. The war also involved troops from Canada, Australia, New Zealand – and ultimately, the United States. But the intensity of fighting and the oceans of blood were concentrated most heavily on the European continent, and its cultural impact may have been even greater there than elsewhere.

Since the bulk of the historiography is fixated on the Western Front and on the major powers, in this book we sought balance by including as much as possible the "small nations" of East Central Europe that are so often marginalized in general histories. We examine, therefore, not only the understudied countries of the Balkans and some of the peoples of the Habsburg and Romanov empires, but also the dispersed people who played such a prominent and distinct role in the cultural life of Central and Eastern Europe – the Jews. The cultural as well as physical experience in this great sweep of territory between the Baltic and Aegean Seas was complicated by alien occupation, among other things. In the West, only Belgium found the majority of its territory, including its capital, under foreign occupation. Small areas of northeastern France, northern Italy, eastern Galicia and Bukovina, and, briefly, German East Prussia were invaded and/or occupied during the conflict; but the residents of Berlin, Paris, London, Rome, Vienna, and Budapest knew nothing of the rigors of occupation that were experienced by Warsaw, Belgrade, or Bucharest (all of which fell into Central Power hands in the course of the war and remained occupied by Germany and Austria-Hungary until the war's end). Vast stretches of land whose names sound so poetic in English – Bukovina, Galicia, Dobrudja, Lithuania, White Ruthenia (as the Germans called Belarus) – were scenes of raging battles as well as foreign rule. The chapters in this volume vividly evoke the kaleidoscopic nature of cultural colonialism, collaboration, and resistance in Belgium, the Ober Ost (German-occupied Lithuania and northeastern Poland), Poland, Galicia, Romania, Macedonia, and the southern Slav lands. A striking feature of occupation policies in the East was the occupiers' obsession with ethnographic, statistical, and other forms of local study of the conquered populations.

It is the word "culture," of course, that generates so many conceptual problems. Some cultural historians, for understandable reasons, focus primarily on the role of intellectuals, with a particular emphasis for the World War I era on their political thought, national consciousness, and racial fantasies. Literary scholars, out of habit, often equate culture with *belles lettres*. And, curiously enough, historians of art, music, and theater have seldom entered or been invited into the broader historical discourse.

Anthropologists, on the other hand – though differing greatly among themselves – have a much wider notion of culture which embraces not only the familiar arenas of kinship, ritual, symbolic language, and religious behavior, but also what some of them call "crystallized culture": the artifacts and products of a given society. In designing this volume, the editors did not wish to exclude the familiar: propaganda in various media, political moods and attitudes, or well-known fiction. But, in order to emphasize what has usually been neglected in the study of wartime culture, we have tried to correct the imbalance on two fronts: first, by including prominently all the arts alongside discussions of literature; second, by enlarging the notion of the arts to include what is called "mass culture" or "popular culture," however it is produced and consumed and whether it comes from inside or outside a given society. Thus, we are concerned with the cultural experience and expression of people, and not just forms of creativity that were invested with the status of "national art."

It is also our hope that this book will contribute to bridging the gap between political/diplomatic and cultural history. Recent work in cultural history has bravely attempted to demonstrate the importance of expressive life – producing and enjoying art, culture, entertainment – in human experience. Unlike older modes of incorporating culture into history (by means of a selective addition of pages and chapters on "literature and the arts"), the newer work has broadened the understanding of the word culture to include folk and urban popular culture; and it has also expanded the utility of that study by linking culture to wider social impulses and values and examining relationships among cultural communities and creators. World War I is an ideal framework for a comparative analysis of such relationships, given that the attempted total mobilization of society, the cooptation of artists into the propaganda effort, the recent emergence of film and other media technologies, and the immersion of many writers and artists in the trench experience all served to make it a turning point in the development of new cultural syntheses.

In diplomatic history, the most interesting recent work has gone well beyond the realm of "what one clerk wrote another" to explore the interconnections among domestic politics, political culture, ideology, and international relations. Crystallized culture has rarely found its way into the analysis of international history. Yet, in time of war, emotions and popular impulses play a great role in the domestic and battlefield efforts of belligerent populations; and much of this emotion is evoked through the use of both formal propaganda, with its relatively direct messages, and the more subtle or indirect approaches of the cultural community at all aesthetic levels: opera, film, spy fiction, theater, spectacle, war novels, graphic art – to name a few. These works of art and artifice feed into the political culture that takes shape in wartime (though almost always grounded in traditions of the pre-war period). And, we must add, they are interesting for their own sake and for their role in the history of art and culture and in the parallel history of social communication.

The convergence of our interests has led us to this project, which is conceived of as an occasion to spur the development of interdisciplinary approaches to history and to highlight the complex web of relations between cultural and political history. We strongly believe that a synchronic approach – which to some minds would imply comparing the incomparable in terms of levels of cultural development – is precisely the one that will allow students and scholars to look at the face of Europe in the 1910s and beyond in a novel way.

In this collection there was no possibility and no intention of imposing uniformity. Contributors have rightly stressed what they see as crucial for their particular case. And the result has been, we believe, a healthy variety. The volume clearly demonstrates what most students would already have surmised about the cultural life of a four-year period in a continent like Europe: namely, that this book might very well have been titled "European Cultures in the Great War." Yet the differences among the experiences of various social and national groups are at least as fascinating as the similarities. This volume is meant, therefore, not only to fill in the missing pieces or complete the record – worthy as that aim may be – but also to sharpen and extend the comparative insights that we have already derived from those histories of the war that focus on combat, occupation politics, the economic sinews of warfare, manpower, hardware, and all the rest.

To be sure, the geographical scope of this volume comes at a price, and we are well aware of the many lacunae in this study. The chapters in this collection focus, of necessity, on a small selection out of the vast array of possible topics for each nation. The general paucity of sources on wartime peasant culture leads to a disproportionately heavy emphasis on urban life in these pages. Much to our regret, we were unable to convince any scholars of Greek or Turkish history to participate in this venture, and those countries have therefore been left out. Our very decision to arrange the book by ethnic groups and nation-states could be challenged as arbitrary. It is our opinion that such an organizational scheme does make sense in so far as – particularly under twentieth-century conditions – shared language and shared political institutions create common media of inter-class communication (and miscommunication) and form common hindrances to relations with people across the political and/or ethno-linguistic divide. It would also be very difficult to explore the connections between wartime politics and culture without taking into account the central role that political-territorial and ethno-national categories played in mediating many people's experience of the war, particularly in the urban settings that form the primary focus of this book. But this should not be taken to mean that we are adopting an essentialist view of nationhood or that we uncritically take it for granted that all members of a given ethnic group necessarily had more in common with each other than with anyone else. On the contrary, two of the themes that interest us are how conceptions of nationhood evolved under the impact of the war, and to what extent patterns of cultural development cut across political frontiers.

In brief, this book should be seen as but an initial step in the direction of a synoptic cultural history of Europe during the Great War. It is our hope that the volume will stimulate other scholars to cross traditional analytical and disciplinary boundaries in their pursuit of historical understanding.

1   Days and nights in wartime Russia: cultural life, 1914–1917

Richard Stites

> Like a prisoner hurled into a deep, empty well, I cannot say where I am or what awaits me. Only one thing has been given me to know; in the fierce and relentless struggle with the devil – the principle of material force – victory will be mine. And then matter and spirit will join in harmonious splendor, and the kingdom of universal will be ushered in.
>
> Anton Chekhov, *The Seagull*, 1896

The wartime culture of Russia has until recently been little studied[1] for several reasons: the Soviet historiographical enmity towards most of those engaged in it; the near exclusion from literary and art history of things that smell of propaganda or popular culture; and – most important – the absence of a real historical memory of that war in Russia, a memory that was buried beneath the remembrance of the revolutions of 1917 and the civil war that followed. A moment's reflection will remind us that this is one of the many historical phenomena that have divided Russia from the West psychologically in our century.

The cultural landscape

The political frame surrounding cultural life in wartime Russia was composed of three blockades: the physical one, political censorship, and the "mental blockade" of boycottism. The first, erected by distances, battlefields, danger zones, and naval forces in the Baltic Sea cut Russia off from most of Europe. The regular flow of cultural products and people virtually ceased. (One interesting side effect of the blockade was that Finnish subjects of the tsar were deprived of European films and began watching Russian ones.) Russian artists and writers were stranded in the West or arrested in the Central Powers countries and often unable to return home. Visiting theater troupes and orchestras were mostly immobilized. Censorship kept bad news to a minimum and stifled anti-war or other protest voices. Frontline correspondents were carefully monitored and the radical subculture of the previous decade was silenced. All of this reinforced the mental blockades erected against the culture of the enemy, past – with some nuances – and present. The renaming of Petrograd and of city streets and the anti-German riots reflected and fueled hatred or fear of enemy influence. Even music by German composers long dead – Mozart, Beethoven – was prohibited in certain concert halls. It became illegal for the German language to be spoken in public places. Dachshund dogs were sometimes killed on the streets.

What were the cultural responses to the war? A few preliminary observations can be stated at once. First, the state played a very small role in culture: its "Skobelev Committee" – named after a chauvinistic nineteenth-century Russian general – had been formed by Skobelev's sister during the Russo-Japanese war. During the Great War, it produced some films, concerts, and unimaginative graphics but remained relatively inactive, in striking contrast to the mammoth efforts made by some of the other belligerent states. The Russian monarchy was uncomfortable with mobilizing mass opinion and sentiment: it had been wary of an upsurge of Panslavism in the 1870s during the Balkan struggle; and its brief experiment with state-directed unions ("police socialism") had backfired in 1905. Unlike the other major belligerent states, the tsarist regime distrusted elements in society that could have worked with it for a major propaganda effort.

A second observation is that Russian high culture writers and artists had difficulty responding directly to the war because of reservations about the programmatic or "occasional" use of art and, for some, because of ambivalence about the war itself. The intellectual idiom of nuances, interior rumination, and transcendent vision fit poorly with such a direct and brutal experience as war. Many who began as fiery patriots became lukewarm after 1915. Conversely, the purveyors of popular culture proved better able and willing to deploy their traditions and forms of expression into propaganda. The gap between high and popular culture was far from complete. High-toned Symbolist poets did write for the popular press and talented artists did make war posters. Yet, the elevated elite could not match the forcefulness and the in-your-face simplicities and distortions of pulp fiction, stage routines, and cinema.

Poetry and fiction

Many literary figures were gripped by agony, ambivalence, or silence: in December 1914, the Symbolist poet Zinaida Gippius wrote that "it is a sin to write poems now" and spoke of the "wisdom of silence." When writers did produce war-related poetry or fiction, it was usually marred by chauvinism or by lack of conviction. A pro-war posture was held by most of the great writers, but it was expressed in essays, journalism, and philosophizing about Neo-Slavophilism, Panslavism, and apocalypse. Writers, artists, and scholars signed a manifesto "to the Fatherland and to the Civilized World," announcing a struggle with the "Germanic yoke" for the freedom of mankind. Maxim Gorky was a signatory. Writers, according to one of them, were enraged at the Germans. From left to right, with a few exceptions, intellectuals initially lined up behind the government. Critics then and now view most wartime literature as banal and monotonous. The darling of prewar salon poetry, Igor Severyanin (1887–1941), allowed himself to end a piece with the words: "Blessed be the people! Blessed be the war!" The marriage of literary creativity with power diminished the value of the former; and the excessive repetition of slogans was almost equivalent to "literary silence." The defeats of 1915 took a severe toll on the optimistic patriotism of the first months. Some writers withdrew "to Parnassus," as a Soviet critic later complained, but others began to evince cautious opposition to the Russian army's wartime treatment of the civilian population – particularly the Poles and the Jews (Segel and Roshwald, this volume). Leonid Andreev, Fedor Sologub, and Gorky used the journal *Shield* for this purpose. Eventually Gorky rallied some writers around opposition to the war itself. Although *Shield* did not improve the literary quality of their output, it did display honorable opposition to anti-Semitism. Sologub in particular described the "fatherland" as a home for all its people, including the Jews.[2]

The most prominent pre-war literary school had been the Symbolists. Their wartime poetry was declamatory and vaguely patriotic in an abstract spiritual sense – but a bit closer to real things and people than their historiosophical speculations. The division over the war itself opened slowly. Andrei Bely, Aleksandr Blok, and Valery Bryusov at varying tempos turned against it; the others either supported it with verbal vigor or remained ambivalent. The most divided was Gippius who privately opposed and publicly – though cautiously – supported it. Vyacheslav Ivanov, Konstantin Balmont, and Fedor Sologub firmly supported the war. Dmitry Merezhkovsky, like his wife Gippius, wavered. Fittingly, the Symbolist poets preferred allegory, allusion, and mystical speculation; and their works in every genre – fiction or not – were enveloped in quasi-religious metaphor. In this respect they resembled others of the religious intelligentsia (often called Godseekers) and occult writers (see below, pp. 26–28).

A few Symbolists wrote in the popular press but their pre-war stance of aloofness from social turmoil for the most part kept them from any kind of direct engagement with the war. Only Bryusov visited places near the front as a journalist, but he never saw fighting and returned to private life after nine months. Blok, escaping the draft through connections, got assigned engineering duty behind the lines in the Pinsk marshes for a short time. The others spent the war in the two capitals and in summer resorts and dachas, thus matching the intellectual remoteness from the real war with physical separation. Symbolists explored the "landscape of the soul" rather than the rational and material world or the fields of battle. Their view of reality is foreshadowed in the Chekhov quotation at the head of this chapter.[3] Avant-garde literary movements proliferated in the 1910s, often descending to mutual antagonism: Acmeism, Imagism, Futurism, Cubo-Futurism and many others produced a brilliant stream of literary art, often in collaboration with the plastic arts. The very nature of their enterprise – abstraction, transrational language, cosmic speculation, *épatage* – flourished well outside the cultural conversation about the war.

Popular fiction functioned in a different way. By this term I mean what critics called vulgar: stories – serialized or issued in cheap paper editions – with simple plots, strong narratives, clear-cut heroes and villains. This fiction said nothing profound or intelligent about the 1914 war or about war itself. Its backtext was newspaper stories and chauvinist journalism rather than religious or philosophical discourse. The racist portraiture of the enemy in cheap fiction hardly differed from that of the intellectual writers – except that its form was physiological and folkloric. It contained no inner exploration and no political agenda except demonization and heroization. Well-trained in etching good and evil and generating suspense, pulp and middlebrow writers easily adapted to patriotic themes during World War I. But the war theme did not predominate. In the first ten months, the genre of popular fiction that led all others in book purchases in the capital was the middlebrow "woman's novel" of sex, love, and career written by Anastasiya Verbitskaya, Olga Bebutova, Evdokiya Nagrodskaya, and Lidiya Charskaya. These writers had long provided a mass readership with scenes of illicit sexual liaisons backstage, on trains, at spas, and in "exotic places"; and this element fitted easily into war tales, just as pre-war spy and war-scare scenarios were easily converted into wartime fiction.[4]

Stage

A similar dichotomy prevailed between "legitimate theater" and the popular stage. Few plays on wartime themes were mounted in the great theaters, considered by many as temples of art. Aside from Andreev (see below, p. 21) and a few Symbolists whose works were mostly unstaged, playwrights steered clear of the topic and the repertories remained classical European and Russian. Konstantin Stanislavsky deepened his work on the "method" in his by-then conventional Moscow Art Theater (MAT). Some claim that MAT was infused with a Tolstoyan pacifism. But this was hardly more than a rarefied and gentle humanitarianism as shown in its production of Dickens' *Cricket on the Hearth*, a protest against war. Aleksandr Tairov's experimental Chamber Theater (founded in 1914) "recoiled from contemporaneity," whether in peace or war. Its doctrine of cerebral and archaic staginess discounted audience and outside world. Said a critic in 1916: "a melancholy and depressed mood pervaded Moscow. But art was being created on Tairov's stage which knew no Moscow, of the past or of the present – did not know or wish to know." Vsevolod Meyerhold moved along two tracks: the mainstream stage with big classics new and old; and his studio where he explored *commedia*, Kabuki, and Spanish baroque – all of them oblivious to the war.[5]

The more commercial theaters staged a few anti-Kaiser potboilers. The best-attended Russian stage was the circus, which supplemented its regular fare with marvelous balletic reenactments of battles, glorifying the Russian forces and maligning Germans, Austrians, and Turks. Appealing more to upper and middle classes were patriotic evening concerts of readings mixed with choirs and folk ensembles that exalted throne and nation. Inspired – and often sponsored by – pre-war right-wing patriotic groups, these events constituted the closest thing in performance art to an official dynastic reading of the war.[6]

Art

Most of the modernist and avant-garde schools of visual art – Cubism, Futurism, Rayonnism, Suprematism – turned to inner visions or to universal ideals, but not to the war. Among the notable exceptions were Vladimir Mayakovsky, Kasimir Malevich, and David Burlyuk who created hundreds of cartoon-like works in 1914, though their patriotic phase was short lived. Only a few artists fought in the war, Pavel Filonov and Georgy Yakulov among them. Mayakovsky went to the front as a war artist. Mikhail Larionov served only a few weeks and was wounded; though inspired by popular soldiers' art before the war, he did not address it during the Great War. Most artists remained in the cities. Marc Chagall, Ivan Puni, Natan Altman, El Lissitzky, and Vasily Kandinsky returned from abroad. During the war years, Russian easel painting became more abstract. Cubo-Futurism reached its peak and Suprematism and Constructivism were born, though the world learned of these last only in the 1920s when an international art network was reestablished. Like the European Dadaists, the Russian avant-garde dwelt in a mood of political uselessness. Its competing schools busied themselves with reinventing art: Futurism, the vision of the outer machine; Constructivism, that of the inner machine; and Suprematism, Malevich's reductionist vision of the world. Publicly, modern artists were virtually impervious to the direct experience of the war.[7]

Popular graphics – post-cards, cartoons, posters – offered narrative propaganda art that resembled pulp fiction and the plebeian stage but with terser messages and more biting wit about the Kaiser and company, Russian heroes, and historical ghosts done up in raw colors and dramatic diagonals with texts resembling those of the folk broadside (*lubok* – a captioned picture). Some of the best cartoons were done by Alexander Lebedev for the covers of the popular weekly, *The War*. Philanthropic societies flooded Russia with patriotic graphics – many of them executed by disciples of the realist Itinerant Movement – which promoted war bonds, hatred of a barbarous foe, and sympathy for the suffering victims at home, on the front, and in allied countries. A 1914 poster by the established artist, Leonid Pasternak, "Wounded Soldier" was adapted by the Bolsheviks after the revolution for their own program. Millions of pictures were produced in a wide variety of styles, often blurring the line between "art" and popular graphics. Artists employed antique Slavonic lettering, Christian motifs, and *lubok* styles on war posters depicting German and Turkish atrocities and Russian war heroes.[8]

Music

Orchestra musicians were not exempt from service as such. At first many avoided the army, and those who went were only nominally soldiers. But in 1916 the draft caught up and one can only wonder if their wartime experience resembled that of Fritz Kreisler who said that in war, "centuries drop from one, and one becomes a primeval man, nearing the cave-dweller in an incredibly short time."[9] The draft, the railroad jam, high prices, and the takeover of some halls for hospitals cut down on symphonic music concerts. All but two big ensembles in Moscow collapsed when war descended: the Imperial Russian Musical society and the private orchestra of Sergei Koussevitzki (Kusevitsky). The latter's bimonthly shuttle between the capitals was reduced due to transport problems. Ironically, audiences expanded. The thirst for Russian and the allied countries' serious music was great in these years (as it would be in 1941). The solemnity and emotionalism of Russian music in particular no doubt played a psychological role – as it often did in times of stress. An ugly debate sprang from the press about performing "alien" music. Koussevitzki received threats for playing older German works in public. His main repertoire was Russian and French. Almost all his concerts were for the benefit of soldiers, their wives, the Union of Cities and – in one case – Jewish relief (Koussevitzki was Jewish). By 1916, the draft had eroded his ensemble and his concertizing declined.[10]

Like many other artists, the major serious composers and performers largely missed the war altogether by staying abroad if caught there or avoiding the draft if at home. In a wider sense, their art – whether traditional or modernist – could not fit a patriotic mold. Their letters are filled with musical and professional concerns, and the war hardly figures at all, though a few did give concerts for war benefits. Igor Stravinsky, stranded in Europe, recalled: "My profound emotions on reading the news of the war, which roused patriotic feelings and a sense of sadness at being so distant from my country, found some alleviation in the delight with which I steeped myself in Russian folk poems." Alexander Scriabin continued working out his modernist or Silver Age mystical themes, religious visions, and experimental sonorities. He saw the war as "spiritual renewal for people . . . even though it destroys them materially." His main preoccupation in the last months before his death in 1915 was planning a monumental performance of his music in India.[11]

Sergei Rachmaninov toured Russian cities with Koussevitzki to raise money for the war effort. Although he produced *All Night Vigil* (The Vespers), *Vocalise*, and some songs, Rachmaninov's depression about the war induced a creative gap for a few years. Sergei Prokofiev wrote some of his greatest early works during the war. Aloof from patriotic rhetoric, he ignited a few minor musical scandals with his Second Piano Concerto and *The Scythian Suite*. One critic vacuously linked the turbulence of his modern music in 1915 to the "ferment" of a world at war. Prokofiev composed, played, and conducted at elite musical sites and theaters and toured the provinces. A lesser known but important composer, Nikolai Myaskovsky (b. 1881) was directly affected by the struggle: serving at the front as an officer, he wrote home in disgust that "everyone is fed up with the war"; although he was productive before and after the war, he wrote no music during it.[12]

In the world of musical theater, the fabled Ballets Russes was scattered and nearly dissolved by the war. Artists assembled and reassembled at the urging of impresario Sergei Diaghileff (Dyagilev) and some members spent a good part of the war across the Atlantic. Though many male dancers were called up, the dancer Sergei Grigoriev missed the draft due to health reasons and joined Diaghileff: he recalls the voyage from the United States back to Europe in a ship bearing "ammunition, horses, and the Russian Ballet." Nijinsky lived under house arrest in Budapest for a while. Those released tended to rendezvous in Europe – not at home because it was simply too hard to get there. In Russia, state theater budgets were cut. The choreographer Mikhail Fokin put on *Stenka Razin*, dealing with a seventeenth-century peasant rebel, set to Borodin's *Prince Igor* music; *Eros*, set to Chaikovsky's *Serenade for Strings*; and Mikhail Glinka's *Jota Arogonese* (from the 1840s) at the Marynsky Theater (later Kirov). Amidst this show of tradition, Fokin did salute the allies in a number called "Dances of the Nations." The nearest that the famed dancer, Tamara Karsavina, got to war was to observe bayonet drill in Theater Square outside the Marynsky. Escape and diversion were the driving force of wartime ballet stage; and its mission, wrote Karsavina, was to "protect the eternal treasure" of classical art.[13]

Opera was no more affected by war than ballet. Indeed the only sign of war in all theaters was the repeated playing of the Russian and allied national anthems to ardent crowds who applauded and bowed to the ambassadors' boxes. The greatest singer of the age, Fëdor Chalyapin (Shalyapin), financed two military hospitals and sometimes sang to the patients. His visit to bombed-out Warsaw and briefly to an empty battlefield produced a photo opportunity and some lachrymose moments in his memoirs. The lofty social circle of Paléologue was probably representative of the capital's elite; their salons featured the nineteenth-century art songs of The Mighty Five composers and other Russians.[14]

In less exalted spheres, music played the war. Anthems and band music – a prominent outdoor genre since the time of Nicholas I – were in full evidence at public performances. Concerts by the Andreev Balalaika Ensemble, founded a few decades earlier, and the recently formed Pyatnitsky Folk Ensemble enlisted stylized "folkish" art in the patriotic cause. But once again, "neutral" genres won out: tango, folksongs, urban romances, Gypsy tunes, and early imported American Ragtime continued to dominate the sheet music and phonograph market and the restaurant and cabaret scenes. I have seen no soldiers' songs that actually emerged from the ranks (see below for songbooks, p. 30); reports and iconography tell us that the men sang at the front as they had in previous wars and brought their accordions with them.[15]

Cinema

The film industry came to Russia in 1896 and the first Russian-made feature was shot in 1908. The movies' familiar blurring of popular and high culture makes cinema art difficult to pigeon-hole. The vast bulk of production in the war consisted of popular entertainment films of various genres – historical-literary epics, comedy, and crime – unrelated to the war. Among the light films that Emperor Nicholas II viewed at the headquarters of the High Command was *Secrets of New York*, a detective serial from Pathé. The biggest entertainment medium of the time, cinema paid scant attention to the war after 1914–1915. Directors of genius – Evgeny Bauer and Yakov Protazanov – lent their talents to popular genres, particularly sexual melodrama, highlighting class and gender cruelty in which a poor female is victimized by an affluent man. Did this generate anger toward the upper classes? Popular media, regardless of the producers' intentions, may have created as much class hatred as anti-foreign feelings. It is still unclear how much wartime resentment at dodgers and dandies fed into the violence of the 1917 revolutions.

Among the war-related films with higher pretensions, three different versions of Lev Tolstoy's *War and Peace* were shot, celebrating the 1812 victory over Napoleon and thus suggesting a successful outcome of the present war. The most original state-sponsored work was the stop-motion film entitled *Lily of Belgium* (see below, p. 21). Popular war films were mostly skilful adaptations of crime or detective stories, with the villains now dressed up as spies, traitors, or brutal German officers. The Skobelev Committee, with only four cameramen at the front, monopolized newsreels and took very little footage.[16] Unlike that of other belligerents, Russian cinema had virtually no impact as foreign propaganda.

The major themes

Disentangling themes from cultural products is an artificial act since most of them were jumbled together. But it may help to examine the treatment of the more prominent topics: enemies, victims and allies, the "Russian soul," and the meaning of war.

The enemy

Ridicule was poured on all Germans, but two "types" invited special abuse: the corseted, monocled, spike-helmeted Prussians: and the Bavarians arrayed in fat beer bellies, sausages, clay pipes, and Lederhosen. Kaiser Wilhelm remained the primary object of scorn and hate. A *lubok* called *Carnival Sideshow: Satan Wilhelm and the German War* contained a malicious rhymed satire attacking all ethnic Germans and a crude cartoon of the Kaiser with insane eyes and twisted moustaches. Whipping up hatred for the enemy, especially the Germans, proved surprisingly easy, since anti-German feelings (often submerged in a generalized

1.1   Germany's Kaiser Wilhelm II choking on the Belgian bone

resentment of the West) were latent among many Russians – common folks as well as intellectuals. Anti-Germanism focussed on national stereotypes and militarism. Cartoons on Belgium showed Prussians with spiked helmets and sabres impaling babies. A full-color poster called *German Barbarism* made its point by showing a Zeppelin airship dropping bombs on a defenseless city – as happened in Poland and Belgium early in the war.[17]

The exalted literary figures had their own version of German barbarism. In instances too numerous to reference, they turned geography and history around and equated the Germans with the Mongols and other "eastern hordes" (Conclusion, this volume). One of the most popular writers of the pre-war period – with a readership much larger than those of Andreev, Gorky, or Blok – was Lidiya Charskaya, who exploited the war in a collection of stories called *Fear Not Your Own Troops*, melodramatic tales with cardboard characters and relatively implausible coincidences. Most of them begin with gentle pre-war idylls which are then shattered in 1914. In one story, a flirtatious young Russian maiden at a Bohemian watering spa (in Austria-Hungary) in the summer of 1914 falls in love with a German who, after the war breaks out, shoots her father and has her stripped at a railroad station. Other tales described the wounds of war, and women burying their dismembered men. There are no real battle scenes, no psychology, and no national insight. But these easily read tales of misadventure at the hands of a devilish people were what sold in the book stalls.[18]

Germans inside Russia were especially hated. Students painted over German street signs; a crowd sacked the German embassy and smashed statues; a reader complained of gothic type in a newspaper. Russians of German, Latvian, Jewish, or Scandinavian descent rushed to adopt Slavic-sounding patriotic names like Romanov or Serbsky (Serbian). Names were changed from Hammer to Molotov, Berg to Gorsky, Taube to Golubev, Schwartz to Chernov, Schmidt to Kuznetsov, and Eiche to Dubnov. The reason was survival: not only were "Germans" being fired without proper vetting of their identity; they were also being beaten up and even killed. When the police rounded up "aliens" in 1915, they took in more non-Germans (including British and French citizens) than Germans! The culture reflected this with a vengeance: stories, plays, and films warned the public against the enemy within. Zinaida Gippius's story "The German," dealt with a little Latvian boy who, because of his foreign name, is taunted by schoolmates who call him "the German." When he discovers his true ethnic identity, the child is happy to learn from his mother that as a Latvian he is also "Russian." Newspapers accused Baltic Germans *en masse* of disloyalty – the evidence in one paper being that Count Zeppelin, German designer of the formidable airship, was married to a Baltic German woman.[19]

The detective thriller was easily adapted to spy stories combining adventure with patriotism. In a Charskaya story, a vindictive German Russian national has his unfaithful wife raped and her Russian lover shot. The film *Amid the Thunder of Cannon* treated the war as a backdrop to an interethnic triangle in which Fritz Müller, the son of a German factory owner in Russia, lusts after the young Vera (Faith) who is loyal to the Russian Sorokin. In wartime Müller and Sorokin are drafted into the Russian army and Vera becomes a nurse. Müller not only shows his true colors by deserting to the Germans, but he tries to rape Vera and kill his rival Sorokin. Villainy is punished and the heroes are rescued by a squadron of Cossacks in the last scene.[20]

The Symbolist Fëdor Sologub – the fiercest of the anti-Russo-Germans – wrote a play, *Edge of the Sword*, which is as racist as anything in popular fiction. In one way it resembles the central premise of the famous Nazi anti-Semitic film, *The Eternal Jew* (1940) because it proposes an essentialist view of the Russo-German residing permanently behind the mask of assimilation. The main character – a Russian German – seems both Russian and civilized in every way; he courts a good Russian girl but turns out to be a traitor and a murderer. The wise Russian characters who see through him are a clairvoyant sister of the girl and some holy pilgrims. The same writer's play *Seeing Off* (1914) displays deep resentment of Baltic Germans and lays on a "natural" brotherhood of Estonians and Russians against the old common foe. This and other works also assaulted home-grown Russian Germanophiles as somehow ethnically blind. These works, brilliantly analyzed in Hellman's work, display the intimate relationship between the late-blooming mysticism of the Silver Age and modern national hatred bred from essentialist philosophical positions.[21]

Austria was seen as a foe of a different order, weaker than Germany, led by a senile old man (Emperor Franz Joseph), filled with ethnic groups who surrendered in droves to the Russians, and the owner of an important Russian war aim – Galicia, populated by Poles, Ukrainians, and Jews, and seen by Russians as theirs by right of ancient Kievan cartography. In the title story of Charskaya's *Fear Not Your Own Troops*, Galician Polish noble girls are frightened by the specter of approaching troops whom they take to be ferocious Cossacks. These turn out to be "friendly" Habsburg cavalry who proceed to rape them. The implication of this and many cultural statements about the Russian army was that Cossacks did not rape – a historical falsehood. In another Charskaya story, a Hungarian spy dresses as a Catholic nun – presumably an act of both cowardice and unmanliness.[22]

A crude and hastily made but exciting film called *Glory to Us, Death to the Foe* (1914) was directed by the talented Evgeny Bauer. News of war darkens the summer love of a young Russian manor-house lady and her officer fiancé, played by the most popular actor of the age, Ivan Mozzhukhin. When he goes off to war, the heroine joins up as a nurse only to find him dying in a *lazaret* (field-hospital). She then crosses the lines disguised as an Austrian nurse and serves in the enemy field hospital in order to spy on them. When a young Austrian officer who has been flirting with her is given by his superiors a secret message to deliver, the nurse lures him to a rendezvous, stabs him, and flees with the document back to her own lines where she is rescued by Russians and decorated with military honors. This theme worked on a genuine social reality – Russian women on the medical front – but also elevated the female gender into heroic modes (on women see below, pp. 23, 25).[23]

The Turks came in third on the list of Russia's enemies. The anti-Ottoman theme drew on "orientalist" memories of the Eastern Question, the nine previous Russo-Turkish wars, and the Great Game involving Muslims further to the east. Since the sultan had declared a jihad or Holy War of Muslim peoples against their foes and slaughtered the Armenians, some films were devoted to Turkish atrocities at the front. But usually the sultan was portrayed grotesquely in cartoons as a running dog and cowardly ally of the Kaiser: a cartoon in Kiev's *Dawn* of 1914 has the sultan urged on by the Kaiser with a sword at his backside. A facile producer of racy stories offered a salacious treatment of the German kaiser in *Wilhelm in the Sultan's Harem* (1914). Olga Bebutova's *Bloody Half-Moon* centered around the seduction and despoiling of "white women" by Turkish agents. Orientalism and the exotic dominated the Turkish theme and produced little of interest.[24]

It need hardly be said that the wartime abuses and atrocities of the Russian army and other authorities got no coverage in any cultural medium. The horrors of the scorched earth and the Great Retreat in Poland, the accompanying rape and murder and pillage of Jews and Poles, the treatment of all Jews as traitors, the death trains, the ugly Russification polices in Galicia, and the repression of the 1916 uprising in Central Asia – none of this was reflected in high or popular culture.

Victims and friends

Loving the allies – the Entente powers, the little Serb Brother, and ravaged Belgium and Poland – offered outlets for the conflicting emotions of hate and love. News of the German occupation policies in Belgium – the false along with the true – came as a shock to Russians as to many others. The invaders looted, shot, raped, and pillaged as they tore through the tiny neutral country and pulverized ancient churches with their giant guns (Schaepdrijver, chapter 11 and Jelavich, chapter 2 this volume). An early response in popular print medium was the first issue of Library of the Great War – a cheap pamphlet series. *The Belgian Victim* (1914) offered vivid descriptions of early outrages by the Germans, the batteries at Liège, shattered buildings and bodies, homes reduced to dust, Zeppelins bombing Antwerp hospitals, German soldiers singing

"Watch on the Rhine," the patriotic song of the early nineteenth century, and "Deutschland, Deutschland, über Alles" to humiliate the Belgians. According to this account they also paraded a bear cub dressed as King Albert on the streets of Brussels. Another account showed a spike-helmeted firing squad executing citizens as women begged for mercy.[25]

Shaming of the Germans was supplemented by admiration of the victims. A Russian circus, in order to show the heroic resistance of the Belgians, performed a spectacle called "The Inundation of Belgium," dramatizing the opening of the dams to drown the German invaders. Andreev wrote a philosophical play on the same theme: *The King, the Law, and Freedom*. Seeing no contradiction to his famous anti-war story of the Russo-Japanese War of 1904–1905, *The Red Laugh* (1908), Andreev accepted World War I as a struggle of "world democracy against Caesarism and despotism." Publicly, he upheld a sacred union of tsar and people; privately he looked at the war as a prologue to a democratic Russia. Andreev did not think much of this play as a work of art; one critic called it "dramatized journalism." An admirer of Maurice Maeterlinck, Andreev modeled his main character on him. A civic-minded writer, this character joins forces with the philosopher king, Albert, in an act to save Belgium: the opening of the dams. Two of its premises were emblematic of pro-war writers: the power of word and thought; and the virtue of sacrificing people in order to save the Nation. Whatever its flaws, Andreev's play drew big audiences in Moscow and Petrograd.[26]

A more striking work of art was the extraordinary stop-motion film entitled *Lily of Belgium*, made by Czesław Starewicz for the Skobelev Committee. It presented Belgium as a forest idyll destroyed by marauding Germanic helmeted beetles, led by a Kaiser-beetle, who are repulsed by Russian pine cones, returning the land to a springtime of blooming lilies. In one regard – depicting Belgium as a ravished land – Symbolist efforts resembled Starewicz's treatment. Shocked by the horrors in this campaign, they produced a rash of sympathetic poems, stories, and plays. Sologub, in the poem, *The Belgian*, somewhat tactlessly made his hero an ivory trader from the Congo. Emile Verhaeren's *La Belgique sanglante* (1915) was translated into Russian, as was an anthology devoted to King Albert with pieces added by Alexander Kuprin and Merezhkovsky, who invoked a biblical commonplace by calling Belgium a Holy Land crucified. The great actress, Mariya Ermolova, joined literary figures in an evening on "The Spirit of Belgium" to honor Verhaeren, George Rodenbach, and Maeterlinck. Balletmaster Fokin used the same title in a dance number at the Marynsky.[27]

Some publicists and writers tried seriously to equate Poland with Belgium, thus projecting Germany as the evil villain of Polish destiny, erasing the Russian outrages then happening in Poland, and obscuring the troubled past of those two neighbors. In the film *Tears of a Ravished Poland* (with the Chopin funeral march played on the piano), patriotic producers mounted an image of German barbarism, Polish suffering, and Slavic solidarity. Certainly the Germans reduced Kalisz to rubble by bombardment and enacted cruel measures in their occupation. But Russian behavior was much worse, especially during the Great Retreat and scorched earth of 1915. The most active Polish patriot, Józef Piłsudski, formed legions to fight against Russia, while the noted cultural figures Henryk Sienkiewicz and Ignac Paderewski sought independence by lobbying abroad (Segel, chapter 3 this volume). And yet, the rightwing Russian Duma deputy, Vladimir Purishkevich, had the audacity to quote the great nineteenth-century Polish poet Adam Mickiewicz in parliament as some kind of proof of Russian–Polish historic solidarity.[28]

The Symbolists, while decrying the brutality of the Germans, were honest enough to air their own feelings of shame about historical repressions and the Russification of Poland and to hope for a glorious Russo-Polish partnership in the future. But they played down Russian cruelties and the renewed Russification efforts in Galicia. Valery Bryusov, with little tact, quoted in his "To Poland" the patronizing words of the Russian poet, Fëdor Tyutchev "On the Taking of Warsaw" (1831), suggesting that now the Polish Lazarus would be raised up by the Russian Jesus. This at a moment when, with half a million Poles fighting in the Russian army, no Catholic chaplains were serving at the front. In all fairness it must be said that Bryusov's well-meant literary atonement met with joy and acceptance among some Warsaw intellectuals. As a whole, the intelligentsia played the themes of brotherhood, forgiveness, and mutual healing, often echoing Mickiewicz's famous formulation of the "crucified Poland."[29]

Panslavism was also, in a sense, a matter of allies – present and future. Panslavism was an old Russian dream of a union of Slavonic peoples into a communion of nations under the Russian tsar. Poland had been excluded in most formulations. Now there arose among a wing of the intelligentsia the vision of a remarriage with Poland, a Galician annexation, a complete Balkan liberation, and the acquisition of Istanbul (Tsargrad in Russian), and parts of Anatolia by the Russian empire. It was no hard passage from the historiosophic smog of neo-Slavophilism (see below, p. 26) to Panslavism: "in the deep Russian sea, all the rivers of Slavia will merge" wrote Sologub. The dream of Tsargrad was nursed

by Bryusov, Sologub, and Vyacheslav Ivanov – though not all Symbolists – and by various liberals and conservatives as well. Though they
evoked no major works of culture, Panslavism and Tsargrad underlay
the appeal of this war among many influential thinkers of the Russian
intelligentsia and even made their way into a war song.[30]

The Russian soul and national bonding

Hovering around the theme of allies and friends and mutually reinforced in all genres was the oldest theme of all: Russia's destiny. Behind it
lay a desperate vision and hope for national solidarity expressed in cultural and social unity. The forms it took were determined by a hundred
years of Russian intellectual history: images of home and nation, concepts of Holy Russia and of Mother Russia, the Russian Soul, and neo-
Slavophilism. In the cultural output of the war, these themes were
wrapped around discussions of history, the folk, religion, cultural heritage, the tsar, and heroes of war.

The yearning for national unity was expressed in various ways – most
of them rooted in ideas rather than realities. The monarch himself,
Nicholas II, thought he saw it in the mystical bond he believed he
possessed with the people, a bond made flesh in the dramatic show of
patriotism on the square in front of the Winter Palace in August 1914.
Duma leaders sought it in a Burgfrieden that they tried to build in the
Progressive Bloc and in the vigorous voluntary associations that sprang
up in the war: the Union of Zemstvos (local government) and Towns,
the War Industries Committees, and the Red Cross. Feminists and
other special interests called for a truce – to support the war effort in
return for a new Great Reform era. Many writers hoped that a solidary
show of patriotism would produce a permanent harmonious union of all
classes and end Russia's enduring problem: the alienation of the elites
from the masses. Bryusov, as a war correspondent, at first saw national
unity embodied in the brotherhood of the front, a front that in a few
years would turn into a line of fraternization with the enemy.[31]

The most colorful cultural expressions of unity were the Patriotic
Evening Concerts. Maria Dolina, a devoted monarchist and singer,
gave hundreds of benefit concerts that offered folk songs, balalaika
bands, martial ensembles, regimental choirs, songs set to the words of
the famous anti-Semitic publicist Pavel Krushevan, and readings of
official edicts and texts provided by the Russian right. Dolina presented
tableaux vivants – actors dressed as Suvorov, Kutuzov, and other commanders of the past, frozen alongside common people for the visual
contemplation of the audiences. The mixture of social orders promoted

all-Russian solidarity and loyalty in a setting of solemn stasis. As Hubertus Jahn so aptly put it, "in this kind of entertainment, patriotism changed not at all; it remained static in the tight-fitting costume of convention and the stiff order of military bands." A remnant of authentic folk art was recruited in 1915 when the 72-year-old folk teller, Maria Krivopolenova, was brought from her native Archangel region to Petrograd. It was one of the last efforts in imperial Russian history to link the culture of the *narod* (peasantry or common people) to a state program. Some artists, giving concerts in military hospitals, avoided Dolina's chauvinism; but they did combine the high culture of the intelligentsia with military bands and folk songs. All of this was a natural attempt to suggest and promote the social-cultural unity of the Russian people in the face of a dangerous enemy – a unity that in 1917 was shown to be fictitious.[32]

The sincere quest for unity in the face of danger helps explain the bitter tone in the critique of domestic life that erupted in the press. Luxury and high life remained in place for the affluent. Although prohibition was proclaimed at the outset of war, complaints resounded in the press and in ministerial chambers about all-night restaurants and illegal consumption of alcohol. And, although motor cars were needed for war, fancy autos careered around the streets of the capitals carrying top-hatted dandies and furred ladies. To the ranks of high society spenders were added speculators and war-profiteers. As in all wars, draft-dodgers abounded and were much resented, whether they were the newly pious who entered monasteries to escape service, or public volunteers – the "Zem-Hussars" – who wore gaudy uniforms and saw no action except during their valiant nocturnal assaults on restaurants and cabarets. With heavy-handed humor, the satirical journal, *Scourge*, and other papers, flogged the draft-dodger in foppish monocle and morning coat, the homefront slacker, the profiteer, and other elements of society who were escaping the horrors of war – all of this highlighting the persistance of privilege in wartime when sacrifice and unity were supposed to be the order of the day.[33]

Bygone heroes were cast in the drama of national unity. The medieval prince Alexander Nevsky, Suvorov, and Kutuzov were regularly featured in cartoon and poster. One of the most interesting examples of historical cooptation was the double pamphlet *How the Russians Took Berlin in 1760*, whose title story presented a falsely optimistic picture of what would happen in the current war on the basis of what happened in 1760. The back-piece was a reprint of an 1882 speech by the nationalist and conservative hero of Balkan and Central Asian wars, General Skobelev. In this scandalous diatribe spoken before a Panslav group in Paris, Skobelev insulted the Germans as a people and foresaw an inevitable war between Teuton and Slav. Skobelev's name, redolent of so many past victories and synonymous with Russian jingoism, was constantly invoked and the state wartime committee on propaganda was named after him. The Russian army, however, produced no Skobelevs in the 1914–1918 war.[34]

Who then were the heroes? Since neither the tsar nor the commanders could qualify, heroic images were fashioned from the exploits of individual combatants: soldiers, Cossacks, flyers. The adventures of the first heroes – Kuzma Kryuchkov, the pilot P. N. Nesterov, and Vasily Ryabov – were put on film. The young Cossack lancer, Kryuchkov, allegedly killed eleven German soldiers in 1915. His face appeared everywhere – in the papers, on posters, on postcards, in the circus – and a rash of verse was poured out in his honor. One representation had him impaling the eleven men on his lance. Nesterov, a 36-year-old daredevil pilot, had made a dangerous loop over Kiev in August 1913; a year later to the day he was killed on the Austrian front by plunging into enemy bombers over Russian positions. As with other air aces of the time, a price had been put on his head by the enemy. Units and battles were also celebrated as in the circus spectacles of "Russian Heroes in the Carpathians" and "The Capture of Przemyśl," a major Russian victory that also inspired a motion picture. Real soldiers, judging from their letters to Gippius, seemed much more human and they wrote in a rather formulaic, coarse, boastful – even folkish – fashion about their wounds, their nurses, and the need for the public to buy war bonds. Although women fought in the war, they received little attention except in women's journals. Much more space was given to nurses, grand duchesses at their hospitals, the sanctity of women, war wives, and rape victims.[35]

War and peace

The intellectuals who greeted the war that proved so utterly destructive could not in 1914–1915 see what was coming. Bryusov, idealizing the Russian occupation policies in Galicia, felt a "geographical patriotism" in the hope of Russian expansion and he saw this "Last War" as a prelude to a New World. Sologub rejoiced about Russian heroism from far away, gathering his information from newspapers. In a play Sologub coauthored with his wife – performed in Kharkov in November 1915 – *A Stone Cast into the Water*, the outbreak of war unravels moral and sexual tangles that are enmeshing good people in a summer "nest of gentlefolk" during their "month in the country." Mechanics and agency are absent and the action is motivated by a transcendent force, a device wholly in keeping with Symbolist esthetics. Other Symbolists, invoking the now exhausted cliché, likened the war to a "cleansing storm." Images of closure, finality, and apocalypse sprang off the pages of almost all the religio-philosophical writers of the time.[36]

The occultist movement, in particular the Russian Theosophical Society of Helen Blavatsky, saw war as a cosmic event of occult meaning – another "cleansing fire" which could weld together a religious East and a scientific West. In the words of a recent historian, they spoke constantly of "crisis of conscience, dark forces, carrying the cross, Russian mission, Godbearing people (*narod-bogonosets*), sacrifice, crucifixions, spiritual renewal, new path, and bright future." Religious writers often utilized a rather watery Christology spiked with Romans and Pharisees, the cross, Golgotha, and resurrection; or they took off into stratospheric metaphysical climes. As a whole, the best thinkers of the time looked backward, upward, or inward rather than peering into the face of battle.[37]

The neo-Slavophiles identifed the Germans with the traditional Slavophile images of Europeans as mechanized, narrow, smug, and affluent – in a word bourgeois. The old East–West dichotomy was reduced to Slav versus Teuton and soul versus machine. Sologub believed that a punitive victory over the Germans would enable the rebirth of Russia. (Interestingly, the new capital of his imagined renascent country was to lie deep in the interior at Yaroslavl on the Volga – considered a stereotypical Russian town.) Conversely, the old Crimean demons and "bourgeois" targets of abuse – England and France – were converted into suitable allies. Abhorring the concrete, the neo-Slavophiles and related thinkers defined reality as potential, essential, ontological – possessing no visible or provable attributes. "Holy Russia" was thus higher and therefore more real than the Russian state, despised by many Symbolists, Godseekers, and neo-Slavophiles. The Great War for them was a prelude to the spiritual regeneration of the Slavic soul, the Russian idea, *vsechelovechnost* (the all-human perspective), and the redeeming power of suffering.[38]

The Acmeist poet Nikolai Gumilëv, going well beyond the usual patriotic motives – hatred of the enemy and national ambitions – embraced war for the sake of war in the manner of Gabriele D'Annunzio and the characters of Ernst Jünger's novels. The sometime husband of Anna Akhmatova (a foe of the war), Gumilëv was later executed by the Bolsheviks for alleged monarchist plotting. His uniqueness stems not so much from heroic participation at the front as from his vision of the fighting as a personal adventure and a "grandiose spectacle" wherein he discovered the "mystery of the soul." Gumilëv's impulse was

1.2 Kasimir Malevich, *Private of the first division*, 1914

psychological and religious – not Panslav or Orthodox (though he was a devout believer), but rather a Nietzschean one of epiphany through danger, a masculine mysticism related to that of the love for the hunt (which Gumilëv possessed), the thrill of the kill, and the risk of being killed in the "cleansing fire" of battle. War for Gumilëv was not so much a sacred cause as a sacramental act. Recording his feelings in 1915 in *Notebook of a Cavalier*, Gumilëv exulted in the scorched earth, "burning everything that would burn." Disciple of the romantic cult of the horse and admirer of "The Turkestan Generals," Gumilëv aspired to be Superman and Conquistador; he saw man as beast among beasts and killing as a supreme work of art, a "festival of the spirit," a religious experience where man communes with God. Gumilëv stood virtually alone. Russia produced no group of well-known "trench poets" like those of other belligerents.[39]

How utterly different was the response of Konstantin Paustovsky, later a distinguished Soviet writer. "Symbolist poets," he recalled, "had completely lost all contact with reality [and] sang about pale ghosts of passion and the fires of otherworldly lusts." About an evening of Futurist poetry in 1914 in which Severyanin regaled a chic audience with sensual and witty verses, Paustovsky wrote: "it was savage to hear those words in days when thousands of Russian peasants were lying in rain-filled trenches, beating back the German armies with rifle fire." Paustovsky did not exult in the war, but he lived amidst the blood and the filth as a medical orderly on hospital trains and then in field medical units. Traveling from front to front through Poland, Galicia, and Russia, breathing in the smoke and stench of war, he began his life as a writer. "The 1914 war did not flood through our consciousness." He wrote years later about the home front in Moscow and elsewhere. "A life was going on in Russia which had nothing to do with the war."[40]

Another form of engagement was the wartime posture of the Orthodox Church. According to archival documents, the archbishop of Voronezh Province in 1916 affirmed the "duty of the clergy to use the symbols of the church to encourage and incite patriotic feelings for the war" through such means as communion masses for recruits, prayers for their safety, patriotic sermons, processions, and the distribution of crucifixes, icons, and religious and patriotic leaflets. Similar programs were preached and practiced all over Russia; and the front was well supplied with Orthodox chaplains who blessed and doused troops and weapons with holy water. Orthodox priests were also brought by train into conquered Uniate and Catholic Galicia.[41]

Not many people, apparently, thought the war funny enough to generate a lot of jokes. There can be little doubt that jokes abounded on the personal qualities of the enemy. One surviving example is about the German army breakfasting in Warsaw, lunching in St. Petersburg, dining in Moscow – and shitting it all out in Berlin. Another is plotted as the familiar dialogue between two Jews, now caught in the battle zone: one a German, the other a Russian, both "patriots." The former brags about the greatness of his Kaiser who rushes from front to front always at the head of the troops (a fiction, of course). The Russian Jew replies in scorn: "Your tsar has no dignity; he runs around like a chicken. Our tsar sits at Headquarters [in Mogilev] and the front comes to him!"[42]

The impact of war

In trying to sum up the scope and meaning of Russian wartime culture, several points seem clear. First, the continuities between old and new expression. Those who addressed the war – whether in accents of high or popular culture – retained the forms and redressed the themes of their pre-war productions. That no great Russian war novel came out of this struggle is no surprise; most masterpieces about war are written out of memory and reflective contemplation. The gap between high and popular culture seems especially revealing. If we can believe that each possessed its own audience or "taste culture," then the division between the intelligentsia and the masses was very real. They saw it through different eyes and eventually divided over support of the war. For the intelligentsia, however removed they were from the war, it remained a burning issue and most of those who exalted a Russian victory maintained that position. For the common people – who suffered far more than the creative intelligentsia – the romance with war ended quickly, even though the common soldiers fought on. Culture as such had much less to do with this than the war's casualties and its economic effects.

In places where art branched off and moved into new directions – as with the avant-garde poets and painters – it had little or no connection to the war. Of all the cultural forms that flourished in the wartime period, none can compare with the glories of Russian visual art. It forms the middle period of a magnificent flowering from the turn of the century to about 1930 with the onset of Stalinism and the end of modernism and the avant-garde. The paintings, collages, studio events, and showings in Moscow and Petrograd in the 1910s have long been considered a peak moment in the history of twentieth-century European art.

The intelligentsia experienced the war largely as a philosophical exercise where moral values reigned supreme and the frontline world of troop trains and mountains of corpses remained in the less important kingdom of phenomenology. Readers of adventure and consumers of the popular arts wanted spectacle and entertainment – including sensationalist violence – that simplified the war as a Manichaean struggle between good and evil. At a deeper level, however, one may discern a striking difference between highbrow and lowbrow (or middlebrow) in their perceptions of the Russian people. The patriotic intelligentsia for the most part saw Russia's strength not in brute force, personal heroism, or material power – but rather in moral fortitude, thus in a sense making a virtue of physical deficiency. Popular culture, by contrast, offered heroes and heroines of physical brawn (for men), courage, and cunning. Cartoon soldiers and fictional female spies are tough and earthy. Their superior morality is assumed because they are Russian and on the "right side" and their inner character is never explored. One of the great political strengths of the Soviet socialist realist culture of the Stalin period was that it managed to weld these two elements into one whole – however fantastic that entity was.

Certain themes correlated well with certain arts or genres of art. Big philosophical dreams cannot be easily articulated in cartoons, songs, movies, cabaret, circus, or pulp fiction. The major thinkers avoided the realia of battle like the plague. Although their barbs at Germany were never expressed in comic low satire, they were full of spite and hatred. The anti-German theme suited the intelligentsia's positions as well as framing plots of adventure, suspense, action, and even love and violence. High and "low" art addressed the Belgium-as-martyr theme because it could be made both complex and simple. But no formula could deliver a satisfying presentation of ambivalence and latent guilt over Poland. The Jewish question got little space in popular culture probably because it would not sell to lower and lower-middle-class consumers.[43] As for the exaltation of the homeland, nothing was more amenable to any form of construction: philosophical, religious, or plain old patrioteering.

Very little research has been published on Russian "trench culture" in the Great War. Physical conditions are a partial explanation: the city-like labyrinths of the Western front had no counterpart in the East; trenches were dug and abandoned quickly until very late in the war. The war of movement in the East offered relatively few opportunities for leisurely creation. Another factor was the relative illiteracy in the Russian ranks. It is possible that many literate soldiers and officers wrote poetically – to themselves or to people at home – of love and death, suffering and despair, perhaps even of hope. But Soviet historiography on the war did not highlight or memorialize it and we have yet to see the literary remains of the Russian Bindings, Owens, and Sassoons. Books of composed songs appeared but they were remarkably similar to nineteenth-century ones. Collections from both eras displayed sentiments of monarchy, loyalty, patriotism, cheerfulness, and bravado. A 1915 songbook was merely updated with a few new items about allies and enemies and verses insulting to the Kaiser.[44]

The wartime use of the arts as propaganda or simply war-related morale building should not be exaggerated; both the producers and the public continued to rivet their attention on purely entertainment genres. Indeed the movie melodrama's popularity increased enormously during the war years. Russian jingoism took hold among all classes for a while – but it did not last long. In all the belligerent countries, culture – high, low, and middle – was enlisted by the state for patriotic purposes. Though hardly novel in 1914, this process was intensified by the technical means of communication. In Russia, one can find in the techniques of patriotic culture a preview of some of those used by the Provisional Government and the Bolshevik regime to legitimize their revolutions: the *tableau vivant*, the historical spectacle, the imaging of enemies in circus, graphics, and movies (which used not only plot, but casting, lighting, and costuming to satanize political and social foes).

Nothing like mass mobilization or nationalization of the arts took place in wartime Russia. A wave of patriotic enthusiasm did arise but did not last very long. To the extent that non-governmental cultural production reflects public opinion, its history shows starkly that enthusiasm for the war – though varying among the classes – sharply declined after the defeats of 1915. Private enterprise continued to churn out lurid graphics, mystical and satanic movies, detective tales, vulgar songs, straight comedy, and dance routines with no political or national content. This went on unhindered and indeed amplified after the fall of the monarchy in March 1917. It was only when the Bolsheviks came to power that state authorities began seriously to regulate the people's taste and then only in 1918 when Russia's war in Europe was ending. Russian wartime culture was wholly transformed after the February Revolution overthrew the tsar. Not that the war ceased being an issue. It was *the* central issue of 1917, but so tightly was it knotted to the revolutionary process that its history belongs to that epic struggle.[45]

2

German culture in the Great War

Peter Jelavich

Among the startling events of August 1914, many German observers were struck by the outpouring of verse from the populace at large. A major Berlin newspaper reported that over 500 poems were submitted daily; during the first month of hostilities, 100 poems on average were published in newspapers throughout the nation every day.[1] Germany seemed to prove that it was indeed the proverbial country of *Dichter und Denker* (poets and thinkers), though the quality of the verse, let alone the quality of the thinking, left much to be desired. The old standbys of patriotic doggerel were resurrected: *Krieg* invariably rhymed with *Sieg*, *Vaterland* with *Gottes Hand*, *Mut* with *Blut* or *Wut*, *Schlacht* with *Wacht* or *Macht*.[2] The language seemed made for militaristic effusions.

Of all of the verses penned in those early days, by far the most famous was Ernst Lissauer's "Haßgesang gegen England" (Song of Hate against England). It was a true "crossover" work: written by a relatively unknown poet with aspirations to elite culture, it became a genuinely popular poem. Reproduced in countless newspapers and handbills, it was declaimed from theater, opera, and even vaudeville stages to thunderous applause. The poem began with a statement that "we" neither love nor hate the French and the Russians; the struggle with those peoples is straightforward and comprehensible – it is a fight between neighboring nations over land. But feelings toward Britain are different:

> Wir haben nur einen einzigen Haß,
> Wir lieben vereint, wir hassen vereint,
> Wir haben nur einen einzigen Feind: England!

> We have just one single hatred,
> We love as one, we hate as one,
> We have one enemy alone: England!

Lissauer's "Song of Hate" expressed succinctly and brutally a sentiment found in innumerable poems, plays, and essays: the belief that England was Germany's most perfidious enemy. The British were cast as a country of insatiably greedy *Krämer* (shopkeepers) who wanted the whole world to themselves. Having the largest empire on the face of the earth was not enough: they actively sought to keep other great nations down. Even though (or rather, precisely because) Germany's industrial production had surpassed that of Great Britain on the eve of the war, the English wanted to deny the young nation its rightful "place in the sun" – its claim to new markets, new colonies, and a new navy. Many Germans believed that England and Germany should have cooperated and marched together (certainly against France, the "historic" enemy of both countries). England's casting its lot with the Entente was regarded as perfidy of the vilest sort. The sentiment was expressed most succinctly in the phrase: *Gott strafe England* (God punish England).

Musicals

Poems such as Lissauer's "Song of Hate" constituted one major genre expressing popular sentiments in wartime Germany; two others were musicals and films. The war had broken out during the traditional summer entertainment slump. Most theaters had closed for vacation, and cinema attendance was low. Over the course of August and September, many stages postponed opening their new season, in part because many actors had been sent to the front, in part out of respect for the gravity of the situation. Indeed, in numerous communities, the police (or the army, which immediately acquired wide authority on the home front) initially banned all comedies and farces "for the duration of the war" – the assumption being that it would last only a few weeks. By October, however, these orders had been rescinded, and almost every stage was back in business. Actresses and older actors, not to mention directors and theater owners, needed employment, and there was money to be made from war hysteria. With breathtaking speed, Germany's top lyricists and popular composers churned out musicals about the war. They were rife with clichés – the English were greedy and perfidious; the French acted macho with ladies but were cowards on the battlefield; the Russians were simply dumb and dirty. With such weak enemies, Germans believed that they would win the war swiftly, just as they had done in 1870 (memories of which were evoked constantly). Another oft-repeated theme was Germany's innocence: the Kaiser, it was said, had asked the French and Russians to demobilize and avoid war. But since they demanded a fight, *nun wollen wir sie dreschen* (now we'll thrash them) – the Kaiser's dictum that was repeated in numerous musicals.

To be sure, Belgium was a touchy subject: the violation of that country's neutrality was a serious blow to Germany's prestige among neutral states. Some German musicals laughed at the issue. In *Extrablätter!*

Heitere Bilder aus ernster Zeit (Get the Extra! Humorous Scenes in Serious Times), a German soldier sings to "Ninette," the "pearl of the Ardennes":

> Mamsellchen! Ach, Mamsellchen!
> Komm laß Dich annektier'n.
> Wir sind ja doch in Belgien,
> Da kann so was passier'n.

> Mad'moiselle! Oh, mad'moiselle!
> I'll annex you, if you please.
> We're in Belgium, after all,
> Where such things are done with ease.[3]

Other works took the issue more seriously, and argued that the Flemish people were actually a Germanic race that deserved either independence from Belgium or incorporation into the Reich. The theme was represented by behind-the-front romances between Flemish lasses and German boys-in-arms.[4]

With respect to domestic politics, the early wartime musicals heralded the *Burgfrieden* (domestic truce), the fact that the Social Democrats had dropped their pacifist rhetoric and had voted for war credits. The Kaiser likewise suspended his public disdain for the Social Democrats with the famous phrase, "Ich kenne keine Parteien mehr, ich kenne nur noch Deutsche" (I no longer recognize any parties, I recognize only Germans). Numerous musicals began with scenes of workers and bourgeois, or workers and nobles, carping at each other, only to stand united on the battlefield at the final curtain. The overcoming of other differences was celebrated as well – Catholic and Protestant, Austrian and German, Bavarian and Prussian (the source of many "comic" scenes). The unity of the nation at war was a theme that inspired some particularly painful verse:

> Mit gleichem Mute ziehn zum Kampf und Tod sie,
> Der Adel und das Zentrum und der Sozi.

> They fight with equal valor till they're dead,
> The nobleman, the Catholic, and the Red.[5]

Obviously, taste was among the victims of the Great War. Romance too was mobilized for the cause: numerous scenes depicted young women rejecting suitors, however wealthy, who failed to head for the front – the spoils of love invariably went to the enthusiastic volunteers.

As the German advance ground to a halt and as casualties mounted, the ebullient mood of early wartime musicals could not be sustained. As early as November 1914, one scene cautioned its audience not to celebrate military victories too loudly or ostentatiously, since at that very moment families would be grieving for those whose death had made victory possible.[6] By the spring of 1915, the flood of military musicals had ebbed, and most stages avoided the theme altogether. As audiences sought distraction from a war that now seemed to drag on endlessly, operettas and fairy-tale plays became preferred genres on popular stages.[7] Those musicals that continued to address current events adopted an increasingly moralistic or didactic tone. One virtue that was stressed was marital fidelity: women were portrayed remaining true to their inducted husbands, and front-line soldiers were shown to be faithful to their wives (despite the flirtations of French hussies); faithfulness to one's spouse and to one's nation became intertwined themes. A whole array of other numbers dealt with the rapidly changing role of women, who were required to assume "men's duties" both at home and in the economy. This was new – and traumatic – to many women and men; thus skits and scenes showing women in traditionally male jobs accustomed spectators of both sexes to the idea that female employment was a wartime necessity. Another theme was donation to the war effort: viewers were encouraged to bring gold and silver, as well as practical metals, to collection points; they were cajoled into buying war bonds; and they were told to keep sending goods to the boys at the front – socks, newspapers, stationery, chocolate.

Those items became increasingly hard to find as the effects of the continental blockade were compounded with each passing month. On the eve of the war, Germany had been importing a third of its food from abroad; now most of those sources were cut off. Bread rationing was introduced in January 1915. By 1916 there were severe food shortages, and the winter of 1916–1917 went down in popular memory as the "turnip winter." The shortfall of coal for domestic consumption reached catastrophic proportions in some areas; indeed, many theaters were forced to close in the winter months. Acute discomfort on the home front, as well as the mounting casualty figures, resulted in deteriorating public morale, and the *Burgfrieden* collapsed. Consumers hated retailers; townsfolk accused peasants of hoarding foodstuffs; workers and many middle-class citizens suspected rampant war profiteering; Bavarians and others throughout Germany cursed the centralizing authorities in Berlin. Part of the population moved to the left, a shift marked by the founding of the anti-war Independent Social Democratic Party (USPD) in April 1917. But others gravitated toward the right, and in particular toward anti-Semitism, as increasingly frustrated chauvinists sought scapegoats for German misfortunes. Jews were accused not only of hoarding and profiteering, but of evading the draft. The most terrible blow came in October 1916, when the imperial army ordered the *Judenzählung*, a tally of Jewish soldiers at the front. It was undertaken ostensibly to counter anti-Semitic accusations; in reality, the racists in the military wanted to collect evidence to feed anti-Semitic fires. That became most evident when army officials refused to publicize the results of the count, which indicated that Jews were represented proportionately on the battlefields. The *Judenzählung* was a monstrous insult to Germany's Jewish citizens, and did nothing to calm the domestic waters; it broke the spirit of many patriotic Jews at the same time that it fanned the flames of anti-Semitism.

By September 1916 the Prussian war ministry could report in its monthly assessment of domestic conditions that among the lower classes, "there is a depressing indifference. Without being an alarmist one can say that the bulk of the population is weary of the war."[8] Musicals tried to wring humor out of this not-so-funny situation, in order to keep up public spirits; as one song proclaimed in February 1917, "Auch lachen ist Zivildienstpflicht" (laughter too is a civilian service obligation).[9] A skit presented in March 1916 depicted robbers who break into an apartment, crack the safe, toss aside money, jewels, and stocks, and run off with the butter that had been locked away.[10] By October 1917 spectators were told not to worry if they did not have enough coal to heat their apartments; they should simply snuggle up with their sweeties to keep warm.[11] Other scenes made light of the social consequences of shortages, as occupations that had formerly been looked down upon acquired new importance: saleswomen now lorded over customers, while mistresses of the house were dominated by their maids and cooks (who had family ties to the countryside, and hence access to agricultural products).[12] By the last year of the war, "humor" was strained to the breaking point. In January 1918 two entertainers at the Wintergarten, Berlin's largest and most prestigious variety theater, joked that ration cards were being issued for *Käsemilbenersatz* (cheese-mite substitute), and they asked whether the ladies of Berlin also had fixed price ceilings, like everything else. The police observer who witnessed that scene deplored not only the tastelessness of those comments in particular, but also "the incessant allusions to food shortages, which make the authorities look ridiculous."[13] The public discontent that was to erupt in massive strikes at the end of that month had already infected the vaudeville stages.

Film

The changing wartime conditions were also reflected on the silver screen. Germany had developed a respectable film industry by 1914, but its cinemas were dominated by works from France in particular, as well as from Italy, Denmark, and the United States. Indeed, German products constituted at most 15 percent of films screened prior to 1914. Ironically, when the war broke out, Berlin cinemas were showing two pacifist films. One was a French production, *Guerre à la guerre* (War on War); the other, *Die Waffen nieder!* (Ground Arms!), was based on Bertha von Suttner's best-selling pacifist book (1889), for which she had won a Nobel Peace Prize in 1905. Needless to say, both works disappeared immediately from the screens.[14] More significantly, the importation of French, English, and Russian films was halted. Many cinemas, like theaters, closed during August 1914, in part out of respect for the war, but also because there was a sudden shortfall of available films. Distributors scrambled to locate feature films with military themes, or recent newsreels with images of the Kaiser, the army, or the navy. Through September, German distributors could offer no new films. But German producers were not idle, and in October the first of numerous wartime flicks hit the market. The conflagration proved a mixed blessing for German filmmakers: they lost most of their lucrative export market, but they enjoyed protection at home. Not only was France – their major competitor – knocked out of the running, but after March 1916 no new foreign films could enter the country, owing to a general ban on importing luxury goods. The result was a boom in German film output. In August 1914, there were only 25 German-owned film production and distribution companies in the country; by 1918, there were 130.[15] This expansion was encouraged in part by an actual rise of attendance during the war; from 1914 to 1917, the number of cinemas in Germany increased from 2,446 to 3,130.

Like the musicals, the feature films and shorts that appeared in the fall of 1914 portrayed war as an exciting adventure and an uplifting experience of national unity. One work that premiered at the end of October was even entitled *Ich kenne keine Parteien mehr*; it depicted how a Social Democratic worker saved the life of his commanding sergeant, a former political foe, on the battlefield, and thus was allowed to marry the sergeant's daughter.[16] Conversely, the enemy troops were portrayed as brutal and gratuitously destructive. By 1915, however, war-weariness was taking its toll on military films, just as it led to a drop-off of military musicals; now entertainment movies returned to cinemas. In August 1914 police and military censors had banned all "frivolous" films. Ernst Lubitsch's *Der Stolz der Firma* (The Pride of the Firm), the second of his numerous comedies set in a Jewish retailing milieu, had premiered on 30 July 1914, but was promptly yanked off the screens. By January 1915 it was allowed to be rereleased, as the authorities succumbed to public demand for light, non-war-related entertainment. Lubitsch proceeded to make some of his funniest films during the war (notably *Schuhpalast Pinkus*, 1916).[17] Genres that had been popular before 1914 were resurrected; fairy tales, as well as sexually risqué works, were in demand (though wartime censorship kept an especially sharp eye on the latter). Even detective films continued to boom, despite their overtly Anglo-Saxon inspiration (the German-produced "Stuart Webbs" and "Joe Deebs" series were obvious knockoffs of Sherlock Holmes). They were so popular that Lubitsch even filmed a parody of them (*Der Fall Rosentopf*, 1918).

To the extent that wartime conditions were addressed, films, like musicals, tried to maintain public humor in the face of mounting short-ages. In Lubitsch's *Das schönste Geschenk* (The Nicest Present, 1916), a young woman announces that she will marry the man who brings her the best gift; she rejects suitors offering her all sorts of jewelry in favor of a man who presents her with a quarter pound of butter. Lubitsch likewise dealt with the entry of women into male professions; *Fräulein Seifenschaum* (Miss Soaplather, 1915) is a comic portrayal of a mother-and-daughter barber team. Other works – particularly shorts screened prior to the feature films – touted patriotic causes like war bonds. *Hann, Hein und Henny*, which advertised the fifth war loan subscription, was considered particularly successful because it starred Henny Porten, the most popular German screen actress of the day.

In the fall of 1914 moviegoers certainly would have been most inter-ested in war documentaries, but such scenes were hardest to film. At the outbreak of fighting camera teams were sent to the front, where they encountered numerous difficulties. A major one was military cen-sorship: concerned with security and espionage, many officers objected to the presence of cameramen (who were, after all, "mere" civilians). But filming a battle would not have been possible in any case, since anyone operating a bulky, hand-cranked camera would have been the easiest target imaginable. That meant, in effect, that no "action scenes" could be shown to hometown audiences. Conversely, views of a "quiet" front were cinematically disappointing. Already at the end of August 1914, the trade journal *Der Kinematograph* reported: "A modern field of battle offers the public . . . hardly anything that can be recognized clearly. The distances are immense, the sharpshooters in the trenches are hard to discern, and the whole field of battle gives the impression . . . of a landscape that is almost completely dead."[18] So what could be filmed? Eventually, the newsreels – all of which were subject to prior military censorship – developed a repertory of themes that included scenes of mobilization; local populations giving soldiers enthusiastic sendoffs; "idyllic" behind-the-front scenes of troops eating, reading mail, or attending concerts; wounded soldiers recovering in hospitals (but never dying); enemy prisoners of war; localities captured by German troops; bridges and buildings (especially churches) destroyed by the "barbarous" French, British, or Russians; and German soldiers rebuilding said structures. Obviously, such "documentaries" hardly gave moviegoers a sense of the reality of war. Indeed, when they were shown in the numerous cinemas at the front, troops howled with laughter or with rage. A surgeon-general in the medical corps reported in a bitterly ironic letter: "The German war news-weeklies may be considered an important therapy for the wounded. My subordinates report to me that they never have heard as much thunderous laughter as when they are shown films about the trenches and the war. But as we all know, laughter is an important medicine."[19]

By 1916 the state of German film was not a laughing matter for the military or the Foreign Office. Whereas Wilhelmine elites traditionally had looked down on film as mere "trash" (*Schund*), after two years of war they finally realized what England and France had recognized from the beginning: namely, that film was a powerful tool of foreign and domestic propaganda. Two major issues were at stake. Neutral countries – Switzerland, Holland, Denmark, and other Scandinavian states, and various Balkan nations – were being flooded with extremely well-made feature films depicting the barbarity of the Teutonic "Huns." German diplomats slowly realized that they were facing an international public-relations disaster of the first magnitude. On the domestic front, military officials, alarmed at mounting public discontent, believed that film could be employed to revive enthusiasm for the war, or at least persuade the populace to *durchhalten* (hold out) until the final victory. By August 1916 the Prussian minister of war wrote to the chancellor, Bethmann Hollweg, that films were needed to inform the populace about the "meaning and purpose of the war"; in particular, they should present to the German people "the heroic deeds of German soldiers on land, on the sea and in the air, and inspire them to adopt a similarly heroic attitude, reminiscent of the war enthusiasm of August 1914."[20]

In August 1916 a film and photography unit was appended to the army's liaison office at the foreign ministry. In January 1917 it was transformed into the *Bild- und Filmamt* (Bufa), which reported to both the General Staff and the Foreign Office (though more to the former than the latter). Bufa encouraged and assisted the production of films about the war. In particular, it employed seven military (rather than civilian) film teams to acquire "genuine" footage from the front. Although its teams, like their counterparts producing commercial newsreels, were unable to film actual battles, they could fudge the issue by substituting scenes of combat training; moreover, they provided much more comprehensive shots of preparations for battles and their aftermath. Most of the Bufa films were shorts, intended to be screened prior to feature films; but some of the "documentaries" were of feature length, such as *Mackensens Siegeszug durch die Dobrudscha* (Mackensen's Victorious Campaign through Dobrudja, 1916) and *Bei unseren Helden an der Somme* (With Our Heroes on the Somme, 1917). The latter was an obvious response to the British film, *The Battle of the Somme*, which had deeply impressed foreign audiences. Though it was successful domestically, the German rejoinder did not fare well abroad; despite its documentary premise, its battle scenes were obviously staged, and not nearly as effective as those in the English work.[21]

Bufa also commissioned a dozen fictional feature films during the war. German diplomats reported that audiences in neutral countries showed little interest in war documentaries, but were very attracted to story films; in that category, England, France, and eventually the United States were beating Germany hands down.[22] Bufa tried to rectify that situation with films like *Das Tagebuch des Dr. Hart* (The Diary of Dr. Hart, 1917), about the kindness of a German military doctor in occupied Russian Poland. The work not only tried to counter the image of the brutal "Hun" by depicting Germans engaged in humanitarian work; it also appealed to the sensitivity of neutral states by dramatizing German support for the creation of an independent Poland (albeit one carved out of Russian, not German or Austrian, territory). Another Bufa feature-length fictional film aimed at both foreign and domestic audiences was *Unsühnbar* (Inexpiable). Starring Adele Sandrock, a *grande dame* of the German-speaking stage, it was a response to *Mère française*, a French production featuring Sarah Bernhardt that had enjoyed great success in neutral nations.[23] But *Unsühnbar* had a clear domestic goal as well. On 16 April 1917, following a renewed reduction of the bread ration, demonstrations and strikes occurred throughout Germany, particularly in Berlin and Leipzig. In response, Paul von Hindenburg, chief of the General Staff, issued a public letter claiming that "every work stoppage . . . is an inexpiable sin against the men in the trenches, who will pay with their blood." The film *Unsühnbar* – whose poster featured a quote from Hindenburg's missive[24] – was a dramatization of the battlefield costs of slacking on the home front.

The ineffectiveness of German feature films compared to the products of the Entente eventually led to the founding of the Universum Film Aktiengesellschaft (UFA), which became the largest German film

2.1   Max Liebermann, Now we'll thrash them: cover of *Kriegszeit: Künstlerflugblätter*, 7 September 1914

production company. The idea had originated with Bufa officials, and in July 1917 it received effective support from Erich Ludendorff, chief aide to Hindenburg and arguably the most powerful man in Germany. In a memorandum addressed to the war ministry, Ludendorff wrote:

The war has demonstrated the paramount power of images and of film as means of enlightenment and influence. Unfortunately our enemies have used the advantages that they enjoy in that area so thoroughly that they have caused us great damage. . . . For the war to be concluded successfully, it is absolutely imperative that film be employed with the greatest force in all places where German influence is still possible.[25]

Ludendorff proceeded to argue that much more effective cinematic propaganda was needed both abroad and at home, and he deplored the fragmentation of effort among the competing film companies. He concluded by suggesting that the Reich buy commanding shares in all major companies, "but it must not be made public that the state is the purchaser."[26]

Over the ensuing months the Deutsche Bank acted as front for the government buyout of the film industry. When UFA was officially founded on 18 December 1917, state participation was effectively obscured by a board of directors that included representatives from a number of major banks and industries. The new corporation subsumed all of the major players in German film, such as the production companies of Paul Davidson and Oskar Messter (who contracted Germany's outstanding directors, actors, and actresses), as well as the Danish-based Nordisk. Since these companies already enjoyed a high degree of horizontal and vertical integration, UFA automatically assumed ownership of cinema chains, distribution services, and factories manufacturing cameras and projectors. The purpose of this government-backed mega-corporation was to bring together Germany's best directors, stars, and scriptwriters to produce works that would promote the Reich's image abroad and stir patriotic feelings among the increasingly restless public. Unfortunately for Ludendorff, UFA had little to show by the time the front collapsed in August 1918. In the Weimar era it was privatized and became the flagship film producer it was intended to be. After 1933, it enjoyed the special favor of Goebbels, who instrumentalized film to a greater extent than Ludendorff ever could have imagined.

Intellectuals at war

Mass culture in wartime Germany reflected a shift from nearly unanimous enthusiasm to a more differentiated situation, where a war-weary population's longing for distraction confronted the desire of certain elites to encourage and sustain enthusiasm for the military cause. It was, indeed, among "high" culture that war hysteria was most pronounced. When the dogs of war were unleashed, it was the *Bildungsbürgertum* – the educated bourgeoisie – that howled the loudest and the longest, and Germany's most exalted writers barked in chorus. To be sure, the ground had been prepared long in advance. Germany's major intellectual currents of the *fin de siècle* regarded war as part of the divine or natural order. Hegelianism, which had dominated German historical, legal, and theological thought throughout the nineteenth century, contended that God had planted struggle into the fabric of history. "Social Darwinism" and "racial Darwinism," which provided ideological justifications for imperialism, postulated a "natural" struggle for existence among nations and races, at the end of which the "best" (European, white, "Aryan") elements would prevail. Writers and artists were especially inspired by Friedrich Nietzsche, who postulated a "will to power" at all levels of material and spiritual existence. Struggle, domination, war – these were willed by Nature and by God.

Nevertheless, the aggressive rhetoric of the pre-war German intellectuals could not hide a fundamental sense of unease; they sensed that their cultural endeavors were increasingly useless in the modern world. Highly respected in the nineteenth century, the *Bildungsbürger* and their artistic spokesmen saw their influence wane in the face of other classes. The nobility continued to have a disproportionate say in Prussian and imperial politics, and its social status was undiminished. The business and technical sectors of the bourgeoisie were increasingly considered the heart and soul of that class, displacing the educated elites. The organized working class, though disparaged, was a potent force, as the Social Democratic Party won a third of Reichstag seats in the elections of 1912. When war erupted, Germany's writers and bourgeois opinion-makers saw a chance to recoup their losses. For all who cared to listen, they packaged and sold the struggle as one of German *Kultur* against Western materialism; it was a spiritual crusade to restore the values of the *Bildungsbürger* to their rightfully dominant place.[27]

Among German writers, the charge was led, quite literally, by the respected poet Richard Dehmel. Though fifty-one years old and lacking any military experience, he begged to be inducted and was sent to the front. Others of his generation demurred, but they dedicated their pens to the national cause. Very soon, the denizens of *Kultur* had a lot of explaining to do. The major problem was, of course, Belgium. Not only was that country's neutrality violated, but the German army – stunned and angered that the Belgians put up any resistance at all – initiated a policy of terrorizing the local population, including mass execution of civilian hostages. Though hundreds of Belgians were murdered in this manner throughout the country, by far the most infamous case was the "sack of Louvain" in late August. German soldiers near that sleepy university town claimed that they had been fired upon by Belgian *francs-tireurs*. Subsequent studies indicated that the troops probably had been subjected to "friendly fire" from other Germans; but in any case, even a guerrilla attack would not have justified what followed. Large sections of the town were systematically torched, and over 200 civilians were shot, some while fleeing their burning homes, others after being rounded up for group executions. Cultural damage was also extensive, as hundreds of manuscripts and incunabula in the university library were reduced to ashes.[28]

On 29 August Germany's Wolff news agency proudly sent a message around the world: "the ancient town of Louvain, rich in art treasures, no longer exists today." After reading that notice in the *Gazette de Lausanne*, Romain Rolland sat down and penned an impassioned public letter to Gerhart Hauptmann. Rolland was a French intellectual who had worked tirelessly for Franco-German cultural rapprochement, while Hauptmann had gained fame as the author of socially critical plays like *Die Weber* (The Weavers). Rolland opened his missive with the sentence: "I am not one of those French who consider Germany barbarous. I recognize the intellectual and moral grandeur of your mighty race." Rolland thereby distanced himself from Henri Bergson, who had claimed in a much-publicized speech of 8 August that the war was one between French civilization and German barbarism. Rolland proceeded to blame the destruction of Louvain on "the political tradition of the kings of Prussia," not on the German people or the German spirit. Hence he called upon Hauptmann to speak out against military excesses. "Are you the grandchildren of Goethe, or the grandchildren of Attila?" Rolland finished by noting that if Hauptmann did not speak out, then he would have to conclude that "the German elite is enslaved to the worst despotism, to one that mutilates masterpieces and assassinates the human spirit."[29]

German writers, who from the outset of hostilities had claimed that Germany was fighting a war of *Kultur* against Western material greed, were cut to the quick and responded with all of the symptoms of a collective defensive psychosis. Hauptmann replied simply: *Krieg ist Krieg* (War is war).[30] Friedrich Gundolf, the most educated among the ultra-aesthetes of Stefan George's circle, wrote: "whoever is strong enough to create, has a right to destroy."[31] In October, ninety-three German writers, professors, and scientists published a manifesto in which they claimed that the destruction of Louvain was a justified reprisal, and that German culture and the German army were a complementary pair, not opposing forces as Rolland had claimed. The signatories included authors like Richard Dehmel, Ludwig Fulda, Max Halbe, Hauptmann, and Hermann Sudermann. In response to such reactions – and horrified by the shelling of the cathedral of Rheims (20 September) – Rolland wrote another open letter to the German intellectuals, in which he concluded: "the vanquished Belgians have robbed you of your glory. You know it. You are furious because you know it."[32]

Many intellectual observers were surprised when one of the most vociferous proponents of the German war effort turned out to be Thomas Mann. Though long an advocate of separating art from politics, he jumped headlong into the fray. To be sure, there were practical limits to his enthusiasm: when called before an induction board, he managed to receive a medical discharge. What he lacked in front-line courage, he tried to make up with verbal bravado. His first major salvo, entitled *Gedanken im Kriege* (Thoughts in Wartime), was published in November 1914. In it he contended that the war was fundamentally a conflict between German *Kultur* and Western *Zivilisation*. For Mann, civilization was characterized by "reason, enlightenment, mildness, good manners, skepticism, resolution – spirit (*Geist*)." Culture was more essential, more fundamental, more cohesive; it was "unity, style, form, bearing, taste." It also was more irrational, and was allied with art, nature, religion, sexuality, and war. Mann contended that art and war were similar endeavors, marked by an "interaction of enthusiasm and order." The problem with pre-war Germany was that it was too complacent, too "civilized." Mann proclaimed: "How could the artist, the soldier in the artist fail to praise God for the collapse of a peaceful world with which he was fed up, so completely fed up!" War was the state most appropriate to Germany. "The entirety of Germany's virtue and beauty – we have seen it now – unfolds only in war. Peace is not always becoming to it – in peacetime one could sometimes forget how beautiful Germany is." Mann mocked those who wanted to bring "the blessings of demilitarization and democracy" to Germany, for which a militaristic and monarchical regime was most appropriate.[33] Once again, Rolland hit the nail on the head when he said that Mann's "monstrous article" was written in "a fit of fury caused by injured pride."[34]

Mann continued to pen combined defenses of German culture and the German war effort right up to 1918. In the process, he resorted to overtly racist arguments. German propagandists never ceased to point out that the English and the French employed colonial troops (from India and Africa) in their armies. Illustrated newspapers like the *Berliner Illustrierte Zeitung* as well as satirical journals like *Simplicissimus* regularly published photographs and caricatures of dark-skinned soldiers in the enemy's armies; the accompanying captions invariably implied that the truly barbarous powers were the Entente, because they dared to unleash such subhuman beasts upon German troops. That became a leitmotif in Mann's works as well, as he continued his crusade to deny any cultural worth to the Western powers. Already in *Gedanken im Kriege*, he called the use of "Kirghiz, Japanese, Gurkhas, and Hottentots" against German troops "an insult, without precedent, monstrous" (*eine Beleidigung, beispiellos, ungeheuerlich*).[35] In an open letter to Stockholm's *Svenska Dagbladet* published in May 1915, he played the racist card to the full: "I'll show you a little picture. A Senegalese negro who is watching over German prisoners, an animal with lips as thick as pillows [*ein Tier mit Lippen so dick wie Kissen*], draws his gray paw [*seine graue Pfote*] across his neck and gurgles: 'One ought to kill them. *They are barbarians.*' Well? I hope that you like my little picture?"[36] In that same essay, Mann claimed that the war would give birth to Germany's "Third Reich." To be sure, at that time the term had not yet been monopolized by the extreme right; Mann himself characterized the "Third Reich" as "the synthesis of power and spirit."[37] Yet the phrase clearly belonged to a camp of millenarian thought that opposed the Enlightenment and democratic politics.

Mann's support of the war and the imperial system was endorsed by most members of his cultured class. The *Intellektuelleneingabe* of July 1915, a petition of intellectuals demanding that Germany fight an expansionist war to annex extensive territories in the west and the east, was signed by 1,347 professors, teachers, artists, and writers. A counter-petition that stressed the defensive nature of the conflict and opposed significant annexations received only 141 signatures.[38] Still, opponents of the war made themselves heard, at least until the censors intervened. Wilhelm Herzog, in particular, took Mann to task in *Das Forum*, the most outspoken pacifist journal of the day; subjected to repeated censorship, the publication was banned permanently in September 1915. In November 1914, Hermann Hesse, who had moved to Switzerland, published an appeal to intellectuals in the *Neue Zürcher Zeitung*; in particular, he criticized "those who take part in the great events by dragging the war into their studies, and at their desks write bloody battle hymns or articles fanning and wrathfully fomenting hatred between peoples. That is perhaps the worst."[39]

The most prominent opponent of Mann was none other than his own brother, Heinrich, an advocate of left-liberal politics. The outbreak of war had halted the serialization of his novel, *Der Untertan* (Man of Straw), a devastating critique of Wilhelmine society. He opposed the war from the outset, but censorship forced him to be circumspect. In November 1915 he published the most notorious of his coded works, a lengthy essay on Emile Zola. The key passage was ostensibly a recounting of Zola's *La Débâcle*, a novel about the defeat of France's Second

Empire in the fall of 1870. The phrasing made it clear, however, that Heinrich Mann had Germany's Second Empire in mind: "An Empire [*Reich*] that was based on force and not on freedom, justice, and truth, an Empire in which people only commanded and obeyed, made money and were exploited, but in which humanity was never respected, could not be victorious, even if it were to march off with superhuman force." Heinrich Mann not only predicted the collapse of the German war effort, but he also foresaw what would follow: "Democracy is a gift of defeat."[40] The essay became an instant *cause célèbre*, and the issue in which it appeared sold out immediately. The scandal was compounded by the fact that Heinrich Mann included some thinly veiled insults of his brother in the essay; the two would not speak to each other for several years. *Die weißen Blätter*, the pacifist journal in which the piece appeared, was shut down soon thereafter; it had long been a thorn in the censors' eyes. Its editor, René Schickele, an Alsatian at home in both French and German culture, moved the publication to Switzerland in April 1916.

The expressionist response

Within the context of "high" art, the greatest concentration of anti-war sentiment was to be found among the expressionists. To be sure, before the war some of them had displayed an unease with the tranquillity of civil life. The poet Georg Heym wrote in 1910: "This peace is so foul, oily and greasy as sticky polish on old furniture. . . . If only someone would start a war, it can even be an unjust one."[41] That same year, Alfred Walter Heymel wrote a poem that exclaimed:

> Im Friedenreichtum wird uns tödlich bang.
> Wir kennen Müssen nicht noch Können oder Sollen;
> wir sehnen uns, wir schreien nach dem Kriege.
>
> Amid peace's richness we feel deathly anxious.
> We know not Must nor Can nor Should;
> We long, we scream for war.[42]

When the desired war finally came, many expressionists flocked to the standards. Their disillusionment was swift. The expressionists belonged to the youngest generation of writers and artists, and hence were the first to volunteer – and the first to die. Among poets, Hans Leybold was killed on 9 September, followed by Alfred Lichtenstein on 25 September. Ernst Stadler died on 30 October; less than a week later, Georg Trakl committed suicide on the Eastern front. August Stramm perished in September 1915.

The most important expressionist forum for anti-war sentiment was the journal *Die Aktion*, edited by Franz Pfemfert. In August 1914, to avoid problems with the censors, Pfemfert decided to limit his publication to art and literature, but the works he printed were as eloquent and explicit as any essays. The issue of 24 October, for example, included "poems from the battlefield" by Wilhelm Klemm, who had volunteered for the front but was overwhelmed by his experiences:

> Mein Herz ist so groß wie Deutschland und Frankreich zusammen,
> Durchbohrt von allen Geschossen der Welt.

> My heart is so large as Germany and France together,
> Pierced by all projectiles in the world.[43]

The grandiose imagery, the conflation of self and world were typical of expressionist lyrics even before the war. Now that style proved well suited to the hymns to peace and humanity that Pfemfert published in his journal, by authors like Johannes R. Becher, Albert Ehrenstein, and Franz Werfel. Klemm's embracing of the enemy also was typical of *Die Aktion*. The cover of the issue in which his battlefield poems appeared featured Egon Schiele's "Image of the Fallen Poet Charles Péguy" – an homage to a fellow writer who just happened to be fighting for the supposed "enemy." In 1915 and 1916 the journal devoted special issues to the literature of Belgium, England, France, Italy, and Russia. The most damning rubric in the journal, inaugurated in April 1915, was entitled "Ich schneide die Zeit aus" (I cut out the times). In it, Pfemfert simply quoted verbatim the worst of the militarist and chauvinist verbiage of his day: songs, sermons, speeches, children's books, as well as essays by professors, authors, and intellectuals.

Theater also became a forum for expressionist works, to the extent that the censors permitted. Expressionist dramas written prior to the war had focussed on the struggles of young people with their familial and social surroundings; father–son conflicts were especially prominent (and parricide was often the "solution" to such problems). As the war progressed, the terrorism of technology, both in the factory and on the battlefield, became an increasingly significant theme. The expressionists sought to dramatize humanity's breakout from its social confines and to depict the birth of a "new man." In his famous definition of expressionist drama, penned in 1918, Kurt Pinthus wrote: "Here man [*der Mensch*] explodes in front of man." One of the first major expressionist works inspired by the war was Reinhard Goering's *Seeschlacht* (Naval Battle). A medical student at the outbreak of hostilities, Goering was assigned to a military hospital, where he soon contracted tuberculosis; he spent the remainder of the war as a convalescent in Switzerland. Inspired by news of the battle of Jutland (May 1916), he wrote a frenetic work that takes place in the gun tower of a battleship. The key figure is the Fifth Sailor – as in many expressionist dramas, Goering's characters do not have personal names – who contemplates mutiny as the play begins, but then is so exhilarated by the ensuing battle that he becomes the most enthusiastic gunner. In a dialogue with the First Sailor, the Fifth Sailor, in his mutinous stage, systematically derides the standard reasons for Germany's naval ventures ("because our country commands us," "for freedom of the seas," etc.). There is something more holy than nationhood and war, he claims, and that is an immediacy of humanity: "Was sein kann zwischen Mensch und Mensch!" (What could be between man and man).[44] Even though the Fifth Sailor is caught up in the excitement of battle, he dies – and the play ends – with these ambiguous words: "The battle continues, do you hear? Don't close your eyes yet. I've been a good gunner, right? I'd also have been a good mutineer! Right? But shooting just came easier to us? Right? It must have come easier to us?"[45] Alarmed by the tone of the play, the censors allowed it to be premiered only as a closed performance for an invited audience in Dresden (February 1918).

Similar restrictions were placed on Fritz von Unruh's *Ein Geschlecht* (A Generation), which was presented first at a private performance in Darmstadt in January 1918; closed performances followed in Frankfurt and Berlin, to great critical acclaim. The descendant of a long line of Prussian officers, Unruh had been trained at an elite military academy along with the Kaiser's sons. He lost his commission in 1911 after the premiere of *Offiziere* (Officers), a play that questioned the glorification of war. *Louis Ferdinand Prinz von Preußen*, written in 1913, was personally banned by the Kaiser, who exercised his legal option to prohibit dramas that depicted any of his Hohenzollern ancestors. Despite these tussles, Unruh volunteered enthusiastically in August 1914, but was soon disillusioned, as his previous qualms about war proved all too real. Though written at the front, *Ein Geschlecht*, unlike *Seeschlacht*, is neither historically nor geographically specific. Set in a graveyard on a mountaintop, it is seemingly timeless. The main character is the mother; caught up in wartime patriotism at the outset of the play, she is happy to send her sons into battle, and she disowns those too "cowardly" to fight. After horrific struggles – both verbal and physical – with her own children, she is transformed into a symbol of regenerative, life-sustaining matriarchy opposed to the destructive, bloodthirsty system that sustains the war. The abstraction from historical specificity, and the unreal quality of its ecstatic language, probably were crucial in allowing closed performances of *Ein Geschlecht* during wartime.

The same did not apply to *Gas I*, written in 1917 by Georg Kaiser, some of whose satires of Wilhelmine society had been banned by the censors even before 1914. Though it too was not located in any particular time and country, *Gas I* hit too close to home. The play deals with a new, superior source of energy (a fictitious "gas") that can be produced in only one factory. After a horrendous explosion, the owner decides that it is too dangerous to exploit, and he proposes to shut the plant down. But his plans are foiled not only by other industrialists, military officials, and politicians; even the workers in the factory are so emotionally bonded to their jobs that they demand it stay open, despite the danger. In the end, the owner is dispossessed, as capitalists and politicians plot a war. Kaiser's dramatization of what later generations would call the military–industrial complex, and his depiction of a working class totally coopted by capitalist values, was too much for the censors, who kept the work off the stage for the duration of the war. It was premiered in Frankfurt and Düsseldorf at the end of November 1918.

The most politicized of the budding playwrights was Ernst Toller. Enrolled at the university of Grenoble when the war broke out, he fled France and volunteered for the Bavarian army. He fought actively at the front, including Verdun, and received medals and promotions; yet he was increasingly distraught over his experiences and suffered a breakdown in 1916. In 1917 he became caught up in the anti-war politics of the Independent Social Democratic Party, and he began to write his first play, *Die Wandlung* (The Transformation). The work dramatizes the metamorphosis of an enthusiastic war volunteer into an artist who leads a popular uprising against the state. Realistic scenes alternate with fantastic dream sequences, including one in which a doctor attaches mechanical limbs to horribly crippled veterans and sends them back into battle. Toller read scenes from that play, as well as his poems, to groups of pacifist students and anti-war workers. He played an active role in organizing the massive munition workers' strike in Munich at the end of January 1918; his ensuing imprisonment gave him the leisure to complete the drama. Obviously, *Die Wandlung* could not be performed until the imperial system collapsed. When it was premiered in September 1919, Toller was in jail once again, this time for having been a leader of the Munich Soviet Republic in April 1919.

Turning to the visual arts, we encounter some of the same dynamics as in other media. It came as no surprise that in August 1914, an academic painter like Friedrich August von Kaulbach painted a large allegorical "Germania" in full battle gear, with eyes blazing in defiance and blond hair blowing in the wind as the countryside behind her burns.[46] What is somewhat more surprising is that similar sentiments were shared

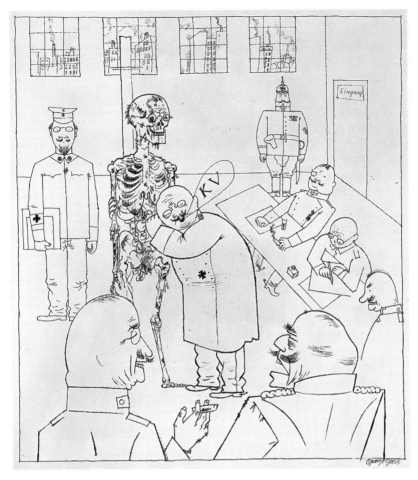

2.2   George Grosz, *Fit for active service*, 1916–1917

by Max Liebermann. The leader of the Berlin "secession" since the
1890s, he had fought numerous skirmishes, direct and indirect, with
defenders of academic art, including the Kaiser. But now he joined the
patriotic fray. When Paul Cassirer, a prominent dealer in modern
art, launched the publication *Kriegszeit* in late August, the cover of the
first issue displayed a lithograph by Liebermann. Entitled "Before the
Palace," it depicted crowds cheering the Kaiser, and was captioned with
Wilhelm's slogan of the day: "I no longer recognize any parties." The
ensuing issue presented another of his lithographs, similarly captioned
with the emperor's "Now we'll thrash them!"[47] (See Fig. 2.1.) In October

1914 Liebermann was among the ninety-three artists and intellectuals who issued the declaration defending German culture and military policies. By then, the impressionist painter Max Slevogt was coming to different conclusions. Like Liebermann, Slevogt was too old to serve, but he received permission to sketch events at the front. On 21 October he noted in his diary: "reluctantly and completely unnerved, I make watercolors of the dead. . . . Impression totally unartistic! [*Eindruck direkt unkünstlerisch!*]"[48] After two weeks he had seen enough and returned home. In 1916 and 1917 he produced a series of lithographs that ridiculed diplomats and military leaders and conjured up horrific visions of war, including one grotesque scene of dismembered men who continue to fight using their severed limbs as weapons.[49]

Not surprisingly, the young expressionist painters went through a similar transformation. Like the poets and playwrights of their generation, many initially welcomed the conflict as a means of cracking the serenity of bourgeois society. The first blow came at the end of September, when they learned that August Macke had been killed. Ernst Ludwig Kirchner suffered a mental breakdown soon after being inducted. Max Beckmann collapsed in 1915 after serving a year in the medical corps, where he sketched numerous pictures of war-wounded men in hospital wards and bodies in morgues. Otto Dix had stronger nerves, as well as luck: he survived the entire war as a machine gunner. In the 1920s he created, retrospectively, the most horrific paintings and etchings of wartime barbarism; but during the war itself, he seems to have enjoyed the thrill of battle at the same time that he recognized its cruelty. His ambivalence was captured in two works of 1915: a *Self-Portrait as Mars*, in which he appears as an angry and determined god of war, and a *Self-Portrait as a Shooting Target*, in which he stares blankly and passively awaits whatever projectile might come his way.[50] A number of graphics in which men merge with the ground and plants sprout from shattered landscapes suggest that Dix considered war part of the natural cycle – in greatly intensified form – of life, death, decomposition, and renewed life.[51]

Even Franz Marc, famous for vibrantly colorful images of animals, could not bring himself to condemn the war entirely; right up to his death at Verdun in March 1916, he sought to find some spiritual meaning behind the carnage. On the eve of the war he had already turned to abstract art: *Fighting Forms*, from the summer of 1914, shows furious black and red swirls raging against each other. A similar abstract imagery of contending forms reappeared in pencil sketches that he made at the front during the spring of 1915.[52] Just as he sensed spiritual forces in the animals that he had painted with such sensitivity before 1914, he now imputed hidden powers to the conflict. On 12 September

1914 he wrote to his wife that "the war does not make me a naturalist – on the contrary: I feel so strongly the spirit that hovers behind the battles, behind every bullet, that the Real, the Material disappears completely."[53] Whereas the war induced artists like Beckmann and Dix to adopt a bitterly incisive realism, it reinforced Marc's growing proclivity for abstraction.

Dada

Expressionism received new impetus from the conflagration, but it had already been well developed by 1914. The only truly novel artistic movement to be born during the war was dada. The term was chosen in 1916 by two Germans, Hugo Ball and Richard Huelsenbeck, to describe the activities of an international group of artists and writers who had congregated in Zurich. When Huelsenbeck moved to Berlin in January 1917, he found there like-minded individuals who had nothing but contempt for bourgeois society and high culture – not just academic art, but expressionism as well. The core of that group consisted of George Grosz and the brothers Helmut and Wieland Herzfelde. Grosz had not shared the war hysteria of August 1914; indeed, his graphic "Pandemonium" depicted the events of those days as an urban riot of crazed lunatics. But in November 1914 he volunteered for the military, since he knew that he would be drafted anyway. He was released from service in May 1915, but was called up again in January 1917; he promptly had a mental breakdown, and after several weeks in an asylum was released again. Though he never experienced battle, he had seen enough of officers and medical doctors, whom he vilified in one of the most bitter graphics to come out of the war: a doctor before a military commissioning board proclaims a decomposing corpse – probably of a soldier who has been killed in action once already – to be "K.V." (*kriegsverwendungsfähig*), that is, "fit for active service" (see Fig. 2.2). In 1916 George Grosz Americanized his first name by adding the final "e" (already as a boy, Georg had been fascinated by American popular culture, gleaned from dime novels and films). At the same time, his poetry and his graphic art underwent fundamental changes. The poems published in *Die Aktion* in 1915 bear strong traces of expressionism; by 1917, however, he was composing works full of lines from vaudeville songs and slogans from commercial advertisements. This dredging of popular culture was paralleled in his graphics, where he developed a harshly angular, seemingly puerile style that was modeled on bathroom graffiti and children's drawings. The bulk of his graphic works during the war depict urban scenes, but for him city life was as violent as any battlefield: riots, rapes, murders abounded.[54]

The activities and attitudes of Grosz were seconded by the Herzfelde brothers. Helmut was so disgusted by the patriotic rhetoric that he privately Anglicized his name to John Heartfield (though he did not use it publicly until after 1918). In July 1916 the brothers launched a journal entitled *Neue Jugend*; to avoid petitioning for the police approval required for new publications, they labeled the first issue "number 7" in order to confuse the watchdogs. The journal, soon printed in newspaper format, had a highly innovative layout, with a confusing mixture of typefaces, and photos and graphics printed askew. The Herzfelde brothers' featured artist was Grosz; indeed, they published two portfolios of his graphic work in 1917. By then the three men had developed a visual and verbal art crafted from snippets of mass media and mass culture. While the *Bildungsbürger* were trying desperately to protect the status of "high" art and literature, Grosz, Herzfelde, and Heartfield recognized that the true optic and acoustic forces of the day emanated from advertisements, popular songs, and illustrated newspapers. By ripping these sights and words out of context and reconfiguring them in new combinations, they satirized commercial and political sloganeering at the same time as they developed what soon would be called "montage."

The efforts of those three prepared the ground for the dada movement that coalesced around Richard Huelsenbeck in the spring of 1918. Until the end of the war, their efforts were generally limited to semi-public readings in Berlin. In his "Dadaist Manifesto," read at the first dada *soirée* in April 1918, Huelsenbeck lambasted the expressionists for being too traditional: their pathos differed only marginally from that of conventional high culture. Ultimately they were as elitist as their supposed foes: "the hatred of the press, the hatred of advertising, the hatred of sensationalism speaks of men for whom a comfortable chair is more important than the noise of the street." Dada turned precisely to such media and to the streets to achieve a new realism, far removed from the naturalism of the nineteenth century: "The word dada represents the most primitive relationship to surrounding reality; with dadaism a new reality gains its rightful place. Life appears as a simultaneous tangle of noises, colors, and spiritual rhythms, which are adopted unperturbedly by dadaist art, along with all of the sensationalist cries and fevers of the audacious everyday psyche, in its entire brutal reality." Huelsenbeck closed his speech, and his manifesto, with the words: "Against the aesthetic-ethical mindset! Against the bloodless abstractions of expressionism! . . . For dadaism in word and image, for dadaist actions in the world. To be against this manifesto, is to be a dadaist!"[55]

The vision of Grosz, Heartfield, and Herzfelde – as well as Huelsenbeck and the other dadaists who came together in 1918 – was an urban one, seemingly distant from the battlefield. But it was born out of a home front rife with discontent. The consumer goods touted on billboards and in newspapers were unavailable to increasing numbers of citizens; the feel-good tunes of popular music mocked those aching from hunger and cold; the political and military slogans rang hollow. The suffering and violence at the military front and the home front, though of vastly different degrees, formed a continuum. In the last months of the war, Grosz painted a monumental work that showed the forces of "order" behind the chaos. *Germany: A Winter's Tale* is anchored at the base by figures of a pastor, a military officer, and a teacher who wields a stick in one hand and a volume of Goethe in the other. In the middle of the painting sits a man contentedly reading his conservative paper, drinking his beer, and eating his sausage (authentic meat ration coupons are pasted onto the painting). He is totally oblivious to the urban mayhem that surrounds him – a prostitute, a pedestrian struck by an automobile, a man carting a coffin, a sailor with a hard and determined look (surely a reference to the mutineers of October 1918). In the upper right, a spiked helmet is paired with a charcoal briquette stamped "Kaiser." The painting was prominently displayed at the "First International Dada Exhibition" in Berlin in the summer of 1920. The Nazis confiscated it from Wieland Herzfelde's apartment in March 1933, and it has not been seen since.

Surprisingly, though the dadaists despised much of wartime politics, society, and culture, they were not intransigent opponents of the war itself. In his "first dada-speech in Germany," given at a closed gathering in February 1918, Huelsenbeck said of the Zurich group in which he had taken part: "We were against the pacifists, because the war actually made it possible for us to exist in all our glory. . . . We were for the war, and today dadaism is still for the war. Things have to collide: there's still not nearly enough cruelty."[56] Paradoxically, for all his detestation of expressionism, Huelsenbeck's welcoming of the war as a means of shaking up bourgeois society was hardly different from the expressionists' attitude in August 1914. Likewise, in the activities of Grosz, Heartfield, and Herzfelde there was an irony that went deeper than any satire they themselves devised: during the last year of the war, all three were employees of Bufa and Ufa, hired to craft anti-Entente films. In late 1917, Harry Kessler, a noted connoisseur of modern art, was the cultural attaché of the German consulate in Bern, as well as the Bufa representative in Switzerland. Struck by the quality of Grosz's work, he arranged through the Foreign Office to have Grosz and Heartfield receive commissions for propagandistic cartoon films. Assisted by Wieland Herzfelde, they created a satire on the American troops that were beginning to appear at the front. Entitled *Sammy in Europa*, the work dragged into the summer of 1918. By then the American forces were no longer a laughing matter for Germany, and *Sammy in Europa*, though completed, was never screened.[57] What made George Grosz, supposedly so enamored of American culture and so hostile to the imperial system, accept employment as an anti-Yankee propagandist? Was it the cynicism that marked so much of his work? Was it opportunism, the desire to make money as well as avoid the chance of being drafted once again? At the very least, it is striking that even Grosz embodied the ambivalence and ambiguities that characterize so many of Germany's artistic and literary endeavors during the First World War.

The aftermath

The significance of the Great War for German culture was profound, though not always in obvious ways. No new major artistic trend developed out of it, aside from dada, which remained a relatively isolated movement until it disappeared after 1920. Nevertheless, the dada spirit and the dada vision – the collapsing of high art and mass culture, and the aesthetics of simultaneity and montage – repeatedly cropped up throughout the twentieth century; variants of "postmodernism" are its latest manifestation. Expressionism, though not new, displayed a burst of fresh energy during the war, and it became the dominant avantgarde of the early Weimar Republic; but it too declined after 1923, to be replaced by a "new sobriety" (*Neue Sachlichkeit*). The most profound changes wrought by the war occurred at levels deeper than artistic trends and styles. One medium in particular was fundamentally affected: film. The ban on foreign imports led to the rapid growth of the domestic industry, and toward the end of the war, its biggest players were consolidated under UFA. Germany continued to enjoy a protected film market until 1924, because foreign producers had no incentive to sell their wares in a country with an increasingly valueless currency. Ironically, it was the film industries of England, France, and Italy – so successful at producing anti-German propaganda – that eventually lost the war, since the cinemas of those nations were swamped with Hollywood movies after 1918. By the mid-1920s, the greatest film producers were the United States and Germany. German film also gained a boost in status during the war. Originally despised as "trash," it came to be recognized as an important medium of mass communication, so that the highest reaches of the German government and military sought to use it for their ends. This too was ironic: whereas the *Bildungsbürger*, the most vociferous opponents of film before 1914, had hoped the war would revive the aura of high culture, it was precisely the medium that they hated most which gained prestige during the conflagration.

Ultimately the war had the greatest impact on German culture in the realm of ideology. A profound polarization took place, which was to frame, to characterize, and to destroy the Weimar Republic. Germany's first democracy seemed, on paper, to be the state that intellectuals like Heinrich Mann had hoped for. Though a small minority during the war, supporters of a republican democracy gained numerous adherents during the 1920s; even Thomas Mann came around, and he was re-united, personally and politically, with his brother. Social Democracy, which had always been republican, proved to be an even greater bulwark of the new state. Pacifism too became a popular sentiment; the resounding success of Erich Maria Remarque's *All Quiet on the Western Front* (1929) indicated that traditional glorification of war rang hollow with large sectors of the population. But the republican middle was fragile and embattled. Worsening domestic conditions during the war, compounded by post-war economic traumas, spurred a left-wing split-off in the form of the Communist Party of Germany (KPD). It enjoyed the sympathy of some notable artists (beginning with Grosz, Heartfield, and Herzfelde), and garnered the ballots of every tenth voter throughout the 1920s (and up to 17 percent during the Depression). Yet the greatest danger to the new democracy was on the right. A significant minority of veterans looked back on the war as a manly, thrilling, invigorating experience – an attitude expressed in Ernst Jünger's *In Stahlgewittern* (Storm of Steel, 1920) and numerous other works. Enthusiasts of the military tended to detest the new democracy, and they subscribed to the anti-Semitism that had gained so much ground during the conflagration. Their political culture and cultural politics soon found a spokesman, and a leader, in a fellow veteran of the Great War – Adolf Hitler.

3   Culture in Poland during World War I

Harold B. Segel

Prelude

The year 1997 marks the two-hundredth anniversary of the founding of the Polish legions by General Jan Henryk Dąbrowski (1755–1818). The event is one of singular importance in Polish history and has a direct bearing on the subject of this chapter. Three partitions, in 1772, 1793, and 1795, erased Poland from the map of Europe. A Polish state was not to come into existence again until after World War I, in 1918. The unwillingness of the Poles to accept the harsh reality of indefinite partition prompted various actions aimed at the total or partial recovery of their lost lands. The most dramatic of these actions were the November Insurrection of 1830, and the January Insurrection of 1863. Both broke out in Russian Poland, and both failed badly.

Prior to the November Insurrection, and indeed within a few years of the defeat of Kościuszko's rebellion in 1794, the Poles turned to France as their best hope for national liberation. French and Polish political interests had converged from 1793, when France faced two of the partitioning powers, Austria and Prussia, in the War of the First Coalition. The first concrete expression of this convergence was the organization in 1797 and 1798 of Polish auxiliary legions to fight under French banners. When Napoleon came to power, the advantage was obvious: thousands of new recruits for his armies. For the Poles, in despair after Kościuszko's defeat and the third partition, Napoleon seemed their only savior. Little wonder that he became at the very least a demigod to them, even in defeat, and that a Polish Napoleonic myth arose that endured well into the twentieth century.

The first Polish legion, which was to serve under General Dąbrowski, was formed in northern Italy in 1797. Two additional legions were raised in 1798 and 1800. The foundation was thus laid for one of the greatest of modern Polish legends, the echoes of which resounded in still partitioned Poland in World War I. What greater proof of the legendary significance of the Napoleonic legions than the fact that their marching song, composed by the legionnaire poet Józef Wybicki and known as the "Marsz, Dąbrowski," became the Polish national anthem. Its concluding verse, "Marsz, marsz, Dąbrowski, z ziemi włoskiej do Polski" (March, march, Dąbrowski, from the Italian lands to Poland), encapsulates the dream the Franco-Polish alliance was meant to fulfill.

Legend has a way of overpowering reality, and so too in the case of the Polish legions. Although they wore distinctive Polish uniforms and bore on their shoulder patches the Italian slogan "Gli uomini liberi sono fratelli" (Free men are brothers), the legionnaires were never used to further the cause of Polish independence. Instead, in a bitter irony, they were sent into action to crush opposition to French rule, to suppress movements of liberation such as their own. The First Legion was soundly defeated by the Russians under Suvorov at Trebbia in 1799; the Second, in the battle of Marengo in 1800. The Legion of the Rhine suffered a similar fate at Hohenlinden. Surviving Polish troops were incorporated into an army of occupation whose task was to prevent further outbreaks of Italian resistance. More ignominiously, new Polish legions were raised and sent in 1802–1803 to the island then known as Santo Domingo to quell black slaves attempting to overthrow French rule.

In cynical recompense for the heroic sacrifices the Poles had made on his behalf, Napoleon, victorious over the Prussians in 1806, saw fit to create a small Polish "entity" from lands taken from the former Prussian partition. "Poland" was deliberately excluded from the name of the state and so it became known as the Duchy of Warsaw. It lasted from 1807, when it was established in accordance with the terms of the Treaty of Tilsit, until, after Napoleon's defeat, it was dismantled by the Congress of Vienna in 1815. Lacking in power, its political system a reflection of French tradition, the Duchy was little more than a symbol to the Poles. To Napoleon, however, it was a recruitment station for thousands of Poles to fight in his campaign in Spain during the Peninsular War of 1808–1813 and, in far greater numbers, in the massive and ultimately doomed assault on Russia in 1812.

If paid in small coin by the French for their loyalty, the Poles who fought under Napoleon's banners in the brief history of the Duchy of Warsaw added new glory to the legend of the legions by their courage. There was the remarkable victory at the defile of Somosierra, Spain, in 1808 by a band of a few hundred Polish light horsemen under the command of Lieutenant Jan Kozietulski that made possible the French capture of Madrid. And there was the gallantry of Prince Józef Poniatowski, the commander of the Fifth Polish Corps of the Grande Armée, who refused to lay down his arms and surrender his men to the Russians after their triumpiant march into Warsaw in February 1813. Instead, he joined the retreating French forces in Germany and met his end in the Battle of Nations at Leipzig on 19 October. Surrounded by Prussian and Russian forces at the River Elster, and mortally wounded, Poniatowski preferred to plunge his horse into the river and drown rather than yield.

The legend of the Polish Napoleonic legions has long overshadowed their exploitation at the hands of Napoleon, who saw in them only cannon fodder for his schemes of imperial conquest. The legend was the creation in part of legionnaires themselves who immortalized their own exploits in song and verse. This body of legionnaires' literature, which runs the whole gamut of emotions of the men who flocked to Napoleon's banners in the mistaken belief that they were the vanguard of a liberated Poland, has more historical than artistic value. Yet whatever its shortcomings, the great Polish Romantic poet, Adam Mickiewicz (1798–1855), devoted ecstatically inordinate length to it in the lectures he gave in 1840–1844 at the Collège de France as the holder of the first chair in Slavic literatures.

Myth Redux: The legions of Piłsudski

The legacy of the Polish Napoleonic legions assumed new life during World War I when it demonstrated once again the tenacity and power of legend. Even before the outbreak of the war, the man of the hour to the Poles was another military figure, this time not a foreigner, as Napoleon had been, but a native Pole, General Józef Piłsudski (1867–1935). A sometime socialist and conspirator against Russia, which he saw as the main stumbling block in the path of regained Polish statehood, Piłsudski went on to become a military hero of legendary proportions and the dominant figure in the political life of the Polish Second Republic until his death in 1935.[1] Remembered for his leadership of the Polish armed forces in the bitter Polish–Soviet war of 1919–1920, and long associated with conservatism and dictatorship, Piłsudski was privately revered and publicly ignored, or condemned, in the nearly forty-five years of post-War II communist rule in Poland. However, with the downfall of communism, Piłsudski has again been reinstated as a national hero. New statues of him have been erected, and a plethora of Piłsudski memorabilia have flooded the market – many of World War I and interwar origin and including postcards featuring Wojciech Kossak's well-known painting of Piłsudski atop his favorite steed "Kasztanka" (Chestnut).

An austere commander and political leader, with little patience for the intricacies of parliamentary routine, Piłsudski none the less commanded nothing so spectacularly as the loyalty of his followers and the affection of much of the Polish populace. When World War I broke out in August 1914, so too did an astonishing array of Polish political organizations, both in the partitioned country and elsewhere in Europe. Convinced that the outcome of the war would bring new Polish statehood, the various political organizations sought to align themselves with whatever side seemed best able to deliver on promises of greater Polish autonomy or even independence.

Polish political opinion at the time was divided into two main groupings. The right-wing nationalists, under the leadership of Roman Dmowski (1864–1939), the other commanding political figure of the time, were affiliated with the National Democratic Movement (Endecja) which Dmowski had founded in 1897.[2] Dmowski believed that German imperialism posed the greatest threat to Polish sovereignty and that for their own salvation the Poles had no choice but to seek Russian protection. In return for their loyalty to Russia, the Poles expected to be granted a greater measure of autonomy within the Russian empire. When World War I came, Dmowski and his followers embraced the Russian cause while at the same time looking to the Western Allies for help. With a strategically different outlook, Piłsudski threw his support to the Central Powers, Germany and Austria-Hungary, in the belief that they woud defeat Russia and in turn would be defeated by the Allies, all of which would eventually work to the advantage of the Poles.[3]

Piłsudski was in a position to offer the Central Powers not only political but also military support. Before the outbreak of the war he had organized paramilitary units innocuously dubbed "Riflemen" (*Strzelcy*). These were formed in Austria with the blessing of the Habsburg authorities who thought that in time of war they might be of advantage. Anxious to keep Piłsudski and his troops on their side, the Austrians also conferred on him the rank of brigadier-general.

When the "great war" that so many people greeted with extraordinary enthusiasm erupted, Piłsudski lost little time in expanding his paramilitary organization and hastening its transformation into a full-fledged fighting force. This he accomplished on 16 August 1914, when he merged his "Riflemen" and other similar organizations that aligned with him politically into the Polish Legions.[4]

Piłsudski's name for his new force was a conscious evocation of the legend and myth of the Polish legions of the Napoleonic era. What Piłsudski sought to convey was the continuity of the Polish armed struggle for independence and the loyalty and heroism for which the

Napoleonic legions had earned justifiable renown. If questions had been raised from time to time throughout the nineteenth century as to the efficacy of the legions – in terms of the Polish liberation struggle – these tended for the most part to become obscured by pride in the legion-naires' nobility of purpose and willingess to sacrifice their lives for the sake of the Polish cause.

Fully cognizant of the place the Polish legions of the past held in the Polish consciousness, Piłsudski deliberately sought to envelop himself and his new legions in the aura of that same legend. Thus the units organized by Piłsudski in World War I were the modern version of the Napoleonic legions, this time sure to achieve what had eluded the legions of yore. By calling his armed units "legions" Piłsudski took careful aim at the Polish heartstrings. The more popular support he had for his cause, the greater the number of troops he could recruit, the more clout he had with the Prussian and Austrian military and polit-ical authorities, and the greater his role in post-war political life in the event the Central Powers won the war. That Piłsudski was already looking ahead to the post-war period at the time he created his legions is manifest, I believe, in the very name he chose for his military organ-ization. The calculation proved wise. Even though the Central Powers were eventually defeated (Piłsudski had broken with them beforehand), the collapse of Russia in the war and the subsequent revolution that gave birth to the new Soviet state meant that the Allies held nearly all the cards in their hands at war's end. President Woodrow Wilson's insist-ence on the absolute need to reestablish an independent Polish state in Europe after the war prevailed, and thus the Second Republic came into existence. As the single most powerful figure of authority to emerge from the war, Piłsudski was naturally thrust to the forefront of post-war Polish politics. The legend, truly the mystique, of the legions had traveled with him and guaranteed his place in Polish history and lore.

Throughout the interwar period, until his death, Piłsudski remained ever cognizant of the mass popular appeal of the association of his legions with the Polish Napoleonic past and never let any appropriate anni-versary go by without public celebration. The centenary of Napoleon's death in 1921, for example, was the occasion for a plethora of state-sponsored solemnities involving processions, public lectures by distin-guished scholars, exhibitions of memorabilia in the National Museum and the Museum of the Army in Warsaw, special issues of news-papers and magazines (*Tygodnik Ilustrowany, Świat, Żołnierz polski*), and addresses by the head of the French military mission (Genral Niessel), the chief of the Polish General Staff, Sikorski, and Count Stanisław du Moriez, a delegate of the Napoleonic committee in Paris. A commemorative volume of the events was published in June 1921 in Polish and French under the respective titles *Księga Pamiątkowa Obchodu Napoleońskiego w Polsce* and *Livre d'Or du Centenaire de Napoléon en Pologne*. The scope, pomp and ceremony of the events, and the mass public turnout were extraordinary.

To understand better the mythicizing of Piłsudski and his legions during and after the war, the particular situation of the Poles on the eve of the conflict should be considered. In addressing the issue of culture in Poland during World War I, it is essential to bear in mind at the outset that no Poland existed at the time. Put differently, there was a Polish nation, distributed over three partitions, but no Polish state. The tremendous enthusiasm for the war, the eagerness to rush into combat, with which virtually the rest of Europe was afflicted, obviously could not be paralleled in whole or in kind among the Poles.

A dispirited, deeply frustrated people, mired for nearly a century and a quarter in the humiliation of partition, the Poles could view the outbreak of the war only as a mixed blessing. The belief was indeed widespread that the outcome of the war, whichever side won, would have to result in some serious change of the Polish status quo. But because the war in the East was inevitably going to be fought mostly on Polish lands, there was considerable anxiety over the toll it was bound to take on Polish cities and towns, on Polish economic life, on Polish culture, and on Polish lives. The last was by far the most immediate concern in view of the fact that young Poles were subject to conscription by opposing armies. Those living under the Prussian and Austrian partitions faced the necessity of serving in the armies of the Central Powers; those living in the Russian partition had to don Russian uniforms. Thus, in a very real sense, for the Poles, World War I was a civil war, with brother opposing brother. This painful dilemma is reflected in one of the most popular poems to come out of the war, "Ta, co nie zginęła" (That which has not perished, composed September 1914) by Edward Słoński (1874–1926), a well-known writer of patriotic soldiers' verses during World War I. Several of Słoński's poems were widely read, reprinted in popular papers and magazines, recited, and memorized. In simple verse, Słoński poignantly captured the true horror of what this particular war meant to the Poles. I will quote just the first stanza in the original so that the poem's simplicity can be appreciated, and then most of the rest of the work in unrhymed English translation:

> Rozdzielił nas, mój bracie,
> zły los i trzyma straż –
> w dwóch wrogich sobie szańcach
> Patrzymy śmierci w twarz . . .

Evil fate has divided us, my brother,
and stands guard –
in two hostile trenches
we stare death in the face.

In trenches full of groaning,
alert to the roar of shells,
we stand opposite one another –
I – your enemy; you – my enemy!

The forest weeps, the earth weeps,
the whole world trembles in flames –
in two hostile trenches,
we stand, you and I.

Hardly has the dawn come up
when shells begin to fly,
with a murderous whistle
you make yourself known.

Down on our low trenches
a hail of shrapnel descends,
and you call out to me and say:
"It's me, your brother . . . your brother!" . . .

Ah, think not of me, my brother,
as you go into mortal combat,
and stand bravely, like a knight,
in the fire of my shots!

And if you spot me from afar,
take me right into your sights,
and fire a Muscovite bullet
Right into a Polish heart.

For I see it now quite clearly,
and dream of it each night,
that That Which Has Not Perished
will grow from out our hearts.[5]

The title of the poem, and the last line, printed always in capitals, are drawn from the opening verse of the Polish national anthem, "Jeszcze Polska nie zginęła" (Poland has not yet perished), originally the marching song of the Polish Napoleonic legions.

The partitioned status of the Poles not only positioned brother against brother in the war, but also imposed a strict censorship that remained in force throughout the conflict. Political demonstrations, public manifestations, like political satire, were permitted only to the extent that they were controlled by the partitioning authorities, obviously for their own ends. Hence, the Prussians and Austrians both fostered and, in a sense, licensed anti-Russian propaganda, while in the Russian partition, the same was true with respect to propaganda aimed at the Prussians and Austrians. To no small degree, the Prussians and Austrians had an easier time in their campaign to win Polish loyalty and turn the Poles against the Russians. While neither Prussia nor Austria were model occupiers in the long period of the partitions, the two great Polish insurrections of the nineteenth century had erupted in Russian Poland and were directed against Russian rule. Both of them, but especially the January Insurrection of 1863, were brutally crushed. Russification, which had not been pursued aggressively before 1863, became oppressive in the Russian partition in the wake of the suppression of the January Insurrection. Polish animosity toward the Russians, notwithstanding their ethnic kinship as Slavs, understandably ran deep and tended to offset hostile feelings toward the Prussians and Austrians. Whatever their dislike and distrust of the Germans, the Poles generally regarded them as more enlightened than the Russians.

The Austrians were also viewed more sympathetically than the Russians, despite the deliberate policy of economic impoverishment long pursued by the Habsburg authorities in Galicia. Moreover, in the last decades of the nineteenth century, Austrian military setbacks coupled with more insistent demands for autonomy on the part of the huge Slavic minorities of the Habsburg empire, resulted in concessions in both the cultural and political spheres. Out of necessity, the Austrian partition became the most liberal by the turn of the century, a fact reflected in the emergence of Kraków as the seat of an impressive florescence of the arts and intellectual life. Thus, although military service in the armies of any of the partitioning powers was loathed by the Poles, above all because it pitted brother against brother, the possible toppling of Imperial Russia in the war excited hopes concerning the regaining of Polish lands as a precondition of Polish independence. Also softening Polish attitudes toward the Austrians was the fact that it was in their partition, and with their support, that Piłsudski had raised his legions.

As the figure of Piłsudski loomed ever larger, and the parallels between his legions and those of the Napoleonic period became more widely drawn, young Poles flocked from all over to enlist in the legions. Eventually, the new Polish legions enjoyed their own mystique and were well on their way to achieving legendary status in their own right. The legionnaire poets of the Napoleonic era, whom Mickiewicz extolled at the Collège de France, had their counterparts among Piłsudski's legionnaires, poet-soldiers such as Józef Mączka, Stanisław Długosz (Tetera), Jerzy Żuławski, Bolesław Wieniawa-Długoszewski, Józef Andrzej Teslar, Marian Dunin-Majewski, Wacław Denhoff-Czarnocki, Feliks

Gwiżdż, and Artur Oppman (who wrote under the name Or-Ot), an indefatigable writer of popular poems on Napoleonic and Piłsudskian themes. Piłsudski's First Brigade also had its own marching song, as had the first legion organized under the command of General Dąbrowski in 1797. And if a country can have only one national anthem – for Poland it was the marching song of Dąbrowski's legions – then in Polish popular culture of the World War I and interwar periods the marching song of Piłsudski's legions enjoyed the stature of a second anthem. The song was written by the legionnaire poet, Tadeusz Biernacki, and comprises the following verses (in translation and minus the refrains):

> We are the First Brigade –
> The Legions are – a beggar's [soldier's, in later editions] song,
> The Legions are – a sacrificial lamb,
> The Legions are – a soldier's boot,
> The Legions are – the fate of desperadoes!
>
> We, the First Brigade,
> Are a troop of riflemen.
> We've hurled ourselves onto the pyre – our fate in life,
> Onto the pyre, the pyre . . .
> On, how much torment, how much suffering,
> Oh, how much blood and tears shed,
> Yet nonetheless, there's not a doubt
> Our wanderings' end has strengthened us! . . .
>
> They shouted that we had grown dull,
> That we no longer believed want and will are one!
> In solitude we poured our blood,
> But our dear Leader was with us! . . .[6]
>
> Today we're looked at differently,
> And they want to join our ranks.
> They tell us that they esteem us,
> But now it's time for our reply! . . .
>
> We don't want your recognition,
> Nor your speeches, nor your tears!
> The time of pleading for your hearts,
> Your purses, has come to an end! . . .
>
> Today it's time to settle accounts
> For the torment of hearts and days of torture.
> Don't ask for pity then,
> The principle is: For blood, seek blood! . . .
>
> Today in unity our strength.
> We are creating Poland – our forebears' myth,
> If you lack strengh in this endeavor,
> You'll earn the shame of your heirs![7]

3.1   A young Polish legionnaire in full dress

More indicative yet of the conscious myth-building taking place around
the figure of Piłsudski during the war was the publication in Wilno in
1916 of a collection of poems in honor of Piłsudski under the title *Pieśń
o Józefie Piłsudskim* (Song of Józef Piłsudski). The first poem in the
anthology is a paraphrase of the actual Polish national anthem that
links the fate of Poland with that of Piłsudski's Riflemen and Piłsudski
himself. I quote the opening lines first in Polish:

> Jeszcze Polska nie zginęła,
> Póki Strzelcy żyją,
> Co nam chciwość wrogów wzięła,

To Strzelcy odbiją.
Marsz, marsz Piłsudski, z Tobą łaska Boża,
Zbudujemy Polskę od morza do morza . . .[8]

(Poland has not yet perished, / So long as the Riflemen live. / What
the greed of our enemies has taken, / The Riflemen will recover. /
March, march Piłsudski, God's grace is with you, / We shall build
Poland from sea to sea.)[9]

Of the writers who fought with Piłsudski, the most prominent was
Juliusz Kaden-Bandrowski (1885–1944). He is best known for his novels
Generał Barcz (General Barcz, 1923) and *Czarne skrzydła* (Black Wings,
1925–1929), the first about a military strong man with political ambitions modeled presumably on the figure of Piłsudski; the second, a grim,
painstakingly detailed picture of conditions in the Silesian coal mine
region. As the chronicler of the First Brigade, Kaden-Bandrowski wrote
a series of eyewitness accounts of the campaigns in which the legions
fought – *Bitwa pod Konarami* (The Battle of Konary, 1915), *Piłsudczycy*
(Piłsudskians, 1915), *Mogiły* (Graves, 1916), and *Na progu* (On the
Threshold, 1928). By and large collections of vignettes devoted mostly
to individual combatants, they give a compelling sense of immediacy
about the events described. Kaden-Bandrowski also published a German article on the legions ("Polnische Legionen 1914–1915") in the
Österreichische Illustrierte Zeitung in Vienna in 1915.

Into the maelstrom: war and occupation

Mobilization in Russian Poland was announced on 30 July 1914. Dark-
red posters suddenly appeared all over Warsaw in the late evening
proclaiming the following day, the 31st, as the first official day of mobilization. Restaurants throughout the city were closed for the occasion
by order of the imperial authorities, but coffeehouses kept their usual
hours and became the principal places of meeting and the dissemination of news. Because of the censorship, Polish newspapers had to be
circumspect in their coverage of the war. In general, they were limited
to reporting "great" Russian victories and "heavy" German and Austrian
losses. However, any incident deemed capable of arousing Polish wrath
toward the Central Powers was given extensive coverage, usually on the
front page. An example of this was the so-called Kalisz tragedy. Shortly
after the Prussian major, Preusker, became commandant of the city, he
imposed a heavy burden of financial "contributions" on the town populace and in this manner collected some 27,000 rubles. More heinous
was his pummeling of the city with shells from artillery batteries emplaced
on the heights above it, setting fires and killing a number of people. As

if this were not enough, Preusker also ordered machine guns to fire on civilians, including women and childen. On 7 August, fires were started at the town hall and other buildings in the city.[10] A film made about the event, *Krwawe dni Kalisza* (Kalisz's Bloody Days), was shown widely in Warsaw. Equally popular was the cabaret satire "Wiluś i spółka" (Willie and Company), mocking, of course, the German Kaiser Wilhelm. The restricted and slanted war reporting in the Polish newspapers created a vacuum for real news as opposed to propaganda. The vacuum came to be filled by the *poczta pantoflowa* (slippers' mail), which made its way from coffeehouse to coffeehouse. Since this was a form of verbal communication the Russians had no way of controlling, before long the true nature of the early course of the war became common knowledge.

In the early months of the war, while still in control of Russian Poland, the Russians made a half-hearted effort to win Polish support and loyalty. Toward this end, on 14 August 1914, Grand Duke Nikolai Nikolaevich, then commander of the Russian army, promised the Poles autonomy as well as freedom of faith and the unrestricted use of their national language. What the Grand Duke expected from the Poles in return for his gesture of Russian magnanimity was for them to extract the "sword of Grunwald" and stand beside the imperial armies which, after the war was won, would bring them the promised freedoms, of course under the "scepter of the Russian Emperor."[11]

But the tide of war turned against the Russians. After the electrifying German victory at Tannenberg in 1914, the Central Powers pressed ahead. A year later, in August 1915, they entered Warsaw. Except for the advance of General Brusilov's army into Polesie and eastern Galicia in 1916, the Germans and Austrians remained in firm control of the Polish lands until the end of the war. It was as if Prussia and Austria had in fact absorbed the Russian partition into their own. But this was no longer the nineteenth century. A war was in progress, its outcome still not a foregone conclusion. Cognizant of the necessity of winning over the Poles to their cause, the Central Powers drummed up as much anti-Russian sentiment as they could while at the same time making lavish promises to the Poles. The territories conquered by the Germans and Austrians were administratively divided under miliary rule, for the time being, into German and Austrian zones. The head of the German zone, with its center in Warsaw, was General Hans von Beseler (1850–1921), a respected siege expert who was appointed governor-general. While, in reality, German and Austrian plans for the post-war political remapping of East Central Europe envisaged no more than a limited reconstitution of a Polish political entity, Beseler presented to the Poles a more optimistic vision of the future. On 5 November 1916, at 12 noon, in the ballroom of the Royal Castle in Warsaw, before an audience of dignitaries representing the Central Powers and the Poles, including the future World War II Polish leader, Władysław Sikorski, then a colonel in Piłsudski's legions, the military ruler of German-occupied Poland pronounced the "will of the allied emperors of Germany and Austria" that from lands liberated from Russian rule, an independent kingdom of Poland would be reestablished as a hereditary and constitutional monarchy[12]. With the Russians presumably on the run, the Germans were counting thereby on Polish assistance in the war against the Allies. Despite the pomp and ceremony of the occasion, the Poles were noticeably unenthusiastic, regarding the proclamation as a transparent ploy. But Beseler was thinking above all as a professional soldier, and the evidence indicates clearly that he was firm in his belief that by creating the façade of an independent Poland he would be able to deliver at least three divisions of Polish volunteers to fight on the side of the Germans. His plan had in fact been presented to General Ludendorff, who viewed it with favor.

To convince the Poles of his sincerity, Beseler followed his proclamation with the unfurling of the Polish flag from the window of the castle as a German orchestra played the Dąbrowski march.[13] Out of deference to the national standard, and on hearing the strains of the national anthem once again, Poles on the street outside the castle removed their hats. But as they did so, they cried out, swept away by the emotions of the moment: "Long live independent Poland!," "Convene the Polish Diet!," and, as they were leaving the scene, "Out with the Germans!" Undaunted, the Germans allowed a performance that evening at the Opera of Stanisław Moniuszko's *Halka* (two acts in 1847, enlarged to four acts in 1858), the Polish national opera. This was a significant gesture in view of the nationalistic and patriotic character of the work. The house was packed and included Beseler himself accompanied by a resplendently attired German retinue, among them the much disliked, and feared, head of the German police in Warsaw, Glasenapp.

The Germans felt secure enough in their occupation of Warsaw to allow the Poles to celebrate a long banned national holiday of great symbolic significance. Under the Russians, any commemoration of the Constitution of 3 May 1791 was strictly forbidden. The Russians wanted no reminder of the liberal constitution whose promulgation became the pretext for the partition of 1793. The Germans saw the matter differently, and, on 3 May 1916, Beseler himself granted permission for the holiday to be celebrated. Out of deference to Polish sensibilities, he also issued an order forbidding any German to be seen in uniform that day. In fact, the only articles of military dress visible in Warsaw on the holiday were the occasional grayish caps (*maciejówki*) of Piłsudski's legionnaires.

If the Poles were glad to see the Russians finally out of Warsaw, and apparently on the run, the German occupation was viewed with mixed feelings. The Austrians and Germans had permitted the formation of Piłsudski's legions, which gave the Poles something to feel pride over. Symbolic gestures such as the restoration of 3 May as a national holiday were similarly appreciated. Of greater importance, two centers of higher education, in which Polish was the language of instruction – the University of Warsaw and the Polytechnical Institute – were opened. Polish feelings about these events were perfectly summed up by the cover of the Warsaw satirical weekly *Muchy* (Flies) for 23 December 1915. Issued a few days before Christmas, the cover depicts a Santa Claus trudging through the snow laden with gifts. The words *Uniwersytet* and *Politechnika* separated by a star between them appear in the sky above. The caption at the bottom consists of four lines of verse: "Old and gray, / through fields and woods, / Santa makes his way. / He's carrying gifts for everyone / In these hard times of ours."

By no stretch of the imagination could the German occupation of 1915–1918 be compared to that of 1939–1945. Nevertheless, the occupiers ran a tight ship. By means of proclamations and poster bills, they made clear their limits of tolerance with respect to the conduct of the Poles during the war. Any assaults on German soldiers, any theft, for example, of military hardware, were punishable by death, which meant the hangman's noose or the firing squad. Pictures of arrested and/or executed violators of the German code of occupation appeared on poster bills, with texts in German and Polish explaining the nature of the particular infraction and the punishment meted out. The German code of conduct extended even to matters of dress and public appearance. Slovenly dress, like signs of intoxication in public, were punishable offenses.

The abandonment of Warsaw by the Russians brought noticeable improvement in the conditions of Polish social and cultural life. Public assembly was less curtailed by the Germans so long as no obvious threat to the interests of the occupiers was evident. Coffeehouses – Lourse, Jackowski, and above all Semadeni – again became vibrant centers of social intercourse and opinion; a cabaret culture also began showing new signs of life. The relatively more liberal policies in the Austrian partition at the turn of the century had made possible a resurgence of Polish cultural and intellectual life which conditions in contemporary Russian Poland could not have accommodated. As a result, Kraków, not Warsaw, was the real center of Polish literary creativity at the time. This is evident above all in the fact that the Polish modernist movement, generally known as Młoda Polska (Young Poland) and counting in its ranks such major figures as the poets Kazimierz Przerwa Tetmajer (1865–1940), Jan Kasprowicz (1860–1926), Leopold Staff (1878–1957), and Bolesław Leśmian (1878–1937), the playwright Stanisław Wyspiański (1869–1907), and the novelists Wacław Berent (1873–1940) and Stefan Żeromski (1864–1925), had Kraków as its center and was integrally bound up with the history, lore, and architecture of the city. But, as if by way of compensation, Warsaw moved to the fore of Polish cabaret life during World War I and never relinquished that position throughout the interwar period. When the famous Kraków cabaret, Zielony Balonik (The Green Balloon) – the first in Polish history – closed its doors in 1912, it was not followed by anything in that city of remotely comparable artistic significance. The balance then shifted to Warsaw where the Momus cabaret, the logical successor to the Green Balloon, had operated with considerable success from 1909 to 1911. Momus laid the foundation not only for the Warsaw cabaret of the war years, but for the effusion of cabaret during the Second Republic.

Wartime wit

The harsh realities of foreign occupation and the devastation of war could not silence the natural wit of the Varsovians. Anecdotes, satire, and jokes made the rounds of the city even in its darkest days. Word of mouth was the easiest and safest way to circulate them, and the coffeehouses were often their breeding ground. Some found their way into cabarets and even into the journals and magazines, legal and otherwise, that continued to be published during the war. The obvious targets of jokesters and satirists were the occupying powers – both Russian and German – and especially the latter because they occupied wartime Warsaw the longest; Poles who collaborated with the occupying powers; and, as one would expect during war, profiteers and speculators. The Russian evacuation of Warsaw on 5 August 1915 unleashed a flood of anti-Russian satire. The following, taken from *Muchy*, are typical. For the sake of space, the Polish has been omitted:

War Communique
To tell the truth, well, there's no Russian front any more. There's just a backside, presented for action by German bayonets.[14]

The Hero
(The poem is accompanied by the picture of a bemedalled Russian officer)

This hero of heroes
Has five orders on his chest,
And stars and medals, too.
But he's always out of powder.
So, as not to lose fame's glory,
Instead of powder, he fires sand.[15]

Girls and Sukin's Sons
(There is an untranslatable pun here in that "sukin syn" in Russian
    means "son of a bitch." The humor of the verse derives from the
    use of "sukin" ("bitch's") as the name of a Russian general.)
Russian generals used to be here,
Old Sukin was among them.
When Ninetka danced for him
He'd tip a hundred off the bat.
Mańka, the girl from the chorus,
Bore Sukin's son, y'know.
Fate plays such cruel tricks these days,
It's not worth kicking up your heels.
The world's made outcasts of us,
Though we're the ones with hearts.
We're caring girls, the lot of us,
And long for you, you Sukin's sons.[16]

When I dream . . . When they dream . . .
That the Muscovites have returned,
Officials, cops, and Cossacks,
That we're the vassals of Asiatics,
It's back to greasing palms again,
That Russian language is back again,
That the young are going down the drain,
That the Pole keeps his hopes up
That the tsar of thieves will reward him . . .[17]

Although made light of by satire, the evacuation of Polish talent along
with the Russian retreat still rankled. In some instances, the evacuation
was politically motivated, as with the editorial staffs of pro-Russian,
anti-German newspapers. The *Gazeta Warszawska* (Warsaw Gazette), for
example, was closely affiliated with the right-wing, pro-Russian National
Democratic Movement of Roman Dmowski. When the Russians quit
Warsaw, most of the editorial staff of the paper went along with them
causing the paper to suspend operations for a long period of time. The
flight of Polish performing artists also took its toll on wartime cultural
life. With the front approaching Warsaw in late fall 1914, theatrical and
other public performances were banned by the Russian authorities until
further notice. Some theater companies (the Teatr Polski, for example)
seized the moment to go on tour in such Russian cities as Moscow and

Kiev. Actors and actresses who belonged to state theaters under the Russian administration were similarly persuaded that the time was propitious for guest appearances in Russia. When the German offensive was temporarily repulsed, theatrical life in Warsaw returned to normal, or as normal as could be in time of war. But when the fortunes of war changed again, and the Russians had to evacuate Warsaw for good, a relatively large number of performers went with them, most seeking what they believed would be the greater security of Russian engagements. The Teatr Nowości (Theater of Novelty), known for its operettas, was particularly hard hit. Not only did most of its artists leave Poland, but its most popular singer, Lucyna Messal, who was also well known in Russia from previous guest performances, went along with them.[18] The resentment that this flight of performing artists might evoke among Poles is reflected in a satirical poem against Messal that appeared in *Muchy*. The poem was chosen as "best" from those ostensibly received by the weekly in response to a competition. The humor of the work derives mainly from an untranslatable pun – the similarity between the singer's name (Messal) and an old Polish word (*mesel, mesal*) for "trowel" or similar tool.

Trowel in Tar

Our diva from the operetta
Had bread, cutlets, sherbet,
And omelettes, and other goodies
To eat in Poland. But Poland
Pleases her no more, and so
She's turned her back on us,
And when Russia got it good,
The diva drowned in tar.
Off she went pretty and young,
But her grief was brief, and the harm small.
The point of this little joke, you see,
Is – a trowel in tar doesn't get hurt at all.[19]

When the extremely popular stage and screen actor, Antoni Fertner, left Warsaw in 1915 to accept a film assignment in Russia about the time the Russians were quitting the city, *Muchy* addressed this little piece to him:

Fertner

He's a stubborn comedian all right, even though he's
already got four medals. He's still full of jokes, as witty
as ever. Today he left for Russia, they can all go to . . .[20]

Nevertheless, when Polish artists began returning to Poland after the Bolshevik *coup* of 1917, Fertner was given a hero's welcome by the Warsaw public.

With the Russians gone, Polish wits trained their sights on Warsaw's new occupiers, who were regarded with only slightly less disdain. But German censorship required no less circumspection than Russian, with the result that most of the jokes and satire aimed at the new occupation relied heavily on puns and other forms of linguistic play. One favorite butt of Warsaw humor was the Council of Regents through which the Germans exercised their authority over the country. Not long after it came into existence, a drawing began making the rounds of the city showing a huge pot with the heads of three cabbages, resembling the three regents, floating around in it. Stirring the soup with a ladle was a cook in the likeness of Jan Kucharzewski, a historian and journalist who became head of the Council of Ministers on 7 December 1917.[21] As he stirred the pot, he kept saying: "Co za cholera – zupa bez selera." This is an untranslatable pun. Seler means "celery" in Polish; the literal translation of the pun would be "What the devil – soup without celery." But the pun lies in the last two words "bez selera," which refer to the German general Beseler. Hence the real meaning of the pun: "What the devil, soup à la Beseler." A satirical "credo" that began circulating through the city at the time also fixed Beseler in its sights:

I believe in the father Wilhelm and in his one and only son Beseler of Warsaw, who was conceived of a lack of Russian ammunition, and came into the world by way of requisition. I believe in the villainy of the German Reich, forced cohabitation with her, constraints on us, betrayal to the Ukrainians, and in the end starvation. Amen.

The wealthy and aristocratic Radziwiłł family also furnished the wit mill with material because of its ties to the occupying powers. Alluding to the prominent positions held by Janusz Radziwiłł, Franciszek Radziwiłł, and Maciej Radziwiłł, an oft repeated song contained the lines "Radziwiłłs, just Radziwiłłs, / Every one of them is beloved of the occupiers, / Every one of them serves the invading states: / The little one, the middle one, and the big one."

Probably the most popular satire of the German occupation came from the gifted poet and cabaret wit, Julian Tuwim (1894–1953). It was a poem called "O, kup pan to!" This is a play on words. As it appears, the words mean "Come on, buy it, mister!" But if the four words are joined together, they spell out "okupant to" ("[it's] the occupier"). The narrator of the poem describes how, when he was a child, he suffered from anemia. His father then took him to Germany for the baths. On a shopping trip, he came across a bunch of toy soldiers. The saleswoman urged the boy and his father to buy the soldiers, constantly repeating "O, kup pan to! O, kup pan to! / Bitte! Bitte! O, kup pan to! (Come on, buy it, sir! Please, buy it, sir! Please! Please! Come on, buy it, sir!)"[22]

The boy got the soldiers, and although he eventually grew tired of playing with them, he never forgot the words of the saleswoman. Now, years later, he observed, dumbstruck, how his toys, ever so much bigger, were marching through his city. Their uniform was the same and they wore the same spiked helmet atop their heads. Was he having hallucinations, he asked himself. Then, all of a sudden he recalled the saleswoman's entreaties and he realized that they were prophetic words that he now understood as "Okupant to, okupant to! / Brrrrr!! / Okupant to!" ("It's the occupier, the occupier! / Brrrrr!! / It's the occupier"! (146)

The revival of cabaret

Riding the tidal wave of enthusiasm for the new form of entertainment that engulfed almost all of Europe from the early 1880s to the outbreak of World War I, cabaret came to Poland, specifically to Kraków, in 1905.[23] This was the year in which the Green Balloon cabaret opened. It lasted until 1912, which was a respectable run at a time when cabarets were usually ephemeral, like much of their art. Following the pattern of its counterparts elsewhere in Europe, the Green Balloon was elitist in nature, run largely by and for artists and their coteries, and was open to the public only by invitation. Because of the Austrian censorship in force at the time, political satire was limited for the most part to local or regional issues. Social satire, however, easily filled the vacuum and, like the Parisian-style *chanson* and dramatic sketch, which were mainstays of the European cabaret in its early history, provided ample outlets for the talents of the participating artists. The most outstanding of them, and for most of its history the prime mover of the Green Balloon, if not in fact its founder, was the medical doctor, Tadeusz Boy-Żeleński, one of the great wits and satirists of his time.

The immediate successor of the Green Balloon was the Warsaw Momus (1909–1911), directed by Arnold Szyfman, who was to make his mark as a brilliant stage director. Momus was extraordinarily successful. Russian censorship drew a tight line around the possibilities for political satire, but the genre was by no means abandoned by Polish cabaret writers. Out of prudence, however, the satirical sketch was set outside Warsaw, usually in Poznań or Kraków, the capitals of the Prussian and Austrian partitions, respectively; audiences were already conditioned to make the appropriate mental transitions. Although indebted in part to the Green Balloon, Momus was open to a paying public, thereby anticipating the commercialization of cabaret in interwar Poland. But Szyfman and such colleagues as Konrad Tom, Leo

Belmont, and Bruno Winawer, among others, never allowed the cabaret's commercial status to compromise its artistic standards.

Small review theaters akin to cabaret arose in Warsaw during the war, and especially after the Russians had been forced to leave the city.[24] The most successful of these was Bi-Ba-Bo, which opened in 1916 under the direction of Andrzej Włast, who became one of the stars of the interwar Polish cabaret. Of the more authentic cabarets that came into existence in 1917, offering regular troupes of performers in familiar cabaret variety-theater programs, the best known were Miraż (on Nowy Świat and the corner of Świętokrzyszka), directed first by Henryk Markiewicz, then by Jerzy Boczkowski; Sfinks (located at Marszałkowska, 116), directed by Wacław Gajdziński; Argus (at Bielańska, 5), directed by Jan Stanisław Mar; and, the most famous of the group, Czarny Kot ("Black Cat", located at Marszałkowska, 125), directed by Kazimierz Wroczyński. They had all closed their doors by 1920 or 1921. Although satisfying the hunger of the public – which now included a large number of soldiers – for this sort of light entertainment, especially during the grim years 1916–1918, these wartime cabarets never achieved the artistic level or prominence of either the pre-World War I Green Balloon or Momus, or of the Qui Pro Quo (renamed "Perskie Oko," Persian Eye, in 1925), the most famous cabaret of interwar Warsaw, and Poland. Qui Pro Quo was founded by Julian Tuwim, Marian Hemar, a prolific provider of songs, poems, monologues, and sketches to the interwar cabaret, and the Hungarian Fryderyk Jarossy, who despite his fractured Polish became the most popular cabaret *conférencier* in interwar Poland.

The wartime cabarets offered much the same fare and even the same entertainers, who wandered from one locale to the other. The biggest hits were military songs, especially those composed by Piłusdki's legionnaires. The biggest hit of all was "My, pierwsza brygada" (We are the First Brigade) as sung especially by Stanisław Ratold whose reputation also rested on his stage portrayal of the elegant, aristocratically mannered man about town. Pola Negri, who won international film celebrity in her roles as a vamp, got her start as a cabaret performer at the Miraż. The kind of artistic experimentation that typified the European cabaret, including the Polish, in its early period of development, from 1881 through 1916, made no appearance in the programs of the wartime Warsaw cabaret. Understandably, given the conditions prevailing at the time, they offered a fare primarily of light entertainment with a strong emphasis on the patriotic. But occasional echoes of major political events were heard in the cabarets. Probably the best example of this is Julian Tuwim's poem on the Russian Revolution of 1917, "Wielka Teodora" (Great Teodora), which was recited at the Black Cat

3.2   Requisition. Prussian troops conscripting Poles into military
service

cabaret by one of its regulars, Maria Strońska. Written for the most part in short, sprightly lines of verse and full of the verbal brilliance for which Tuwim has long been admired, the poem reviews in broad strokes the violent, destructive nature of Russian revolts and concludes with the prophesy that when the current revolution has run its course nothing much will have changed. As if predicting the emergence of a Stalin-like leader, Tuwin declares that when everything has been destroyed, cities leveled, the "great harvest of centuries destroyed by a bloody hand" and "the mouths of prophets silenced by black fists," "HE who has been longed for," the "coming BOOR" will arise and "you will begin praying to the new deity." He continues: "The ancient spirits will assume the forms of new thugs, / Peter the Greats and Ivan Groznys will emerge, / The beast of the old 'idols' will arise on the black steppe, / Where not long ago Lev of Yasnaya Polyana beamed."[25]

The cabaret *szopka*

Despite the witty chansons Boy-Żeleński wrote for the Kraków Green Balloon, the most popular form of entertainment offered at the cabaret – and one unique to the Polish cabaret – was the *szopka*. This was an elaborate puppet show based on the Kraków Nativity puppet theater and noteworthy for its humorous intermixing of biblical and local contemporary personages. The *szopka* served primarily as a vehicle for satire aimed both at well-known members of the Kraków artistic and academic community and various aspects of Kraków and Galician society. The dialogue was written by Boy (as he is generally referred to) and other Green Balloon writers, while the rod puppets (which were used exclusively in performances) were the work of artists and local craftsmen. The *szopka* became the principal link between the pre-war and interwar Polish cabarets. Puppet shows called *kukiełki warszawskie* (Warsaw Dollies) and modelled on the *szopka* of the Green Balloon ran for a three-month period in the second season of Momus in Warsaw, but were less elaborate than their Kraków forebears. Their satire, which was often bold, also followed the Green Balloon pattern of being targeted at literary and artistic figures. In the interwar period, when the numbing censorship of the former partitioning powers had been lifted, Tuwim, Hemar, and other collaborators devised a variation on the prewar cabaret *szopka* in the form of an outright political satire in dramatic form known generically as *szopka polityczna* (political szopka). This new type of *szopka*, which satirized mostly Marshal Piłsudski's political opponents (whose number was anything but small), was the creation primarily of Julian Tuwim, Marian Hemar, and Antoni Słonimski.

The ongoing cultivation of the *szopka* as well as its transition from social and artistic to political satire is evident in what may well be the first post-Green Balloon *szopka*, the *Szopka warszawska* (Warsaw Puppet Show) by Adolf Nowaczyński (1876–1944). A satirist and playwright who was active in cabaret life both before and during the war, Nowaczyński made his literary debut in 1902 with *Małpie zwierciadło* (Monkey's Mirror), which he used to deflate various aspects of Polish modernism. Nowaczyński's barbs, delivered often with stunning verbal acrobatics, earned him a legion of enemies in his native Kraków. Their number must surely have increased, at least in some quarters, after World War I when he placed his considerable literary talent at the disposal of the right-wing, anti-Semitic National Democratic Movement of Roman Dmowski.

Written during the war, in 1916, when Warsaw was under German military administration, and published under the pseudonym Halban, Nowaczyński's *Szopka warszawska* already gives ample indication of the direction his wit was to take. Its title notwithstanding, the *szopka* is, atypically, not dramatic in form. It is instead a fairly long verse work which may not have been intended originally for cabaret performance. But since there were four cabarets in existence in Warsaw during the war – Sfinks, Miraż, Argus, and Czarny Kot – it is possible that parts of the poem were read in at least one of them. The reading of poetry, above all humorous poetry, was often part of a cabaret program.

Nowaczyński's *Szopka* is essentially a Dmowski-inspired lament over Poland's lost greatness and current humiliation. He grieves over the wartime German occupation, not only because of its harshness but because of Prussian deception and treachery that threaten the very foundations of Polish society. The threat, as he sees it, is twofold: the Germans themselves, and, under the protection of Poland's Prussian masters (which, to be sure, Piłsudski's wartime policies helped bring about) the Jews (including such distinguished scholars as the historian Marceli Handelsman and the literary historian Juliusz Kleiner) who would run rampant and bring about a Judaization of Polish culture:

> In the Warsaw "Alma Mater" in quotation marks,
> Handelsman lectures on Polish history, and
> Kleiner drills romanticism into students' heads.
> Let's hope that even
> The new faculty of theology
> Will soon become circumcised and Jewified . . .
>
> Then every one of these fine gentlemen
> Will advise the Polish people
> The simplest way even for a million
> To emigrate, in order to leave the country
> To Israel with no arrears at all.

You Jews are going to pine for Dmowski!
And you'll come to the Endek Canossa,
O Israel, barefoot and emaciated!
What was the point of stirring up
Polish youth against the Russkis the whole time
Just so that it would be led astray in the end?

Now I've got to sober you up, Hebrews!
The Germanic furor is beginning to awaken
And will find its sacrificial lamb,
And it will be you . . .

Whoever said the Germans
Are the brothers of us Sarmatians
I'll break all his bones in front of
The Church of the Franciscans.[26]

The anti-German and anti-Jewish nature of Nowaczyński's *Szopka Warszawska* was also echoed during and immediately after the war in popular pamphlets and brochures, usually published anonymously. That they originated in Dmowski's camp is beyond doubt. The chords struck are familiar: the Germans pose a worse threat to the Polish nation than the Russians; the Jews are machinating in any way they can to insure a German victory in the war since they will align themselves with whatever side they deem of advantage to their own interests and in any case feel closer to the Germans than to the Poles. Representative of this kind of literature is an anonymous pamphlet titled *Żydzi podczas wojny* (Jews during the War), probably published in 1918:

Russia has withdrawn. Her place has been taken by the Germans. The Jews are always very consistent. Now it would be very much in their interest if, with their help, Berlin weakened us. A German policy aimed at restraining the immigration of Jews into Germany suits them greatly. In the German Jews they have, after all, powerful guardians, since these guardians also do not want Polish Jews flowing into Germany and creating competition for them. So they work toward an improvement of the conditions of Jews here, naturally at our expense.

The result of all of this is that, in the new scheme of things, that is, when the Kingdom of Poland is falling under German influence, the Jews in Poland represent a privileged element. German goals coincide with Jewish goals. And the slogan of increased assimilation, or the greater entry of Jews among us and the introduction in our ranks of dissension, similarly coincides with this policy . . .[27]

Echoing Nowaczyński's complaint about the Judaization of institutions of Polish higher learing, the anonymous author of "Jews during the War" attributes this to the turmoil of the war which the Jews lost no time in turning to their own advantage:

Taking advantage of the turmoil of war and of the bizarre circumstances prevailing among us under the German occupation, Jewish members of the intelligentsia thrust themselves into chairs of universities and polytechnics, where they teach Polish history and literature and, in short, make sure that the Polish spirit remains constantly under their control. (p. 28)

Works such as Nowoczyński's satire and the anonymous "Jews during the War" might suggest that there would have been no lack of anti-Jewish barbs in other Polish arts at the time, for example, cabaret. But this was not the case, and it remained true throughout the interwar period. The reason, simply put, is that almost from the beginning, in Warsaw, Jews were prominent in cabaret culture, both as contributing artists and directors. Szyfman, the founder of Momus, was a Jew, as was Tuwim, without whose presence it would be difficult even to imagine the Warsaw cabaret both during and after World War I. When we find anything that seems outwardly anti-Jewish in cabaret numbers, it either typifies a self-deprecating type of Jewish humor or satirizes contemporary anti-Jewish arguments and attitudes. The Polish cabaret before World War II was a venue of close collaboration between Jewish and ethnic Polish artists, and this tended to keep expressions of genuine anti-Jewish sentiment from the cabaret stage.

The cinema

The war dealt the fledgling Polish film industry a serious blow. Although cinema was still in its infancy, Warsaw in 1915 could boast of twenty-five movie houses and two filmmaking companies, Kosmofilm and Sfinks.[28] After the war, they merged into a single company under the name Sfinks. Because of the links with German-language cinema, the technical level of Polish filmmaking was higher in Austrian Poland. But conscription drastically reduced the ranks of technicians. Most were drafted into the Austrian army, but some enlisted in Piłsudski's legions where they organized film units whose purpose was to record the exploits of the brigades.

Until the war, the European market in general had been dominated by such French companies as Gaumont and Pathé. But with the outbreak of hostilities the Central European market was cut off for them. So too was the Russian market because of the problems of transport and communication. The vacuum left by French and Russian companies began to be filled mostly by the Germans. As German filmmaking developed, the lands occupied by the German and Austrian armies emerged as a new market.

The years 1914 and 1915 were the hardest ones for the Polish film industry. The moment war was declared, Kosmofilm stopped production.

Although Sfinks continued to operate, it was forced to cut its ties to French Pathé and the resultant loss of financial backing hurt the quantity and quality of films it was able to turn out. The loss of camera operators and other skilled personnel to military service or foreign assignments from which they were unable to return also sharply curtailed film production. Of negative impact as well was the relatively large number of actors and actresses who, as we have seen, were either forced to evacuate Warsaw with the retreating Russians, chose to leave voluntarily, or could not make their way home from guest appearances in other countries. It was because of these and other hardships that Kosmofilm and Sfinks merged, pobably some time during 1915. As the German occupation sank deeper roots, close ties between Sfinks, as the combined Polish company was known, and such major German film organizations as Projektions A.-G. Union and UFA were forged, assuring the Poles vital technical as well as financial backing.

What kinds of films were available to the Poles during the war? For obvious reasons, documentaries proved the most popular. They were also the easiest to supply. News companies representing the occupying powers were, of course, major sources. The most important of such companies were Bild and Filmamt in Germany and the so-called Skobolev Committee in Russia. These in turn served as the model for a film unit that arose in Kraków and supplied camera operators to the Polish legions who covered most of the campaigns Piłsudski's forces fought in from 1914 to 1916. In the area of documentary, Sfinks concentrated primarily on the Warsaw scene, including the first film reportage of the breakup near Warsaw of Hindenburg's offensive in October 1914.

During the German occupation, a number of documentaries were made reflecting the new liberties enjoyed by the Poles under the Germans. Among these were: *Uroczystość otwarcia Uniwersytetu w dn. 15. XI. 1915 r.* (Celebration of the Opening of the University of Warsaw on 15 November 1915); *Pochód 3 maja* (Procession of the Third of May, 1916); *Na stokach Cytadeli* (On the Slopes of the Citadel, 1916); *Historyczny dzień Polski* (A Historic Day for Poland, a reference in the film's title to Beseler's proclamation of November 1916); *Uroczyste wkroczenie Legionów do Stolicy* (The Ceremonial Entry of the Legions into the Capital, 1916); and *Zwołanie Rady Stanu i pierwsze jej posiedzenie* (The Convening of the Council of State and its First Session, December 1917). Two films turned out by Sfinks sought to portray everyday life in Poland during the war: *Warszawa w chwili obecnej* (Warsaw at the Present Time, 1916), and a similar film with Kraków as its subject and filmed in 1917.

In the spring of 1917 a film bureau (Urząd Filmowy) attached to the Polish legions was established in Warsaw. Sfinks collaborated with it, and their first joint film was devoted to the 3 May celebrations in 1917. Its opening was a gala occasion, as was the premiere of the German–Polish film of February 1918, *Pod jarzmem tyranów, 125 lat niewoli Polski* (Under the Yoke of Tyrants. 125 Years of Polish Servitude).

When the Russians quit Warsaw, Polish patriotic sentiment exploded and was reflected in several films of an anti-tsarist nature, among them *Ochrana* (The Okhrana [the Russian Political Police]), *Carat i jego sługi* (Tsardom and its Servants), and *Carska faworyta* (Favorite of the Tsar). Also popular were films of erotic and criminal content such as *Studenci* (Students), *Bestia* (The Beast), and *Tajemnice Warszawy* (Secrets of Warsaw). Although the public flocked to see these films, churchmen and political conservatives denounced them as demoralizing. The last film produced by Sfinks during the occupation was *Carewicz* (Tsarevich), which was based on a work by the feminist novelist and playwright, Gabriela Zapolska. It was coproduced by Globus of Berlin.

Whatever the vicissitudes experienced by Polish cinema during the war, it did produce a genuine international star, Apolonia Chalupec, known best as Pola Negri (1897–1987). Trained as a ballet dancer from an early age, she set her sights on a stage career and made her debut in 1912 in a comedy by the nineteenth-century Polish dramatist, Aleksander Fredro. Although she appeared in other stage productions, her irritatingly raspy voice was regarded as a serious detriment to a flourishing theatrical career. But she proved a great success in non-speaking roles beginning with that of the lead dancer in a Polish production in 1913 of the Austrian director Max Reinhardt's well-known Eastern pantomime spectacle, *Sûmurûn*. This led to her first movie part, that of an exotic dancer in the film *Niewolnica zmysłów* (Slave of the Senses); however, this premiered only toward the end of 1914, by which time the war had drastically shifted the focus of public interest. Although Negri appeared in a few other films produced in Poland in 1915, her star began to rise only after she broke her contract with Sfinks and left Warsaw for Berlin, in 1916, in order to work with Saturn-Film A. G., a second-rate company once known for its pornographic films. Negri, however, was sued by Sfinks for breach of contract, lost the case, and had to return to Poland for several months to shoot an additional four films for the Polish company.

Pola Negri's first big role in Germany was in the film *Zügelloses Blut* (Unbridled Passion, 1917). By then she had quit Saturn and was affiliated with Projektions A. G.-Union, which not long afterward merged with the giant German film company, UFA. After an unfinished film based on the life of Mata Hari, Negri made four other films for Projections A. G.-UFA in 1918. The last was a version of *Carmen* directed by the legendary Ernst Lubitsch. It was the first major German film for both actress and director and launched their international careers.

The end of the war

On 12 November 1918, as the war was drawing to an end, General Beseler had abandoned Warsaw, and German soldiers were being disarmed on the streets of the city (the subject of a number of drawings and cartoons), the Miraż cabaret premiered a new review that had been secretly prepared in advance to celebrate liberation. It was called, appropriately, "Wiwat wolność" (Hail freedom). Its finale contained the lines:

> Hail the free nations of the world!
> Hail the people of France and England!
> Hail Poland, who for four long years
> Endured ruin and hunger . . .[29]

Other cabarets quickly followed suit, Sfinks staging "Niech żyje pokój" (Long Live Peace) and Czarny Kot, "Legioniści i filuty" (Legionnaires and Rogues). Whatever the suffering of the war years, the death and destruction, the conflict was finally at an end. The dawn of Polish independence after nearly a century and a quarter of partition and profound national humiliation was at hand. The sadness of the fratricide in which the Poles had been caught up through no fault of their own was tempered by the collapse of the three partitioning powers, Germany, Austria, and Russia, and the prospect of statehood regained. The Poles had acquitted themselves with bravery in the fighting, but took particular pride that in Piłsudski's legions a Polish fighting force had been able to serve under a Polish commander, a commander who had become a national hero and was destined to control the fate of interwar Poland until his death in 1935. The euphoria gripping Warsaw that November 1918 was splendidly captured in one eyewitness account:

It was already evening when I went out of the main hall of the railroad station onto the Aleje Jerozolimskie. Warsaw was going crazy! People who didn't know each other were embracing and were cheering the Polish army. Girls were throwing themselves at the officers and men, while young people kept on waving banners taken from the Germans as well as the spiked helmets removed from their heads. Extra editions of newspapers were also stirring up the city from one end to the other with their reports of the cease fire on the Western front at Compiègne. In Warsaw, the Citadel had already been taken over and Polish flags were flying over the guardhouse on Saxon Square and over the Belvedere Palace.[30]

The euphoria of 1918 would be dissipated before long by the stark realities of political instability and economic hardship in the interwar years. But for the time being, Germans, Austrians, and Russians were at last out of Poland, and the country was free. The people were entitled to celebrate.

An overview

World War I was a mixed blessing for the Poles at best. The excitement with which the outbreak of hostilities was greeted elsewhere in Europe was paralleled on a less exuberant level among many Poles who expected that the outcome of the conflict would finally bring about a restoration of Polish independence. The military and political reversals suffered by Austria-Hungary in the second half of the nineteenth century had resulted in a significant amelioration especially of Polish cultural life in the Austrian partition and understandably whetted the appetite for an extension of these gains throughout the Polish lands. Events such as the Russo-Japanese war of 1904–1905 and the Russian Revolution of 1905, which were taken as signs of the weakness of the Russian empire, buoyed hopes even more. The dismal outcome of the January Insurrection of 1863 had sounded the deathknell of romanticism and prompted the Poles to reconsider armed revolt against Russia as the most efficacious means of achieving freedom, at least within the context of the Russian partition. Emphasis shifted instead to a new program of organic work intended to strengthen the fabric of Polish society throughout the partitioned country. Efforts were undertaken to break down traditional barriers between social classes and between the majority of the Poles and other ethnic communities, especially the Jews, to raise the level of literacy, and to lay the bases of a sound national economy that would enable a future independent Poland to stand on its own legs and even flourish.

The literature of modernist Poland from the 1880s to World War I sought to reconcile the lofty ideals of the Polish Romantic tradition and the more modest but achievable goals of organic work. As the embodiment of the Romantic ethos, the legacy of the Napoleonic legions understandably fell subject to the greatest deconstruction. From the perspective of the turn of the century, the entire episode of Napoleonic Poland was seen as one of false gods, noble but vain sacrifices, and delusions of grandeur. No text of modernist Poland encompasses this view of the past more compellingly than Stefan Żeromski's historical novel, *Popioły* (*Ashes*, 1904–1905).

War, and more realistic expectations concerning Polish independence, breathed new life into the legend of the Polish Napoleonic legions. And when Piłsudski organized his own legions on the model of those of General Dąbrowski, a new legend was born. It was carefully nurtured by Piłsudski and his followers throughout the war and even more aggressively during the Second Republic, to the point where Polish neo-Napoleonism acquired the virtual status of a state institution. But the sense of relief and joy that greeted the end of the war and the rebirth of the Polish state soon yielded to a somber awareness of the terrible devastation World War I had brought to Poland and the extraordinarily difficult road that lay ahead. Grave political, economic, and social problems plagued Poland throughout the interwar years. Moreover, the peace that made possible a new Polish state also contained the seeds of future conflicts over territorial disputes. The worst of these was the Polish-Soviet war of 1919–1920. So the end of the Great War in 1918 was merely a pause between conflicts on a variety of battlefields, external and internal. Sandwiched between the enormous costs of World War I and the unspeakable horrors of World War II, the twenty years of the Second Republic seem a pitifully small period of time for meaningful national reconstruction. The independence that Poland had finally achieved after 120 years of partition came at a heavy price.

In Piłsudski, the war had produced a hero to whom the Polish people looked for leadership in the troubled years of the peace. But Piłsudski was a military man who seemed more comfortable in the circumstances of war than in those of peacetime parliamentary politics. And when the complexities of such politics seemed to immobilize the country and became insufferable to him, he staged a successful *coup d'état* in May 1926. From that event until his death in 1935, when the reins of political power passed to a clique of right-wing army officers, Polish democracy was in a state of suspended animation. Revered as a national symbol, the focus of a variety of popular cultural artifacts during and after World War I, Piłsudski became a progressively more remote figure, ill-adapted to the trappings of power yet discontent with those who would wield it in his name.

Behind the glittering façade of the military pomp and ceremony of interwar Poland, and the careful nurturing of the Napoleonic legend, lay a national mood of anxiety, apprehension, and weariness with martial clamor. This is reflected, I believe, in the pacifistic fictional writing of the period. Polish literary anti-militarism made an early appearance in works by Andrzej Strug (real name Stefan Gałecki, 1873–1937), a former participant in Piłsudski's legions who had become disillusioned with war. But the distinction of having written the best anti-war novel in interwar Poland belongs to Józef Wittlin (1896–1976). In his major work, *Sól ziemi* (*The Salt of the Earth*, 1936), Wittlin tells the story of an illiterate Polish peasant who is conscripted into the Austrian army, experiences the full measure of the madness of war, yet remains incapable of understanding how men could inflict such torment on one other.

World War I coincided with the flowering of the modernist movement that sanctioned the appropriation of popular culture by "high art." As commonly defined, popular culture had never attracted serious attention in Poland; the war changed that by creating a new set of cultural values. Satire, especially as practiced in pre-war elitist cabarets, was forced to give up the myopic concerns of small cliques of artists and intellectuals in favor of the life and death issues confronting the populace as a whole; from the fratricidal nature of the conflict from the Polish point of view to the hardships of daily life under the different occupying armies. With reliable press coverage impossible owing to censorship, satirical journals of one sort or another became a conduit for covetously consumed scraps of information. Coffeehouses, which had been popular meeting places for artists in the turn of the century, also became venues of fact and rumor, "living newspapers" in a sense. Light verse, long spurned as beneath the dignity of the serious writer, provided the forms and rhythms for easily memorized and recited wartime songs and poems of a patriotic and military character. Short forms in general – from poems and anecdotes in satirical journals to cabaret skits and personal campaign vignettes such as those by Kaden-Bandrowski – became the order of the day. Reportage, now the spirit of modern journalism, challenged the primacy of imaginative literature in the interwar era, in Poland as in much of Europe, and became the medium of choice of leading literary figures. As in the documentary film that came to prominence during the war, immediate experience trivialized the inventions of fiction.

4 Jewish cultural identity in Eastern and Central Europe during the Great War[1]

Aviel Roshwald

Ask the generation past,
Study what their fathers have searched out . . .
Surely they will teach you and tell you,
Speaking out of their understanding.

Bildad the Shuhite
Job 8:8–10

. . . Truly it is the spirit in men,
The breath of the Almighty, that gives them understanding.
It is not the aged who are wise,
The elders, who understand how to judge.

Elihu son of Barachel
Job 32:6–9

Two central issues dominated the evolution of European Jewish culture during the nineteenth and twentieth centuries. One was the age-old question of how to maintain some sense of unity and faith in the face of dispersion and adversity. The other concern – not altogether separate from the first – was to what extent and in what ways ancestral traditions should be retained, discarded, or adapted in the face of modernity's challenges and opportunities. Both these issues, in turn, raised fundamental questions about the nature of Jewish identity. The cataclysm of the First World War intensified the struggle over Jewish self-definition in a rapidly changing world and accelerated the crystallization of new, competing forms of cultural expression and political action among the Jews of Europe.

Unlike any of the other peoples examined in this volume, the Jews had neither a state of their own, nor a geographical region where they constituted a majority of the population. Jews were a minority group wherever they lived. Their population was dispersed across the length and breadth of the European continent (not to speak of other continents), and Jews accordingly served in the armies of each of the belligerents during the war. Yet although nearly every country had a Jewish minority, it was in the lands of the former Polish-Lithuanian Commonwealth that the majority of European Jewry lived. This was also the region where

Jewish cultural and communal life was most distinct and separate from that of local majority populations. I will accordingly focus my attention on the Jews of East Central Europe, focussing in particular on Polish Jewry, whose wartime experience and post-war prospects became a central source of concern and topic of debate among Jewish communities throughout Europe and the United States. Moreover, the wartime conquest of the Russian portion of Poland by the armies of the Central Powers transformed the region into a zone of cultural and political contact, conflict, and experimentation on an unprecedented scale. Within this dynamic new framework, rapid changes were wrought in Jewish cultural life as well as in the mutual perceptions and self-definitions of Eastern European Jews, Central European Jews, and non-Jewish groups alike. This region can be viewed as the cockpit of self-consciously Jewish cultural life and the primary wartime zone of encounter among competing visions of Jewish identity. Hence, its study affords the best opportunity for developing a relatively integrated analysis of such a kaleidoscopic topic. Needless to say, significant communities of unassimilated and semi-assimilated Jews resided in other parts of Europe, and much work needs to be done on their cultural history during this period. Such a broadly inclusive survey is simply beyond the scope of this chapter, however.

Introduction

The greatest concentration of European Jewry in 1914 lived in the territories of the former Polish-Lithuanian Commonwealth, which had been partitioned among the Russian, Austrian, and Prussian (later German) empires in the late eighteenth century. The redistribution of these lands at the Congress of Vienna in 1814–1815 had left the lion's share in the hands of Russia. While the regions of Posen (Poznań) and Eastern Pomerania remained under Prusso-German control, and Galicia was ruled by Austria's Habsburg rulers, the rest of Poland was incorporated into the Russian polity. The eastern reaches of the former Polish state – including what we know today as Lithuania, much of Belarus, and a large chunk of Ukraine, along with Bessarabia and parts of southern Russia – comprised the Pale of Settlement, the geographical zone to which the bulk of the Russian Empire's Jewish population was confined by law. Jews also lived to the west, in the heartland of the conquered state – a region designated as the Kingdom of Poland or Congress Poland, whose sovereign was the Russian tsar and whose putative autonomy had been whittled down to nothing by the second half of the nineteenth century.[2] Only a relatively small minority of Jews – those who possessed substantial financial means, some students, those who were skilled in certain specialized crafts, and women in possession of the notorious "yellow ticket" that identified its holder as a registered prostitute – were authorized to reside to the east of the Pale in the Russian heartland; including illegal residents, the Jewish population east of the Pale numbered no more than 300,000 at the turn of the century.[3]

The roughly 4.5 million Jews of the Pale and Congress Poland comprised over 10 percent of the region's total population. Most Jews lived either in cities, where they often constituted as much as 25–50 percent of the population, or in small to medium-sized towns (*shtetlach* – plural of *shtetl* – in Yiddish), where they frequently formed a majority of the population. The high concentration of Jews in particular neighborhoods and towns, their juridical designation as a discrete social category, and their tendency (reinforced by legal restrictions on Jewish land ownership) to occupy specific economic niches as middlemen, petty traders, and artisans, as well as their common experience of discrimination and persecution, all served to reinforce the survival of a very distinct and all-embracing Jewish cultural identity. This identity was anchored in a tripartite foundation: the traditional religious community and way of life; the Hebrew language, which was the primary medium of men's prayer and study; and Yiddish, the *mame-lushn* (mother tongue), which served as the main medium of daily communication for men and women as well as the language in which most women prayed, wrote, and read.[4] Modern political and cultural movements advocating radical change in the form of assimilation, religious reform, socialism, or Zionism had sprung up in the main cities of the Pale and Congress Poland during the last two decades before the war, but these remained confined to relatively small Jewish elites with exposure to a modern education. Each of these elites aspired to transform the masses in its own image, and under the tsarist regime it was the assimilationists (who advocated that Jews modify their traditions and learn to blend into the Polish cultural mainstream) who tended to hold dominant positions as intermediaries between the Jewish community and the state authorities. But among the Jewish masses, the cultural impact of these movements had barely begun to make itself felt; in general, options such as emigration to the New World (which would not be possible during 1914–1918) or participation in mystical or charismatic forms of Hasidism were the favored forms of escape from their material and psychological plight.

The confinement of the bulk of Russian Jewry to the Pale of Settlement, along with limitations on Jewish land ownership, discriminatory restrictions on sundry forms of economic and cultural activity, denial of equal access to state-run educational institutions and to jobs in the administrative sector, and provisions that disproportionately limited

Jewish electoral influence in the Duma (imperial parliament) and local municipalities and councils, represented the juridical face of Russian state anti-Semitism. (The Jews of Congress Poland were emancipated in 1862, but, in practice, continued to be discriminated against.) The tsarist government's repeated failure to intervene effectively on behalf of Jewish communities victimized by violent pogroms (anti-Semitic riots) was the major unofficial manifestation of the regime's hostility toward its Jewish subjects. Although anti-Semitic prejudice was also widespread in the popular and elite cultures of Germany and Austria-Hungary, Jews had enjoyed full legal and civic equality there for almost half a century by the time the Great War broke out. By contrast with Russia, those states seemed like havens of dignity and security for Jews.[5]

From its outset, World War I reinforced this perceived contrast between conditions in Russia and the Central Powers. While German and Austrian propaganda promised the Jews of Poland liberation from the oppressive practices of the tsarist regime once the Central Powers' armies had rolled back the Russian forces, the Russian military authorities treated the Jewish population as a treacherous element whose presence near the front lines was a potential liability to their war effort. During the spring and summer of 1915, well over half a million Jews were deported from their home towns near the front and forced to flee into the interior of the country. The scale of the crisis overstrained the resources of Jewish relief organizations. The situation was aggravated by the Russian army's harsh and arbitrary treatment of the Jews of eastern Galicia during its occupation of the region in 1914–1915. Then, as the Germans and their Austrian allies advanced deep into Russian Poland and Eastern Galicia in the summer of 1915, the retreating Russian forces adopted a "scorched earth" policy that took the form of ravaging, looting, and burning countless Jewish *shtetlach* and Jewish urban neighborhoods before abandoning them to the enemy. This systematic military pogrom inflicted thousands of casualties and further aggravated the refugee problem, the breakdown in public health, and the economic mayhem that the war had already unleashed among the great Jewish population centers of Eastern Europe.[6]

Responses to catastrophe

Much of the Jewish cultural response to this cataclysm was expressed in terms and images that harked back to traditional theological themes. As David Roskies has pointed out, the encounter with the horrors of the Great War did not necessitate the development of radically new modes of thought and expression among Jews.[7] The encounter with collective catastrophe and the questioning of religious faith in the light of apparently meaningless brutality were well-established themes in the Jewish experience, as a cursory glance at Lamentations, some of the Psalms, and various segments of Rabbinical literature will demonstrate.

Traditional treatments and commemorations of collective disaster fell into two categories. One was the conflation of the specific tragedy with earlier massacres and atrocities suffered by the Jews. The most clear-cut manifestation of this approach was the use of pre-existing days of mourning (such as Tish'ah be-Av [the ninth of Av], the anniversary of the destruction of the First and Second Temples) to honor the memory of more recent martyrdoms.[8] In this frame of reference, a tragic sense of meaning was imparted to a particular calamity by associating it with an archetypal martyrdom that transcended the ephemeral flow of history.

The historicist version of traditional responses to national catastrophe focussed on the Covenant between God and the Jewish people. In this framework, a sense of meaning was created by suggesting that Jewish suffering must be the consequence of a specific breach of the Covenant – the implication being that redemption might ultimately be found through repentance and good deeds. Jewish history could be seen as an unfolding dialogue between God and his people, a relationship which gave the Jews a certain influence over their own fate. The other side of this coin was the calling to account of God, the questioning of His own commitment to the Covenant – a cry of outrage articulated most boldly by the eighteenth-century Hasidic leader, Rabbi Levi Isaac of Berdichev (1740–1809).[9]

Elements of both these approaches to catastrophe were interwoven into the modern genre of pogrom poetry that arose in the wake of the 1903 Kishinev (Bessarabia) massacre and that continued to evolve during World War I. In his Yiddish poem, "Have Pity," S. Frug linked the victimization of Kishinev's Jews to all the other disasters of Jewish history:

> Our misfortune, great and timeless,
> Has laid its hand on us once more.[10]

Sung with musical accompaniment, "Have Pity" called on Jews to contribute to relief programs for the Kishinev community, and was later revived as a fund-raising song for the relief efforts of World War I. The Hebrew poet Chaim Nachman Bialik's "About the Slaughter," also published in the wake of the events in Kishinev, struck a more jarring note, parodying liturgical themes in its rageful indictment of God's indifference to His people's suffering. A number of Yiddish works composed during and just after World War I took the bitter mockery of

Covenantal promises and lurid descriptions of atrocity scenes to new extremes. In "A Night" (1916), Moyshe-Leyb Halpern, a Galician *émigré* living in New York, utilized Judeo-Christian apocalyptic imagery to suggest that the world war and the accompanying destruction of Jewish lives was the work, not of the Grim Reaper, but of the much-awaited Messiah who had chosen thus to end history. *The Heap* (1921) by Peretz Markish, who had fought in the Russian army during the war and subsequently witnessed horrific pogroms in the Ukraine, described the heap of Jewish corpses as having risen higher than Mt Sinai (where the Ten Commandments had been handed down). These poets sought to shock their readers by writing in a defiantly sacrilegious style; yet, as Roskies suggests, in their very preoccupation with iconoclasm, these bitter modernists could not free themselves altogether from the referential framework of the Covenant.[11]

While secularized Jewish urban intellectuals may have expressed their anguish through modernist literary inversions of traditional theological themes, the battered masses of the war zones clung to more reassuring images. The detailed wartime observations of S. An-sky (pen-name of Shlomo-Zanvill Rappoport, 1863–1920), the noted Russian Jewish writer and amateur ethnographer who travelled extensively in Congress Poland, Galicia, and Bukovina on relief work during the war years, suggest that the victimized inhabitants of *shtetlach* turned to familiar biblical archetypes and religious beliefs as sources of solace or hope at a time of widespread despair. Biblical stories could even serve as precedents or models for pragmatic action. This, according to An-sky, was the case in Ger, the hometown of the Gerer Rebbe (the head of a major Hasidic movement), which found a garrison of Russian troops stationed in its midst early in the war. When two Polish military engineers who were members of the unit began to stir up anti-Semitic feelings among the soldiers, incidents of random violence, harassment, and theft began to multiply. The engineers accused the Jews of treachery and espionage, and forced them to dig trenches for the garrison on the Sabbath. In response, the Rebbe is said to have advised one of his confidants to invite the Russian commander and his fellow officers, including the two engineers, to a lavish feast. Once the Russians were thoroughly drunk and merry, the host would suddenly fall to his knees before the commanding officer and denounce the deeds of the evildoing pair before the assembled company in the hope that the commander would take action against them.[12] This story clearly calls to mind the biblical fable of Esther, the Jewish queen of Persia, who threw a feast for the king and his evil minister, Haman, who was plotting to exterminate all the Jews of the Persian Empire. There too, the occasion was used as an opportunity for denouncing the villain and securing the support of the higher authority.[13] In the biblical story, the plan works out perfectly. In the case of the latter-day incident, short-term success was achieved, as the Russian commander ordered that the Sabbath be respected by members of the garrison and that no further harm come to residents of the town. (Part of the dramatic effect was lost on account of the engineers' failure to show up at the banquet; perhaps they too had read the Book of Esther.) A few weeks later, however, this military unit was replaced by another one, which promptly fell into the familiar pattern of looting and violence.[14]

Many people clung to Hasidic mysticism during the worst periods of wartime affliction. It was widely believed that the advent of the Messiah would be preceded by a time of great suffering for the Jewish people and the world as a whole, and it was accordingly common to refer to any time of trouble – and the period of the Great War in particular – as *meshiach-tseitn* (Messiah times). Such beliefs could take very concrete form, as in the pre-war story of the Hasid whose Rebbe was arbitrarily imprisoned by the tsarist authorities. Upon his release, the Hasid secluded himself in apparent dejection while his fellow Hasidim celebrated the liberation of their leader. When asked why he did not join in the festivities, the Hasid answered that he had believed the suffering of the Rebbe was an indication that he was the Messiah about to reveal himself. Now that the Rebbe had been anticlimactically released from jail, it was clear that he was not the Messiah after all, hence the Hasid's downcast spirit![15]

If Jews tended to think of their persecution within a traditional frame of reference, wartime anti-Semitism elaborated upon traditional stereotypes and themes of its own. The widespread view of the Jew as an alien being whose very presence defiled the Christian community was readily incorporated into the patriotic worldview of wartime Russia. Rather than being accused of poisoning the wells, Jews were now accused of spying for the Germans, but the basic theme of the Jews as insidious enemies of the people remained the same. Treachery was regarded as intrinsic to the character and identity of Jews. Such views were widespread among the Russian officer corps as well as among the Polish and Ukrainian peasantry. They were also actively propagated in urban middle-class and intellectual circles by the right-wing Polish National Democrats, whose pre-war development into a mass movement had culminated in an anti-Jewish economic boycott begun in 1912. The result was a self-perpetuating pattern of innuendo, slander, and false reports about Jewish agents using various signaling devices to communicate information about Russian troop placements to the Germans. Jews were routinely accused of being in secret telephone contact with the enemy. German Zeppelins that bombed behind Russian lines were referred to as "Beilises" – a particularly vivid illustration of how readily the traditional blood libel was transposed into the rhetoric of war.[16]

Although some liberal and left-wing intellectuals, such as members of the Polish Socialist Party (PPS) and the progressive Russian intellectuals grouped around Maxim Gorky[17], remained outspoken advocates of tolerance and equal treatment for Jews, the perception of Jews as the enemy from within grew more intense and widespread as the fighting dragged on. The Russian military seemed eager to blame its increasingly poor performance on a Jewish fifth column, rather than assume responsibility for its own mistakes. Apart from the general policy of deportation referred to above, such accusations also resulted in innumerable cases of arbitrary arrests and summary executions of Jews who had been denounced as spies. (Jews were similarly accused and abused in Romania following that country's entry into the war on the Entente side in 1916.[18]) The Russian army's habit of looting and destroying Jewish homes and shops became so consistent that non-Jews would routinely place icons in their windows on the approach of Russian forces, to spare themselves the attacks that would inevitably be visited upon their Jewish neighbors.[19]

In grappling with these circumstances, Jews did not rely exclusively on religious faith and historical archetypes; their panoply of defense included a formidable array of fables and tall tales as well. In the face of total war, the Jews of Eastern Europe armed themselves to the teeth with jokes. According to An-sky, one story that made the rounds turned the ubiquitous telephone libel into a story of eleventh-hour exoneration and rescue. In this tale, the Jews of Zamość are accused by local Poles of using clandestine phone lines to maintain illicit contact with the enemy. Just as they are about to be sent to the gallows by a military tribunal, someone (in some versions, a Catholic priest) rushes in and convinces the authorities to stay the execution while he presents them with vital new evidence. Having been led to the mansion of the local nobleman, the authorities are astounded to find the nobleman's wife in the basement, where she is busy relaying secret information over the phone to the Germans! The innocent Jews are promptly released, and the true culprit is taken into custody. In one particularly fanciful version of the story, the treacherous Polish noblewoman is surrounded by a group of men in Hasidic garb who are likewise chatting with the Germans over the phone lines. In the dramatic finale, these men are unmasked as Poles who have disguised themselves as Jews, presumably so as to mislead the authorities into blaming the wrong community in the event they are caught.[20] Such ostensibly lighthearted legends may have served an escapist function, while at the same time the very out-landishness of their plot twists constituted a bitter commentary on the hopelessness of the actual situation: it required an outrageous exercise of poetic license to save the Jews of Zamość from their unjust fate.

Tales of high melodrama and intense pathos were, of course, more directly reflective of the Jewish wartime experience. Yiddish folk-songs during these years dwelled on universal themes such as the separation of mobilized men from their loved ones, as well as on the more specific suffering and moral decay of Jewish soldiers as Jews. Thus, a song entitled "Oy Vey in 1915" highlighted the essential incompatibility be-tween Russian military service and the Jewish way of life by focussing on the unavoidable wartime violations of the Sabbath and, more omin-ously, hinting at the passive or active participation of Jewish conscripts in the rape of Jewish women:

> *Oy vey* in one thousand nine hundred and fifteen
> A new order, oh, order, came out
> Oh, every father must lead his child
> Like a slaughterer the cattle.

> *Oy vey*, Friday, Friday, Friday night
> Oh, our lips were pale, oh, pale
> We would have liked to go to a Jew for the Sabbath
> If they hadn't had an inspection, an inspection.

> *Oy vey*, Saturday, oh Saturday, oh Saturday, very early
> –Out on maneuvers, out
> Have we eaten, have we drunk?
> And you get slapped too.

> *Oy vey* brothers, we're lost
> We are in murderous hands, *oy vey*
> We took Jewish girls
> And wasted their lives.[21]

Another poignant aspect of the Jewish war experience was the fact that there were Jews serving in each of the rival armies, which meant that Jewish soldiers were unintentionally but unavoidably killing each other on a daily basis. (Poles faced a similar dilemma.) An oft-repeated story that captured this bitter truth told of a Russian Jewish soldier who had just fatally wounded a German soldier. As he lay dying, the Ger-man soldier cried out "Shma' Yisrael" ("Hear O Israel") – the opening phrase from the Jewish credo, commonly uttered as a Jew faces death.[22] Realizing that he had just hurt a fellow Jew, the other soldier cradled the injured man in his arms, but it was too late and the man expired. In one variant, the dying man asked his killer to send his money to his wife, but then gasped his last breath before he could communicate her address. Whether or not such an incident ever really occurred, it was seized upon by An-sky as a quintessentially folkloric expression of a fundamental truth about a war in which Jews were not only part of the cannon fodder, but were in effect forced to take up arms against one another. In this and other ways, the traditional powerlessness of Jews in the face of arbitrary government was magnified and assumed tragic proportions in the context of Europe's general descent into the murderous frenzy of 1914–1918.[23]

In the zones of Russian rule and occupation, the war seemed to threaten the physical and cultural existence of the Jewish people at one and the same time. A tsarist decree in July 1915 banned the mailing of all printed matter in Yiddish and Hebrew, followed up by a complete ban on Hebrew-scripted printing in 1916. For its part, the Russian army uprooted entire Jewish communities, desecrated cemeteries, burned towns and synagogues, and destroyed countless books and artifacts. This was a situation that forced intellectuals to become *engagés* in the most concrete sense of the term. A number of Polish-Jewish and Russian-Jewish intellectuals became actively involved in public relief work while at the same time making efforts to salvage what they could of a culture that seemed on the verge of annihilation; never before had it been more difficult to distinguish the demands of the body from the needs of the soul. Y. L. Peretz (1852–1915), the noted Hebrew and Yiddish author who had become a leader in the movement to elevate the common folk's tongue – Yiddish – to the status of a national literary language, now became even more intimately involved with the Jewish masses. He turned his Warsaw literary club, ha-Zamir (The Nightingale), into a refugee center that rapidly became crammed with hundreds of hungry men, women, and children who had been forced from their homes in the war zone.[24] Confronted in the last year of his life with the bitter suffering of simple people in an uncaring, bloodthirsty world, Peretz despaired of his earlier belief in secular education and liberal, democratic values, calling instead for a return to the synagogue and religious faith as the only possible sources of spiritual salvation for the Jewish people. (Just as he had earlier contended that Yiddish was the best vehicle for conveying worldly values to the masses, Peretz now argued that Yiddish could serve as an effective medium for fostering a popular religious revival.[25]) At the same time, Peretz was joined by the writers S. An-sky and Jacob Dinezon in issuing a manifesto calling on their fellow Jewish intellectuals to collect whatever information they could on the Jewish wartime experience for fear that if the recording and writing of history were left to others, the Jewish experience would be utterly obliterated.[26]

It was An-sky who did more than anyone to fulfill this difficult object-ive. The noted Yiddish author and playwright had mounted an ethno-graphic expedition to Jewish *shtetlach* in the Ukraine in 1912 in order to record folklore and gather artifacts from what he already feared was a fast-disappearing way of life. The war made such an effort all the more urgent. An-sky became a leading figure in an officially authorized Russian-Jewish relief organization based in Kiev. His status as a well-connected Jewish intellectual who had a permit to live outside the Pale, combined with his new role as a uniformed officer of a government-accredited relief organization, gave him *entrée* to official circles in both the government and the military. He succeeded in using his connections to gain permission to travel on a relief mission to Russian-occupied Galicia in 1915, and then again during the brief reoccupation of east-ern Galicia during the 1916 Brusilov offensive. His official uniform and fluent Russian enabled him to pass himself off as a non-Jewish Russian on occasion, while his command of Yiddish facilitated an ease of com-munication with the Jewish inhabitants of war-ravaged Galicia.[27]

While focussing his efforts on the overwhelming task of trying to put together programs of material assistance for the beleaguered popula-tion, An-sky also strove to fulfill his own call for the creation of a Jewish record of the war. His wartime diaries, edited and published in book form after the end of the conflict as *Der yidisher khurbn fun Poilen, Galitsye un Bukovina fun tag-buch 1914–1917* (The Jewish Catastrophe in Poland, Galicia, and Bukovina from the 1914–1917 Diary), reflect his compul-sion to write down every anecdote, every tragic tale, every wry comment, and every observation that was in any way related to the Jewish experi-ence of the war or expressive of the outlook of the masses. At first glance, there is little concern here with a search for broad theological or philosophical meaning; the main thrust of the work is simply directed at fulfilling the objective of the writers' manifesto – preserving a specific-ally Jewish memory of the war.

Yet by the same token, the incidents and narratives selected for inclusion in *Der khurbn fun Poilen* reflect An-sky's particular fascination with Hasidic lore and mystical folk beliefs. He seemed to regard the apparent irrationality of the masses as an expression of a deep, spiritual, inner life and religious faith of the sort that a cultured and worldly man like himself might never fully experience, but could nevertheless learn to appreciate. Thus, he was struck by a story told him by a follower of the Kopyczynecer Rebbe. The Rebbe, who was stranded in Hamburg when the war broke out, asked his Hasid to make his way to a location in his Galician home town of Kopyczynec, where he would find two letters written by the eighteenth-century founder of Hasidism, the Ba'al

Shem Tov. He was to hide the letters in a safe place so as to save them from possible destruction at the hands of the invading Russian army. The Hasid managed to conceal the letters just hours before the arrival of Russian troops. Later, after the pillaging soldiers had passed through the town, he retrieved the documents from their hiding place only to find that the letters had "flown away," leaving the pages blank! While technical experts insisted that chemical processes could reveal the handwriting, the Hasidim refused to subject the letters to any such scientific treatment, insisting that the episode had a mystical meaning (that remained unspecified). While An-sky clearly did not believe in magic, he did find the symbolism of the story more powerful than any logical explanation of the event. He went on to link the tale of the disappearing writing to the legend about the letters flying back to heaven as Moses broke the tablets of the Law, turning this positive Talmudic image of God's redemptive intentions into a pessimistic metaphor for the destruction of the Jewish spirit: In 1915, at the time of An-sky's first expedition, the tablets were broken but the letters were still intact – the physical existence of Galician and Polish Jewry was disrupted and shattered, but there was still an epic, heroic quality to their spiritual resistance and dignity. By 1916–1917, the time of his second trip through the region, Jewish morale had been crushed and the population had been reduced to a state of abject beggary – the letters had flown from the fragmented tablets.[28] In yet another play on the image of broken tablets, An-sky told his readers of the destroyed synagogue he saw in Dembitz, where among the broken tablets of the law he found fragments of the two commandments, "Thou shalt not covet" and "Thou shalt not murder," with the word "not" missing from each one!

The image of Eastern Europe as nothing but a physical and spiritual graveyard for Jews was also captured in the wartime drawings of Abel Pann (1883–1963), a Russian Jewish painter who looked to the Zionist enterprise in Palestine as offering the only chance of redemption for a Jewish population that was being brutalized and destroyed in its native towns and villages. Residing in Paris during most of the war years, Pann was not an eyewitness to events in his native land, but in 1916 he produced a series of harrowing images of the persecutions, hoping to draw public attention in the West to the plight of Russia's Jews. Many of the etchings bore ironic captions: "The Traitors" depicted a group of Jews hanging from the gallows as alleged spies; "Hiding from their Protectors" showed a group of terrified Jewish women and children seeking cover in a forest while Russian troops marched by; "The Son's Return" portrayed a young man arriving home to find his father lying in bed with a bullet hole in his head. Most disturbing of all to the eye

4.1   German soldiers in Poland seek lodging in a Jewish house

of a post-Holocaust observer is the print entitled simply "Cattle Cars," which shows emaciated refugees stuffed into cattle cars, hands and arms bent at sharp angles as they reach out in desperation, while a soldier with a bayonet at his side stolidly stands guard, his back turned to the supplicants.[29]

A new framework in Eastern Europe: German occupation

A critical turning point in the war on the Eastern Front took place in the summer of 1915, when the German army not only pushed Russian forces out of most of Galicia, but occupied the Polish heartland itself as well as lands to the northeast. Cities such as Warsaw, Vilna, Kovno (Kaunas), and Bialystok all came under German control. The entire region was divided into zones of German and Austro-Hungarian occupation. The northernmost German zone, roughly corresponding to the old Grand Duchy of Lithuania, was designated the Ober Ost (Upper East). Administered directly by the German Supreme Command in the East (under Generals Hindenburg and Ludendorff), the Ober Ost included urban centers such as Vilna and Kovno and was populated by a mixed Lithuanian, Polish, Jewish, Belorussian, and Baltic German population. The rest of German- and Habsburg-occupied Poland came to be designated as a notionally sovereign Polish Kingdom in November 1916. In practice, the Kingdom was run by a Provisional State Council (later a Regency Council) that had little freedom of action and that essentially functioned as a fig-leaf for German authority. None the less, the creation of structures and institutions symbolizing the principle of Polish national self-determination had a significant (if in some ways unintended) impact on the development of ethnic politics and national consciousness among the peoples of the region.[30]

The widespread depiction of Jews as hostile to the Russian cause had obviously been somewhat self-fulfilling, and among many Jews, the German military advance was initially welcomed as a potential liberation from the systematic persecution they had suffered at the hands of the Russian military. This perception was reinforced by German and Austrian Yiddish-language propaganda pamphlets that highlighted the contrast between the civic equality enjoyed by Jews in the Central Powers with the oppressive conditions prevalent under the tsar. The October 1914 issue of *Kol Mevaser* (The Heralding Voice), a Hebrew- and Yiddish-language propaganda publication produced by the German Jewish Komitee für den Osten (KfdO, of which more below) and distributed by the German army, featured a front-page cartoon of Tsar Nicholas II standing in the Jewish cemetery at Kishinev (site of the 1903 pogrom), draped in a prayer shawl, and calling on his dear Jewish subjects to rise up from their graves and help him in his hour of need.[31] The wartime circumstances of East European Jewry also served as material for German propaganda in neutral countries such as the United States. Photographs taken by the German military documented the destruction of Jewish towns by the retreating Russian army in 1915 and contrasted these images with pictures of German soldiers providing Polish Jewish children in cholera-ravaged neighborhoods with clean drinking water, German troops engaged in friendly commerce with Jewish storeowners in recently occupied towns, and the like. Such photographs were disseminated to the German and international press as part of an effort to convince world opinion that the German drive eastwards represented the advance of civilization in the face of barbarism.[32]

In reality, German attitudes toward Jews were not as uniformly enlightened as this propaganda suggested. The anti-Jewish prejudice that was so deeply ingrained in the culture of the German officer corps manifested itself ever more openly as frustration mounted over the elusiveness of a decisive and victorious end to the war. Indeed, in 1916 the

Prussian war ministry conducted a notorious survey of German Jewish participation in the war effort in a transparent attempt to represent the Jews as not contributing their fair share to the nation's struggle; the resulting statistics, which actually established that Jews were proportionately represented both in the army as a whole and among frontline soldiers, were duly suppressed until after the war. Such incidents – along with the growing anti-Semitic sentiments awakened by the wartime influx of Jewish forced laborers and refugees from Eastern Europe – highlighted the fact that, for all their juridical equality, German Jews were still far from being accepted as integral members of the German national community. This awareness, in turn, contributed to the strengthening of Jewish national consciousness among many members of the younger generation, who questioned the assimilatory impulses of their parents' generation.[33]

German occupation turned out to be a mixed blessing for the Jews of Eastern Europe (or *Ostjuden* – East Jews, as Germans and German Jews alike referred to them). The German occupation authorities introduced basic principles of civil equality and the rule of law to the Russian territories that fell under their control, and Jews clearly benefited from the elimination of the legal discrimination and systematic persecution that had been directed against them under the tsar. (The German military authorities in the occupied regions of Romania, by contrast, refrained from dismantling that country's institutional anti-Semitism, in part out of concern that to do so would disrupt their attempts to negotiate a separate peace with the Romanian government in unoccupied Moldavia.)[34] Yet the equality experienced under the Germans was a harsh equality of arbitrary military edicts, strict rationing of basic supplies, onerous economic exploitation, and rapacious requisitioning.[35] Some of the German commercial restrictions hit Jewish middlemen particularly hard. The forced labor quota that Jews along with other ethnic groups had to fulfill was deeply resented. (Jews were housed in separate labor camps in order to accommodate their observance of the Sabbath, but this did not alleviate the extremely difficult physical conditions under which they, like all forced laborers, toiled.) The lower strata of Jewish society continued to suffer tremendous hardships throughout the years of German and Austrian occupation, while the renewed Russian incursion into Galicia in 1916 inflicted an extra measure of devastation on the population of that province.[36]

The perception of a steady moral decline under the impact of these afflictions was the focus of much Jewish reportage and literature during and immediately after the war. The steep rise in the incidence of female prostitution was commonly addressed in the form of apologias, especially by sympathetic German Jewish observers. Such authors either minimized the extent of the phenomenon, or stressed that Jewish women's readiness to sell themselves was a measure of the desperation to which the most vulnerable members of the community had been reduced. In their eyes, destitute Jewish mothers, whose husbands were either dead or off in German labor camps, were not to be condemned or viewed as having lost their spiritual integrity if they resorted to prostitution in their effort to provide for their hungry children.[37] A number of young Yiddish writers in Poland introduced a more hard-hitting, realist style to the depiction of wartime communal collapse and moral disarray. Most notable among them were Leyb Olitzky and Oyzer Varshavski (1898–1944), who depicted the moral disintegration of *shtetl* communities under the impact of wartime shortages and German commercial restrictions. In Varshavski's *Shmuglars* (Smugglers), the livelihood of an entire *shtetl* comes to depend on black market commerce and smuggling, which absorbs the energies of men who had in yesteryear been hardworking artisans and respected merchants. Backbiting among partners, fear of informants, the employment of prostitutes to smooth passage through German checkpoints – these and other evils associated with the illicit trade lead to violence, sexual anarchy, the breakdown of social hierarchies, and intergenerational clashes that tear apart the social and cultural fabric of the *shtetl*.[38]

The cultural dimensions of German occupation

The wartime reconfiguration of much of Eastern Europe into a German-dominated political-military sphere created new challenges to ethno-cultural identities, novel occasions for cultural conflicts, and fresh opportunities for cultural cross-fertilization and redefinition. Among German soldiers, officers, and administrators, the *Ostjuden* aroused a variety of reactions and impressions. The similarity between Yiddish and German created an apparent ease of communication which led to the cooptation of Jews in disproportionate numbers into the lower, clerical ranks of the German administrative organs.[39] At the same time, though, the widespread perception of Yiddish as a debased dialect of German reinforced the German sense of cultural superiority over East European Jewry.[40] Some of the images of East European Jewish life recorded by German military photographers suggest a superficial interest in traditional Jewish culture as an exotic phenomenon, an object of Orientalist fascination.[41] By the same token, for many Germans who spent the war years in the East, the contact with the region's Jews reinforced their negative perception of *Ostjuden* (and, by extension, of Jews in general) as strangely dressed people with bizarre customs, who lived like vermin in unsanitary conditions, and who could hardly be considered members of the same species as the Germans.[42]

Indeed, the problem of hygiene was the most prominent among a number of administrative issues that highlighted cultural differences and created tensions between Jews and Germans. The German authorities tried to impose strict sanitary standards both as a public-health measure and as an expression of their cultural superiority and of the far-reaching nature of their control. In many instances, as soon as the German army had occupied a town, its residents – and Jews were frequently singled out in this respect – were required to clean up its streets and public areas. Strict new regulations were introduced governing the use of public latrines (evoking a wave of bathroom humor among the Jewish population). Jews were even required to bathe in their *mikvoes* (public baths used for ritual cleansing) in shifts spread over the course of the week, a measure which was seen by Jews as threatening to the unique ceremonial status of the religiously ordained pre-Sabbath visit to the *mikve*. German regulations requiring the burial of the dead in wooden coffins (rather than just in shrouds, as was the general Jewish practice) at a time when wood was in very short supply due to the German army's own requisitioning, led to the accumulation of unburied corpses for days on end. This was a flagrant violation of Jewish law, which requires that a body be laid to rest on the day after a person's death.[43] A somewhat more trivial, but nevertheless irksome, instance of the friction between German bureaucratic norms and Jewish culture arose with the introduction of German-issued photographic identification cards for the entire population: the requirement that all adults remove their headgear for the official snapshots was an insult and humiliation for religious Jews.[44]

Germany's eastward expansion also inevitably led to a broadening of contact between German Jews and East European Jewry. This sharpened pre-existing divisions within the German Jewish community over the nature of its relationship to the *Ostjuden* – a debate that was itself a manifestation of deep-seated uncertainties over how to define German Jewish identity. The German Jewish establishment was largely assimilationist in outlook, embracing a Reform Judaism that separated religious identity from ethnicity and that regarded German Jews as "Germans of Mosaic faith." Fully espousing mainstream German nationalist ideals, most Jewish public figures, newspapers, and institutions endorsed the German war effort as a righteous struggle, and viewed the expansion into Eastern Europe as part of a grand civilizing mission. The Jews of Eastern Europe were commonly regarded as uncultured cousins (several times removed) whose mentality and way of life had, due to unfortunate circumstances, not changed since the Middle Ages.[45] The erosion of the political boundaries between German Jews and *Ostjuden* thus presented an opportunity for German Jews to carve out a special niche for themselves within the broader framework of Germany's civilizing mission. At the same time, the sudden sense of proximity to these unwashed masses also provoked profound discomfort among German Jews who were at pains to distance themselves from any direct association with the *Ostjuden*. Above all, it was feared that an influx of Jewish refugees and jobseekers from the East would provoke an intensification of German anti-Semitism that would target all Jews indiscriminately.[46]

It was in this ambivalent spirit that institutional offshoots of the Hilfsverein der Deutschen Juden – the most prominent German Jewish relief agency – launched relief operations among the Jews of Poland and the Ober Ost. Their main objective was to enable the Jews of the occupied lands to survive the wartime material shortages while staying put in the East. The relief committees associated with the Hilfsverein also sent instructors and administrators to establish modern schools and promote German-language education among the *Ostjuden*, whose native Yiddish was considered an unseemly jargon rather than a distinctive Jewish tongue in its own right.[47]

Yet this paternalistic approach to relief work did not go unchallenged. The Zionists had constituted a vocal, dissenting minority within the German Jewish community since the turn of the century, and their leadership questioned the assumptions and goals of the Hilfsverein. Shortly after the war's outbreak in 1914, a coalition of liberal and Zionist Jews led by Max Bodenheimer had formed the first organization specifically committed to relief for, and lobbying on behalf of, East European Jewry – the Komitee für den Osten (Committee for the East), or KfdO. Contesting the Hilfsverein's goal of leading the *Ostjuden* as individuals toward Western enlightenment and modernity, the KfdO insisted that Polish Jewry be recognized as an organic community with an intrinsically valuable culture and tradition of its own. This community needed to be assisted in redeeming itself on its own terms, and its integrity was to be enhanced through the fostering of Jewish national-cultural autonomy in the occupied lands. The KfdO tried to link its goals to German war aims by arguing that the Yiddish speakers of the East were already linguistically tied to Germany and hence ideally suited to serve as propagators of German cultural, commercial, and political influence in the occupied territories.[48]

The German occupation authorities, however, were more inclined to endorse the position of Germany's Orthodox community on the

Polish Jewish question – a position which was much closer to that of the Hilfsverein than of the KfdO. The German Orthodox rabbinate was vehemently anti-Zionist, and its representatives ran relief and educational services of their own in Poland, using their influence to try to steer the religious masses away from Zionism and toward a distinctive political consciousness of their own – a consciousness focussed on the achievement of full civic equality combined with the preservation of religious values. These efforts culminated in the creation in 1916 of a Polish branch of Agudat Israel, the Central European Orthodox political movement whose main base of operations up to that time had been in Germany.[49] The German authorities indicated their support for this conservative form of Jewish activism by inviting representatives of the German Orthodox rabbinate to serve as advisers on the Jewish question to the German occupation administration in Poland. It was no surprise, therefore, when in November 1916 the German authorities dealt a blow to the KfdO's lobbying campaign on behalf of Jewish national-cultural autonomy in Poland by issuing a statement formally recognizing the Jewish population of Poland as a religious rather than national minority.[50]

The Germans also instituted curial elections for *kehillah* (community) councils, which were entrusted with authority over Jewish communal institutions in Poland. The introduction of electoral politics to the *kehillot* (plural of *kehillah*) undercut the long-standing control of Jewish communal boards by the small elite advocating Jewish assimilation into the Polish mainstream, and opened the door to Agudat Israel's emergence as a key player in Jewish affairs at the local level. Agudat Israel's powerful position in the new councils was, in turn, to become a vital component of the party's political machine in the interwar Polish republic.[51] This is just one example of the many ways in which the the German occupation authorities' institutional and juridical improvisations helped shape the longer-term development of ethnic and cultural politics in interwar Eastern Europe.

While the German authorities' approach to the Jewish question had important institutional ramifications, an official decree could not resolve the matter of Jewish identity no matter how ponderously it was phrased. Debates among both German and Polish Jewry continued to intensify over the nature of Jewish culture, its relationship to modernity, the desired form Jewish education should take, and whether or not Yiddish and/or Hebrew should be cultivated as Jewish national languages. Among the keenest observers of these debates was a small group of German Jews posted as censors and translators to the press section of the Ober Ost administration in Kovno. Referring to themselves as the Intellectuals'

Club (and with an extra dash of sarcasm after the war as the Club of Former Intellectuals), this group of writers, poets, and artists was part of a tiny but vocal movement of cultural and political dissent that had begun to stir within the German Jewish community in the decade preceding the war. These figures espoused a more radical and assertive form of Zionism than was common among the leaders of the KfdO – a Zionism that was to be based on the cultivation of a completely distinct, authentic, and holistic Jewish cultural and national identity, rather than an armchair Zionism that was little more than a Jewish version of nineteenth-century German liberal nationalism. This quest for cultural authenticity was intimately linked to a fascination with the lifestyle, language, and customs of the *Ostjuden*. Martin Buber's (1878–1965) translations and interpretations of Hasidic tales and legends, published from 1906 on, had a particularly strong influence on this intellectual coterie, which saw the Hasidic *Gemeinschaft* specifically, and East European Jewry generally, as repositories of spiritual wisdom, religious spontaneity, and social commitment – qualities that seemed sadly absent from the overly structured, formalized, and hence alienating, norms of Western modernity.[52]

Many avid readers of Buber's rather romantic work were unsettled and disturbed by their wartime encounter with the living, breathing Hasidim of Poland, whose apparently uncouth manners and unhygienic living conditions shocked them.[53] Others, however, found the encounter with *Ostjuden* in their native surroundings to be refreshing and invigorating, and it was in this category that the members of the Intellectuals' Club fell. These men embraced the opportunity to learn more about, interact with, and even intervene on behalf of, East European Jewish communities. Many of their experiences and impressions were recorded in a collection of bitingly funny sketches by Sammy Gronemann, published in 1925 under the title *Hawdoloh und Zapfenstreich* (Havdalah [Jewish ceremony marking end of Sabbath] and [Military] Tattoo).[54]

The Intellectuals' Club constituted a miniature counter-culture movement in the very bosom of the German occupation administration. Among Gronemann's companions in the group were fellow Zionist intellectuals such as the novelist Arnold Zweig and the artist Hermann Struck, as well as a few non-Jewish philo-Semites such as the modernist poet Richard Dehmel.[55] Gathering together at a *Stammtisch* (a regulars' table) on a weekly basis, these keen observers – and, often, mordant critics – of their social and cultural surroundings, exchanged impressions, read poetry and essays, and debated political and intellectual issues. They shared a common scorn for the pompous militarism and mindless bureaucratism of the Prusso-German officers under whom they served. More broadly, they looked to East European Jewish culture as a vibrant, spontaneous expression of folk spirit that contrasted sharply with what they regarded as the stiff formality and artificiality of German Jewish culture – be it of the assimilated or Orthodox variety. The often chaotic appearance of East European religious services appealed to them as an expression of the synagogue's function as a public gathering place and a civic forum; even the Orthodox synagogues in Germany seemed sterile and alienating by comparison. They regarded the apparently incongruous presence in *batei midrash* (small, neighborhood houses of prayer and study) of weary laborers curled up in corners asleep alongside intensely engaged study groups, as an indication of the fundamentally egalitarian, inclusive ethos of authentic Judaism. Hermann Struck's wartime drawings, later published as illustrations for Arnold Zweig's *Das Ostjüdische Antlitz* (The East-Jewish Countenance), portrayed the Jewish men, women, and children of Poland-Lithuania as physically battered and weary people whose eyes and facial expressions bespoke an inner resilience, an uncompromising ability to remain true to themselves.[56]

Writers such as Gronemann and Zweig depicted the *Ostjuden* as a people who contended with their burdensome material existence by living their real lives in the world of the mind and spirit. This was most clearly visible on the Sabbath, the day of rest, when the mask of the material world was cast off and the light of the soul shone forth from the eyes of the humblest Jewish workers and peddlers. In Gronemann's eyes, the very war that marked the moral collapse of the West brought forth the noblest qualities of the East European Jews, whose spiritual inner life remained intact amidst the turmoil despite their political and military powerlessness. (As we have seen, An-sky's view from the Russian side of the front was far more pessimistic by 1916–1917.) The ability to distinguish clearly between the holy and the profane constituted the inner power of these authentic Jews – hence the title of Gronemann's book, which juxtaposes the evocative image of the Havdalah ceremony (separating the sacredness of the Sabbath from the profanity of the work week) with the self-important posturing of the *Zapfenstreich* – the military tattoo. Avigdor Ha-Meiri, a Zionist writer who served as an officer in the Habsburg army and fell into Russian captivity in 1916, independently developed a similar theme as he described the uncanny ability of the impoverished, oppressed Russian Jew to turn the prosaic into the sublime. In his account of his time spent with a Jewish family while on labor service in Ukraine, Ha-Meiri wrote of how the ordinary Russian samovar became a manifestation of the divine in the eyes of his host, who compared the steam billowing forth from the utensil to the divine "cloud of honor" that enveloped the cherubs in the Jewish temple in Jerusalem.[57]

The wartime spread of this "cult of the *Ostjuden,*" as Steven Aschheim has called it, among scattered groups of Jewish intellectuals in Germany and the Habsburg Empire was stimulated by their contact with East European Jewish refugees and exiles. The young Gershom Scholem (1897–1982), whose father had expelled him from his home (in a formal letter sent by registered mail to his own address) on account of his Zionism and his opposition to the war, took up residence in 1916 at a Berlin boarding-house run by a distant relative of Hermann Struck. Here he came into close contact with a group of East European Jewish intellectuals – among them, the Hebrew writer Shmuel Yosef Agnon (Samuel Josef Czaczkes; as an Israeli citizen, Agnon was to become the 1966 Nobel Prize winner in literature for his fictional portrayals of Jewish *shtetl* life) and Zalman Rubashoff (a Zionist activist who was later, as Zalman Shazar, to become Israel's president). Powerfully drawn to the mental world of these men, Scholem was reinforced in his conviction that traditional Jewish culture contained elements that were vital to the moral regeneration of Western Jewry. Unlike many Zionists, he embraced Yiddish as a language that expressed a uniquely Jewish worldview. Moreover, he attacked the KfdO's contention that Yiddish-speaking Jews were natural agents for the dissemination of German culture and influence in Eastern Europe. This propaganda line not only threatened to compromise the Jews' relations with other nationalities in the region; it also flew in the face of the identity of Yiddish as a language that might have evolved from German, but that had come to constitute a distinctive medium for the expression of humanistic values that could not be further removed from the cold and alienating norms of German society.[58]

For their part, many of the exiled East European Jewish activists and intellectuals hoped to take what was best about Western civilization and apply it to the betterment of East European Jewish conditions – and above all to the construction of a cohesive, mass-based, socialist Zionist movement. They contributed to the overall evolution of the "cult of the *Ostjuden*" in a socialist direction, as did the encounter of Zweig and others with the abject poverty of the Jewish masses in the East. The idea of synthesizing Western civilization (i.e., science, technology, modern political institutions) with socialist values and elements of East European Jewish cultural consciousness led to the creation in 1916 of the Jüdische Volksheim (Jewish People's Home) in Berlin. This school was designed primarily for the education of East European Jewish children, but it also sponsored cultural programs and lectures designed for the general Jewish public. *Ostjuden* were to be provided with educational advancement and means for self-improvement, while German Jews were to be exposed to the look, sound, and feel of East European *Yiddishkeit* (Jewishness).[59] Among the organizers and supporters of this institution were S. Y. Agnon, Chaim Arlosoroff (a refugee from the Russian Empire who was to emerge as the major inter-war ideologue of labor Zionism before his assassination in Tel Aviv in 1933), Franz Kafka (1883–1924), and Martin Buber.[60]

The intersection of the war experience and the encounter with the *Ostjuden* stimulated the development of influential critiques of Western modernity on the part of a number of Central European Jewish intellectuals. Thinkers such as Martin Buber did not unconditionally reject the legacy of the Scientific Revolution and the Enlightenment, but they looked to the apparent social intimacy and spiritual *Innerlichkeit* of the East European Jewish communities as an example and inspiration for social and moral reform among Jews as well as non-Jews in the West; the influence of the neo-romantic German cult of *völkisch* authenticity was clearly discernible in these ideas, but, under the impact of the war, this element was linked to a strongly humanistic, even cosmopolitan, agenda.[61] The war strengthened the conviction of those in Buber's intellectual orbit – notably, the members of Prague's Zionist Bar Kochba society – that science, secularism, and the streamlined, impersonal state were morally bankrupt values and institutions presiding over a soulless society, and that the culture of the *Ostjuden* offered some meaningful alternatives. Buber himself, who had moved from an early optimism about Germany's role as a liberator in the East to deep disillusionment in the face of rising wartime German anti-Semitism, wrote his first draft of *Ich und Du* – his seminal work on the nature of genuine dialogue – in 1916, under the direct impression of the utter breakdown in human communication that the Great War represented. During the same period, the monthly journal he edited – *Der Jude* – served as a forum for Zionist writings, sympathetic accounts of the *Ostjuden* as "moral reservoirs" for world Jewry, and impassioned debates about the *Grenzsperre* proposal (legislation that would bar immigration into Germany by East European Jews, implemented by executive order in Prussia in 1918),[62] which Buber vehemently opposed. While developing his ideas about dialogue among humans and between man and God, Buber also refined his conception of the fundamental spiritual and historical unity of the Jewish people within the framework of their Covenant with God – a unity that transcended political boundaries and internal disputes and whose significance as an example and inspiration to a broken world was universal.[63]

For his part, Scholem's wartime discovery of the spiritual world of the *Ostjuden* led in later years to his scholarly work on Jewish mysticism, work that shaped his philosophical critiques of modernity.[64] Likewise, Franz Kafka, who had been enchanted by his discovery of Yiddish theatre in 1911–1912, deepened his engagement with Jewish culture and Zionist ideas during the war, studying Hebrew and writing pieces such as "The Trial," "The Great Wall of China," and the so-called Zürau aphorisms that reflected his preoccupation with the contrast between *Gesellschaft* and *Gemeinschaft*, his interest in religion as a source of social cohesion, and his growing fascination with Kabbalistic mysticism as a framework for exploring the meaning of human suffering. His strengthened Zionist sympathies were quite pungently expressed in "A Report for an Academy," published in Buber's *Der Jude* in 1917, which can be read as an allegory for the trauma and ultimate futility of Jewish efforts at assimilation.[65]

If the German advance into Eastern Europe led to a sharpening of differences among rival German Jewish cultural and ideological currents, it also generated stimuli and opportunities for the development of diverse East European Jewish artistic, educational, and political movements. Their November 1916 statement about Jewish religious identity notwithstanding, the German occupation authorities cannot be said to have maintained a coherent or consistent policy line toward the Jews; the Jewish question, after all, did not constitute an all-consuming ideological obsession for them in this conflict, as it was to do in the Second World War. Attitudes and priorities varied from one bureaucratic apparatus to another. The idea of Germanizing the Yiddish-speaking Jews was widespread, but never systematically implemented. Local commanders with whom Jews were most likely to come into direct contact tended to be more anti-Semitic than the top-ranking officers who laid down general policy guidelines. Even General Ludendorff – later to become a political ally of Hitler's – seems to have taken a relatively benign interest in Jewish welfare during the war, supporting the establishment of a Jewish soup kitchen named after him and meeting occasionally with selected Jewish artists.[66] The relatively tolerant atmosphere of the German occupation – compared to that of the Russian – facilitated a revival of the Yiddish and Hebrew press and the inception of open activity by Jewish political parties. The segmented and multilayered character of the German military-bureaucratic apparatus, combined with its unfocussed approach to Jewish issues, created opportunities for

German Jewish army chaplains, uniformed Jews in the Ober Ost apparatus, and representatives of German Jewish communal organizations to use their official connections to obtain facilities or at least freedom of operation for various local Jewish charitable, artistic, and educational initiatives.

The result was a veritable blossoming of competing visions of Jewish culture and identity. In the political sphere, Jewish parties whose operations had been severely limited or altogether suppressed under Russian rule, were allowed openly to canvass for popular support and to hold public meetings. The introduction of universal manhood suffrage (albeit within the framework of a curial system that distributed electoral power unevenly among various income brackets and religious groups) in Warsaw's and other cities' municipal elections increased the pressures and opportunities for the conversion of elitist political coteries into mass movements. Relief work also presented an opportunity for rival Jewish parties to reach out to the common people. The Zionists were particularly successful at winning hearts and minds among the common folk, as reflected in their gathering of 238,000 signatures on a 1917 petition calling on the Great Powers to support the Jewish claim to Palestine. Money was even collected on behalf of aid to the beleaguered Yishuv (Jewish settlement) in Palestine during 1917, and the anniversary of Theodor Herzl's death was widely commemorated in urban centers as well as provincial communities around Poland. To be sure, other parties competed with the Zionists for popular support. Notable among these was the Bund – an anti-Zionist socialist party which embraced Yiddish as the language of the proletariat, and the Folkspartei (Folk party, or Folkists) – a populist grouping created in 1916 by a group of writers and journalists championing Yiddish language rights and Jewish cultural autonomy.[67]

The Zionist leaders soon discovered that the sudden expansion in the scope of their activities was accompanied by an intensification of doctrinal disputes within the movement. The religious Zionist Mizrachi movement came into its own as an autonomous faction during the war, and was later to break off from the General Zionist umbrella organization to form a separate party. The Folkists' success at winning away some support from the Zionists' potential electoral base contributed to the heightening of inter-generational tensions within the secular mainstream of the General Zionist movement. A group of younger members challenged the leadership's long-standing indifference and even hostility toward Yiddish, accusing it of adhering to a self-defeating intellectual elitism. While these ideological dissenters, first known as the Youth Center and later as Tseire Tsion (the Youth of Zion), shared Zionism's

4.2   Yiddish placards publicizing the SS (Socialist Zionist) electoral list, on a municipal election day in Częstochowa, German-occupied Poland, during World War I

general commitment to the revival of Hebrew as a spoken language among Jewish immigrants to Palestine, they contended that Yiddish had to be recognized – and even cultivated – as an authentic expression of Jewish popular culture and identity in Eastern Europe. This unprecedented debate over a possible role for Yiddish in the movement ended with a grudging concession by the majority at the Third (Polish) Zionist Conference of October 1917 that Yiddish could be considered "a supplementary language, from which one must pass in stages to Hebrew."[68] Meanwhile, the Germans' establishment of an institutional framework for a nominally independent Polish state, accompanied by a rising tide of Polish ethnic nationalism, fueled demands among Zionists (as well as some other Jewish parties) that Poland's Jews be guaranteed some form of non-territorial national autonomy. While maintaining its vision for a Jewish national revival in Palestine, then, the Zionist movement was beginning to define a role for itself in the ongoing cultural and political life of the Diaspora and to modify the socio-cultural elitism that had characterized its early years.[69]

The growing restlessness among the younger generation of Zionists also manifested itself in the development of socialist Zionist youth movements, most notably Ha-Shomer Ha-Tsair (The Young Guard).[70] Established by members of two small pre-war Zionist youth movements who met as refugees in wartime Vienna, Ha-Shomer Ha-Tsair's ethos reflected the influence of diverse intellectual and cultural currents. These included ideas its founders came into contact with during their stay in the Austrian capital, such as Buber's humanistic interpretation of Judaism and the romantic nationalism of the German Wandervogel scouting movement. The result was an ideological synthesis that combined socialist values with a voluntaristic, pioneering ethos, and universalistic, secular utopianism with an emphasis on the cultivation of Jewish culture and identity.[71]

As with the "cult of the *Ostjuden*" and radical Zionism in Central Europe, then, the momentum gained by these cultural and political trends among East European Jewry during the war years was closely associated with a generational divide. Zionism's transformation into a mass movement was spurred in part by the growing activism and political initiative on the part of youth organizations within it. As the fabric of traditional Jewish society was being torn to pieces, the older generation of cultural and political leaders seemed bereft of responses to the afflictions of the war; in the eyes of politically engaged young people, the task of creating a new social and cultural framework in place of the demolished communal structures of yesteryear fell to their generation. Even the Orthodox Zionist Mizrachi movement saw the rise within its ranks of a youth organization. Personal commitment to political activism and *hachsharah* (training for agricultural labor in Palestine), belief in some form of collectivism or socialism, a sometimes incongruous mixture of naive utopianism and pragmatic engagement with concrete problems – all these ideas, values, and qualities had been propagated and had manifested themselves before the war, but they gained much broader appeal in the course of the conflict and struck a particularly resonant chord among members of Zionism's "generation of 1914."[72]

In the world of Jewish letters and arts, the German occupation also marked a dramatic shift from conditions under tsarist rule. Although many of their regular contributors and correspondents were left stranded in Russian-held territory to the east, and despite severe paper shortages, most of the major Yiddish and Hebrew dailies in Poland – suppressed by the Russian government in July 1915 – were able to resume production on a modest scale by early 1916. If original copy proved hard to come by, the papers printed war news from German and Austrian news agencies and translated editorials and opinion pieces from the German Jewish press.[73]

The cultural implications for Jews of German hegemony in Eastern Europe formed a major topic for debate in these newspapers. While the removal of tsarist oppression was greeted with relief, it was also widely feared that the new regional dominance of German language and culture could threaten the autonomous development of Jewish culture. This common perception was given various ideological spins. *Ha-Tsefirah* (The [Horn] Blast, Warsaw) – Poland's leading Hebrew Zionist daily, which catered to an educated elite among the Jewish reading public – reprinted an article from a Zionist publication in Berlin which contended that the prospect of individual advancement through the German educational system combined with the relatively easy linguistic transition from Yiddish to German would tempt many young Jews to slide down the slippery slope of cultural assimilation. Only by cultivating Hebrew as their tongue could Poland's Jews ensure that they retained a truly distinct identity in the face of Germanizing pressures and temptations.[74] For their part, advocates of Yiddish argued that the belief of some German officials that Yiddish-speaking Jews were natural candidates for Germanization should simply be used to gain official support for the creation of a Yiddish-language school network. This, in turn, could form a precedent for the establishment of non-territorial national-cultural autonomy for the Jews of Poland (as well as for other national minorities).[75]

Linguistic and cultural assimilation was portrayed as a threat to moral values in a short story by Reuven Fahn, serialized in two successive issues of the Galician Hebrew Zionist weekly, *Ha-Mitspeh* (The Watchtower, Cracow). Entitled "The Guest," the tale revolves around the Grosskopf (literally, Big Head) family, which has fled wartorn Galicia for the security of Vienna. While other Jewish refugees live in poverty but hold fast to their religious tradition and identity, the Grosskopfs have enriched themselves through black-market trading while embracing a shallow and dissolute Viennese life-style. When an uncle – a pious rabbbi from Galicia – comes to stay with the family for a few weeks, he is shocked to learn that the boys' names have been changed from Moshe and Leyb to Moritz and Leon, while the daughter is now Mitzi instead of Miriam. Things go from bad to worse as the rabbi learns that Mr. Grosskopf now belongs to a Reform temple, and then goes on to discover that talk of a possible early end to the war brings anxiety rather than joy to this family of hoarders and profiteers. Cultural assimilation and moral decay were thus presented as two sides of the same hollow coin.[76]

As is clear from some of the newspaper articles discussed above, it was widely felt that the primary arena in which the Jews' linguistic and cultural future would be determined was that of education. Limited efforts to establish modern Jewish schools had been made before the war, but these had been seriously limited by the suspicious Russian authorities. The educational norm for most Jewish males was still the *cheder* – the traditional religious primary school where young boys would be taught the Torah by rote and perhaps exposed to a smattering of Talmud. A small number of adolescents and young men might go on to serious study of the Talmud in a *yeshivah*. Girls would generally be taught in separate girls' *chadarim* (plural of *cheder*) or at home, the scope of their education often being limited to the religious fundamentals and the ability to read and write Yiddish.[77] For the tiny minority of the Jewish population with the means for and interest in the pursuit of a modern education, Russian-language high schools and universities – which severely limited the number of Jewish entrants – or study abroad had been the only real options before the war.

The German occupation opened up possibilities for the development of a Jewish-run, modern educational system designed for both sexes. By the same token, it generated conflict over what languages should be used in secular Jewish schools. In Poland, German was declared to be the official language of instruction for Jews, but this policy was enforced very haphazardly and abandoned altogether in 1917 in the face of widespread teacher strikes and the establishment of a clandestine Yiddish school network. The Ober Ost administration was more ecumenical in its linguistic policies, presiding as it did over such an ethnically heterogeneous population; in fact, it set out to understand, control, and "civilize" this bewildering welter of nationalities by fitting them into neatly defined ethno-linguistic frameworks that would serve as media for the propagation of German values and cultural forms, and that would lend themselves to a divide-and-rule strategy.[78] Its official line, applied inconsistently, was that children of various ethnic groups should be educated in their respective native languages, with Yiddish recognized as the Jewish language. The Ober Ost authorities even used Yiddish on the identification cards they issued to Jews. They also permitted the establishment of schools that employed Hebrew as their primary language of instruction, including a Gymnasium in Vilna. This Zionist educational network went on to grow and flourish as the Tarbut (Culture) school system in interwar Poland. Even the Orthodox Agudat Israel party undertook a modernization of religious education with the establishment of boys' and girls' schools in Cracow (in Austrian-ruled western Galicia) in 1917.[79]

Vocational education for disadvantaged Jewish youth was also expanded, the most dynamic institution in this field being Vilna's Hilf durch Arbet (Help through Work) school. First established in 1903, this work-school sought to train its students in modern artisanal techniques. During the German occupation its programs were greatly expanded thanks to the active intervention of *Feldrabbiner* (German army chaplain) Sali Levi of Breslau, who helped arrange for German instructors to be brought in to teach students the latest styles and methods. Similar institutions, including an agricultural school, were created in smaller towns with the support of Levi and Hilf durch Arbet. Students from Hilf durch Arbet were featured as the Jewish representatives at an ethnic craft show organized for propaganda purposes by the Ober Ost authorities in January 1917.[80]

The goal of establishing Yiddish as a legitimate, national language in its own right – which had been articulated as an official program by the 1908 Czernowitz conference of Yiddish writers – was advanced not only through the creation of Yiddish-language educational institutions, but also through the progress made during 1915–1918 toward fixing uniform standards for the language. This effort may have been stimulated by the wartime publication of several German–Yiddish dictionaries in Germany, including one compiled by a non-Jewish scholar. The Ober Ost authorities may also have indirectly spurred interest in the standardization of Yiddish orthography and vocabulary through their own obsession with cataloguing and systematizing their knowledge about the various ethnic groups under their control and with determining how exactly to translate decrees and proclamations into local languages.[81] In any case, it was during the war that the editorial staff of Vilna's Yiddish-language daily, *Letzte Najes* (Latest News), undertook the first serious effort at defining a common set of rules governing the writing of Yiddish. This initiative was followed up systematically by the YIVO Institute for Jewish Research established in Vilna after the end of the war. (Of course, it could be argued that to attempt to impose consistent rules on Yiddish was to undermine the very qualities of spontaneity and scorn for authority that lent the language its authenticity as a medium of popular expression.)[82]

Thus, in the face of often unpredictable and arbitrary German policies and despite the sometimes presumptuous or condescending nature of German Jewish assistance programs, East European Jewish cultural and educational leaders were able to make the most of the constructive opportunities created by the German occupation. Rather than becoming the passive objects of German cultural imperialism, they were able to turn the feudalistic pluralism of the German military bureaucracy to their advantage through the mediation of well-placed German Jewish supporters and sponsors.[83] Perhaps if Berlin had succeeded in establishing long-term hegemony over Eastern Europe, German assimilatory pressures and temptations would have posed a greater threat to the autonomy and vitality of Yiddish culture. (Even some of the apologists for Yiddish in the KfdO believed that in the long run Yiddish would pave the way for the Germanization of Poland's Jews.) As it was, despite sporadic efforts at Germanization of Poland's Jews (including a short-lived Austro-German policy in 1915–1916 of issuing proclamations to the Jewish population in Hebrew-scripted German instead of Yiddish), the overall impact of the occupation was to facilitate a consolidation and institutionalization of both Yiddishist and Hebraist cultural movements on an unprecedented scale; for their part, the Polish Jewish assimilationists found their pre-war position as leading communal representatives, and their image as pathbreaking modernizers, undermined.

The post-1915 reinvigoration of Jewish cultural expression and activity in Poland and Lithuania was not confined to intellectual circles; it manifested itself in a variety of spheres and among segments of every social stratum. The years of German occupation witnessed a proliferation of Jewish reading clubs and discussion circles in all the major towns and cities of the occupied lands. These ranged from small groups of Zionist intellectuals committed to the study and propagation of Hebrew letters, to well-attended public fora such as the "trial" of a popular novel staged over a succession of evenings by the Bialystok Cultural Union. Designed to foster debate about the relative virtues of tradition and modernity, this event allowed the audience to participate in the judgment of the novel's female protagonist, whose quest for personal liberation leads her to abandon her husband and children.[84]

Not all forms of popular entertainment were so high-minded or ideologically focussed. Jewish audiences filled cinemas, eager to catch the latest products of the German and Polish film industries.[85] Even a movie whose plot (about a disillusioned young Hasid who seeks refuge in a monastery from the spiritual oppression of Orthodox Judaism) seemed to have Christian missionary overtones was screened night after night in Bialystok before a packed house, to the accompaniment of a Reform synagogue choir; the proceeds went to benefit a Jewish charity.[86] The German occupation did put an end to the tsarist censors' wartime exclusion of any and all Jewish themes (including stories from the Hebrew Bible!) from the silver screen. Film versions of two Yiddish plays were produced in 1915–1916 by Sfinks, the Jewish-run film company that had been founded in Warsaw in 1910 and that also produced features that were not specifically Jewish in content. The Polish-born film star, Pola Negri (the screen name of Apolonia Chalupec), who was first "discovered" by Sfinks and starred in seven of the company's films during 1914–1918, went on in 1918 to play the leading role in a German-produced movie (based on a pre-war Yiddish play) entitled *Der Gelbe Schein* (The Yellow Ticket). Filmed in the Jewish quarter of

Warsaw, this picture indicted tsarist anti-Semitism by telling the story of a young Jewish woman whose only chance to escape the Pale and obtain an education in St. Petersburg is to work as a prostitute.[87]

Yiddish theaters, which had been closed down by the Russian authorities soon after the outbreak of war, reopened in Warsaw, Vilna, and other Polish and Lithuanian cities in the wake of the German advance. Their most crowd-pleasing features were schmaltzy melodramas and heavy-handed comedies from the pre-war repertoire. The plays of Avrom Goldfadn (1840–1908), a pioneer of Yiddish theater, and Jacob Gordin (1853–1909), an *émigré* who wrote for the New York Yiddish stage, were still the most popular hits.[88] The contrast between big city life and the *shtetl* and the tension between forces of assimilation and tradition provided much of the thematic content for these productions, which were peopled by an array of stock characters. Moralistic themes as well as elements of social radicalism were integrated into some of these plays as well (most notably in the work of Jacob Gordin). Yiddish operettas were also well attended, and some producers even succeeded in drawing German officers into their audiences by hiring popular German singing stars to play the female leads.[89]

While the war lasted, the international world of Yiddish theater was fragmented; new plays being written abroad for the New York and London audiences were not readily accessible to producers for the Warsaw stage. Yet it was precisely during this period of relative isolation that modernist experimentation in Poland's Yiddish theater received its greatest impetus. Yiddish literature had already been established as a form of high culture directed at a mass audience by writers such as Y. L. Peretz, Sholem Aleichem (Solomon Rabinovitz, 1859–1916), and Mendele Mocher Sforim (Shalom Jacob Abramowitsch, 1836–1917), all three of whom passed away during the First World War. (Peretz's 1915 funeral in Warsaw drew a crowd estimated at 100,000.) But attempts at elevating Yiddish theatre to the status of serious drama had only just begun prior to the war. Peretz himself had sounded a militant call in 1910 for the creation of a new Yiddish art theater that would supplant the low-class *shund* dramas – the hastily assembled patchworks of plagiarism and improvisation that served to reinforce the image of Yiddish as a degraded jargon.[90] Peretz, Sholem Aleichem, Sholem Asch (1880–1957 – a disciple of Peretz), and others, began writing Yiddish plays, some of which were produced in the years before 1914 by young amateurs who drew their inspiration from Stanislavsky's Moscow Art Theater. Ester Rokhl Kaminska's (1870–1925) renowned Warsaw-based theatrical company also staged a number of these more serious dramas.[91]

It was in 1916 that these tentative initiatives came together and gained momentum through the creation of the Federation of Yiddish Dramatic Actors (FADO), soon to be known as the Vilna Troupe. Formed as a company of committed young amateurs, the Vilna Troupe found a group of eager spokesmen among the Ober Ost's "Intellectuals' Club," which was delighted to see the distinctive culture, tradition, and language of the *Ostjuden* presented in a dignified, artistic form on the stage. Hermann Struck, Arnold Zweig, and other members of that circle were able to convince the military authorities to grant the troupe exclusive use of an old circus building in downtown Vilna. In its performances, the diversity of accents and dialects that pervaded the typical Yiddish theatrical ensemble was replaced by a uniform Lithuanian (Litvak) pronunciation of Yiddish. FADO took its plays seriously as literary works that were to be interpreted line by line and rehearsed thoroughly; its audiences were expected to remain quiet during performances rather than engaging in the raucous behavior that was tolerated at other Yiddish theaters. German military officers, who could comprehend snatches of Yiddish dialogue, were drawn in increasing numbers to the Vilna Troupe's productions, joining everyone else in rising in honor of the Zionist anthem "Ha-Tikvah" (The Hope) when it was played at the end of performances. Early efforts by the military authorities to discourage this trend gave way by the end of the occupation to their proud showcasing of the Vilna Troupe as an example of the cultural refinement of Eastern Europe under Germany's tutelage.[92]

With the support and encouragement of its German sympathizers, the Vilna Troupe transformed itself into a professional theater that staged plays by the likes of Sholem Asch and Peretz Hirschbein (another young member of Y. L. Peretz's circle who had founded a Yiddish art theater in Odessa in 1908), as well as producing translated versions of major Western plays by the likes of Molière, Arthur Schnitzler, and Eugene O'Neill. At a time when travel within Poland and Lithuania was tightly restricted, Zweig, Struck, and Gronemann were able to arrange for the Vilna Troupe to go on tour. The company gained broad recognition and rave reviews in 1917 during its stay in Warsaw, where Ester Rokhl Kaminska appeared on stage to endorse and acclaim its efforts as heralding the advent of "a new age and a new art."[93] The Vilna Troupe developed a highly visual, symbolist style that took themes and images of traditional Jewish life and exoticized them by transposing them into expressionist stage designs and choreography.[94] This was to culminate in the production of An-sky's *The Dybbuk* in 1920, just one month after An-sky's death; this mystical story of possession and exorcism had itself been inspired by the playwright's pre-war ethnographic research. With the dissolution of the wartime barriers between countries and continents, the Vilna Troupe was free to go on world tours and to introduce plays like *The Dybbuk* into the international Yiddish theatrical repertoire. In so doing, it also won a greater measure of recognition for Yiddish as a legitimate medium for artistic expression.[95]

The Russian Jewish avant-garde's quest for modernist authenticity

Experiments in the synthesis of Jewish folk culture with modernist artistic forms were also under way on the Russian side of the ever-shifting Eastern Front. These efforts were spearheaded by a highly creative and productive group of semi-Russified Jewish artists – a number of them educated in Paris – who were able to gain recognition and support among members of the wealthy Jewish elite that was allowed to reside in St. Petersburg (Petrograd from 1914) and Moscow. Inspired by similar trends in the Russian art world, members of this coterie had for years been discussing how to create a secular Jewish culture that would be in the forefront of modernity and progress while at the same time expressive of the Jewish national spirit. In their eyes, a critical step in this cultural rebirth would be the development of painting and sculpture among the People of the Book, whose engagement with these media had historically been limited by the biblical ban on idolatrous graven images.

This call for the production of Jewish visual art echoed all the more loudly during World War I, when the tsarist ban on publications in Hebrew script imposed a sudden silence on Hebrew and Yiddish literature, theater, and journalism. While individual Jewish artists had begun to produce works before the war, it was in 1916 that some of the first steps were taken toward the creation of an institutional framework specifically designed to encourage and support Jewish art in Russia. In that year, the painter Nathan Altman (1889–1970) and the sculptor Ilya Ginzburg (1860?–1939) joined with others in founding the Jewish Society for the Encouragement of the Arts (JSEA), headquartered in Petrograd with branches in other cities. The JSEA mounted a retrospective exhibition of works by Jewish artists in the same year, and its Moscow affiliate followed suit in April 1917. The JSEA's efforts were reinforced by An-sky's success in founding a Jewish Museum in Petrograd to house the collection of ethnographic materials from his pre-war expedition. This could serve as a ready-to-use archive of materials for painters and sculptors eager to integrate motifs from Jewish folk art into their own work.[96] These institutional initiatives helped spur a flurry of creative activity by artists such as Marc Chagall (1887–1985), El Lissitzky (1890–1941), Issachar Ryback (1897–1935), and Robert Falk (1886–1958), whose paintings, graphic art, and stage sets (for the Yiddish and Hebrew theaters that flourished during the early revolutionary years) combined Cubist, Expressionist, and Futurist styles with elements drawn from careful study of synagogue interiors, tombstone decorations, and traditional illustrated manuscripts.[97]

With the overthrow of the tsar and elimination of all discriminatory restrictions on Jewish culture in the spring of 1917, Russia witnessed an explosion of Jewish cultural production in every domain. The Jewish Theatrical Society, established in December 1916 by a group that included An-sky, promoted the professionalization and modernization of Yiddish theater along lines similar to the efforts of the Vilna Troupe.[98] The foundation of a Hebrew theater – Ha-Bima (The Stage) – followed in 1918. Jewish film studios, which had produced a handful of wartime dramas portraying Jewish loyalty to the tsarist cause before being shut down in 1915, resumed their activities in 1917, turning their attention to portrayals of the oppression of Jews under the tsarist regime.[99] The Kultur Lige (Culture League), established in Kiev at the end of 1917, assumed responsibility for organizing an autonomous Jewish educational and cultural life in the newly self-governing Ukraine (where Yiddish was recognized as an official language). The Kultur Lige sought to foster the development of a democratic Jewish national identity that would integrate folk culture with high culture, an aspiration expressed in its motto: "Make our masses thinkers. Make our thinkers Jewish. . . ."[100]

Ryback and Lissitzky were both active in the Kultur Lige, as they strove to develop a distinctly Jewish type of artistic modernism in which abstract forms would serve as the ideal media for the encapsulation of popular culture – a variation on a theme that pervaded Russian avant-garde circles during these revolutionary years. Their efforts to articulate the essence of this process in an intellectual doctrine took on an increasingly formulaic and dogmatic quality, however, as in Ryback's and Boris Aronson's assertion in 1919 that modern Jewish painting should be characterized by "analytic-synthesized grayness of pigment in deep-dark polychromaticism."[101] Eventually, most of these artists abandoned the experiment in abstract-ethno-cultural synthesis, directing their main efforts toward unequivocally abstract painting, while occasionally producing illustrations or decorations intended for specific use in Jewish publications, stage designs, or buildings. By the early 1920s, freedom of artistic experimentation had been severely restricted by the communist authorities. Many Jewish (as well as non-Jewish) artists left the country

(Ha-Bima relocated to Palestine in 1926), while others found an artistic refuge in designing sets for the Soviet Union's officially sponsored Yiddish theaters, whose repertoire and management became the object of ever more disruptive intrusions by organs of the state.[102]

Conclusion

The First World War was a double-edged sword that devastated traditional *shtetl* life and culture in Eastern Europe while simultaneously cutting away age-old obstacles that had hampered Jewish cultural and political self-expression. The events of 1914–1918 stimulated efforts to transform and restructure Jewish culture. New opportunities were created for Yiddishist and Zionist intellectuals seeking to lend a modern voice and secular form to Jewish national identity. At the same time, the war intensified the sense of disillusionment with European civilization among a number of Jewish intellectuals in Germany and Austria-Hungary, and spurred them to explore ways of reconnecting themselves with the rhythms of traditional Jewish life. The Central Powers' occupation of Poland and Lithuania heightened the intellectual and cultural cross-fertilization between these movements, which seemed to be moving toward similar objectives from opposite directions. Meanwhile, in Russia, the toppling of the tsarist regime in 1917 led to a blossoming of cultural experimentation among semi-Russified Jewish artists and intellectuals who were committed to a synthesis of European high culture and Jewish folk culture. Of course, the successful British military campaign against the Ottoman Empire and the November 1917 Balfour Declaration opened up all sorts of new possibilities for the Zionist enterprise in Palestine – but that important topic lies beyond the scope of this chapter.

It would be a mistake to suppose that World War I gave rise to any semblance of a consensus about the nature of Jewish identity or the direction cultural development should take. If anything, the accelerated pace of change brought about by the war led to a sharper delineation of differences among various cultural and ideological currents. The sudden erosion of boundaries between Germany and Eastern Europe did not just foster warm encounters of the sort experienced by Gronemann's Intellectuals' Club; it also engendered defensive reactions on the part of East European Jews fearful of Germanization and of German Jews loath to be associated with *Ostjuden*. The politicization of Jewish cultural currents in Poland (e.g., the formation of the Folkspartei and Agudat Israel by Yiddishist and Orthodox Jews, respectively) and the crystallization of factional differences within pre-existing politico-cultural movements (e.g., the consolidation of the Orthodox Mizrachi group within the Zionist organization) both reflected and contributed to an intensified competition among rival – sometimes even mutually exclusive – conceptions of Jewish cultural identity. This tendency was even manifest in the world of letters, where the literary generation that had included in its ranks bilingual (Hebrew and Yiddish) writers like Y. L. Peretz gave way to a new generation of authors who wrote exclusively in one language or another (be it Yiddish, Hebrew, or Polish). This was accompanied by a more clear-cut difference in intellectual orientation between Hebrew and Yiddish authors during the interwar period, as the former seemed to focus largely on the spiritual crisis associated with the *shtetl*'s decline, while the latter (many of them oriented toward the Bund) developed a more social-realist style that concentrated on concrete socio-economic dilemmas faced by the working masses.[103]

Yet it is precisely this multiplicity of educational and artistic institutions and the rapid growth of mass movements agitated by feverish ideological debates and intense political competition, which indicates that a fully formed, modern, Jewish national culture had come into its own in Poland-Lithuania during the war. Each movement – from Agudat Israel on the right to the labor Zionists and Bundists on the left – was convinced it held the key to the modern expression of Jewish identity. Many of these movements achieved a remarkable degree of vertical integration, developing and deploying impressive arrays of organizations and institutions – youth groups, newspapers, school systems, communal associations, relief services – as they vied with one another in the struggle to define and embody Jewish collective identity. The very diversity of rival views spoke to the vitality of Jewish culture as it emerged from the war – a phenomenon all the more impressive given the massive violence to which large segments of Eastern Europe's Jewish population had been subjected during the war, and which grew worse rather than better amidst the ethnic conflicts, revolutions, and civil wars that lasted in parts of the region until 1921.[104]

One of the essential ingredients of this vitality was the construction of bridges between high and popular cultures, an endeavor that lent cohesion to the various cultural and political currents of Eastern European Jewry. Although some of the more radical experiments in Jewish artistic modernism failed to appeal to a broad audience, examples such as the popular success of the Vilna Troupe or the Zionist movement's ability to garner unprecedented support among the Yiddish-speaking masses while still retaining its long-term commitment to the revival of Hebrew suggest that Jewish intellectual elites' attempts to reach out to the masses were not doomed to failure. The example of Russian populism clearly had a molding influence on many of these efforts; but perhaps their relative success in communicating across lines of class and education was partly rooted in the still-living legacy of traditional Judaism, a way of life in which the Torah had served as a common reference point around which social and cultural life among all classes had revolved.

In his wartime journal, An-sky observed that Russian soldiers' anti-Semitic violence had an irrational and unpredictable quality which made it particularly dangerous and destructive, and which was all the more disturbing in light of their capacity for equally spontaneous manifestations of good will toward Jews. The German military, by contrast, employed violence in a ruthlessly goal-oriented manner, as in the torching of a disease-infested, captured Russian barracks with all 192 of its occupants in order to prevent the possible infection of German soldiers. This methodical approach, in An-sky's view, seemed at least to have the virtue of rendering the worst abuses comprehensible and hence more avoidable.[105] In subsequent years, new regimes in both Russia and Germany achieved a synthesis of method and madness that spelled doom for the Jewish culture that had blossomed so remarkably amidst the chaos of World War I. In the Soviet Union, over the course of the 1920s, Jewish culture was either suppressed or coopted for propagandist purposes by the Bolsheviks; its most notable leaders and institutions were eventually destroyed by Stalin. For their part, the Germans returned to Eastern Europe in the Second World War with a new and expanded conception of hygiene that marked out all Jews as vermin, to be slaughtered as systematically as the sick Russian soldiers of An-sky's World War I anecdote. It is mostly in the State of Israel and here and there in the Western diaspora that fragmentary elements of Eastern European Jewish culture live on today.

The tragic carnival: Austrian culture
in the First World War

Steven Beller

A question of identity

In the 1 October 1918 issue of *Der Merker*, Egon Friedell reviewed a
performance of a play at the German People's Theater (Deutsches
Volkstheater) in Vienna. The play was not new, but rather an Austrian
classic, Grillparzer's *Ottokars Glück und Ende*. Friedell began his review
as follows: Grillparzer's patriotism is, as with Austrian patriotism in general, a problem. For the German this emotion is summed up in the words
"Deutschland über alles!," for the Frenchman in the sentence "Vive la
France!" These are simple formulae, incapable of misinterpretation.
But the Austrian views his fatherland with a sort of Strindbergian love-
hate, in which the word "fatherland" itself appears to him as something
ridiculous, which he cannot utter without a slightly sarcastic tone creeping
in.[1] Friedell was only too accurate. A month later the "Austria" of which
he spoke was to disappear, to be replaced by a series of successor states,
including the rump state of "German-Austria,"[2] without ever having
found a "simple formula," a clear identity, around which its peoples –
and its culture – could rally for the war effort, indeed for the state's
very survival.

A state which, in the early twentieth century, was still trying to find a
"national" identity was headed for trouble. For anyone trying to piece
together the cultural history of "Austria" during the war years, this
contemporary problem of even identifying what is "Austrian" adds an
extra, complicating dimension. While histories of the other "national"
cultures can more or less take the question of national identity for
granted, and concentrate on the social, economic, ideological, and political aspects of cultural experience in the war, a history of "Austrian"
culture cannot. Even if the cultures of the other nationalities within
the Habsburg Monarchy are dealt with separately, on national lines,
this still leaves the history of "Austrian," that is to say Vienna-centered,
culture to be addressed, a culture whose very nature makes any simple
assumption of "national" identity impossible, as Friedell indicated. It

also makes the story of Austrian culture during the war more intriguing, just as it made the culture itself less centered, less stable, less consistent, more erratic, more frivolous, and potentially more liberated from convention.

In this chapter I look at the problems posed by Austrian identity for the war effort; the reciprocal ways in which culture and war interacted; and the ways in which culture responded to and mirrored the larger developments of the war. I then sketch the main ways in which members of the cultural world reacted to the fact of war, culminating in a discussion of the greatest anti-war text of Austrian literature, Karl Kraus's *The Last Days of Mankind*. Kraus's critique of wartime popular culture leads to a discussion of the part played by the leading Viennese form of popular culture, operetta, during the war. I end with some comments about the nature of Austrian culture as revealed by the wartime experience.

The starting point is the question of Austrian identity. The extent of the problem can be gauged by the wartime career of one of the very centers of Austrian official culture: the Burgtheater. It served a dual purpose. It was the imperial court's theater; at the same time it had the reputation of being "the premier *German* stage," despite the 1866 political separation of Austria from Germany. One might have thought that the tension inherent in this dual Habsburg–German role would have been subsumed by the sense of unity, the *Nibelungentreue* (bond of the Nibelungs) evoked by the Dual Alliance, and common destiny, of Germany and Austria-Hungary. The director of the Burgtheater, Hugo Thimig, certainly thought so. Hence, when he persuaded his boss, the imperial court chamberlain, Count Montenuovo, to reopen the theater (after the initial plan of keeping it closed for the duration of the supposedly short war was given up), he suggested for the reopening the performance of one of the classics of German dramatic patriotism, never before performed at the Burgtheater, Kleist's *Die Hermannschlacht*.

This did not go over well. The play had not been performed at the Burgtheater before for good reason, for it was a hymn to German nationalism rather than Austrian, Habsburg patriotism. As Thimig himself records, Montenuovo asked him "whether the play is not too German, that is solely German. One has to take account of the Hungarians and the Slavs, who are standing together with us in the field of battle." Consequently, Kleist's play did not reopen the wartime Burgtheater. Yet *Die Hermannschlacht* was the first major Burgtheater premiere of wartime, to the continued annoyance of the court authorities. As Thimig reported, Montenuovo and the whole court regarded the play as "a quite unnecessary indication of Germany's unity under Prussian leadership."[3] Moreover, the main enemy in Kleist's play is the Roman

Empire, whereas the Habsburgs claimed to be the heirs to that imperial inheritance and the protectors of the *Roman* Catholic Church. The fact that the court theater's director could have chosen such a play thinking it a patriotic gesture speaks volumes for the confusions inherent in the German Austrians' cultural and political situation.

Thimig's successor in spring 1917 was Max von Millenkovich, but his distinctly German nationalist and indeed anti-Semitic sympathies did not go down well with the liberal press; nor did they sit well, more-over, with the plans of Franz Joseph's successor, Emperor Karl, to reconstruct the Monarchy as a multinational state. Millenkovich there-fore lasted only until July 1918.[4] By then the man in charge of the court theaters, as general intendant, was Leopold von Andrian-Werburg. He set about giving the two theaters a "great Austrian" rationale. This meant for the Burgtheater a radical makeover, and the admission that, because of Austria's expulsion from German affairs in 1866, it could not really be the premier German stage, but had instead to become the center of *Austrian* culture, that is of the multinational empire. More-over, it should not be just for the elite, but rather be the centerpiece of an "effective system of cultural and social policy" which would create the sort of mass patriotism which could counteract separatist national-ism in a way which dynastic loyalty could no longer do. Andrian was thus prepared to consider having the Burgtheater stage plays in dialect, and even by authors from the other nationalities of the empire, a policy which had not hitherto been followed. It was too late in the day, how-ever: the Monarchy collapsed almost before Andrian had started imple-menting his plans.[5]

The conflict inherent in the idea of *an* Austrian identity is made equally clear by a parallel attempt at creating a workable, attractive "Austrian" patriotism, which could convey Andrian's vision of the "ab-stract beauty and sublimity" of the "great-Austrian idea," this time by Andrian's close friend and ideological ally Hugo von Hofmannsthal.[6] Hofmannsthal, working in collaboration with the Habsburg authorities, was the editor of a series of twenty-six volumes, the *Austrian Library*, which Insel published during 1915–1917. He wanted the newly dis-covered patriotic Austrian poet, Anton Wildgans, to publish a selection of his poems as a volume in the series. Thinking to speak to a fellow believer, Hofmannsthal asked Wildgans to write a poem to conclude his collection which would sum up what "Austria" meant. Following his own idealised "Austrian idea," of Austria as "the special task given to the German spirit in Europe," to create an organic synthesis between German and Slavic "being," which would overcome national difference, Hofmannsthal asked Wildgans to write a poem which would celebrate the "beside each other – in each other" and the "living with each other" of the Austrian peoples. Wildgans refused. He could only believe in "the ethical strength of a state of many nations, when one of them has clear hegemony. And therefore I have to hope, that this leading role in our fatherland is given to the German people." Instead Wildgans offered Hofmannsthal a poem, "The German spirit," which identified the Austrians as the true upholders of the *German* spirit. Hofmannsthal in turn rejected this as far too Germanocentric. As a compromise, Wildgans and Hofmannsthal settled on "Infantry! A poem dedicated to the people-at-arms" (*Volk in Waffen*), as the final poem in the volume, set in the first person plural. Austria was thus not mentioned by name, but substituted by the army, and patriotism was replaced by "us," leaving the question of ultimate loyalty – whether to fatherland, nation, *Volk*, or collective self – open.[7]

The huge ambivalence in the German/Austrian identity shown in both these examples was not just a product of ideological confusion, or a psychological inferiority complex. It had roots in a disjuncture between political history on the one hand, and cultural and economic reality on the other. Politically, as already touched upon, Austrian had been replaced by Prussian hegemony in Germany, and Austrian Germans divorced from German politics. Culturally and economically though, Austrian German artists had become increasingly dependent on the German market for their livelihood. The awareness of Austrian artists of the importance to them of their German public could result in what looked like abject self-denial, but might have been sound economics. The director's book for the "patriotic" operetta *Gold gab ich für Eisen*, for example, explicitly allowed for the replacement of the word "Oestreich" [sic!] by the word "Deutschland" "on all German stages," and the replacement of Austrian localisms by German ones.[8]

The difference between German and "Austrian" art was never clearly spelled out, perhaps because it could not be, and the role of the other, non-German "Austrian" nationalities in "Austrian" culture never properly accommodated. The result was that the Austrian authorities' efforts to use cultural means to strengthen the war effort were hobbled by a lack of an unambiguous focus for the loyalty of the populace. The unresolved conflict between a German and a multi-/supra-national "Austrian" identity severely hampered any effort at cultural mobilization in the Austrian state.

The uses of culture

This is not to say that the Habsburg authorities did not try to use culture to bolster the state's image. Culture was often used as a surrogate

for both political power and ideological clarity. The cultural campaigns –
"Austrian Weeks" – in the neutral countries in 1917 were set in motion
with political aims in mind: not only to allay the Entente's claims about
Austrian barbarism and stress its character as a "flourishing land of
modern high culture, which even in wartime does excellent peacetime
work," but also, more to the point, to counteract the impression of
Austrian material and spiritual exhaustion.[9]

There was a distinct tendency in leading Austrian circles to rely
on art as compensation for a lack of political or military power. In
1917, Vienna's leading newspaper, the *Neue Freie Presse*, juxtaposed the
epoch-making and disastrous news of the American entry into the war
with a cultural weapon: an extensive article by the doyen of Austrian
architects, Otto Wagner, on "Vienna after the War."[10] The plastic arts
were held to be particularly valuable to the Austrian state, for they did
not rely primarily on language or require clear, intellectual articulation,
and could therefore function on a plane above the national divisions,
and beyond the problems of national identity. Austria had an officially
organized "artistic war propaganda," in the form of the Art Group
(Kunstgruppe) within the War Press Office (Kriegspressequartier). In
this organization were the artists who had volunteered for service –
about 120 in all – whose job it was to go with reporters and record their
impressions of the front, so that they could represent heroism in art.[11]

Yet, for all the attempt to use art to improve and indeed create an
Austrian self-image of cultured refinement, the state was remarkably
maladroit in its use of art as propaganda. If the anecdotal memoirs of
Karl Hans Strobl are to be believed, the Art Group was in the hands of
military officers with absolutely no artistic sense. Hauptmann Rabl
thought, for instance, that if he sent out his artists to the tops of mountains at the Italian front they would come back with a set of paintings
which could then be stuck together to form a "battle panorama."[12]

Having obtained some heroic art from the Art Group, the army
authorities then insisted that the official Austrian art exhibitions of 1917
in the neutral countries show some of these pictures, interspersed with
the "paintings of peace." Given that the exhibitions were linked to
Emperor Karl's peace-seeking policy and were intended to convey an
image of Austria as a peace-loving country only reluctantly at war, these
interspersed examples of heroism no doubt confused the message. When
the various Viennese art associations sent a joint letter of protest to the
army about its intervention, the War Press Office replied by threatening
to disband the Art Group and send all its members to the front.[13]

There were also efforts to use popular culture in the service of the
war effort. The Education Ministry distributed postcards, at heavily

subsidised prices, to try to instill patriotism in the populace. The Interior Ministry, trying to get a head start in indoctrination, published in 1916 the picture book *Wir spielen Weltkrieg! Ein zeitgemässes Bilderbuch für unsere Kleinen* (Let's play World War! A contemporary picture book for our little ones).[14] At the beginning of the war the most famous venue of mass popular culture in Vienna, the Kaisergarten Amusement Park in the Prater, was confiscated as enemy property. (It had been owned by a British-registered company.) Its new owner, a merchant and reserve lieutenant, was ordered by the War Ministry in 1916 to set up a War Exhibition, which showed life at the front, including a field, the Galitzinwiese, given over to barbed wire and trenches. An operetta theater was also built, the Bundestheater in der Kriegsausstellung, which showed some war-related operettas. Naval games were staged, first in the Prater's Rotunda, and in 1917 on the Galitzinwiese, while in May of that year war-related art, including paintings by Egon Schiele and Albert Paris Gütersloh, was shown in the Prater as part of the War Exhibition.[15] Even the Panorama of the Battle of Bergisel, celebrating one of the most famous examples of Austrian patriotism, Andreas Hofer's (temporary) success over Napoleon's armies in the Tyrol, was brought from Innsbruck and exhibited in the park in a purpose-built building.

Film was eagerly utilized as a medium to show the victories and feats of heroism of the men at the front. The two leading film companies, Wiener Kunstfilm and Sascha-Film, competed to bring their newsreels of the war to the public, with Sascha having the advantage that its boss, Sascha Kolowrat, was from 1915 the head of the Film Office (Filmstelle) of the War Press Office. Both weekly news programmes enjoyed great success, giving the viewers what they wanted: scenes of heroism and the certainty of victory. Perhaps because of the dramatic nature of the terrain, films of the Italian front, including War at 3,000 Metres, A Day at War with the Tirolerjäger, and film of the "Battle of the Isonzo," were particularly popular. Censors controlled the footage, removing anything that might evoke sympathy for the enemy, such as footage of an Italian soldier bandaging the wounds of a comrade. Along with these "news" films, the cinemas showed many "patriotic" films, such as *Der Nörgler* (The Grumbler), where a skeptic is converted to support of the war by dreaming about the war effort. Such films, together with the newsreels, made film "a central factor in the propaganda effort of the war."[16]

Even more central was the close control exercised by the authorities over the press, who from the start were almost entirely cooperative in feeding their readerships what the authorities wanted them to read. The War Press Office kept the war correspondents – domestic, allied, and neutral – at some distance from the headquarters of Army High Command. They also were sparing in permitting journalists to go to the front, waiting until success had been achieved before letting them come. Reporters were usually only able to report *faits accomplis*, and most of the time had to imaginatively "elaborate," in the best Viennese feuilletonistic manner, the dryly factual daily bulletins of the Army High Command. The journalists' reports were then subject to censorship by the War Surveillance Office (Kriegsüberwachungsamt), before publication.[17] Parallel to this system of tight control of news from the front, there was an office in the War Archives (Kriegsarchiv), staffed by writers such as Stefan Zweig and Rainer Maria Rilke (for a short time), with responsibility for recording the heroic exploits of the war for posterity and for public consumption, as well as for the troops. It produced collections of battle descriptions and poetry, military propaganda, an official journal, *Österreich-Ungarn in Waffen*, and from March 1917 a patriotic magazine aimed at the members of the military, *Donauland*.[18]

With such a bureaucratic apparatus, and such a collection of literary talent, one might have expected Austrian propaganda to be of the top rank, but the prevailing opinion among historians now is that the Austrian propaganda effort was almost a complete washout. The authorities proved incapable of mounting an effective propaganda campaign. Only in March 1918 was the Enemy Propaganda Defense Organization (Feindespropaganda-Abwehrstelle) set up to launch a defensive campaign against *foreign* propaganda *within* the Monarchy.[19] Part of the reason for this failure has to do with the position of the army in the Monarchy, and its collective worldview.

The army held a central place in the Habsburg Monarchy; indeed, because of the constitutional structure of Austria-Hungary, it was, next to the emperor-king himself, the most important institution common to the empire's two halves. A symbol of this importance was that, in the Austrian half of the empire anyway, the apparatus of censorship and propaganda was under military control. There was no equivalent to a civilian Ministry of Information. In the view of the military leadership, this was as it should be, for it was the military which would win the war, and the loyalty of the troops which was of paramount importance in preserving domestic order as well. The propaganda effort thus concentrated almost exclusively on military matters and military morale.[20] The War Archives, similarly, concentrated on recounting the *military* glories of the war, primarily for military consumption. The military leadership was simply not very interested in what the domestic front thought.[21] When, as early as September 1914, Hugo Ganz, a prominent journalist, told the authorities about the outrage caused among the populace by the strict censorship, he got the reply: "the people's job in wartime is to shut up and obey."[22] As for ideological questions, questions about the Monarchy's political meaning left the army, still loyal to the dynasty alone, cold. As Plaschka puts it: "For the army, the guiding image of the multinational state did not have much political charisma."[23]

The net effect of the army's propaganda effort in the army itself is hard to assess. Although the Habsburg military held together as a fighting force far longer than might have been expected, this might well have been due more to residual loyalty to the dynasty, one's nationality, or to one's comrades than any form of propaganda. One eyewitness account of what the Austrian soldier was reading suggests a certain imperviousness to propagandistic force-feeding: "What I found here most widespread were detective stories, erotica and Ullstein books."[24]

What the military handling of information meant domestically was an information and meaning vacuum, into which rumors of all sorts, and the views of other ideological parties, especially those of the various nationalisms, could creep.[25] There was an "absence of a political and strategic goal which would have an effect on the masses." The army, given its self-image, might have thought that loyalty to such concepts as the emperor-king and fatherland sufficed, but in the course of the war they increasingly appeared "meaning-impoverished."[26] Partly due to the army's own political culture, so anachronistic by 1914, and partly due to what was in any case, as we have seen, a practically insoluble crisis of the cultural and political identity of "Austria," let alone "Austria-Hungary," there was no set of convincing or cogent ideas forthcoming about what it meant to be "Austrian," which could either stand the test of veracity, or outweigh the attraction of the seductively simple, Entente-backed idea of national self-determination.[27]

The suggestion of an empire-wide patriotic propaganda campaign had been made before the war, by Conrad von Hötzendorf, who had promptly forgotten about it again. Arz von Straussenburg, Conrad's successor as chief of the General Staff, introduced the idea late in the war, but for the troops only. Any prospects for such a campaign on the domestic front were in any case small given Emperor Karl's distaste of and lack of faith in propaganda, which he dismissed with the words: "Thoughts and ideas cannot be recommended like laxatives, toothpaste and foodstuffs."[28] Unfortunately for him and his Monarchy, he was quite mistaken.

The period of draconian censorship and political repression in the first two years of the war so poisoned the atmosphere of the domestic front, that the liberalization of Austria under Karl from the end of 1916, *à la* Gorbachev, simply made matters worse. The German press was relatively pliant, and relatively well treated by the military censors, but the Czech press, even though Bohemia was not remotely in any war zone, was clamped down on hard by the War Surveillance Office, and forty-six Czech newspapers banned in the first months of war. Those that remained published were not quite as collaborative as most of their German counterparts, choosing not to close up the large white spaces left by the censor's excisions. This led to the Czech papers' street vendors on Wenceslas Square shouting out: "What is white is the truth – what is black is lies!" Many German newspapers – even Karl Kraus's *Fackel* – did try to hide the effects of censorship, but even they often found it hard to cover up the often large distance between the story which the military wanted told, and the true state of affairs.[29] This situation left the field free for all sorts of rumours to spread, especially when the evidence from refugees and soldiers on leave flatly contradicted what were often intentionally mendacious news stories.[30]

By the time of the return to constitutional government and political liberalization under Emperor Karl, much of the non-German Austrian public relied more on the underground networks of rumor than on the deeply distrusted press, and the same, to a lesser extent, was true of the German Austrian public. The loosening, though not removal, of censorship powers under the new regime and the reconvening of the Reichsrat, with the immunity from censorship of the reporting of deputies' questions, opened the floodgates of information, often confirming the greater veracity of rumor over the previous official version.

Moreover, even parts of the German press, which had all along resented the military's rough treatment while nevertheless complying to their strictures, increasingly began reporting the course of events as they saw them. The military authorities looked on, increasingly frustrated by the state of public opinion, chastising the civilian authorities for not cracking down on the press, but with the lifting of the emergency decrees in October 1917 and the return of constitutional niceties, the censors' powers were now much more tightly delimited than before.[31] Even Karl Kraus, who by 1918 had turned his *Fackel* into a radical anti-establishment, as well as anti-war and anti-militarist, mouthpiece, was not touched by the authorities.[32] The sequential combination of ruthless suppression, followed by half-hearted and erratic liberalization was a perfect recipe for the destruction of any trust between governing and governed, that condition of complete lack of authority – political, legal, or moral – which Kraus was to sum up as the "tragic carnival."

The uses of war

If the Austrian authorities found using culture for propagandistic ends problematic, the cultural world was not averse to using the authorities and war for its own ends, if it could. While the members and institutions in some cultural spheres suffered immensely from the war's vicissitudes, others profited. A few individuals were able to take full advantage of war's opportunities. The exigencies of war also allowed some new (and not so new) cultural media and intellectual movements to come into their own.

There were clear losers under the novel political and economic conditions of wartime. The members of the Wiener Freie Volksbühne, a center for avant-garde theater in Vienna, had suspended performances for the duration of the war, and, as that duration proved much longer than expected, they eventually voted to dissolve the organization.[33] The court theaters: Burgtheater and Court Opera, were eventually reopened, but under special conditions, which included the halving of ticket prices and of performers' salaries, and the reduction of the number of performances. Both theaters' directors also had the problem that much of their personnel had been called up for the military, and they had to exercise their own brand of *Protektion* to have members of their staff excused from war service. At the Opera, stagehands who had been called up were eventually replaced by prisoners of war.[34]

One other official wartime condition was the prohibition on performing works by the enemy. The ban on the performance of works by French, British, Russian, and Belgian artists affected cultural media variably. For some of Vienna's theatres, which had specialized in French farces, such as the Theater in der Josefstadt, there was clearly a large problem, which was only partially solved by the substitution of German and Hungarian comedies and Austrian operettas.[35] The ban cut variety theaters such as Ronacher's off from much of the international scene, thus depriving the shows of much of their international exoticism. On the other hand, this left many more opportunities for home-grown talent to emerge.[36] Similar effects could be seen in the nascent Austrian film industry. While the ban deprived cinemas of their staple – French movies – this gave Austrian filmmakers a huge, captive audience.[37]

At the Burgtheater the ban was not so harshly felt, especially as the prohibition was interpreted to refer only to living authors, making performances of classics such as Molière and Shakespeare acceptable.[38] At the Opera, given the nature and history of the institution, the idea of banning works by the enemy was completely impractical, especially once Italy had entered the war on the side of the Entente. Gregor did limit works premiered during the war to those by German or Austrian composers, such as Alexander von Zemlinsky and the inevitable Richard Strauss, with a couple of works by composers from the neutral countries as well, but it would have been making a travesty of the Court Opera to insist on the exclusion of Italian, or even French, works. Gregor was, in fact, only asked to keep the performance of enemy works to a minimum. Even so, the 1915–1916 repertoire of the Opera shows works by Verdi, including *Ernani*, as basic to the repertoire. Puccini, then very much a living composer, is also well represented. Of French operas, Bizet's *Carmen* remained a favourite of the public. The 1916–1917 season saw the return of *Eugene Onegin*, 1917–1918 the revival of Rossini's *Wilhelm Tell*, not exactly a pro-Habsburg piece. One of the leading singers in the ensemble was an Englishman, Alfred Piccaver. The Court Opera clearly kept its international character despite the pressure to exclude enemy works.[39]

The exigencies of wartime did eventually take a large toll on both court theaters, with the curtailment of tram services forcing performances to be brought forward and coal shortages in 1917 often threatening to force closure for lack of heating.[40] Even in fields where the war had been initially beneficial, such adverse economic conditions increasingly impinged. Publishing had experienced a huge fillip from the start of the war, with a vast increase in book publication, and many authors made the most of the demand for patriotic and uplifting texts.[41] By the latter part of the war, though, economic conditions had led to some of Vienna's top authors, Schnitzler and Hofmannsthal among them, having to protest in early 1918 against their Berlin publisher, Samuel Fischer, for not publishing their works due to a shortage of paper.[42]

The two cultural media which did best in wartime conditions, much to the disgust of many in the cultural elite, were film and operetta. The nascent film industry provides, indeed, one of the best examples of how individuals in a cultural medium could profit from wartime. Sascha Kolowrat was already a prominent filmmaker in Vienna before war broke out. At the beginning of the war he was called up to serve in the automobile corps on the Galician front, but with his aristocratic connections he was able to get a transfer in 1915 to the War Press Office, where he became commander of the Film Office. Once established there, he was able to have film people serving at the front assigned to his office, and Kolowrat's *Protektion* thus saved a great many members of Austria's film world from a hero's death, a fact gratefully remembered by many after 1918. The dual development of the rapid development of film's popularity during the war, both with the public and with the state, and at the same time the industry's consolidation, most dramatically in the foundation of UFA in December 1917, the giant German film conglomerate, left Kolowrat and his Sascha-Film by war's end in a dominant position in the Austrian film world, even if in effect a subsidiary of UFA.[43]

The change in status and fortunes of film during war was particularly marked, going from being seen by the authorities as a danger to youth to being recognized fairly quickly for its great potential for propaganda.[44] Together with film's relative novelty and its replacement of the need for live performers by a machine, and hence its cheapness, this meant that it thrived. In the spirit of an age where German technological ingenuity was being called upon to overcome the Entente's economic blockade through the invention and introduction of synthetic substitutes, *Ersatzmittel*, the cinema acquired the pejorative name of "Theater-Ersatz," and in a way this is exactly the function it performed, at a time when elite theatre was struggling to make ends meet.[45]

Next to the newcomer, film, the cultural medium which did best during the war was much more established and "Viennese": operetta. The war years saw an even greater dominance by operetta of the Viennese theater scene. By 1918, out of sixteen theaters in all, there were six theaters in Vienna dedicated to operetta alone, the same number as played serious drama.[46] Part of the reason for this was that operetta was completely in the domain of commercial theatre, and run accordingly as an entrepreneurial business. It was thus far less hidebound than the institutions of official high culture, and could get around the problems of supply more easily. The new performance plan, not of performing a repertoire of works, but rather having serial runs, also clearly cut down on costs. Moreover, by being very much a home-grown product, operetta had no problem adjusting to the prohibition of enemy works. The most straightforward explanation, though, for operetta's great success is that it "appealed to a new wave of escapism, just as it had done amid the economic and social problems of the 1870s and 1880s."[47] Going to the operetta was a way of evading an increasingly harsh and depressing reality.

Ironically, the scientific movement set up to combat the ill-effects of such suppression of reality, psychoanalysis, was also among the big winners of the war. Freud's movement had been largely dismissed before the war as either quackery or, worse, a "Jewish science." The extraordinary number of shellshock victims of the war led to a large body of empirical evidence of trauma, as well as a large incentive to search for ways to cure the condition, at least to the extent that the patient was well enough to be sent back to the front. Psychoanalytic techniques, called on often as a last resort, proved to be surprisingly effective, so that by the end of the war the Habsburg authorities were actively courting the psychoanalytic movement, laying on a large banquet for the delegates to the International Congress of Psychoanalysis in Budapest, in September 1918, at a time of acute shortages. In many ways it was the war which gained Freud's movement international and official acceptance.[48]

General cultural patterns and the course of the war

The makers of Austrian culture, generally speaking, reflected the ups and downs of wider public opinion in their response to the war's course of events. There was the ubiquitous initial manic enthusiasm in the summer of 1914, and writers from Austria did their bit to fuel the war hysteria in both Austria and Germany. It was a resident of Vienna, Ernst Lissauer, originally from Berlin, who wrote the immensely popular *Hassgesang gegen England* (Song of Hatred for England). The most popular wartime poem, *Das Reiterlied* (Song of the Cavalryman) was written by the Austrian, and Zionist, Hugo Zuckermann, one of the few writers of any prominence to actually die at the front.[49] Other, unlikely poetic celebrators of war in the first moment of conflict included the proletarian-poet Alfons Petzold, and the super-refined aesthete Rilke.[50]

The number of those affected by the surge of patriotic feeling in 1914 was surprisingly large. Sigmund Freud discovered a loyalty for the Austrian and German cause which he had long thought dead and buried.[51] Stefan Zweig, despite his later denials, was swept up by the enthusiasm for war, and at one time even wanted to go to the front, only to fail the medical inspection.[52] Arthur Schnitzler was less xenophobic than most, but his diary for 1914 shows that even he was caught up in the excitement of the first wave of German victories.[53]

A few prominent artists and intellectuals did not even wait to be called up but volunteered for front-line duty. These included Ludwig Wittgenstein, who enlisted in the artillery in August, and Oskar Kokoschka, who joined a cavalry regiment in early 1915.[54] An all too common response among the cultural elite was a strong public enthusiasm for the war, but a private striving to use their connections (*Protektion*) to "fix" their call-up (*sich richten*), or at least to get out of any possible front-line service. The most prominent example of this blatantly hypocritical behavior was provided by none other than Hugo von Hofmannsthal, who, at the same time as he was proclaiming his enthusiasm for "doing his bit" on the front line, was frantically trying to get himself transferred from the prospect of front-line service to a safe office job in Vienna.[55] Robert Kann has explained the super-patriotism displayed by writers and journalists during the war, their subservience to the wishes of the military, as overcompensation for their guilt at avoiding front-line duty, although there are other, less charitable interpretations.[56]

Other figures were genuinely enthusiastic to be called up. Robert Musil viewed the war as an opportunity to solve the Austrian problem of not being serious, and served dutifully for three years as a lieutenant in South Tyrol.[57] Arnold Schoenberg, a Hungarian citizen, German chauvinist, and Austro-Hungarian patriot, was an enthusiast for the war effort. He set Otto Kernstock's poem "Der deutscher Michel" to music, and in 1916 composed a march "The Iron Brigade" as his cultural contribution to the fight. He also tried to volunteer in May 1915, but his was a case where the genuine wish to serve was eventually thwarted by his own ill health and the efforts, unbeknownst to him, of his colleagues to have him released from duty.[58]

Usually, as in Hofmannsthal's case, the strings were pulled with the full knowledge and cooperation of the subject. Sometimes the army itself, or rather some officer within the hierarchy, would cooperate in accommodating the otherwise harsh logic of the Austrian military to the needs of the particular artist. Rilke, whose war enthusiasm was almost over before it had begun, was called up in November 1915, and he immediately set about using his exquisite connections within the Austrian aristocracy to get him out of this bind. His *Protektion* obtained a place for him in the War Archives. There he was treated with kid gloves by the commandant of the Literary Department, Colonel Alois Veltzé, who told Rilke's immediate superior, F. K. Ginzkey: "For form's sake we'll have to give him something to do – but it won't be particularly burdensome." Rilke was duly released from military service in July 1916.[59]

Rilke's position, that as a cultural monument he should be above military service, was shared by Egon Schiele, with similar results. Schiele, as Whitford puts it, believed "that artists were too important to be put in danger." When he was, nevertheless, called up in June 1915, he tried, in vain, to use his connections to get posted to the Art Group of the War Press Office, but his efforts to avoid the front did result in his being transferred at the end of 1915 to a position in Vienna dealing with Russian prisoners of war, and by 1917 he was in a sinecure in the Army Commissary in Vienna. Schiele was thus able to paint while still in military service, indeed under a sort of military patronage. Yet he took no interest whatsoever in the war, and the closest he got to any war painting was portraits of Russian prisoners. When he was invited to exhibit at the War Art Exhibition in May 1917 he chose to display a pre-war work, *Resurrection*, which he retitled *Resurrection, Fragment for a Mausoleum* to make it appear more related to war. Yet this fairly obvious failure to produce martial art was, by 1917, not at all frowned upon, and the authorities sent Schiele abroad as one of the cultural ambassadors to accompany the art exhibits in Stockholm and Copenhagen. Schiele's immense success in the last years of the war was thus due partly to the army's support.[60]

By the time Rilke and Schiele were conscripted in 1915, the initial enthusiasm for the war, both among the public at large and the cultural elite, had dropped off precipitously. In some cases the change was more or less immediate. Arthur Schnitzler, although hoping for the victory of the Central Powers, refused from the outset to profit from the war by indulging in the spate of patriotic literature, and his position soon changed to one of utter disgust for what was happening. On 13 October 1914, as a trained physician, he observed the treatment of the war wounded by his friend Otto Zuckerkandl, and recognized the full horror of what was happening: "Here is the meaning of war. Everything else can be forgotten – diplomacy, world history, fame, enthusiasm, even death. The only thing that counts is suffering. And I am seeing only the millionth part of a millionth of it." At a dinner party on 6 October 1915 he heard stories of atrocities committed by the Austrians in Serbia. He commented: "Horror upon horror! Injustice upon injustice! Insanity upon insanity!"[61]

Even someone as initially committed to the war as Oskar Kokoschka was so damaged by it both physically and mentally that he ended up wanting nothing more to do with it. He volunteered, in the midst of his torrid affair with Alma Mahler, for a dashing cavalry regiment. Kokoschka was by all accounts a brave soldier and effective NCO, seeing plenty of action in the summer of 1915 on the Eastern front, where actual use of the cavalry, of lance and sabre, was much more common than on the static Western front. On 29 August he was severely wounded at Lutsk, but survived. He had still not had enough. Volunteering for the front again, he was given the relatively safe posting of press liaison officer. On 28 August 1916, however, he was wounded by a grenade, and suffered shellshock and nervous collapse. He now "had no further desire to solve his emotional problems by flirting with death." After his convalescence he moved to Berlin, and then to a sanatorium in Dresden, where he made sure of avoiding a recall to duty for the rest of the war.[62]

The change in atmosphere from the initial months of heroic élan to a more realistic sense of the nature of modern warfare can be seen almost in caricature in the work of Albin Egger-Lienz. The braggadocio of his work, *Helden 1915*, where the soldier-heroes swagger fully upright into battle, was by 1916 replaced by the much humbler *Der Namenlosen 1914*, where the troops now advance in a crouch. (See Fig. 5.1) By 1918 Egger-Lienz was painting monumental battle scenes, *Missa Eroica* and *Finale*, not of living heroes, but of dead ones.[63]

5.1   Albin Egger-Lienz, *Den Namenlosen, 1914* (To the nameless ones, 1914), 1916

The watershed for Austria-Hungary in the war came in the autumn of 1916. In September the Austrians were forced by their inability to handle the Russians, the Italians, or the Romanians, to agree to a Joint High Command with the Germans, in which the Germans were the senior partner. There followed the assassination of the prime minister, Stürgkh, by Friedrich Adler on 21 October, and then the death of Franz Joseph on 18 November 1916. While Franz Joseph had already begun to move in the direction of some liberalization and an early peace, Karl moved much more rapidly toward these goals over the winter of 1916–1917, exploring the possibility of an early peace and moving to a constitutionalization of the Monarchy.[64] As we have seen, these changes did not have the desired effect, indeed were only to speed the eventual dissolution of the Monarchy; but they did take some of the pressure from the authorities off the backs not only of the populace but also of the makers of culture, and provided new opportunities which were eagerly grasped by many.

Artists such as Schiele and Kokoschka were only too happy to get out of Central Europe in 1917 to attend the openings of the art exhibitions in the neutral Scandinavian countries.[65] Writers such as Stefan Zweig and Franz Werfel were sent to Switzerland in 1917 and 1918 also to improve Austria's image abroad and get over the message that Austria was interested in peace. Both Zweig and Werfel took advantage of their distance from the Austrian authorities to display a far more extreme form of pacifism than they had dared to hitherto.[66] Zweig's story in particular indicates how far things had changed by 1917 in the Monarchy. When his pacifist drama, *Jeremias*, was published at Easter 1917, what would have been anathema when he had started writing it, in March 1915, was now, in 1917, a massive popular success. Even more indicative was the enthusiastic agreement of his boss at the War Archives, Veltzé, to Zweig's attendance at the play's premiere in Zurich.[67] Simply put, it suited Austrian policy to have one of its leading writers in Switzerland represent Austria as a peace-loving land. Once there, Zweig was able, through a deal with the *Neue Freie Presse*, to obtain release from military duty, and permission to stay in Switzerland, which he did until the war's end.[68]

In the last year of the war, Austria-Hungary began to fall apart economically and politically. Culturally, although there were some striking advances, events took a similar course. On the positive side, the 49th Secession exhibition, in March 1918, saw the dawn of a new era in Austrian painting, led by Schiele. Andrian's intendancy also promised to inject some ideological backbone into Austrian official culture.[69] Yet the prevailing atmosphere was one of doom and despair. The deadly influenza epidemic, which robbed Austrian culture of Klimt, Schiele, Kolo Moser, and Otto Wagner, among many others, severely deepened the gloom. Even much of what was achieved in 1918 was less innovation than the settling of old scores: the two major premieres at the Court Opera of that year were stagings of relatively old works to satisfy political or personal goals, and both, in retrospect, appear symptomatic of a deeper cultural and moral crisis.

Leoš Janáček's *Jenufa*, based on a story "from Moravian peasant life," received its Court Opera premiere in February, 1918, more than a decade after its Czech premiere. This was supposed to be a sign of the opening up of official Austrian culture to the other nationalities, yet its storyline, of paternal irresponsibility and grandmotherly infanticide, hardly presented an uplifting picture of the Czech or Slovak peoples.[70] Richard Strauss's *Salome* may have been the first truly modern opera, and its performance at the Court Opera a belated triumph of Gregor's persistence against the censors over almost a decade, but it too, with its bloodlust and its anti-Semitic undertones, was not exactly conducive to civic virtue.[71] It seems particularly inappropriate that the premiere at the Opera on 14 October 1918 was given "by order of his Majesty for the benefit of the Imperial-and-Royal Military Widows' and Orphans' Charity."[72] But by mid-October things had reached such a point that virtually anything was possible.

Individual responses to the war

If the cultural elite's general mood swung more or less in time with that of society at large as the course of the war unfolded, there were as many individual cultural responses as there were members of that elite. These responses, for all their complexity, fall into three main categories: collaboration, retreat, and opposition.

Collaboration

It is clear that working in the environment of the War Press Office and the War Archives meant providing what the authorities wanted, rather than staying true to one's artistic calling. It is difficult to gauge at times how much cynicism this required of those involved. The most prominent war correspondents, such as Alice Schalek and Roda Roda for the *Neue Freie Presse*, reported the news from the front in as heroizing a way as possible. In Schalek's case she probably believed what she was writing, but in the case of Roda Roda it is not at all clear that he really believed that war was "a means for becoming human" as he claimed.[73] The extent to which the journalists themselves knew how much what they were reporting was at variance with reality is suggested by a report in Schnitzler's diary on Christmas Eve, 1914, of an interview of Archduke Friedrich, the Austrian commander-in-chief, by Ferenc Molnár, the journalist and playwright. According to Molnár: "If I had reported the whole conversation, rather, if I had been allowed to do so, the war would be over the day after tomorrow." He cites Friedrich as saying that Austria would not have a great victory, and that the Serbian campaign was a catastrophe, and then he reports him as adding: "but don't worry – write: the necessary measures have been taken."[74] It was this sort of suppression of the facts – and at the same time the leaking of the truth to friends – which ensured the huge success of the rumor mill in Austria during the war.

The extent of cynicism involved in collaborating in the war effort should not be exaggerated. While Zweig or Werfel, Albert Ehrenstein, or Egon Erwin Kisch, did most of their propaganda hack work believing little of what they wrote, there were many others who were truly committed to the Austrian cause, or at least to the cause of the Central Powers. The most obvious example of Austrian loyalty was Hofmannsthal.[75] Peter Rosegger, formerly a pacifist, greeted war in 1914 as an ardent Austrian nationalist and, though far too old for active service, saw himself as being a "meaning-soldier" (*Sinnsoldat*) in the war effort.[76] Richard von Kralik, from a conservative Catholic perspective, could view the war as "my war," and at one point in 1915 could equate "culture" with "war" with "everything."[77] Richard von Schaukal was even ennobled for his poetic services to the war effort.[78] Writers such as Rudolf Hans Bartsch or Karl Hans Strobl, or painters such as Joseph

Engelhart, were heavily politicized before the war began, and the experience of war only strengthened this.[79]

Playwrights wrote consciously patriotic plays specifically to spur the war effort. The Burgtheater premiered Thaddäus Rittner's *Kinder der Erde* in December 1915, and Hans Müller's immensely successful *Könige* opened in October 1916. This latter play, which dramatized an episode in the Middle Ages, when a German (Bavarian) emperor had shared sovereignty with a faithful Austrian archduke and erstwhile imperial rival, ran to fifty-two performances before the war's end, making it one of the most popular wartime productions at the Burgtheater. (It was also accepted for performance at fifty-eight theaters *before* its premiere.)[80] Another major success, though not without controversy, was Karl Schönherr's *Volk in Not*. This tried to rally Austrian patriotism around the story of Andreas Hofer and the Battle of Bergisel against the French in 1809. It provided a completely uncritical account of the Tyrolean hero, but, even so, fears that it conveyed too much of the reality of warfare almost prevented Thimig from putting it on at all, and led to the premiere being at the Deutsches Volkstheater in July 1916, before it was eventually premiered at the Burgtheater in January 1917.[81]

There was also a clearly political agenda in many of the more successful historical novels of the time, but the problem of Austrian identity appears yet again, for the political message in these novels was not one reassuring to a "great-Austrian" such as Hofmannsthal. If writers such as Karl Hans Strobl were politicized, they were so as German Nationalists, with an "ambivalence" about Austria made even stronger by, as often as not, their origins in the provinces, on the border of "Germandom." Adam Müller-Guttenbrunn, for instance, a German from the Banat, published in 1917 his *Joseph der Deutsche*, which stressed (fallaciously) the German nationalist programme of Joseph II, and his aim to conquer Belgrade.

This German identity was especially true of German writers from the Bohemian crownlands. (Jewish writers such as Werfel, Kafka, Brod, and Kisch are an exception in this respect.) Strobl, a Sudetenländer, wrote as his wartime magnum opus a trilogy about Bismarck. Walter von Molo, from Moravia, published *Fridericus* in 1918, a novel about Frederick II of Prussia. Friedrich Winterholler, a Moravian from Brno, returned in his novel, *Laudon* (1917), to the ideal of the Holy Roman Empire of the German Nation. In these novels the war was described through historical surrogates as an inevitable, world-historical force of nature, in which super-heroes such as Joseph II or Frederick the Great could only ride fate, and in which endurance was the sole goal and victory the only moral criterion. Moreover, it became here a *German* war above all, in which the rest of the Austrian populace, especially the Slavs, were ignored. This was not only so for German nationalist historical novelists, but was also true of supposedly Catholic conservative German-Bohemian writers such as Kralik. It was Kralik who wrote, affectionately: "It is your war, O German People!"[82]

Retreat

If collaboration accounted for a very large number in the cultural elite, some of the most prominent stars in the Austrian-Viennese firmament chose the reverse of this: retreat, silence, escape into the private world of art, as they saw it. Gustav Klimt's art, for instance, appears completely untouched by the war.[83] This is in a sense not surprising, because Klimt had never been all that politically engaged. In Schnitzler's case, on the other hand, the writer had often involved himself in political controversy; his silence on the war was one based on principle: the refusal to get involved with the "dilettantish busy-bodying" of collaboration in the war effort, and this initial decision was increasingly confirmed by his horror as the war proceeded.[84] Although he carried on writing during the war, he studiously ignored war-related topics. In his public readings he did include passages from *Hirtenflöte* and *Young Medardus*, both with anti-war and anti-heroic themes. Otherwise, Schnitzler kept his private thoughts on the war to himself, recording in his diary dreams which reflected his fears about it, and keeping notes on his feelings about the war, which were published posthumously in 1939. It was for this silence that Kraus, an erstwhile enemy, marked Schnitzler out for his respect as almost the only Austrian writer to behave decently during the war.[85]

The most extreme form of retreat from the "great times" of the war was suicide, there being perhaps no more tragic case than that of Georg Trakl, Austria's finest expressionist poet. His zeal in volunteering as a medical orderly in 1914 was soon enough more than matched by his despair at the horrors of what war did to human beings, recorded in his last, searing poems: *Klage* and *Grodek*. It was during the battle of Grodek, in Galicia, in early September, that he was left to look after ninety severely wounded men in a barn, without a doctor present for two days and without enough drugs to ease their pain. One man under his care shot himself before Trakl's eyes. Stepping out to recover his equilibrium, he was faced with the corpses of suspected "traitors" (local Ruthenian peasants) hanging from trees. The experience first drove him insane, and a few weeks later drove him to take his own life in Cracow on 3 November 1914. Franz Kafka wrote of Trakl: "He had too much imagination. That is why he could not stand the war, which arose from a colossal lack of imagination."[86]

Ludwig Wittgenstein had been hoping to visit Trakl in hospital, but arrived in Cracow only on 5 November. Wittgenstein also had contemplated suicide as a response to his war experience, but instead he found his retreat from the war spiritually, in the form of what amounted to a religious conversion. Already attracted before the war to the stoic idea that, whatever happened externally, nothing could happen to one's innermost being, Wittgenstein was greatly strengthened in such beliefs by his experience of the war and by his reading of Tolstoy's *The Gospel in Brief*. His experience of the war and his philosophical work during it are a study in stoic separation of the inner and the outer life. While he was serving courageously in the Austrian army, he was reading Russian authors, Tolstoy and Dostoevsky, and still corresponded with his very close English friend, David Pinsent. While the war went on around him he concentrated all the more on philosophical and ethical matters. Thus the main effect on Wittgenstein of the Brusilov offensive of June 1916 was for him to alter radically the structure of his philosophical work, later published as the *Tractatus Logico-Philosophicus*, so that it became as much a Schopenhauerian thesis on the nature of ethics and aesthetics as a work on the nature of language. It was the war, therefore, which prompted Wittgenstein to add that spiritual, almost mystic dimension to the *Tractatus* which later anglophone philosophers found so puzzling.[87]

A similar reaction can be seen in the work of Arnold Schoenberg. Initially an enthusiastic supporter of the Central Powers' cause, he became disappointed by the course of both the war and his own career during it. By 1918 things were looking up for Schoenberg professionally and financially, yet the war years had been tough, and in response to the harsh realities of his wartime experience Schoenberg increasingly sought solace in religion, what he called the "faith of the disillusioned man."[88]

Schoenberg had already had the idea of writing a piece based on Richard Dehmel's "new belief in God" before the war, but it was only in January 1915 that he started to compose *Jacob's Ladder*. By 1918 the text and most of the music had been completed, but Schoenberg never finished the score. The text and the music that *was* composed show a remarkable parallelism: while the text shows Schoenberg's increasing religiosity, which was to lead on to *Moses und Aron*, and, one might argue, Schoenberg's rediscovery of his Jewishness, the music shows large advances on the way to Schoenberg's post-war method of serial, twelve-tone composition. His return to the Jewish religion and his resorting to the method of serial composition were thus not only bound up with each other, but also with the war.[89]

Many others shared Schoenberg's disillusionment with the war. Freud had the questionable consolation of having had his theories about the imperfectibility of human nature confirmed. His *Thoughts for the Times on War and Death* reflected his deep disappointment not so much with the fact of war itself, as with the way it was conducted, barbarically, showing just how thin the veneer of civilization was. The war thus encouraged the pessimistic strain embedded in psychoanalytic theory.[90] Hermann Broch came to similar conclusions. Excused from active duty due to medical unfitness, he spent the war managing both his family's factory and a military convalescent hospital. Yet most of his intellectual energy was spent observing "the disintegration of values," of the Western system of ethics, a process which he was to set out so brilliantly in his post-war novel, *The Sleepwalkers*.[91] Even less directly involved in the war was Franz Kafka. He was excused from military service due to ill health and his "indispensable" work as an insurance clerk, and so the war had little direct effect on him. Yet, while his personal crises, such as the failure of his engagement and his suffering from tuberculosis, clearly had a huge influence on his writing, the war also had major indirect influences on him. The Russian advances in Galicia caused a flood of Galician Jewish refugees to Prague (and Vienna) in early 1915. The presence of these traditionalist Jews in his city may well have played a role in Kafka's "crisis" about his own Jewish identity, expressed in two stories, *Jackals and Arabs* and *Report to the Academy*, published in *Der Jude* in October and November 1917 respectively.[92] The millenarianism which marks the Zürau aphorisms of 1917–1918 has also to be understood in the context of the general crisis of that period, involving not only the war, but also the Russian Revolution and the almost simultaneous Balfour Declaration of November 1917.[93] Kafka's response to this crisis was to explore the idea of the responsibility of the individual to society and to "life," and to seek to renew religious faith in an age when traditional authority was seriously decayed. The concept of "the indestructible" which dominates the Zürau aphorisms thus brought Kafka's response to the war uncannily close to that of Wittgenstein, an affinity partly explicable by their mutual reading of Schopenhauer.[94]

Opposition

The third option, after collaboration and retreat was to speak up against the war, to take a stand for pacifism. The most notorious expression of pacifism in Austria was hardly in the cultural sphere: the assassination of the Austrian prime minister, Count Stürgkh, by the sometime theoretical physicist and socialist, Friedrich Adler, in the autumn of 1916.[95] Most pacifists in the cultural elite were not prepared to go that far. Indeed some pacifists, such as Franz Werfel, were effectively cowed by the Habsburg authorities from voicing their true convictions until very late in the day.[96] Some, such as Stefan Zweig, were extremely circumspect, collaborated with the authorities, and cloaked their private pacifist convictions in historical and biblical allegory for their public pronouncements. Yet others, most famously Karl Kraus, attacked the war from very early on, although Kraus himself did not attack the authorities or the military until well into 1917. For all the circumstantial shortcomings, Austrian pacifism produced at least two works of particular note: Stefan Zweig's *Jeremias* and Karl Kraus's *Die letzten Tage der Menschheit.*

Jeremias   Zweig's pacifist record was not as spotless as he claims in his memoirs: despite his swift turn to private pacifism, he continued to write propaganda pieces for the Austrian press. He cannot escape charges of time-serving and opportunism.[97] One suspects that his releasing *Jeremias* for publication at Easter 1917 was also not quite as courageous as he leads one to believe, but had at least something to do with Zweig's fine sense of the changes in the Austrian political atmosphere.[98] Nevertheless, *Jeremias* remains a powerful statement against war, and took some courage to publish, for it can easily be read on one level as an indictment of the leadership of the Central Powers.

Zweig essentially reconstructs the origins of the First World War in the form of the biblical war against Nebuchadnezzar. Instead of the Dual Alliance with Habsburg's nemesis, Prussia-Germany, Zweig has the Jews debating whether to ally with their old enemy, the Egyptians, or stay out of the war, for "our battle is not theirs."[99] He also has public opinion and the crowd swaying the decision-making process, with the crowd drunk on the vision of absolute power, "Israel über den Völkern" (Israel above all peoples).[100] The old king, Zedekia, clearly has the traits of Zweig's image of Franz Joseph, an old man swayed by hawkish advisors and his own sense of honor to wage war even if it means almost certain destruction, an identification made even plainer by Zedekia's very title, "König zu Jerusalem," king of Jerusalem, one of the many titles which the Habsburg emperor still claimed from the dynasty's glorious past.[101] To this are added some traits of William II – Zweig has Zedekia say of the war "I did not want it" (Ich habe es nicht gewollt).[102] As for the leadership, Zweig has them dealing with the problem of food shortages by agreeing to keep the people ignorant of the problem: "We must be united against Nebuchadnezzar and united against the People."[103] There is even a scene in the play which deals with the power of rumor and the pernicious influence of the media.[104]

Against this the pacifist message of Jeremias is impossible to misinterpret: "an evil and fierce animal is war"; "better to be wise than strong, better to be God's slave than the master of men"; "no war is holy, no death, only life"; "peace is better than honour, suffering better than death."[105] In one scene, Zweig implicitly appeals to the "people" to reconsider if they really want war.[106] Yet again, though, it is never really clear to which "people" the allegorical message is addressed: is it the German "Volk" that is spoken to, or the "Austrian" "Volk," or neither? The play ends on a rousing note of consolation in defeat and of national spiritual defiance: "One can kill human beings, but not the God that lives in them. One can conquer a people (Volk), but never its spirit."[107] Yet when the play was first published this would have sat oddly with both Germans and Austrians, who, if disillusioned with the war, were not defeated.

The play clearly has a pacifist message, but on a deeper level it is more about this spirit of defiance against superior might, even the acceptance of suffering as the sign of divine love, and the road of exile as the way to God. In other words the "People" about which *Jeremias* concerns itself is, in the end, neither the Germans, nor the Austrians, but the Jews, both the Jews of the biblical time in which the play is set, but also the Jewish situation of the time when the play was written. The play starts as pacifist allegory, but turns into a Jewish theodicy, an attempt to explain the chosenness of the Jewish people precisely in terms of exile, persecution, and alienation. There are even Zionist undertones in the piece, but it is ultimately the Central European, emancipatory interpretation of Judaism, of the "temple in your hearts," which becomes the dominant theme. "World-wandering is our abode, suffering our field, and God our home [*Heimat*] in time."[108] The most famous work of Austrian pacifism published during the war was thus a work without an Austrian identity, which put national identity on a spiritual level, above any national identity associated with a particular geographical location. This was about as far from the "Austrian idea" as one could get.

The last days of mankind   Karl Kraus was also taken with using biblical Jewry as an allegorical equivalent, not for Austrians, but for Germans, a parallel which he discusses explicitly in *Die letzten Tage der Menschheit*.[109] Kraus also shares with Zweig the prophetic stance, although there is no positive lesson at the end of his prophecy, only the

Last Day of Judgment. There is also not the same sort of ambiguity of Zweig's biblical allegory: Kraus's play is perhaps the most searing indictment of the Central Powers' conduct of the war it is possible to imagine.[110] Any passingly comprehensive account of Austrian culture during the war cannot help but be deeply influenced by the war's portrayal in Kraus's play.[111]

It is a truly remarkable, at times almost surrealistic, account, written in a whole panoply of dialects, with an overwhelmingly large cast of characters. The play begins in Vienna, and concentrates at the start on the Austrian experience of the war, which consists of the stupidities and mendacities of the authorities, of the jingoistic crowds, of "public opinion," and most of all of the press. As the play and the war proceed the Austrian experience becomes ever more bizarre, illogical and frivolous, ever more devoid of moral authority. Kraus develops an image of Austria at war as the "tragic carnival," a world turned upside down, in which the social order has been destroyed and the sense of propriety which comes with legitimate authority has disappeared.[112] It is a society falling apart at the ethical seams. Kraus has even his "optimist" cede to the "grumbler" the horror of the Austrian war experience when he is shown a picture of the hanged Cesare Battisti (an Italian patriot/ Austrian "traitor"), with the hangman smilingly posing for the camera along with the execution's witnesses, craning to get in the photo. This picture, which Kraus held to symbolize the "Austrian face" of absolute evil, was made into a postcard and distributed by the Habsburg authorities as propaganda – supposedly for their side. (See Fig. 5.2.) Kraus's "tragic carnival" is a doomladen anticipation of the theory of "the banality of evil," which was to be applied to an even greater Central European moral disaster a few decades later.[113]

Yet, the main target of Kraus's play comes to be not the unraveling Austria, but its extremely powerful and well-organized German ally. It is the "techno-romantic adventure" of the German war effort, the tragic perversion of German idealism into a justification for war, which comes to dominate Kraus's polemic. "Obsolete conceptions of power" and a wilful romanticization of war – using metaphors such as "drawing the sword" when the actual weapons being used are howitzers, flamethrowers and poison gas – collude with and cloak the materialism of "predatory greed," to create a demonic, insatiable imperialism that is the real driving force behind the German war effort. The heralds of armageddon, Gog and Magog, turn out to be two fat, philistine North German tourists on holiday in Switzerland.[114]

Kraus's indictment of the Central Powers, all based on accurate documentation, is brilliantly devastating; but much of it is deeply

5.2   The execution of Cesare Battisti

problematic, and at times neither fair nor accurate. Kraus spends a large part of the play blaming the press for starting the war and keeping it going through self-serving mendacity. Yet, as we have seen, the Austrian propaganda effort was one of the least successful among the combatants. Moreover, Kraus's favorite target, the *Neue Freie Presse*, which he casts as a major warmonger throughout the war, was arguing throughout 1918, despite German pressure, for a compromise peace to save Austria-Hungary.[115] Yet the problems with Kraus's work lie much deeper than just superficial inaccuracies or exaggerations, and stem from a fundamental ambivalence.

Recent research has shown that the post-war play is actually a conservative, "romantic anti-capitalist" critique, written during the war, overlaid with a radical, republican gloss, which was added after 1917. It was only then that Kraus realized that the real villains were indeed the military and political authorities of the Central Powers rather than the "enemy within" of media and economic interests.[116] Underlying the attack on the turpitude and moral failure of the Central Powers is thus a far more questionable attack on modernity itself.

In many ways Kraus's critique of modernity, using Germany as the exemplar, is eerily prophetic. The war, for Kraus, has shown how a twofold conquest – of nature by technology, and of "Kultur" by materialism – has left the spiritual side of Man and the World yoked to purely material concerns, with devastating ethical consequences.[117] In a Weberian, "disenchanted" world, structures and numbers create distance between people, which in turn leads to amorality and brutality, as "*Menschen*," human beings, are recast as "*Menschenmaterial*," human material. From here it is only a short way to viewing "human material" as expendable, as not even really human.[118] In this despiritualized, deindividualized world, German nationalism is the obverse of German materialism and both are embodied in the concept of the national god, so that the ethical purity of Kant's categorical imperative becomes a justification for national, material self-aggrandizement.[119]

The catch with this otherwise suggestive analysis comes when Kraus identifies the root cause of this creation of the materialist, national god, for it is precisely here that Kraus uses the parallel with the "ancient Hebrews." The Germans are seen as the direct heirs to the *Jewish* ideas of a national God, of a Chosen people, and of a worshipping of money: "For in both cases they operate in terms of a *Gesamtkunstwerk* of a *Weltanschauung*, which sees the things of the world run by the things of the spirit, so that wars can be run just like business ledgers, namely 'with God.'"[120] Kraus went even further in the poem which was his favorite for public readings until late in 1917, *Gebet an die Sonne von Gibeon*, in which the Jews, with their false, national god Jehovah, are seen as the destroyers not only of other nations, but also of nature itself, and are the root of all evil.[121]

Kraus was far from being alone in holding such views. Some form of anti-Jewish prejudice seems to have been endemic in Austrian society, including in the cultural elite. The composer, Julius Bittner, for instance, was not known as an anti-Semite. Yet his main wartime opera, *Das höllisch Gold* (Hellish Gold), looks today like a psychogram of the anti-Semitic, Austrian mind.[122] Its characters include: the Man, the Woman, the Devil, the Old Hag, a Jewish Usurer (the off-stage villain), and Ephraim, the latter's son, whose goodness is achieved only by the complete denial of his heritage, symbolized by money.[123] This work indicates just how widespread the identification of "Jew" with money and with the materialist destruction of true spirituality and Christianity was in Kraus's world.

Such anti-Semitic images in the elite were paralleled in an endemic anti-Semitism in the Austrian, particularly the Viennese, masses. This was kept in check at the beginning of the war, as the sense of social unity which the war engendered almost everywhere also included the Jews as, again, good Germans/Austrians. Yet, in the course of the war, as thousands of Jewish refugees from Galicia came to the Austrian capital seeking refuge, as the increasing shortages of food and supplies started to pinch, and as Austrian fortunes in the war took a turn for the worse, Viennese public opinion turned to its favorite scapegoat: Jews. The refugees were attacked as parasites on society, the lack of success at the front was attributed to the Jewish "enemy within," an amalgam of journalists, bankers, profiteers, and revolutionaries. Shortages were explained as the result of Jewish blackmarketeering. By 1918 the Christian Socials and the German Nationalists were competing in the fierceness of their anti-Semitic rhetoric, and even the Social Democrats occasionally joined in against "Jewish" capitalists.[124] Kraus was wrapped up in this sort of mindset. He also thought in terms of an "enemy within" who was clearly Jewish, and the main targets of his wartime attacks, such as Moritz Benedikt, "the lord of the hyenas", were Jews. With the rise of anti-Semitism and his realization that the authorities were, after all, the real culprits in the war, Kraus did replace *Gebet an die Sonne von Gibeon* at his public readings with his *Lied des Alldeutschen*, but he did so only very late in the day, in November 1917.[125]

Operetta and the war

Of a piece with this hatred of the "judaization" of Germany was Kraus's equally vehement dislike of the main forms of mass, popular culture. We have seen what he thought of the press, and he was as wary of the power of film to influence, and hence mislead, the masses.[126] What Kraus clearly saw as the epitome of evil in Viennese popular culture was the operetta. He did not dislike all operettas, far from it. He was a great devotee of Jacques Offenbach, and would often read Offenbach operettas at his public readings.[127] But the Viennese operetta, especially that of the "Silver Age" of just before and during the war, was seen by him as aesthetically hollow and morally corrosive.[128]

Kraus held operetta in contempt partly because he saw it as a mode of frivolous escapism, by which the Austrians could yet again ignore the moral immensity of the war, and he was disgusted with the behavior of composers such as Franz Lehár, who collaborated with the authorities, going on tours of the Western front. The wartime operettas, those that were explicitly patriotic, but also those which were just frivolous, were seen by Kraus as an amoral, hedonistic pillar of the war effort, a true opiate of the people, "a narcotic to transmute the ugliness of war into agreeable fantasy," and hence keep the war gong.[129] But he also disliked operetta, I think, for more conservative reasons – because it was aimed at satisfying the mass market: just like the press, the musical stage had been turned into a business, art had been turned into just another part of the capitalist world.

This detestation of operetta was shared by others. Alban Berg spoke of the philistinism, amorality, and "impurity" of operetta.[130] The theatre critic, Paul Stauber, spoke of the "operetta plague" which was taking over Vienna's theatres, and blamed the huge success of cinema, "with its uninhibited pandering to the lower instincts," on the Viennese public having been prepared for such immorality by the equally base operetta.[131] Yet it was not only the baseness or frivolity of the medium that was objectionable, but also its commercialism: what mattered in the operetta world was money, marketing, and hype, not quality or artistic integrity.[132] The Stauberian/Krausian protest was not only against the Viennese frivolity of operetta, but, more broadly, against the intro-duction of modern mass culture, of the entertainment industry, into the Habsburg capital.[133]

Yet one might ask at this point: what was wrong with operetta being frivolous; what was wrong with there being a mass-cultural entertain-ment industry alongside high culture? As Stieg points out, operetta was supposed to be easy to digest aesthetically, without the ethical function of high drama, and was "a recreation spot like Bad Ischl."[134] Was Kraus's critique fair? Was he justified in seeing operetta as symbolic of Austrian moral degeneration? Or was there something more here, which, because of his narrow, Malvolian perspective, he missed?

There was more than enough evidence to confirm the Krausian view of operetta; but there is also evidence, patchy though it might be, that points to another conclusion. Operetta did act by and large as an opiate and a vehicle of escapism; a cursory study of the operettas produced for the Viennese stage from 1914 to 1918 shows an art form that was indeed hyper-conservative in its structures, usually without any serious content, and trying hard to avoid social reality.[135] Yet such accusations are not universally valid: some, indeed a surprising number, do have a serious message, reflecting the preoccupations of the public during the war years. Some operettas dealt directly with class relations and social issues, such as Robert Stolz's *Das Lumperl* from 1915, which contrasted Viennese decadence with Styrian provincial industry.[136]

There were operettas with a cultural-critical message against the very entertainment industry of which they were a part, such as Oskar Straus's *Nachtfalter*.[137] Many operettas sent a message of multinational harmony in the Habsburg Monarchy. The most successful of all wartime operettas, Emmerich Kálmán's *Die Csardasfürstin* of 1916 celebrated both the usual crossing of social barriers and the political coming together embodied in the Austro-Hungarian Compromise or *Ausgleich*.[138] Oskar Nedbal's *Die Winzerbraut*, also of 1916, handled similar themes, but between Vienna and Croatia.[139] In another cross-national operetta, though, Edmund Eysler's *Wenn zwei sich lieben!* of 1915, what appears to be an operetta celebrating multinationalism turns into a celebration of the constancy of the Hungarian peasantry, with almost a Magyar nationalist message.[140] Similarly, in one of Lehár's most successful wartime operettas, *Wo die Lerche singt*, from 1918, it is the naturally beautiful Hungarian peasant girl, Margit, who is seduced and then rejected by the big city artist, Sándor, only to be rescued by her salt-of-the-earth former peasant fiancé Pista, so that she escapes back to the countryside, "where the lark sings."[141]

Lehár's operetta was clearly an essay in escapism, offering a rural idyll as a solution to the problems of the city and, implicitly, the war. The charge of escapism cannot be denied for the vast bulk of operettas. Many produced between 1914 and 1918 would be set in "the present" in Vienna or the Monarchy but make no mention of the war at all, or of the oppressive wartime conditions being suffered by the populace. There is no lack of food or champagne at the inevitable balls and banquets where so many operettas were set.[142] Yet this escapism was often consciously acknowledged by the operettas themselves. *Die Csardasfürstin* is redolent with admonitions to forget the horrors of the world around you, and live instead for the moment: "The whole of existence is a nonsense . . . / In this vale of sobbing, I'd rather be nightclubbing"; or "In this familiar atmosphere, / where we dance and kiss and play, / I cock a snook at the world so drear, / and make the night into day."[143] There were few illusions that operetta was doing anything but offering momentary relief from the world outside the theatre.

Operetta was also clearly aiding the war effort. Especially at the beginning of the war there were obviously war-related patriotic operettas, such as Kálmán's *Gold gab ich für Eisen* (I Gave Gold for Iron) and *Komm' deutscher Bruder!* (Come, German Brother!), a joint effort by Edmund Eysler and Franz Lehár, and, although the wave of patriotism subsided fairly quickly, war operettas did appear later, such as Leo

Ascher's *Der Soldat der Marie* of 1916.[144] Operettas supported the war and the military in more indirect ways as well. Their heroes are often not only aristocrats, but also army officers, usually lieutenants; the favorite theme of sexual promiscuity, often associated with the "handsome" hussars and officers, was also occasionally given a patriotic "justification" as a way to provide more soldiers for the fatherland.[145] The wave of historical operettas set in the eighteenth century offered many opportunities for a sort of dynastic, Austrian patriotism without all the complications of the modern era.[146] In all these ways and more operetta bolstered morale and the image of the military.

Yet there was, for all its apparent supineness, a subversive streak in operetta, which occasionally peeks out from behind, or rather through, the frivolity. From the title of Eysler's *Frühling am Rhein* (Spring on the Rhine) one might expect that this operetta was a pro-German, pro-war piece of propaganda. There are elements of this, yet patriotism is not the main theme of the piece. The title is deceptive. It does not refer primarily to spring on the Rhine, but rather to Moritz Frühling, a Jewish merchant, whose Jewishness is made explicit at various points, and who speaks in a form of Jewish German. Even more intriguingly, Frühling, for all his uncouth manners and lack of aesthetic sense, is a positive figure, indeed the hero of the operetta, for it is his Jewish cleverness and his good-heartedness which saves his foster-daughter, Trendl, from the clutches of her refined, but completely amoral uncle, a German baron. The ethical Jew defeats the German aesthete, and the happy ending – the union of Trendl with her true love, Heinrich (Heini for short) – is celebrated on a steamer called "Die Loreley."[147]

Even overtly patriotic works such as *Gold gab ich für Eisen* have their intriguing aspects when it comes to judging their value as propaganda. There is more than enough jingoistic bluster in Kálmán's operetta, especially the scoffing at Entente propaganda, but most of it is given to the comic characters, Vitus, the idiot-farmer, and his much younger brother, Xaver, to express, and the latter is in an incestuous affair with Vitus's daughter, Walpurga.[148] This is a sub-plot, but even the main storyline is of dubious propaganda value: it stresses the horrors of war, and ends up questioning the primacy of duty. After not having had the heart to tell his comrade-in-arms's mother, Karoline, that her son, Franz, has been killed in battle, Alwin allows himself to be mistaken for Franz by Franz's mother and his sister, Marlene. When the real Franz turns out to be alive after all, his mother forgives Alwin for his ruse, saying that he was right to lie to her about her son's death, because she would have died of a broken heart at the news: "You have behaved like a good human being (*Mensch*). You listened to your heart, not the call of duty. You have given me gold instead of iron."[149] What sort of patriotic propaganda justifies a soldier not doing his duty?

One of the really big hits of the war was Leo Fall's *Die Rose von Stambul* (1916–1917), with text by Julius Brammer and Alfred Grünwald,. This operetta tapped into the fascination with the oriental Turkish allies, and one might have thought had some propaganda value, but the Ottoman authorities were not flattered by the attention; rather, the Turkish ambassador in Vienna lodged an official complaint about the operetta being disrespectful to Islam.[150] He was right: the operetta is a propaganda piece, not for Turkey, but for the cause of Turkish women's rights.[151] Moreover, although it is set in "the present," there is no reference to the war, a Hamburg millionaire is a figure of fun who has to accept the inter-racial marriage of his son to a Turkish woman, and included in the music is a can-can and the barcarolle from Offenbach's *The Tales of Hoffmann* – French music.[152] Despite this, or probably because of it, *Die Rose von Stambul,* was a runaway smash of the war years.[153]

Brammer and Grünwald's next operetta libretto was Leo Ascher's *Bruder Leichtsinn*, with a denouement that amounts to an ideological defense of operetta. There is hardly any reference to the war. Any references there are are rather indirect, and often subversive. In the quasi-French setting of Brussels, can-cans are danced, and even the Marseillaise is smuggled into a scene.[154] Most curious of all, the operetta, which premiered on 28 December 1917, several months after America's entry into the war, has an American as its hero, Jimmy Wells. Not only is he an American: "he is an impeccably elegant young man – but with chocolate brown skin. He is an American, the son of a mixed marriage – he speaks with a funny accent, and often flashes a brilliantly white smile; there is absolutely nothing of the 'nigger' about him, rather he is a very intelligent, quite charming gentleman, who is at ironic ease among Europeans – in short, someone who knows his own worth. He behaves as the complete man of the world."[155]

It is Jimmy Wells, who is the anonymous letter-writer, with whom the operetta's heroine has fallen in love, and whom she is allowed to marry, despite the objections of her natural father, the Count Dunoir[!], because "brother light-heartedness' (*Bruder Leichtsinn*) commands it. Leichtsinn reassures Dunoir that Jimmy will be good for his daughter: "Jimmy will protect her like a jewel – he is a pearl." Dunoir: "Does it have to be a black pearl?" Leichtsinn: "Those are the dearest."[156]

This is an extraordinary conclusion. One could argue that it is meant ironically, yet the daughter, Musotte, and Jimmy, are clearly, explicitly portrayed as sympathetic characters, and the whole operetta stresses again and again that it is *good* to go where the fancy takes you, not to worry about the consequences, but to follow your heart, and appeals to the Viennese on that level.[157] The prospect of racial miscegenation is clearly seen as a positive within the operetta: "a little *noire* – a little *blanche* – that is the right *mélange*."[158] The most straightforward interpretation is that the librettists, in the midst of a tragic and seemingly never-ending war, actually were defending their craft, as exponents of light-hearted entertainment, and stressing not only its ability to divert from life's realities, but also its emancipatory and even assimilatory potential. That the librettists and the composer were Jewish, products of an emancipatory and assimilatory ideology, would help to support this conclusion. After all, if half-black Americans should be, and can be accepted in the operetta world, Jews must surely be included as well.

The two sides of modernity

What *Bruder Leichtsinn* points to so clearly is that the frivolousness of operetta had a positive side missed by cultural critics. Operettas such as *Die Csardasfürstin*, *Die Rose von Stambul*, and *Bruder Leichtsinn* promoted an optimism, which suggested, that, if one took a chance and challenged social convention, then one could realize one's dreams. If one embraced the carnival, the "world turned upside down," then there could be a happy ending.[159] Moreover, one could also change society. Perhaps because of the earth-shaking events going on around them, these operettas were not socially conservative, as is usually assumed about operettas. Rather, they promoted and exemplified social change. The *Csardasfürstin* not only ends up getting her aristocrat, but it turns out that the feudal order, symbolized by her princely fiancé's family tree, is itself falling apart. The Turkish "Rose of Stambul" gets her man, and by implication has struck a blow for reform in Turkey. Jimmy Wells and Musotte are symbols of a new age in inter-racial understanding. Such optimistic operettas expressed, perhaps in a clichéed way, a confidence in the future, which was not so much the spirit of frivolity as the spirit of the new entertainment industry, and ultimately of liberal modernity.

In contrast, the post-war Krausian culture-critics and socialist cultural theorists looked on the new mass, popular culture with immense distrust, and indeed contempt. There was little attempt to coopt it. Instead the socialists sought to spread German high culture from the top down, while Krausians in the cultural elite looked to the cultivation of authentic modern art for the dedicated few.[160] Modernist culture in Vienna was thus fated to remain largely a matter for a small elite, intent on authenticity rather than popularity, while popular culture's entertainment industry carried on developing.

When the Viennese operetta world was destroyed in 1938, with the disappearance of its heavily Jewish personnel, many of its members found their way to Broadway or Hollywood, if they were not there already. Once there they helped in the development of the modern world of commercial mass culture, which dominates modern consciousness, and still insists on the optimism of a happy ending. Alfred Grünwald settled in New York, where his son Henry was raised. Henry Grunwald went on to become editor of *Time*, and eventually American ambassador to Vienna.

Kraus was not entirely wrong in calling the Austrian experience of the war the "tragic carnival." The lack of a settled Austrian self-understanding, the resultant lack of legitimate authority, and the anachronistic and at times chaotic nature of the Austrian bureaucracy ensured, as we have seen, more than enough confusion, absurdity, and brutality, to justify the appellation, and Austrian popular culture undoubtedly played a large part in this. On another level, though, Kraus – and many others like him – failed to see that the "carnival," tragic or not, also offered large opportunities for change and experiment, risk-taking and opening to new ideas, which the world of operetta could, on occasion, grasp. What he failed to see was that his world of "critical modernism,"[161] holding the world accountable to the stringent moral and aesthetic code of a quasi-biblical prophet, had as its inevitable and necessary counterpart, the commercial, often frivolous, but equally "modern" world of mass popular culture.

More often than not in Vienna this argument between elite, "critical modernist" high culture and commercial, popular mass culture was an internal Jewish debate, with Jews predominant on both sides. Perhaps this is the reason that Kraus failed for so long to realize that he was utterly mistaken to see the "Jewish" worlds of the liberal press, finance, commerce, and the entertainment "industry" as the main culprits in bringing about the "last days of mankind."

He did finally see that it was the German and Austrian political establishments, with their complete perversion of German idealism on the one hand, and a ruthless amorality disguised by old-world cordiality on the other, who were really to blame, and the final, post-war version of his play reflects this adjustment accordingly. He could even see that this war was probably not going to be the end of the matter:

It has not taken place on the surface of life, but rather has raged at life's core. The front has spread into the hinterland. It will stay there. And the transformed life, if there still is one, will be teamed up with the old way of thinking. The world will go under, and we will not notice. We will have forgotten everything that happened yesterday; not see what is gong on today; and not fear what is coming tomorrow. We will have forgotten that we lost the war, forgotten that we began it, forgotten that we waged it. Therefore it will not stop.[162]

This would turn out to be tragically perceptive, but what was to happen a couple of decades later was beyond what even Kraus could have imagined. He could not know in 1922 that the absolute evil he had thought to discern in the war was only the prologue to something even more hideous. Nor could he know that when the "last days of mankind" really came with the Holocaust, "Jewish" Central European modernity, in both its "critical" and "optimistic" forms, would not be the perpetrator, nor the prophet, but the victim.

6　Ambivalent patriots: Czech culture in the Great War*

Claire Nolte

Despite years of growing international tensions and warnings about the inevitability of war, the population of the Czech lands, as elsewhere in Europe, was taken by surprise when war erupted in 1914. The duration of the war was likewise unexpected, since most people at the time, including many leading statesmen, suffered from the illusion that modern war could not last more than a few months.[1] However, the Czechs faced additional problems in adjusting to the war. On the one hand, they wanted to support their soldiers at the front, but on the other, they nursed long-standing political grievances against the empire which had sent them there. This ambivalence was widespread in the population, as the anti-war and anti-Habsburg slogans on the sides of troop trains and in the songs sung by departing soldiers indicated. Resentment toward the war, along with traditions of Russophilism, fueled mass surrenders of Czech troops to the Russians in 1915.[2] Ultimately, most Czechs overcame their ambivalence, as the war and the deteriorating economic situation eroded the last remnants of their loyalty to the Habsburg state.

These Czech attitudes were reflected in the culture of the war years. Ever since the days of the National Awakening in the early nineteenth century, when scholars and linguists undertook to revive the Czech language and culture from its submersion in a Germanized Central Europe, Czech intellectuals had been closely associated with their nation's political establishment and regarded it as their duty to support its program. This imperative became more compelling during World War I, and culminated in the last years of the war when cultural leaders challenged Czech politicians to assume a more defiant stance. The politicians, however, had reason to be cautious. The war had brought the suspension of constitutional rights, including parliamentary immunity, along with the closing of all representative bodies in the Cisleithanian, or Austrian, part of the Dual Monarchy.[3] Several leading

* The research for this chapter was undertaken with the generous assistance of a grant from the International Research and Exchanges Board.

Czech politicians had been imprisoned and two of them, Karel Kramář and Alois Rašín, had been sentenced to death for treason, a punishment that was delayed because of the impending death of Emperor Franz Joseph in 1916, and eventually lifted by his successor, Emperor Karl. For this reason, there was little overt support for the efforts of the Czech *émigrés* gathered around Tomáš Garrigue Masaryk and Edvard Beneš to create a new state of Czechs and Slovaks.

Despite the political turmoil, daily life in Prague seemed to go on unchanged, at least during the early years of the war. One journalist wrote, in 1915, that Prague was fortunate for having been spared the horrors of war. He bemoaned, however, the fact that popular celebrations, such as the beloved carnival balls, had disappeared from the social calendar.[4] The American consul in Prague affirmed this view in a dispatch in January 1916:

I am compelled to say that life here seems absolutely normal. The streets are crowded with well-dressed people and coffee houses, cinematographs, theaters, and cabarets are going full blast. Of course, I am not speaking of underlying conditions but of the general appearance of things.

The Bohemian national spirit which was so rampant before the war has absolutely evaporated . . . whatever the cause may be there is no questioning the fact that on the surface at least there is loyalty to the Government . . . It is not safe to say whether this attitude of the Czechs is due to official pressure, but the Czechs are certainly showing no spirit in defending what I had been led by the Germans to believe was the political creed of all of them, that is, the separation of Bohemia from Austria.[5]

If the American consul's view of Czech enthusiasm for the war was exaggerated, his observations about daily life in Prague were not. When the war first broke out, many cultural journals suspended publication, some of them declaring, with the avant-garde journal *Moderní revue*, "Inter arma silent Musae."[6] Most, however, resumed publication as it became clear, after a few months, that the war would not be over soon. Although some newspapers and journals fell victim to wartime censorship or economic problems, most continued publication, if on a reduced scale. It is indicative of the relative normality of the cultural world at this time, that three new cultural journals appeared in the midst of the war.[7] The lecture series at the Cultural Union also continued through the war years, although the speakers avoided current events.[8] Apparently, the muses were not silent in the Czech lands, although they often had to speak softly, since, as one observer noted, the war formed a "gloomy background that could not be dismantled."[9]

The Czech literary world continued its impressive productivity, despite an occasional skirmish with the censors. Czech writers debated whether it was appropriate, given the nature of the conflict, for Czechs to celebrate wartime accomplishments in literature. As a result, the influence of the war on the literature of the time was, in the words of one literary scholar, "reflected primarily through intellectual and moral inspiration rather than through artistic ferment."[10] Czech writers, like those in other countries, attempted to find meaning in the conflict, their search often causing them to abandon the individualism of pre-war art in favor of an emphasis on the collective. There was a renewal of interest in the writing of the *Ruch* (Activity) generation, writers on nationalist themes who had gathered around the journal of that name in the late nineteenth century. Previously discredited as anachronistic by a younger, more cosmopolitan, generation, the few remaining members of this group enjoyed their last moments of literary respectability during the war years.[11] This sense of connection to an earlier time was described in a contemporary account: "[T]he war warmed and deepened our love and respect for our mother tongue . . . and we understand today the joy that filled the thought of the national awakeners and heralds a century ago whenever a valuable new Czech book appeared."[12]

The work of Viktor Dyk (1877–1931) – which encompassed poetry, prose, and drama – is representative of this trend. Although, as a young man, Dyk had been deeply affected by the government's crackdown against a progressive youth movement called the *Omladina*, he joined the *fin de siècle* trend toward titanism, which the cult of Nietzsche had inspired, and was close to the circle around the avant-garde cultural journal, *Moderní revue*, that propagated the new literary trends of symbolism and decadence. He mocked these enthusiasms in his later years, commenting in a poem from 1915: "We were stormy and rebellious youth / full of skeptical talk. / We were derisive and somber, / we, the generation of negation."[13]

Dyk's transformation from a modernist to a traditionalist had already begun before World War I.[14] He joined the State Rights Progressive Party, which alone among Czech parties advocated war to achieve national independence, and ran unsuccessfully for parliament on its ticket in 1911. When the long-awaited war of liberation did break out, Dyk was perfectly situated to express the longing for national community of a generation cut adrift. Although Dyk contemplated joining Masaryk in exile, he ended up staying in the country to work with the domestic opposition. He continued to publish (although some of his writing was banned), and to work as a translator, specializing in the work of Victor Hugo, whose opposition to the Second Empire and to the German conquest of his country could serve as a metaphor for the Czech situation.[15]

Dyk's political work earned him imprisonment in Vienna during 1916 and 1917, where he wrote perhaps the most famous expression of the nationalist trend in Czech wartime literature, an ode to the national homeland entitled "The Land Speaks," that concludes:

> What did you fear?
> What is death?
> Death means coming to me.
> Your mother, the land
> Is opening her arms to you; possibly, you have despised her?
> Come, you will know, how the land has soft arms
> For the one, who has fulfilled what awaits him.
> I ask you, as your mother, defend me, my son.
> Go, though you may go to your death unwillingly.
> If you leave me, I live on.
> If you leave me, you will die.[16]

Dyk's activity as a translator of Victor Hugo and other writers, French and German, highlights another trend in the literary world of Prague in the Great War, the flourishing book trade.[17] Publishers continued to offer a dazzling array of new publications, and even launched some new ventures. The Borový publishing house began a series called "Zlatokvĕt" (Golden Blossom) in 1916 for Czech *belles lettres*, and Topič publishers inaugurated a similar venture for Czech and foreign literature.[18] Translations abounded, and even writers from enemy lands were acceptable to the censors if they carried an anti-war message. As a result, the Czech public was able to keep abreast of the latest works by the Norwegian writer Knut Hamsun, as well as to read one of the most famous anti-war novels of World War I, *Le Feu*, by the French writer, Henri Barbusse, along with the books of his countryman, Romain Rolland, and of the Belgian, Émile Verhaeren. The Czech politician, Jan Herben, found the fine distinctions of Austrian censorship amusing, as he wrote in his wartime diary:

Miss Casonová may sing in English in the National Theater because she supposedly will sing American English, she may sing in Italian because she will sing Austrian Italian. She may not sing in French, because it did not occur to her to declare that she will sing Swiss French.[19]

Any discussion of Czech wartime literature would not be complete without mention of the best-known writer of this era, the anarcho-socialist and all-around bad boy of Czech literature, Jaroslav Hašek (1883–1923). Although Hašek's account of the life and adventures of his famous creation, Josef Švejk, was actually written after the war, Hašek had introduced the Švejk character in some of his pre-war short

L   E   T   Á   K   57.

Eduard Bass:
Ó LOUČENÍ, Ó LOUČENÍ...

S karikaturou Zdeňka Kratochvíla. Cena 40 haléřů.

6.1   Zdeněk Kratochvíl, cartoon depicting "Citizen Coudenhove,"
a reference to the last imperial governor of Bohemia, Count
Maximilian von Coudenhove, carting away the defunct
Habsburg eagle. Cover of an Eduard Bass cabaret poem, 1918.

stories. His novel reflected some of the ambiguities of the Czech situation, and was coolly received in the new Czechoslovak Republic after
the war. In it, Hašek pillories the incompetence of the Austrian government and bureaucracy, but also shows the loyalty, along with the
exasperation, of its Czech officers. Lieutenant Lukáš, for example, is
described as

a typical regular officer of the ramshackle Austrian monarchy . . . who equated being Czech with membership in some sort of secret organization, to which it was wiser to give wide berth. Otherwise, he was a decent man, who was not afraid of his superiors and looked after his company at manoevres, as was seemly and proper.[20]

After the war, most Czechs preferred to forget that there had been loyal Czech soldiers like Lukáš. Rather, they viewed their service in the Austro-Hungarian army as involuntary, as in the wartime joke: three soldiers, one French, one German, and one Czech, all die at the same time and appear at the pearly gates. St. Peter asks the French soldier why he fought in the war, and he replies, "For the republic and the nation!" When he asks the same question of the German soldier, he asserts, "For the emperor and the fatherland!" But the Czech soldier, faced with the same query, responds, "For eight kreutzers a day."[21]

Hašek as an erstwhile socialist embodies the other collectivist trend in Czech wartime literature.[22] Socialist doctrine had won many adherents among the European intelligentsia before World War I, and the suffering of the war years, along with the utopianism of the new Bolshevik regime in Russia, only strengthened its appeal. In the Czech lands, this enthusiasm often overlapped with older traditions of Slavism and Russophilism, outgrowths of the peculiar situation of the Czechs in a German-dominated Central Europe. Hašek is representative of these trends. Although he was not in the school of socialist writers concerned with proletarian problems, his sense of Slavic solidarity facilitated his conversion to the Bolshevik cause.

Like the Good Soldier he immortalized, Hašek was called to military service. Taken prisoner by the Russians, he ended the war as an apparatchik in central Russia. In the interim, his peregrinations brought him into contact with another arena of Czech wartime culture, the Czech Legions. Although the Russian tsar had contemplated enrolling the large numbers of Czech prisoners of war into a legion to fight alongside Russian forces, little was done in this direction until the revolutions of 1917. Masaryk came personally to Russia to organize this new force of Czech and Slovak soldiers, but the Legions he founded were soon caught up in the Russian Civil War. Their struggle to leave Russia via Siberia, whence they traveled by ship to join the Western armies in France, is celebrated in Czech national history as their Anabasis. Hašek volunteered for the Legions, and wrote stirring anti-Austrian articles and speeches for its Propaganda Section, but did not accompany them to France, offering his services to the new Bolshevik government instead.[23]

Already in the prisoner of war camps, Czech prisoners had launched some fledging cultural enterprises, aided by the Czech *émigré* community in southern Russia. The creation of the Legions brought in financial support to expand these efforts, culminating in a complex of activities that not only chronicled the events of the Anabasis, but also provided information and diversion to its participants. The most important arena was publishing, carried out in local printing facilities or on a mobile press in a train car, that produced periodical literature, along with book-length fiction and non-fiction. In addition, amateur theater and music groups flourished, artists designed insignia, sculptors erected monuments in Siberia to honor fallen heroes, and a special division for film and photography was created to document the struggle.[24] Although Czech prisoners of war and legionaries in the West undertook similar efforts, they were fewer in number and did not match the productivity of their compatriots in Russia.[25] The legionary culture established an heroic legacy that was central to the mythology of the new national state. It superseded the much larger participation of Czechs in the Austro-Hungarian army, whose bravery and courage was overshadowed during the war by the mass surrenders on the Eastern front, and forgotten altogether after the war in the euphoria of national independence.

The search for meaning, for absolutes, that the war had engendered in Czech literature faded rapidly once the war had ended. The literati who emerged as spokespeople for the new Czechoslovak state were neither former legionaries, Bolshevik enthusiasts, or even nationalist dreamers, but rather a new generation of pragmatists who, shaken by the experience of war, disavowed the search for absolute values in life and in art.[26] Karel Čapek (1890–1938) is the most representative writer of this generation. His first independent collection of short stories, *Wayside Crosses*, appeared during the war, and expresses his skepticism about man's ability to achieve spiritual understanding.[27] In addition to rejecting the ideological trends of its predecessors, this new generation also rejected many of their thematic and stylistic emphases, favoring prose over poetry, and drawing inspiration from more popular literary forms, like the detective novel, which older, more elitist, writers, had scorned. Čapek, who spent most of the war years as a literary and art critic in Prague, came into his own in the new Czechoslovak Republic, where his pragmatism and skepticism reflected the mood of the 1920s more accurately than the impassioned faiths of the war years.

If literary output continued unabated during the war, the same cannot be said for the visual arts. Although "Prague by 1912 had become the leading center of cubism in the Austro-Hungarian Monarchy," artistic output plummeted during the war years, as commissions dried up and artists were drafted or volunteered for Czech armies abroad, like the painter František Kupka (1871–1957) and the sculptor Otto Gutfreund (1889–1927), who were both studying in Paris when the war broke out.[28] Although exhibits were mounted and articles analyzing them appeared in cultural journals, they appeared less regularly and on a far smaller scale than in the pre-war years.[29]

The American consul's comment about the popularity of public forms of entertainment is reaffirmed by a contemporary observer, who noted that the more deprivation the war caused, "the more we listened to music and went to the theater to drink the ambrosia of familiar Czech ideas."[30] Theatrical life had been expanding in the Czech lands before the war. There were several permanent theater companies, including three outside of Prague, along with an estimated sixty traveling companies and numerous amateur groups.[31] Although the initial shock of the war caused paralysis, the theaters rebounded and were soon packed to capacity. Even the military authorities recognized the positive impact theater could have and arranged for acting groups to tour the front.[32] The war years were not marked by theatrical innovation, since the few attempts to present new expressionist works met with indifference from an audience looking for escape or searching for meaning in troubled times. Rather, light comedies, many foreign in origin, and Czech historical plays, formed the foundation of the theatrical repertory. Among Czech performances, a nineteenth-century folk opera, *Fidlovačka* (Spring Festival), played to great acclaim during the war. Performed by both professional and amateur troupes, its audiences regularly rose to join in the singing of its most famous song, "Where is My Home?" a nationalist ode that became the official Czech anthem of the new postwar state.[33]

The center of dramatic life was the National Theater, built by the nineteenth-century nationalist movement as a symbol of Czech cultural revival. With the renewed respectability of nationalist culture during World War I, the theater again became a "temple of rebirth."[34] Its artistic director, Jaroslav Kvapil (1868–1950), was well suited to further this role. Like Dyk, he had been a supporter of the *Omladina* movement in his youth and went on to become active in the underground opposition during the war. His trips abroad on theater business were often a cover for him to contact *émigrés* close to Masaryk and Beneš. His approach to theater had been criticized as overly conservative even before the war, and he had little feel for the newer trends that were sweeping the theatrical world. Nevertheless, he managed under difficult circumstances to maintain a regular performance schedule, undertake new productions, and even launch several new Czech works. His most important accomplishment in those years was the presentation of a cycle of Shakespeare plays honoring the 300th anniversary of the death of the bard. Kvapil had long favored Shakespeare, but the political overtones of his new enterprise caused the Bohemian governor to ban it at first. Although works by Richard Sheridan or George Bernard Shaw were acceptable, Shakespeare had been regarded by Habsburg authorities as politically tendentious ever since nineteenth-century Czech national-ists had promoted his plays as an alternative to the German culture of Central Europe. In the end, Kvapil managed to overcome the resist-ance of the governor's office and present fifteen Shakespeare plays, some of them new productions, during March and April of 1916.[35]

In the more popular theaters of Prague, Shakespeare was often re-placed by operettas, then at the peak of their popularity. Since Czech composers only began to write operettas after 1900, the bulk of the repertory originated outside the Czech lands. This hardly affected their popularity, as one participant recalled: "This time...was the most fortunate for the Arena theater. Every day was sold out, and the theater groaned under the presence of the Sunday audiences."[36] The success of operettas helped to bail out financially troubled theaters, and inspired others, like the Municipal Theater that had opened in the Vinohrady section of Prague in 1907 as a counter-force to the National Theater, to add operettas to their performance schedules. This activity would never have been possible without the benevolence of the military authorities, as one performer recalled:

I must truthfully say that the *k.u.k bewaffnete Macht* [imperial and royal milit-ary] was very generous toward actors, even Czech ones. Active duty officers Vodílek and Šlemr...arranged cushy jobs for themselves in an engineering barracks in Vršovice, where they fought for the emperor and his family...they performed daily in the theaters and happily rehearsed as necessary. Along with their income from the theater (even if modest), they also got food from the imperial and royal mess hall and *Löhnung* [military wage].[37]

In addition to plays and operettas, theaters also hosted puppet per-formances. Puppetry was an established art in the Czech lands, whose roots went back to the national revival of the previous century. The war brought both disruption and opportunity, as many puppet theaters, especially those that lacked a permanent home base, failed, while others found new performing opportunities at military hospitals or even at the front.[38] The craft of puppetry also flourished in the Czech legions and among Czechs in POW camps.[39] Czech puppetry was, and remains, an art form, with a repertory that mixes serious plays and traditional folk theater with the Czech version of Punch and Judy. Puppet theaters joined the National Theater in commemorating Shakespeare in 1916

6.2   A group of Czech legionaries in Italy commemorating their
performance of the Czech folk play, *The Bagpiper of Strakonice*, 1918

with performances of *Hamlet*, *Macbeth*, and other classics, while at the
same time entertaining children and adults alike with the antics of the
comic character Kašparek.

Honky-tonk, or beer hall, entertainment, was another form with deep
roots in the popular culture. The first venture of this type had appeared
in Prague in the 1870s, and was still going strong after World War I.
It featured a variety of acts overseen by a master of ceremonies, along
with group singing of songs called *kuplety* (couplets), which had easily
remembered verses and simple melodies. Prague honky-tonk culture
spread throughout the Czech lands, carried by touring groups and,
especially during the war, by soldiers. The songs sung by the Good
Soldier Švejk demonstrate Hašek's familiarity with this aspect of the
underside of Czech culture.[40]

The American consul in Prague also took note of the popularity of
another, relatively new, form of entertainment in wartime Prague, the
cabaret. The so-called "literary cabaret" was an international form,
which had grown up in major cities like Paris and Berlin before the war.
The first cabaret of this type in Prague opened in the Lucerna building
on Wenceslaus Square in 1910. Initially bilingual, it hosted stars of German cabaret, such as the chanteuse, Thea Degen, and the comedian,
Jean Paul, along with Czech performers.[41] The new cabaret was more
refined than the older forms of beer hall entertainment, featuring sentimental ballads in place of the more bawdy *kuplety*, and satirical revues
that often, especially during the war, carried pointed political messages.[42] It is indicative of the high tone of this new enterprise, that the

artistic director of the National Theater, Jaroslav Kvapil, was among the founders of the Lucerna cabaret.[43] The war years undermined the international spirit of the early cabarets, while rising national sentiment led to the founding of more Czech-oriented enterprises, like Cabaret Rococo, which opened in 1915.

Czech cabaret produced its own stars, among them Karel Hašler (1879–1941), a member of the National Theater ensemble whose songs of old Prague became cabaret classics, and Eduard Bass (1888–1946), whose hallmark was his performance of satirical songs of his own composition from sheets called *Letáky*.[44] Both Bass and Hašler were Prague Jews, whose anti-Habsburg political sentiments made their cabarets successful during the war years. The Red Seven, originally a student group that gained prominence in the Rococo cabaret, cultivated a similar style, which is evident in their ballad about the brave Austrian German soldier named Huber, who suffered various injuries in the war each resulting in the loss of a part of his brain. After each incident, he begs to return to his unit and is immediately promoted for his valor. In the last verse, one final shell rips away all that is left of Huber's brain and

> in a true miracle of science
> . . . having lost his entire brain
> into the skull, now emptied
> they stuffed a bunch of hay
> so that it would not sound hollow.
> Returning with an empty head,
> but also with great renown,
> he immediately wanted to fight again.
> The emperor came personally to him
> and declared: "Even I have heard about you.
> Huber, I make you now a general!"[45]

On the periphery of more mainstream cabarets like Lucerna and Rococo, lay the bohemian netherworld of Prague. In the Montmartre cabaret, literati such as Egon Ervin Kisch, Max Brod, and Jaroslav Hašek gathered to view, and participate in, free-form performances in German, Czech, and Yiddish, that ranged from tangos and Apache dances to ragtime. It should come as no surprise to those familiar with Good Soldier Švejk that Hašek's speciality at these events was improvising pseudo-scholarly lectures, like the "mystifications" of Dada artists, with such titles as "On the Training of Police Dogs," or "The Saints from the Point of View of National Economics."[46]

Honky-tonks and cabarets were eventually superseded by the most modern form of mass entertainment, the film industry, which came into its own during World War I. It is a testimony to the popularity of the genre that the number of permanent movie houses in Prague rose from eighteen in 1910 to thirty-five during the war.[47] Films were also brought to soldiers at the front in so-called movie trains.[48] The nascent pre-war Czech film industry fell apart once the war began, and was not revived until the last years of the conflict.[49] As a result, most of the films shown to Czech audiences were not Czech in origin, rather foreign imports. Viennese distributors controlled the market in the Czech lands and purchased most of their films from foreign sources, since the Austrian film industry was also just emerging. These sources, however, were rapidly drying up, since the war brought a ban on the import of films from England, France, or Russia and, after 1915, from Italy.[50] American films were effectively banned during most of the war because of the difficulty in obtaining them. Since the ban did not affect films from enemy countries that had been imported earlier, the Viennese branch of the French film distributor, Pathé Frères, was able to supply audiences with French films from their large stockpile. The main beneficiary of these bans was the Danish film industry, which became the main provider of entertainment films to the Central Powers in the early years of the war. As the war progressed, the ban on Italian films was evaded by purchasing them in neutral Switzerland and similar methods brought the occasional American film to the Czech lands. While Viennese newspapers debated the propriety of showing Italian films while the empire was at war with Italy, they were widely shown in the Czech lands, where censorship was less stringent than in German Austria.[51]

In addition to entertainment films, the governments of all countries, including Austria-Hungary, produced documentaries of the war that were a staple in movie houses, and also underwrote propaganda films. One, entitled *The Dream of an Austrian Reservist*, featuring thousands of soldiers, had over 1,500 presentations in the Czech lands, making it the most successful film of the war years.[52] To undermine the dominance of Danish films, German authorities encouraged the formation of a native film industry, which soon gathered a large market share in the Austro-Hungarian empire. Although some 55 percent of the films imported into Austria-Hungary in 1916 came from Germany, the Czech public favored Italian, French, and Danish films, which "perhaps could be understood as [expressing] the anti-Austrian and anti-German spirit of the Czech population."[53]

As is evident from the experience of the film industry, the war had a politicizing effect in many cultural arenas that was not offset by the meager efforts of government authorities to drum up support through pro-government propaganda.[54] In the Czech lands, the increasingly desperate situation galvanized Czech cultural leaders to more overt actions. If they had quietly accepted the ban on lavish celebrations of the 500th anniversary of the death of Jan Hus in 1915, they were less acquiescent as the war dragged on.[55] In response to the Two Emperors' Manifesto in 1916, which called for the formation of a Polish state, Czech representatives to the long-adjourned parliament formed the Czech Union, which soon caused a storm of controversy in Prague when it declared its loyalty to the government in Vienna and undercut the legitimacy of the *émigré* movement around Masaryk and Beneš. To counter this action, Jaroslav Kvapil, the artistic director of the National Theater, organized a group of literati behind the so-called Writers' Manifesto, that was signed by 222 Czech writers and presented to the Czech Union in May 1917. The manifesto, which was vague enough to evade the censors, demanded a return to full constitutional freedoms, including parliamentary immunity.[56] It came at a time of rapid political change in the empire, after the new Emperor Karl, fearful that the ideas which had fueled the overthrow of the Russian tsar could spread, had reconvened the parliament and amnestied political prisoners, including Kramář, Rašin, and Dyk.

As it became increasingly clear that the war was lost, Kvapil continued his public initiatives, organizing a celebration of national loyalty in the Smetana Hall of the Municipal House in April 1918, where the aged writer, Alois Jirásek (1851–1930), a veteran of the *Ruch* generation, read a declaration that pledged its political representatives to continue the fight for national independence.[57] The culmination of these cultural-political manifestations took place in May 1918, when Prague played host to an influx of Slavic guests, including over 100 South Slavs, 60 Poles, and 18 Slovaks, along with smaller ethnic Italian and Romanian delegations, for a massive celebration of the fiftieth anniversary of the laying of the foundation stone for the National Theater.[58]

With the anniversary celebration of the National Theater, described as "the greatest revolutionary manifestation of the resistance on the homefront," the Czech national movement had come full circle.[59] Following the premise that the Czechs, as a small nation, could only justify their existence through culture, the intelligentsia had always been expected to articulate the national program. The laying of the foundation stone for the National Theater in Prague in May 1868 had been the high point in the national awakening of the nineteenth century, and the largest Czech demonstration to that point in the history of the city. It was, therefore, only fitting that the fiftieth anniversary of that event should take place as the Czech nation stood on the verge of a new era, and that its artists and writers, through such forums as the National Theater, had helped lead them to this point.

Nevertheless, the passions that had shaped Czech culture during the war faded rapidly after it ended. In order to place their new country in the vanguard of European trends and legitimize its existence, artists and writers set aside the nationalist prisms of the war years to return to a more cosmopolitan orientation.[60] The plays and stories of Karel Čapek, along with the modern art of František Kupka and Otto Gutfreund, brought worldwide recognition to the new Czechoslovak state. On the other hand, the work of Viktor Dyk, little known outside his homeland, was largely forgotten, while Jaroslav Kvapil's theatrical realism seemed stodgy at a time when Czech theater, swept by avant-garde trends, began an "exuberant, richly inventive phase."[61] Although Czech cultural leaders discarded the old-fashioned nationalist tone of the war years, they did not abandon their commitment to the nation. Rather, their efforts to create a modernist culture after the war represented a continuation of their traditional nation-building role in the changed political and social circumstances of the new Europe.

7   Culture in Hungary during World War I

Joseph Held

The term "culture" is amorphous. Not surprisingly, dictionaries offer varied definitions for it.[1] One way to circumvent the amorphousness of the term is to divide it into low, high, and intermediate categories. But such fragmentation is artificial. It takes away the subtle inter-relations that exist in real life. Consequently, culture should be described as a whole, its components subtly shading into one another, almost mysteriously, combining individuals into families, neighborhoods and, finally, nations. Culture is like a fine Persian carpet; its intricate individual patterns provide for the completeness and beauty of the whole. Take away a pattern – or even part of it – and it is no longer a carpet. To put it another way, civilization is but the external condition of modern man; culture, on the other hand, is the soul, the spirit.

Therefore, it would be somewhat misleading if this chapter were to divide Hungarian culture during the First World War into "high" and "low" segments. If one can speak of divisions – some of which did indeed exist – these would be running along rural and urban lines, both containing plenty of "high" and "low" elements. Yet, these parts were interdependent and often complementary. One of the best examples of such interdependence was the fact that all social strata in Hungary ate the same kinds of food. It was true that, for instance, chicken paprikash was prepared in a coarser way in the villages than in the cities, and the better-to-do ate more of it than the poor. Nevertheless, the same kind of food was consumed by peasants and aristocrats alike.[2] One should remember that Hungarian culture was, in many ways, similar to the cultures of the surrounding East European peoples. This was ensured not only by the ethnic composition of the Hungarian state, but also by the fact that Hungarians freely intermarried with other ethnic groups.

If categories must be set up – and this can hardly be avoided – they will be pursued under concepts of "rural" and "urban" cultures. Rural culture in Hungary was, on the whole, more traditional than its urban counterpart. This meant reliance on a host of village customs

176

derived from centuries of community life. But innovation and efforts at modernization were not lacking, especially in the rural towns that dotted the countryside.[3] In 1914, Hungary included a diverse population with several nationalities (Hungarians, Romanians, Serbs, Carpatho-Ukrainians, Germans, Jews, Croats, Slovaks, and Slovenes). Ethnic Hungarians (Magyars) made up little more than half of the total population of 20 million people. Yet I cannot deal with the cultures of the various non-Magyar nationalities and nations in this chapter for lack of space.

The fact must also be mentioned – a fact that is so obvious that it is often taken for granted by scholars – that Hungary was still part of the Habsburg Empire. In that empire the new century produced a rebellious generation of artists, painters, and other intellectuals, chiefly among the bourgeois stratum of society. The atmosphere was heavy with the effects of a new industrial revolution that began in the 1890s; its consequences included not only a surge in living standards, but also nostalgia for a simpler way of life.[4] In fine arts this was the age of the "decadents," that is, of artists who broke the bonds of traditional restrictions and standards, and proudly embraced all sorts of innovations. They explored the depths of perception, searching for the supernatural through the irrational. This was also the beginning of rebellion among women, seeking a way out of the rigid family structure, and freedom of choice in occupations as well as individual life-styles. There was also constant interaction among intellectuals in the empire. Consequently, the Austrian and Hungarian elites knew each other well. We must also emphasize, however, that the stirring of the new age was felt mostly among the narrowest stratum of intellectuals.

The majority of the Hungarian people were peasants living in villages in 1914.[5] As Tekla Dömötör explained, "Besides the eye-catching, dramatic holy day customs, there were many more everyday habits and rules governing the behavior of individuals and families."[6] Such customs formed the bases of behavior and morals, the order of eating, of dressing, of addressing one another, of the tempo of work, of the rights and duties of the sexes and age-groups, of those of inheritance. During World War I, these customs and rules hardly changed. The most important element in the four years of war was a negative one, that is, the removal of nearly half of the adult male population to serve in the armed forces.

A few examples will provide illustrations of these customs. When a child was born, it was not yet automatically a member of the community. Such membership was bestowed through a series of acts, including baptism, which provided occasions for the strengthening of family ties, and also created new family relationships.[7] Customs described the manner in which the baby had to be swaddled, fed, and cleaned. The baby's name was kept a secret in order to protect it from malevolent spirits.[8] Baptism meant acceptance by the community.

Marriage customs varied from region to region. Some were more elaborate than others. Even at the beginning of the twentieth century, some marriages were arranged between the respective families. However, by the beginning of World War I, such cases were restricted more and more to better-to-do households, and the marriages were the result of love between couples.[9] The marriage ceremony was performed with elaborate rituals. Peasant families often went into debt to finance a wedding.[10]

Village children had to be protected against evil spirits and magic. This was accomplished by incantations, and the use of various plants with magical properties. When a child or adult became ill, it was often attributed to malevolence by an enemy and was "cured" by turning to an "expert," usually an old woman, who then "lifted" the curse.[11] She, of course, had to be paid for her services. The celebrations and commemorations of life's turning points represented a significant part of village culture. Other customs and rules were attached to the agricultural seasons, the seasons of the year, and religious holy days.

Religion played a major role in village life. The local clergy were important authorities and advisors, supervising the local school (usually located in a church building) and participating in the most important events of village life. Going to church on Sundays and holy days was an unspoken requirement. Those who did not go incurred the condemnation of the community.[12]

The six months of the agricultural season required very hard labor from the entire community, men, women, children, and old folks. The time of the grain harvest was especially difficult. Agricultural machinery was still largely absent in the villages, although the threshing machine had already made its appearance. The physical demands of farm life were aggravated during the Great War, when the work in many villages had to be performed by women, children, and old folks. Nevertheless, ancient customs were continued under the persisting limitations; although merriments were fewer, and perhaps less exuberant, they continued to be held nevertheless.

Only during 1917, when the bloodletting on the fronts became overwhelming, did discontent become widespread. The war disrupted rural life to some extent, but not fundamentally; the news of casualties created grief in the families affected, but it did not alter traditional customs. In fact, a great many peasant families benefited from the war; food prices increased, and peasant speculators (including men and women) grew rather prosperous. There were no food shortages in the villages, and life went on as usual. Undoubtedly, the poor suffered more during the war than those with some means, and a disproportionately large number of them served in the army. Yet, those who were left at home lived better because wages increased.

But rural culture was not only village culture; the towns located in the countryside were centers of a different, often vibrant cultural life.[13] For instance, in the town of Esztergom, northwest of Budapest, there was a very lively performing arts group, made up of amateur players. The engine of cultural life was provided by the many civic societies which, by 1914, were well developed. These were often headed by priests or ministers who paid a great deal of attention to the education of their membership. Their programs consisted of concerts, readings of religious and/or scientific texts, and of poetry. When the regiment of the army stationed at Esztergom during peacetime, left for the front, the important role played by the officers of the regiment stationed in the city ended for good. Their balls, concerts, and amateur theater productions ceased. The regimental band which regularly played in these productions left with the regiment. The balls that usually followed the concerts or plays were suspended. The local Jewish intelligentsia, which had its own club, but whose membership also participated in other cultural programs, was also drafted.[14]

The larger rural town of Miskolc, located half-way between the northeastern border and Budapest, was a commercial center, providing a transition point for goods between the mostly agricultural south and the mining centers and wine-producing regions of northern and eastern Hungary. Not surprisingly, the leading citizens of this center were merchants or descendants of merchants. Cultural life in Miskolc was different from that of Esztergom. It was more secular in character, no doubt because the city was a commercial center, and its citizens engaged more in trades and commerce than those of the other city. Miskolc had a considerable educated stratum which dominated banking and financial institutions and government offices. There was a large Jewish presence in Miskolc, whose members took a very active role in the business and cultural life of their city.[15] During the war, many of the active citizens obtained exemption from military service, and continued their activities under the conditions of mobilization and war. Nevertheless, the war sapped the energies of the citizens, most of whom were increasingly preoccupied with procuring the everyday necessities of life.

A somewhat different situation prevailed in one of the great centers of Calvinist culture in Eastern Europe, the city of Debrecen. Located in eastern Hungary, this city had long been a market town. The atmosphere of the city was deeply nationalistic and Calvinist; in 1849, it harbored the last independent Hungarian government of Lajos Kossúth, fighting against Habsburg rule. By the end of the nineteenth century, however, the city had received large numbers of migrants from the surrounding countryside, many of whom were not able to adjust to the religious/oppositional atmosphere created by the traditional citizens of Debrecen. The fact that most of the newcomers were either Jewish or Roman Catholic contributed to this.[16]

Cultural life in Debrecen was based on the Reformed church. The grand old Calvinist church was the focus of holy day gatherings, where cultural programs were presented and supervised by the local ministers. Yet, by 1914, there were many secular organizations such as reading circles and amateur theater groups that pursued non-religious programs. In addition, the city had a university, which added a certain boost to secular cultural activities. The immigrants had their own supporting associations and these helped them to adjust to city life. Nevertheless, Debrecen remained until well into the war a semi-urban area, whose ties to the surrounding countryside were felt deeply in cultural life. The customs and habits of the peasants, newly become urban dwellers, remained a determining factor, and the village customs described above were certainly part of their existence.

There were twenty-three rural towns in northeastern Hungary, generally referred to as the "storm corner" because of its history of poverty and unrest. This region contained the poorest peasant population in the country, which, before 1914, became a major source of overseas emigration. The emigration ended in 1914. Yet the discontent of the poor did not boil over, not least because large numbers of them were serving in the army. The culture of these northeastern rural towns was based on a strong sense of independence fueled by the Protestant ethic; they were usually anti-Habsburg and self-reliant. In almost every town in the "storm corner," education, both on the elementary and secondary level, was an important means of development. Literacy was relatively high; printing presses and occasionally a publishing firm found ready acceptance.[17] This contributed to the proliferation of posters, advertisements, and political flyers. The local newspapers were eagerly read, and they often published highly inflammatory political articles and disputes.

Similar to other regions of Hungary, the population of the towns of the "storm corner" adopted the dress and behavior patterns of larger cities, and established all sorts of civic associations. Some of these were religious, and therefore, exclusive; others were more general. But there was a great deal of cooperation among these institutions in organizing poetry and story-readings, joint dinners and other public events. These activities continued during the war albeit on a reduced scale.

One other factor in rural society must be mentioned, namely, the surge in the establishment of civic associations. These associations provided a framework for local initiatives, and, although they had to be approved by the government, they were semi-autonomous. During the war the government used some of these societies to contribute to the building of nursery schools and to help the poor.[18]

The people of the countryside maintained a façade of normality in the difficult four years between 1914 and 1918. The war had created less hardship in the rural areas – food was more available, and the transformation of the economy, which began only in the second year of the war, affected the industrial regions more.

The increase in the size of the army, depending heavily upon the rural population, removed large numbers of peasants from their homes, especially the village poor, and this was the real hardship for local communities. In most villages, women, children, and old folks had to assume the burden of work in the fields. At the same time, it became more difficult for wealthy peasants to hire laborers. This, in turn, limited their ability fully to participate in the agricultural boom. However, because of labor shortages, those poor who were left out of the draft could obtain better wages. This certainly improved their living standards. On the whole, since peasant culture consisted of customs that were not gender-dependent, these went on as before, albeit on a reduced scale.

In summary, cultural life in the villages did not change fundamentally during the war, although, from late 1917 on, shortages of manufactured goods and implements did appear. Soldiers who were wounded at the fronts returned home to recover. They helped to lessen the labor shortages. Prisoners of war – mostly Italians and Russians – also contributed labor to the countryside. However, village culture was resilient; centuries of changing fortunes over which they had little control had immunized the peasants, and they were ready to profit from wartime conditions at the expense of the urban citizens.

In the first half of the nineteenth century, most, if not all, public education was in the hands of religious denominations. In 1868, however, a law established compulsory elementary education for all children regardless of gender, and began a process of extending government scrutiny over the schools. In 1869, no state schools existed as yet; 96 percent of all elementary schools were controlled by the religious denominations, and 4 percent were sponsored by municipalities. By 1914, the state controlled 19.55 percent of elementary schools, 8.36 percent were in the hands of municipalities; the Catholic church maintained 30.92 percent; the Greek Catholics and Calvinist churches together 20.99 percent; the Lutherans 7.69 percent; the Greek Orthodox church 8.27 percent; and other religious denominations 2.60 percent; 1.46 percent were in private hands; and associations maintained 0.16 percent of elementary schools. The language of instruction in 79.78 percent of the elementary schools was Hungarian; in 2.65 percent German; in 2.24 percent Slovak; in 13.24 percent Romanian; in 0.35 percent Ukrainian; in 1.60 percent Serbo-Croat; in 0.07 percent Italian; and in 0.06 percent "other" (mostly Hebrew). The state schools employed 26 percent of the teachers, and 25 percent of all school children attended state schools. By 1914, 54 state-sponsored secondary schools existed, while the number of religious high schools numbered 127.[19] However, these numbers did not tell the whole story. In fact, by 1914, almost all schools received state support, and at least partial state supervision. By 1918, most schools were under direct state control or supervision.

The number of students at Hungarian universities rapidly expanded in the first decade of the twentieth century. Parallel with this development, new disciplines were introduced and departments established. At the outbreak of the war, there were over 8,000 university students in Hungary. In the ancient Transylvanian city of Kolozsvár (Klausenburg; today Cluj) a new university was established, and, by 1914, it had 2,500 students. In 1912, two other universities, one in Debrecen and one in Pozsony (Pressburg; today Bratislava) were created.[20]

Budapest acquired – and maintains to this day – overwhelming weight in the urban culture of Hungary. The city was united in 1867; the two halves, spreading on the left (Pest) and right (Buda) banks of the Danube river, acquired the name by which it is known today. In 1892, an imperial decree proclaimed its equivalence with Vienna, designating the city as an imperial/royal seat.[21]

During the last decades of the nineteenth and well into the twentieth century, Budapest grew rapidly. Its population increased by nearly 50 percent, it became the center of manufacturing and trade, and it acquired overwhelming domination in most areas of Hungarian life, except agriculture. During much of the previous century the Buda side was *gemütlich*, the home of spacious houses, rural-style inns and restaurants, restrained manners, and was the center of royal administration. Pest, on the other hand, was more exuberant and vulgar, its theaters and other public amusement places and industries multiplying by the hundreds. A huge city park was constructed on the eastern edge of Pest, which included an amusement park and a permanent circus. Thousands of apartment houses as well as individual villas of the affluent were constructed. By 1910, the city had become a modern metropolis.

Budapest represented many new departures in Hungary's cultural life. It was the center of new and old educational institutions, including universities and colleges; it was not only the seat of the government of the Hungarian half of the Habsburg Empire, but also the hub of such reform efforts as represented by the leading hospitals and medical institutions in the country. Industrial workers were provided health- and accident insurance, and child labor was regulated and restricted. As a consequence of these efforts – that eventually trickled down to the rural towns – general life expectancy increased and the ratio of deaths decreased by nearly 20 percent.[22]

The city comprised several social strata. The highest level consisted of the aristocracy. It was divided into at least two segments, the born aristocrats and the financial aristocracy. Of these two, the first possessed the greater prestige, but not the wealth. Many of them lived in magnificent palaces, although not in a separate district. In some areas their houses predominated, but they did not exclude dwellings of lesser folk. The aristocracy provided most of the higher ranking officers and generals for the Habsburg armies, and they suffered proportionately higher casualties than other segments of the population. (In real numbers, of course, this concerned only a small number of individuals.) The financial aristocracy consisted of a large number of Jewish entrepreneurs. Many of them converted and mingled with and married into the other aristocracy, but this did not lessen the differences between their social prestige. During the war the two segments of the aristocracy maintained their separation from the rest of society, except for some activists, such as the Counts Károlyi, Andrássy and Prime Minister Tisza, who were deeply involved in politics. Of the financial aristocrats, several contributed to liberal causes, among them Baron Hatvanys and Miksa Fenyő.

The city's other social strata included a growing number of industrial workers, craftsmen, and petty merchants who made a living by catering to the workers as well as to the bourgeoisie and the gentry. The government found out soon enough that industrial workers were worth more for the war effort in the factories than in the armed forces. Thus, concerted efforts were made to keep them at home. Their wages, compared to the wages of other workers, increased considerably during the war.

The gentry constituted a typical Hungarian social stratum, consisting of the descendants of impoverished nobles who had lost their land holdings. They obtained jobs in the state and local bureaucracies. They considered themselves the "real Hungarians." Comparable only to the Polish *szlachta*, the Hungarian gentry often dominated public opinion.[23]

The ethnic composition of the city was complex. By 1910 the majority consisted of ethnic Hungarians, and about 20 percent of the population was Jewish; there were also a great many intermarriages, helping in the quick assimilation of Germans, Jews, Slovaks, Serbs, and others.

Among the numerous opportunities for public entertainment, there were about 600 coffeehouses, and a large number of restaurants, inns, and other houses of amusement. In the coffeehouses merchants exchanged business news, intellectuals argued about ideas, and authors wrote poetry and novels. Projectograph had been distributing foreign films in Hungary since 1898, and the first Hungarian film, directed by Mihály Kertész, was made in 1912. However, the modern cinema emerged from a coffeehouse in Budapest.[24]

The other institution of popular amusement was the *kocsma*, a plebeian pub, a combination of drinking parlor and restaurant, serving all sorts of alcoholic beverages. The *kocsma* was strictly male-oriented; its location, of course, determined its clientele. In the suburbs it was a gathering place for workers; in the inner city the clientele was mixed. The owners served food; their major function was similar to that of the coffeehouses, that is, to provide a meeting place for people, mostly workers. The *kocsma* often provided back rooms for union organizers and for the meetings of various political groups, including the Social Democratic Party. It was often the center in which singing groups of workers met and practiced.

Then there was the new entertainment center, the cinema. By 1912, there were 270 cinemas in Hungary, 92 of them located in Budapest, with an aggregate of 26,332 seats.[25] Although many rural towns also established movie houses, the institution had not yet penetrated rural society, especially the villages. During the war years, cinema became the cheapest form of entertainment favored by the workers and the lower bourgeoisie. At first, the films were procured abroad but, increasingly, they were being made in Hungary. Here the new art/entertainment form was based on the best novels and was considered complementary to the theaters. Millions of people attended, and the cinema became the first institution of true mass-entertainment in Hungary.

During the war, the cinema also served propaganda purposes. Its newsreels showed the heroism of front soldiers, although missing from it was the debasement of the enemy. Going to the movies on Sundays became a regular pastime during the war and, especially during wintertime, a more popular entertainment than attending the amusement park. By 1914, there were some exquisite cinemas in Budapest, catering to the *haute bourgeoisie*. The leading film director was Sándor Korda, later Sir Alexander Korda. Mihály Kertész, later Michael Curtiz, director of the famous film, *Casablanca*, was also a well-known director. He had to leave Hungary after 1919, because he made propaganda movies for the post-war communist government of Béla Kun. By 1918, there were forty-five Hungarian film directors, some of them foreigners. An independent studio and famous cinema, the Corvin, named after King Mathias Corvinus, was established.[26]

The sporting scene developed rapidly. Soccer clubs had emerged by the turn of the century and were attracting large crowds, especially from among the workers, but also from the other social strata. Rivalries developed that were to last throughout the century, including the years of the war. Although some star players were called up, most of the others remained in the hinterland, and the championship continued until 1917 without interruption. After 1917, however, the championship competition was shortened, and it ceased altogether during 1918–1919.

Special entertainment was provided by the theaters in Budapest. At the turn of the century, there were six repertory companies and the opera, all with their own buildings. The National Theater produced plays, including the classics, on a very high level; others were dedicated to mass culture, showing comedies, operettas, and even burlesque. In addition, as John Lukács remarked, there were twenty-one houses of prostitution in Budapest in 1906, and this number probably remained constant. Criminality was not widespread, and alcoholism was not a universal problem.[27]

The cultural scene of the Hungarian capital was rounded off by myriad discussion groups, reading associations, poetry-reading circles, as well as choirs and other clubs. A large number of people regularly took advantage of the nearby mountains and forests in Buda and made Sunday excursions into the area.

The outbreak of the war did not immediately affect the city's cultural life. Food remained plentiful, entertainment continued unabated, the theaters and cinemas remained open. Budapest was better supplied with provisions than Vienna; restrictions began to appear only in late 1915, early 1916. As the war progressed, newspapers increasingly assumed the role of entertaining the public. War stories, descriptions of public charity events to benefit the wounded and maimed soldiers or to help war orphans, and stories of ordinary and extraordinary scandals filled their pages. There was little censorship during the first two years of the war, as far as reporting from the front was concerned.[28] The government of Prime Minister István Tisza cared more for keeping the lid on domestic discontent, and especially on agitation for democratic reforms. Yet the deep fissures in political life which had developed before 1914 between the progressive intelligentsia and the conservatives continued unabated.[29]

Intellectual culture in Budapest was shaped by these deep divisions. The dividing lines went back at least to the turn of the century. In 1900, a new journal, *Huszadik Század* (Twentieth Century) signaled a generational and ideological break with Hungary's immediate past. It represented the views of the leading members of the Társadalom-tudományi Társaság (Association for Social Science), most of whom were political liberals. Iván T. Berend, comparing the liberal writers' journal, *Nyugat*, with *Huszadik Század*, has remarked:

Similarly to *Nyugat* in literature . . . *Huszadik Század* struggled for a special place for sociology in the intellectual and political life of the age. The first [journal] meant more than literature, and the latter more than pure science. Together, they expressed complete opposition to traditional Hungary, and they demonstrated the need for complete change not only in the existing political and economic structures, but also in the structures of culture, morals, life-style, and the arts.[30]

Most members of the Association for Social Science wanted to understand the workings of society, and to use the "science of sociology" to change it. All changes had to come through knowledge, otherwise they would be harmful. Some of them, such as Ervin Szabó, a librarian, and Gyula Pikler, a professor at Pázmány Péter University, were Marxists. Others professed different ideologies, but they were all left of center in their political convictions. They recognized the necessity to change the uneven distribution of land; they wanted to eliminate the domination of political life by an alliance of the gentry and the aristocracy; they sought to end corruption in public life. Above all, they wanted to transform Hungary to resemble post-revolutionary France, where – as they believed – notions of liberty, equality, and social harmony prevailed.[31] The outbreak of war contributed to their disillusionment.

The time has come, however, to place the "radicals" in Hungarian history, those who "manned the barricades" at the Association for Social Science and were major contributors to the *Nyugat*, in a broader perspective, because in the past eight decades their roles have been seriously distorted. First, the post-war regime of Nicholas Horthy needed scapegoats for the terrible fate that had befallen Hungary through the Treaty of Trianon. This regime was able to misdirect the anger of the people against the "radical Jews and their allies" who "stabbed Hungary in the back." The possibility was not explored that, if the reforms advocated by the radicals had been enacted, there would have been no need for revolution. On the other hand, after 1947, the radicals were proclaimed to have been true internationalists, the "flag bearers of the workers' cause," the heroes of the pre-Bolshevik revolutionary era, and therefore the forerunners of the Hungarian Communist Party. The fact was, however, that the radicals represented many varieties of liberal thought. The Marxists were, of course, for revolution, although Leninist totalitarianism was, with a few exceptions, not really to their liking.[32] The non-Marxists did not want revolution, but a fundamental reform of society, in order to make it a more humane, more flexible organism. They wanted to provide equal opportunity for all, to reduce the political influence of a sinfully wealthy Catholic Church, and to introduce free and universal suffrage for all, including women. They were aware of the risk of granting the suffrage to the nationalities, but they hoped that an agreement with them would preserve Hungary's territorial integrity.[33]

It seems, however, that most citizens of Budapest in 1914 were more interested in enriching themselves, or at least providing a decent living for their families, and having their children educated to their highest potential. They wanted entertainment of various kinds. Relatively few people attended the meetings of the Association for Social Science, or wrote articles for *Nyugat*, and other radical journals. The "radicals" of the early twentieth century in Hungary represented a generation whose fate was very similar to that of the populists of the 1930s. Both of these groups observed the ills that beset Hungarian society and proposed remedies that were either ignored by the masses of citizens or were brushed aside by those in power.[34] The "radicals' " failure was already evident when, in 1913, they sought an alliance with the Social Democratic Party, whose call for a general strike for universal suffrage failed. When they established a Radical Party in 1914, they were mostly unsuccessful in recruiting membership.[35]

There were, indeed, some towering figures among the "radicals." These included, among others, the poet, Endre Ady, the great musicians, Béla Bartók and Zoltán Kodály, the writers Dezső Kosztolányi, Pál Szende, and Gyula Krudy, the painters Moholy Nagy and Károly Kernstok, and, not least, the journalist Ignotus, Oszkár Jászi, and the budding anti-Semite, Dezső Szabó. However, their true impact was delayed until after the war. In fact, the dominant culture of Budapest was bourgeois.

This urban culture included disparate elements, some deeply conservative,[36] some truly liberal,[37] and some politically neutral. When speaking of bourgeois culture in Budapest, we are dealing with a many-sided phenomenon, which was in some ways very cosmopolitan, but certain features of which remained linked to rural culture. Nowhere was this more evident than in the musical life of the city.

Even in the second half of the twentieth century the prevailing popular misconception in the West is that Hungarian music equals Gypsy music. But nothing could be further from the truth. Up to the mid-nineteenth century, Hungarian music was based on martial music used for the recruitment of soldiers for the Habsburg armies, before general conscription was introduced. Variations on this music were raised to a very high level by outstanding Gypsy violinists, such as János Bihari, the world famous *primás* (first violinist). Other gifted Gypsy musicians invented countless variations while entertaining rural or urban audiences. Gypsy musicians performed at weddings, at country and urban fairs, rural inns and *kocsmas* of the towns and cities. They produced exotic music, with sentimental lyrics, and easily remembered songs. Their violins and *cimbalom* (dulcimer) were supported by the deep sounds of the viola. Nobody cared much about the mostly inanely sentimental lyrics of the songs. But this was not Hungarian music. It was artificial, and it did not reflect the attitudes of the usually taciturn rural folk who kept their feelings close to their chest. Gypsy music catered to the romanticism of the rural and urban gentry.

Serious classical music had long traditions in Budapest. The greatest Hungarian musical genius was Franz Liszt. In 1875, he became the first president-director of the Hungarian Academy of Music in Budapest, and his symphonies and other compositions were the celebrated occasions of musical life in the capital city. Ferenc Erkel was the first composer who embarked on the development of a true Hungarian operatic language. He also composed the music for the Hungarian national anthem. But the emergence of truly popular music in Hungary owed its development to others.

Gypsy musicians continued to entertain millions of the common people during the war, but change was on its way. It had already begun at the turn of the century when two young musicians, Béla Bartók and Zoltán Kodály, embarked on a journey of discovery. They started collecting tunes in the villages which, as they were able to determine it, were original Magyar folk songs. They discovered over 10,000 such songs whose tunes and words derived from ancient times. These songs were based on pentatonic melodies – akin to Chinese musical structure – and they were beautiful in their simplicity. They expressed the joys and sorrows of the simple Hungarian people.

The two musicians used these melodies to elevate folk music to a very high level, and to integrate it into serious music. Kodály organized children's choirs and he also composed phenomenally successful musicals such as *Hári János* (the stories of a typical soldier, hilariously unreal, comparable to those of the Baron Münchausen), and the magnificent religious compositions, *Psalmus Hungaricus* and the *Te Deum of Budavár*.[38]

Bartók was the more original thinker of the two, an ingenious innovator. He was also very successful in depicting the often elementary passions of the people by using the ancient tunes and rhythms discovered in the old folk songs. He created folk-ballets such as the *Csodálatos Mandarin* (The Magical Mandarin) and *Fából faragott királyfi* (The King's Son who Was Carved from Wood), several compositions for quartets and the opera, *A Kékszakállú Herceg Vára* (The Castle of Prince Blue-Beard). The latter was first performed in the Budapest Opera house in 1917. Bartók realized that by doing away with traditional tonality and using often clashing atonal combinations, he could achieve surprising results.[39] Yet, neither Kodály, nor Bartók, were able to achieve the immediate success in Hungary that they so truly deserved. Bartók was especially misunderstood, and his atonal compositions were derided by the conservatives as senseless cacophony.

By 1910, the progressive members of the *new* generation were in full revolt against traditional culture. Artists, actors, writers and other intellectuals were all affected by this process.[40]

In 1919 Moholy Nagy noted in his diary that he realized during the war that he had responsibilities to society and, as a painter, he was indeed capable of "serving the meaning of life."[41] Yet it is a common mistake to identify the revolt of the artists and intellectuals with the proletarian movements in Hungary. They had mutual sympathies, but most of the artists recoiled from the often primitive and destructive nature of the workers' movements, especially of those on the far left.[42]

There was no sharp division separating mass culture and intellectual culture in Budapest. The educated elite attended the theater, the opera, art exhibitions, and concerts; they read the new literature produced by young writers and journalists; but so did the less educated and less affluent. They visited the musicals (operettas), the folk-plays (*népszínmű*), the cabarets and the orpheum (burlesque). Intellectuals as well as the common folks could be found in the circus or the zoo on Sundays, and reading cheap paperback novels. The masses in Budapest were now literate; they read the daily newspapers, and especially the lavishly illustrated magazines, and attended the cinema. The scientific worldview, based on the Copernican–Newtonian heliocentric universe and Darwinian notions of evolution, became part of mass consciousness. Religion was also changing; open atheism emerged, and skepticism spread not only to the elite, but also to the masses. The transformation was equally evident in literature. The writers – and their reading public – moved toward rationalism, the realistic portrayal of the individual in an increasingly impersonal society, and the conflicts between individual morals and social ethics. The nationalistic tone of story-telling characterized by Géza Gárdonyi and Mór Jókai, the revered poetry of János Arany and Sándor Petőfi, gradually gave way to the psychological novel whose heroes struggled with their fate. Zsigmond Móricz and Kálmán Mikszáth, Dezső Kosztolányi, Gyula Krúdi, to mention only a few of the new writers, strengthened this tendency during the war; the bloody reality of the conflict was faithfully reflected in poetry and other writings.[43]

Many representatives of the new intellectual currents came from rural towns. The journal *Budapesti Napló*, published by József Vészi and Ede Kabos, originally provided space for Endre Ady, as well as for Lajos Bíró, Dezső Kosztolányi, and Menyhért Lengyel. (Bíró and Lengyel became screenwriters for Hollywood films in the 1930s.) Professor László Négyesi's seminar on literature attracted a heterogenous crowd of students, some of whom were interested in the new culture.

Endre Ady, the outstanding Hungarian poet of the early twentieth century, was a provincial journalist in the city of Kolozsvár where he attracted the attention and condemnation of conservative critics. He found an outlet for his angry poetry at the *Budapesti Napló*, and soon became a target of the critics of the capital city. In 1904 and again in 1906–1907, Ady spent time in Paris, where he absorbed the atmosphere of anti-clerical French liberalism. He also became acquainted with modern French literature.[44] He was a true path-breaking, pioneering poet whose verses provided a devastating criticism of Hungarian realities. He believed that Hungarian society was hopelessly corrupt and it was ready for revolution. Yet, he did not reject all traditions; he cherished those that showed the vitality of the simple Hungarian folk, especially those who rebelled against Habsburg rule. However, in contrast to contemporary liberalism, Ady was skeptical of the possibility that society might peacefully be transformed.

After the outbreak of the war, Ady's radicalism assumed a new intensity. However, as the war progressed and he became more and more convinced that it was lost, he slid into nihilism. He lost all hope for the eventual transformation of Hungary into a progressive society. Ady saw the war as an unprecedented cataclysm, one that would produce the most barbaric conditions ever seen by mankind. In 1916, he wrote: "The future is so uncertain that I would advise those who wish to see it, to return to the past, as if I were a reactionary."[45]

When scanning the literature of World War I, especially the journals of the "radicals," such as *Nyugat*, one is struck by three facts. One is the moderate tone that permeates reports dealing with the war. The other is the virtual absence of censorship in the first two years. (It is likely that self-censorship played a role in this.) Only in the third year is there evidence of government intervention.[46] The third is that alongside the critical articles about the Entente, especially the Russians, there is little of the vituperative hatred that spewed forth from most of the yellow press – and even from respectable mass publications – in Germany and in the Entente countries, especially France. Even when speaking about Russia, the tone was surprisingly moderate.[47]

On the other hand, there were critical articles expressing disappointment with French progressives such as Anatole France and the Irish George Bernard Shaw who willingly lent their pens to war propaganda.[48] Zoltán Ambrus also condemned Hungarian journalists who glorified war, charging that they did not know what they were writing about.[49]

Others described the horrors and terrors that soldiers felt under fire.[50] There were articles about the crisis in Germany following the fruitless battles in the West,[51] and about the changing public mood in the Habsburg Empire, creating despair after military disasters, affecting the mind of soldiers at the front.[52] Throughout 1914 and 1915, one journal published letters by the "English correspondent Harry Russel-Dorsan," whose "eye-witness" reports purported to provide an objective view of the war "from the other side." However, in 1918, after the publication of these "letters" in book form, it was admitted that the author of the correspondence was none other than Dezső Szomory, a well-known Hungarian writer.[53]

In the last two years of the war, more and more space was devoted to internal Hungarian affairs.[54] This may have been a last-ditch effort of the radicals to direct the public's attention to issues at home. There were also discussions of the relations between the Habsburg Empire and the United States, as well as articles about the first opera of Béla Bartók, and an evening of Kodály's music. A theater critic gladly noted that, in the third year of the war, the playwrights finally gathered enough courage to abandon themes based on the war, and devote time to other topics. This certainly signaled disgust with the war.

There were signs that people were tired of the war. The publication of a new volume of Endre Ady's poems, mentioned above, showed this clearly. A reviewer noted that this volume "showed that the poet, once known for his vitality and engagement in the life of the nation," was now standing on the sidelines as a neutral observer, becoming uninterested in events.[55]

In 1918, when the war was over, the historian of literature, Aladár Schöpflin, provided an impressive analysis of the causes of the defeat, citing first and foremost the irresponsibility of the intellectuals and the gentry. He also stated – as it turned out mistakenly – that the revolution (of November 1918) could not be reversed. He asserted that the program for rebuilding Hungary was ready. It was provided by the radicals of the pre-war era, and the intellectuals were willing to implement it.[56] Ignotus wrote about the "new Hungary," asserting that it was ready to take its place in the world among the progressive nations. All this was, of course, whistling in the dark. The country was yet to face a short-lived but destructive communist revolution, and its dismemberment had already been decided by the victors.

When looking at culture in Hungary, it seems clear that the war did not so much produce a break with the immediate past as intensify pre-existing elements of change that had originated in the pre-war years, while at the same time creating new obstacles to the fulfillment of socio-cultural and political reform efforts. The great cultural upheaval occurred before 1914, and the generation which believed that Hungary could be turned into a democratic society had laid the foundations for its program – in vain as it turned out – by the outbreak of hostilities. The vibrant, lively debates of the first one-and-a-half decades of the twentieth century were not repeated after 1918. The nation's defeat and its consequences cast a pall on Hungary which it did not succeed in dispelling until well past the middle of the century.

8   Culture in the South Slavic lands, 1914–1918

Andrew Wachtel

When World War I began, the lands that would in 1918 be united as the Kingdom of the Serbs, Croats, and Slovenes (officially renamed Yugoslavia in 1929) were part of three separate states. The Kingdom of Serbia controlled primarily Serb-inhabited lands south of the Sava and Danube rivers, as well as Kosovo and the bulk of Macedonia (the latter two, with their mixed Serbian, Macedonian, Albanian, and Muslim Slav populations, had been taken from the Ottomans in 1912 during the First Balkan War). The Kingdom of Montenegro held sway over traditional Montenegran territory, as well as areas with a primarily Serbian and Muslim populace that it had acquired as spoils of the same war. Finally, Serb-inhabited territory north of the Danube, Bosnia and Herzegovina, as well as all the Croat and Slovenian lands, were under the rule of the Austro-Hungarian Empire, with some areas ruled directly from Budapest, some from Vienna, and Bosnia under joint administration.

The proximate cause of World War I, the assassination of Archduke Franz Ferdinand, took place, of course, in Sarajevo, on Bosnian territory. And the first battles were fought between Austrian and Serb units in July and August 1914. The South Slav lands remained a battlefield throughout the war. Major campaigns included the initial Austrian offensive against Serbia, the combined Austrian, German, and Bulgarian attack on Serbia in 1915 which led to the total defeat of the Serbian army and its epic winter march through Serbian and Albanian territory to the safety of the island of Corfu, the battles on the Soča front near the Italian/Slovenian border (these remain to this day the largest-scale mountain campaigns in the history of warfare), and the breakthrough on the Salonika front in 1918 which led to the final collapse of the Austro-Hungarian army.

As one can imagine from this list, dislocation in the South Slav lands was intense, and the effect it had on cultural life was staggering. The Serbian government evacuated from Belgrade to Niš (some 200 miles to the south) at the beginning of the war, and remained there until the

193

retreat of 1915, when it was forced to relocate to Corfu. The Serbian capital, Belgrade, was occupied from 1915 until almost the last days of the war, and the Serbs were treated as an occupied and humiliated enemy to whom no avenues of cultural expression were allowed. Under these conditions, organized cultural or public activity inside Serbia, either of high or popular variety, could not flourish.[1] Most of the leading Serbian cultural figures found themselves either in the army or abroad, and in so far as Serbian cultural activity continued, it did so in London, Paris, Geneva, Nice, and other centers of Serbian emigration. Serbian citizens of the Habsburgs were treated no better. Arrests of Serbian political and cultural figures marked the first weeks of the war, and officially approved pogroms were common, especially in ethnically mixed Bosnia. Serbian cultural organs disappeared completely: in the primarily Serb Vojvodina region, for example, all thirty-one pre-war Serbian-language newspapers and journals were suppressed as soon as the war began, including *Ljetopis Matice Srbije* (The Journal of the Serbian Cultural Society), the oldest and most prestigious Serbian cultural organ.

The Croats and Slovenes of the Habsburg lands were not exactly treated as enemies, as indeed they should not have been considering the large numbers of loyal troops they provided for the Austro-Hungarian army. Nevertheless, cultural activity in the Croatian capital Zagreb (which was ruled by authorities appointed in Budapest) and, particularly, in the Slovenian capital Ljubljana (called Laibach and ruled directly by the Austrians) was subject to suspicion and censorship. In both Slovenia and Croatia, a portion of the cultural leadership had traditionally been provided by conservative clericals. These men were generally loyal to the Catholic Habsburgs, and they provided a core of loyalist cultural support for the empire's policies. In the immediate pre-war years, clerical cultural leadership had been increasingly challenged by liberal parties more partial to some form of Yugoslavism, generally one that envisioned not an independent Yugoslavia but rather the reconstitution of the empire as a triune kingdom, with an autonomous Slavic entity added to the existing Austro-Hungarian units. Members of these groups were regarded with great suspicion when war broke out, and were treated with varying degrees of severity. At a minimum, they were not allowed to express pro-Yugoslav views, which were seen as tantamount to abetting Serbia. By 1917, however, the Austrians and Hungarians began to recognize that they could not win the war without redoubled support from the Slavs in the empire. One result of this recognition was that Yugoslav cultural and even political sentiment began to be seen as acceptable (providing it was, at least implicitly, kept within the bounds of triune sympathies), and by 1918 even Croatian and Slovenian conservative elements had embraced some form of Yugoslavism.

Despite the obstacles of war, conscription, and censorship, however, a surprisingly rich cultural life continued in the South Slavic lands, particularly in Croatia and Slovenia. The war years saw the first major publications of both Ivo Andrić and Miroslav Krleža, the greatest Serbian and Croatian writers of the twentieth century respectively, and, even more important, these years saw the crystallization of a vision of Yugoslav culture that would dominate the cultural policy of the first post-war Yugoslav state. According to this vision, Yugoslav culture was to be a supranational synthesis of the best elements of each of the separate national cultures.

Cultural life in Croatia

Perhaps because of its position as a ward of Budapest rather than Vienna, Croatia experienced the least disruption of cultural life during the war years. Institutions like the Croatian National Theater continued to perform nightly, major literary journals published uninterruptedly, new journals and newspapers, many of a decidedly Yugoslav character, were founded (especially after 1916), the first locally produced movies on South Slavic territory were made and screened, and a lively popular press produced illustrated magazines primarily devoted to war news, but also including serialized fiction and cultural news. A closer examination of these outlets should give a better idea of day-to-day cultural life in wartime Zagreb.

Theatrical life

During the 1915–1916 season the Croatian National Theater presented 159 dramatic, 105 operatic, and 65 operetta performances. Naturally, under wartime conditions the theater had to walk a fine line between presentations of an overtly patriotic (i.e., pro-Habsburg) nature and more neutral or even potentially oppositional shows. This was particularly true because, while its audience was primarily Croatian, the theater could operate only because it continued to receive substantial official subsidies.[2] For the most part, the National Theater avoided controversy, presenting politically neutral dramatic works that lacked any connection to the war, by Croatian authors, such as Milan Begović's *Laka služba* (An Easy Post), Milutin Nehajev's *Spasitelj* (Savior), Fran Galović's *Před smrti* (Before Death), and Marija Zagorka's *Grička vještica* (Grichka the Witch). Major works by foreign authors included productions of Ibsen's *Hedda Gabler* designed by the leading Croatian painter of this period, Tomislav Krizman, as well as Chekhov's *Cherry Orchard.*

The opera scene, also, was for the most part politically unproblematic during the war, with the bulk of the repertory devoted to light and comic works: staples included Johann Strauss's *Die Fledermaus*, Imre Kálmán's *Princess of the Czardas*, Georges Bizet's *Carmen*, and Otto Nicolai's *Merry Wives of Windsor*. More serious opera could be heard as well: Bedřich Smetana's *Bartered Bride*, Jules Massenet's *Werther*, the major operas of Giacomo Puccini, and Richard Strauss's *Salome.*[3] Notable new productions of the period were Wagner's *Tristan and Isolde* (with sets and costumes by Krizman), Tchaikovsky's *Queen of Spades*, and Mozart's *Marriage of Figaro*, all of which debuted in 1917. At the same time, particularly at the beginning of the war, the opera theater presented some overtly pro-Habsburg works, most obviously an opera by the little-known Croatian composer and dramatist, Djuro Prejac, entitled *Za Kralja i dom* (For the King and the Fatherland). This dubious masterpiece appeared in the repertoire on 3 October 1914 and received 23 performances through the end of the 1916–1917 season when it was mercifully retired.

Simultaneously, the theater was involved in a number of enterprises that were interpreted as anti-Habsburg. While none of these involved overt allusions to the contemporary situation, most could be understood as in some way opposing the regime's military policies or promoting South Slavic unity. Perhaps the most notorious instance of oppositional theater was Josip Bach's staging of Aristophanes' *Lysistrata*, which debuted at the National Theater on 7 February 1915, an official day of prayer for military victory, as it happened.[4] This "coincidence," as well as the subject matter of the play itself, immediately drew the attention of the clerical newspaper *Novine* (News) which, on 25 March published a vitriolic attack against the production on the grounds of immorality. Even earlier, on 18 March the paper had sponsored a delegation to the Croatian Ban (governor) asking him to forbid further performances and complaining that "the National Theater has been propagating immorality for a long time. It has become a breeding ground for all sorts of unrefinedness, including anti-religious tendencies, and following in its lead are all the cinemas and much of the press."[5] According to the mostly liberal journal *Savremenik* (The Contemporary) this complaint was merely a cultural power grab on the part of the clericals. Their dislike of Aristophanes' play, it was asserted, was not prompted by its anti-religious character so much as its pacifist orientation.[6]

A certain degree of Yugoslav nationalism appeared in the opera theater by 1917, as well, with the premiere of Petar Konjović's *Vilin veo* (The Vila's Veil), a romantic opera in three acts to a libretto by D. Ilić. This opera was a typical example of what might be called synthetic Yugoslavism, in which Serbian thematics – in this case the folk poem in which the *vila* (witch) Ravijojla kills the hero, Miloš Obilić, and is forced to bring him back to life by Prince Marko – are presented using all the techniques of modern European culture – in this case an aria-less "Wagnerian" opera in which Yugoslav folk melodies were woven into the fabric of music and singing.[7]

Provincial theaters in Croatia also operated during the war, and their repertoires appear to have been even less adventuresome than that of the National Theater in Zagreb. The Croatian People's Theater in Osijek performed more or less normally, presenting a large selection of uncontroversial classics and a few new works. The Municipal Theater in Varaždin was actually founded during the war, opening on 11 December 1915 with Imre Kálmán's operetta *Der Gute Kamerad*. The first dramatic performance there took place on 16 December 1915 with a play by the then unknown Nikola Kos, *Seljaci u gradu* (Peasants in the City).

Visual art

In the period just before the war, one visual artist towered over all others in Croatia: the sculptor Ivan Meštrović. The son of a Croatian shepherd, Meštrović displayed artistic talent early, and by dint of hard work and some good luck, made it to Vienna, where he studied sculpture and mingled with the artists of the Secession School. Meštrović burst onto the Yugoslav national scene with his controversial exhibition at the Rome Exposition of 1911. Although he had been expected to exhibit his work at the pavilion of the Hapsburg Empire, he refused to do so unless a separate pavilion was provided for South Slavic artists. When this was denied, he and his compatriots offered to exhibit at the Serbian pavillion.[8] The mere fact of an already-well-respected Viennese-trained artist turning his back on Central European culture to throw in his lot with the Serbian "barbarians" was sensational enough. But the work he exhibited in Rome, his so-called Kosovo or St. Vitus Day temple (it was on St. Vitus Day in 1389 that the fateful Battle of Kosovo was fought), was even more sensational. From the outside, the temple had a monumental, classical feel, although it was embellished by such typical secessionist touches as caryatids and sphinxes. In form, it combined Catholic and Orthodox elements (it was built on the pattern of a Roman Catholic cross, but the dome looked like that of a Byzantine rather than a Catholic church). On the inside were displayed Meštrović's figures inspired by the heroes of the South Slavic oral poems: Marko Kraljević, Miloš Obilić, the Mother of the Jugovići, a guslar. These sculptures, even today, have a monumental presence, and, in the case of the male figures, a pent-up strength that seems ready to move from sculpture directly into life. For many of Meštrović's contemporaries, for whom these figures symbolized the entire spirit of the Yugoslav awakening, the works seemed nothing short of miraculous.

Meštrović left Croatia just before the war began, and spent the war years in exile in Italy and England. He was perhaps the most visible and certainly the most famous of the members of the "Jugoslav Committee," a group of exiled Habsburg South Slavs who did as much as anyone to secure Allied backing for a post-war Yugoslav state. In 1915, Meštrović was given a solo show at London's Victoria and Albert Museum, the first living artist to be so honored. His work, not surprisingly, was interpreted as much politically as it was artistically. The following wartime description was typical:

Meštrović's temple has deep national significance. In this sense it towers above all previously existing artistic monuments from ancient times until today. What the pyramids were for the Egyptians, the pagodas for the Indians, the Parthenon for the Greeks, the Coliseum for the Romans; what the Gothic cathedrals were for the Middle Ages, the luxurious palaces for the Renaissance, what the National Gallery is for today's Englishmen and the Louvre is for the French, that is what Meštrović's temple is for the Southern Slavs. But it must be pointed out: not a single one of the monuments mentioned above is in as close touch with the national soul as the Temple is with our soul, the Yugoslav soul.[9]

Literary life

Literary life in Croatia appears to have gone on more or less oblivious to the surrounding war. Of course, a number of important Croatian authors served in the army, including most notably Miroslav Krleža. Some others even gave their lives at the front, including the talented poet and dramatist Fran Galović and the promising young prose writer Branko Knežović.

Savremenik (The Contemporary) was the leading pre-war Croatian literary journal. Published by the Association of Croatian Writers, this monthly continued to come out regularly throughout the war, paying as little attention to the war as possible. The only concession to wartime conditions was the frequent publication of double issues, with, for example, only six issues covering the twelve numbers in 1915. Even before the war, the editors of this journal were known for their liberal, unitarist views, but, because of censorship, these were rarely expressed overtly. When attempts were made to publish works that could be considered anti-Hapsburg or anti-war, the offending issues were censored. Thus, in August 1914, *Savremenik* tried to publish a play by Srdjan Tučić entitled *Osloboditelji* (The Liberators), devoted to the Serbs in the Balkan wars. Although it was set in type, the play was not allowed to appear, and was published only in 1918 as the empire collapsed. And in 1915, when the journal tried to publish *Ratni Adagio* (Wartime Adagio) by Knežović, they were again refused permission.[10] As a result, the journal stuck primarily to literary work of extremely high quality on non-military and non-national themes. Thus, for example, 1915 issues included poems by such major authors as Vladimir Nazor, Ljubo Wiesner, Dragutin Domjanić, Tugomir Alaupović, Krleža, Miloš Crnjanski; and stories by Viktor Car-Emin.

Also published throughout the war in Zagreb was the journal *Hrvatska prosvjeta* (Croatian Enlightenment). Although it was announced as a monthly, it generally published in double or even triple issues. As opposed to the liberal *Contemporary, Croatian Enlightenment* was sponsored by clerical interests and numbered more than a few priests among its contributors. Not surprisingly, the journal was pro-Hapsburg. Although it lacked any important writers, the journal published work by Croatian authors from many provincial cities as well as from Zagreb, including Ema Božičević (Split), Rudolfo Franjin Madjer (Osijek), Sane Kurjaković (Karlovac), Iv. Ev. Šarić (Sarajevo) – all of whom had work published in the final issue of 1914, for example. Overall, the literary work was more oriented toward war themes than was the case with the major liberal journals in Ljubljana or Zagreb. One can find many poems like "Hrvatskim junacima" (To the Croatian Heroes) by one Jovan Hranilović, which begins: "Hail to you, Croatian heroes / who do honor to our race / Hail to you, grey falcons / Our youth, our hope."[11]

By 1917, censorship in Croatia appears to have become far less aggressive. Among other important work to see the light in that year was Krleža's bleak anti-war story "Hrvatska rapsodija" (Croatian Rhapsody).[12] Cultural life in general appears to have become much freer by 1917, and some major events of an overtly Yugoslav character took place. Among the most important were the celebration of the fiftieth anniversary of Bishop Josip Strossmayer's Yugoslav Academy of Sciences, in July, and the sixtieth birthday of the pro- Yugoslav writer Ivo Vojnović, which was marked on 9 October in the National Theater with a performance of his *Ekvinocij* (The Equinox). The latter event was dubbed an unofficial national holiday, and tributes to Vojnović appeared in all the newspapers and journals. The extent to which Yugoslav-oriented topics had become permissible by this time can be seen in *The Contemporary*'s *feuilleton* on the occasion:

Vojnović's success is our national success, particularly because he is equally Croat and Serb. There is no Croat who is more Serbian than Vojnović and no Serb who is more Croatian. He is the expression of the entire people, the artistic incarnation of the folk epic combined with antique culture (like Mažuranić), a European and a guslar, an orator and – recently – the comrade of all who endure, struggle and remain quiet.[13]

The war years also saw the appearance of several important new journals. One that had nothing to do either with the war or the awakening Yugoslav consciousness was *Ženski svijet* (Woman's World), one of the first publications devoted specifically to women's issues anywhere in the South Slavic lands.[14] It began publication in September 1917, edited and published by a Slovenian woman writer living in Zagreb, Zofka Kveder-Demetrović. More important pro-Yugoslav cultural journals were *Hrvatska njiva* (Croatian Field), which began publication in December 1917, and, the most influential of all, *Književni jug* (The Literary South), which first appeared on 1 January 1918. This latter journal was edited by Niko Bartulović, Vladimir Ćorović, Ivo Andrić, and Branko Mašić. The art editor was Tomislav Krizman. In his first editorial, Bartulović laid out the journal's gradualist, synthetic Yugoslav philosophy:

We see hundreds of practical tasks: the question of a united literature, as well as a single language with a single alphabet and orthography ... If we get to know each other better, popularize Slovenian writers among Croats and Serbs and vice versa, if we encourage our public really to see our literature as a unity – that would be a great thing. By this route a still-greater assimilation and purification of our language will occur all by itself, as will our pride in a single great literature that includes Njegoš together with Prešeren, Župančič with Kranjčević.[15]

In subsequent issues the journal proved true to its word, publishing Serbo-Croatian works in both the Cyrillic and Latin alphabets, as well as untranslated pieces in Slovenian. All of the best authors of the day contributed to this flagship of gradualist Yugoslav cultural orientation.

Although by 1917 the Austro-Hungarian authorities were willing to allow strong statements of Yugoslav sentiment as long as they were couched in at least implicitly triune terms, even as late as 1918 there were some expressions of Yugoslav patriotism they were not prepared to countenance. In February 1918, *Croatian Enlightenment* announced plans to celebrate the 100th anniversary of the birth of the "Illyrian" poet Petar Preradović.[16] The commemoration was to be very public, including songs, flower laying, and speeches. But, when the day arrived, most of the public tributes, as well as a performance of Preradović's play *Prince Marko*, were banned. Despite the ban it appears that the citizens of Zagreb celebrated in their own way. Stores in the city were closed and many roofs displayed Yugoslav banners. People flocked to the poet's grave to leave flowers. People placed Serbian, Croatian, and Slovenian ribbons at the feet of the poet's monument (the ribbons were quickly removed by the police) and sang Yugoslav patriotic songs.[17]

In addition to journals, book publication continued apace in Croatia during the war. As was the case with journal publications, books about the war tended to be pro-Habsburg, such as R. F. Madjer's *Crveni križ i drugi zapisci sa sela uoči rata* (The Red Cross and Other Notes from the Countryside just before the War, Osijek, 1915), and Pero Dupor's *Sa južnog i sjevernog ratišta* (From the Southern and Northern Battlefields, Zagreb, 1915). But the vast majority of books had nothing to do with the current war, including major new translations of *Don Quixote* (1915), *A Christmas Carol*, and Zola's *La Débâcle* (the latter two in 1916).

Among Croatian authors, the most prolific was Vladimir Nazor, who published collections of lyric verse and short stories during the war, as well as his romantic epic *The Gold-Winged Duck*. Nazor's career, however, had begun well before the war. Undoubtedly the major writer to debut in these years was Miroslav Krleža who published extensively during the war, including his first book of lyric verse *Pan*, and his *Tri simfonije* (Three Symphonies).[18] The young author also wrote a number of dramas during this period, including *Cristoval Colon* (Christopher Columbus). By the end of the war, Krleža had established himself as the leading figure of twentieth-century Croatian literature, a position he was never to relinquish.[19] His most striking work published during the war, however, and the only piece that made direct reference to it, was "Croatian Rhapsody."[20] Krleža's reference to a musical rather than a literary genre in his title is not accidental, for the "Rhapsody" is a highly experimental, generically heterogeneous work which reads now like a prose poem, now like a drama, now like a film script. The ambitious and complicated style is motivated by the young author's desire to depict in some thirty pages the nightmare of the war in all its aspects, concentrating primarily on the chaos of the rear, rather than the terror of the front. In Dostoevskian fashion (and Krleža undoubtedly learned a great deal from the Russian master), he focusses on a closed universe, the inside of a railroad car hurtling through the Croatian countryside. The car is populated by a motley collection of mutilated, dying, and hopeless people, who fight, wallow in blood and filth, and argue about Croatia's destiny. This whole nightmarish kaleidescope is constantly filtered by an overarching narrative consciousness, whose commentary evokes the full horror of the war years. The "Rhapsody" ends with a vision borrowed not from Dostoevsky but from Gogol; the railcar goes hurtling metaphorically through the air, carrying its denizens to an unknown and ambiguous destiny, a kind of chthonic inversion of the ending of *Dead Souls*.

Popular culture

Of course, the high culture of the National Theater and the leading literary journals was not the fare consumed by the majority of the Croatian bourgeois population. They, it appears, favored the cinema. Despite the fact that films made in Britain, France, the United States, and Russia were banned, at least four cinemas were active in Zagreb for most of the war (by 1918 six were in operation).[21] The largest of these, the Metropol, boasted a capacity of more than 1,000.[22] A ticket cost from one to three crowns.[23] Based on their advertisements in the daily newspapers, Zagreb cinemas appear to have changed their offerings every three or four days, an indication of both the huge filmmaking capacity of the Central Powers and neutral countries during wartime and a healthy appetite for cinema on the part of Croatians.

Advertisements sampled at random from *Jutarnji list* (The Morning Paper) for January 1917 give an indication of the kind of fare that was proffered here. Early in the month the major hit was a documentary showing the coronation of King Carol and Queen Zita of Romania. It played at four theaters in Zagreb simultaneously. In late January, however, one could have sampled *Othello* at the Apollo Theater and *Judgement Day, or the End of the World* at the Metropol. The latter was advertised as "a sensational drama in five acts, with a scene of a *colossal* never-before-seen effect: an earthquake and a falling meteor."

The war years also saw the first feature films made on Croatian territory.[24] Although none of these survive *in toto*, much information is available about the first, a comedy entitled *Brcko u Zagrebu* (Brcko in Zagreb), which was shown in Zagreb in the fall of 1917.[25] The story was simple and pure entertainment. A salesman from the province of Brcko (Arnošt Grund; he was also the film's director) comes to Zagreb on business. There he meets a diva from the operetta (Irma Polak). Brcko has a good time squiring her about, visiting various places, taking her to the public swimming pool on the Sava, buying her a new outfit. But someone writes to Brcko's wife about all that is happening to him in Zagreb. While Brcko and the diva sit in a café on Zagreb's main square, Brcko's wife arrives and makes a scene. The diva runs away, and the wife grabs a soda water siphon from the table and sprays Brcko in the face. The end![26] The shooting of the film appears to have been far more complicated than the plot. According to the recollections of one participant, "there were various adventures in filming the movie, including the fact that when they were filming a scene in a carriage they could not stop all the little boys in Zagreb from tagging along to see this 'unusual sensation.'"[27]

A more ambitious film was the drama *Matija Gubec*, based on August Šenoa's 1877 novel *The Peasant Uprising*. Gubec's sixteenth-century struggle for fairer treatment for the oppressed peasantry of Croatia and Slovenia had nothing to do with South Slavic independence, but in its nineteenth-century treatment by Šenoa it acquired such overtones. The Hungarian authorities in Zagreb did not interfere with its screening, however, and the premiere, which took place on December 10, 1917, "called forth a storm of approbation and awed amazement."[28] Interestingly enough, and an illustration of the heavier cultural censorship in Slovenia under the Austrian authorities, this film was banned when Ljubljana's Kino Central tried to show it in January 1918.[29]

The cultural scene in Slovenia

While the Hungarian authorities overseeing cultural life in Zagreb proved relatively tolerant, the Austrians in Ljubljana were far less so, especially through 1916. One reason is historical and geographical: Croatia always had its own institutions, political and cultural, but the Slovenian lands were traditionally treated as the private property of the Habsburgs, and oppositional or proto-nationalist cultural expression was potentially more dangerous and certainly more visible in the Slovenian capital than in Zagreb. The second is the large German-speaking population of Ljubljana, which could be and was counted on to step into the gap caused by the virtual disappearance of Slovenian-organized cultural events in the first years of the war. There was, of course, no analogous Hungarian population in Zagreb. The face of cultural life in Ljubljana changed dramatically in the summer of 1914. Many leading cultural figures, especially those associated with the Slovenian Social Democratic and Liberal parties were interned, and many others were drafted. Slovenska Matica, the center for literary publishing and literary life in general, was closed, not to begin operation again until September 1917. Pro-Yugoslav journals appear to have been banned.[30]

Even more severe was the change in the situation relating to public performances (theater, concerts, and lectures). The 1913–1914 cultural season had seen some 273 non-institutional events, including lectures, concerts, and dances.[31] Of these, most were sponsored by the Liberals (36 percent), the Clericals (44 percent) and German-speaking groups (12 percent). During the same season, there were 324 institutional events: 235 theater and opera performances and 89 concerts. Theater and opera performances were 36 percent Slovenian and 64 percent German. A plurality of vocal and instrumental concerts was sponsored by Slovene groups, but the majority were by private German institutions or the government (military band concerts, primarily). The first war year saw a gigantic drop. Non-institutional events declined from 273 to 24, institutional ones from 324 to 52. Not all groups of the population lost cultural ground equally, however. German-speaking groups saw their share of the cultural pie grow from 33 percent to almost 40 percent, while the Slovenian share slipped from 58 percent to 42 percent. What is more, Liberal-sponsored events almost disappeared entirely.

The content of cultural offerings changed as well. The Slovenian National Theater closed and remained dark through 1917. Even in the German theater, serious plays were removed from the repertory, replaced by fluffy pieces with titles like *Wartime Idyll*, and *The Colonel's Wife*. Only one cinema functioned during the first war year, but features, which before the war had been imported primarily from England, France, and Russia, were replaced by patriotic war documentaries such as *The Taking of Przemyśl* and dramas like *The Nurse from the Red Cross*.[32] A few serious symphonic concerts could be heard, mostly performed as benefits for wounded.

In 1915–1916 the number of events rose in comparison to the previous year, mostly because the German theater got back on its feet. The raw number of cultural events of all kinds in the city expanded to 175, but this was barely 30 percent of the total of the last pre-war year. Even more significant, the Slovenian share of the cultural scene dropped to 15 percent with German-sponsored or military events (band concerts) taking over the rest. In 1916–1917 the number of events increased again, to 227. The Slovenian share of cultural activity rose a bit, as war setbacks forced the Austrians to be more accommodating than they had been during the first years of the war.

Literary culture

Against the background of a hugely diminished public performance scene, Slovenian print culture (both high- and lower-brow) continued to be nurtured in a few major journals as well as in mass-media publications designed specifically for a wartime audience.

Overall, *Ljubljanski zvon* (The Ljubljana Bell), the most prestigious literary organ in Slovenia at this time, was remarkably unaffected by the war. Issues appeared regularly once a month, with no change in graphics, almost no change in content, and no official mention of the war. The first indication that the war was having an effect on the intellectual and cultural life of the country was a selection of poems by Pavel Golia, *Iz cikla: 1914/15* (From the Cycle: 1914/15).[33] These four lyrics, the first material the journal published with a military theme, were dedicated to "My friend Egon Gabrijelčič, corporal in the K. and K. army" who "fell, awarded the highest medal for bravery on Feb. 9, 1915 in the Carpathians." The poems themselves are not of the highest quality, but they contain some good lines as well as a fair amount of banality. Still, the friendship of the two men and the immediacy of the war does come through in "Bojišče" (Battlefield)

> Fallow lands, fallow fields.
> One thousand men, a single will.
>
> Broken roofs, empty towns.
> Cannons, rows of cannons, tanks.
>
> Open sky above the front. At the front
> endurance, courage, death at hand.
>
> Blood, thunder, shouting, groans
> Heroism, toughness, ruin.
>
> Long and shallow graves:
> Our strongest sons within.
>
> Hero after hero leaves us.
> Mass death forges the future.
>
> From beyond the pyramid of martyred corpses
> a new day dawns, still young and bewildered.

Regarding politics, *The Bell* was basically liberal, but it seems to have been tolerated because it rarely published anything other than imaginative literature and articles on cultural topics. Still, occasionally it was able to make its disdain for clerical-sponsored (and therefore pro-Habsburg) Slovenian culture. Thus, in a review of a collection of "soldiers' songs" designed for a mass audience, *The Bell* noted: "we leave discussion of the musical merits of this new volume to the experts; looking at the words, one must remember that the editor has no understanding of the concept of folk songs, otherwise he would certainly not have treated our people's heritage so cavalierly and with so little respect."[34] At the same time, *The Bell*'s editors were not openly anti-patriotic, as a review of a competing collection shows; *Slovenske vojaške narodne pesmi* (Slovenian Military Folk Songs), edited by Fran Marolt, was considered to be beautifully published and "will be welcomed by all who love music, by singing groups, schools, and in today's circumstances, by all soldiers in their free time, especially on watch, in hospitals and sanitoria."[35]

Under the editorial direction of the poet Oton Župančič, starting in 1917, *The Bell* took on a much more openly Yugoslav character. One can see the turn to Yugoslavism first and foremost in the obituaries, which begin to talk about what a loss the deceased would be to Slovenia and Yugoslavdom.[36] Reviews, too, become overtly Yugoslav in this period. Thus, in an article about the Croatian writer Matoš, *The Bell's* reviewer claimed that his work was particularly important "today . . . when all Slavs without regard to political, religious, or cultural background have united behind the Yugoslav idea."[37]

Although *The Bell* continued to publish throughout the war years, a glance at its book review section shows that the publishing industry in Slovenia was severely affected by the war. The number of new books reviewed in the 1915 edition of the journal was only about 66 percent of the 1914 number, and by 1916 it had dropped to little more than 50 percent of the pre-war average. What is more, the percentage of German-language books grew steadily. Nevertheless, the war years saw the publication of a number of major works by Slovenian authors. The first was a collection of children's poetry, of all things, entitled *Ciciban in še kaj* (Ciciban and Other Stuff) by Župančič. These charming poems have nothing to do with the war, indeed, they can be seen in some sense as a defiant refusal to have anything to do with it, and they remain to this day among the best-loved children's poetry in Slovenian. That same year saw the publication of *Padajoče zvezde* (Falling Stars), the first book of lyric poetry by Alojz Gradnik. Gradnik's is primarily love poetry, although it contains a morbid, even decadent streak that must have been particularly attractive during the war years. Completely oblivious to the war was the wartime work of one of Slovenia's greatest prose writers, Ivan Tavčar. In 1917 Tavčar published *Cvetje v jeseni* (Autumn Flowers), a lyrically tragic love story. His masterpiece, *Visoška hronika* (A Chronicle of Visoshka), a family novel set at the end of the counter-reformation that combines realist and modernist techniques, was not published until 1919, but it was mostly written during the war as well.

Undoubtedly the most powerful Slovenian literary work to appear during the war years, and one that deserves a worldwide audience, was the collection of prose poems entitled *Podobe iz sanj* (Dream Pictures) by Slovenia's greatest twentieth-century author, Ivan Cankar. Cankar, who was to die in December 1918, just after the Kingdom of the Serbs, Croats, and Slovenes was proclaimed, had become a confirmed supporter of political Yugoslavism in the early teens. He was jailed just before the war for his beliefs, and was drafted in 1914. Released from the army for reasons of health, he spent the war years in Ljubljana. The stories in *Dream Pictures* are varied, but taken as a whole they succeed in depicting such universal emotions as fear, love, and personal and national responsibility through a luminous, deceptively simple symbolist prose that captures Cankar's personal and Slovenia's national anguish. The narrative is always filterered through Cankar's lyrical "I," as, for example, in the story "Gospod stotnik" (Captain Sir). Here, the poet watches from behind the captain's back as the latter gives his troops a final parade-ground review. The captain walks through the ranks, ignoring some of the men and asking the others, noted by the narrator as the finest of them, a few personal questions: "He reached the end, raised his baton for the last time, and turned around. Then I saw his face and my heart skipped a beat. His face was without skin or flesh, and in place of eyes there were two deep holes, sharp teeth stuck out of his strong, naked jaw. The captain's name was Death."[38]

Visual art

While theatrical performance and literature were curtailed in Ljubljana, visual artists appear to have been less affected. June and July 1916 saw a major exhibition devoted to contemporary Slovenian art in Ljubljana. War themes were conspicuously absent in the show's five rooms, which displayed 122 paintings, as well as the sculptures of Lojze Dolinar, "the Slovenian Meštrović." Rihard Jakopič, the outstanding Slovenian modernist painter, was represented by ten major canvases. Other contributors included Matija Jama, Ivan Vavpotič, Maksim Gaspari, Hinko Smrekar and Matej Sternen, whose three nudes were singled out for praise. Overall, one reviewer called the show "the biggest cultural event in Slovenia in wartime."[39] A similarly ambitious exhibition of Slovenian art took place in October 1917 in the Jakopič Pavilion in the center of Ljubljana.

Popular culture

Just as the war was starting, a new weeky newspaper, *Tedenske slike* (The Illustrated Weekly) began to appear in Ljubljana. At a cheap subscription price of 10 crowns per year, it was clearly meant to attract a large audience. In its opening number, the paper declared itself a "completely loyal, patriotic, openly Austrophilic paper, as we will show in both words and pictures."[40] The paper was chock full of photographs of mobilization, generals, and Emperor Franz Joseph. Each week the latest battlefield photographs (always showing triumphs of the armies of the Central Powers) were presented with optimistic commentary. In addition, the paper provided advice on housekeeping, a cultural calendar, classified advertisements, and, at least in 1914 and 1915, obituaries. This practice had stopped by 1916, most likely because it was bad for morale.

Although not primarily a cultural organ, *The Illustrated Weekly* did publish sections of serialized novels in most issues. Typical was *Usoda špijonova* (A Spy's Fate), which graced the paper's pages through most of 1916. Set in Vienna, Trieste, Slovenia, and the Tyrol, this was a racy and adventure-filled tale of abysmal literary quality. It concerned an Italian officer, son of a Venetian patrician who spies for Italy against Austria. Lest readers get carried away by the dashing spy, the anonymous authors of the tale provided a moral message that ran at the beginning of each installment: "Watch out for home-grown spies. Their sordid profiteering puts the lives of thousands and thousands of our brave soldiers at risk." In addition to serials, the newspaper also subsidized the publication of novels of a middle-brow character including Florijan Golar's *Kmečke povesti* (Peasant Tales) and Milan Pugelj's *Mimo ciljev* (Off Target).

One remarkable book published in Slovenia in 1917 was a short novel on war themes meant for juvenile readers: Ivan Lah's *Dore*. Lah himself was a writer who was wounded while fighting in the Austro-Hungarian army. The book was evidently popular: according to *The Illustrated Weekly* more than 1,000 copies were sold in the first week it appeared. It told the tragic story of a young peasant boy (Dore) who goes to search for his father at the front (his mother died before the war). He practically freezes to death on the road amidst the military trains, which take him to a base hospital. When he recovers, he works for Sister Selma in the hospital kitchen, and searches constantly for his father among the wounded and ill. When he is fully recovered he goes back to his home village, but soon becomes restless and lonely again, and leaves to search for his father and Selma. He cannot find them and is eventually badly wounded by bombs dropped from an Italian airplane. Although he never finds his father, in his dreams Dore imagines that he was killed during the war. At the end of book, Selma finds the boy on his deathbed in the same hospital where he had worked earlier, and he is buried in the soldiers' cemetery. The narrator provides a number of hypotheses about the fate of the father, but this is left unclear.

As in Zagreb, the cinema was undoubtedly the most popular form of entertainment in Ljubljana during the war. Unlike Croatia, however, no films were actually made in Slovenia, so Ljubljana's citizens had to content themselves with documentaries and feature films made mostly in Austria and Germany. The only live public performances of a popular nature were those of military bands, which appear to have become increasingly frequent as the war ran on.

Serbian culture during the war

As noted earlier, the war years were a disastrous time for public as well as popular culture in Serbia. Belgrade had been the only real cultural center in the Kingdom of Serbia, and when the government was evacuated to Niš in the first months of the war the main cultural organs simply stopped functioning. *Srpski književni glasnik* (The Serbian Literary Review), the dominant literary and cultural journal of pre-war Serbia stopped publishing in 1914, and did not resume until after the war. As far as public performance goes, the situation was no better. The Serbian theater in Belgrade closed at the beginning of the war, not to perform again until March 1918.

Once the occupation of Belgrade began, things got even worse. The one Serbian-language newspaper published during the war, *Beogradske novine* (The Belgrade News) printed little more than heavily censored war reports. Although it did provide a kind of daily chronicle, there is no report of any cultural activity in the city until an article dated 13 February 1916. Here, readers were informed about a film series at the former "Colosseum" building. A daily program was offered for soldiers, a Wednesday program for officers, and Tuesday and Friday screenings for the general public. At the time of press the cinema was offering *A Trip to China* followed by the drama *The Black Diamond*. A military band also performed after the program. Clearly, the performances were popular in the culture-starved capital, especially among Belgrade's children. As a result, on 27 February the newspaper was compelled to announce that children under fourteen were no longer to be allowed in unless accompanied by parents.

As far as can be ascertained, no regular theater performances occurred in wartime Belgrade, although visiting troupes evidently appeared from time to time. For example, *The News* on 19 May 1917 announced a performance of *Hasanagica* by one Milan Ogrizović, played by Mme. Taborska and Mr. Gavrilović. From the description, it appears that the actors were on tour from the provincial town of Osijek. In all likelihood, the only frequent cultural events in the occupied capital were performances by Austrian military bands, announcements for which appear from time to time in the newspaper.

With the entire country occupied from 1915 to 1918, the primary concern of the reeling Serbian government in exile was clearly not the preservation of Serbian culture. Nevertheless, some officially sponsored cultural activities were undertaken. Thus, for example, the artist Kosta Miličević, who had served in the army and taken part in the retreat to Albania and Corfu, was hired in 1916 by the Serbian General Staff to travel with the army as an official painter. He produced a number of works depicting Corfu landscapes and Serbian officers. The Topographic Department of the Army's Supreme Command sponsored the shooting of a great deal of film footage by Dragiša Stojadinović. Immediately after the war, this footage was used to make a number of documentary films. In addition, theatrical troupes, staffed mostly by refugee actors from the Serbian National Theater, performed under the auspices of the Serbian Army in Solun, North Africa, and on Corfu.

Serbian culture in exile

Equally important for the preservation and advancement of Serbian culture was the work of various non-governmental *émigré* groups. Many exiled Serbs contributed to the Yugoslav-oriented newspapers, almanacs, and other publishing ventures that sprouted all over the European diaspora.[41] Typical was the *Prosveta Almanah za godinu 1918*. Edited by Pero Slepčević, the almanac was assembed in 1917 and published in Geneva. It is filled with secessionist-style woodcuts, reproductions of Meštrović sculpture, and plenty of Yugoslav unification propaganda. Although it is hard to know exactly who published and who consumed Yugoslav propaganda during the war, one way to measure the extent of Yugoslav feeling in the exiled Serbian community is by tracking publications in Cyrillic of the Croatian author Ivan Mažuranić's *Death of Smail-Aga Čengić*. This work had been identified with Yugoslavism from its appearance in 1846, but had always been more popular among Croats. Nevertheless, in 1916, an organization of Serbian students in Virivil put out a hand-written and lithographed version of the work, as did another group in Northern Italy. Excerpts were published in an anthology that was put together in Nice in 1917. The wartime government also sponsored new editions of this work,[42] as well as publications of the great nineteenth-century Serbian epic, Petar Petrović Njegoš's *The Mountain Wreath.*

Serbian literature

Although publication inside Serbia was impossible, many individual Serbian writers remained active during the war years. Some were attached to the army, like the poet Vladislav Petković-Dis, who participated in the epic retreat of 1915. His simple but emotional poem "Posle Albanije" (After Albania) captures the despair of a once-proud army: "We were wonderful, glory's favorites / Instilling fear in our foes. / We had the soul and blood of a healthy race. / And now? Who are we now? And where is our home?"[43] Dis was not to experience the rebirth of Serbian military glory: he died on a boat that was torpedoed off Corfu in 1917. The Herzegovinian Serb poet, Aleksa Šantić, remained in Mostar throughout the war, and published a number of pro-Yugoslav works in *The Literary South.* The war years also saw the first important publications of Miloš Crnjanski. Crnjanski's family, though Serbian, were loyal citizens of the empire, and Crnjanski himself had grown up in Timoşoara where he received an education comparable to that of his contemporary, Krleža. During the war, Crnjanski served in the Austro-Hungarian army, and saw fighting on the Russian front. At the same time, he published lyric poetry regularly in the Zagreb monthly *The Contemporary.*[44]

But the most important Serbian writer to appear during the war years was the Bosnian-born Ivo Andrić.[45] Andrić, who was studying in Cracow when Franz Ferdinand was assassinated, hurried home as soon as he heard the news. He had been associated with the Young Bosnia group whose members carried out the assassination, and was arrested by the Austrian authorities just days before the war began. Although he was released from prison in 1915 due to lack of evidence, he was interned until 1917. The experience of being an actual or virtual prisoner for three years had a profound effect on the tubercular, hypersensitive young writer. His first substantial work, a series of prose poems entitled *Ex Ponto* (published in the summer of 1918) can in fact be seen as a kind of extended meditation on the theme of loneliness, exile, and suffering.

Today, as on all the other difficult days of imprisonment, I pity everyone who is alive, those who do evil as well as those who suffer it. I pity myself and my fading strength. But most of all I pity the mothers . . . Do people ever think what the night is like for a mother who knows that her only son is fettered by iron and a stranger's merciless hand?[46]

Visual art

Although public culture all but disappeared in Serbia during the war, individual artists were nevertheless able to work. An excellent example is the painter Ljubomir Ivanović. When the war began, Ivanović was mobilized, but because of his poor health he was made a hospital orderly. He stayed with the Serbian army through much of its retreat, stopping in Prizren in late 1915. After this he returned to Belgrade. His wartime painting consists of genre scenes unrelated to the war for the most part. He did, however, produce a line drawing entitled *Beg* (Flight) in 1915, that captures something of the feeling of the retreat of the defeated Serbs. Equally powerful is his *Fallen Soldier* from the same period.[47] Perhaps the greatest Serbian artist of the period, however, was Nadežda Petrović. Although she was already a well-known and successful painter, she worked as a volunteer nurse during the Balkan wars of 1912–1913. She volunteered again after the outbreak of World War I and died in the typhus epidemic of 1915. Not surprisingly, she had little time to paint in the last years of her life, but she did manage to produce a few canvases, including her *chef d'oeuvre*, the highly postimpressionist *Valjevska Bolnica* (The Valjevo Hospital – the hospital in which she herself was to die). In bold brushstrokes and bright colors, it depicts a series of white tents against an expressionistic, almost Fauvist, landscape of green, orange and red.[48]

Conclusion

World War I was, by any measure, a disaster for the territories that would become the Kingdom of the Serbs, Croats, and Slovenes in 1918. It has been estimated that the war cost Serbia one-third of its prewar population and one-half of its national wealth. Although casualties were nowhere near as high among the Habsburg South Slavs, they were numerous, and it has been estimated that these territories lost one-fifth of their pre-war wealth.[49] All cultural institutions in Serbia were suppressed during the entire conflict, while those in the Habsburg territories functioned under various degrees of censorship and self-censorship.

Nevertheless, it was during the war years that sentiment for cultural and political Yugoslavism grew to a fever pitch. Although the idea that the South Slavs (with the exception of the Bulgarians) should all live in a single state had been gaining momentum since the turn of the century, it was only during the war that this notion became the common property of the majority of educated South Slavs. The growth of Yugoslav sentiment during wartime can be seen in the gradual Yugoslavization of officially pro-Habsburg publications like Ljubljana's *Illustrated Weekly*, as well as the founding of prestigious, openly Yugoslav journals like *The Literary South*. It is, of course, extremely difficult to ascertain how far and to what extent a feeling of Yugoslav unity had trickled down to the masses, especially to the peasants. There is a great deal of evidence to support the belief that the formation of a unified Yugoslav state did have widespread popular support by the war's end. Thus:

in August 1918 General Stjepan Sarkotić, the last imperial governor of Bosnia, estimated that 100 percent of Dalmatia favored Yugoslav unification, and about 60 percent of Croatia, Slavonia, Bosnia and Herzegovina approved unification. It can be assumed that Sarkotić referred to the non-Serbian population, as the Serbs in the Monarchy were assumed to favor unification with Serbia.[50]

The promulgation of the Kingdom of the Serbs, Croats and Slovenes, which occurred on 1 December 1918, was greeted by waves of celebrations all over the territory of Yugoslavia, as the Kingdom came to be popularly known. On 3 December 1918, banner headlines in *Slovenski narod* (The Slovenian People), Ljubljana's most important newspaper, announced: "Proclamation of Union with Serbia." Commentary on the subject was unanimously favorable: "They [the Serbs] want full union with us. All will be absorbed in a new creation. The first step of the heir to the throne Alexander, his first speech, is the best guarantee for the peaceful evolution of our new state." Articles in the same paper filed from Zagreb described large crowds in the streets of the Croatian capital. They were said to be singing national hymns and demonstrating in favor of union. An important national demonstration took place in the National Theater as well. "The actors and audience sang national songs together."

Whether such sentiments reached the countryside, however, is another question. Certainly, the success of Stjepan Radić's populist Croat People's Peasants Party in the elections of 1920 (they took the biggest bloc of Croat votes and swept rural areas overwhelmingly) indicates that Yugoslav sentiment was far weaker in the Croatian hinterland than in the cities or on the coast. Furthermore, Yugoslav nationalist euphoria did not last long even where it had existed, and for various reasons, both political and cultural, the South Slavs never succeeded in creating a long-term stable state or Yugoslav national identity.[51] Still, Yugoslavia in one form or another existed through most of the twentieth century, and the contribution of wartime culture to its creation cannot be ignored.

In addition, the war years saw the publication of at least three individual works that can stand with the most powerful literature to grow out of this or any war. Ivo Andrić debuted with *Ex Ponto*, a prose poem which gives voice to the imprisoned individual, powerless to affect the course of events, and desperate to retain sanity and life itself in extreme circumstances. Miroslav Krleža's first major work, the lyrical, almost surrealistic "Croatian Rhapsody," captures the collective insanity and desperation of the Croatian nation in wartime. And Ivan Cankar's final completed book, *Dream Pictures*, a miniature epic composed entirely of brilliant brief prose poems, expresses both personal and national anguish in the face of implacable death and destruction. Although Yugoslavia is gone, seemingly forever, these three works, so similar in spirit, can stand as a kind of epitaph both for the viciously fratricidal battles of World War I and for the Kingdom of the Serbs, Croats, and Slovenes that rose from their ashes.

9   Between apology and denial: Bulgarian culture during World War I

Evelina Kelbetcheva

Introduction

Bulgaria's involvement in World War I was relatively late and came after much hesitation and vacillation. Bulgaria remained a marginal member of the Central Powers' alliance system primarily because it had little in common with the overarching strategic interests and war aims of the Austro-German bloc. During World War I, Bulgaria's old enemy – the Ottoman Empire – became its new ally, while Russia was now its enemy. Bulgaria's military and political aims – which had been frustrated during the two Balkan wars of 1912–1913 – were practically achieved by the end of 1916 with the defeat of Serbia and Romania, and the establishment of Bulgarian control in both Macedonia and Dobrudja. The collapse of the Central Powers in 1918, however, brought about a reversal in Bulgarian fortunes.

Over the course of the Balkan Wars and World War I, the basic paradigm of Bulgarian culture changed. The altered forms of artistic expression and the attitudes of the artists towards the wars were especially symptomatic. The burden of the national ordeal and the wartime experiences led to the formation of a new worldview and a new self-awareness. The intelligentsia were the most sensitive to the changes and their reactions were the most intense. On the one hand, the Great War became a touchstone for the humanistic yearnings of the intellectuals. On the other, it acted as a catalyst for new aesthetic directions. This process challenged the established pre-war value system. In this chapter, I argue that World War I brought an end to the National Revival period in Bulgaria.

The coupling of the struggle for national unification with the transformation of Bulgarian culture was unavoidable, because in a small country with a disrupted cultural-historical continuity, the idea of national destiny becomes the catalyst for almost all cultural, intellectual, and artistic creativity. The intellectuals were the vanguard of the national-liberation movement which climaxed with the three consecutive wars. This interconnection was fostered by a lack of an established avant-garde or a tradition of *l'art pour l'art* in pre-war Bulgarian culture, as well as by the strong civic involvement of the Bulgarian intellectuals. It was only after the defeat in 1918 that we witness what Ivan Berend calls "the revolution of art [becoming] the art of revolution."[1]

In the Balkan Wars, the intelligentsia had participated spontaneously and *en masse*. Writers and poets, professors and scientists, musicians and artists, actors and journalists were at the frontline as ordinary soldiers as well as officers. During World War I, the country's cultural life changed significantly. For the first time, there appeared a clearly defined institutionalized and centralized structure in Bulgarian culture. The cultural environment was mostly dominated by military and political aims. This is clear when we look at the new subordination of the most prominent cultural institutions to the Ministry of War and the creation of a Cultural Department (Kulturno Otdelenie kam Staba na Deistvashtata Armia) under the General Staff. The most influential cultural institutions were the Ministry of Popular Education, the Bulgarian Academy of Sciences, Sofia University, the National Theater, the Opera, the National Library, the Archeological and Ethnographic Museum, the School of Arts and Industry, as well as the newly established Military and Historical Museum, which all operated in cooperation with the Ministry of War and the General Staff of the Army. Many Bulgarian scholars, professors, artists, writers, and journalists were attracted to work in these institutions. This resulted in a program of broad, but centralized and heavily controlled, cultural activities.

Scholars of those official institutions focused on studying the history, everyday life, culture, traditions, and language of the inhabitants of the newly acquired territories of Macedonia and Dobrudja (seized from Serbia and Romania, respectively), with a view to establishing their "true" identity as Bulgarians. Surveys of monuments, and other cultural artifacts were carried out. On the homefront, books on the Bulgarian historical and cultural heritage were also published. Support for Bulgarian poetry, prose and drama was also provided by the state. The extent to which Bulgarian wartime culture was subject to the military aims of the state is shown by the very nature of the lectures, poetry readings, and commemorations that were organized wherever Bulgarians were living. This is also valid for the most popular forms of entertainment: theater, cinema, and the open air brass band concerts. News from the front and other patriotic themes were an integral element of all of them. Very rarely did any art form distance itself from the war theme – either at the front or at home.

Most patriotic literary creations were directed at the audience on the home front, and were written there. Even a new derogatory term was coined, "the home front heroes," that described the "patriotic" poets who filled the newspapers with their poems and articles, "marked by barren pathos and banal tendentiousness, which emits ecstasy."[2] Soon, however, the reaction of Bulgarian intellectuals against this trend grew stronger and became a major trend in Bulgarian culture. At first it was expressed only in art and literary criticism. However, it soon became a movement to fight against the abridgment of free and creative expression and against the dogmas of state and military institutions. It was soon considered a violation of intellectual creativity to try to impose political conformity – and thus mediocrity – on the intelligentsia. A significant number of Bulgarian intellectuals was accused of having no distinctive civic position, thus betraying the principles of humanism. In contradistinction to the official propaganda productions, then, stand the achievements of dissident artistic circles such as the Modernists and the innovators in traditional art forms. This is what I refer to as the second, or non-official, trend in Bulgarian wartime culture.

Another theme involves the role of the homefront and the different initiatives designed to further political and military objectives. Many newly established charitable organizations arranged theater and opera productions, concerts, lectures and shows, the proceeds of which went to support the soldiers' families.

Finally, popular folklore during the war expressed the hardship (to the point of starvation) experienced by common people in rural regions – especially women left behind to work the land while their husbands were fighting and dying at the front. (During the last stages of the war, widespread starvation in the countryside led to the so-called Women's Revolts.) However, traditional folklore was confined largely to the countryside and was quickly becoming alien to the modern city-dwelling Bulgarian, who was mainly influenced by the official propaganda or the more sophisticated urban art forms. As we shall see, though, some avant-garde artists began experimenting with syntheses of folk imagery and modernist styles during the war.

Folk culture, official culture, and popular entertainment

During World War I, folklore, and especially folk songs, initially expressed patriotic feelings typical of the Balkan Wars. The world war was viewed as a continuation of the previous wars and the widely shared opinion was that people were fighting for the liberation of their fellow-countrymen. But even at the very beginning of the war there was the realization of a future contradiction that would develop between Bulgaria and its current ally Germany. Songs described this with bitter irony: "Ganyo [nick-name for a Bulgarian] is carrying the back pack, Doycho [nick-name for a German] is eating 'banitza' [traditional Bulgarian cheese pastry]."[3]

Folk wisdom had noticed and had already captured these contradictions, which were also expressed in the discontent and the complaints of many leading intellectuals in Sofia. Soon, relations between the Bulgarian army command and the higher German General Staff became very tense, mainly because of the fact that Germany refused to send support to the southern front.

A major theme of folk songs was that of the fate of the family, and especially the loss of the father or son. One of the most interesting is the song about the widow Milkana. It begins with the Balkan war, and it tells us the story of a young woman who has lost her husband, the father of her seven children. She suffers greatly. Four years later, in 1916, she has to send off her oldest son, Ivancho, to the front, where he is later killed by the French, near Dobro Pole. The singer denounces "these terrible wars, which ruin human destiny." After the death of her son, Milkana condemns the war and bemoans her fate.[4]

This is in contrast to the spirit of the Balkan wars when pride and glorification of heroism predominated. Denouncing the war became the most typical theme in Bulgarian folk songs from the second phase of the world war 1916–1918. After 1918, folk songs were full of sorrow, despair and pain for the loss of the war, along with the many victims – orphans and widows – who remained as a result. This suggests a significant shift in the attitude of common people toward their own experience in the Great War.

Of course, this shift in attitude was not reflected in officially sponsored popular entertainment, which sought instead to incorporate folk motifs into pro-war propaganda. The theater was the most popular and influential wartime entertainment at the front line. Despite the attractiveness of the quickly developing cinema, the guest performances of Bulgarian acting troupes and the lively interaction with the audience turned front line theater into a distinctive genre of entertainment, which went beyond the bounds of traditional amusement. At the end of 1917, the famous playwright, director, actor, artist, and wag, Boris Roumenov, known as Boryo Zevzeka (Boryo the Joker), proposed to the General Staff that a special institute be created for "military entertainment." Very popular at that time was the German Balkan Theater in Niš, in occupied Serbia. But it was most of all the tremendous success of the performances among soldiers which helped Roumenov justify his proposal that all this would be "of great importance to raise the morale of the soldiers, and to contribute to their education, entertainment, and courage."[5]

It was not until the summer of 1918 that the General Staff created a statute book for theater activities. According to its regulations, a theater group had to be formed in each infantry and cavalry division. The repertoire of the groups was to include plays written by Bulgarian authors in literary Bulgarian or in dialect form, depending on the make-up of the regiment. The plays had to be approved by the Cultural Department. The field theater groups included a small choir and orchestra of twelve musicians. The theater manager had to select the repertoire and to attract professional actors and authors who were paid by the General Staff to write the "appropriate plays." Among the biggest hits were *Balkanska Komedia* (Balkan Comedy), the farce *Borislav na fronta* (Borislav at the Front), *Sveti Ilija v plen* (St. Elijah Captured), *Sofianzi pred Bukurest* (Men of Sofia at the Gates of Bucharest), and *Zhiv kinematograf* (Live Cinematograph).

The audience influenced not only the genre of the plays, which were predominantly comedies and farces, but also the way performances were presented. In some of the regiments, the enthusiasm was so great that the soldiers themselves constructed a theater. This happened on the southern front, close to the Anglo-French battle line. At the end of February 1918, the Voinishki Dramatichen Teatar (Soldiers' Drama Theater) was built in less than two months by a small group of volunteers from the 51st Infantry Regiment of the IV Division. The theater was a marvelous heated structure that seated nearly 400 spectators.[6]

Pomoravia, the first Bulgarian wartime theater during World War I, was established at the end of 1917 by a group of Plovdiv actors who were not mobilized. In Niš, in occupied Serbia, where the group adopted its name and officially announced itself as a wartime theater, two Serbian actresses joined it, Bunichka and Popova. Notwithstanding the enemy status of France and Russia, the repertoire of Pomoravia included Beaumarchais, Gogol, and Ostrovsky. The group maintained its professional pre-war level. This was highly appreciated by the citizens of the areas recently occupied by the Bulgarian army, where the quality of the theatrical performances contributed to the prestige of Bulgarian culture as a whole. The audience coming to watch Pomoravia included army officers and citizens from the occupied territories on the southern front. Similar to Pomoravia was the Sborna Patuvashta Trupa (Combined Traveling Group), formed in 1916 by a group of actors from the National Theater in Sofia. Only occasionally did the group visit occupied

Bucharest, where they staged *Po stapkite na voinata* (Following in the War's Steps) by I. Balkanov, which later became a must in theater repertoires because of its ardent patriotism.[7]

The most popular of all divisional groups was Frontovi Teatar na Parva Sofiiska Divisia (Field Theater of I Sofia Division) founded in 1917 and financed by the Ministry of War. This group began back in 1913 and it was established as a traveling theater known under the name of Barabanchitsi (The Drummers), from the name of the humorous weekly magazine *Baraban* (Drum), which published one-act scenes from plays of the group's repertoire. During the war, the group endeavored to become a humorous wartime theater. Its manager was Boris Roumenov. In less than two days the actors were assembled and after less than two weeks of rehearsal the first performance was ready. The group traveled across the front line in a cart and staged its plays in a tent, made up of three pieces of canvas and a few spikes. The curtain hung on two telephone cables. Sometimes, instead of cables, two soldiers were happy to contribute to the success of the performance by holding on to the curtain.[8]

The favorite play and one which was most often staged, was *Balkan Comedy* by Sava Zluchkin. Its comically endearing protagonist was the simple-hearted and naive traditional Bulgarian folk character called Ganyo. He was contrasted with the "sly and cowardly Greeks" and the insidious Serbians and Montenegrins – a theme from the Second Balkan War, since the Great War was associated with and recognized as a natural continuation of the Balkan Wars and of the unsuccessful Bulgarian attempt to achieve national unification. There, on the battlefields of Macedonia, strong feelings of patriotism and hatred for the enemy were rekindled through the constant reminder of the anti-Bulgarian behavior of Serbians, Montenegrins, Greeks, and Romanians during the earlier war. Roumenov's description of *Balkan Comedy*, a play he directed, gives the best sense of the atmosphere at the time. During one performance, exactly at the moment in the play when Ganyo was attacked by his Serb and Montenegrin adversaries, the makeshift curtain fell down. Shouting was heard on the stage – some soldiers jumped in to help Ganyo, who was being treacherously surrounded. At the end of the performance the actor who played the role of the Montenegrin was taken to the chief officer because he had jumped through the window to escape the vengeance of the angry audience.[9]

This scene reminds one of the classical description of the performance of Miserable Genoveva from the novel *Pod Igoto* (*Under the Yoke*) by Ivan Vazov, which was so typical of the theater of the Bulgarian

Revival. In this theater, the audience and the actors come together in their unconditional acceptance of the action. However, in the case of the wartime theater, the tacit involvement of the spectators was not sufficient; their spontaneous reaction was deliberately provoked. To some extent, the theater both looked to the audience for inspiration, and actively encouraged a popular spirit of vengeance against former allies who had turned into enemies. This performance did not distance itself from the audience by the conventionality of stage illusion. It sought exaltation and had the effect of active patriotic stimulation.

Another example of a farce displaying the sense of humor and self-irony typical of Bulgarian wartime theater, Roumenov's *Borislav na fronta* (Borislav at the Front), was a parody on Ivan Vazov's famous play, *Borislav*. The original play had been staged at the National Theater and dramatized episodes from medieval Bulgarian history as lessons for the contemporary generation. The wartime version, narrated by the prompter, discredited the play's historical myths and ridiculed all of its characters.

The main comic element was the constant confusion between the theatrical characters and the performers. The latter were ordinary soldiers who played both the male and the female roles. This effect was sought deliberately. It was widely used in other parodies as well, such as in *Figaro at the Front Line*. Various thematic elements were removed or adjusted so as to match the real-life situation, which was so close to the audience at the front. Roumenov's theatrical realizations were subject to the conditions of the soldiers' daily life. They had to be part of their leisure time, they could not bother them with problems, but must simply entertain them and make them laugh wholeheartedly. Despite the fact that such theater was not of high artistic quality and that it was closer to popular stage performance as a genre, it was not an easy job for a professional actor to take part in it. None of the other field theaters were able to compete with the success and the popularity of Roumenov's "sincere" theater, which represented a natural mix of popular stage and classical stage elements. The effort to make the actors and the spectators equal was some form of a searching for trust and equality between them – an idea which was later developed by the disillusioned post-war generation. This approach emerged for the first time in the performances of the wartime theater.

On the eve of the war, the cinema became very popular, mainly in the big cities. Foreign comedies, thrillers, and vaudeville shows were shown. As a logical continuation of the rapid advance of movie making, Bulgarian movies were born. According to one reliable newspaper report, the most prestigious cinema hall in the capital, Modern Theater, did not have the capacity to seat all the people who crowded in front of the box-office.[10]

The wartime repertoire was dominated by scenes depicting the victory of the armies of the Central Powers, and especially the battles on the Macedonian front and the victorious marches of the Bulgarian army against the Serbs. Military men recognized the great potential of the cinema as a popular art form which could be used for the purposes of propaganda as well as entertainment for the soldiers and officers. Moreover, the cinema developed rapidly and became the best contemporary method for documenting the wartime effort. General Zhostov, head of the General Staff, pointed out that the actors who were sent to the wartime theater to depict Bulgarian victories against the Serbians in November 1916 "were not able to portray the last convulsions of Serbian agony." That was why the general asked that a cameraman be sent to the front lines.[11]

The movie house Vardar, on the southern front, was provided with films by the German Ministry of War. But there were many other places where films were shown. An article on the development of the arts on the front pointed out that "in many places next to the battle line there were projectors and there were all the additions and newly constructed buildings where theater performances could be presented as well." It should be noted that these combined cinema and theater performances, which usually ended with folk music and dances, were particularly popular with allied troops from Germany and Austria-Hungary.[12]

Along with the rapid advance of the cinema as a method for documenting military victories and as a propaganda tool, the first Bulgarian feature movie was created: *Bulgaran e gallant* (Bulgaran is Gallant, 1915). It is very likely that it was directed by the actor, Vassil Gendov, who played the main character. He is also considered to be the author of the script, the director, and the cameraman of a second film called *Lyubovta e ludost* (Love is Madness). Both films were melodramatic comedies with a vaudeville character. Meanwhile, another director, Kevork Kuyumdjian, shot a film called *Chada na Balkana* (Children of the Balkans), a tearful story about love overcoming the obstacles of war. This was a film designed to inspire a pompous form of patriotism.[13]

Unfortunately none of these films are preserved and there remain only newspaper accounts and reviews with which to reconstruct these productions. It is obvious that the newly born Bulgarian cinema followed the old-established tradition – well accepted by the audience – of comedies, vaudevilles, and thrillers. But it also exploited another topic, very important for the country – the war.

High culture in the service of official nationalism

During the Bulgarian National Revival in the eighteenth and nineteenth centuries, literature dominated Bulgarian culture. This continued through the entire pre-war period, when its significance in the formation of social consciousness was most strongly felt. It is interesting that during this epoch the fine arts (e.g., the ethnographic genre, music – still at the stage of adapting folk-songs; architecture – constructed along the lines of European eclecticism, baroque, or Art Nouveau; and theater – rambling between Romanticism and shy attempts towards modern psychological analysis) did not carry the impact of the written word.

Poetry was widely appreciated among all strata of Bulgarian society. Before the wars there were ninety-nine literary magazines in Bulgaria (sixty-seven of them published in Sofia). During the war their number was reduced to twenty-four (twenty in Sofia).[14] It is important to note that the literacy level among the Bulgarian population was very high. According to statistical records, 89.9 percent of inducted soldiers in 1915 were literate. This ranked Bulgaria eleventh in the world![15]

World War I brought into being a fundamental division among intellectuals into two groups, which I will call "the apologists" and "the humanists." The apologists supported the official state and military propaganda. Most of them were already known for their traditionalism, defense of realism in literature, and fierce opposition to modernism or the avant-garde. The apologetic themes of their poetry, novels, and journalism were constant. The apologists lacked any sense of hesitation about the conflict or desire for impartial judgment of the war and its impact on Bulgarian society. This attitude seemed to go hand-in-hand with their conservative political views and their traditional aesthetics. Although they sometimes showed compassion toward the enemy, mainstream traditional realists in both literature and the arts possessed no adequate vision to describe or judge the Great War.[16] The following lines of D. Babev can serve as a fitting critique of the traditional poetry of the home front's "heroes of the rear": "Some day, when the war is over, amidst the numerous interesting memories, there will remain one not so interesting – the poems written on the homefront. This jejune memory will resemble the rambling sound of a deserted windmill that does not feed a single creature but only flaps for show its white wings against the wind."[17]

Ivan Vazov, who was seventy during World War I, was the most famous Bulgarian poet and novelist, often called the patriarch of Bulgarian literature. His works expressed an unswerving sense of recognition for national achievements, heroism, and the virtues of the Bulgarian people. His treatment of the cause of justice and future happiness after a run of suffering and misfortune was a cornerstone theme in his voluminous work. He remained firmly rooted in the moral principles of the Bulgarian National Revival: diligence and tenacity. Among the currents that flowed through Vazov's works from the wartime period was what might be termed a battlefield naturalism that was used to articulate impassioned attacks against the Serbs, British, and French. His work, sometimes naive, was also so highly emotional that much of its social and artistic impact was lost.[18] The awkward and contrived quality of his verse, the elaborate epithets, trite comparisons, and images devoid of originality all reveal an outdated artistic taste which, despite frank and patriotic feelings and even the occasional flicker of sympathy for the enemy soldiers' suffering, makes it difficult to consider Vazov's wartime poetry as a major artistic achievement. The vocabulary of the National Revival no longer seemed able to produce anything other than clichés.

Kiril Hristov's wartime works brought him questionable fame as a champion of Bulgarian chauvinism. One of the most popular poets of post-liberation Bulgaria, a highly gifted and original lyricist, Hristov as a person gained notoriety as a vainglorious and vengeful man, who made unscrupulous use of the political situation. During the wars he was very prolific and in this respect rivaled Vazov, although he surpassed him in his mastery of a variety of genres. His first collection of poems, *Na Nozh* (With Bayonets Drawn, 1912), is an example of straightforward, declarative, battle-cry poetry, inspired by militant exaltation. From this book comes the famous wartime slogan, "Mushi, Koli, Sechi" (Stab, Butcher, Slay).[19] The preface to his collection of poems *Pobedni Pesni* (Songs of Victory, 1916) calls for authors to write about war while it is taking place and not later. Wartime literature, according to him, can assist in the attainment of national unity. It reinforces the attitudes relating to the deeds of revolutionaries from the past and particularly from the Bulgarian National Revival. One of the most significant themes is that of Macedonia: this object of irredentist claims was regarded as Bulgaria's open wound and, by the same token, as a unifying symbol of Bulgarian aspirations.[20]

Kiril Hristov was persistent in his indiscriminately apologetic attitude to war. Although he felt kindred ties to European culture, he showed little concern over the sufferings and misery that war would inflict on the peoples of Europe. He was a stranger to the idea that war could be a disaster for civilization, a collapse of age-old values, an upsetting of social norms. This is indicated very clearly in such poems as "Na kovarna Serbia" (For Treacherous Serbia), "Molitvata na poeta" (The Poet's Prayer), and "Zub za Zub" (A Tooth for A Tooth).

In the above cited preface, Hristov utilized vulgar abuse to characterize the younger poets and their modern themes, which he found artificial. He advocated "not refined, imaginary moods – but life; not mythical creatures – but real people, in flesh and blood." He openly portrayed "the young modernists" as apes! In order to explain this attack against the modernists, we should not forget that these were the very authors who opposed most firmly the concept of war. Modernists, even if they did not denounce the war, did not write a single verse in praise of it. Kosta Todorov, a contemporary of Hristov, writes in his "Outline of Culture During the Wars" that Hristov's collections of verse were not only a "pitiful social and literary failure," but also "a sign of a poetic gift that was exhausted."[21] This is still a valid assessment of Hristov's wartime poetry.

Apologists like Vazov and Hristov were fully encouraged by the cultural institutions that played a major role at the time. The Ministry of Education was the most influential for the formation of cultural policy in Bulgaria and supported all spheres of cultural life. On 16 January 1916, it issued a remarkably tolerant document concerning national education. The interesting fact about this document was that although the ministry was associated and cooperating with the General Staff and its Department of Culture, it nevertheless maintained a sober, defined, and tolerant position. It said that "lectures have to inspire a modest, measured, and impartial tone, without exaggeration, bragging, or deprecation of the national character, strength, or heroism. The same approach should be used for our enemies as well, in order to influence favorably the views and feelings of the Bulgarian youth."[22]

The wartime cultural productions illustrate the extent to which this was wishful thinking. The ministry began the difficult task of building schools in the newly acquired territories, providing additional support to financially strapped communities, and organizing lectures and commemorative celebrations. The number of middle schools and students increased in spite of war, epidemic, cold, and hardship. At Sofia University, students were mobilized and professors were involved in all sorts of cultural and propaganda activities, but professors over forty were not drafted. This allowed for continuity, so that in 1916 all disciplines were still taught at the university.[23] University professors protested actively when some of the university buildings were appropriated for a German Officers' Club. The professors complained that nowhere else did the Germans act like this. On the contrary, they claimed that the Germans supported the activities of the universities in occupied cities such as Ghent, Brussels, and Warsaw.[24] This exemplifies the strained relations between Bulgaria and its allies and the implacability of the university professors against the violation of their autonomy. It was also an expression of resolution and national pride.

The National Library was expanding rapidly at this time. It was especially active in creating a "wartime collection" of military archives, memoirs, stories, jokes, literary criticism, photos, and songs. Copies of these collections were intended for the libraries in Vienna, Munich, and Jena; however, they were never sent. The Library engaged in a hectic gathering and preservation of documents, archives, and publications deemed to be of value for Bulgarian history and culture. Bulgarian scholars involved in the nationalist cultural enterprise were indignant over the difficulty they encountered in gaining access to archives in Austrian- and German-occupied regions of the Balkans that contained materials of interest to them. At the same time, they rejected the idea of undertaking joint scientific expeditions with their colleagues from the Central Powers, fearing that valuable documentation and artifacts would ultimately end up in German museums and collections.[25] Contemporary records show the shameful involvement of Bulgarian National Library officials in the appropriation of the contents of the captured University of Belgrade library (which had been evacuated to Niš before the final collapse of Serbian resistance). After the war, the books were returned to Serbia.[26]

The National Theater was also under the auspices of the Ministry of Education. Regular artistic life was interrupted – the theater was closed for the season in 1916–1917. During the war, the actors who did not perform in the front-line traveling troupes were involved in charity. In contradistinction to the pre-war period, the plays now performed were mainly by Bulgarian authors. The best loved and most often presented play was *Borislav* by Ivan Vazov, which proclaimed the traditional values of the people: honesty, dignity, and mercy. The repertoire also included some foreign plays with patriotic themes, such as *Motherland* by Hermann Sudermann. The National Theater hosted guest performances from several theatrical groups from Germany, Turkey, and Austria-Hungary. A German–Turkish Theater from Istanbul, the National Hungarian Opera, several German troupes, and the famous Vienna Volksoper performed in Sofia.[27] Although there were no regular opera productions during the war, opera singers were among the most active participants in charity concerts. Their repertoire was similar to that of the National Theater: *Makedonia e Svobodna* (Macedonia is Free) by D. H. Georgiev (1917) and *Gergana* with a libretto by the well-known "apologist" L. Bobevski and music by G. Atanasov. Musicians and singers went to continue their studies in allied countries.[28]

All front-line cultural life was organized by the Cultural Department of the General Staff that was established according to the German model. It had the same objectives: to introduce wartime censorship, provide soldiers with suitable literature, organize scientific expeditions to the "liberated" territories, facilitate educational programs, open bookstores and libraries, preserve historical monuments within the ethnic Bulgarian borders, use art to document military actions and inspire the soldiers, deliver university lectures at the front, and organize theater performances.[29] An important achievement was the fact that professional lecturers, heads of expeditions, artists, actors, and musicians were attracted to carry out its activities. The head of the department, Pavel Oreshkov, himself was a prominent scholar.

A survey of the fifty-five book titles published for the "Pohodna Voinishka Biblioteka" (Front Library for Soldiers) indicates that short stories and novels by Bulgarian authors were the most common texts produced. Among them were classics by I. Vazov, L. Karavelov, Elin Pelin, A. Konstantinov, and P. Yavorov. Second in number were Russian authors such as Pushkin, Gogol, Chekhov, and Turgenev. Their inclusion is a striking indication of the continued prestige of Russian high culture, given that Bulgaria was at war with Russia. (Emblems of Russian cultural influence were not altogether immune from wartime passions: at the onset of the conflict, the name of the largest Orthodox church, built in honor of the Russians who fought for the liberation of Bulgaria from the Ottoman Empire, was changed from Alexander Nevsky to Sts. Cyril and Methodius.) The Front Library also contained the works of Cervantes, Mickiewicz, and Mayne Reid. German literature was represented by the brothers Grimm. The literature of the neighboring Balkan countries was left out, mainly because of the accumulated animosity of the Second Balkan War.

The Cultural Department appointed photographers not only to document the wartime action, but also to record the historical and architectural monuments in the captured lands as well as the daily activities, costumes and traditions of the people in the "liberated" territories. Because of the growing importance of photography for the representation of the wartime effort, the selection process was very careful.[30]

Wartime artists were also under the Cultural Department and were appointed by the General Staff after they had been approved by a committee of professors from the School of Arts and Industry. These artists were allegedly given "absolute freedom in their professional work."[31] What was the real situation? Wartime art was in many respects similar to that of literature of the so-called official line. For the first time, major national cataclysms – the three consecutive wars – presented Bulgarian artists with the need to interpret front-line heroism and preserve it and pass it on to the next generation.

Artists assigned to military divisions were to "present war in its multifaceted aspects in an artistic form. Artistic works will be the most valuable material both for the history of the war and for our art." A special statute regulated the rights and obligations of wartime artists: they enjoyed freedom of artistic activity and two months' leave of absence to work in their studios with the obligation to report regularly. The paintings remained their property but had to be at the disposal of the General Staff for exhibitions and charity purposes. Twice a year they had to take part in competitions, one of which had to be foreign. The so-called "free artists" – unattached to the army – were also allowed to work close to the front line if they observed the statute. Sixteen artists were chosen to take part in a wartime exhibition in Berlin in 1916, but, by the following year's exhibition, only six still cared to be showcased in the German capital.[32]

Critic and artist Sirak Skitnik described the battlefield artworks of the time with remarkable insight:

A wartime artist cannot see the frightening face of war that transforms the whole landscape, distorts the people, deforms expression, and creates its own laws and psychology . . . The artist did not grasp that . . . war in its essence is a blind movement and a clash of crowds . . . The artists did not see ordinary man called up from the peaceful fields, spurred on, weak-willed among the multitude, wailing and obedient – driven by a faceless force to useless painful suffering and death. This is why the wartime works will be remembered as [productions of] . . . the immature and poor-sighted artist.[33]

Modernism as a medium of dissent

The humanistic trend in Bulgarian culture was represented in both artistic productions and art criticism. In their approach to the themes of the wartime crisis in Bulgarian society, the humanists' sharpened critical sense stands out. Their revolt against the ethos of official literature and art is reflected in their revaluation of terms like patriotism, duty, and defense of national pride. Humanists were convinced that during the war there originated "a corrupt and poisonous literature – a banal and ordered art, which is disgusting to all honest and thinking minds."[34]

The official artistic productions were criticized by humanists both as aesthetic failures and as expressions of spineless submission to the political establishment. They argued that the tendentious glorification of heroic deeds did not allow the artists to recreate truly the tragic image of war. As in literature, the authors of patriotic art were criticized for not being familiar with battlefield life and were ironically called "the heroes of the rear" and accused of mindless aping of foreign models devoid of links with authentic indigenous culture.[35] The critics were convinced that the lack of great talent was a result of a tragic bifurcation of national creative thought. The disruption of the organic connection with the folk tradition could not be compensated for by the absorption of highly developed European literary and artistic forms. This, they said, is why there were no significant works about the war.[36]

The social reasons for the failure of wartime poetry and art were no less determining. The critics were fully aware of the late development of the Bulgarian national state and society. It had led, according to them, to the emergence of intellectuals with no firm civic foundation or political position. Submission to the will of the ruling elite and subordination to officially controlled cultural politics inevitably led to banal, formal, insincere, and shallow works.[37] Humanist writers, poets, critics, and scholars revolted against the glorification of heroic battle deeds, though some of them had romanticized war during the Balkan conflicts of 1912–1913. For them, writers were the most delicate barometers of social mood, heralds of the struggle for humanism and culture. There were no truly sophisticated or educated persons who did not stand against the absurdity of human slaughter. The war provoked, alongside a sense of revulsion towards the "old world," a feeling of liberation from the burden of prejudices and self-contempt associated with the mediocrity of existence in the pre-war era. This attitude was the cultural extension of their overall disappointment with the Bulgarian model of democracy and parliamentarism. Thus the sharpened critical sense of the Bulgarian humanist intellectuals towards their own artistic creation during the war became the first manifestation of the crystallization of their civic and artistic consciousness. Despite the subjectivity and maximalism of parts of the evaluation, this cultural critique can be seen as the expression of a new self-knowledge engendered by the war.

Among these dissident intellectuals, a new attitude toward Europe was clearly evident, a change in the mode of engagement with the "foreign" and in the way of counterposing the "native" to it. This peculiar social and spiritual dialogue between indigenous and imported themes was critically intensified by the war.

Although lines of distinction among the new stylistic currents remained blurred, two elements of the European avant-garde – Symbolism and Expressionism – clearly left their mark on the development of a distinctively Bulgarian modernist aesthetic. The specificity of Bulgarian

Symbolism consists of the unity of realistic, romantic, and symbolic elements in it, which distinguishes it from the more philosophical and lyrical French prototype. Bulgarian poets enriched their national culture with new spiritual positions – a brilliant psychological range, spiritual contrasts, and deep dramatism (P. Yavorov, D. Debelianov, N. Liliev). These writers gave voice to the revolt of the individual personality as well as the seething collective discontent of society.[38] Under the influence of the wars on their ideas and poetics, important changes occurred. They began to sound at times reconciled and lyrical (N. Liliev, D. Debelianov), at other times proud (T. Trayanov), at other times passionately life-asserting (H. Yasenov, E. Popdimitrov). The motifs of compassion with Bulgarian national destiny, of the connection with the native land and nature, and of the ineradicable faith in the spiritual mission of the artist as true leader of his people, began to dominate their work.[39]

One of the most talented young modernists was Dimcho Debelianov, who was killed at the front in 1916 and did not live to see his collection of verse published. He was a proofreader, reporter, stenographer, student, and officer. But above all he was a poet. He died leaving forty-three poems that were published posthumously. We know of six wartime poems, but in the memories of his front-line comrades these were no less than thirteen. The work of Debelianov suggests that Bulgarian Symbolism was a complicated artistic reaction to the world, a revolt of the individual, and an inevitable clash with reality that led "to an irrevocable tragic decision." It was symptomatic of the perception of war on the part of all humanistically minded intellectuals. Resistance to the horrible reality of war was swept away by the "sweeping wave of the multitude," the inertia of mass feeling. "There blended joy and sorrow, there joined the petty and the great."[40] Humanism made the young officer and poet regard with sympathy the tension of the soldiers' routine. One can trace the theme of resignation, expectation of "the feast of the bloody laugh" and of the same deep existential loneliness that we sense in Geo Milev. Here the symbolic imagery of the early poems is most precise in matching the poet's perception of the war. He succeeds in capturing both the hidden grief of the soldiers and their outward show of cavalier hilarity.

Particularly suggestive are "Edin ubit" (One Soldier Slain) and "Tiha pobeda" (Silent Victory). In these poems one can outline a unique (for Bulgarian wartime poetry) tenderness of feeling, a strangely fatalistic resignation before the powerful call of the earth's bosom, a feeling for "*branna sueta*" (the vanity of battle), the pointlessness of sacrifice, the absurdity of death. The strengthening of "earthly love" is in strange contrast to the reproach: "Comical pity, / absurd pity, in thunderous cruel times / no, not a life to take / he gave his own instead."[41]

The ideological transformation and the new aesthetic dimensions of Symbolist poetry can best be judged from the words of Teodor Trayanov, the most faithful of the Symbolist poets and critics of the pre-war period: "The development of Bulgarian Symbolism was happening at breakneck speed . . . Not the history of the Bulgarian people, but the destiny of the Bulgarian national spirit were the problems which agitated the artists to the point of self-immolation. Bulgarian individualism lived in those who gave birth to it only for it to be transformed into superindividualism."[42]

The poetry of T. Trayanov presents a new "turning of the spiral". The concept of war, death, self-sacrifice – the basic themes in "Bulgarski baladi" (Bulgarian Ballads) – leads to a comparison with the *haidouski* epic[43] and with the best in the work of Hristo Botev, the greatest poet and national revolutionary of the Bulgarian Revival period. One can trace, through the lyric genius of the Bulgarian poets, a deep national symbolic opposition which marks the intensity of the changing epochs. Botev's hero Hadzhi Dimitur, the guerrilla fighter for Bulgarian national liberation, is an expression of the apogee of Bulgarian idealism and patriotism. For example, on the top of the Balkan mountain the dying hero becomes immortal through his deed and through the empathy of the beasts, nature, and the bards. Almost half a century later in the lowlands, in the middle of nowhere, dies another hero – unknown, anonymous, lonely, one of the multitude – who will not be buried. This is the unknown hero of Trayanov. The poet's insight offers an image of one of the most painful contradictions in the psychology of the new Bulgarian intellectual. This is the contradiction between patriotic duty, the deep belief in the just cause, and the pointlessness of sacrifice on such a horrendous scale. This is where the drama of the new "Bulgarian ballads," the drama of the downfall of age-old national yearning and battles, emerges. Trayanov, this "Pilgrim in Black", this Messiah and theomachist, nurturing the confidence of a citizen of Europe, diplomatic and erudite, became one of the most prominent poetic articulators of the tragic clash of two epochs in Bulgarian history.

The impact of the war on the modernists was inescapable. Even Nikolay Liliev, the most popular and "pure" among the Symbolists, who never wrote anything directly connected with the war, translated Henri Barbusse's *Le Feu*, one of the most outspoken of European anti-war books. This work was an outcry of pain not only over the destruction of harmony between society and the individual, but also over the role intellectuals themselves had had in unleashing the war machine.

The other powerful artistic medium to take hold among Bulgarian modernists during the war was Expressionism. The emergence of this current in Bulgarian literature was directly related to the experience of the authors' closeness to the front line and the extremely sharp perception of a new nightmarish existence. In the writers' renditions of their experiences, the unleashing of the dark, latent instinct for destruction of the enemy was portrayed as unstoppable; it outlined new, so far unsuspected, traits of human psychology. The exaltation in the strength of the victorious side unchained the will for revenge; it excited in a weird way, and aroused a lust for death.

All this finds its synthesis in the last frontline diary "Karvavi petna" (Blood Stains) by Vladimir Musakov. Abhorrence of the essence of war and an incessant anger at its pointlessness underline the pathos of his book. They account for the choice of form and for the peculiar nature of the narration and the blending of naturalistic style with romantic digressions, expressionistic breathlessness of experience, of memory, of dream and reverie. In the form of a personal diary, written almost at random, unsystematic, and eschewing finesse of form, V. Musakov depicts the madness of war. At the same time he lovingly creates its antithesis – nostalgia – and the relentless hope for a normal, quiet, ordinary life full of tenderness and caring. Through his character, V. Musakov poses his final rhetorical question: "What if all this is a lie?"[44] This small book becomes one of the most conspicuous proofs of the humanistic pathos of the Bulgarian intellectuals and the rejection of war. Besides, it is one more proof of the power of the psychological turning point associated with the front-line experience and the search for new forms of expression, adequate to the tragedy.

Georgy Raichev was under the strong influence of the psychological realism of Dostoevsky and affected by diabolic prose. He advocated the psychoanalytical Freudian line in literature. All these conceptual and artistic influences blended in a peculiar way in his works, dedicated to the wartime experience. But his main emphasis was on psychological imagery and detailed expression of emotion and experience. The author drew on themes and images from contemporaneous world literature in his depiction of the pointless horror of war and the destruction of the human psyche as a result of war's nightmarish essence. He chose to turn to the dark side of the psyche and to dream-visions in order to represent the frontline experience.[45] In 1919 in Sofia, when Stanisław Przybyszewski, a very popular Polish "Freudian" author, was criticized, Raichev was the only one to stand in his defense, probably because his personal experiences from the war made Przybyszewski's words sound valid: "This is a time of mass psychosis when the contagious hystero-epilepsy spreads like wild fire round the world, when the end of the world is expected at any minute . . ."[46]

In all of his works Raichev stood against the lunacy of war. It accounts for the new artistic elements in his short stories and the fierce humanistic passion of his message. Similar to many from his generation for whom wars were the touchstone of artistic and civic conduct, he confessed in his diary: "Let my country forgive me but I would not allow even ten tsars like Ferdinand, nor ten prime ministers like Radoslavov to decide for me when, where and at what hour of the day I should be shot 'for the good of my fatherland.'"[47]

Raichev's kinship with Geo Milev's attitude towards the fatherland is more than obvious. But it was soon to be transformed not only into a kinship of doubt and new self-consciousness but into a common search leading directly to the Expressionist experience and the recreation of a terrible reality. Towards the end of 1914 Geo Milev came back to Bulgaria from Germany full of ideas, eager to share his cultural experiences and to find followers among the young Modernists. He befriended – and this was no accident! – D. Debelianov, N. Liliev, L. Stoyanov, and N. Rainov. They had undertaken a sober but painful reassessment of the war. In a letter to Debelianov, Stoyanov wrote that "war will discredit the military and . . . one will witness heaps of unforgivable faults, thefts, repulsive speculations, stupid and fatal orders, while numerous black crepes of mourning on people's doors will bring disillusionment."[48]

When Geo Milev published his *Lyrichni hvurchashti listove* (Lyric Looseleaf Sheets) – a translation of works by eminent contemporary European poets, Nietzsche among them – dedicated to his friends, he had already graduated from the Military Academy for Officers for the Reserve and was called to join the Ninth Division as an interpreter. He was filled with disgust and skepticism – this is what he felt before leaving for the front-line. "Off to make war – this is where I am going! No one cares what you think . . . Someone puts the uniform on you and drives you to the front-line. Go there and die! You have not read your book, you have not finished your verse . . . Who cares . . . Go there and die! . . . Die for the fatherland!"[49] All the more frightening is the metamorphosis of the "fatherland" concept. There is no doubt that it was felt as a painful dilemma. N. Rainov finds a single name for what they had been fighting for – Chimera. And Geo Milev would come to the fateful question in September 1923, after an uprising in Bulgaria: "That's wonderful, but what is a fatherland?"[50]

The reassessment of the traditional values was intensified during the war as was the sense that the world urgently needed to change. This was the "overture" to Milev's wartime works written on the southern front. "Pri Doiranskoto ezero" (At Lake Doiran) and "Uzhasut na ognenia bich" (The Horror of the Fiery Scourge) are undoubtedly unique in the strength of their denunciation of this slaughter. At the same time, traditional writers such as Vazov, Hristov, Bobevski, and dozens of others competed to praise the legendary heroism of front-line soldiers and describe death as "a kind person decorated with flowers," while refraining from any mention of the exhaustion, the despair, the doubts, the pain and horror, starvation, cholera, and humiliation.

It is only with Geo Milev that one finds the intertwining of the three knots: craving for peace, deep existential loneliness, and the quest for a "superhuman essence of the mind." This philosophical introspection was interwoven with the aesthetic search for a new form of expression, not only modern, but precisely adequate to the new routine rhythm of a man hurled to the front-line. This is the reason why only in Geo Milev's works can one find a changed lexicon, submitted to the extreme torture of experience, and an incessantly accelerating poetic rhythm which strongly suggests the power of his indignant cry. (It was then that he assigned Ivan Hristov to translate Leonid Andreev's *Red Laugh*, the Russian anti-war novel of 1908 that had already become the byword for a fierce anti-military stand.)

In this train of thought one can also regard Milev's poem "Moyata dusha" (My Soul) as a programmatic work. In Bulgarian literature during the war one can hardly find a stronger and more innovative work that focuses on the spiritual reaction to the war and the defeat. The poet identifies with the war-torn existence of thousands. The use of battle lexicon lends a remarkable expressiveness to the work: tearing limb from limb, laceration, spurting of blood, ripping, burning, breaking, fracturing of bones, boiling, blazing, destruction – a full spectrum of images from the self-destruction of human civilization. All the more frightening is the spiritual self-alienation, also caused by the war – "my soul is not my soul."[51] Hell is not the final destination, though. War is over but there follows "the raging advance of a multitude" – the revolution.

The year 1918 saw the publication of the *Grozni prozi* (Ugly Writings in Prose), eleven pieces in which the horror and denunciation of war emerge as actual consequences for the human individual, as he is turned into a spiritual and physical cripple. In these works there is a strongly imposed symbolic image, a comprehensive biblical image of human tragedy. This is the image of Christ crucified. Geo Milev, who was the first translator of *The Twelve* by the Russian Symbolist, Alexander Blok, could not fail to be influenced by the poet's interesting transformation into an ardent supporter of the October Revolution who cast its leaders in a Christ-like mold. The frame of reference here is much more universal – a generalization of the sufferings of all people and a sense of responsibility before the entire world. Likewise, in the deformed crucifixes of the artist Ivan Milev, and in the works of Y. Yovkov, such universal themes were expressed in a new Bulgarian biblical imagery.

In Geo Milev's later works – *Zhestokiyat prusten* (The Cruel Ring) and *Glavata mi – kurvav fener* (My Head – A Bloody Lantern) – this imagery, so suitable for a war experienced as an apocalypse, finds new dimensions. There appears, roaming throughout the world, dying, lost in the wind, rain and mist, a dark figure of a beggar – Oedipus. He is the symbol of the fallen but undaunted human spirit, the suffering of a mind in revolt against the senseless bestiality of war.

In all of his work and cultural activity during and after the wars Geo Milev was undoubtedly a philosopher, poet, and publisher with a decidedly anti-militarist stance, given to prophetic generalizations and symbolic treatments of human suffering who, despite everything, continued to nurture an intuitive belief in a future harmony between man and the world around him.

Led by the desire for spiritual revival and for a suitable expression of their changed conception of the world, these shell-shocked Bulgarian artists turned not only to Expressionism but also to the diabolic and fantastic. But these tendencies were alien to prevailing currents in Bulgarian culture. The exploration of these modes of expression can be seen as an attempt to overcome traditional artistic barriers in favor of a global outlook, and, by the same token, a bold breaking of taboos surrounding the innermost feelings of the individual.

In Bulgaria, Expressionism appeared as a result of the experiences in the war which led to a turning point in the individual consciousness of the intellectuals in conjunction with a sharpened social and spiritual crisis. The unusual emotional compression and the flouting of traditional forms make this poetry as "chaotic as time, from whose broken up, bloody soil it is born."[52] It was a way unknown till this moment of combining the themes of native reality with the modern. The Expressionist artistic form developed by Geo Milev during and after the wars proved that the moment had come for a new way of combining the "native" with the "foreign" – i.e., the use of a new artistic form born in Western Europe for the recreation of a national tragedy.

The most important manifestations of Expressionistic aesthetics are seen in authors like Geo Milev, V. Polyanov, and G. Raichev among others. Under the influence of Expressionist ideas, they were oriented toward crisis, peak experiences. Expressionism became the most adequate form for the presentation of their changed worldview – a result of the Great War, of the apocalyptic experience of the front line, and of the destruction of the former world. Thus, it also appeared as one of the bridges to the revolutionary avant-garde of the 1920s.

Folk motifs and artistic rebellion

The inundation of foreign influences in the area of politics and culture presented Bulgaria with the enormous task of processing them. The change in attitude of Bulgarian authors toward the war took place through innovations introduced in the traditional art forms. A new trend in art was born – original and deeply based in folklore – which later crystallized in the spiritual movement of Native Art in the early 1920s. Its most prominent figures were already known for their unique artistic achievements during World War I.

In the sculpture of Ivan Lazarov, we find the representation of the psychological reaction of Bulgaria to its participation in World War I. "Pak na voina" (To War Once Again – see Fig. 9.1) is a title that contains both refusal and resignation, a sense of duty and disapproval, that is to say, all those mixed feelings in response to the new national trial. Once again the main characters are peasants, a man and a woman. The man, called to the front, is shouldering his gun, straggling along, staring forward as if unwilling to succumb to the grief of parting. His handsome face is haggard, brows are puckered by the same tenacious hard thought. His wife is close by, small and stooping, lagging a few steps behind him; her look is one of expectation, fear, and bewilderment. Her expression reflects her inability to confront fate, this new misfortune that the war will bring. This work is the last in the wartime cycle and in it Ivan Lazarov still defends his concept of a humanist denial of war. The entire cycle has one and the same aesthetic interpretation – psychological realism, alien to any kind of purposefully sought heroism and aesthetization of the war scenes. Romantic idealization, so widespread in the battle genre, is not present in the artistic principles of the sculptor. Vivid and natural are the faces of these worn, peasant figures, parched by the sun and wind, carrying this new burden with the same old conscientiousness and sense of duty, alongside their never-ending work in the fields. This is a portrayal of the nobility of silent suffering and stolid endurance. This is precisely the sort of perspective that also allows the artist to develop sympathy for the enemy who is himself a man like the Bulgarian peasant – a soldier doing his leaders' bidding. This is how the sculptor achieves the humanistic depiction of war and its impact on the psychology of the common man.

The internationally renowned painter, Vladimir Dimitrov-Maistora, named the First World War "imperialistic slaughter," in contrast to the Balkan War in which he enlisted as a volunteer, deeply convinced in the righteousness of the cause. In 1915–1918 he was an artist at the First Separate Army and presented many of his works at regularly organized

9.1 Ivan Lazarov, *Pak na voina* (To war once again), 1915

exhibitions in Sofia and Berlin.[53] His attitude toward the war remained unchanged, though suppressed by his sense of duty. The deep and insurmountable uncertainty of the situation is precisely what called forth the aesthetic will of the artist. During the First World War he worked incessantly. The drawings left by this gifted artist even nowadays are much more impressive and modern in presentation than the

9.2   Vladimir Dimitrov-Maistora, *Raneni* (The wounded), 1917

dozens of huge, detailed, pompous battle pictures by more conventional painters. Among the most successful attempts at drawing scenes of life between battles, finished in 1916, are *Voinitsi v pohod* (Soldiers on the March), a multitude of faceless people, frowning but striving forward, and *Raneni* (Wounded – see Fig. 9.2), where the wounded are depicted marching head-on with bent heads, bandages all over their faces and arms, eyes hidden (like the women veiled in mourning in the works of Ivan Lazarov and Ivan Milev). A strange tranquility and wish for peaceful repose streams from *Zhazhda* (Thirst), *Pochivka* (Rest), and *Rodna pesen* (Native Song). Especially strong in their effect and suggestion of the idea of the pointlessness of war are the graphic series *Ubiti* (Killed), *Invalidi* (Crippled), and the drawings *Uzhasite na voinata* (Horrors of the War). In his best works, having already established his own style, Maistora proves again and again that, even when depicting war, the artist can combine his humanistic conviction and resentment of war with aesthetic imagery.

In the background, for the movement of innovation in the traditional art forms, one of the biggest names is Yordan Yovkov. His brilliant career began during the Balkan wars, where he served as an officer.[54] For his wartime prose he received the most distinguished award. In his work he presents the perception of war as an "ominous and dark uncertainty" ("Pred Odrin" [At the Gates of Adrianople]). Elsewhere it is both a human and a natural calamity: "A storm more frightening, more fierce and devastating than all the storms of a hot summer. The land is deeply furrowed by grenades, meadows and hills are washed in blood, the sky is in flames, slumbering valleys are awakened by hellish thunder and everywhere – the thick sheaves of a harvest, lifeless bodies."[55]

Another peculiarity of Yovkov's work reveals an urge for biblical imagery. It shows, beyond doubt, that he had reached a level of even-handedness within humanistic themes – good and bad, justice and injustice, blindness and insight, life and death, annihilation, punishment, power over people, destiny. In Yovkov's work the citations from the Apocalypse, chapters 5 and 6, are verbatim. The very choice of this apocalyptic vision is a result of a direct analogy to the war: "There it is, terrible, merciless war! There is no greater disaster on earth. . . . Harvest is coming, harvest! – there it is, harvest. Before these numerous sheaves even the most greedy of harvesters would shudder!"[56]

Yovkov was most closely connected with the life of the ordinary people. Most of his characters were peasant prototypes from Dobrudja and soldiers on the front line. But he had one more "secret," which, to a great extent, determined the character of his work, and its artistic originality – and this was his use of folklore. There was an innate connection between his own artistic perception and the poetics of folk literature. The folklore model helped him avoid the danger of going too far, of introducing an unnatural situation. Prior to the wars, folk tradition existed in its classic form as an overall existential conceptual and aesthetic system, although already shaken by the new economic and political conditions. Its destruction is brought about by these very wars and the following national disasters which changed the life-style and ideological stereotype of the Bulgarian people and defined the beginning of a new era. Yovkov's work represents an attempt at one and the same time to salvage elements of the folk tradition and to draw on its strengths through the creation of an organic synthesis between popular culture and poetic aestheticism.

Yovkov's poeticism, as early as his first public appearances, was related to the extraordinary, the "exceptional," perceived as a harmony between man and nature undaunted even in the hardest of times. His innate feeling for life, his sense of the forces binding land and man, inspiring in him adamant tenacity and unbreakable will for victory, underlie the intensity and innovation with which he depicted war. What is unique with Yovkov is his "battle lyricism," a characterization coined by Vladimir Vassilev.[57] This is the feeling that inspires all his short stories, introduces tenderness in the bloodiest of themes. It is rooted in a deep humanism and in an effort to reveal beauty and good in each peasant soldier in time of war. And if Yovkov is a psychological realist in depicting human emotions and an epic poet in painting a battle, he is a lyricist in his overall perception of people, animals, land, and sympathy for soldiers and officers, for their mothers and loved ones, and even for the defeated enemy. Yovkov's lyricism and the search for eternal human values, even during the war, creates the originality of his style and the impact of his prose.

The movement for native art, arising amidst the apparent catastrophic collapse of a folk-based Bulgarian cultural identity, created a distinctive ideological-aesthetic center, around which the efforts of some of the most talented Bulgarian artists were united. They became the creators of a new national art which was fertilized by the avant-garde experience in Europe. This cultural phenomenon was initiated during the Great War.

Turning toward the folk tradition at this fateful moment for the nation was an expression of persistent faith in the value of a distinctively Bulgarian artistic genius; the resurrection of the old tradition boosted a weakened national self-confidence. At the same time, its integration with avant-garde, Western and Central European techniques served to legitimize the enterprise as modern and progressive. Trained academically, but also familiar with the novelties in the European modernistic circles, the artists of the new generation searched for a new national artistic style through which they wished to make an original contribution to European culture. The resurrection of the old Bulgarian folklore tradition was itself deeply connected with general European trends that idealized the primitive, natural, and exotic as antidotes for disease-ridden urban civilization. Thus, in their very call for the revival of native art, Bulgarian artists incorporated the most up-to-date trends in the art of the twentieth century.

Conclusion

The war brought Bulgaria to a cultural turning point. Its essence was the destruction of numerous aspects of the Bulgarian socio-cultural self-image, formed during the National Revival period, which had been vigorously defended during the pre-war period. This turning point was primarily existential. For the first time, after nearly five centuries, the Bulgarian was forced for years to leave his village, land, and family, and obliged to be content with a reality that was absolutely alien to his prior, peaceful existence. A strenuous battlefield life, the accumulation of physical and mental hardships, the confusing alternation of allies, the unstable military fortunes, all profoundly disrupted the patriarchal outlook of the Bulgarian soul. Furthermore, the battlefield way of life brought with it a new collectivism and a new equality in the face of death. The war not only changed the Bulgarian mental landscape, it provoked a new self-consciousness among intellectuals.

The war brought about a collision between two cultural trends in Bulgarian society: an officially institutionalized "order" and the older tradition of free civil and artistic expression. The Cultural Department of the General Staff advocated, by direct control and official subsidy, a battle art of an old-fashioned, banal, and mediocre aesthetic. Significant achievements were rare. Its art was dominated by unreserved apologetics. Legitimate and thoughtful patriotic concerns degenerated into national chauvinism, expressed in pallid and unpersuasive phraseology and ineffective art precisely when it had became clear that the traditional realistic method provided an inadequate figuration for representing radically altered individual and social existence. The official artistic program also resulted in a collision with Bulgarian humanism. Displays of coarse chauvinism, national bitterness, and warlike ferocity had previously been rare phenomena in Bulgarian art.

The change in artistic emphasis from concern with the individual to stress on the group reflected a profound wartime shift in intellectual consciousness. This shift manifested itself in changed patterns of artistic figuration. Depending on individual temperament and stylistic community, artists explored various modes for expression of the war's hardships. It is fascinating to note how the primary representatives of humanism in Bulgarian culture during the war belonged to the Modernist artistic movements. Thus the significant cultural and generational opposition between "old" and "young," or traditionalists and modernists during World War I turned out to be a struggle between the official patriotic agenda and universal human aspirations. The most talented Bulgarian artists, humanists, and intellectuals transformed the horrors of the war into spiritual statements. They transcended formulaic patriotic ecstasy, and in this way voiced a cry of anger against human slaughter. An enormous conflict between humanistic values and a nationalist yearning for belonging, justice, and Bulgarian heroism, was produced by the reality of war.

As a result of the war, a spiritual commitment to endurance and new metaphorical employment of biblical figurativeness in Bulgarian art was born. It was directly influenced by the thinking of humanistic intellectuals, who perceived this war as an apocalypse and a revelation, as a collapse of culture and hope for human coherence. In this way, the work of Bulgarian artists became equal to the best achievements of European thought and artistic creation. The wartime reevaluation of the "native" and "foreign" in Bulgarian culture resulted in a new national style – the vast artistic and intellectual movement of Native Art. It was described as a new spiritual phenomenon, with innovative philosophical and artistic dimensions. The wars and the collapse of national aspirations reconfigured Bulgaria's relationship with the rest of Europe, culturally as well as politically, bringing an end to the era of the National Revival, and opening the door to new experiments in artistic representation of national experience.

10   Romania: war, occupation, liberation

Maria Bucur

As latecomers to the Great War, the Romanians initially experienced vicariously its unfolding drama.[1] None the less, in the two years of neutrality (1914–1916) cultural life in this country was far from passive *vis-à-vis* the events outside its borders. Journalists, writers, musicians, and theater companies became engaged in debating the merits of neutrality versus participating in the war on the side of the Triple Entente rather than the Central Powers, with whom Romania had a defensive treaty. These manifestations helped construct both the general attitude of the population regarding the importance of participation in the war and powerful myths about Romania's friends and foes. The experience of the war, occupation, and retreat to Iaşi during the 1916–1918 period unsettled many of these myths and helped create others. The entrance into the public arena of a great number of soldiers and civilians who had not been considered consumers of culture up to then modified the language and meaning of the various cultural artifacts produced during this period. Cabaret and other forms of variety show surged in popularity. Moreover, these cultural productions brought together dramatic actors and comedians, classical virtuosos such as George Enescu, and equally popular Gypsy musicians.[2] Their performances defied the established boundaries between low and high culture and invited the audiences of these different tiers of cultural life to interact with each other in the realm of the arts. This transformation became the opening act in the quest for Romanian identity during the interwar period. The experience of the war created not only new avenues for cultural manifestation, but also new rules, a new language and a series of symbols of Romanianness. The ideal of unifying all lands inhabited by speakers of Romanian had been dreamed up by writers and other intellectuals before 1914. However, in the course of the war various cultural artifacts helped expand the appeal of these myths and reconstruct their significance in keeping with the popular tastes. By 1918, high and popular culture found wider and more varied audiences that engaged in the making and consumption of these artifacts. The new make-up of cultural

243

producers and consumers in the public arena guaranteed that, far from being unified, Romanian identity and nationality meant increasingly different things to those encompassed by the borders of Greater Romania.

The historiography of cultural life on the Western front during the Great War has grown over the last few decades.[3] By contrast, Romanian historiography has been uninterested in anything that did not pertain to the military, political, or diplomatic aspects of the war.[4] There have been no substantial analyses of the social and economic effects of the war as total war on the home front. Attempts to deal with the arts have been schematic and have followed the overarching teleology of Romanian historiography on the war – that all events from 1914 to 1918 represented an inexorable process leading to the union of the Romanian Kingdom with Transylvania, Bukovina, Bessarabia, and the Banat on 1 December 1918.[5] Therefore, this chapter represents a first attempt to discuss the significance of cultural life in Romania during the war beyond the nationalist clichés. As such, my analysis cannot be either exhaustive or a true synthesis. Rather, it combines research on some crucial primary sources with the limited amount of secondary sources available on Romania. This chapter represents the starting point for what I hope will become a greater interest in the cultural aspects of World War I in Romania.

The artifacts and types of cultural production on which I focus differ from period to period and run the gamut from opera and literary journals to cabaret, variety shows, and cartoons. In 1914 high culture received far more press than did any form of popular culture. The invisibility of popular culture has been reinforced by many historians of literature, who take into consideration only the quality of the literary content in their evaluation of the pre-1918 period as an incipient stage in the development of an authentic indigenous novel and drama. In his analysis of the work of Mihail Sadoveanu, one of the most prominent writers of the twentieth century with significant publications before 1918, literary critic Nicolae Manolescu writes that there was "no Romanian novel until after World War I."[6] According to such accounts, conservative anti-modernism dominated high culture. The scant commentary on the aesthetics of popular literature suggests that it was equally traditionalist.

A similar evaluation pervades the discussions about Romanian art – painting and sculpture in particular – before 1914. Although a few important names had begun to challenge the old established academic schools, their impact had been marginal before the beginning of the war. Few were the patrons of high art interested in the avant-garde art currents of the day. The sculptor Constantin Brâncuşi had sought refuge in Paris because of the conservatism of the Romanian art scene at the beginning of the century. The type of modernist effervescence that fermented in the avant-garde art circles in Paris, St. Petersburg, and Berlin, barely reached Romania. The changes that occurred in high art during the war must be evaluated against this backdrop of artistic conservatism.

New forms of popular culture had entered the mainstream of cultural life before 1914 even less than avant-garde modernist works: a small film industry had begun to develop, but it could not compare to production in Germany, Russia, or even its neighbor, Austro-Hungarian Transylvania. Film had become, however, one of the favorite pastimes of the populace, alongside circus performances and fairs. Cabaret and variety shows had not yet become as popular as they were at that time in Vienna, Munich, or Paris. The urban population patronized operetta and film. Urbanites recently transplanted from the countryside preferred the weekly neighborhood dances, replicating the village Sunday folk dances (hore).[7] However, the position of popular culture within the larger spectrum of the arts changed drastically during the war.

My emphasis on these different types of cultural production shifts with their changing significance from one period to the next in the narrative of the war. I have divided the 1914–1918 period into several phases: (a) the years of neutrality, August 1914 to August 1916; (b) the early phase of the war, 14 August–24 November 1916; (c) the German occupation in Wallachia, 24 November 1916–5 March 1918; (d) the retreat to Moldavia, 24 November 1916–5 March 1918; and (e) the resurgence of the Allied forces, 5 March–1 December 1918. My analysis will underline the main avenues for cultural life during each of these periods and the most prominent themes, focussing on the shifting relationship between high and popular culture from 1914 to 1918.

The years of neutrality, August 1914–August 1916

During the two years of neutrality, Romanian culture was driven by three important underlying themes: defining national ideals, identifying which allies presented the best guarantee for the fulfillment of these goals, and attempting to preserve a sense of normality in the hurricane that seemed to engulf the entire continent. High art occupied center stage in the debate over national ideals, while more popular forms of culture, from weekly journals to cartoons and variety shows, provided the bulk of the propaganda about alliances. The producers and consumers of high culture – drama, literature, music, and art – were more concerned with preserving a sense of normality in the midst of the growing bellicose excitement, while more popular forms of art began to incorporate some of the realities of the war into their entertainment material. They did not confront these realities head on, but rather took them as a given and either put a humorous spin on them, or portrayed the war's harsher aspects as a hardship placed by the haves on the shoulders of the have-nots – the consumers of popular culture. These forms of entertainment offered an escape from the sense of helplessness *vis-à-vis* the inevitable entry into the war. However, they did not ignore this impending event; they simply tried to make it more palatable.

Since the first decade of the twentieth century one of the most important avenues for constructing national ideals in the cultural realm and connecting them to a political agenda had been the Cultural League, an organization founded by intellectuals from both sides of the Carpathians, and whose spiritual father was historian Nicolae Iorga. This organization had provided a forum for nationalist-irredentist voices among the educated public and had funded various forms of national-ist cultural propaganda, from periodical publications such as *Neamul Românesc* (The Romanian Nation) to festivals of folk music and poetry and cultural evenings celebrating the writings of Romanian poets, play-wrights, and novelists from Transylvania. Starting in 1914, the Cultural League intensified its nationalist activities. It sponsored the defection from the Austro-Hungarian Empire of a number of important Roma-nian writers, among them Octavian Goga, Vasile Lucaci, and Ioan Slavici. All three men blended nationalist ambitions in their writing and went on to political careers. Goga in particular came to be revered during the war, both as a writer and as a political personality. By con-trast, Slavici became *persona non grata* after he expressed his support for the Central Powers. The League did much to sustain some of these writers financially, except for Slavici, and provide them with a market for their writing. However, some of its supporters felt betrayed by what they regarded as the cowardly stance of the League's leadership *vis-à-vis* the crown's decision to remain neutral. Some members resigned in protest over the unwillingness of the League to begin an all-out cam-paign for entry into the war on the side of the Entente powers.[8]

The League's leadership had come to see itself as the paragon of patriotism and the most powerful judge of true nationalist culture and activities. However, the disgruntled membership's opinion was far from unanimous on this issue. In other observers' opinion the League was too radical in nationalist rhetoric and aspirations. According to the Jewish newspaper *Infrățirea* (The Brotherhood), the League identified Romanian culture and identity only with the ethnic Romanians living in the kingdom, purposely excluding Jews from this community.[9]

In spite of the ambitions of its members and leadership, the League was far from embodying the nationalist aspirations of all Romanians, and offering the main cultural outlets for such feelings. In the summer and fall of 1914 virtually all newspapers and literary journals exploded in an avalanche of passionate nationalist rhetoric, not only in their political commentaries, but also through the types of poetry, short stories, and illustrations they published. From the most popular daily, *Universul* (The Universe), to the left-wing *Adevărul* (The Truth), the press became adorned with patriotic poems and editorials. More sophisticated literary journals, such as *Flacăra* (The Flame) and *Convorbiri Literare* (Literary Conversations), also offered their share of patriotic literature. Moreover, although newspapers published mostly pulp fiction, *feuilletons*, and syrupy poems, some of the same authors who contributed to literary journals began to write more prominently in these dailies – among them Gala Galaction, Victor Eftimiu, and Ioan Agârbiceanu. The presence of pieces by Transylvanian writers such as Agârbiceanu and Goga was especially powerful in intensifying irrendentist tendencies.

A wave of enthusiastic nationalism took over theater performances as well. A larger number of Romanian plays were chosen for the repertoire of the National Theater, which usually performed French, German, or English plays. The spectators seemed animated by the prospect of a war for Greater Romania especially after the performances of historical plays, such as *Apus de Soare* (Sunset) by Barbu Delavrancea, which depicted the life of the fifteenth-century Moldavian voivod, Stephen the Great. The public came to expect the singing of patriotic hymns at the end of these shows.[10] Even performances of fairy tale plays, such as Queen Marie's *Ilderim* and Mihai Sorbul's *Trandafirii Roşii* (The Red Roses), began to take on more nationalist connotations during this period.

During the early months of the war the nationalist literature spoke of war as a necessary process, the price to pay for achieving the grandiose dream of Greater Romania. (See Fig. 10.1) Many authors celebrated violent and rugged heroism as the highest virtue to emulate: "Awaken your victorious soldiers / The pride, the strength, our age-old pageantry / Let the Carpathian peaks shiver / From your triumphant assault."[11] However, while this poem tried to stir patriotic feelings, it also betrayed a sense of disappointment about the current state of preparedness among Romanians to fight a war: "You tremble abjectly and weakly / Before the ocean that is coming? / Where are you, children of Basarab / To wash away our nation's shame?"[12] Other writers concurred in questioning the patriotic élan of the average Romanian, emphasizing the need for leadership, for role models in this matter, starting with King Ferdinand,

10.1   "Towards the ideal," *Flacara*, October 1914

to stimulate the population's zeal: "A good Romanian? . . . Sire, forgive me / I do not wish such a misfortune / On this people that awaits silently, / Gazing towards the Throne, a ray of justice."[13] The author, and others with him, suggested that too many Romanians were satisfied with a passive patriotism and were driven by narrow financial interests in their decision to support the nationalist cause. Throughout the two years of neutrality, both elite literary journals and more popular publications used this type of propaganda to reinforce the noble aims of the

Romanians on entering the war and the need to sacrifice one's personal interests for the sake of the greater good.

This public wave of patriotism began to decrease over time among theater-goers, as audiences attended often expensive performances more as an escape from their concerns about the war than as a way of showing support for the conflict. At the same time, theater critics, writers, and performers began to publish more articles about the need to understand culture, especially high culture, as a vital form of instilling patriotic virtues: "Because theater tends to be free in expressing emotion, it can become a school for heroic virtues."[14] Manifestos on behalf of the theater betrayed two other worries. First, the state had not clarified what impact the country's entry into the war might have on government subventions for theater performances, this at a time when the revenues of most theaters depended heavily on a theater tax administered by the Ministry of Culture. Second, they wanted to appeal to an elite public which was becoming more interested in other forms of entertainment of lesser patriotic zeal, such as film and operetta. By identifying attendance of theater performances as a form of education and even as a patriotic duty, critics were attempting to entice more members of the educated elite toward the theater.

Two years of neutrality eroded some of the bellicose enthusiasm in the literary world as well. The poems, front page editorials, and cover illustrations that had depicted nationalist goals, the need to enter the war, and the heroism of the Romanian people began to thin out. More news and commentaries about the ravages of the war started to take over both newspapers and literary journals. By 1916, after watching on the sidelines and observing the horror of total war on the Western front for two years, the minstrels of Romanian patriotism were starting to lose some of their élan. War did not appear as worthwhile a price to pay as it had seemed in 1914. The drama of the war was becoming all-encompassing and beyond comprehension. In June 1916, right before Romania's entry into the war, one poet published these dark, disillusioned verses: "Black weapons on blooming meadows . . . / Tomorrow will turn to ashes . . . / Fortresses tomorrow will be a bloody path . . . / There is blood, and fire, and budding / Life pushed into death."[15]

Even during the initial outpouring of nationalist propaganda some important differences became obvious among writers. Some were disappointed in Romania's neutrality and spoke with distrust about the government's ability to lead the country towards greater irredentist aspirations. Others were more moderate in their patriotism, satisfied with the prudent decision of the Brătianu government. Still others believed an alliance with the Central Powers guaranteed the best chance for Romania's interest in the future, although, or perhaps because the Hungarian irredentists would be on the same side as the Romanians. According to this view, it would be easier to negotiate a settlement favorable to the Romanian interests in Transylvania and Bukovina if the Romanians fought on the same side as their Austro-Hungarian rivals. During the years of neutrality proponents of all these views went to great pains to describe the virtues and vices of all of the belligerent countries. The cultural production that focussed on the war discussed the qualities of the French, the Germans, the Russians, and the Austro-Hungarians more than those of the Romanians. The literature, whether popular or high, the variety shows and graphic art, all helped construct images of the various enemies and allies.

Debates over who Romania's "natural" allies were took place very prominently in a few literary journals.[16] *Viaţa Românească* (Romanian Life), led by the Bessarabian *émigré* Constantin Stere, argued consistently on behalf of an alliance with the Central Powers. The articles published here ranged from detailed discussions of Germany's aims in the war to discussions of German art and literature to illustrate that country's superior level of civilization. One such article supported Germany's participation in the war as a form of "defending their culture" against the "crime, egotism and decadence" that dominated Western Europe.[17] Literary reviews and cultural commentaries in general focussed almost exclusively on the music, philosophy, poetry, and theater produced in Germany since the eighteenth century, as a reminder to readers of the enlightened qualities of the German people, whom they identified with the achievements of Goethe, Schiller, and Beethoven.

At the same time, *Viaţa Românească* published a series of articles criticizing the Entente powers as barbarous.[18] This was not a direct critique of the French or English. After all, much of the Romanian population harbored a deep sympathy for the French, and Marie, the Romanian queen, very popular both in elite circles and among the populace at large, was the granddaughter of Queen Victoria. Rather, Stere and his collaborators were petrified about the prospect of fighting on the same side as Russian Empire.[19] Stere's own experiences in Russian-annexed Bessarabia had shaped his deep distrust of the Russians. Other Romanian writers, such as Gala Galaction, also saw their choice in terms of being at the mercy of the Germans or the Russians, both of which were much closer to the Romanian borders than the French or the English. Their perception that the Germans possessed a level of civilization and culture superior to the Russians persuaded these writers that the Central Powers would protect Romania's interest more than the Entente would. Cultural arguments had high currency in these political debates.

Most other literary journals were pro-Entente, however. From *Flacăra* to *Rampa* (The Stage) writers and artists loudly voiced their Francophile feelings. Their depictions of French culture and civilization were a mirror image of *Viaţa Românească*'s portrayal of Germany. As the war progressed, these journals began a litany of all the cultural artifacts destroyed by the Germans in Belgium and later in France. They published photographs of prominent architectural monuments taken before and after the German attacks, already a powerful commentary on the war, accusing the Central Powers of barbarism against civilization and culture.[20] Francophile feelings became fused with anti-German ones. Articles describing the history and significance of these monuments often accompanied the photographs. By equating the moral character of the two opposing forces with their treatment of each other's cultural patrimony, these authors reinforced the central role of art in defining the moral fiber, the integrity of a nation.

By contrast, few of these discussions about German destruction in the war showed pictures of or described the human carnage. Even when doing so they used drawings rather than photographs, unlike the illustrations of the cathedrals that had been destroyed. These drawings filtered down the immediate violence of the war with two significant results: on the one hand, they made it harder to perceive the senselessness of the killing (e.g., unidentifiable bodies stacked on top of each other); on the other hand, the villains could be identified more clearly as the Germans.[21]

Some of the pro-Entente literati were less interested in vilifying all that was German than in identifying the war itself as the agent of violence. Eugen Lovinescu was one of the few balanced thinkers during this period, locating his sympathies clearly in the Entente camp, but refraining from identifying the actions of the Germans during the war with the character of that entire nation or with their culture. Lovinescu was weary of the nationalist fanfare which was growing to a deafening level, obscuring the hardships of the war and the equally violent behavior of all parties in this war.[22] Other producers of culture concurred. Composer and conductor George Enescu continued to play a repertoire of classical music that crossed wartime boundaries. When confronted by a journalist about including the Hungarian Rákoczy March in his performance of Hector Berlioz' *Damnation of Faust*, Enescu responded that "from now on our chauvinists must think and listen silently . . . I cannot massacre Berlioz simply because of these events."[23]

Artifacts in the realm of popular culture, be they cartoons, humorous literature, or variety shows, were less subtle in their depictions of the enemy and the potential allies. Two of the most popular variety shows in the summer of 1914 were *Ultima Oră* (The Last Hour) and *Intrăm Sau Nu Intrăm?* . . . (Are We Entering or Not? . . .), both focussing much of their material on the international developments during the previous few months and on Romania's stakes in the war.[24] The themes most prevalent among these forms of popular culture were Romania's tempting location and resources for all of the belligerents and the violent, barbarous nature of the Central Powers, with special emphasis on the Germans. Many cartoons and comedy skits in variety shows depicted Romania as a prize over which the Great Powers were fighting with greed. One popular image was that of Romania as an attractive young woman, courted persistently by four older men in military uniforms – France, Russia, Austria-Hungary, and Germany.[25] This image pitted the innocence of Romania's demeanor against the almost obscene poses of these representations of the Great Powers' desires. Such depictions showed great faith in Romania's strength and pride in its qualities, while betraying a sense of distrust toward the Great Powers, somehow ready to rob this country of its virtue. This portrayal was designed to reinforce popular xenophobia and feelings of superiority.

If these images showed unease about the aims of all the Great Powers, they overwhelmingly sided with the Entente powers in the conflict. The Central Powers were depicted as natural enemies and increasingly barbarous as the war developed. The Kaiser appeared alternatively as a dirty old man or as a greedy, grotesque caricature, eager to take over the entire world and devour it with his claws.[26] The Austrians appeared most often weak, decrepit – the very image of the aging Emperor Franz Joseph. The Hungarians, however, received the worst press, particularly because of the long-standing animosity between Romanians and Hungarians. (See Fig. 10.2) In many of these depictions Hungarians appeared as criminal rapists of Romania.

The violence of these images of the enemy grew over time, while representations of the potential allies, France in particular, became more positive, more committed as time passed. France was depicted more clearly as Romania's natural ally, its protector against the barbarism of the Central Powers, and the only Great Power which did not have any direct vested interests in this country's future.[27] The unwritten implication in these descriptions was that the Russians were not to be trusted, but that the French could be counted on to protect Romania's integrity during and especially after the war.

CONCESII MAGHIARE

10.2 *Hungarian concessions*, cartoon published in the literary journal *Flacara*, 1914

If cultural life became an avenue for discussing Romania's national goals, its potential allies and enemies, most consumers of culture still looked towards theater, music, art, and literature as a way to escape the vicissitudes of daily life. This desire to preserve a sense of normality in the whirlwind of the war characterized works and performances of high art in particular. As much as theater companies tried to switch to Romanian patriotic plays after August 1914, audiences seemed more interested in romantic plays and comedies. One theater critic noted this desire in a sarcastic poem: "The public wants to rejoice / Wants operetta . . . as in the park / One moment to forget the carnage / And to imagine war / As a simple bad dream."[28] Theater journals published far more news on the fashionable theater world – the affairs, the trips, the lamentations of Romanian actors and actresses – than articles dealing with the war. One journal in particular, *Gazeta Ilustrată* (The Illustrated Gazette), focussed almost exclusively on the whereabouts of Romanian high society. The war seemed a distant, abstract event in the pages of this glossy and richly illustrated journal, which displayed prominently photos of the latest fashions, balls, and horse races. Similarly, the important art exhibitions during this period displayed no works that dealt with the war, or even social and political subjects. They were overwhelmingly personal in nature – still-lifes, portraits, landscapes. The repertoire of the symphonic music concerts at the Athenaeum, the favorite hall for such performances, frequently crossed the wartime frontiers. Most of the reviews made no reference to the possible political connotations of the musical selections, an indication that such issues did not interest the public at these performances.

The consumers of popular culture were similarly interested in escaping the realities of the war, although perhaps not as preoccupied as the audiences of high culture in preserving an image of undisturbed, peaceful normality. Cinema-going was a favourite pastime in Bucharest, where most movie theaters in Romania were located.[29] One of the biggest hits in the summer of 1914 was an imported film, *Excelsior*, an extravagant metaphor of the relationship between progress and war. The movie had elaborate sets that showed the forces of light, of beauty, of the civilized world pitted against the misfortunes of war, a melodramatic story of good versus evil – enlightening peaceful progress through civilization versus the dark, destructive forces of war. Audiences rushed to see the special effects "displayed lavishly for the first time," and especially the brief cameo by a famous Romanian pilot, Aurel Vlaicu.[30] These features were the main attraction rather than any connection to the war, but the movie still engaged that issue, if only indirectly. Other popular movies such as *The Gold Conqueror*, *The Black Gang*, or *The Last Tango* had no connection with the contemporary international situation.

None the less, one particular feature of these performances tied them more closely to the events of the war. Theater owners were beginning to introduce comedy stand-up routines as the opening act of movie showings. Most of the humor presented in these performances was derived from the daily news and touched on the war on a regular basis. This new form of performance proved increasingly popular, for movie advertisements began to feature prominently acts such as "Opening Act *Coana Manda* by Iulian."[31] Thus, although popular culture performances provided an escape from daily hardships, they did not marginalize the reality of the war, but rather tried to mediate its horrors through the lens of comedy. They were less intent upon constructing an image of normality than works of high culture in all the arts, from painting to theater.

The early months of the war (14 August–
24 November 1916)

Any desire to escape the reality of the war became futile after 14 August 1916, when Romania declared war on the Central Powers. Mobilization was rapid and it left civilian life, its cultural aspects included, in a frantic and powerless state. Schools, theaters, concert halls, night clubs closed within weeks of entry into the war. Most of the personnel employed in these places were mobilized and were not replaced. Moreover, the revenues on which some of these institutions had come to depend (the National Theater and the orchestra of the Ministry of Instruction in particular) were transferred to the war budget. Cultural life was especially affected by the German bomb attacks on Romanian territory via zeppelins, which first struck at night but increasingly made their "deliveries" during the daytime as well. These raids interrupted most public civilian life and made attendance at any kind of performances life-threatening.

Three important features came to dominate the cultural features in the handful of periodicals that survived during this period. First and foremost, they stood as a witness to the lack of preparedness of the Romanians for the war, in spite of the two years spent watching the war on the sidelines. The army had no organized news or propaganda service. Instead, communication between the front and the civilian population took place exclusively through occasional military communiqués from the trenches. The army had not contemplated the issue of the troops' morale either, and no propaganda cultural services were set up to deal with this issue. In fact, some writers repeatedly noted with great frustration the urgent need to cater to the intellectual and emotional needs of the soldiers in addition to the strict military aspects of life in the trenches.[32] A corollary of this criticism was the complaints about censorship. The state had begun to interfere with the freedom of the written word and of any public gatherings or performances. Some writers argued that these actions by the state were hindering efforts to improve the morale of the civilians, and especially of the soldiers.[33]

Finally, almost all publications and performances, whether pertaining to high or popular culture, turned from negative critiques to vicious attacks against the Germans. This attitude intensified especially after the zeppelin attacks began. As the daytime bombings intensified, cartoons depicted the Germans as baby killers. These representations went to the point of identifying the Germans as inhuman beasts, whose cruelty was only surpassed by their deviousness. It came as no surprise that most of the population of Bucharest started to panic and pack up as soon as news of a German invasion came through in November. By 23 November only a fraction of the civilian population and a handful of officials were left to confront the advancing armies of the Central Powers, while the king, the government, and the bulk of the administrative officials, had retreated to Moldavia, with the interim capital in Iaşi.

The German occupation (24 November 1916– 5 March 1918)

Romanian historians predominantly depict the German occupation as a cruel and self-indulgent presence which seized all of the material resources of the Romanian population in order to fund a cosmopolitan artistic scene and night life. One oft-cited anecdote is that when German officers wanted to get away from the horrors of fighting on the Western front, they would try to get transferred to the Romanian front, rather than ask for leave to travel home for a short time. Bucharest had become their spa. Conversely, Romanian historians depict the occupied population as helpless victims of the cruel occupation and of the forced separation from their loved ones, who had gone into exile in Moldavia. On closer examination, opinions are split on the question of whether those who stayed behind and became engaged in the administrative and cultural life under the German occupation were martyrs or traitors. A heated debate ensued after the war on whether writers such as Liviu Rebreanu, Tudor Arghezi, or Gala Galaction should be imprisoned for having worked for publications subsidized by the German occupation. These writers and other artists and intellectuals defended their activities as necessary to keep alive Romanian culture and its artistic patrimony throughout the occupation period, pointing out the difficulty of publishing anything at all critical of the Germans, because of the strict censorship. They defended their actions by asserting that they did what they had to in order to at least publish some news in Romanian and keep alive a consciousness of Romanian language and culture.

The German occupation did, indeed, aim to drastically change cultural life for the benefit of the Central Powers' troops. A few weeks after Bucharest was occupied the building of the National Theater was requisitioned for use by a German-language troupe. Subsequently, the cafés, luxurious restaurants, cabarets and other night clubs were also claimed for the officers of the Central Powers, and took on German names. However, the occupants had their own hierarchy. The German and Austrian officers had access to the most luxurious spots, where the only language used was German and the entertainment was provided by German, Austrian, Romanian, and sometimes Jewish performers, while the Bulgarian and Turkish officers had to contend for the use of second-rate restaurants and taverns, entertained by local Gypsy bands. Overall, however, for the occupying troops night life was inexpensive and offered a great deal of variety, from cabaret shows to brothels.

Other forms of "requisitioning" offended the Romanian public even more. In May 1917 the German authorities decided to take the bells from all the churches in Bucharest in order to obtain bronze for the manufacture of ammunition.[34] For the sake of expediency this operation was done in broad daylight, by breaking all the bells in full view instead of lowering them intact and carrying them away to be melted. The cultural significance of this action was tremendous for all inhabitants of the capital, who perceived the German action as an expression of brutal, intentional disregard for all that was sacred and closest to Romanian spirituality – the Orthodox Church.

Evicted from their theaters, the Romanian-language ensembles had to seek other locations for their shows or start performing in German for the occupiers. A few alternative Romanian-language theaters did open up in the spring of 1917, with performances that had to end early because of the curfew, but which were still well attended, in spite of economic hardships. Their repertoire was heavily censored and could very rarely include plays or operettas by French, Italian, Russian, or English authors.[35] However, the German censors were not averse to performances of Romanian plays, so long as they did not have a political/historical character or tinges of Germanophobia in them. The occupation authorities seemed eager to lift the morale of the civilian population through such small tokens. Therefore, although debilitated, Romanian culture was able to survive under the Germans, not so much in spite of the occupation, but rather because of the pragmatic outlook of the German administration.

For the audiences eager to attend performances of high theatrical quality, the German groups that performed at the National Theater offered a blend of plays by classical German authors such as Schiller or Goethe and more modern playwrights such as the Norwegian, Ibsen. This theater also hosted a number of troupes from Germany and Austria throughout the period of the occupation. The Theater an der Wien visited Bucharest on a tour showcasing famous Austrian operettas, followed by the Gastspiele der Darmstadter Hofoper. The Athenaeum hosted many classical music concerts, especially by German and Austrian chamber groups, as well as a number of exhibits of Romanian and German art collections from the occupied territory. These venues of high culture catered exclusively to the tastes and interests of the occupation's elite officer corps, although they were not closed to the Romanian public.

Some Romanians did attend these performances. However, they were few and far between, for political as well as economic reasons.

The German administration paid attention to the reading interests of its officer corps as well. Throughout the occupation it published a lavishly illustrated weekly magazine, *Rumänien in Wort und Bild* (Romania in Words and Images). Although clearly a propaganda tool subsidized by the German authorities, this magazine sought to educate its audience about Romanian culture, history, geography, and economic resources in a positive light. One could read about some light topics and keep up on the tours of the Darmstadt Hofoper, but such items made up less than 10 percent of the material. Most of the magazine was taken up with illustrations and descriptions meant to familiarize the German officers with the particularities of the people they were occupying.

Popular culture offered a greater opportunity for the Romanian population to escape the dreadful reality of the occupation. In general, while the venues for high culture became more restricted, the diversity of offerings among various forms of popular culture increased. One German and three Romanian dramatic companies operated during this period. By contrast, three cabarets, one operetta, and fifteen movie theaters functioned in Bucharest throughout the year, with a few additional variety gardens during the summer months. The Romanian dramatic companies occasionally offered variety shows as well.[36] Although the cabarets were attended exclusively by German officers and their guests, the performers were often Romanians. Some of them were ex-circus performers, while others were musicians and actors in search of a lucrative contract. While this form of entertainment had been almost absent from Romanian night life before 1916, the presence of the demanding German audiences and of some experienced traveling Austrian and German cabaret artists provided the ground for developing a few thriving clubs that survived and grew after the war, such as the Trocadero.

Movies remained the most prevalent form of popular entertainment for the Romanians. During the German occupation all public gatherings and performances were forbidden without prior approval from the censorship office, even when they involved only a small band of Gypsy musicians at a local tavern. Therefore, most people either read at home or, if they wanted to socialize, went to the cinema. Movies had become heavily censored as well. Many of the shows started with film clips from the Western front, showing the victories of the German troops. However, most movies were either comedies, thrillers, or melodramas unconnected to the war. One could choose from titles such as *The*

Mysterious Telephone or *The Tragedy from the Falcon Villa*. Furthermore, comedians such as Iulian continued to perform stand-up opening acts before movie showings. Their material could no longer make reference to the war because of the German censors, but they still tried to use material from the current events in Bucharest, focussing on the troubles and shortcomings of various categories of civilians, such as enterprising young women or doctors turned small owners of convenience stores.

These types of subjects came to dominate variety shows as well. The *nouveaux riches* of the war were a favorite target, although both the authors and the public seemed to enjoy poking fun at the women who had maintained a high social profile in the company of the Germans. Not only were such stories spiced up with details that delighted the male audiences, but these were also both vulnerable and safe targets. These "easy" women could not defend themselves and the Germans were not singled out as their seducers.

Exile in Moldavia (24 November 1916–5 March 1918)

Cultural life in the unoccupied territories developed in an *ad hoc*, highly improvised fashion, in response to the inadequacies and priorities of the war. By contrast with the occupied territories, where the distance between high and popular culture became greater, mirroring in many ways the gap between the occupiers and the occupied, cultural artifacts and performances in Moldavia saw an increasing blend of elite and popular forms of art. Although initially this trend brought together audiences of very different cultural and social backgrounds, by March 1918 the producers of high culture attempted a certain reinstitutionalization of performances that catered exclusively to the tastes and expectations of the elite. To their surprise, however, some of these audiences had come to enjoy variety shows and operettas more than classical theater and operas.

During the first few weeks of the retreat, not only cultural institutions, but newspapers and other periodicals, as well, ceased to function. The entire population mobilized to accommodate the large influx of refugees into Moldavia, and especially the needs of the army. Soon, however, artists and intellectuals persuaded the military and civilian authorities about the importance of entertainment for the morale of the civilians and especially the soldiers. As a result, the army agreed to finance the publication of *România*, the only newspaper that circulated both at the front and at home, with a daily run of at least 15,000 copies. This newspaper became very influential in cultural life because it served both soldiers and civilians, was published with overt propaganda goals, and was written exclusively by a staff of prominent writers. The editor-in-chief was Mihail Sadoveanu, a well-known prose writer, with the help of Corneliu Moldovan, a playwright, and the famous poet Octavian Goga. Other prominent writers, such as Delavrancea and Iorga, also published here often. As a result, the most popular tool for information came into the hands of nationalist intellectuals whose concept of writing was closer to the notion of inspiring nationalist idealism and constructing role models for patriotism than to professional journalism.

The most prominent themes in this publication were all tied to the war. One of the favorite topics was the aggressive vilification of the Germans, along with their cultural patrimony. This functioned as a form of morale building, to justify the flight from Wallachia as a way of preparing a strong counter-attack against the Central Powers. Conversely, veiled attacks against the Russians ceased and the articles describing the long-standing cultural and emotional ties between the Romanians and the French increased.

The most visible issue in *România* and other forums of cultural life, such as theater and music concerts, was the need for concerted mobilization of all individuals – civilians and soldiers, men and women, businessmen and teachers – behind the nationalist ideals that could be fulfilled only through the current war. In the pages of this publication fictional reportage of heroic acts in the trenches alternated with normative descriptions of the ideal role of the Romanian mother in raising true patriots. These representations reflected more the desire to create a normative national ideal, than the real unity of all Romanians behind such a notion. For instance, *România* repeatedly advertised cultural events that were fund-raisers for the war effort, especially for the wounded and the prisoners of war. These advertisements most often mentioned the donations made by prominent figures – the queen, Prime Minister Brătianu, George Enescu – in order to encourage generous contributions by other members of high society. The tone of these announcements ranged from hopeful to imploring, betraying the frustrations of the fund-raisers in actually mobilizing existing financial resources behind the war effort. Indeed, most of the events in the realm of high culture that took place in Iaşi and the other main towns in Moldavia during this period were somehow tied to fund-raising efforts. To their credit, most actors, musicians, and other artists involved in the performing arts worked very hard to organize theater, opera, operetta, symphonic and musical review performances which mostly benefited the war effort. By contrast, affluent Romanians needed to be entertained, and intimidated by the generosity of other famous names into showing their patriotism.

The transient conditions under which most of these performances operated made any long-term repertoire impossible to prepare. In addition, performers were liable for mobilization at any moment, and props as well as buildings could also be requisitioned without warning. As a result, the most prevalent form of performance that developed was the "smorgasbord" show: the first part could be one act from a Romanian historical drama, such as Delavrancea's *Apus de Soare*, followed after the intermission by a musical recital by George Enescu with a chamber music group, or an operatic singer, such as Jean Athanasiu, accompanied on the piano. Such shows were a great success, since they brought together a large number of famous names from various areas of Romanian cultural life in the span of less than three hours.

These performances were not without their critics, however. The tension between the refugees and the local population was bound to mount as the war continued, and it was reflected in cultural life as well. The actors and musicians from Bucharest came to dominate these performances very quickly. Some artists from Iaşi found themselves relegated to secondary roles and perceived as unsophisticated provincials by their very guests. In addition, refugee actors and musicians from other cities such as Craiova were altogether unable to perform their craft and found themselves in dire straits.[37] With fewer resources for cultural productions and smaller audiences for paid performances, these artists had to find other forms of entertainment to sustain themselves, from musical reviews to performances in hospitals and on the front.

Literary life produced few works by comparison with the performing arts. A few volumes of poetry by Nicolae Iorga, Vasile Voiculescu, and a few other young writers appeared during this period. Sadoveanu published a collection of short stories on the war, while a few playwrights, most prominently Mihail Sorbul and Corneliu Moldovan, attempted to produce a new form of theater – war drama. Sorbul's *Dezertorul* (The Deserter) focussed on the plight of a Romanian family under the German occupation. The play depicted the increasingly brutal attitude of a German officer toward a family with which he had been friends before the war. The play premiered with some success in the spring of 1918, as its melodramatic characters, the tragic outcome, and the depiction of the enemy entertained even the staunchest nationalists. A less successful attempt to entertain and represent the realities of the war came from Corneliu Moldovan. His drama *Pe aici nu se trece!* (No One Passes Through!) attempted to represent life on the front and the common, anonymous heroism of the average soldier during the famous battle of Mărăşeşti. The language and action were too schematic and had insufficient entertainment value for critics and public alike. Still, at the suggestion of Sadoveanu, the interim director of the National Theater, a short version of this play was incorporated into propaganda shows on the front and in hospitals.

It was in the realm of popular entertainment that the war brought together high and popular culture more successfully. On the one hand, reviews became the favorite form of entertainment among the common folk and members of high society alike. Many people sought release and escape from the hardships of the war through laughter. On the other hand, artists themselves became less concerned about their own status as legitimate versus popular performers. Some were simply concerned with being able to make a living, while others began to see their role less in relation to the purity of their craft and more in relation to the healing and educational value of their performances. One of the most prominent of such performers was George Enescu. Since the beginning of the war he had refused to abide by narrow nationalist political considerations in making his repertoire choices. During exile in Iaşi, Enescu performed extensively, organizing many very successful cultural fundraisers for the elite public with the same gusto that he offered to play for the wounded and to perform at the front for the troops. He was one of the main initiators of performances that combined various forms of entertainment which crossed the boundaries between high and low culture, and he took these shows to the soldiers in the trenches. His very presence at these events legitimated them as "true" cultural manifestations, rather than pseudo-patriotic performances, as many other review shows were labeled at that time by literary critics.[38]

Although Enescu had become a celebrity among all Romanians on his own merits, his performances in hospitals and at the front became famous because of his association with the popular comedian Constantin Tănase. Tănase had already gained notoriety with his stand-up routines in variety shows and had become a true hero with the soldiers because he volunteered to fight at a time when most other artists preferred to stay on the home front. During the performances they put together for the soldiers in the trenches or hospitals, the two often alternated music with comedy stand-up routines. Sometimes Tănase would even sing some of his numbers accompanied by the virtuoso violinist. Enescu's partnership with Tănase was based on the genuine respect each performer had for the other's talent, and produced a large number of electrifying performances that remained prominent in the mind of some soldiers many years after the end of the war.[39]

This relationship illustrates very well a turning point in Romanian culture: high and popular culture could blend successfully. The artists themselves believed in the quality of these productionss, and the audiences found them very appealing as well. Tănase's efforts at legitimizing his form of performance as a cultural artifact of high quality bore fruit especially after the war, when he opened, with great success, his own variety show theater. However, the foundations of his popularity were laid during his wartime performances on the home front and among the troops.[40]

Not all art critics and producers of elite culture felt positive about these changes. In order to supplement its earnings, the National Theater decided periodically to rent out its building to a film distributor. Some critics loudly voiced their disagreement with this pragmatic policy. Since they identified this form of entertainment with a moral epidemic, using the building of the National Theater to show movies seemed like a sacrilege.[41]

By the fall of 1917 the unanimity in the voices being heard on stage, in print, and on canvas was cracking. Even with all the censorship imposed to control the morale of the civilians and soldiers, the problems at the front with the Central Powers, in Russia, and among the Romanian civilian population could not be contained any longer even in the censored cultural sphere. A series of new publications appeared, critiquing directly *România* and the other ultra-nationalist publications, such as *Drum Drept* (Straight Path). A group of younger writers and journalists, who had served on the front and were fed up with the current depiction of the war experience and internal situation, began to publish the weekly *Deşteptarea* (The Awakening), which later appeared as *Chemarea* (The Call). The ideological bent of this publication was clearly leftist, while its articles on cultural issues showed a great deal of difference vis-à-vis *România*'s contributors in tastes and approach to patriotic values alike. For instance, in December 1917 *Chemarea* published a devastating review of a volume of poetry by Nicolae Iorga. The unnamed author accused Iorga of cheap, superficial patriotism. According to the reviewer, these verses were "trench songs . . . which contain nothing moving beyond the real situation in which they were written [i.e., in the comfort of Iorga's home]." He went on to comment that "Mr. Iorga's role appears immoral and cynical."[42] The man who had been for a good part of the war "the voice of the nation" was coming under heavy criticism.

This was not the only voice that commented negatively on the facade of united patriotism of the "official" nationalist writers and painters. In January 1918 the Supreme Command of the Romanian army helped organize a collective exhibition of mobilized artists on themes related to the war. Some pieces attempted to depict the heroism of the common soldier rising above the suffering of the war, to the delight of Iorga, whose notion of artistic creativity was closely intertwined with his nationalist feelings. However, to his disappointment, most artists in this exhibit were "too modernist," too much interested in representing the emotions of the soldiers in a more abstract, analytical manner.[43]

A subsequent art exhibit by B'Arg (Ion Bărbulescu), a promising young painter and cartoonist, showed other current preoccupations that veered away from the normative patriotism envisioned by Iorga and Sadoveanu. His work focussed on social themes – the devastation wrought by the war in the lives of the soldiers and the families they left behind and the dehumanizing impact of captivity on the prisoners of war. Along with B'Arg, a number of other members of the group Tinerimea Artistică (The Artistic Youth) also exhibited works highly critical of the war. Among them were Viorel Lascar and Nicolae Tonitza, who embraced an expressionist technique to depict the dehumanizing impact of the war on the peasant soldiers.[44]

Likewise, variety shows began to poke fun not only at the enemy without, but also at the enemy within, from the *nouveaux riches* to the "inflation of generals" that had been plaguing the country since the end of 1917. Theater critics and nationalist writers alike fretted about the effects of such performances on the morale of the civilians, but could do little to control this phenomenon, since these reviews were very popular. Such concerns became even greater after the humiliating peace of Buftea on 5 March 1918.

From humiliation to victory (5 March– 1 December 1918)

With the Russian Revolution next door and no guarantee for additional help by the French allies, the Romanian leadership signed a preliminary peace with the Central Powers on 5 March 1918. The peace was humiliating to the Romanian army and devastating for the prestige of the kingdom, since it *de facto* leased out for an extended period of time all economic resources in Dobrodgea (Dobrudja) to the Central Powers. The population wavered between resentment on account of this defeat and a sense of release and even joy at the thought of seeing some family members for the first time in two years.

Cultural institutions such as theater companies, periodical publications, and orchestras began their own process of demobilization. Many refugees wanted to return swiftly to their homes, leaving behind any contracts for further performances or publications in Iași. The news-paper *România* ceased publication, since its foremost *raison d'être* had been to inform and educate the mobilized soldiers. Some publications continued to appear, but were clearly in a period of redefinition, espe-cially those that had appeared in Bucharest during the German occupa-tion. *Rampa*, a weekly theater publication, invited new writers to submit independent articles for publication. Corneliu Moldovan, one of the main contributors to Sadoveanu's *România*, began to write for this pub-lication, lending new legitimacy to a periodical that had come under attack in Iași for collaborating with the German occupation.[45]

By the summer of 1918 a series of cultural events signaled the attempt to restore normality. Enescu returned to Bucharest at the beginning to July to give a series of concerts benefiting the Red Cross. Although still banished from their regular performance halls by the German authorities, the National Theater and a few other pre-war Romanian companies began a regular season in the fall. High society was thrilled to attend performances of such "elevated" artistic quality. At the same time, musical reviews were seeing full houses throughout the summer. Censorship had become more lax since the peace, and performers and public alike enjoyed the new, if limited freedom to criticize the internal situation. However, some of the more daring vari-ety acts, especially by comedians returning from exile in Iași, crossed the line still held up by the censors. Tănase, for instance, was forced to leave the stage and leave for Iași because of a veiled attack against the Germans in one of his stand-up routines.[46]

In October, when news about the German defeats on the Western front began to come through, a new wave of excited aggressive patriot-ism began to sweep through both literary publications and perform-ances. By 1 December, when the remobilized Romanian armed forces marched through Bucharest, the entire cultural life was dominated by one voice – that of enthusiasm for the nationalist ideal of unification with the Romanian-inhabited provinces of the Austro-Hungarian Empire. Only after the dust from these celebrations settled, did the significant differences that had developed during the war resurface. Cultural life during and after the war showed that between 1914 and 1918 the discourse over national identity had been raised to a new level of intensity in both politics and the arts, but had not become unified, as some nationalists had hoped. In fact, the ideals and tastes of the Roma-nian public had become more diversified during this period. Toward the end of the war, some producers and critics of high art sought to regain greater control over the identification of "authentic" culture with certain forms of nationalism. However, the public had become less interested in these norms than in the new forms of entertainment that took off during the war, especially variety shows. The distance between high and low, "serious" and "pseudo"-culture was being renegotiated more openly by writers, actors, artists, and their audiences.

Conclusion

The Great War did not produce the Great Romanian novel or bring into the limelight a new artistic movement. The years of neutrality and the following two years of fighting, occupation, defeat, and remobilization kept cultural life in a state of flux. In this regard, art became less of a faithful reflection of the general situation in the occupied and free territories than a tool for mobilizing civilians and soldiers alike, as well as a means to allow some release from the daily stress of warfare. Because of this function, during these four years the performing arts excelled more than writing, painting, or sculpture. Most literary historians identify this period as the age preceding the rise of the authentic Romanian novel. Similarly, they pass quickly over the poetry and short prose published during the war as a marginal phase in the career of prominent writers such as Mihail Sadoveanu or Vasile Voiculescu.[47] Yet it was because of the very saturation of literature and art with depictions of heroism and sacrifice in an overbearing nationalist language that the currency of realist forms of expression decreased after 1918. Following in the footsteps of Tristan Tzara, the post-war generation became more interested in abstract and shocking forms of expression, borrowing some of their language from popular culture – cabarets, movies, or variety shows. Furthermore, the vicissitudes of war and the very tastes of the public created the opportunities for the tremendous growth of several types of popular culture. Such forms of entertainment, from cabaret to variety shows and comedy stand-up performances at the cinema had been few and far between before the war. Their growth in popularity during the war laid the foundations for the golden age of the Romanian review theater, which flourished during the interwar period.

Occupation, propaganda and the
idea of Belgium

Sophie de Schaepdrijver

Invasion

At nine o'clock on the morning of 4 August 1914, the neutral kingdom
of Belgium was invaded by the armies of the German Empire. Twenty-
six hours earlier, the Berlin ultimatum demanding unimpeded passage
through Belgium had been rejected by the Belgian government. Germany and Belgium were consequently at war. Within days, the armies
clashed at the fortresses of Liège; the town suffered the first aerial
bombing in history; and, as the German armies advanced, the first
mass executions of civilians followed, blurring that neat distinction between combatants and civilians that the Hague agreements of 1899 and
1907 had so confidently decreed in a quest to align future warfare with
nineteenth-century notions of civilization and progress. "A strange war,"
one of the bewildered survivors of the Dinant massacre was quoted as
saying, "in which the soldiers are less exposed than the children, the old
folks, and the sick who are left at home!"[1]

As it turned out, the brunt of "exposure" during the Great War was
still very much borne by the soldiers. Yet civilians were drawn inexorably into the war experience. The civilians of the belligerent states "lived
in the war" (as Marcel Proust said, likening it to the way "people used
to live in God").[2] And they were constantly exposed to the formidable
force of war propaganda, which itself blurred the combatant–civilian
distinction, in that it required all without exception to take sides.

The invasion of Belgium had overnight become *the* burning international question, pointing so unwaveringly as it did to the role of
Germany in the European conflict.[3] A judgment on the Belgian question was automatically a judgment on Germany. Justifications of the
invasion implicitly endorsed the view of Germany's conduct of the war
as self-defense; condemnations of it contained assumptions of Germany's war guilt. A phalanx of academics and journalists in Germany
began arguing that the neutrality of the invaded kingdom was merely
a thin cover for Belgium's pre-war subservience to French and British

interests; British propagandists, meanwhile, used to the hilt the notion of Britain's defense of a rightful international agreement that Berlin had so cavalierly tossed away as a "scrap of paper." Naturally, judgments on the invasion rose to shriller pitches as word of its excesses spread. The luridness of Entente atrocity propaganda, in which authentic accounts of mass executions were drowned in false exaggerations about toddlers with hacked-off hands and nuns impaled on bayonets, found a German counterpart in grisly descriptions of Belgian *francs-tireurs* (armed civilian snipers) treacherously attacking the German troops, of Belgian children driving rusty nails into the skulls of sleeping soldiers, priests cutting off the fingers of the wounded to retrieve their rings, and so on.

In the midst of all of this, the Belgian government-in-exile – unsure of its future, mistrustful of and mistrusted by its Franco-British guarantors, clinging to its right to steer an autonomous course, and desperately strapped for cash – raised its own voice, especially for the benefit of the non-belligerent neutral states.[4] Although some of it was characterized by the same type of *Boche*-bashing found in the Entente discourse, much of the propaganda of neutral Belgium formed a genuine "third party" in the discussion. Away from the hyperbole of atrocity propaganda, and against the formidably entrenched German channels of opinion, a few Belgian scholars produced analyses of remarkable levelheadedness and solidity.[5] The Belgian propaganda effort was described by one of its officials as preferring "the normal means of intellectual persuasion (that is to say, historical and legal argument) to the mechanical methods [and] the formulae of advertising, and the tricks of political propaganda."[6] Yet, for all that, this being the age of total war, the Belgian question was being fought out internationally with exactly those "tricks of political propaganda," and this largely without consulting the Belgians themselves.

Before long, the theater of the paper war between the Entente and Germany shifted from the invasion of Belgium to the very existence, the *significance*, of Belgium. "Belgium" became shorthand for the moral issues of the war. On the Entente side, and more particularly in Britain, the small state was elevated to the status of living embodiment of the right-against-might values that the West was ostensibly fighting for. Around Christmas of 1914, for example, a lavishly illustrated "Tribute to the Belgian People from Representative Men and Women Throughout the World," assembled statements from the likes of Sarah Bernhardt, Edith Wharton, Ignacy Paderewsky, and Claude Debussy (who contributed a *Berceuse héroïque* incorporating strains of the *Brabançonne*, the Belgian national hymn), all equally dithyrambic on what had by now become "Brave Little Belgium." Joseph Hertz, chief rabbi of the

United Hebrew Congregations of the British Empire, even went so far as to state:

> Only that nation can be called cultured . . . which by its living, and, if need be, by its dying, vindicates the eternal values of life – conscience, honour, liberty. Judged by this test, two of the littlest of peoples, Judaea in ancient times and Belgium to-day, and not their mighty and ruthless oppressors, are among the chief defenders of culture, champions of the sacred heritage of man.[7]

On the other side, German voices were raised to question Belgium's very right to independent existence. Within months of the invasion, the Belgian state was widely dismissed as an accidental product of nineteenth-century European diplomacy: a mere construction that – so the argument implied – could be undone again. The German economist Werner Sombart famously called Belgium "a still-born product of European politics."[8] Arguments as to Belgium's artificiality soon proliferated.[9] An avalanche of pamphlets, books, newspaper articles, and magazine essays pounded on the *Leitmotiv* of Belgium's essential non-existence, its necessary lack of history, traditions, and collective will, a makeshift state with a Gallophile government.[10] In its emphasis on the superiority of essential, almost "organic" definitions of existence over mere legal notions of international agreements and recognized statehood, this discourse mirrored the German wartime insistence on the over-riding importance of authenticity and self-assertion.[11] Belgium's *insignificance* thus vindicated the German conception of war aims in the same way that its *significance* sanctioned those of the Entente. Over the course of the war, the cultural politics of the German military authorities in occupied Belgium would take these notions to their logical consequence, in an attempt to establish a more permanent domination over the conquered country.

Occupation

The German occupation of Belgium[12] was, as it were, an unplanned by-product of the Schlieffen Plan, or rather, of the failed attempt to implement it; Belgium had not been invaded with the express aim of annexing it.[13] As the initial chaos subsided, occupiers and occupied perforce settled down into a frail, makeshift *modus vivendi*, fraught with harsh repression and resentment, and characterised by a great deal of mutual icy distance.

By December 1914, nine-tenths of Belgium was under German occupation.[14] Authority was in the hands of the German governor-general, who, being under direct orders from the emperor (and not answerable to the *Reichstag*), functioned somewhat like a colonial viceroy.[15] At the highest level, the Belgian state no longer functioned in the occupied country. Parliament had dissolved; the government was in exile in France (near the Norman port of Le Havre), and the king had taken up residence at the Belgian front. The only ongoing "Belgian" authority under occupation was local. As had obtained in earlier centuries, it now devolved upon the country's 2,633 *communes* to defend their citizens against the encroachments of invading powers. Four years of occupation would see an unending series of clashes between the German military and local Belgian powers. In a steady stream, hundreds of recalcitrant burgomasters, aldermen, and councilmen joined what Brand Whitlock, the US minister to Belgium, called "that patriotic colony in German prisons."[16] A constant level of low-key resistance was to be kept up for the duration of the war, even as occupation life settled into a makeshift routine.

Within weeks of the invasion, the problem of food provisioning for the occupied population emerged. As famine threatened, a consortium of Belgian and American businessmen in Brussels set up the first food aid operation. This impromptu solution eventually developed into the largest and most continuous international food relief operation witnessed until then. Over the course of the war, the international Committee for Relief in Belgium, led by Herbert Hoover, shipped a total of 5 million tons of foodstuff into the occupied country, worth $880 million (a sum larger than the pre-1917 US state budget). In the occupied country, the Comité National de Secours et d'Alimentation/Nationaal Hulp- en Voedingscomité, which distributed and administered foreign aid and assumed central responsibility for indigenous charitable endeavors (drawing heavily upon local authority structures as it did so), acquired great symbolic importance as the only nationwide Belgian institution still functioning, in this capacity clashing more than once with military authorities. The relief operation was able to maintain a modicum of food supply at least until the winter of 1916/1917, when material life took a sharp turn for the worse.[17]

Routine was restored with great difficulty, as the war had broken up pre-war communities and as military occupation paralyzed communication. Invasion and *furor teutonicus* had caused a mass flight of civilians: in early November 1914, an estimated 2 million Belgians out of a total population of 7.5 million had fled the country. Most of the refugees eventually returned (after express promises by the occupation authorities that they would not be harmed in any way). Others, however, stayed away, so that until the end of the war almost 600,000 Belgians remained in exile (most of them in France, Britain, and the Netherlands).

This situation in the words of a contemporary, the historian Henri Pirenne, created what were in effect "two Belgiums."[18]

The relations between those two nations would soon turn sour, each party claiming it was shouldering the brunt of the war hardships. The refugee press repeatedly referred to the occupied Belgians' supposedly snug accommodation with German rule. The Belgians who were "stuck inside," as the claustrophobic expression went, felt abandoned by those who had fled to safety abroad; anti-refugee resentment in occupied Belgium was to find expression in venomous doggerel, comics, and cartoons – the whole gamut of pre-war charivari.

Resentment was exacerbated by mutual ignorance, as communication between the "two Belgiums" became next to impossible. For Belgium soon became virtually sealed territory, surrounded by German forces on three sides, and on the fourth (i.e., the Belgian–Dutch border) a 10 foot high, 50,000 volt electric fence erected in the spring of 1915 by German military engineers. Postal communication between the occupied country and the outside world ground to a near-total halt, so that most of the Belgians "within" remained ignorant of the fate of their compatriots abroad, and, tragically, of their spouses, sons, and brothers in the Belgian army along the Yser front. Over the long years of occupation, many were to experience the lack of information as maddening, alternating between bouts of black pessimism and periods of hope, depending on the scraps of information that came their way. Gradually, "many people had become neurasthenics," as a local memoir reported. "One heard of sudden deaths, of heart failures caused by pressures, hardships, and anxiety over one's dearest, that one had no news of. . . ."[19]

Information from abroad not controlled by the German authorities became exceedingly scarce. Having been completely suppressed in the first weeks of occupation, the Belgian press was subjected to heavy censorship from October 1914 onward.[20] The vast majority of pre-war newspapers refused to submit to German control and stopped appearing. Eventually, several new German-approved papers appeared on the market. This *emboché* press, as it was commonly called ("infested by the *Boche*"), was received by the public with suspicion, but read none the less, given the scarcity of other sources of information. What scraps of Allied papers could be smuggled into the country were passed from hand to hand avidly. Thus, for instance, did denizens of Brussels during the first months of occupation shell out the enormous sum of 10 francs (one-third the price of a pair of men's shoes) for the privilege of perusing a fortnight-old copy of the London *Times*; crowds gathered in parks to hear street peddlers read and comment upon (real or invented) excerpts from the Entente press. Before long, an underground press flourished. Next to the most famous clandestine journal, *La Libre Belgique*, whose editors for four years managed to elude the military police and once famously had a copy of the paper delivered to Governor-General Von Bissing's office, several dozen others emerged, such as the ephemeral *Motus!* (*Journal des gens occupés*), the Ghent periodical *Het Nachtlichtje* (The Night-light), *De Vrije Stem* (The Free Voice) in Antwerp, the Brussels *Satirische Zeitung* (a francophone paper, despite its title), *De Patriot*, *L'antiprussien*, *La caricature antiboche*, etc. For the duration of the war, this clandestine press would keep up its campaign of casting systematic doubt on the *emboché* press's assertions of German military superiority, of diffusing (and often inflating) bits of good news culled from smuggled Allied sources, of blasting war profiteers and the unpatriotic generally, and overall keeping up a steady stream of exhortations toward patriotic endurance, peppered with dramatic drawings – with titles like "*Kultur* was Here" and "Before the Shooting" – by the Dutch-born Antwerp artist Louis Raemaekers, as well as satirical cartoons and much anti-German doggerel ("Fire! Boom! Wham! / Still more Prussians *Kaput!*").[21] A steady level of cultural resistance would thus be kept up all through occupation, keeping alive a basic non-acceptance of German authority.

This non-acceptance was fanned by the circumstances of military occupation, which cut deep into daily life. Letters were subjected to censorship (envelopes could not be sealed), causing many Belgians to shun the postal service – delivering their own letters if within town or giving up correspondence in all but the most urgent cases. Travel was heavily restricted. Citizens felt virtually "immured alive" in their localities,[22] which they could not leave without all manner of passes and bureaucratic stamps. And, in the second half of the war, as the forced deportation of labour to German factories and Western front defense lines started (a total of 120,655 Belgians were forcibly deported), men between the ages of seventeen and fifty-five were subjected to military controls of their whereabouts.

Life as it was lived under occupation was slower and poorer than in pre-war days, the lack of stimuli deeply felt even in the capital. "Truly," as the Flemish poet and journalist Karel Van De Woestijne expressed it (in his customary putting-a-brave-face-on-things banter), "we have become simpletons, and gape in wonder at things banal to others, but which to us possess the thrill of the new, as people do who live in an atmosphere of dull isolation."[23] Many of the great names in Belgian culture had left. Nobel Prize laureate Maurice Maeterlinck toured Entente and neutral Europe on an unofficial mandate from the Le Havre government to defend the Belgian cause. (In Milan in early December 1914, he rather hyperbolically eulogized Belgium as an emblem of honor in a profit-obsessed epoch: by throwing itself in the path of the "barbaric" advance, and being nearly "trampled to death" in the process, Belgium, Maeterlinck told his audience, had "saved Latin civilization from its greatest threat ever.")[24] Belgium's most illustrious poet, Emile Verhaeren, died tragically in a railway accident in Rouen in 1916, in the midst of a lecture tour; from his exile years he left a series of elegies on Belgium's plight and impassioned indictments of its invader ("Germany! Germany! / You bringer of dusk!").[25] The biologist and advocate of the Flemish Movement Julius Mac Leod, was in Britain, as were Emile Waxweiler, the founder and director of the Sociology Institute in Brussels (who died in an accident in London in 1916),[26] and Eugène Ysaÿe, one of the most famous violinists of his time. The musicologist, Maurice Kufferath, director of the *Monnaie* opera in Brussels and the author of important studies on Wagner, had gone to Switzerland, where he took what a witness described as a "very alert, very 'Belgian'" stance.[27] And the great fauvist painter and sculptor Rik Wouters, who had fought in the Belgian army and had crossed the border after the fall of Antwerp in October 1914, died in Amsterdam in 1916 at the age of thirty-four.

In the occupied country, the absence of so many brilliant minds was keenly felt. Although the Brussels art market resumed its workings from the spring of 1915 onward, the lack of communication with the foreign art world was widely felt to stifle creativity, and exhibitions were rendered even more morose by the absence of much of the *beau monde* (now in exile) as well as by the silence of the critics (who due to the closure of the Belgian press no longer had an outlet for their opinions). Yet, in a faint echo of the intense prewar art economy, production continued (with, incidentally, little or no work that reflected war themes), exhibitions were held apace, and sales took place – even if many of those sales were motivated by charity, or by a desire to invest wartime profits.[28] By all accounts, Belgium's enforced and unaccustomed seclusion from foreign cultural life (except, of course, the German) weighed heavily: museums and galleries were open, but ignorance reigned as to what was going on abroad; research libraries became accessible again, but their periodicals sections remained closed; book sales continued (second-hand bookshops especially proliferated, due to middle-class impoverishment), but the newest books from France or Britain were no longer on offer (nor were most of those appearing in the Netherlands or Switzerland). Belgians "within" had little idea of how other European cultures were living through the war experience: "Brussels no longer knew what London or Paris were reading, writing, thinking," as Whitlock observed.[29] During the second half of the occupation, the dearth of intellectual stimulation was compounded by deepening material hardship. A report smuggled out of the country in the summer of 1917 noted: "As the population becomes more exhausted physically, serious intellectual work is no longer undertaken. For the majority, life has narrowed down to the purely physical. People's thinking has become sluggish."[30]

What added to the sense of deafening silence was the fact that so many Belgian writers stopped publishing rather than submit their work to censorship[31] – or see it abused by German propaganda, as happened in the case of Stijn Streuvels, a Flemish novelist who specialized in peasant themes. Streuvels, who had been strapped for income since the outbreak of the war, in early 1915 had published his wartime diary with an Amsterdam publisher (as was still possible before the closing of the Dutch border). The ironic, detached tone in which the diary related the events of September 1914 in Streuvels' rural West Flemish home region (an area which, though it had experienced its share of suffering during the invasion, was not among Belgium's dramatically "martyrized" regions like Louvain or Dinant), coupled with some sarcastic remarks about the French as Belgium's new friends, had upset patriotic opinion. All the more so as the German press had eagerly seized upon the diaries as expressing the Belgians' "true" and friendly dispositions towards the *Reich*, in the process twisting its contents so as to offer proof of the existence of Belgian *francs-tireurs*. Belgian patriots abroad were incensed: the poet Marie Gevers accused Streuvels of having betrayed "the spirit of Tyl Uylenspiegel," an accusation over which Streuvels was exceedingly piqued ("Oh, go ahead, Miss Marie Gevers," he wrote in his private diary – which remained unpublished during his lifetime – and groused that "before the war one could so to speak kill one's parents just to get famous whereas *now* . . .").[32] Tensions subsequently abated, but the question "to publish or not to publish" remained burdened with connotations of patriotism and civic treason – so much so that when, years later, the novelist Georges Eekhoud, who was known to be critical of chauvinist clichés, cautiously suggested that choices in publishing best be left to writers' own conscience, this statement could be hailed by the censored press (which for obvious reasons advocated a return to normality in all domains) as "a noble example of tolerance and openmindedness".[33] Yet, meanwhile, Eekhoud himself kept his silence during the war, as did the overwhelming majority of Belgian writers, unwilling to address their audience under a regime of harsh censorship and military might. Literary production went private.

One example is the five-act historical drama *Egmont* (on the sixteenth-century martyr of the Netherlands uprising against Philip II's regime), written by the symbolist poet and playwright Iwan Gilkin during the first year of the occupation. In this play, Gilkin deliberately set out to rewrite Goethe's 1788 *Egmont* – which he deemed "too dry and cold", too classical and abstract to arouse passion – in a more historical and place-specific, indeed nationalist vein. *Egmont* was not staged until 1930, six years after Gilkin's death.[34]

Patriotic honor mandated the shunning of German-sponsored events. In March 1915, the non-conformist Brussels philosophy professor, Georges Dwelshauvers, had the temerity to attend a German concert given at the Monnaie Opera. Having been spotted entering the hall by one of the "patriotic spies" who were on the lookout, he was subsequently ostracized by polite Brussels society. This led him to draw closer to German company, isolating him from Belgian society altogether; he finally felt obliged to leave Belgium after the war was over. The audience for the May 1916 performance of Wagner's *Ring der Nibelungen* contained virtually no Belgians (although Wagner's work had been remarkably popular in prewar Belgium). In general, the Occupation Government cadres and officers kept to themselves in cultural matters, converting, for instance, the Brussels Théâtre du Parc into a German establishment with its own troupe.[35]

As military censorship extended to plays and even concerts, it was considered patriotic not to go out at all, especially in the first months of occupation. Yet the need for distractions made itself felt, and soon enough theaters reopened, staging rehashed prewar fare with an emphasis on light material, *variétés* and *revues* of every description, popular comedies with song-and-dance numbers, reassuringly hackneyed blood-and-thunder plays and, in urban neigbourhood theatres, broad variety shows performed in dialect. More demanding material was seldom staged, innovative plays not at all, as audiences expected to be entertained first and foremost, and as a large part of the intelligentsia continued to avoid the theatre. By some unwritten rule, concert-going was not considered unpatriotic among the upper middle class (by contrast to the theater, and of course the cinema), and a humble musical "season" was restored with much chamber music, organ concerts in churches, and even the occasional opera (the first full production being Gluck's *Orphée*, staged in Brussels in May of 1916).[36]

Not all amusements were so sedate. The laments of the patriotic-minded notwithstanding, cinemas, music-halls, and dance-halls soon restarted business. By the end of November 1914, some of the *cabaretiers* of the working-class *Marolles* quarter of Brussels had already reopened

11.1   "She'll end up loving me," *Fettered Belgium*, 1915

their dance-halls (complete with "mechanical organs" and polka bands), to the public. The relief volunteers who distributed soup in the neighborhood instantly made it known that they would henceforth patrol the dance-halls and strike patrons off the food aid rolls. Their efforts were in vain. (But they did point to local governments' desire to maintain what was seen as the patriotic propriety that the war called for – a paternalistic desire also attested to by refusals of assistance to Belgian soldiers' wives suspected of dalliance with Germans.)[37] In vain, too, did municipalities try to keep the assisted out of cinemas by threatening a withdrawal of food aid, while *La Libre Belgique* urged its readers to boycott the movie theaters, since going to the movies meant spending money on the Germans (the Occupation Government having sequestered the cinemas, many of which belonged to the French distributor Pathé).[38] Inexorably, cinemas became more popular. By December 1917, Brussels had 140 movie theaters, from an estimated

90 before the war; the entire country (the German front included) had 1,500. Between June 1916 and June 1917 alone, an estimated 50 million cinema and theater tickets were sold in the occupied country, a proliferation partly due to the patronage of newly wealthy war profiteers.[39] Yet the cinemas also attracted a wider clientele, avid for some distraction, offered in the guise of prewar French comedies, wartime vehicles for the Danish star Asta Nielsen, or the newer German UFA extravaganzas such as Ernst Lubitsch's *Carmen*. (The "educational" fare offered by the relief organization found fewer enthusiasts.) One fan of Asta Nielsen, the young Flemish expressionist poet, Paul Van Ostaijen, offered the following irreverent comment on cinema-going: "You will be forgiven much / for / you have seen many movies."[40]

Meanwhile, more traditional popular entertainments suffered setbacks because of scarcities and restrictions. Thus did thousands of local brass bands – a staple of prewar Belgian local life – lose their trumpets and trombones to German quarter-masters' ferocious quest for copper; the Belgian popular pastime *par excellence*, pigeon-contests, was rudely suppressed when the German authorities started requisitioning and killing the homing pigeons with the argument that the birds were used for military spying. Local carnivals were forbidden, the ban enforced by the German military police. Urban peddlers of toys, knick-knacks and pictures, who from August 1914 onward had cashed in on the demand for national symbols – selling penny portraits of national heroes like Cardinal Mercier, picture postcards of King Albert with his soldiers, texts for new patriotic songs (to be sung to the tune of pre-war popular hits), or even black silk caps with tricolor tassels, a headgear much in fashion among Brussels prostitutes – saw their business crushed by a German ban on Belgian national emblems.[41]

Other pursuits, by contrast, took off, such as outdoor sports for men; all over the country, local notables funded and sponsored soccer clubs in order to provide youths with a healthy pastime. The originally Basque pelota ball game, already much beloved in the Charleroi region, spread to the rest of Wallonia and to the working-class and lower-middle-class suburbs of Brussels. Generally, under occupation, Belgians exhibited a marked predilection for outdoor company – at mass picnic outings, in public parks, and at curbside café tables (defiantly hauled out every spring despite the military ban). "The Belgians need to gather together," as an August 1917 report stated: "so they seek out curbside tables where they drink little and talk little, yet manage to put some heart into one another. The need for encouragement is urgent, for people atrophy and become anemic."[42] Freedom of assembly, however, was suppressed – increasingly so in the second half of the occupation, especially in the provinces nearest the front, where for long periods of time 3 p.m. curfews were imposed. As a result of enforced idleness, the reading habit spread, as some observers happily noted (before the war, the Belgian reading public had been very restricted, and functional illiteracy, especially in Flanders, had been higher than in neighboring countries), even if much of the fare consisted of romance and adventure novels – although the demand for classical French authors also soared. Relief committees set about organizing popular libraries (in addition to the 1,176 existing ones, 313 new ones were set up in the space of a few months) as well as literacy classes and vocational training for adults. Yet these successful initiatives were snuffed out in 1916 by a military ban (which aimed at forcing unemployed or underemployed Belgians into the German war economy).[43]

The religious service turned into practically the only organized public meeting not subjected to German control, and churchgoing increased as a result, even among known agnostics. All the more so as openly political words were spoken from pulpits, such as Cardinal Mercier's patriotic exhortations (widely circulated in underground editions). Religious practice, moreover, provided some much-needed comfort; shrines of the Blessed Mother Mary – where pictures of faraway soldiers took their place alongside traditional votive offerings – attracted more pilgrims than they had before the war; new ones were set up all over the country.[44] And finally, the relief organization stimulated much ongoing cultural activity: charitable concerts, fancy-fairs, and benefit art exhibitions, by organizations such as *Art et Charité* and *Aide aux Artistes*. In these, work by major artists like Armand Rassenfosse, Anna Boch, and Jakob Smits was presented alongside artfully crafted lace doilies, batik work, embroidery, and other expressions of textural art – the output of which had multiplied enormously since the war began, for young middle-class women were observed to have forsworn their prewar enthusiasm for tennis and other strenuous sports in favour of fancy needlework, a pursuit deemed more demure and feminine and hence more patriotically appropriate.[45]

This reigning emphasis on proper patriotic behavior (especially among the bourgeoisie), which sometimes verged on the hysterical, could not but engender reactions, especially as the war wore on. Resentment rose against continued ostracism of Belgians suspected of "fraternizing" with Germans. (This ostracism, though heaviest in the early months, persisted all through the occupation, focussing on women especially.) During the second half of the occupation, young urban intellectuals, many of whom resented being made to feel they ought to be in the Belgian army, openly started criticizing the patriotic certainties that had so far dominated Belgian–German "cohabitation," and struck up friendships with German fellow artists. Thus did the graphic artist and minor Dada poet, Clément Pansaers, befriend Carl Einstein, the expressionist writer of "anti-novels" and a regular contributor to the expressionist magazine *Die Aktion*, which was widely read among the Belgian avant-garde. (Einstein worked as an administrator at the *Zivilverwaltung* in Namur until early 1918, when he was transferred to Brussels, where in November 1918 he was to become the spokesman of the Revolutionary Soldiers' Council.) Pansaers tutored the children of the dramatist Carl Sternheim, another occasional *Aktion* author, who had been living in Belgium when the war broke out. In the salon of Sternheim's grand villa in the countryside south of Brussels, an atmosphere reigned that may have permitted greater rapprochement between Belgians and Germans than obtained elsewhere under occupation (Sternheim and his brilliant wife Thea Bauer had come to Belgium in 1913 to escape what he called "Deutschlands Tingeltangel"; his plays were banned in wartime Germany). In December 1917 Pansaers launched an illustrated literary monthly called *Résurrection* (Brussels, 1917–1918), the first issue of which was dedicated to Romain Rolland. *Résurrection*, which described itself as "a consistently expressionist and emphatically international magazine," offered wood-cuts by *Der Sturm* artists and covers by Pansaers himself, and published politically engagé essays by Einstein and other Germans, together with excerpts from Pansaers' own, vaguely Taoist, *L'Apologie de la Paresse*, texts by the lyrical-expressionist playwright Michel de Ghelderode, pacifist-internationalist manifestos, and lastly, as the poet Robert Goffin was later fondly to recall, some "incomprehensible poems, written according to the formula of words-thrown-in-a-hat." It circulated widely among the tiny Brussels avant-garde, where literati friends of Einstein's, like Fernand Crommelynck – who after the war was to revolutionize the Belgian theater with *Le Cocu Magnifique* of 1920 – convened in a cabaret by the name of *Le Diable au Corps*. *Résurrection*'s left-wing and pacifist-humanist message meanwhile was probably funded by the Germans and left intact by the censors, which is not surprising, given the fact that the civil arm of the Occupation Government was much inclined to further the desire for peace ("Friedenssehnsucht," as the *Politische Abteilung* called it) in the occupied country, together with criticism of a Belgian government supposedly beholden to a warmongering France.[46]

The Antwerp avant-garde movement, the liveliest of all such cultures in occupied Belgium, concentrated around the aforementioned Paul van Ostaijen, who in the course of his short life was to become the most important literary figure of Flemish modernism. His 1916 *Music Hall* showed distinct expressionist influence, even if the overall tone of the poems remained lyrical (and vaguely Whitmanesque). Van Ostaijen was a central figure among the town's avant-garde painters. Cut off from direct contact with developments abroad as they were (having to rely on reproductions in magazines like *Das Kunstblatt*), they welcomed whatever theoretical nourishment came their way, such as the pre-war manifesto *Du Cubisme* by Gleizes and Metzinger (1912), to which they were introduced by Van Ostaijen. Their output meanwhile remained relatively modest – partly because of the dearth of material (especially oil paints), which prompted radicals like Paul Joostens to come forward with large non-figurative *collages*. Joostens' "pasted-paper paintings" were first shown in the Brussels Galerie Giroux in early 1917, and caused some dismay among what his circle gleefully referred to as "the bourgeois." Eminently bourgois and eminently rejectable, too, was the whole idea of Belgian heroism, especially with Van Ostaijen, who, at the outbreak of the war, at age eighteen, had gone out of his way to take dancing lessons – thus defying, in a gesture both dandyish and Dadaist, August 1914's heavy atmosphere of war volunteerism and sacrifice – and in later years openly criticized what he called "Patriotism, Inc." (Again, it should come as no surprise that utterances such as these were left unmolested by the *Zensurstelle*.)[47]

Among the wider population, however, a low-key yet resilient sense of patriotic attachment seems to have endured all through the occupation. The enthusiastic "Belgians" acclaiming the kaiser's troops on newsreels shown in Germany therefore had to be impersonated by soldiers in fancy-dress;[48] and Governor-General Von Bissing's attempts somehow to anchor German rule in Belgium by means of widely publicized "improvements" met with indignant rejection.[49] Although chauvinist posturing abated considerably with time – by 1916, Belgians no longer ostentatiously plugged their ears whenever German military bands played Von Suppé overtures in town squares – distances between the civilians and the occupying forces continued to be observed. The blunt fact of military occupation precluded socializing. Memories of the invasion lingered; daily vexations could not be ignored, especially in the second half of the war, when requisitions of household goods were stepped up (occasioning brutal house searches); and, more importantly, the military compulsory-labor program led to ferocious manhunts on streetcars, in cafés, and in cinemas. The list of Belgians arrested, deported, or executed for acts of "treason against military authority" grew longer. In vain did officials at the Government-General note that this draconian policy was bound to cripple attempts at fostering long-term acceptance of the occupation regime.[50]

Non-acceptance of German rule was famously expressed in the dogged refusal to acknowledge the transition to Central European Time imposed by the military. Germans and Belgians thus effectively lived in different time zones, an unspoken rule that gave rise to a whole array of baroque arrangements of alternating "Belgian time" and "German time," but which was maintained for the duration of the war as a sign of that invisible partition which most Germans in Belgium knew better than to attempt to break through. In his diary of 1916, the German-Alsatian officer and novelist Otto Flake (who at that time held a position at the censors' office in Brussels) called it "an honest and clean divide – me as German, the others as Belgians. . . . The feelings of the vanquished are a fact of life that I completely understand; the presence of the victors is another. Each has to bear his wartime fate on the side that the August catastrophe has found him on."[51] Yet Flake, like many Germans in occupied Belgium, could not but suffer from his situation, and even he ultimately succumbed to the complacent notion that Germany was somehow fulfilling a *mission*. In his notes, he mused about the day when Germany was to become "big brother" to "the smaller Germanic nations" in Europe: "the brother who has made good and presents them all with his . . . culture." In this context, "the Flemings will seek the [German] support they will need." Thus could some good result from the German presence: "In this matter, at least, is it easy to do good work."[52] Flake was referring to a cultural program that had been underway for a while: that of *Flamenpolitik*.

Flamenpolitik[53]

The German wartime *Flamenpolitik* (Flemish Policy) was aimed especially at privileging the Flemish in Belgium. More specifically, it sought to accommodate the agenda of the Flemish Movement.[54] This cultural politics did not proceed according to a strategic blueprint, prepared in advance; it was a makeshift program, its grander aims usually formulated *ex post facto*, proceeding by fits and starts, the initiative coming now from Berlin, now from the occupation authorities in Brussels.[55] Conceptions of tangible German profits ranged from ambitious plans for a Germanic Flemish satellite state to more modest schemes of a permanent disintegration of Belgium through the creation of a friendly Flemish outpost (in case Germany was defeated and Belgium had to be relinquished). For all that, none of the advocates of *Flamenpolitik* formulated particularly precise notions of its practical uses within the context of Germany's war aims, which were themselves in a constant state of flux.

The *symbolic* value of a Flemish cultural policy, however, seemed beyond dispute. On the international stage, it countered atrocity propaganda much more effectively than *francs-tireurs* hyperbole could. It redefined Germany's invasion of Belgium in flat contradiction to Allied propaganda: the Flemings' plight transformed what the Allies decried as the invasion of a *nation* into an act of liberation of a *nation* from the clutches of a *state*. Germany's selfless support for its Flemish kinsmen served the notion of Germany's wartime mission; the Flemings' putative pre-war plight in francophone Belgium served as a small mirror-image of what had supposedly obtained on the wider European stage, to wit, the stealthy suffocation of the Germanic element.

This new vision won over German intellectuals with amazing rapidity. The historian Karl Lamprecht, who before the war had introduced Pirenne's monumental *Histoire de Belgique* to the German public, presently produced blueprints for a German confederacy including Flanders – Flanders, which, history showed, was *essentially* German, while the notion of Belgium had always been a hollow one.[56] Predictably, Lamprecht's state-loyal stance cost him his longstanding friendship with Pirenne; but it won him some new contacts in the occupied country. On 29 December 1914, he received a letter from a student of Pirenne's by the name of Leo Picard, with the request to "tell us, us Flemings who feel Germanic, tell us our task . . ."[57] The 26-year-old Picard was among the older members of a small radical Flemish-nationalist group constituted in Ghent in October 1914 with the express aim of breaking with Belgium. The group, which was headed by a Dutch Protestant minister with pan-German leanings, called itself *Young Flanders*.

For quite some time, these *Young Flemings* remained the sole recruits of the *Flamenpolitik*. The latter's aim as far as the immediate circumstances of occupation were concerned, was to offer a program for organizing, mobilizing, and controlling civilian life in the conquered country by latching on to the Flemish Movement and, through it, the Flemings. Yet the pre-war leaders of that very Flemish Movement vehemently refused wartime German advances as incompatible with Flemish dignity, and indeed would keep up this unconditional rejection all through the occupation.[58]

Still, indignation was not the sole *flamingant* reaction. In diffuse circles of the *flamingant* rank and file, where over long years of militancy a certain fetishization of linguistic rights had taken hold, German kindnesses (which initially consisted mainly in favoring Flemish over French on cinema posters, on army placards, etc.) were received warmly. Thus, perversely, did the February 1915 appointment of a German military censor who knew Dutch (before that time, the *Zensurstelle* had permitted correspondence in French or German only) "immerse certain *flamingants* in ecstatic bliss . . . [and] fill them with undying gratitude, as if this were some kind of precious favour," as Van De Woestijne sarcastically noted.[59] The German and censored press meanwhile did its best to inflate, and in some cases actually forge, francophone anti-Flemish slurs.

Meanwhile, among Flemish refugees in the Netherlands, and with crucial contributions from Dutch–German circles, a separate identity was fashioned for those *flamingants* who accepted German support: refusing to stay silent while the Belgian state, with French support, was allegedly plotting to trample their rights, and choosing true nation over imposed state as they did, they were crowned with the title of *activists*. By contrast, the majority of *flamingants*, who persisted in refusing German support, were disdainfully termed *passivists*. The self-styled activists in Holland found their first "martyr" in the Flemish poet René De Clercq, a teacher in a Belgian refugee school, who had been fired in October 1915 because of his editorship of the Dutch-Flemish daily *De Vlaamsche Stem* (The Flemish Voice), which was paid by Berlin to attack the Belgian government. The activist press in occupied Belgium explained De Clercq's dismissal as punishment for his *flamingant* beliefs, thus generating some indignation among younger Flemish literati, such as Van Ostaijen. De Clercq's topical poem *Aan die van Havere* (To "Those of Le Havre") versified and thereby elevated the new activist paradigm of the essential difference (and tendential opposition) between the Flemings and official Belgium – a paradigm ratifying the notion of Flemings' *conditional* loyalty to Belgium (a notion heretofore considered shockingly cynical). The poem instantly became the ultimate activist *credo*:

> We like neither tricks nor frills,
> Lords of Le Havre, bear in mind:
> We are Germanics, not Latins,
> Open of heart and pure of blood!
>
> If I've no rights, then I've no country,
> If I've no bread, I've no disgrace,
> Flanders, Flanders, tooth and claw
> I stand up for you
> Fight for you! . . .[60]

The question of conditional loyalty rose with particular ferocity over the German-sponsored Flemishization of the university of Ghent. "Ghent" was meant as the *Flamenpolitik*'s trump card, granting as it did the *flamingants*' dearest wish: higher education in Flemish. It exposed the powerlessness of the Belgian government in exile (which in the absence of parliament was unable to make unequivocal promises as to post-war university reforms), a powerlessness easily interpreted as unwillingness – and hence as essential malevolence *vis-à-vis* the Flemings. The Flemishized university moreover won over certain hearts among *flamingant* soldiers at the Belgian front, who expressed sympathies for those Flemish intellectuals in occupied Belgium who had accepted chairs.

These, meanwhile, formed a rather mixed group of some forty political appointees, ambitious schoolteachers, and a few bona fide *flamingant* academics. The pre-war standard-bearers of the Flemish University Movement had refused to offer their support to wartime Flemishization, especially after the arrest and deportation to Germany of Pirenne (who had been singled out in the German reports as a leader of the opposition) and his colleague, the Flemish historian Paul Fredericq (a particularly rebellious "passivist") – an act of clumsy (and embarrassing) brutality.[61] In the sense of significantly widening societal acceptance of activism, the *Von-Bissing-University* (as townsfolk called it, referring to the governor-general), then, turned out not to be a success after all – especially as its solemn opening in the fall of 1916 coincided with the first wave of deportation of forced laborers from Ghent.

Confidential reports by Occupation Government officials by now recognized the isolation of the activists, whom one sceptic called nothing but "generals without an army" bent on personal advancement.[62] Yet despite the odd internal acknowledgment of the "enormous stumbling-block which the Belgian national character, including the Flemish one, represents for the [German] administration,"[63] the *Flamenpolitik*, having become a goal unto itself (not to mention an attractive career ladder for German academics), proceeded apace. And so, between October 1916 and March 1917, the occupied country was divided along linguistic lines, with Brussels as the Flemish, and the provincial city of Namur as the Walloon, seat of administration.

This administrative division, incidentally, called for a Walloon cultural policy, which however remained very modest – a virtual residual category alongside the *Flamenpolitik*. The Walloon activism engendered by this *Wallonenpolitik* remained equally marginal. This is not to say there was no Walloon collaboration with the occupying powers; yet this collaboration was not buttressed with nationalist-separatist arguments to the degree it was among Flemings. The physician Arthur Limet, the major figure in Walloon *Deutschfreundlichkeit* – a pan-Germanist of sorts, he had publicly started hailing the German invasion from January 1915 onward – failed to create a Walloon Council, and was to state at his post-war trial that his actions had owed nothing to any *wallingant*

11.2 *Unfettered Flanders*, 1918

conviction whatsoever. Few if any of the employees and directors at the new "Walloon ministries" at Namur had belonged to the pre-war Walloon Movement. In fact, this new Walloon administration was so evanescent that up until the end of occupation most Namurois remained completely ignorant of the fact that their town was now the seat of a "Walloon government."

"Namur," then, was a marginal byproduct of "Brussels." Likewise, German Walloon cultural policy was a mere afterthought. Still, officers in the Occupation Government pursued it conscientiously. Efforts were made to promote interest in Walloon folklore and dialects as keys to the "Walloon national character."[64] The Press Bureau created such ephemeral journals as *L'Avenir wallon, L'Écho de Sambre et Meuse,* and *Le Peuple wallon,* which somewhat halfheartedly polemicized with the

Flemish activist press over far-fetched subjects such as the pre-war Flemish "domination" of the Congo, while – in unison with Flemish activism – lambasting Belgium as a destructively centralizing amalgam of two essentially different "races." The sometime writer Paul Ruscart conducted interviews with leading Flemish activists such as De Clercq – "this poet of a race both stubborn and sensitive" – which appeared in the censored press. Ruscart was among the nine members of a Walloon Defense Committee, which in March 1918 called upon the Walloons to defend the "interests of their race" against Belgian-Flemish domination. For all that, Walloon activism, such as it was, did not spawn noticeable cultural manifestations. Walloon regional and dialect literature seems to have been more readily harnessed for patriotic than for separatist purposes, as is attested by the existence of wartime protest songs such as "Li casque di pruchin" (The Prussian helmet) and the Liégeois "Poqwè q'nos d'vans hère les Allemands" (Why we must hate the Germans).[65]

Meanwhile, for the benefit of German and world public opinion, the Occupation Government remained bent on presenting the breakup of the conquered state as the disinterested implementation of the Flemings' own thirst for self-determination. This prompted the creation of a fifty-member activist "parliament," which called itself the Council of Flanders. This Council made its presence known in February 1917 with a manifesto, *To the Flemish People*, which clamored for Flemish "national liberation" – a goal not further elaborated upon. [66] Among the occupied population, the Council's conceit engendered heated indignation. Despite the ban on "passivist" utterances (enforced by fines, arrests, and deportations), Flemish – and *flamingant* – public opinion vehemently denied the Council the right to speak on its behalf.

Council members, Ghent professors, and officials in the new Flemish ministries were, as is abundantly clear from their correspondence and their press, stung to the quick by "passivist" accusations of dishonor – accusations which rankled all the more as most activists, far from being revolutionaries flouting convention, were essentially claiming status within the bourgeois world. To counter their compatriots' hostility, they tended to justify their collaboration with the enemy by painting a lurid picture of Belgium's immutable hostility toward the Flemings. The ever-expanding breakup of the Belgian state structure under the occupation, then, did not just implement the German authorities' wishes, but also fitted in with activist tunnel vision. As a result, the notion of the essential opposition of "Belgium" and "Flanders" continued to be elaborated, eventually culminating in a January 1918 declaration of "Flemish independence" from Belgium.

But, as sceptics in the Occupation Government had feared, this open declaration galvanized the public into a renewed demonstration of resistance (and this at a time when apathy in the face of seemingly unending occupation had started to spread together with resentment over what the censored press interpreted as the exiled Belgian government's indifference to the population's sufferings). All over Flanders, pageants hailing the proclamation of independence were met with massive counter-demonstrations. Arrests and deportations of protesters followed, which did nothing for activist popularity. "The situation has *never been worse*," wrote one *Young Fleming* to his contact in the *Reichstag*. "If the war lasts another year, there will not be a single friend of the Germans left in Flanders."[67]

At this point, the occupation authorities stopped taking the Council seriously. All pretense of it being a "Flemish Parliament" was dropped, and its sole function became that of a propaganda machine. As a result, the last year of the war saw a remarkable expansion of the Council's Propaganda Bureau (which, not coincidentally, was part of its "ministry" of National Defense).[68] Between January and September of 1918, the 4 million Flemings of occupied Belgium were flooded with 2.5 million activist pamphlets, and a typical week offered 30 to 40 activist gatherings all over Flanders – in small towns often the sole source of public amusement.

In the process, the whole repertoire of prewar middlebrow *flamingantism* – popular meetings, community singing nights, celebrations of "leaders," dramatic performances, lectures, pageants, and so on – was mobilized to excess. The rich patrimony of traditional *flamingant* battle songs was drawn upon extensively: examples are anthems like "Mijn moederspraak" (My Mother-tongue) and "Mijn Vlaandren heb ik hartlijk lief" (Dearly Do I Love My Flanders), or paeans to medieval Flemish glory like "Artevelde's Geest" (The Spirit of Artevelde), referring to the fourteenth-century Ghent popular leader, and "Groeningergrootheid" (Groeninger's Glory), referring to the field where Flemish troops defeated the French nobility in the 1302 Battle of the Golden Spurs – an event immortalized in *De Leeuw van Vlaanderen* (The Lion of Flanders), the fantastically popular Flemish historical novel of 1838. Wartime additions were De Clercq's indictments of the Belgian government set to music, and other protest songs like "Aan die van Antwerpen" (To Those of Antwerp), which darkly hinted at the Belgian state's supposed willingness to sacrifice this great Flemish harbour to French interests. (Choral works by the famous *flamingant* composer Peter Benoît, such as the 1877 *Rubens Cantata*, had however to be struck from programs after objections from the heirs to his estate.[69]) New plays like *Waarom?* (Why?) and *Het Einde* (The End) – in which actors brandished a sign reading "Down with Le Havre!" – dramatized the theme of Flemings' persecution by the Belgian state in none-too-subtle mode (as even an activist theater reviewer on one occasion had to concede).[70]

The activist dailies fueled the self-replenishing frenzy with exultant reports on all manifestations. Alongside this press, which the German Press Bureau had granted a virtual media monopoly in Flanders, activist literary-political magazines took the place of prewar ones (which had all stopped publication). The illustrated weekly *Vlaamsch Leven* (Flemish Life), the most important cultural magazine of wartime Flanders, which appeared from 1915 to 1918, offered much neoromantic lyricism (often with a distinct Catholic bent), Flemish folklore, humoristic novellas, and *flamingant* hero worship. *De Goedendag* (The Mace, referring to the medieval Flemish weapon), run mainly by Ghent students, presented wistful poetry on love, nature, and generic longing, as well as hymns on *Young Flanders*, on the Flemish student movement, and, predictably, on the Battle of the Golden Spurs, next to indictments of "*Fransquillon* Tsarism" (*fransquillon* being the traditional term of abuse for Flemings who spoke French: 4.7 percent of the Flemish population according to the census of 1910), "The Great Scam of 1830" (the date of the Belgian Revolt), and calls for "a more authoritarian state." In the last year of the occupation, more modernist titles appeared, such as the ephemeral *De Regenboog* (The Rainbow) and *De Beiaard* (The Carillon), and the Antwerp monthly *De Stroom*, where Van Ostaijen established his reputation as art theoretician with an important essay on expressionism in Flanders. As it happened, among the Flemish literary avant-garde a particular form of humanitarian expressionism merged with activism – or, to be more precise, *Aktivismus*, the left-leaning political-expressionist creed advocated by the widely read *Die Aktion*. A comparable though modest development obtained on the Walloon side: in the last issue of *Résurrection* (May, 1918), Pansaers called for artists' political engagement, and in this context advocated an active Walloon militantism. *Aktivismus'* emphasis on national self-determination, as well as its claim to a central role in society for the writer – as expressed in Rubiner's 1916 poem *Hören Sie*, published in *Die Aktion* ("Es lebe der Führer! / Es lebe der Literat!") – could not but strike a receptive chord, even if Van Ostaijen, probably the most brilliant mind of his generation, was later to dismiss much of this vogue, his own early work included, as "extra-lyrical pomposity" and as "adolescent ideals, lopsidedly hypertrophied by the events of the war."[71]

Those modernist stirrings remained fairly marginal: overall, activist public culture was steeped deeply in the universe of pre-war romantic *flamingantism* – what one perceptive "passivist" abroad called "the subsoil of the Flemish language rights movement, where the dregs of resentment . . . and turbid romanticism lay fermenting, [and where] the plant of Flemish activism could not fail to shoot up as soon as the heat and rain of German instigation and generosity began to stimulate its growth."[72] Pennant-waving pageantry, rhetoric, and medieval imagery assumed even more central importance than they had before the war, and so did the idealization of Flemish peasant culture. A particularly powerful example of the latter is the 1916 novel *Pallieter* by the thirty-year-old Felix Timmermans, one of the very few Flemish novels to be published under the occupation: a hymn to peasant piety and innocence, with the title figure, a kind of unspoiled *Ur*-Fleming, as the embodiment of artless happy-go-lucky *joie de vivre. Pallieter*, still probably the best-known book in Flemish literature, became extremely popular with German audiences as the putative expression of the "true Flemish national character." Needless to say, it is no coincidence that the most famous literary product of the occupation years in Flanders should be this ostensibly apolitical, defiantly anti-intellectual *Heimat* novel: Timmermans, a member of *Young Flanders*, in his denial of the contemporary reality of the world war, obliquely endorsed the activist view that but for the bellicose Belgian state, Flanders would have been spared all its calamities. With his customary studied *naiveté*, he expressed his own view of the future thus: "The Flemings to have their very own Kingdom! And to be friends with all!"[73]

Activist propaganda, then, continued to draw heavily on the traditional stock of mid-nineteenth-century *flamingant* themes and techniques. Efforts toward using more modern means of propaganda seem to have remained half-hearted at best; a consistent cinema strategy never took off, and what little movie production there was concentrated on documentary footage of activist speeches – and, of course, filmed re-enactments of the Battle of the Golden Spurs.[74] The commemoration of the latter became an ever grander affair, its anniversary (11 July) replacing, in Flanders, the Belgian national holiday (21 July), celebration of which was strictly forbidden throughout the country.

Little was left to chance as regards the organization of these commemorations, as indeed was the case with activist public events generally, all of which were prepared with painstaking care. Local propaganda representatives would report on the nature of the local public before each planned event: social composition, mean household income, and level of previous exposure to activism. Precise suggestions were added as to what type of pamphlet would be most likely to catch the local mood. Information was given on appropriate lecturers, singers, or subjects. One rural schoolteacher warned Brussels not to send too sophisticated a speaker in front of peasant audiences: "the villagers are extremely shy when confronted with city folk."[75] The Central Propaganda Bureau was flooded with requests for pianos, slide projectors, and, relentlessly, money. When in doubt, quantity counted: "I rely on the use of flyers especially to poison the minds of the population with our arguments, and on such a scale that some of it at least has to linger," as a local representative informed the Bureau with (presumably) unintended candor.[76]

With great zeal, ample finances, and the invaluable support of the occupying forces, the Council and its administration thus set about the task of persuading the Flemish public of the rightness of the activist cause. Minds had to be won over, moods had to be swung, loyalties turned around, resentment against Belgium fanned, a new imagined community presented for mass consumption. Far from being a frustrating diversion from tangible power, this symbolic activity seems to have been rather congenial to the activist community. Professional or amateur literati to a man, most of the activists were experts at handling symbolic goods. Indeed, language had always been their medium, their vehicle, their *raison d'être*, and their main political issue; words, in the activist universe, *were* action; language substitued for power quite satisfactorily.

Defining national interests beyond the purely linguistic ones, then, was not the activists' forte. In long years of pre-war militancy they had acquired a particular linguistic myopia, a fetishism of language couched in traditional incantations on "Flanders' Agony," "Systematic Enslavement of the Flemings," etc.[77] Indeed this fetishism of language had made activism possible in the first place, as neither pan-German convictions (virtually non-existent) nor the mere attraction of war profiteering can account for its emergence; activists suffered from the distorted perspective of the grade-school teachers, the struggling writers, the lifelong "language-lovers" (*taalminnaren*), the passionate philologists, in short, the linguistic militants that they were.[78] For them, linguistic discrimination was fully as horrible as genocide – indeed it *constituted* genocide. A 1918 study of the pre-war linguistic regime of the Brussels primary schools could thus be applauded as a demonstration of "how our people have systematically been assassinated."[79] *Fransquillon* became the generic term for whoever disagreed with activism, whatever the opponent's language – for attacks on activism could not but be

attacks on the *flamingant* cause. Accusations of national betrayal were
accordingly reversed. In fact, "the cunning and wealthy *fransquillons*,"
as a 1917 *People's Catechism* categorically stated, were the true traitors
of "their *country* and their *people*," for they had "betrayed their language, and, with that language, the national character, and, with that
character, the national interest. And by thus betraying their people they
have betrayed Flanders, which is their *true* Fatherland. They are, therefore, not merely *traitors to the state*, they are true *traitors to the Fatherland*
and doubly *traitors to the people!*"[80] Conversely, as René De Clercq
exclaimed, those who "at the risk of losing everything, fight for the very
survival of their race, for the preservation of their mother-tongue," were
the very opposite of traitors.[81] The activists' linguistic efforts, then,
were redemptive – more than that, they showed them to be the true
people's champions.

In terms of tangible linguistic advancement, meanwhile, activist zeal
– implemented as it was with German military support – was counter-
productive in the extreme, since it reinforced prewar criticisms of linguistic legislation as illiberal. "Passivist" *flamingants* observed with dismay
that among the wider Flemish population, the Flemish-nationalist themes
brandished in activist rhetoric were becoming tainted with the stigma
of collaboration, the very *word* "Flemish" in some cases acquiring an
odious sound. Among the Flemish middle classes, using French became
a sign of patriotic resistance; and Flemish working-class skepticism
over the use of the "mother-tongue" (as opposed to familiar dialect, or
upwardly mobile French) as an act of social emancipation was mightily
strengthened.

Activist reaction consisted of a permanent discarding of pre-war
notions of political persuasion. Editorialists called for more coercion
and openly advocated the enlisting of military might, all of it in the
unshakeable conviction that the "Flemishization" of Flanders hinged
on the partial or total breakup of the Belgian state, which alone could
create the possibilities for a top-down eradication of "French" influences. Flanders' only chance for linguistic homogeneity – the *sine qua
non* of national survival in the activist mindset – thus lay in total
separation from "Frenchifying" Belgium. The notion of a monolithic
"Belgium," essentially foreign and hostile to the Flemings' natural
fatherland, was significantly hardened in the process. As a Ghent orator
declared in July 1918: "Belgium is an invention of diplomats! Flanders
is God's creature!"[82]

This called for a turning-around of patriotic imagery. Years earlier, at
the outbreak of the war, René De Clercq himself had joined the choir
of Belgian patriots with singular vigor, sounding the theme of crucified

Belgium (a cliché of Entente propaganda) in his early 1915 poem *Als de Heiland* (Like the Saviour):

> Young and fair
> You have let Yourself be nailed to the Cross
> To Save the World.
> Beads of Your pure blood glisten
> In Your black crown of thorns,
> O Belgium, God's dearest son!...[83]

After De Clercq's conversion to activism, he kept the theme but shifted the accent: by Easter of 1918, *Flanders* had become the Saviour. "Did not our people suffer and fight as the Saviour? Has it not been bitterly persecuted, oppressed and trampled down ... by those that were supposedly its own ... and that not merely threefold, but seven times seventyfold? Oh, the heavy cross that our people has had to bear, and to which it has shamefully been nailed!"[84]

These, of course, were words. Messianic metaphors alone could not sway public opinion, and patriotic redefinition among the wider population still had a long way to go. "Naïve, stupid folk," lamented one propagandist.[85] As the post-Armistice scenes in the Flemish cities would show, these folk were very much in the majority. (In all, over the course of the occupation, an estimated 20,000 Flemings, at most, were involved in activism in one way or another.)[86]

And yet, the cultural politics of occupation would leave a legacy. Among the young Catholic Flemings of the *petite bourgeoisie* – the traditional breeding-ground of *flamingant* cadres – *Flamenpolitik* and activism had, as the novelist Gerard Walschap later testified, forced a separation "between Flanders and Belgium, two fatherlands, which for us, until then, had been one and the same, and which to our bewilderment turned out to be implacable enemies."[87]

Conclusion

The wartime uses and abuses of "Belgium" were to leave differing legacies. Allied hyperbole soon sank without trace, as indeed it had started to do during the war, when exasperation over atrocity clichés had risen with the body count that dwarfed Belgium's 5,500 civilian dead of 1914. (By late 1915, as Robert Graves noted, "we no longer believed the highly-colored accounts of German atrocities in Belgium; knowing the Belgians now at first hand.")[88] "Brave Little Belgium" rhetoric, which over four years of warfare had become a hollow trope, trotted out with increasing cynicism, eventually turned in on itself in anti-Belgian resentment, as became clear at the peace conference;[89] indeed this rhetoric partook of the overall rejection of the right-against-might pieties of 1914, and Belgian international status suffered accordingly. (That Geneva was chosen over Brussels as the seat of the League of Nations was no coincidence.)

In the liberated but impoverished country, the rejoicing over the end of occupation – the triumphal entry of King Albert, the return of Pirenne and other deportees, the near-canonization of Mercier – was short lived, and the patriotic cultural resistance themes of the war years soon lost their relevance; heroic notions of Belgium went the way of all war heroics. Official studies of the invasion, of life under the military regime, of the deportations and the other miseries of Belgium's war years, received little notice, solid though they were;[90] the newly created War Archives Commission disbanded after a few years – unmourned, as few historians showed interest. The war experience became devoid of meaning; the notion of Belgium's existence somehow carrying a deeper significance for European culture became a slightly embarrassing, and therefore soon discarded, memory.[91]

For all that, the Allied victory had restored Belgium in its 1914 form. Overnight, the German authorities had vanished from the conquered country. By the middle of October of 1918 its officials had started leaving Belgium, without further ado, in the full knowledge that whatever inroads the occupation regime had been able to make on the subject population's basic non-acceptance of its legitimacy had been few and far between. Within months of the Armistice, at least one of these officials – the Social Democrat and university lecturer Heinrich Waentig, an erstwhile member of the *Politische Abteilung* in Brussels – would publicly acknowledge as much. But his acknowledgment went hand in hand with a reiteration of the basic premise of *Flamenpolitik*: the insistence on the "racial question" that lurked behind Belgian "official state wisdom" – in other words, the inescapable impossibility of Belgium.[92] Indeed the German-propagated notion of Belgium's essential insignificance was to endure far longer than the Allied image of Brave Little Belgium.

This obtained foremost in the now liberated country itself, where the notion of total and necessary equation of language and nation, as developed under the auspices of *Flamenpolitik*, was increasingly to sway the purveyors of symbolic goods. Within the Flemish Movement, the activist notion of implacable opposition between "Belgium" and "Flanders" imperceptibly took root as memories of military occupation and repression gradually faded and as linguistic reformers faced an uphill battle against francophone hostility now readily couched in triumphalist patriotic phrases. The notion of common fatherland took a beating, as Belgian chauvinism henceforth spoke French, *flamingant* militantism acquired decided anti-Belgian overtones (which would eventually carry large segments of the Flemish Movement into World War II collaboration), and *wallingant* resentment of the centralized state was infused with a heavy dose of distrust of a Belgium supposedly hijacked by the Flemish, who were considered to be both demographically dominant and essentially disloyal. Dispassionate commentators on the language issue had a hard time of it. Although the center held – language and federalist reforms, democratically arrived at, continued apace – it had been drained, so to speak, of much of its content, becoming more narrowly pragmatic than it had been. The language struggle was henceforth loaded with grand notions and accusations – betrayal, martyrdom, historical choices, Wilsonian self-determination – it was never designed to withstand. Language had been a problem in Belgium; now it was *the* problem *of* Belgium. In this sense, August 1914, the finest hour of the idea of Belgium, was also the beginning of its end.

12   Cultural life in France, 1914–1918*

Marc Ferro

One of the features of the First World War in France is that, once it had broken out, those who took part in it did not seem to evince any doubts or reservations about its meaning, significance, and objectives; they enthusiastically cried "on to Berlin!" even though, just a few weeks earlier, many of them had just as strongly expressed their love of peace by calling for a "war on war." But this image would be left incomplete were we not to note that, once the war was over, it was generally judged to have been an exercise in absurdity of a sort that no one could ever be persuaded to participate in again; this was supposed to have been the "war to end all wars." Cinematographic images and phonograph records have conserved the traces of that double illusion. In 1914, the presence of cameras stimulated *poilus*[1] to employ exaggerated gesticulations to express their joy over the departure "for Berlin." In 1918, celebrating the armistice, they sang in derision, "Oh, we should never have gone there."

It was, in effect, the culture of an entire society that was thus taken hostage by a conflict that became a total war (even if use of this term to characterize the 1914–1918 conflict may seem out of place in light of the even more extreme "totality" of the Second World War).[2]

Rupture or crystallization?

At the level of ideas, this notion of a culture hijacked by war seems borne out by what some of the most elevated spirits of France wrote at the time. For example, the *Bulletin des armées de la République* published the following words by the philosopher Henri Bergson in its 4 September 1914 issue: "The conflict before us is between two opposing forces – the (German) force, which wears itself out because it is not supported by a higher ideal, and the (French) force, which can never be spent because it rests upon an ideal of justice and liberty." Henri Lavedan –

---

* Translated from the French by Aviel Roshwald.

a painter of Parisian society, dramatist, and occasional philosopher in his own right – gave vent to his nationalist frenzy in delirious prose:

I believe in the courage of our soldiers, in the wisdom of their leaders . . . I believe in the power of our just cause, in this crusade for civilization. I believe in the blood of wounds, in the water of the benediction; I believe in the prayers of women, in the heroism of brides, in the calm piety of mothers, in the purity of our cause, in the unblemished glory of our flag. I believe in our great past and our greater future. I believe in our fellow citizens, alive or dead; I believe in ourselves, I believe in God. I believe, I believe.[3]

This patriotic mysticism constitutes one of the most striking features of cultural life in these war years. It penetrated the most rational of souls, such as that of Félix Sartiaux, who wrote in *Morale kantienne et morale humaine* (Kantian Ethics and Human Ethics): "One of the most subtle traits of the German character is its hypocrisy, which appears in the guise of a naive sincerity. The judgment of the Roman historian Velleius Paterculus has often been noted. He considered the Germans to be a race of born liars."[4]

Uttered as they were by independent spirits, disciples of the Enlightenment and of a European intellectual culture that had seemed committed to the principles of reason and science, such remarks are suggestive of a cultural rupture with the past brought on by war. This was certainly the perception of the philosopher Henri Bergson, writing in March 1917:

Overnight, the war has fixed the exact value of everything on the face of the earth. Many things that appeared important to us, have now become insignificant; others, to which we paid but little heed, have become the essential things. It seems to us that the veil of convention and custom interposed between our spirit and reality has quickly fallen away; a scale of value has manifested itself to us, attached to every object, every nation, every person. Every idea of every person now appears to have an indefinable yet unmistakable label or mark that indicates its absolute value, beyond the bounds of custom or convention, beyond space and time, in eternity.[5]

Does this diagnosis not smack of the spirit that was later to reign in the totalitarian regimes?

"The war fixed the value of everything . . ." writes Bergson. But were the elements of this development not already in place, ready for crystallization under the pressure of war? The wartime spirit had already manifested itself before 1914 in an anti-scientific backlash among the likes of the literary critic Ferdinand Brunetière (1849–1906), who contended that science no longer offered intellectual satisfaction now that it had become so internationalized. He already spoke of the bankruptcy of science, whereas Ernest Renan (1823–1892) had still evoked its future.

The fact was, that in the name of progress and modernization, the pre-war years had witnessed the ruin of landscapes, the disappearance of age-old occupations, the death of crafts and professions. For this very reason there had been a certain reassertion of traditional values during this period, as a defensive response to perils which sometimes remained faceless, as in the fluctuations of prices or fashions, and sometimes took the form of a clearly identifiable rival and enemy – a role played by Germany from the 1870s on. Hence the success of nationalist novels such as *Colette Baudoche* by Maurice Barrès (1862–1923), whose dramatic tension revolves around the love affair between a German man and a young woman from the severed province of Lorraine, or moralistic, Catholic fiction such as *Le démon de midi* (The Demon of Noon) by Paul Bourget (1852–1935), which excoriated married men who allowed their mid-life crises to shatter their family lives. In truth, while the intensity of the chauvinistic explosion of 1914 may have made it seem like a break with the past, its origins can be traced in part to the widespread teaching of history according to the patriotic paradigm of the historian Ernest Lavisse (1842–1922) by instructors who preached a synthesis of socialist and nationalist values to their students in schools around the country. (It was only in the course of the war itself that this synthesis began to break apart, as divisions grew within the educational establishment over the objectives, if not the meaning, of the war.) This patriotism seemed to suffuse all major intellectual currents, ranging from Paul Claudel (1868–1955) – that "warrior poet," as he was stigmatized by the more or less anarchist Gil – to the writer and poet Guillaume Apollinaire (1880–1918), a rebel of the avant-garde whose brief stint in the wartime censorship administration earned him the lash of the pacifist (and future radical socialist) Guilbeaux's pen.[6]

Apart from a handful of pacifists such as Romain Rolland, who produced a stream of publications from the neutral refuge of Switzerland, it can be said that, irrespective of official censorship, the wartime spirit of patriotism "sealed off" (to borrow Christophe Prochasson's term) any possibility of intellectual dissent, and even transformed the behavior and conduct of individuals. In his *Carnets de guerre* (War Notebooks), Georges Renard recalls the social type of the

elegant intellectual, refined to excess before the war, who pays one a visit, having arrived from the front the week before. He stretches out with his boots on the bed, and the following morning, when one wakes him and asks whether he would like hot water, he bursts out laughing, passes his hand through his hair, curls his moustache, and declines any further toilet. The civilized being has reverted to savagery.[7]

It is striking that Henri Barbusse's (1873–1935) celebrated indictment of war, *Le feu* (first published in 1916; later published in English translation under the title *Under Fire*), was initially understood simply as the naturalist reportage of a combatant familiar with death, before it was recognized as the work of a future militant pacifist.[8]

The art world was not immune to the nationalist reductionism of the war years. Many painters and sculptors associated with the Parisian avant-garde bent before the storm of criticism from politicians and journalists who derided all modernist art forms as degenerate inventions of the German mind. Figurative art inspired by the traditional folkloric prints known as *images d'Epinal* or by classical portraits, pushed controversial genres such as Cubism to the sidelines, expecially in the wartime work of foreign-born artists such as Picasso, vulnerable as they were to the charge of being unpatriotic.[9]

Another aspect of wartime culture was its preservation of certain taboos. The global criminality of the war was emphasized much more than the specific acts of cruelty that every individual was capable of committing in the course of combat. The First World War was wedged between two long periods of pacifism during which people sought to outdo each other in moralizing and the expression of fine sentiments. Clearly, the period 1914–1918 was marked by a barbarization of individuals – a phenomenon that was not limited to the German side of the front. Yet, by a sort of act of omission, the cameras that recorded the war never show men in the process of dying, stabbing each other, sneaking up on each other, and finishing one another off. They only show the image of the dead – a much calmer, if also more tragic, image. Are the rare scenes in which British or French infantrymen fall under enemy fire authentic or recreated? In any event, they are rare. Certainly, the images at our disposal convey a sense of the horrors of war, but never of any specific person's cruelty.[10]

"The civilized being reverts to savagery," wrote Renard, in the passage cited above. In fact, the war of 1914–1918 took a society that believed the future belonged to the progress of civilization and turned it into something brutal. This was, indeed, a cultural turning point (analyzed in recent years by George Mosse), a societal transition into a totalitarian mindset that could not tolerate the notion of the golden mean. The statesman Joseph Caillaux experienced this, much to his own detriment. In the face of his country's massive human losses (which he dared to denounce), caught between the bellicosity of most and the pacifism of a minority, this former advocate of Franco-German rapprochement searched for a third way of reconciliation and compromise – and was branded a traitor. All social classes and all age groups were swept up in this *ensauvagement*, and, for the first time in history, even children were enlisted culturally into the ranks of a society geared for war.[11] Set apart and supervised in the framework of the educational system, they came to be construed as a sort of stake in the conflict: the war was being waged "for" the children, in order to guarantee them a beautiful future; thankfully, "they would not have to go through any of this." Children's education was suffused with a militaristic culture designed to achieve the moral and intellectual mobilization of childhood. Stéphane Audoin-Rouzeau has studied the methods of this program. It involved both classroom teaching, which placed the war at the center of pupils' attention, and pedagogical tools, such as short texts with exercises designed to expose "the vandalism and destructive rage of the Germans," and posters, prints, and books designed for leisure reading. Among the latter were publications such as *Fillette*, *Bécassine*, and *Lili*, whose heroes took their place alongside the patriotic characters and drawings of Hansi (pseudonym of Jean-Jacques Waltz, 1873–1951), the Alsatian-born satirist and caricaturist who had never ceased to mourn the loss of Alsace and Lorraine during the 1871–1914 period. Such images and texts were designed to create the concept of a heroic childhood. The protagonists of these narratives engaged in a variety of noble exploits: furnishing false information to German occupation troops; uttering courageous words after having been wounded in an artillery bombardment; dying under a hail of fire with the words "Vive la France" on their lips. These heroic storybook children, these infant martyrs, reached back to the tradition of those diverse miraculous episodes that were reported by the propagandist publications of the revolutionary and Napoleonic wars. This was how one revived believing hearts, adherents of the various mystical ideologies with which the new century was to become all too familiar, a flock of faithful nationalists that the veterans' leagues were to reanimate after 1919.[12]

Ideological journeys

"Three little marionette acts"; that is how Hubert Bourgin – graduate of the Ecole Normale Supérieure, Dreyfusard, democrat, and Durkheimian, who was to become a quasi-fascist and anti-Semite in the 1930s – begins his description of the conduct and itinerary of the intellectual class during the war:

During the war, concern and anxiety brought them back to the patriotic fold. I would find all of of them – from the Sorbonne, the Collège de France, the academies, and the *lycées* – attending meetings of the Civic League presided over by Ernest Denis . . .

These great professors, these sages, these men of thought, reason, and wisdom, turned out to be as light, inconsistent, thoughtless, frivolous, narrow-minded, and miserable as the most mediocre of their fellow citizens. Their union, their discipline, their understanding lasted just as long as their fears, and the very first hours of Victory in 1918 marked the signal for their dispersal. When the difficulties of a bad peace reignited the heady and unwholesome political passions that had been carefully kept alive by their partisans during the war, the educated elite – reconquered by their old habits as well as their interests – withdrew one by one from an enterprise that had supposedly subordinated all that to the Fatherland . . .

Thus, in their third act, these ridiculous puppets returned to their separate little boxes, lined with errors, prejudices, and pretensions, thereby assuring tranquility and lasting power to the political clique whose harmfulness they had so solemnly borne witness to during their fleeting civic rebellion.[13]

This text has a double significance. First, it clearly shows that the war constituted a sort of parenthesis, and that after 1918 the world of ideas resumed the course it had been on before 1914. In this fashion, it serves as something of a corrective to the texts quoted in the previous section, which capture both the rupture caused by the war and the fact that the culture of war was rooted in elements that predated the conflict.

Beyond that, it provides a good sense of the two modes of intellectual production of this period: the one that was rooted in the idea of progress, of rising socialism, of scientistic analysis of society's future, and the other approach, which rallied to the defense of self-interest. In Italy, Benedetto Croce had written that socialism was an "idea" and fatherland an "instinct." The conflict between these two tendencies tore apart many citizens, as a number of intellectual itineraries suggest.

On the eve of the war, French cultural life was indeed divided into two camps: the former Dreyfusards, who defended the rights of the individual, and the anti-Dreyfusards, who claimed to speak in the name of the state and the nation. With the outbreak of hostilities, patriotism brought together all these currents, including that of the socialists who rallied to the Union Sacrée (Sacred Union – the pro-war consensus) and swept away the manifestos issued by their German "comrades."[14] The struggle for the rights of the individual was transfigured into a battle for the victory of human rights as incarnated by the Republic and by the Republic alone.

Retrospectively, a great deal of importance was ascribed to the first "pacifist swallow" – Romain Rolland's *Au-dessus de la mêlée* (Above the Fray), but it does not seem to have evoked any echo at the time.[15] None the less, a small group of intellectuals did gather around him as of 1915, including former members of the "Vitalist" circle which had included figures such as Georges Sorel, J. R. Bloch, Georges Duhamel, and the Belgian, Emile Verhaeren. In their eyes, before the war, Romain Rolland had been the purest of the pure, and quite a number of socialists had adhered to this intellectual current which looked favorably upon the working-class world.

During 1914–1915, these pacifist groupings were not able to make themselves heard at all. While they may have felt, in Jean Guéhenne's words, "that the most honest people could not hold their tongues," their voices were drowned out by the din of warmongers, whose "Grand Marshal," Maurice Barrès, president of the League of Patriots, wrote no less than 269 articles glorifying the war in 1915 alone. Countering the Nobel Peace Prize winner Romain Rolland were figures like René Benjamin, militarist and winner of the Prix Goncourt, who weighed in with sales of 150,000 copies of his pro-war publications.[16]

Nevertheless, as the war dragged on, and as anti-war socialists from various European countries gathered at the conferences organized by Lenin and others at Zimmerwald and Kienthal, Switzerland, in 1915 and 1916, an internationalist movement reconstituted itself. A militantly pacifist and socialist literature began to take shape, through a myriad of small journals and reviews which often expired after brief runs. Among their number were *La caravane*, in which Raymond Dorgelès published several poems on the trench experience as early as 1914, *L'effort libre*, *La Forge*, and others. By far the most influential of these was *Demain* (Tomorrow), founded by Henri Guilbeaux, friend of the anti-war author Barbusse. *Demain* became the journal of the Zimmerwaldian left, around which gathered figures ranging from the Russian socialist internationalist revolutionaries Martov and Trotsky to Français Merrheim. These publications constituted the nuclei of "workers' libraries" which served as foyers of a socialist counter-culture that disseminated the writings of men who went on to become pioneers of the proletarian revolution. One rediscovers in this milieu the heritage of the Capri school, that intellectual circle which resurfaced in Paris just before the war and then coalesced around *Demain*, but whose voice was also heard, despite the censorship and thanks to the assistance of Séverine and others, in daily papers such as the *Journal du Peuple* and *Le Bonnet Rouge*. By the end of 1916, a certain critical mass and sense of direction had been gained by these radical socialist and anarchist circles, leading to the emergence of a true anti-war current that commenced its drive "against the mainstream." This was to climax with the explosion of the Russian Revolution in 1917.[17]

A cultural stew

It has become banal to draw a contradistinction between elite and popular cultures that breaks with the political establishment's vertical division of society into ideological categories. This contradistinction certainly has merit when applied to the period leading up to the war, although it needs to be modified by the addition of a third component – namely, working-class culture, with its libraries of "approved" authors, its newspapers, and, in the last years before 1914, its films. This wave of proletarian culture ebbed during the war, not so much because of the nearly unanimous rallying of all classes to the country's "defence," as on account of the attrition among the primary disseminating agents of this culture – primary-school instructors. Out of 65,000 teachers, over 35,000 were called to arms, of whom more than 8,000 were killed in combat. The furrow traced by the war ran particularly deeply through this social cohort, and hence socialist or worker culture was the most severely damaged cultural sphere (though, to be sure, not all schoolteachers had been involved in its propagation).[18]

In fact, the field of artistic creation was itself dried out by the departure for the front of those who sustained French cultural life; and many of them died in the war, including the poets Péguy and Apollinaire (who succumbed to influenza two days before the armistice). Censorship and paper shortages alone cannot account for the precipitous decline in cultural production and intellectual activity: whereas 141 philosophical publications appeared in 1914, no more than 49 came out in 1918. The total number of printed works dropped from 9,000 in 1914 to 4,274 in 1915.[19] But not all aspects of cultural life were affected to the same extent.

The case of the cinema illustrates the situation. Georges Méliès ceased film production, his company having gone bankrupt in 1914. Max Linder, gassed at the front, never resumed production, and ended up committing suicide along with his wife, just after the war. The large companies – Gaumont, Pathé, Eclipse – were able to survive, thanks to their production of war news. The Eclair company engaged in similar coverage, but finally went out of business as practically all its managers, directors, and producers were called to the front.[20] Newsreel scenes shot under the supervision of the Service Cinématographique des Armées

(Military Cinematographic Service) were dominated by a stock set of propagandist themes: battle footage (be it authentic or staged), portraits of commanding officers, the role of France's allies, and the military power of France. This last theme also formed the subject of fictional movies such as Léonce Perret's *Les héros de l'Yser* (The Heroes of the Yser), produced in 1915 by Gaumont. As far as one can tell from the spotty statistical record, the cinema audience declined less than did theater attendance during the war, at least in Paris. The cinema had became the popular diversion *par excellence* for all those *poilus* of rural background, for many of whom the first exposure to film had probably come in the wake of their first train ride. They re-encountered the medium at the front, where military cinemas screened films that served as an emotional outlet despite their conformist style, and were capable of unleashing laughter, though not as effectively as commercial releases such as Charlie Chaplin's *The Champion* (1915).

The French commercial cinema of this period corresponded quite closely to the negative image that educated people and artists had of it. This "machinery for Helots," as Georges Duhamel termed it, was not considered capable of creating works of art worthy of notice. When cinema was not vulgar, it was reproached for its slavish imitation of the theatre and castigated for being "recreative" rather than creative.

As soon as war had been declared, cinema wrapped itself in the flag, producing patriotic movies such as *Frontières du coeur* (Frontiers of the Heart) – a pastiche of scenes based on the great songs of French history ("Sambre et Meuse," "Le chant du départ" "Le clairon"). Gaumont tried its hand at less pompous films that combined the comical with the patriotic, such as *Bout de Zan patriote* (Bout de Zan the Patriot). The popular appeal of such chauvinistic films declined continuously over the course of the war. Attempts were made to draw the educated public to the cinema by producing screen adaptations of famous plays, starring stage actors from the renowned Comédie Française, but these met with no greater success. When Sarah Bernhardt first saw herself on the silver screen in *La dame aux camélias*, she fainted at the sight of how ridiculous the whole thing seemed. Thus, it was the escapist genre, especially grotesque or risqué films, that came back in force, films such as the eternal Rigadin series: *Rigadin trompé* (Rigadin Fooled), *Rigadin heureux en ménage* (Rigadin in Domestic Bliss).

It was espionage and detective films that drew a portion of the French intelligentsia to the cinema, at least during the war. The director Louis Feuillade (1873–1925) was a craftsman of successful serials such as *Fantomas* (1913–1914); his verve also comes through in the episodes of the detective series *Judex* (1916), whose hero, flaunting his black cape and wide-brimmed hat, comes to the aid of just causes and oppressed innocents in the manner of Zorro. Such films, transposed onto the screen from the serialized fiction of the press, attest to the fact that French cinema – unlike its German, Italian, or American rivals – had not yet found its own tempo and identity. It would acquire its own rhythm with the advent of René Clair and Abel Gance (who began filming *J'accuse* [1918–1919] – a powerful indictment of society's complacency amidst the slaughter of war – several months before the Armistice).[21]

But high culture itself became sterile during the war. The fate of the Grasset publishing house gives one a sense of this. Called to the front, Bernard Grasset was obliged to suspend publication. During the periodic leaves which he was granted for medical reasons, he returned to his publishing work surreptitiously, fearful of being branded a shirker. This was how he managed to organize the reissue of some editions, most notably of Jean Giraudoux's (1882–1944) works, to organize tours of the front by major authors, and to publish magazines such as *Lisez-ça* and *Le fait de la semaine*. He refused on principle to publish new works that did not deal with the war, turning down manuscripts such as Montherlant's *Exil* and *La relève*, while publishing war-related material such as *Lettres de prêtres aux armées* (Priests' Letters to the Armies). The two major works that emerged during this period and found a broad market, from the Salons to the train-station libraries, were Paul Reboux's *A la manière de . . .* and André Maurois' *Les silences du Colonel Bramble*, a humorous depiction of the British allies that appeared in the spring of 1918 and became an instant success in the bookstores.

It is none the less significant that in the great, standardized compilations of French literature, such as the volume edited by Lagarde and Michard (which retained semi-biblical status in academic circles until the 1980s), literary history practically disappears for the period 1914–1918. It halts in 1914 and resumes where it left off in 1919. Only four wartime texts have made it into these compendia: Apollinaire's *Calligrammes*, Paul Valéry's *Civilisations*, Barbusse's *Le Feu*, and, of course, Marcel Proust's (1871–1922) *A la recherche du temps perdu* (published over the years 1913–1927). The volume of this work entitled *Du côté de chez Swann* had been published at the author's own expense after all the major publishers had turned down the manuscript. But the journal *Nouvelle Revue Française* began publishing a series of extracts until the war interrupted the process. Proust stopped publishing, but carried on with his writing. He felt suffocated by his ill health, his soul ready to drift away – and yet, knowing that the time left him was short, he made the most of his last years and wrote prolifically.

The fact is that most writers and artists were mobilized and found themselves in the trenches along with everyone else. This made for a cultural stew – a melange of sensibilities and manners of living such as history has seldom witnessed. Thus it was in the case of André Mare, cubist designer and painter, a patriot as rebellious and caustic as his fellow artists from the Beaux-Arts school in Paris. Leaving for the front with a devil-may-care attitude, he soon discovered the smell of cadavers, men overcome by melancholy, others who went mad. This intimate dialogue with death led him to recognize the inanity of official propaganda and "eyewash" (*bourrage de crâne*); he exploded with anger over the useless offensives, those misguided efforts which finally provoked mutinies in 1917, not as an expression of pacifist sentiment, but because troops demanded that the war be conducted more effectively.

Accordingly, Mare wrote less and less in his *Carnets à Charlotte* (Notebooks for Charlotte, his girlfriend); instead, he painted. Why did he choose Cubism as his medium – an art form which was being denounced as "Boche"[22] in Paris? Because he found it to be best suited to capturing the essence of this abstract and industrialized war. Designated as a camouflage artist, he was sent to Italy, where he was dazzled by what he described as a country "whose people love life too much to do battle." Upon his return to France, he abandoned Cubism in order to depict life in his art – that life which he knew would soon abandon him.[23]

Mare's work thus expresses a sort of intellectual counter-culture, but it is not different in spirit from the odds and ends of text written by his companions in misfortune, plebeians condemned like him to endure the living hell of the trenches before dying – and who, far removed from both official propaganda and revolutionary illusions, were the first to speak the truth about the war. Indeed, one of the most unusual aspects of the culture of the Great War was that it produced, doubtless for the first time in France, a kind of anonymous counter-narrative, a collective stammering that called into question the official story.

Certainly, alongside the official view of the war, which Maurice Genevoix expressed so ably in *Sous Verdun* (Under Verdun), there did exist an institutional counter-narrative which was promulgated by the war's opponents – socialists and pacifists, mostly. But this version had a very specific, carefully developed, ideological content. The agony of trench warfare brought into being another form of history, the anonymous, straight memoir recorded in the form of an attestation free of any political or polemical agenda. The letters and other rough compositions of soldiers that are available to us were collected and organized only after the war; they need not be suspected of reflecting a desire to propitiate higher authorities, as is the case with some of the trench journals, and – just like Mare's paintings and sketches – they reflect as faithfully as any form of documentation can, the lived experience of the men on the front line. Norton Cru's volume is the most widely known of these collections, but it essentially consists of the writings of educated combatants who had at least completed secondary school and who at a minimum held the rank of non-commissioned officers.[24] J. Meyer and Ducasse put together a more eclectic, if shorter, collection.[25] But to really get a sense of how combatants experienced life at the front, one needs to refer to the 1,000 first-hand accounts gathered by Jacques Péricard in *Verdun*.[26] Here one rediscovers that horror which the men lived through every day in the trenches, as Germans and Frenchmen piled on top of each other, carpeting the soil with their corpses and coloring it with their blood. These rough narratives are the only ones that allow us to live the daily experience of war at ground level. Another example of this counter-culture is to be found in the notebooks of a day-laborer by the name of Louis Barthas. Published sixty years later, they evoke everything a simple corporal could feel, understand, and know of this war. In his eyes, Prime Minister Clemenceau – the "Tiger" who rallied France's forces after the setbacks of 1917 – remained nothing more than the suppressor of the 1907 populist uprising in Narbonne; the socialist and former anti-militarist Gustave Hervé was a chameleon who had become a war-monger in 1914; for that matter, the great Napoleon had been not so much the victor as the butcher of the Battle of Austerlitz. Barthas was a socialist, he quoted Goethe and Victor Hugo, considered that those who thought they were dying for their country were actually dying for the industrialists, and felt that the great poet was being abused when his words were quoted in the context of this war: "Those who die piously for the fatherland."[27]

Here, then, the anonymous narrative converges with the opposition narrative. Were anti-war sentiments primarily a manifestation of popular culture or of elite culture? Perhaps in this camp, as in the majority, pro-war camp, such horizontal distinctions were eroded by the war.

In any case, in the aftermath of the war, the horizontal fractures among different types of cultural life reappear: popular culture, proletarian or socialist culture, elitist culture. The Dadaist explosion represented an attempt to embody all three; but that is a story in its own right.

Finally, the war gave rise to a new hierarchy of merit, which society accepted without a murmur of protest. At the head of this new elite of victims (second only to the dead) were the blinded veterans, followed by the gassed, the amputees, and those whose faces had been disfigured. The lads of the trenches came next, with survivors of the nightmares of

Verdun, the Somme, and the Champagne ranking higher than veterans of the Dardanelles or of other fronts. If aviators were "flying aces," artillerymen counted for nothing: operating from behind the front lines and beyond immediate danger, they soon came to be known as *planqués* (skivers, drawers of lucky numbers), though they were not deemed as bad as the general staff officers, who were considered outright *embusqués* (shirkers). Indeed, in this war, everyone was a shirker in someone else's eyes. Finally, at the very bottom of the list, were the various categories of civilians regarded as war profiteers, who were objects of public contempt. In France, the right-wing veterans' leagues and diverse fascist organizations were nourished by the resentment that animated the *poilus* against the home front. When, at the hour of victory, they sang in unison, "Oh, we should never have gone, we should never have gone [to the front] in the first place," they were trying to exorcise an anger which could explode at the slightest provocation.[28]

This hierarchy of merits explains why, during the war, in the world of clothing and fashion, the nurse's uniform (associated with solicitude for the common soldiers) gained pride of place over the worker's garb (associated with themes of emancipation and revolt), and why colors were predominantly somber and subdued, with grey and beige prevailing even in the realm of high fashion.

But the most striking revolution in dress during these years when women liberated themselves through their involvement in new spheres of social and economic life was the shortening of skirts and dresses, which no longer came lower than half-way down the calf. From 1914 to 1918, Paul Poiret, the master of pre-war fashion design, was able to adapt to such novel tastes along with the founding father of haute couture, Charles Worth. But it was Coco Chanel (then still known as Gabrielle Chanel) who introduced the world to the cardigan and who embodied the fashion of the liberated woman of the Roaring Twenties.

And yet, for all that, it was not until after the Second World War that French women won the right to vote. Indeed, the rancor and bitterness with which many veterans of the Great War responded to their encounter with this transformed society gave rise to an anti-feminist ideology that triumphed during the 1930s and that compounded all the other social and ideological resentments of those years.

The end of the war held little promise of a better future.

13   The impact of World War I on Italian political culture

Walter L. Adamson

Italy in 1914 appeared on the verge of becoming a modern liberal democracy. It had industrialized rapidly since 1896, though with pronounced regional unevenness.[1] The cities, where about four out of every ten Italians lived, had department stores, movie theaters, and other manifestations of an emerging mass society of consumption. Near-universal manhood suffrage was adopted in 1913, instantly tripling the electorate, and a parliamentary system had been operative for five and half decades without a serious threat of military rule or a reassertion of the monarchy, now largely ceremonial. Yet, just eight years later, Italy would opt for Mussolini's authoritarian and ultimately dictatorial, fascist regime. Obviously there is some temptation to argue that it was World War I which produced this result, for, although Italy entered the conflict in May 1915 on the side of the Entente, it emerged from forty-one months of an unpopular war with the psychology of a de-feated nation, a sharply polarized electorate, and a host of social and political problems connected with massive mobilization and sudden demobilization.

Yet such a conclusion would be oversimple, even misleading. Especially during the final year of the war – between the disastrous defeat at Caporetto in October 1917 and the victory at Vittorio Veneto in November 1918 – state policy took an unprecedented turn toward "nationalizing" the Italian peasant masses, above all peasant men serving in the armed forces. And there was widespread hope, especially among intellectuals, that a fusion of popular and elite culture might create a renewed national community. The fact that such a renewal ultimately proved impossible within the framework of liberal-democratic institu-tions had more to do with patterns of political choice rooted in the state from its beginnings in 1861, and with cultural reactions to those pat-terns in the 1911–1915 period, than with the war itself.

It is not possible here to review the problems of the Italian liberal tradition in any detail.[2] Suffice it to say that it was decisively shaped by the largely "diplomatic" character of the national unification experience;

308

the lack of mass support for unification, especially in the south, and the divisive regionalism that persisted; the antagonism of the church toward the new state; the outmoded, elite-based organization of the army, which weakened still further in the decade and a half after the defeat in Ethiopia in 1896; and the failure to pursue domestic policies that might have integrated and educated a citizenry which, even in 1914, remained about 40 percent illiterate and incapable (except for a minority of 20 percent) of speaking a standard Italian. What all this produced was the notorious division between the "legal" and "real" Italy. Legal Italy's deeply rooted fear of the lower classes – a fear symbolized by the ultimately repressed Garibaldian undercurrent of the Risorgimento – had always foreclosed the possibility of creating inclusive democratic institutions that would politicize the real Italy.

Thus, in those mostly northern regions where agricultural modernization was attempted in order to create a national market, traditional social patterns of aristocratic control and peasant submissiveness were retained, whatever the cost to efficiency and potential innovation. In Rome, parliamentary institutions became dominant over the king largely because of their progressive, Piedmontese origins, but little was done to create a popular basis for those institutions by nationalizing the masses though education, expanded suffrage, and civic-religious ceremony.[3] Rather than allying with their counterparts in the south, who wanted a strong state, northern liberals preferred to conclude backroom deals with the southern landed oligarchy; even after the left came to power in 1876, the dominant political pattern remained elite manipulation. In the years 1910–1911, the liberal political class finally agreed to pursue a significant expansion of the suffrage. But political parties – including the Italian Socialist Party (PSI) – remained small, elite institutions.[4]

Between 1903 and 1914 – when Italian liberalism's most consummate practitioner, Giovanni Giolitti, dominated national politics – socialists, Catholics, and the mass constituencies they represented were brought more fully into the political arena than ever before. But Giolitti engineered these inclusions through the traditional means of a now merely wider network of inter-elite alliances rather than by reconstructing the system as a genuinely competitive democratic process with mass-oriented political parties. None the less, cautious as it was, Giolitti's strategy might ultimately have succeeded in building a mass base for democracy had he avoided the temptation of a war in Libya (Tripolitania and Cyrenaica). Though he went to war largely for diplomatic rather than domestic reasons, his policy gave a big boost to the Nationalists (ANI), who had made the Libyan campaign the centerpiece of a vociferous challenge to the Giolittian liberals and whose apparent success unleashed forces that could not be contained within the old, elitist framework. By 1912 the war had mobilized and polarized the nation's political culture along fault lines roughly corresponding to those that would characterize Italian debate in the intervention campaign of 1914–1915 and that would persist throughout the war and post-war years that culminated in the March on Rome.

In part because of his dexterity in practicing what many intellectuals viewed as a cynical politics of mass manipulation, Giolitti had, already by 1910, excited a vast array of cultural opposition groups including nationalists, futurists, syndicalists, and the *vociani*, a Florentine circle around the journal, *La Voce*. Yet, when he sent his warships south in the fall of 1911, he had the support of the first two of these groups; the syndicalists and the *vociani*, then under the influence of Gaetano Salvemini, opposed the war on the grounds that it would worsen (rather than relieve) the appalling economic conditions in the south of Italy. But the war quickly proved to be a powerful vehicle for unleashing urban, popular energies and disrupting a politics of business-as-usual. By 1912 all the activist elements in the cultural opposition had turned in its favor – with the exception of the radical faction of the PSI led by Mussolini, newly ascendant within the party. Over the next several years the pro-war elements would become so enamored of the myth of war as a vehicle for ousting the liberal political class that they would persuade Mussolini to join them.

With the Libyan war, then, Giolitti unwittingly strengthened an eclectic but potent anti-system opposition of nationalist and culturally modernist elements. But he also undid his alliance with the socialists. Moderate socialists like Filippo Turati opposed the Libyan war as a colonialist adventure that took the nation's eyes off domestic problems – a position Giolitti had shared with him during Prime Minister Francesco Crispi's African adventures twenty years before. Now Turati's association with Giolitti discredited him and his fellow moderates within the PSI, and a radical faction, with whom Giolitti could not work, took over. When Giolitti was forced to resign in March 1914, after having revealed the huge financial cost of the Libyan operation, Italian politics was polarized between anti-system extremes as never before.

In one respect, however, the extremes of Italian politics stood together: they were wholly urban and mostly northern phenomena. Culturally, the two great, complexly interconnected divisions in Italian life were between city and country, and north and south. The divisions had deep roots in Italian history which, since the demise of the Roman Empire, had been a predominantly agricultural peninsula divided into numerous regions by many small city-states, occupying foreign powers, and an anti-national papacy.[5] No centralizing monarchy that might have worked against these divisions had ever developed.

Rural life in the new Italian state remained much as it had been for centuries. By the turn of the century, however, major improvements were being made in conquering the diseases of malaria and pellagra, and some rural areas registered dramatic population gains.[6] None the less, with industrialization, economic opportunity became urban, and, after 1896, the northern cities swelled with new residents from nearby farms, producing a housing crisis and many related social problems. Despite them, local peasants continued to pour into these cities by the thousands every year. In the south, where the cities offered far less opportunity, many rural residents chose to cross the Atlantic: some 2.5 million left for good between 1891 and 1910.[7]

Cultural life in this period was transformed by the beginnings of mass-circulation journalism and a culture industry of opera, theater and cinema, but this was almost entirely urban and northern.[8] Indeed, in mass journalism, the pace was set by a single man, Luigi Albertini, editor of Milan's *Corriere della Sera* from 1900 to 1921. Under his leadership its print run increased from about 75,000 to over 600,000.[9] Made possible by the financial backing of major Lombard firms, Albertini's *Corriere* became the model not only for other city-based papers like Turin's *La Stampa*, Rome's *Il Messaggero*, Bologna's *Il Resto del Carlino*, and Florence's *La Nazione*, each of which used corporate financing to multiply its circulation many-fold, but also for expressly partisan newspapers like the socialist *Avanti!*, which had a circulation of 400,000 in 1914; the nationalist *L'Idea Nazionale*, which was transformed into a major daily in 1914; and Mussolini's *Il Popolo d'Italia*, which was created late in 1914 and soon became a major daily.

Italians had traditionally placed opera at the apex of a hierarchy of theater arts; below it, in descending status order, stood spoken plays, equestrian spectacles, acrobatic performances, and circuses. During its nineteenth-century heyday, opera was mostly an entertainment for the upper classes, who owned their theater boxes and came every evening during the six weeks of winter carnival to gamble, socialize, and enjoy the performance, which was expected to be new and sophisticated even if it was sometimes ignored in the generally rowdy atmosphere.[10] Some servants and other members of the popular classes attended, standing or sitting on a few wooden benches on the floor below the boxes, but there was no notion of a standard price of admission or of a democratic "right" to it. By contrast, the decade and a half before the war saw the increasing emergence of operas aiming at a mass audience, such as Giacomo Puccini's *Madama Butterfly* (1904) or *La fanciulla del West*

(1910). Increasingly opera houses became state-run, private boxes were sold off, and theater prices were standardized. What made this possible, above all, was the growing acceptance of repertory opera, which meant that the opera season could be based, year in and year out, on the same fifteen or twenty "classic" operas.[11]

Broader audiences for a more commercial and democratic theater also made possible more theaters. Their number tripled to about 3,000 in the three decades before 1914. In that year, 131 Italian towns – some of them very small indeed – had opera seasons. Moreover, traditional opera and spoken plays utilized traveling companies and a "soloist" or "great actor" who could attract audiences wherever the performance was staged. After 1905, new *teatri stabili* became the rule.[12] Such permanent repertory theaters with fixed locations and a company of regular actors were made possible by grand productions, such as the plays of Gabriele D'Annunzio, which featured the dynamic actress Eleanora Duse, and elaborate staging and costuming that attracted large audiences and much notoriety. The creation of such *spettacoli* also encouraged theater owners to host traveling shows of a more populist nature, like Buffalo Bill Cody's Wild West Show, which made a tour of major Italian cities in 1906. By the time of the First World War, some of these entrepreneurs, like the Chiarella brothers in Turin, had succeeded in building a large-scale theater consortium based on a number of *teatri stabili*.[13]

As *teatri stabili* doing blockbuster *spettacoli* became increasingly successful, related entertainments catering to more focussed audiences also emerged. Thus, by 1914, many Italian cities also had *teatri minimi*, which did lower-cost productions such as one-act plays of a more serious artistic nature. Many producers of *teatri minimi* were also artists themselves, and they commonly also worked in film. An example is Nino Martoglio, who founded the Teatro Metastasio in Rome in 1910 and directed the film *Sperduti nel buio* (Lost in the dark), usually considered the best naturalist film of the silent Italian cinema.

Similarly, in opera the commercialized productions of Puccini stimulated a more modernist or avant-garde variety of opera, typified by Ildebrando Pizzetti, who was a music critic both for Florence's avant-garde *La Voce* and for *La Nazione*, and whose *Fedra* opened at La Scala in March 1915.

Increasingly, however, both opera and spoken plays faced stiff competition from the most popular of all new entertainments, the silent cinema, today judged by many to have had its golden age in the Italy of the immediate pre-war yeas. The Italian film industry developed gradually from 1895 to 1908, by which time every major city had a movie theater and some provincial ones did too.[14] Over the next few years films began to get longer, to take more interest in narrative rather than simply shooting scenes, and to become controlled by large production companies as well as equally large but separate distribution companies. And, as in theater, the transformation of filmmaking into an industry meant that large blockbuster shows with wide appeal began to appear. In 1913 alone, came Mario Caserini's *Last Days of Pompeii*, Enrico Guazzoni's *Quo Vadis?* and, most ambitious and successful of all pre-war Italian films, Giovanni Pastrone's *Cabiria*, which ran for six months in Paris and for a year in New York.

These films were the basis of a huge export market. The peak year for exports to the United States was 1912 when Italian films earned nearly 1.4 million lire. After that there were tariffs, but increases were still registered between 1912 and 1915 in exports to Spain, France, Argentina, and Brazil, and they remained large, though decreasing, in Great Britain, Russia, and Switzerland. Exports continued during the war, except to Austria and Germany, but by 1918 revenues were only 25 percent of what they had been in 1912.[15] Yet it is important to recognize that even in the years of its greatest success abroad, the Italian film industry never accounted for more than a third of its own internal market.[16] Among the main causes of this anomaly is that Italian film companies never achieved the vertical integration of production, sale, and distribution that their foreign, particularly American, competitors did. In addition, as even cursory reflection upon the history of Italian film suggests, its appeal has often been to a largely intellectual audience, more numerous outside Italian territory than within it.

Finally, alongside these developments in the press, theater, and film, were other indications that industrial prosperity was being translated into increased leisure, especially for the middle classes. Sports like gymnastics, marksmanship, fencing, and mountaineering became popular, and for the masses, bicycling and organized soccer. Any observer of Italian life in 1914 could hardly have failed to take note of the quite extraordinary changes that such developments in cultural life had registered over the past two decades and especially over the last half decade. Yet in two important respects the changes were superficial. First, they affected only urban residents; peasants were as unlikely to be aware of what was happening in the news or in film as their counterparts a century before (unless, perhaps, they had been to America). Second, the techniques of advertising and promotion bound up with mass culture had no impact whatsoever on Italian public institutions like the state and the army. This would become starkly apparent during the first two and a half years of the war when neither the state nor the army made even the most minimal effort to "sell" the conflict to those being called upon to fight it.

In contrast, one group in civil society would prove fully conversant with the techniques of modern mass culture: the avant-garde intellectuals and students who provided the backbone of the ten-month campaign to force Italy's entry into the war, which culminated on May 23, 1915, with a declaration of war on Austria. It would be too much to say that the barrage of propaganda and raucous street demonstrations that the futurists, nationalists, syndicalists, and other interventionist groups deployed was alone responsible for pushing Italy into the war. Prime Minister Antonio Salandra and his foreign minister, Sidney Sonnino, had been secretly negotiating with the major powers during these same months to extract territorial advantages in return for Italian entry, and their apparent success with the Entente early in the spring ultimately persuaded the king to support intervention. Yet, given that Giolitti and the majority in parliament resolutely opposed Italian entry, it is unlikely that the government would have been able to engineer intervention in the absence of a vocal mass movement favoring it.

To appreciate what a remarkable event the intervention campaign was, it must be recognized that parliament never really consented to the war and voted for it only when it was clear that to do otherwise was to threaten the continued existence of the institutions of the monarchy and parliament. In the months after Giolitti resigned, in March 1914, Italy's politics had become increasingly polarized along the lines first evident from the Libyan War in 1911–1912: between nationalists and cultural avant-gardists opposed to Giolittian liberalism, on the one hand, and the liberals and their former allies, the socialists, on the other. When Mussolini switched camps in October 1914, all the activist elements were now on the same side. Thus, when after months of ecstatic campaigning the interventionists achieved success, the event had the appearance and feel of a *coup d'état* at the end of a civil war, and it certainly made a mockery of liberal institutions. Moreover, during the next half decade, Giolitti's liberals would become increasingly irrelevant as the interventionist/neutralist divide gradually hardened into a nationalist/ socialist one, with each side fervently opposed to the status quo.[17]

Ideologically, the interventionists spanned the full spectrum from the nationalist right to the revolutionary left, and included many democratic leftists. Yet their preponderant weight was always on the right, a fact that would have important implications at the end of the war. Partly because of their diversity, the interventionists often thought of themselves as the "second Italy" or "real Italy," in contrast to the "legal Italy" of *giolittismo*.[18] Yet the *real* "real Italy" – the peasant-soldiers who

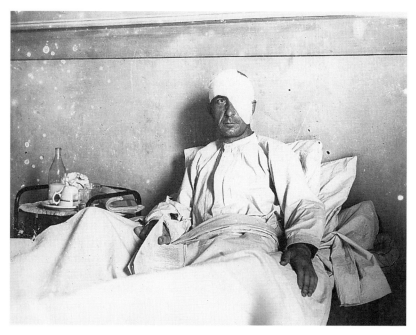

13.1   Ardengo Soffici, August 1917

made up about half the infantry troops – emerged only after war on Austria was declared.[19] Like most ordinary citizens in cities, they had been wholly uninvolved in the intervention campaign, but, unlike the former, they were only barely aware of it. Almost none of them volunteered for the war, and they approached military service with an apolitical resignation that would become increasingly embittered as the war dragged on from the predicted "weeks" to the reality of three and a half years.[20]

To understand the Italian experience in World War I one must begin with its army and the man who led it, an austere Piedmontese general of the old school, Luigi Cadorna.[21] Like the northern liberals who controlled the state, the Piedmontese aristocrats who led the army feared a nation-at-arms model of the military, preferring rigid hierarchy and severe discipline over conscripts. Clinging to the old ways proved difficult: the humiliating defeat at the hands of the Ethiopians in 1896 and a simultaneous industrial takeoff that would change the nature of modern warfare suggested a need to test new approaches. Unfortunately, instead of encouraging the officer corps to innovate, industrialism weakened it still further as richer bourgeois families who had made officers of their sons in the 1870s now pursued other opportunities, and their places were increasingly taken by less-educated recruits from the south. Between 1898 and 1908, as military salaries fell relatively and promotions slowed, ten different war ministers presided over the embarrassment, and relations between the army and the state hit new lows. While the relative success in Libya under army chief of staff General Alberto Pollio improved the situation somewhat, he died in 1914 and had to be replaced by Cadorna just before World War I erupted in August. When Pollio was selected in 1908 over Cadorna, Giolitti had reportedly said: "Pollio I don't know, but I prefer him to Cadorna whom I do know."[22]

Between August 1914 and the Italian intervention the following May, preparations were appallingly meager. Some arms and ammunition were purchased (ironically, Krupp made a spring delivery), but in the early weeks of war troops still had to be told to fire only when necessary, and many were using extremely antiquated rifles. Still more alarming was the fact that little had been learned from studying the experience of the British and French armies. Cadorna's orders were to press relentlessly forward and upward (the Austrians had most of the favorable mountain positions), hurling massed infantry against entrenched positions and absorbing whatever losses were incurred. The first six months of the war cost Italy 62,000 combat deaths and 170,000 wounded, in an army of 1 million men, and no significant advances were made.[23]

In the early days of the war, an infusion of interventionists into the reserve-officer ranks had helped create a mood of *sacro entusiasmo*, but, by December 1915, when Cadorna granted the troops a fifteen-day leave, morale problems were already becoming serious. Besides Cadorna's military tactics, the main sources of these problems were the absolute lack of information provided to soldiers (either from military sources or newspapers) and the virtual absence of moral support beyond company chaplains, alcohol before offensives (which the troops dubbed *benzina*), and a few improvised brothels. When the war resumed in January 1916, Cadorna coolly announced as his main weapon against poor morale the threat of "decimations" (on-the-spot executions of a randomly selected, fixed percentage of troops from units that refused orders).[24] The policy was first carried out in May, after an Austrian offensive known as the *Strafexpedition*, and it became increasingly common over the next year and a half – until Cadorna was relieved of his command in November 1917 after the rout at Caporetto pushed the Italians back 80 miles in three weeks, nearly to the gates of Venice.[25]

In this atmosphere of authoritarianism and persistent disappointment, several varieties of internal-organizational conflict prevailed. One was between Cadorna and the other generals. Failure bred unpopularity and controversy, but most generals quickly learned that to cross Cadorna by sending realistic reports to Rome was to lose out in the bureaucratic politics of assignment and promotion. A second conflict was between Cadorna and Prime Minister Salandra. This came to a head after the *Strafexpedition*, with Cadorna prevailing and Salandra replaced by a technocratic nonentity, the 78-year-old Paolo Boselli. Yet prime ministers mattered little: Cadorna ran the war with the king's backing, while Rome had little to say about it, and keen observers of politics in Rome concluded that Italy was governed by no one.[26] Finally, and perhaps most significantly, there was a fierce rivalry between career officers and newly recruited reserve officers, many of whom had been active in the intervention campaign and were often better educated, more intellectual, more northern, more bourgeois, more interested in the welfare of the troops, and more likely to be leading them than the careerists, many of whom headed for safe posts in the backlines shortly after the war began.[27] In this way the poisonous conflict of the intervention campaign between militant pro-war insurgents and the more passive incumbents of the political class came to infect the upper ranks of the army.

What then of the reaction to all this among common soldiers? The overwhelming evidence from the many first-hand accounts we have of the Italian trenches along the Austrian frontier is that they fought bravely and tenaciously despite their utter lack of patriotic ideals and of even the most elementary understanding of why the war was being fought.[28] Their primary, even exclusive, concern was with simple survival in order to be able to return home. They were completely free of political rhetoric, either nationalist, anti-interventionist, or pacifist. They were little identified with groups (except in the case of regionally based brigades), and sought neither to be heroic nor insubordinate. They coped primarily by believing that the war would end soon ("next spring" and, when that turned out to be wrong, "next fall").

Naturally, however, as the war slogged on through the mud and ice of three winters, infantrymen in particular became increasingly embittered. As an army nurse wrote in her diary of 1917, "when the soldiers say the *Government*, one always has the impression that they are talking of an enemy."[29] Yet, paradoxically, it was not contact with the government but with the homefront that most stimulated this bitterness. For to return home on one of the leaves Cadorna reluctantly granted was to be reminded that many there were ignorant of "the mud, lice and blood of the front lines," that many there were *imboscati* – literally, hidden away in the woods rather than exposed to danger.[30] The notion of the

imboscati or "war-shirkers" was, arguably, the most famous and enduring political effect of the Italian combat experience. For the front-line
soldier, anyone in a less risky position was *imboscato* in relation to him,
whether that be the career officer working the supply trains, the politician in Rome, or, most notoriously, the worker in the munitions factories of Turin or Milan. Even the soldier who remained in the trenches
might be considered *imboscato* by his fellows returning from a night
patrol.[31]

What made the concept of the *imboscato* political, and insidiously so,
was the contrast it implied between the soldiers at the front, often
southern and peasant, bleeding and dying for their country while earn-
ing half a lira a day, and the workers, northern and socialist, working
hard but in safe surroundings and for fifteen times the wages.[32] Moreover, the concept was political because the peasant-soldiers shared it
with the interventionist intellectuals, many of them reserve-officers at
the front, who now saw their socialist antagonists of 1915 as having
transformed themselves into worker-*imboscati* cynically allied with the
regular-officer-*imboscati* whom they supplied with munitions. From
this point of view the pre-war political and military elites were morally
equivalent to the socialists, and infinitely less admirable than the
peasant-soldiers to whom the pro-war intellectuals now felt themselves
spiritually allied.[33] Many of these intellectuals would join with peasants
in the post-war ex-combatant movement that became one of the main
early sources of fascism.[34]

Beyond their shared admiration for peasant-soldiers and contempt
for *imboscati*, however, Italian intellectuals took quite diverse views of
the war experience, as even a rapid look at the very rich war literature
they produced confirms.[35] Sometimes the war is presented as a specific
cultural or human experience to be savored for the sake of "life." Such
literature often exudes an aura that is ecstatic, aristocratic, and intensely private. The same aura pervades the (mostly futurist) literature
that sees in the war an occasion for a socio-cultural remaking in its
totality. Less grandiosely, the war is sometimes presented as a specific
political event that provided a fundamentally democratizing experience
not only by mixing classes and regions but by making possible their
mutual recognition and bonding. This experience may be understood
as an opportunity to be seized upon and developed in the post-war
period, or it may be treated more ominously as a key event in the
larger story of the failure of the Italian political class. Finally, the war
is sometimes treated still more grimly or cynically as a necessary or unavoidable political event without likely positive consequences, an event
to be endured or despised and escaped.

Probably the Italian literary intellectual most famous for his role in World War I was Gabriele D'Annunzio. Returning to Italy in 1915 after five years in French exile, D'Annunzio spearheaded the intervention campaign with theatrical speeches that presaged his later self-presentation as the "first Duce" at Fiume.[36] When the war came, the 52-year-old poet adopted the most dramatic role possible, that of military aviator.[37] His daring flights over Trieste, Trento, and even Vienna were great publicity stunts and won him considerable notoriety. On one such flight, in January 16, 1916, his plane crash-landed on the sand dunes of the Gulf of Trieste, and he was blinded when his face struck the plane's forward machinegun on impact. Though he would eventually recover sight in his left eye, it was in a condition of total blindness over the next three months that he penned his reflections on the war on over 10,000 notecards, later transcribed by his daughter, and published as *Notturno* in 1921.

Notturno presents the war as a theatrical backdrop for an exercise in audacity, a ritual of chivalry, a relentless self-glorification – but, as the title implies, its vision is dark and brooding. In his blindness, the poet's vision is interior, focussed above all on the memories of fallen comrades, especially his early flying partner, the young aristocrat Giuseppe Miraglia, who died in an accident in December 1915. Yet the book is more concerned with the writer's experience of memory than with memories *per se*, and with his desire for death more than with the death of others. Interspersed with poetry, it is a survivor's plea to join his fallen companions. "Death appears to me only as the form of my perfection."[38]

Another, quite different aestheticization of the war experience can be found in the war diaries of the Tuscan painter, Ardengo Soffici, whose trained eye focusses reverently on the sublimity of the Alpine landscape as the scene for so much destruction and death.[39] In time, his gaze shifts from natural immediacies to the troops, whom he regards with both disdain and fascination. Yet he remains intent on the war as an extraordinary experience to be savored, rather than as an event with political consequences to be pondered and assessed.

With a similar appreciation but with a much more intense interest in the fraternization of the troops and a correspondingly more jocular and populist style is Paolo Monelli's novel *Le scarpe al sole* (1921), indicatively subtitled a "chronicle of the happy and sad adventures of *alpini* (Alpine soldiers), mules, and wine."[40] Monelli was a journalist, and he gives us an endless string of humorous anecdotes and a dictionary-writer's grasp of soldierly slang. Thus the title – "shoes toward the sun" – means "in the slang of the *alpini* . . . to die in combat." Yet the point of the book seems to be that in this absurd world one can do little to avoid such a fate, thrust as we are on to a stage as "puppets in the hands of an unknown puppeteer."[41] We do best to try to enjoy in the meantime the little entertainments of language and ritual and the countless encounters in which they unfold.

Far more ecstatic in their sense of military spectacle, and more cosmic in their estimation of its consequences for a reshaping of cultural life, are the war diaries of futurists like F. T. Marinetti and Ottone Rosai.[42] The most famous and best of these is Marinetti's "lived novel," *L'alcova d'acciaio* (*The Steel Alcove*), which is set in the Veneto during the war's final six months in 1918, and was first published in 1921.[43] Unlike his war writing from the Libyan years – "The Battle of Tripoli" (1912) and "Zang Tumb Tumb" (1914) – the book is a highly readable account of festive but often also grotesque episodes, rendered with a mix of lyricism and satire, and with his "words-in-freedom" poetry used only occasionally as a decorative special effect. Among the episodes are a gas attack treated as a moment of divine revelation, a fantasy of a firefight by (Italian) American "cow-boys," and, while he is on leave, a futurist evening in Milan at the opulent home of the Marchesa Casati. But it is at the "*guerra-festa*" that Marinetti is most at home – with his dog Zazà, his lover "74" (a machine gun), and his smart-talking, fast-shooting comrades.

Even more poetic but with a completely different aura, outlook, and intent, are the reminiscences of Piero Jahier, like Marinetti a participant in the Florentine futurism of 1913–1914. For Jahier, what was decisive about the war experience was the emergence of the *popolo* into its proper place at the center of national life, an event he symbolized in his poetic "portrait of the soldier Somacal Luigi."[44] Somacal is depicted as a "cretin" from birth ("neglected as a child, malnourished, allowed to run wild") and, until he was called up with others in his birth-year (the "class of '84"), a manual laborer (someone who "is nothing but does everything"). Offering himself willingly, Somacal the soldier is endearingly idealized as having a "rump that eternally expects to be given weight to carry," "a head that crouches on his shoulders like something bulky, because for a man who carries things, the head gets in the way," "hands of stamped leather that forever hold a shovel," and a "glance that is always down at the earth so as not to stumble." He is, in short, a dutiful beast of burden, but he cannot be a proper soldier because the position of attention – body and feet straight, eyes forward – is the "negation of his life." None the less, he does well at all the little things that matter at the front, like being among the first to run forward, digging a trench, or keeping his rifle clean. But can he shoot straight? Not at first. Somacal has always lived with both eyes open, so he finds it difficult to close one eye and squint with the other. This inability so endears him to his captain that the latter calls him "friend," a gesture Somacal smilingly returns. He is an *alpino* – not out of love for the *patria* (he doesn't know what that is) but because he likes mountain air and feels the need to stay the course. The honor of Italy is in the Italian *popolo*, concludes Jahier, and Somacal is their exemplar.

Other novels that seize upon the populist dimension of the war experience are Mario Puccini's, *Il soldato Cola* (1927), and Emilio Lussu's *Un anno sull'Altipiano* (1938).[45] Like Jahier's Somacal, Puccini's Cola is a bit the laughing-stock through whom the interventionist intellectual, who had known of the peasant only at a distance when he had campaigned for the war in 1914–1915, could now express his profound remorse for the havoc wrought in peasant lives. But his book is absolutely without editorializing, and Italy is barely mentioned. What we witness is a scene of constant fear and incessant repetition in which the soldiers dream of going home and plot constantly and without scruple to do so. If Somacal is an object of admiration, Cola wants to lose a limb (and does lose an arm) in order to be granted a discharge and a pension. What is Italy's honor to him?

Lussu's book is a first-person account by a reserve-officer. He shows us how the resentment of the soldier against the officers begins, as the latter ride horses on long marches and watch the troops like inquisitors. They can be paternal (providing liquor to their men as they themselves get drunk) but also arrogant and authoritarian in their hopeless drives to gain territory, which is why the men say, "better a dead general than one who's wide awake." The narrative builds to a climax of mutiny and attempted decimation, but what lingers most in the reader's memory are men like "Uncle Francesco," a southern peasant with five children who sends home every lira he makes.[46]

Finally, there are those texts focussed on the politics of the war in a still more sinister light. Attilio Frescura's *Diario di un imboscato* (1919) is a fresh and spontaneous but also unrelentingly detailed documentation of the many modes of dissent (self-wounding, desertion, mutiny) expressed by common soldiers toward their officers who are depicted as uncaring and incapable. Giuseppe Prezzolini's *Dopo Caporetto* (1919) and Curzio Malaparte's *La rivolta dei santi maledetti* (1921) are reflections on the disaster at Caporetto, which we will consider momentarily. Carlo Emilio Gadda's war books reflect repentently on the pain of the former interventionist, now faced with the unending horrors of combat, who lives the experience as a gap between his ideals and his nervous system.[47] Finally, Giovanni Comisso offers an utterly cynical portrait of war as "every man for himself," of officers so inept that they cannot read maps

13.2   "Three hundred thousand dead Germans in a month, General," *La Ghirba*

and so immoral they steal from their fellow officers, and of troops so completely in the dark that, at the war's end, they "smile stupidly as if they didn't know themselves what they had been doing and why."[48]

Grim estimates of the war by intellectuals had come as early as 1915, as the reflections of Renato Serra remind us.[49] But what gave the cutting edge to most of them was the defeat at Caporetto, so cataclysmic as to divide the Italian war experience literally into two. Naturally, with Cadorna's policies and massive evidence of morale problems, there was a tendency to assume that the rout had been caused by some sort of "soldiers' strike." Indeed, it was Cadorna himself who first seized upon this explanation, one that was then quickly assimilated by interventionist critics like Prezzolini and Malaparte who sought to use the experience as leverage in overthrowing Italy's liberal political class.[50] Yet subsequent research has shown that the strike was largely mythical and that the overwhelming cause of the debacle was military. Cadorna was caught by surprise (he took evidence of a German–Austrian buildup as a bluff), and the enemy used new offensive tactics based on rapid infiltration of confined areas to blow holes in the Italian lines, tactics that were used elsewhere with equally devastating results against the British and the Russians.[51]

After Caporetto the Italians were fighting a different war, one on Italian soil in which the nation's survival was suddenly at stake, and this seems to have enabled them to make some necessary adjustments. Cadorna was dismissed and replaced by a new army chief of staff whose policies were more cautious and civil; a new and somewhat stronger government took over in Rome; new tactics like those that had been used against them were devised, and a new elite corps of *arditi* (assault regiments) were created to use them; and, most importantly, a major effort was made to boost troop morale both materially, with better equipment and provisions, and culturally, through education, entertainment, more humane policies, and more promises of post-war happiness. In the latter effort Italian intellectuals played a key role.

For all these reasons, the year from Caporetto to Vittorio Veneto amounts to a second phase of the war. In this phase, Prezzolini later wrote, "Italy was united as it had not been for centuries – in fact, in law, and in common consciousness."[52] Before Caporetto the government had feared a propaganda campaign lest it alarm the population that the war might be less than short and decisive; now an institutionalized propaganda service (*il Servizio P.*) launched a major campaign to win back the troops.[53] Led in part by Giuseppe Lombardo-Radice, a student of Salvemini and Italy's major pedagogical theorist, the *Servizio P.* aimed to avoid "Lectures" to the troops by talking one-on-one with soldiers in casual settings, reassuring them that their needs were being met, and informing them of the many new cultural opportunities being developed for and by them.[54] Among these opportunities were new recreation facilities (sixty-three *case del soldato* were created in the 5th Army alone), theaters run by the troops for their amusement and without propaganda, "film evenings," gymnastic competitions (with prizes going to the families at home), improvements in mail service, distribution of newspapers from home, and encouragement of new "trench journals" on which many common soldiers collaborated.[55]

Among the best and best known of these journals were *La Ghirba*, edited by Soffici (a future fascist), and *L'Astico*, edited by Jahier (a left-democrat) and the only one of these journals literally edited in the trenches. *La Ghirba*, which published 29 issues with a circulation of about 40,000 each (ten times what *La Voce* ever sold during the days when Soffici wrote for it), featured humorous illustrations of familiar combat scenes (though no deaths were depicted) and was replete with earthy, insider slang. Written material was minimized and rendered at an elementary level, in keeping with an audience that was at best barely literate. In contrast, *L'Astico*, which offered thirty-nine issues to a similarly sized readership, featured articles stressing a simple morality of duty, and aimed to educate its readers, even as it recognized their present deficiencies. But it too was very interested in the folklore of the war, and encouraged the soldiers to submit transcripts of their songs, poems, and stories. Rather than allow this material to speak for itself, however, Jahier's tendency was to incorporate it into stories in which he supplied the moral. The result was a not always smooth fusion of intellectualism and populism, of abstract thought and concrete images. Though less than *La Ghirba*, *L'Astico* gave new voice to a mass culture more visually illustrated, spoken, and sung than written and read.

The staple cartoon in *La Ghirba* simply vilified the Germans. The issue of April 21, 1918, for example, carried one labelled "German Strategy" which depicted a soldier asking, "Three hundred thousand German deaths in one month, General? Did you figure on this in your plans?" "But of course," he replies. "The piles of cadavers help to block enemy counterattacks." Toward the end of the war, however, *La Ghirba* felt freer to turn its irony against targets closer to home. Thus, in its final issue of 31 December, it parodied an "extremely reserved" circular from the Italian Supreme Command of the "hellish forces" regarding the "overly meek" behavior of "some of its devils" who don't kill enough. To this the sector commander is depicted as replying to the Supreme Command that he has sent some of his "young devils . . . to attend special training courses in Germany and Austria."

An example of Jahier's very different approach is the story he tells based on soldier accounts of the *pignoli* among them – those overly meticulous soldiers who tend to arouse the contempt of their earthier comrades.[56] There was a certain lance-corporal, he writes, whom everyone referred to as a *pignolo*. But why, asks the narrator? Because he sounded roll-call precisely on time and made sure everyone cleaned the dirt from under their cots. Then there was another officer in camp, a medical lieutenant, who was also considered a *pignolo*. His offense? He gave no one a rest leave unless they were truly sick; men who had merely got drunk the night before could not get the morning off. Finally, there was a general called a *pignolo* because he insisted on snooping about making sure that every little thing was done to the letter. But what these examples show, Jahier concludes, is that to be a *pignolo* is simply to be diligent and dutiful. If this is what a *pignolo* is, we should all be *pignoli*. "We will win the war if we all become *pignoli*."

The contrast between *La Ghirba*, which accepted the limitations of its readers and sought to entertain them, and *L'Astico*, which insisted upon trying to educate them for democratic citizenship, points to a larger feature of the politics of the war's second phase. Immediately after Caporetto, the old interventionist groups rallied to produce new national-unity coalitions. In November 1917 a "Committee for a National Self-Examination" was founded by a broad coalition of intellectuals that would soon include Benedetto Croce, Giovanni Gentile, Gaetano Salvemini, Giuseppe Prezzolini, Sergio Panunzio, and many others from both left and right. At about the same time, a "Parliamentary *Fascio* of National Defense" was put together by the nationalist Giovanni Preziosi; it too included representatives from the full spectrum of interventionist forces. Such groups certainly helped promote a more democratic conduct of the war and more progressive policies, including "leaves" for peasant-soldiers to return home during planting and harvests, promises of land to the peasants, insurance policies for the troops, and improved disability and discharge benefits. Yet the democratic or left interventionists remained the junior partners of these coalitions, as they had been in 1915. Despite a heyday in 1918, when the end of the war came they proved politically impotent, remembered more for their initial sponsorship of the enterprise than for re-steering its direction. Thus, the greatest legacy of the *Servizio P.*, though supported by many left democrats and operated with considerable independence from partisan politics, was, in the words of Adrian Lyttelton, that it "helped to form the cadres of politicized young officers who were the backbone of the Fascist movement."[57]

To understand the legacy of the war, and of its final year in particular, we must also appreciate the cultural and social conditions at home. These were complex and ambiguous in their implications. On the one hand, it appears likely that the public did not really understand the conditions at the front. They did of course hear the stories of their returning sons, but the government made a systematic effort to censor visual images from the war zone in newsreels, films, and print media so that the public would be left as unperturbed as possible.[58] Fearing total censorship, newspapers in fact partially muzzled themselves already in May 1915, offering guarantees to the government that they would limit the number of correspondents on the scene, keep them circumspect in their reportage, and allow articles to be reviewed by authorities before being printed.[59] All films produced during the war likewise had to be reviewed by the state, and its censors allowed no bloody or otherwise macabre scenes and no images of anti-war politics (acts of mutiny, insubordination, desertion). Ironically, then, as one historian has recently pointed out, while painters in the Risorgimento could immortalize its battles in all their grisliness, no photos or films accurately portraying World War I were permissible.[60] This did not prevent such images from being captured, mostly in private photos, but it did mean that the newsreels and movies of the day were confined to scenes of troops marching off, ceremonies in the *piazza*, and detached, mostly aerial shots of the landscape and trenches. Even the best films, such as Pastrone's *Maciste alpino* (1916), tended to operate in a comic style in which its heroes "taught lessons" of Italian military superiority to the bumbling enemy.

On the other hand, the public certainly understood the conditions at home, and these were increasingly disruptive, though not without new opportunities as well.[61] The fundamental fact was the enormous cost of the war, which had to be deficit-financed (government debt quintupled between 1914 and 1919), and which produced spiraling inflation (wholesale prices quadrupled in those same years) as well as huge increases in military-oriented production despite shortages of coal and steel.[62] This production certainly increased employment, but such increases were mostly confined to the northern industrial triangle, and the conditions of work there were certainly arduous: very long hours, falling wages, and a prohibition on strikes. Some professions, like medicine, also expanded substantially, although, obviously, this expansion reflected hardship.[63] As the war dragged on, food shortages became increasingly common in cities. In 1917, amidst rationing of bread and pasta, food riots broke out in several cities in August, most famously in Turin where soldiers were used to restore order. Significantly, the (mostly peasant) soldiers did not hesitate to shoot at a citizenry they suspected was full of *imboscati* and that, in any case, was facing relatively fortunate non-combat conditions.

Despite these difficulties (or perhaps as an escape from them), the new urban culture industries were relatively unaffected by the war, even if the number of productions declined somewhat. Puccini continued to write new operas – *La rondine* appeared in 1917, *Il trittico* in 1918 – and if their débuts were now in New York or Monte Carlo rather than Milan, this only continued a trend toward the internationalization of opera that had begun before the war. Arturo Toscanini, who (unlike

Puccini) was fervently pro-war, conducted some concerts in the war zone. La Scala proceeded normally during the war and even added some "patriotic evenings" with speeches by political figures and musical programs. Indeed, in 1918, three leading Milanese theaters were putting on operas simultaneously. Major changes came only after the war: La Scala closed down for three years to modernize, and when it reopened in 1921 the city's socialist mayor had succeeded in making it state-operated; during the 1920s many opera houses of lesser fame were converted into cinemas.

Peasant life was less affected by the food shortages of the cities, though few men were left to work the fields. Inflation even allowed some peasants to save, and rising expectations were also fueled by government promises of land after the war. Yet the consequences of this were far from salutary. New hope among the peasantry scared the landlords, and long-standing arrangements based on custom and trust became suspect to both parties, each of which suddenly demanded that its contractual rights and obligations be taken literally. When this new atmosphere of mistrust is considered alongside the general expectation after the war – by workers, intellectuals, ex-combatants, and women, as well as by returning peasant-soldiers – that some new set of political arrangements, some "new order," would have to be put in place, its full explosive potential becomes apparent.

Moreover, even the seemingly positive changes provoked by the war often proved unsettling. Production increases to meet the demand for military *matériel* were little short of miraculous, but this huge expansion made adjusting to the peace more difficult. One historian has even argued that the transformation of manufacture from small workshops to the huge factories of the war mobilization system made a "decisive" contribution to the "authoritarian developments of the following decade."[64]

Changes in women's lives too were often both positive and unsettling.[65] There was an enormous increase in women working in industry, a phenomenon receiving close attention already by 1916.[66] By 1918, women numbered 196,000 or 22 percent of the total industrial labor force.[67] This made them major wage-earners even as it made their lives more difficult. Peasant women also had new opportunities, even as they shouldered enormous new responsibilities.[68] With the strongest and most active men away, they now did the farmwork their brothers and fathers had previously done, along with their own traditional chores. In addition, they often had to turn to supplementary work in factories to make ends meet, and they were obliged to undertake public transactions, like buying and selling livestock, that men had formerly done.

This brought them into the public realm, but it also made them more vulnerable to its dangers, sexual predation foremost among them. Finally, women of the urban middle classes sometimes enjoyed new cultural opportunities. One example is Maria Ginanni, a Florentine poet who directed *L'Italia futurista* for long periods while her futurist comrades were in combat.[69] Yet such opportunities were short-lived, brought no significant political changes for women in the postwar world, and may even have contributed to a backlash against the "new woman" in the Italy of the 1920s.[70]

Reflecting upon "the effects of the war on Italian culture," an astute observer at the time summed them up as follows: "confusion of spirit, bitterness about the ratio of sacrifices to the apparently small results, general suspicion of all other nations, fear of every idealism, a greater gravitation toward practical interests, a general bewilderment and indecision in conduct."[71] Soon spirits would sink still further as Italy walked out of the Paris Conference, a renegade regime was established at Fiume further delegitimizing the state, and worker unrest in cities and agricultural strikes fully polarized an already fearful citizenry.

Yet, to revisit the point made at the outset, the fact that fascism proved to be only four short years away cannot be understood primarily as a function of the war. The war began the process of nationalizing the peasant masses that would be realized only after World War II, and it profoundly unsettled the country. It increased inter-class animosities and suspicions, and made old cultural and political practices appear as archaic as they were. It exacerbated inter-elite conflicts, and created expectations no elite could fulfill and an emotional climate which increased the likelihood that whatever political solution was undertaken at war's end would be an extreme one. And it provided the fascists with some of their most potent myths and symbols: the ideal of the nation, the mysticism of blood and sacrifice, the cult of heroes and martyrs, the community of the trenches, the symbolism of death and resurrection.[72] Yet for the political system, these cultural changes were like so much unkneaded dough. The fact that they were ultimately baked into a fascist loaf had a great deal to do with factors that preceded the war: the failure to bring the peasant masses into the political system after 1861, the polarization of political forces toward anti-system extremes bequeathed by Libya and the intervention campaign, and the relative preponderance of the nationalist right within the interventionist bloc. Without these factors, the nationalization of the masses and the disorientation and hardships of the war might have provoked a sense of shared suffering and fueled a progressive renewal of the national community based on the new camaraderie of 1918. As it was, mass nationalization came much too fast and in circumstances that were out of control. So it was that Italy won the war and yet lost the peace by losing faith in itself at the moment in which it most needed it.

14   Popular culture in wartime Britain

Jay Winter

In terms of domestic – though not imperial – institutions, the British state in 1914 was perhaps the weakest in Europe. Concomitantly, no country boasted a civil society as strong and diverse. This contrast gave to popular culture a critical role. It ensured that in wartime Britain propaganda from below would dominate the war of words and images. And it created a vocabulary of a simplicity and immediacy that made that propaganda effective.

During the war, a chorus of voices, some on their own, some organized, some in it for the cash, condemned things German as embodying "Prussianism," shorthand for everything that "Englishness" or "Britishness" was not. In this discourse, to defeat Germany was to preserve a different way of doing things, a supposedly "British way of life," wherein an army and state power were marginal to what really mattered to the vast majority of the population.

The roots of this language of national pride and anger at the enemy were deep and well grounded. Pre-1914 Britain was the home *par excellence* of the Protestant voluntary tradition.[1] It underlay the social contract, the very strength of which helps account for Britain's endurance in the war. Popular culture sang of a task assumed voluntarily. That voluntary cause was the cause of a volunteer army. Even after conscription had come in 1916, the war was configured still as the effort of a nation acting not out of compulsion but out of choice and conviction.

One of the ironies of the war is that the very effort waged to preserve civil society helped bring about its transformation, if not its demise. After 1918 state and society in Britain overlapped in ways they had never done before; the state took on tasks previously done by local authorities or voluntary organizations, and the taxpayer footed the bill. The local state was progressively eclipsed by the central state, and Britain has never been the same since then. At the same time, expressions of popular culture became more national, more located in what may be termed mass entertainment, than ever before. These "concentration effects"[2] of war touched many parts of British social life. But virtually none of those rallying to the cause in 1914 or thereafter had any clear vision of this, one of the salient costs of victory.

This chapter will examine facets of the wartime culture of voluntarism, its strengths, its weaknesses, its glaring contradictions. It will do so in two parts. The first considers the impact of popular culture on the war effort, in terms of its unifying effects, its capacity to bond front and home front in an inextricable embrace. The second focusses on the impact of war on popular culture, and its parallel and subsequent development.

Front and home front

Through popular song, verse, and imagery, entertainers and artistes told the British public between 1914 and 1918 what they were fighting for. They did so neither at the behest nor under orders of the government. Entertainers acted independently, though profit and patriotism went hand-in-hand.

Their message was clear. On one level, the cause they boosted was that of "poor little Belgium" and the sanctity of treaties; Britain was drawn into a war not of its own making and was fighting for "Right." These issues mattered intrinsically, but their power derived from the fact that they revealed a deeper and more immediate danger that directly threatened Britain and was not just confined to the Continent. That threat to Britain was German power, thrust into France and Belgium and soon camped on the shores of the English Channel itself. Here was a clear and present danger to what contemporaries saw as the British way of life, a very local way of life, a life of pubs and clubs and a host of associations drawing people to activities of an astonishing diversity. Now in 1914 the strongest army in the world, the German army, was at the gates. It was challenging a nation whose inhabitants unthinkingly believed that Britain was the pre-eminent world power, the envy of what Charles Dickens had called "Lesser Nations." In light of this threat, and in response both to the harshness of the treatment of Belgian civilians and to the high casualties among the professional army and the volunteers who served in the Territorial forces, public opinion in Britain was united behind the war effort.

National pride drew men to the colors in 1914, but so did a sense that the "nation" was a very local place. Popular culture – understood as the codes, gestures, and forms of voluntary associations, elaborated not through the state but in civil society and through the market – expressed these sentiments, and a host of entrepreneurs sold artefacts, songs, images, and entertainments that transmitted them.

This was where cultural codes and commercial strategies came together. Artists, actors, comedians, minstrels, and a host of others spoke to and for civil society in Britain. The state did not orchestrate their words or work, or treat these people like puppets. And once millions of men had joined up, the armed forces drew on the same vibrant cultural life shared by their families at home.

A long way to Tipperary?

The division between war front and home front is a vexed issue in the historiography of the First World War in every European country. Some veterans believed fervently that they and their generation in uniform had been initiated into a cult that was theirs and theirs alone.[3] The gap between soldiers and civilians, they held, was a yawning one, bridged neither before nor after the Armistice. When they tried to speak of the war on leave, some ex-soldiers recalled, no one at home wanted to listen. Instead, civilians sang blithely of abominations they knew not; tortures slighted by their levity. So wrote Siegfried Sassoon of his disgust of the language of music halls, the tunes of which "mocked the corpses round Bapaume."[4]

There was a shrill tone to much wartime popular entertainment. Here Sassoon's words have been used justifiably to point out the crudities of what the French call *bourrage de crâne*, or the eyewash of press and other propaganda. But this interpretation of the divide between soldiers and the country for which they fought holds only part of the truth. To some soldiers, music hall, popular songs, and theatrical displays did tend to trivialize the war and the hardships they faced at the front. But millions of other soldiers knew why they fought in part because their instinctive loyalties were touched by the sentimentality of these voices and images. The message they took from them was clear. They could (and did) put up with the awfulness of trench warfare in part because of their commitment to the world they had left behind, a world conjured up in vivid terms by popular entertainments.

Here is the key to the history of popular culture in wartime Britain and among that part of the nation in action on the Continent. A civilian army brought its civilian entertainments with it.[5] Music hall celebrated a code of ordinary life which reminded soldiers that they were in uniform only "in parentheses," as it were.[6] In song and stylized stage buffoonery, millions of soldiers saw the "before" and dreamed of the "after." The vast majority believed that this period in uniform was a hiatus in their lives, a period with a clear end: victory and demobilization. Defeat hardly entered their minds.[7] After the war, they would return and resume the course of their lives. These men in effect never left home; they brought it with them in their imagination as cultural baggage which saw most of them through the worst of what they had to face.

The sounds of home

Popular culture gave voice to the reassuringly familiar images and memories of "Blighty" – the Urdu word for "home" borrowed from British India – in a disturbingly alien world. It offered a host of images and phrases infusing a myriad of makeshift strategies of coping with the war, contrived in a hurry and soon to be gone without trace. Many of the sounds of home were carried on gramophones. This part of the entertainment industry went through a massive restructuring in wartime. Its history shows clearly both the strength of the links between front and home front, and how those links were forged.[8]

The outbreak of war in 1914 was a disaster for the gramophone industry in Britain. More than half its equipment and records were produced in Germany. The German assets of the major player in this field, the British Gramophone Company, were confiscated, sold by the state, and never recovered. Three years later, the Russian Revolution stripped the company of its holdings there. In effect, the domestic market was all that was left; and that market thrived. One reason for success was greater purchasing power among the manual working class; another was the market in uniform. Gramophones were commonplace on the Western front, and their products blared out over no man's land whenever conditions allowed. We can learn much about popular culture in wartime by surveying this market and its products.

Initially, the Gramophone Company released a series of "patriotic records." Stewart Gordon offered "Our United Front," "Sons of Old Britannia." and the "Little Mother." For those interested in verisimilitude, there were the recorded sounds of "British troops passing through Boulogne" and (believe it or not) "A drill sergeant's words of command." But these records did not sell well. The market that mattered was for other kinds of music. As one British Gramophone Company official put it in 1915: "The demand for the so-called patriotic popular number has practically passed into oblivion, the boys at the front calling for the straight popular number."[9] About 50 percent of the trade was in music hall ballads; the rest was in "standard selections and operatic numbers" up to and including recordings of the renowned Italian tenor, Enrico Caruso.

Later in the war, one of the soldiers' favorites was "Roses of Picardy," words and music by Robert Weatherley and Haydn Wood. Its central lyrics catch the romanticism of much of popular culture, a kind of sentimentality through which the ties between front and home front were expressed and reinforced:

> Roses are shining in Picardy.
> In the hush of the silver dew.
> Roses are flowering in Picardy.
> But there's never a rose like you.
> And the roses will die with the summertime.
> And our paths may be far apart.
> But there's one rose that dies not in Picardy.
> 'Tis the rose that I keep in my heart.

It is certainly true that the character and ironic bite of many songs varied according to the artist's inflection, but one would be hard put to squeeze irony out of this song. It became a fixture among men who had fought in Picardy on the Somme and elsewhere, and has entered the lexicon of Great War lyrics sung to this day. The sweet sadness of the melody made it more appropriate for campfires than for the march, but that sedentary location was a time for reflection anyway. Kinfolk at home responded to its cadences too. It should hardly surprise us that music of the "Roses of Picardy" variety offered connection or consolation to millions of divided families in Britain.

So did an earlier song, "If you were the only girl in the world," released in April 1916 by Columbia Records almost immediately after it was first aired that very month in the London review "The Bing Boys are Here."[10] The song, written by Clifford Grey with music by Nat D. Dyer, captured the same non-martial and nostalgic air as did "The Roses of Picardy." This is the refrain, sung as a duet by George Robey and Violet Loraine:

> ROBEY   If you were the only girl in the world.
> LORAINE And you were the only boy.
>
> ROBEY   Nothing else would matter in this world today.
> LORAINE We could go on loving in the same old way.
>
> ROBEY   A garden of Eden just made for two.
> LORAINE With nothing to mar our joy.

The production and sales of songs like "If you were the only girl in the world," "It's a long way to Tipperary," and "Roses of Picardy" expressed the world of sociability imbedded in pre-war music halls and theaters, a world of safety and affection that soldiers had joined up to defend. Political ideas or abstractions had little to do with their motivation or staying power. When a soldier in the London Regiment was asked if he was fighting for the empire, his response was an emphatic "yes." What he meant, he later told a friend, was the Empire Music Hall in Hackney, a working-class neighborhood in north London.[11]

Those neighborhoods sang songs about the war and replayed them in their own homes. In wartime popular entertainment was more domestically centered than ever before. The reasons were straightforward. From 1915, pub life was curtailed in the interests of munitions production: limited opening hours were strictly enforced. Music halls were restricted and controlled. The Football Association (see below) suspended its fixtures for the duration. In 1917–1918, virtually all extra-domestic forms of entertainment were subject to a heavy tax, doubling the price of entry tickets. Furthermore, throughout the war, and especially after the carnage on the Somme and around Ypres in 1916–1917, there was an ambience of austerity, which befitted a world awaiting news of survival or worse every day of a war that lasted through 1,500 dreary days.[12]

The same was apparently true among French families. Many were in mourning, an official of the French gramophone company noted in September 1915, but "there will be a reaction among those people which will tend to make them seek a healthy and moral diversion from the nightmare they have lived through." That "diversion" was located within the home. As the historian of the British gramophone industry has remarked: "Under the pressure of war people appear to have reacted introspectively, retreated into their own homes, and sought entertainment and solace from gramophone records rather than pubs and other public places of entertainment."[13]

The commercial effects of this extraordinary marriage between the civilian and military markets were spectacular. After an initial dip due directly to the rupture of trade with Germany, record sales in Britain boomed. From a pre-war level of about 4 million records, the Gramophone Company boasted about 6 million sales in 1918–1919. After the war, sales went on all-year long, instead of clustering around the winter gift-buying season as in the pre-war period. There was a serious shortage of new gramophones in wartime, since the British Gramophone Company retooled its plant on the western outskirts of London to produce munitions. But as soon as the war was over, 60,000 new machines were put on the market and sold. This was twice the level of sales before the war.

I have already noted the fragmentation of the international market for these musical products. In effect, the overall business done by the

14.1   British troops plucking turkeys for Christmas

Gramophone Company in 1920 was *lower* than in the pre-war period. But that aggregate decline masked a massive increase in *domestic* activity and profits. Here is a classic case of import substitution, but in unusual circumstances. Most of the effects of the war on British export markets were negative. Pre-war customers in Africa, Asia, and South America started to produce their own products in the absence of British goods. But in the domestic sphere, with the sudden disappearance from the scene of German production machinery, the British gramophone industry stepped into the breach and made a fortune.

The business history of one corner of the entertainment industry reveals two essential features of the role of popular culture in wartime Britain. First, it demonstrates how music (among other entertainments) bridged civilian and military tastes and markets; they were reciprocal, not antagonistic. Second, it shows that the production of popular culture was a business, whose history reflected many of the same pressures afflicting other parts of the domestic economy. Here the flair and instinct for adaptation shown by the managers of the British Gramophone Company reflected a more general phenomenon. Businessmen in many fields knew that production of certain goods and services boomed in wartime precisely because front and home front were part of one cultural continuum.

The "thriller" comes of age

The publishing industry did its "bit" for the war too. As in the case of phonograph records, here is another tale of commercial success and popular propaganda from below. Once again, privately initiated and produced items made a fortune for their creators while affirming the Allied cause and celebrating the men in uniform defending it. Here too, soldiers were consumers as well as defenders of the home front.

As in the case of the gramophone industry, the most popular messages were indirect. The best-selling fiction in wartime Britain was the "thriller."[14] This category includes fiction centering on crime, espionage, and mystery, not set in war *per se*, but illustrating abundantly those features of strength and determination that would see Britain through to victory. Soldiers loved these stories; so did their families.

The "thriller" is a genre, with its own characteristics. The internal tension is physical rather than emotional, providing a formulaic spectrum of action and detection leading to the resolution of the initial or hidden danger. This formulaic character separates such publications from the "high-brow" novel, the province of the educated elite, or the "middle-brow" novel, produced by writers of some ability but with a commitment to more than formulaic prose.[15] "Thriller" writers have no such inhibitions about the use of formulae. In more recent years, the genre has been modified, to incorporate elements of other kinds of fiction. The novels of John Le Carré, for instance, are more than formulaic. When the "thriller" was young, though, it was much less sophisticated and complex.

The war was the moment when the "thriller" became the dominant form of fiction, with an enduring mass market. Thrillers enabled a cheap stylization and streamlining of the format of popular publications. Drawing on the early success of the spy scare literature of the pre-war period, wartime novels could easily be slotted into the preoccupations of the time. *The Riddle of the Sands*, a pre-war best-seller written by Erskine Childers, created a model for many later efforts. These series of books could also be extended *ad infinitum*, since their production was not a time-consuming affair.

The key agent – and beneficiary – of this process was the publishing firm of Hodder & Stoughton. Again, entrepreneurial improvisation was the key to success. In wartime there was not only a paper shortage, since wood pulp was diverted to the production of acetone for gunpowder, but an author shortage, due to military enlistment. The result was the shelving of older lines of publication, and in particular the middle-brow "three-decker" novel central to the pre-war trade. These were works of moral improvement as much as adventure: Sir Walter Scott's *Waverley* was an early, three-volume mainstay of this trade, conducted profitably through circulating libraries run by Charles Mudie and W. H. Smith. Instead of aiming for these circulating libraries as the core of their sales, Hodder & Stoughton went for a mass market of a different kind. Formulaic novels had certainly antedated the war, but now they were classified according to genre, the best selling of which were the "thrillers."[16]

The vagaries of war, therefore, created conditions for the transformation of popular publishing. The vision behind this change was provided by Ernest Hodder-Stoughton, a man whose European education may have eased the passage from a non-conformist to a more populist approach to publishing for the people. He inaugurated the "Yellow Jacket" series in 1917, which became a dominant force in British trade publishing for four decades thereafter.

In contrast to the gramophone industry, mass publishers sold thrillers which took the war as their direct setting. Hodder-Stoughton not only ran the company which bore his name, but wrote some of its most profitable titles. His *Jack Cornwall V.C.* was a stirring tale of the Battle of Jutland, with heavy echoes of Tennyson's "The Charge of the Light Brigade" and Kipling's "Gunga Din." This kind of "boys' own" tale of daring was aimed at a domestic market; here the publishing trade was less successful in marrying front and home front than was the gramophone industry. But other thrillers, less full of swagger and remote from the war, did reach the men in uniform. E. W. Hornung, author of the "Raffles" series of detective thrillers, opened a lending library in the reserve camps of the British army. The demand was for tales of rakish characters like Raffles or the French equivalent, Arsène Lupin, who chased criminals, not storm troopers.[17]

The war was the moment when popular literature turned into mass fiction.[18] This kind of publishing benefited from economies of scale due to the popularity of novels with interchangeable parts. The genre – adventure, spy, or Western – once fixed, could go on and on forever. All one needed to do to renew it was to change the names of the protagonists, and a few details of the milieux, and – presto! – a new "Yellow Jacket" appeared. The genre was a "safe standard" of assured mass sales, a commercial "blue-chip" which germinated during war, and flowered in the two decades following the Armistice. Thus clever marketing and product differentiation increased the demand for popular fiction radically, an outcome of wartime cultural production with lasting consequences.

The sporting life

So far I have shown the appeal of some popular entertainments in wartime, some of it in uniform, some of it behind the lines. Wartime conditions forced adjustments in presentation, production and marketing of these services and goods, but the changes merely redistributed the goods of popular culture among a shifting and mobile population. This was especially true of sports.

The premier focus of sports in 1914 was association football (or what Americans call soccer).[19] In origin an elite pastime, by 1914 soccer was the national game. Recruiting for the army went on at half-time of football matches, but the sport's popularity made some mandarins worry that the working-class taste for it could diminish munitions production. In 1914, most workers had a $5\frac{1}{2}$-day week, with Saturday afternoon given over to recreation. It was those few hours, central to the working-class week, that seemed to the gentlemen of the London *Times* to stand in the way of the munitions effort. Nothing could better demonstrate elite incomprehension of the mores and manners of the 80 percent of the population that earned its living by manual labor. When calls came from on high to scrap the schedule of the Football League, clubs answered that their players had led the way in responding to the call for men to join up. The West Bromwich Albion team had formed a company in the 5th South Staffordshire Territorials (that is, locally raised volunteer soldiers): most were fans, but eight players had enlisted too.

But the pressure to desist from football continued. By December 1914, newspapers stopped printing sporting news, limiting their coverage to results only. There was no municipal celebration when Sheffield United returned to the city as winners of the Football Association cup, but 2,000 fans turned out all the same. Given the headaches of railway timetables and the wartime dispersion of families, in 1915 the Football Association called off its activities for the duration of the war.

Football did not stop; it just went overseas. The 1st Battalion of the 18th London Regiment "kicked off" the Battle of Loos with a football. A year later it was the 8th East Surreys' turn to "play the game." Each of the four platoons of the company commanded by Captain W. P. Nevill went over the top with a football. He offered a prize to the first unit to reach the German lines. A neighboring battalion witnessed what happened. "As the gun-fire died away," recalled Private L. S. Price, "I saw an infantryman climb onto the parapet into No Man's Land, beckoning others to follow. As he did so he kicked off a football; a good kick, the ball rose and traveled well towards the German line. That seemed to be the signal to advance." Captain Nevill never got to hand over the prize; he was killed, but two of the footballs made it. One is in the National Army Museum in London; the other, at the Queen's Regiment Museum in Canterbury.[20]

These relics of war are also emblems of the enduring linkages between British popular culture and the world of sociability invented by the infantry in France, Flanders, and in a host of other theaters of military operations. These activities emerged from below, and presented the staff with a ready-made answer to the question as to what to do with millions of bored soldiers in the extended periods they spent behind the lines. Let them play football was the reply, and play they did.

The obsession with the game baffled the French, who "wondered why our soldiers played so much instead of practicing warfare."[21] The answer was that they played because they were British. The game symbolized a certain lightheartedness, a defiance of circumstances, as well as adhesion to a collective code of sportsmanlike behavior. Cricket and rugby reflected similar codes, though these sports never matched soccer's universal appeal.

The rhetoric of sportsmanship was everywhere, but it should not be taken too seriously. Yes, British soldiers believed in "playing the game," but not in the sense of the muscular Christianity of the English public schools. Solidarity yes; piety no. The trench newspaper of the Glasgow Commercial Battalion derided the image that soldiers fought battles just as they played games. "Is it true? IS IT HELL!!! Anyway the moral is that you should play football."[22] It was a moral shared by Dominion troops, from countries settled by men and women of British extraction. This is hardly surprising, given the fact that roughly 50 percent of the men who joined up from Australia, Canada, South Africa, New Zealand had been born in Britain. British sports were in their blood.

The world of Harry Lauder

And so were theater parties and concerts of popular music, organized either by amateurs in military uniform to pass the time, or by visiting celebrities who crossed the Channel to cheer the men in the ranks. One of the most popular was Harry Lauder, whose persona as a bekilted Scots vaudeville minstrel was instantly recognized world-wide. In 1916–1917, he performed in a London review, a highlight of which was his rendition of the song "The Laddies who fought and won," as a prelude to the appearance on stage of a contingent of the Scots Guards. On 1 January 1917 he received word that his 22-year-old son, John Lauder, a captain in the 8th Argyll and Sutherland Highlanders, had been killed in action at Ovilliers on the Somme three days earlier. The review closed down temporarily, but Harry Lauder decided to go back to the stage, and to sing the same songs and with the same determined message. In June 1917 he brought his portable piano and his review to the troops in France. His name brought out the crowds: 5,000 soldiers in one evening alone in Arras.[23]

This kind of celebrity presence at the front reinforced similar tendencies of a less professional kind toward the configuration in song of the bond between soldiers and civilians. The efflorescence of concert parties and amateur vaudeville performances was a mainstay of life behind the front. Unlike performances of the Harry Lauder variety, which were organized from on high, these entertainments were very much *ad hoc*, but none the less popular for that. Trench newspapers are full of comment about this amateur theatricality, and in particular about the ingenious ways soldiers compensated for the absence of female performers. Drag was not invented during the war, to be sure, but it took on a very ecumenical form during the conflict.

The "little fellow"

The genius of Charlie Chaplin was brought to the trenches too. This was hardly surprising, given the origins of his art in pre-war music hall, and the voracious appetite of soldiers in every army for cinematic comedy. But, in the case of film, we confront another element in the transition from popular culture to mass entertainment: the American wave. By the middle of the war, the film industry emerged as both the centerpiece of popular entertainment and the most important vehicle for projecting the meaning of the war as a struggle of Good against Evil. Not surprisingly, the Allies were better at exploiting this medium than the German High Command, whose concept of the consent of the governed was their silence and obedience. In the last year of the war, when Germany was deprived of American film imports, Ludendorff saw the light, and, with friends in the Deutsche Bank, bankrolled the creation of a German national film consortium. But these actions came too late to make a difference in terms of wartime propaganda.[24] As Professor Jelavich has noted in his essay in this volume, the Germans tried to replicate Allied initiatives, but with little success. Their film *Bei unseren Helden an der Somme* of 1917 evoked little of the sensational public interest in Germany that the British film *The Battle of the Somme* had done in Britain the previous year. With some staged photography, and much real footage, this British film toured the country to massive audiences. One estimate has it that 20 million people saw it in 1916:

14.2   British soldier writing home

half the population of the country. There never was a box-office success like it before or since.[25]

The Allies were particularly successful with this medium. American film imports, both before and after 1917, made it very difficult to speak of a specifically British film product. British- and French-made films were available, but they were simply eclipsed by the power of the Americans, and especially of that British expatriate, Chaplin.

A London-born music hall performer, Chaplin had joined Mack Sennett's Keystone Company in Hollywood in December 1913. He was already a celebrity in 1914, and contributed to the war not by joining up but by staying put in California and making films. Chaplin's service to the Allied war effort on the screen far outweighed the advantages of putting him in uniform. He was an iconic figure, a man both terribly vulnerable and somehow able (sooner or later) to plant his boot on the seat of authority. He was the great survivor, "the tramp" – the title of one of his most successful films of 1915 – the little guy whose decency almost gets trampled, but whose resilience is indefatigable. No wonder some British Highland Light Infantryman stole a cardboard figure of Chaplin and brought it over to the Western front.[26]

More unusual was the effect Chaplin's photograph had on shell-shocked soldiers. A physician serving with the US army said that an autographed photo of Chaplin did wonders for the men in his care.[27] "Please write your name on the photos," Dr. Lewis Coleman Hall wrote to Chaplin, "the idea being that nearly everyone has seen you in pictures. I will show your picture to a poor fellow and it may arrest his mind for a second. He may say 'Do you know Charlie?' and then begins the first ray of hope that the boy's mind can be saved."[28]

Some of his films were explicitly propagandistic, but most wore their patriotism lightly. In *Shoulder Arms*, he dreams of an adventure in which he manages to capture virtually the entire German General Staff, including the Kaiser, played by his brother Sidney. He represented the amalgam of American and British popular culture which emerged as the hallmark of mass entertainment during and after the conflict. Similarly popular was the Canadian-born American actress Mary Pickford, "America's sweetheart," whose 1917 portrayal of an American patriot facing a German firing squad was just the thing to rally American opinion on their entry into the war. On 8 April 1918, Chaplin's appearance with Mary Pickford and Douglas Fairbanks on Wall Street in New York drew an estimated 30,000 people.[29] After clowning with Fairbanks (and standing on Fairbanks' shoulders), Chaplin told the crowds that "This very minute the Germans occupy a position of advantage, and we have to get the dollars. It ought to go over [*sic*] so that we can drive that old devil, the Kaiser, out of France."[30] In Washington, he repeated the same pitch: "The Germans are at your door! We've got to stop them! And we *will* stop them if you buy Liberty Bonds! Remember, each bond you buy will save a soldier's life – a mother's son! – will bring this war to an early victory!" He then promptly fell off the platform and (in his words) "grabbed Marie Dressler and fell with her on top of my handsome young friend, who happened to be then the assistant secretary of the navy, Franklin D. Roosevelt."[31]

Chaplin's career brings out one of the central features of the impact of the war on popular culture in Britain. The conflict both created opportunities for the domestic production of goods and services in the entertainment industry and shifted the geographical center of much of that industry across the Atlantic. From 1918 on, it was simply impossible to speak of European cinema as a discrete entity; it could not resist the American invasion and American ways of doing things.

The business of the sacred

Cultural history is a messy subject, full of unevennesses and inconsistencies. By no means all aspects of popular culture can be located within the framework of analysis adopted in this chapter. Much of associative life and collective activity in the 1920s ploughed the same furrows as had been ploughed decades earlier.

That was literally the case with the allotment (or home gardening) movement, though the effort to increase domestic output of foodstuffs may have helped encourage the time-honored and apparently unstoppable tendencies of the British public to get their hands and feet dirty in the garden. Continuities may be observed in other pastimes as well: horse racing, cricket, rugby, ballroom dancing. Pub life was changed by the war, but many of its key features were resumed in the 1920s. It is true that you could no longer get a drink all day – licensing hours continued to apply until 1985. It is also true that the consumption of hard liquor had gone down in wartime due to rising prices and falling supplies, and that there were grumbles about the taste of wartime beer, which had a lower specific gravity.[32] But by the 1920s, most features of pub life were very much like those of the turn of the century.

With religious activity, we enter a complex world not at all reducible to church attendance. It is true that church enterprise took on many ingenious forms before, during, and after the war. For many women, sociability of a respectable kind was safely located only in such activities. But popular religion is not at all the same as institutional religion,[33] and here the variety of religious experience was too protean to enable the war to channel it in a specific direction.

Some claimed that military service turned soldiers away from religious observance. This is highly unlikely. Soldiers were probably little interested in the first place in denominational forms or theological precepts. As one chaplain remarked to a Scots theologian, "the British soldier has certainly got religion; I am not so sure, however, that he has got Christianity."[34] Superstition, spiritualism, a sense of the uncanny: these were the quite understandable forms through which soldiers and their families sought the sacred in wartime and after. These phenomena flourished everywhere before the war, though during the conflict, the urge to contact the dead naturally grew.[35]

There were those who cashed in on bereavement. Some ran séances; others sold spirit photography. Other forms of commemoration also entailed production, distribution and exchange. Street or church shrines proliferated, and these too were made by artisans and amateurs alike.[36] There were village pilgrimages and vigils, as well as charitable activities among the men at home and at the front. The YMCA was particularly active in providing reading matter and entertainment, no doubt of a suitably sober kind. In a host of ways, the search for the sacred went on as before, a central and enduring facet of popular culture that historians neglect at their peril.

"High culture" and popular culture

To differentiate rigidly between "high" and "low" is an outmoded practice in the study of cultural history. Still, it is necessary to point out a number of features of artistic activity with a bearing on the trends described in this chapter. One is the *Kulturkampf* over music and literature. In performances, Elgar replaced Beethoven, whatever the cost in quality and power. The study of Schiller and Goethe were supposedly compromised by their writing in the Kaiser's language. Thus the lecturer in German at Oxford had his salary cut in half, so that French and Italian could be taught in the university. Much of the fruitful field of scientific collaboration so profitably cultivated before the war was left fallow. To a degree, British–German scientific cooperation never recovered from the caesura of 1914.[37]

In other respects too, cultural historians have interpreted the 1914–1918 war as a major discontinuity. The most influential of these scholars is Paul Fussell, whose *The Great War and Modern Memory*[38] set in motion an entire industry of scholarly activity. Fussell's claim is that the Great War destroyed the cadences of Georgian writing in poetry and prose which could not accommodate the sense experiences of trench warfare. In direct reaction to the war, Fussell argues, a number of writers created a new "paradigm," an ironic mode of writing which dominates war memoirs and has served as the grammar of later literary encounters with catastrophe in this century.

This argument has much to recommend it. But its central claim that the war was a discontinuity in cultural history cannot be sustained. In part this is because it rests on a narrow range of sources.[39] But a deeper difficulty is in Fussell's reluctance to see the war as soldiers did: full of love for the old ways, they regarded it as an interval in a life to which they very much wanted to return. What Fussell terms "modern memory" did exist; the irony of the trench poets and novelists was a reality, and an enduring one at that. But it was not the only cultural form in which representations of war were framed. Above all, soldier-writers and artists retained the use of sacred forms and images as they attended to the universal tasks of bereavement. The elegiac and the lyrical were there too, and harked back to an older set of languages – the romantic, the classical, the religious – through which grief was expressed and in which mourning was lived and (for most people) transcended.[40]

In this sense, the work of many elite writers and artists paralleled that of their less talented but more widely read and heard contemporaries. Some new ground was broken in cultural history during the war, but much old ground remained to be ploughed. To change the metaphor from agronomy to astronomy, older forms of cultural expression flared up, nova-like in wartime, with a brilliance that belied (and foretold) their eventual demise.

From popular culture to the entertainment industry

Most of this essay has considered the unity of wartime cultural history in Britain. Soldiers did not spin off into a world of their own. It is true that they saw things that civilians never saw, and those who did not, might thank God for that. But the men who came home in 1919 were distinctly civilian in their language, their aspirations, their comportment. Perhaps this is one reason why their reintegration into peacetime society was much smoother than many in authority had feared at the time. They had won a war to defend their way of life, in their villages, towns, and cities, and it was to those neighborhoods and local landscapes that they returned after the Armistice.

To a degree, though, the world to which they returned was different. Most of those who had fought did not have the vote in 1914; all did in 1918. Some women got the vote too; within a decade, all did. Before 1914, many were not covered by national insurance; after 1920, all were. Many had had blessedly little to do with the state; after the war, the tentacles of the political realm stretched further than ever before.

The war also accelerated markedly a change in economic life of great significance for the employment prospects of part of the returning army and navy. The war effort had increased the size and economic power of large units of production. Amalgamation was the order of the day. The big five high street banks emerged after the war. So too did United Dairies, the chemical giant ICI, and the successor company of British Gramophone, EMI.[41]

Those in the service sector, including the entertainment industry, followed this path where they could. The bad times inaugurated by the trade slump of 1920 hit heavy industry but not the service sector. There, bigger was better, or at least safer. In the 1920s, the biggest cinemas in Britain were built.[42] The Gaumont Palace in London seated 5,000 people. Every large city had its equivalent, though on a lesser scale. More capital was required to operate in the entertainment trade. More money was made in it than ever before.[43]

The inevitable outcome of this increase in scale was a homogenization of products offered to a sophisticated, demanding, and increasingly national public. Local dialects and accents remained, but a national market emerged for the light consumer durable goods of the culture trade. The nationalization of taste was the way to economic success in this area, and the war marks a point at which that process took a major step forward. Once more, unevennesses and irregularities survived the war intact. Regional accents and preferences persisted then as they do now, but the 1914–1918 war, in part through the creation of a national army defending a national way of life, helped marginalize them.

The British Broadcasting Company soon got into the act of cultural nation-building. In the early years, under the leadership of Sir John (later 1st Baron) Reith, a man who had been severely wounded in 1915 at the Battle of Loos, the BBC incorporated a self-appointed national mission not only to inform the British public of what was happening in the world, but also to tell both the British public and the world at large what "Britishness" was and what it sounded like.[44] Popular culture was swiftly becoming national culture; and local entertainments, with any luck, became national ones.

Some, like Lauder and Chaplin, became international ones too. The trade went in both directions across the Atlantic, though the tide running east was always the stronger. In part, this was an outcome of the robust character of the American export market in the entertainment industry. The demands of a more racially and ethnically heterogeneous population presented different problems and prompted different solutions there, but the scale and dynamism of American developments made it impossible to separate fully the post-war European and American entertainment industries. In particular, the film industry crossed boundaries, and created a set of staple products and stars which helped turn national markets into international ones.

Conclusion

The interpretation offered in this brief survey rests on a view of war as releasing centripetal forces which helped transform elements of pre-war popular culture into post-war mass entertainment. To establish the validity of this hypothesis, a much more comprehensive survey of leisure activities and collective behavior would have to be provided. Some features of popular culture in the 1920s had not changed, but the context in which they operated had.

This story raises a central paradox. The great strength of British society in the late nineteenth and early twentieth century was its decentralization. A weak state and a strong set of voluntary institutions – which we now term "civil society" – gave to British popular culture a particular flavor, one which marked all wartime forms of collective expression. That cultural repertoire was an essential resource in wartime; it was mobilized not primarily by the state but by the private sector, either to "do their bit for the war," to profit from it, or both. Governmental propaganda activity helped orchestrate messages originating in the private sector, but the state never dominated it. That is why, despite anger at profiteering and weariness at the shocking casualties, the British public consented to seeing the war through to victory. They knew the ugliness of the war; how heavy the losses were; and how grim the accounting would be. Nevertheless, the overwhelming majority believed in staying the course until victory was achieved.

This commonality of purpose fused home front and battle front. Popular entertainments linked those in uniform and their families and made this extraordinary feat of endurance possible. But the very effort to win the war helped undermine some of the crucial cultural conditions which made that victory possible. The cultural ties to towns, villages, and neighborhoods, the expression of regional loyalties completely compatible with national and imperial ones, had given the British nation – in uniform and at home – a set of reasons to believe that winning the war was a necessity. But the industrial character of the conflict and its tendency to draw into the cauldron everything and everyone useful to the war effort irreversibly shifted the balance between state and civil society. In 1918, the Britain about which so many songs had been sung was a thing of the past. Under a cloud of bereavement, though relieved by victory, the British public was unaware that a fundamental prop of the older order had gone. But gone it had. A lot more than the roses had indeed died in Picardy.

Conclusion

Aviel Roshwald and Richard Stites

A perusal of the cases in this volume suggests, not surprisingly, that in all the belligerent countries during the Great War, government propaganda, the arts, and entertainment were deployed at varying levels of consciousness to glorify the homeland and reinforce a personal attachment to its values (real or mythical), to demonize the enemy, to honor one's leaders and one's allies, and sometimes to induce support for expansionist war aims. Yet one must avoid the equation of wartime culture with propaganda as if that were the pre-eminent, or only, mode of cultural expression of a nation at war. Readers will conclude, we believe, from the chapters in this book that propaganda was only one of many such modes of expression. Wide realms of high culture and mass entertainment, independent of the state, flourished in many places, sometimes supporting, sometimes opposing (within the constraints of censorship), and sometimes ignoring the nation's war effort.

The content of the belligerent powers' propaganda was so diverse as to defy classification. All the unoccupied states created some kind of machinery for disseminating selected information, and all of them enlisted the services of citizens considered to be endowed with the gift of persuasion, ranging from journalistic hacks to distinguished professionals such as Dr. Edgar Berillon (not to be confused with the better known Dr. Bertillon of forensic medicine fame), who lectured all over France on the excessive defecation and distinctive body odor of Germans and on the fact that their large intestines were nine feet longer than normal.[1] Propagandists coopted all levels of discourse but probably had the greatest demographic impact through the use of images and stereotypes taken from folklore and pre-war popular culture. The perfidious British shopkeeper, the impotent Gallic lover, the Bavarian sausage eater, and the savage Cossack all appeared in the graphic pandemonium of wartime villains and buffoons. And, in imagery and imagination, they were easily bested on the field of battle by the propagandists' own heroes and demigods.

349

The success or failure of propaganda for foreign consumption – Britain being the leader in this enterprise – had little to do with its veracity, and its content rarely had much connection to the actual conditions or prevalent sentiments within a given state. As Sophie de Schaepdrijver's chapter demonstrates, one of the most revealing examples of the conflict of competing propaganda campaigns is the case of Belgium, whose imaging ran from the sugary Entente slogan of "Brave Little Belgium" (a trope repeated for Norway, Holland, Finland, and Czechoslovakia during World War II) to the depiction of Belgium as the monster creation of misinformed diplomats – a view embraced not only by the German occupiers but also by the "activists" among the Flemish nationalists inside the occupied state. These propaganda battles seemed to evoke little response from the Belgian populace as a whole during the war years. Yet the legacy of these campaigns, and the related tensions over patterns of collaboration and resistance during the occupation, contributed to the polarization of politics in post-war Belgium. The clashing propagandistic clichés of 1914–1918 were thus to color the political discourse within the country for decades to come.

The scale and form of official efforts to entertain the troops varied considerably. British troops in France and Belgium were constantly exposed to a familiar home-oriented culture that boosted morale and frequently crossed the class divide. The German military authorities in occupied zones of Eastern Europe sought to reinforce their troops' sense of superior cultural identity and civilizing mission by staging theatrical productions for them, while also catering to their taste for the less prestigious but more popular *Frontkino* (front-line cinema).[2] Little of this seems to have existed in the ranks of the Russian army. Bulgarian troops, who seldom fought far from native soil, were regularly regaled by folk performances and popular entertainers. The Italian authorities did not begin their campaign to "nationalize" the front-line troops in earnest until after the defeat at Caporetto in 1917. Trench journals – usually composed and edited by junior officers – were employed in the French, British, and Italian armies as a medium for the expression and venting of troops' frustrations, and to a certain extent also as an instrument of propaganda and morale-boosting.[3] In general, soldiers who had access to front-line entertainment preferred the lighter forms to those infused with politics or high art. As to the political implications of troop culture, the war certainly engendered what the Italians called a *generazione bruciata* and a brotherhood of violence. But the fact that the British Tommy, the French *poilu*, the Italian *trincerista*, the Russian *frontovik*, and the German *Frontkämpfer* traveled very different political roads in the post-war years – from peaceful civilian, to Red Guard, to Freikorps volunteer – surely cannot be attributed to the cultural offerings brought to or produced at the front. They were determined rather by the nature of the war itself, the mode of its termination, and the character of the peace that ended it. And, of course, the variety of individual responses within each army belies simplistic generalizations about the experience of each nation's "front generation." Indeed, at least in the German case, members of the immediate post-war generation – those who just missed being conscripted in 1918 – seem to have had a more marked tendency to draw unidimensional political lessons from the war than did the front generation itself.[4]

If one were to write a history of European cosmopolitanism, a bewildered halt would have to be made in 1914. We say bewildered because, although it is natural for nations at war to look inward with devotion and outward with hostility, the constricting force of the parentheses of the Great War was almost unprecedented. And it was particularly forceful within that element of society – the intellectuals – where internationalism and cosmopolitanism had been, with some important exceptions, fairly commonplace. The magnet cities of Munich, Vienna, and Paris were now off-limits to those "on the other side." That international galaxy that had haunted the prewar Café Rotonde in Paris – Apollinaire, Cocteau, Picasso, Modigliani, Rivera, Chagall, and a dozen others – was now largely dispersed.[5] Concert stars, dancers, painters, writers, as well as intellectuals, scholars, and professors – if not stranded – ended their sojourns and made their way home or gathered in neutral states. This cross-continental retreat from foreign soil was a kinetic parallel to the intellectual abandonment of "alien" inspiration. Everywhere – but especially in France, Italy, Germany, and Russia – nationalist intellectuals exalted a "sacred hatred" as well as a *sacro egoismo*.

Two themes leap off the pages of their writings and manifestos: one historical and one essentialist. The historical one was the hoary semi-Orientalist mythos of one's nation as the bastion against Eastern barbarism. Russian historians frequently invoked their struggle against the Mongols in the Middle Ages as the exploit that saved Europe. The Poles saw themselves as the guardians of Western Christendom, protecting it and sacrificing themselves in the struggle against the uncivilized, Orthodox, semi-Asian Russians. The German version constructed the Eastern menace as Slavdom. As both Marc Ferro and Peter Jelavich note, the French philosopher Henri Bergson moved the frontier of "civilization" back one more country when, in the first days of the war, he proclaimed that it was a struggle between French civilization and German barbarism. As if completing the picture, the Belgian writer Maurice Maeterlinck went so far as to claim that Belgium had "saved Latin civilization from its greatest threat ever."[6]

The other theme involved a claim to innate or genetic "culture" or "spirit" that was seen as the antithesis of the enemy's. The German *Bildungsbürger* and the Russian intelligentsia were especially eloquent on this subject. The parallels were striking but not surprising in view of the fact that Russian intellectual discourse was suffused in this period with German philosophy – and that German thought in turn had been heavily influenced by Russian literature and social thought.[7] German thinkers postulated the notion of *Kultur* – manly, organic, authentic – as against civilization as embodied in the decadent French. The Russian intellectualized notion of *dusha* (spirit or "broad Slavic soul") was set against Western materialism. These formulations had great appeal, and were often also used by smaller peoples as a way of preserving a culture while seeking a place in the modern world. For example, Jewish thinkers, including German Jews stationed with the army in Eastern Europe, sought to draw on elements of traditional *shtetl* culture in their search for a spiritual dimension for modern Jewish national identity.[8] The ugly irony – often enough lost on or denied by intellectuals – was that the most assertive voices proclaiming a spiritual essence or a higher culture arose in states whose troops were among the most brutal in their occupation policies: Russia, whose Cossacks ran roughshod over the Jews of Poland and Galicia; and Germany, whose forces pillaged and killed civilians during the fight for Belgium, where a favorite anti-German slogan was "*Kultur* was here."[9]

A less visible theme, one that perhaps has been exaggerated because of the theatrical nature of its proponents, was the love of war for its own sake: war as a manly test of atavistic warrior blood, or simply as a Nietzschean act of will. Modris Eksteins speaks of a fascination with "an act of assertion, of conquest, of victory, of struggle, and of dynamic life in war" as a motive force for certain combatants.[10] The view of war as a spiritual test took on many shapes. From behind the lines, Italian intellectuals, yearning for their country's intervention in the war, spoke lyrically of the world's need for a "bath of steel." Thomas Mann, also writing from the home front, equated war with art: "The entirety of Germans' virtue and beauty . . . unfolds only in war." A particularly bloodthirsty example of literary cruelty is to be found in the wartime oeuvre of the Bulgarian writer Kiril Hristov. The examples of this kind of thinking among fighting men are well known and possess the mark of sensationalism: the German *Frontkämpfer* heading for the trenches with a copy of Nietzsche or Stefan George in his field pack; the adventurous aviator-poet Gabriele D'Annunzio; and the Russian soldier-poet Nikolai Gumilëv.[11] But it does not appear that these self-styled adventurers in the "storm of steel" (the title of Ernst Jünger's 1920 memoir of his front experience) were typical of the soldiers who fought and died by the millions in this war. The camaraderie of the military unit, the snippets of home-front culture and popular entertainment available to troops during their intervals behind the lines, and cynical gallows humor, seem to have done more to sustain morale (such as it was) on the various fronts than any romanticized notions of heroic self-sacrifice.[12]

The mosaic of avant-garde cultures that emerged, continued, or metamorphosed during the war reflected intellectual and creative energies that bore a variety of complex and evolving relations to the war itself. There was an early burst of enthusiasm for the war among avant-garde artists in all of the major belligerent countries. Most German Expressionists initially greeted the conflict as an opportunity for realizing their Nietzschean fantasies. Italian Futurists, whose creed was suffused with militarism, played an integral part in the successful political campaign on behalf of Italy's intervention in the war. Russian Futurists and Suprematists briefly set aside their involvement with abstract art as they engrossed themselves in the officially sponsored revival of the old-fashioned broadsides known as *lubki*; the images they produced for this medium were essentially crude propaganda cartoons. Likewise, in France, *imagerie d'Epinal* (roughly speaking, the stylistic equivalent of Russian *lubki*), classical portraits, and patriotic themes became all the rage among some former Cubists, forced by public pressure to abandon their supposedly German-inspired experimental style.[13] In quite a number of instances, a marked bifurcation arose between artists' independent work and their officially commissioned production. Stefan Zweig, among many other writers, produced propagandistic eye-wash for the Austrian government long after he had despaired of finding any positive meaning in the war; a fair number of avant-garde painters in France, Britain, and Germany were gainfully employed producing camouflage designs for military equipment;[14] several of the Dadaists – who considered themselves so radically anti-establishmentarian that they denounced the Expressionists as elitists – produced propaganda shorts for the government-controlled German film industry.

If cooptation by propaganda machines led the avant-garde to explore more figurative styles, so did the growing impulse to question the war. As disillusionment crept in among many of these artistic circles, they sought to express their critique of the debilitating conflict in a manner that would be readily grasped and understood by the general public. The result was the employment of figurative techniques to convey what

Paul Fussell or Samuel Hynes would call a modernist message. This was true, for example, of the British artist Christopher Nevinson, whose employment by the Ministry of Information as a war artist led to clashes over the potentially demoralizing impact of some of his work. His abandonment of Futurism in favor of a more accessible style was welcomed, but his tendency to use this style to articulate a bitter commentary on the horror and futility of trench warfare awakened controversy. When the War Office forbade the inclusion of *Paths of Glory* (1917), which portrayed two dead Tommies lying face down in the mud, in Nevinson's 1918 exhibition, he turned it into an even more powerful image of protest by displaying it with brown paper marked "Censored" pasted over the image of the soldiers' corpses.[15]

The common theme among all these conflicting trends and images was the intense politicization of art during the war. Neutrality or indifference toward the ongoing conflict was virtually impossible during these years, and even the escapism that came to dominate popular entertainment was in large measure a response to the war. A comparison of the chapters in this volume suggests that the various wartime trends in the development of modernist art can be linked to the diverse political contexts within which their producers operated. The modernist medium was always associated with resistance to the cultural mainstream, but the message conveyed by this medium – and the perception of what constituted the mainstream – varied according to the circumstances of time and place. In Italy and Germany, Futurist and Expressionist artists initially embraced the war as an opportunity for collective catharsis and national reawakening; many of the German Expressionists soon reversed course, and devoted their canvases to portrayals of the horror of war. In countries where avant-garde art was perceived as a foreign import, it tended from the first to be associated with indifference or even resistance to mainstream patriotism. In such cases, those radical artists and intellectuals who wished to express their solidarity with nationalist sentiment generally did so by turning away from modernist styles. This was the case in France for the duration of the war and in Russia for its first few months. In the Czech lands, likewise, modernist writers reverted to hackneyed, neo-romantic themes that lent themselves more readily to the expression of Czech nationalist or pan-Slavic opposition to Habsburg-Germanic oppression. In Belgium, conversely, some Flemish nationalists, pacifists, and radical intellectuals cultivated artistic and literary modernism precisely in order to escape the constraints of a stifling, pro-Allied, Belgian patriotism; they were tolerated and even encouraged by the German occupation authorities, who hoped to cultivate an alternative, pro-German, Flemish patriotism.[16]

In Bulgaria, disenchanted artists rebelled against the crudely militaristic chauvinism of the cultural establishment by trying to develop a progressive variant of patriotic culture that fused Symbolist and other avant-garde techniques with indigenous folk motifs in its depiction of the common people's suffering. Similarly, leftist artists in the free zone of Romania introduced experimental styles into popular modes of entertainment such as variety shows as part of their effort to expose the evils and sufferings brought on by the war.

One of the dilemmas of those engaged in avant-garde theater, music, painting, sculpture, and literature was that, although they were members of educated elites, they often claimed and even believed that their work was in fact the only true expression of popular culture. Some made the connection by draping their works in the garments of folklore, fairground shows, and mass entertainment – circus, cinema, the comics, even the detective novel. In this, the avant-garde differed from cultural elitists of the older generation, and the approach was fairly successful in attracting an audience.[17] But the majority of avant-gardists who despised the modern market could rarely meet the desires of ordinary people who actually preferred commercial mass entertainment. In many cases, therefore, the iconoclastic artistic ferment of the avant-garde either antagonized the masses within their countries, or remained altogether isolated from them. In such instances, the gap between avant-garde and popular culture may well have widened during the war, as the commercialization of popular entertainment and the growth of cinema (both as a medium for officially inspired propaganda and as an avenue of escape from the realities of the war) proceeded apace on the one hand, while the alienation and self-absorption of the avant-garde grew on the other.

Inter arma silent Musae was a cry often heard in 1914. While the intellectual elite and creative artists may sometimes have seemed tongue-tied, the same did not apply to the popular arts. The very birth of modern melodrama had occurred in the turbulent years of revolutionary and Napoleonic France. During every interval of violence and war since that time, "the unembarrassed muse"[18] had raised its clamorous voice in the service of Mars, as pure distraction in time of trouble, or both. One of the intriguing questions about popular culture in each of the belligerent states is: how soon did the forces of mass entertainment desert the first in favor of the second? There is no neat pattern of periodization, of course, since both functions overlapped almost everywhere. But there certainly was a striking difference between, for example, Britain, where popular entertainment remained infused with patriotism through the duration, and Russia, Austria, and Germany, where its content turned rather quickly away from martial concerns and expectations of an early victory for one's own side, to attacks on the "internal enemies" (profiteers and shirkers), and on to the familiar terrain of escapism. Perhaps autocratic regimes were too brittle in their approach and heavy handed in their methods to maintain effective hegemony over popular culture. Censorship that indiscriminately banned all negative images could only deepen people's suspicions and fears and enhance the credibility of rumors, as Steven Beller's chapter on Austria suggests. For their part, the British authorities' willingness to permit some glimpses of the misery and frustration of trench warfare to seep through into propaganda films and officially sponsored war art may have served to strengthen the public's sense of solidarity with the Tommies.[19] Of course, despite various half-hearted government and civic attempts to maintain general restraint and sobriety during wartime, all countries witnessed a rapid growth in "dissolute" forms of escapist entertainment, such as night-clubs, dance-halls, and, last but not least, prostitution.

Virtually all the cases point to an enormous wartime growth of those technical means of communication that were central to the development of modern mass culture. In those days, this meant pulp publishing, cinema, the gramophone, graphic reproduction, photojournalism – and the streetcar, metro, automobile, and train that could convey patrons to places of entertainment or bring folk ensembles and film projectors into small towns and to the soldiers at the front. In fiction, nothing was easier than to convert the old themes of Nick Carter, Maurice Leblanc, Emilio Salgari, Karl May, or Mór Jókai into wartime espionage or sabotage adventures which neatly combined propaganda and entertainment. The same applied to the other popular arts. Of these, the movie industry quickly became king, with national cinemas developing rapidly in an environment of blockade and import restrictions.

Whenever it did deal with war-related issues, popular culture tended to adopt a polarized perspective that recognized no gray zones between the love of motherland and hatred of the enemy. The most venomous attacks were often directed at countrymen seen as not contributing their fair share to the common effort. Worse than the cowardice of outright deserters was the hypocrisy of those who trumpeted their patriotism while engaging in privileged draft-dodging through medical excuses, exploitation of bureaucratic connections, the fulfillment of ostensibly vital functions in the war economy or propaganda effort, etc. While the image of womanhood was elevated as a symbol of national purity in propaganda posters, soldiers derided women for supposedly taking advantage of the war to indulge in infidelity, sleep with the enemy, or steal men's jobs.[20] Combat troops saw their own staff officers as shirkers. In one country after another, this binary vision of the front line was readily adopted by the popular press (which was itself denounced on the gritty pages of trench journals as incapable of honest reporting). The *imboscato* in Italy, *embusqué* in France, and Zem-Hussar in Russia were subject to barbed criticism as were the Bulgarian "heroes of the rear" who sat behind desks firing off patriotic poems.[21] Jay Winter and Jean-Louis Robert have vividly shown how condemnation of profiteering and other examples of unfairness became a basic feature of wartime domestic community codes.[22] Although widely and variously represented, especially in satirical press cartoons, in practice, the abuses were not subject to much real control or punishment. This gap between words and actions accentuated the sense of disillusionment and betrayal of ideals and reinforced the widespread tendency to castigate entire segments of society (politicians, officers, Jews, industrial workers, women) as parasites and traitors.

Commercial culture was generally much more successful than the avant-garde in incorporating and homogenizing selected folk motifs in a manner that was appealing to mass audiences and that lent it a veneer of national authenticity. The intense growth of commercial entertainment during 1914–1918, its strong association with patriotic themes, as well as its attraction as a form of diversion from wartime troubles, contributed to its legitimization as a national cultural arena for people of all classes and regions. In many instances, however, this created little more than a façade of unity, an illusion of national integration that did little to resolve the very real socio-economic, ethnic, and ideological divisions and conflicts that were seriously aggravated by the war.

Conversely, attempts by isolated figures such as Romain Rolland and Stefan Zweig to revive the pre-war ideal of a progressive, cosmopolitan culture that recognized no national boundaries and embraced pacifism went against the current of both popular sentiment and official culture in wartime, although the idea that all those millions had died in order to secure everlasting peace for the survivors was to gain currency in France and Britain after the war. For many among those (be they intellectuals or factory workers) in search of a serious alternative to aggressive nationalism, it was the Bolsheviks' militantly revolutionary, anti-liberal brand of internationalism that beckoned as the most appealing mirage from 1917 on. Those who looked to Wilsonian liberal internationalism as an attractive alternative were to be dismayed in 1919–1920 by President Wilson's own apparent inability to implement his vision. For those who remained wedded to the propagandistic ideal of national unity transcending all internal differences of class and region – an ideal that had seemed on the brink of sudden realization in many a land during the first days or weeks of war only to fade away in subsequent months and years – a purer, harder, more demanding and hence more liberating form of nationalism was the only conceivable remedy. And to many of those who had grown altogether weary of bombastic phrases and evanescent ideals, a retreat into cynical skepticism seemed like the best way of saying "good-bye to all that."[23]

Notes

INTRODUCTION

1 For a concise, introductory discussion of the war's impact in a range of socio-political spheres, see Jack J. Roth, ed., *World War I, A Turning Point in Modern History: Essays in the Significance of the War* (New York: Knopf, 1967).

2 Paul Fussell, *The Great War and Modern Memory* (New York and London: Oxford University Press, 1975). Samuel Hynes has further developed this theme, arguing that, as the war dragged on, it engendered dismay and disgust among intellectuals over what they saw as its criminal misconduct, the betrayal of the front soldiers' idealism by Britain's self-satisfied social and political elites, and the hollowness of the "official version" of events. The result was the crystallization of a vigorous modernist counter-culture that was intimately linked to a myth of the First World War as the great divide that separated an age of romanticism and innocence from the twentieth-century world of disillusionment and alienation. Though the general public was initially resistant and even hostile to this seemingly un-patriotic perspective, the modernist myth of the Great War soon displaced the official version in popular consciousness as the primary interpretive framework for the events of 1914–1918 (Samuel Hynes, *A War Imagined: The First World War and English Culture* [New York: Atheneum, 1991]).

3 Modris Eksteins, *Rites of Spring: The Great War and the Birth of the Modern Age* (New York: Doubleday, 1989).

4 On Nazism and kitsch, see also Saul Friedländer, *Reflections of Nazism: An Essay on Kitsch and Death*, English trans. (New York: Harper and Row, 1984).

5 Tipping his hat to Fussell, Eksteins does acknowledge that "irony . . . became for many the rhetorical mode and mood" (ibid., 219). For a compelling argument about the alienation of West European intellectuals of the "generation of 1914" from liberal values – and their all too common attraction to neo-conservative and fascist ideas instead – see Robert Wohl, *The Generation of 1914* (Cambridge, MA: Harvard University Press, 1979).

6 Jay Winter, *Sites of Memory, Sites of Mourning: The Great War in European Cultural History* (Cambridge: Cambridge University Press, 1995). For interesting discussions of how elements of cultural continuity manifested themselves among front-line soldiers and helped sustain their willingness to fight,

see J. G. Fuller, *Troop Morale and Popular Culture in the British and Dominion Armies, 1914–1918* (Oxford: Oxford University Press, 1990) and Stéphane Audoin-Rouzeau, *Men at War 1914–1918: National Sentiment and Trench Journalism in France during the First World War* (Oxford: Berg, 1992).

7 See George Mosse, *Fallen Soldiers: Reshaping the Memory of the World Wars* (New York: Oxford University Press, 1990).

8 Leonard Smith has pointed out that intellectual historians and students of "high" culture tend to see the Great War as a watershed of modernism, whereas social historians tend to emphasize elements of continuity (Leonard V. Smith, *Between Mutiny and Obedience: The Case of the French Fifth Infantry Division during World War I* [Princeton: Princeton University Press, 1994], 244–247).

9 For a highly stimulating exception to this generalization, see Hubertus F. Jahn, *Patriotic Culture in Russia during World War I* (Ithaca and London: Cornell University Press, 1995). Also, Richard Cork's spectacular volume on avant-garde art during the war – of which more in the conclusion – makes a point of including Russian works (Richard Cork, *A Bitter Truth: Avant-Garde Art and the Great War* [New Haven: Yale University Press, 1994]).

10 Michael Howard, *Oxford History of the Twentieth Century* (Oxford University Press, forthcoming).

1   DAYS AND NIGHTS IN WARTIME RUSSIA

1 There is a very old pioneering Soviet work on literature: Orest Tsekhnovitser, *Russkaya literatura mirovoi voiny* (Moscow, 1937). But the best studies have been done by non-Russians: Hubertus Jahn, *Patriotic Culture in Russia During World War I* (Ithaca, 1995); Ben Hellman, *Poets of Hope and Despair: the Russian Symbolists in War and Revolution (1914–1918)* (Helsinki, 1995).

2 Mikhail Heller, "La littérature de la Première Guerre mondiale," in Efim Etkind *et al.*, eds., *Histoire de la littérature russe: le XX siècle – l'Age d'argent* (Paris, 1987), 641–648; Tsekhnovitser, *Russkaya literatura*; Hellman, *Poets*, 80–84 (Gippius qu. 148); *Shchit: literaturnyi sbornik*. ed. M. Gorky, L. Andreev, and F. Sologub (Moscow, 1915), tr. as *Shield* (New York, 1917). Polish Jews were subjected by Russians to brutal deportation during the great retreat of 1915.

3 The best study is Hellman, *Poets of Hope and Despair*.

4 See Jeffrey Brooks, *When Russia Learned to Read* (Princeton, 1985) for the whole genre of popular reading and its audience; and Richard Stites, *Russian Popular Culture: Entertainment and Society Since 1900* (Cambridge, 1992), ch. 1. On war-scare fiction, see Stites, *Revolutionary Dreams* (New York, 1989) ch. 1.

5 Jean Benedetti, *Stanislavski* (London, 1988); Konstantin Rudnitsky, *Russian and Soviet Theater 1905–1932*, tr. R. Permar and L. Milne (New York, 1988), qu. 16, 17; Benedetti, *Meyerhold the Director*, tr. G. Petrov (Ann Arbor, 1981), 210; Eduard Brown, *Meyerhold: a Revolution in Theater* (Iowa City, 1995), 110–149. A light survey of *The Theatrical Gazette* (*Teatralnaya*

gazeta) for the war years suggests that the war was wholly absent from high level comedy, avant-garde, and absurdist theater. Moscow and Petrograd were not unique: the Odessa *Theater and Movies* for December 1914, when war interest was still high, advertised classical opera, ballet, and drama; contemporary melodramas (only one of which sounds like it had a military theme [*On Manoeuvres*]); and Yiddish theater (*Teatr i kino*, 52 [24 December 1914]); *Epokha* in Kiev reveals a similar assortment, without the Yiddish component (2 [8 February 1915]).

6 For circus and other popular performances, Jahn, *Patriotic Culture*, is indispensable.

7 Arnold Haskell, *Diaghileff* (New York, 1935), 269–270; Jahn, *Patriotic Culture*, 14; Camilla Gray, *The Russian Experiment in Art, 1863–1922*, rev. ed. (London, 1986). Kandinsky, of course, was internally bruised by being forced to vacate his second "homeland," Germany, and by the loss in combat of two of his German friends: August Macke in 1914, Franz Marc in 1916: Peg Weiss, *Kandinski and Old Russia* (New Haven, 1995), *passim*. For a sampling of avant-garde utterances in 1915, see John Bowlt, ed., *Russian Art of the Avant Garde: Theory and Criticism*, rev. ed. (London, 1988), 112–135.

8 Postcard Collection in the Slavonic Library (Helsinki). The best treatment by far is in Jahn, *Patriotic Culture*, 11–85, with illustrations. I sampled fifty-six issues of *The War* (*Voina*) for the years 1914–1916.

9 Fritz Kreisler, *Four Weeks in the Trenches* (Boston, 1915), 64.

10 Arthur Lourié, *Sergei Koussevitzki and His Epoch* (New York, 1931), 140–148; Moses Smith, *Koussevitzki* (New York, 1947), 87–95. In Kiev, for example, Beethoven, Schubert, and Wagner were banned at the outbreak of war: Michael Hamm, *Kiev: Portrait of a City, 1800–1917* (Princeton, 1993), 221–222. At least one critic tried for balance among allies and enemies: "the highest development of contemporary music," wrote Alexei Losev, "is that of Skryabin [Scriabin] and Wagner. Compared with it, [Verdi's] *Traviata* is vulgarity" (*Studenchestvo – zhertvam voiny* [Moscow, 1916], 120).

11 *Stravinsky: an Autobiography* (New York, 1936), 83 (the folk material was from the collection of the early nineteenth-century Slavophile, Pëtr Kireevsky, and later formed the basis of *Les Noces*); Faubion Bowers, *Scriabin*, 2 vols. (Tokyo, 1969), II, 265–266.

12 Geoffrey Norris, *Rachmaninov* (London, 1976), 51; Barrie Martyn, *Rachmaninoff* (Aldershot, 1990), 253–287; Israel Nestiev, *Prokofiev*, tr. Florence Jonas (Stanford, 1960), 98, 111; Harlow Robinson, *Sergei Prokofiev* (New York, 1987), 101–120; Aleksei Ikonnikov, *Myaskowsky* (New York, 1946). The last of the Mighty Five, the aged Tsezar Kyui [César Cui], wrote some Panslav songs and a few war-related choral works: *Izbrannye pisma*, ed. I. L. Gusin (Leningrad, 1955), 692–693.

13 S. L. Grigoriev, *The Diaghilev Ballet 1909–1929*, tr. Vera Bower (London, 1953), 101–112; Romola Nijinsky, *Nijinsky* (New York, 1934), 276–298; Elizabeth Souritz [Surits], *Soviet Choreographers in the 1920s*, tr. L. Visson, ed. S. Barnes (Durham, NC, 1990), 28–38; Tamara Karsavina, *Theater Street* (New York, 1931), 309–325. There are a few details of concert life in Maurice Paléologue, *An Ambassador's Memoirs*, 3 vols. (New York, 1923), *passim*. The Imperial Ballet did give a rare performance at the front in 1916.

For other frontline entertainment, see Jahn, *Patriotic Culture*, 120–122 and Jahn, "Patrioticheski motivy v russkoi kulture perioda I mirovoi voiny," in *Patrioticheskie traditsii russkoi kultury* (St. Petersburg, 1992), 139.

14 Feodor Chaliapin, *Man and Mask: Forty Years in the Life of a Singer* (New York, 1932), 214–219; Paléologue, *Memoirs*, II, 209–220.

15 Stites, *Russian Popular Culture*, ch. 1; Starr, *Red and Hot*, chs. 1–2. For one accordion photo of many, see *Solntse rossii*, 299: 44 (November 1915), 6.

16 The best treatments: in English, Jahn, *Patriotic Culture*, ch. 3; in Russian, S. Ginzburg, *Kinomatografiya dorevolyutsionnoi Rossii* (Moscow, 1963), 155–385. See also Peter Kenez, *Cinema & Soviet Society, 1917–1953* (Cambridge, 1992), 18–27 and Jay Leyda, *Kino: A History of the Russian and Soviet Film* (1960; Princeton, 1983), 72–89. For the false analogy with 1812, see Bruce Lincoln, *Passage through Armageddon* (New York, 1994), 152 and, for the tsar's taste in film and light reading, 170–171.

17 *Raëk: Vilgelm Satana i nemetskaya voina* (Moscow, n.d.), in the Slavonic Library, Helsinki. See discussion in Jahn, *Patriotic Culture*, 31; he also shows how vituperation against the Kaiser, a crowned head after all, was sometimes controlled by the censors (89). Virtually every other issue of *Voina* contained a withering depiction of the Kaiser by Lebedev. The airship poster, "Barbarism of the Germans" is reproduced in Frank Kämpfer, *Der rote Keil: das politische Plakat* (Berlin, 1985), 163.

18 Lidiya Charskaya, *Svoi, ne boites i drugie razskazy iz sovremennykh sobytii* (Petrograd, 1915).

19 J. N. Westwood, *Endurance and Endeavor*, 4th ed. (Oxford, 1993), 218–219 and Lincoln, *Passage through Armageddon*, 138 for anti-German actions; Andrew Verner, "What's in a Name? Of Dog-Killers, Jews, and Rasputin," *Slavic Review*, 53:4 (Winter, 1994), 1046–1070; Gippius in Hellman, *Poets*, 150. A cartoon in *Voina*, 65 (November 1915) identifed Russo-Germans with fat top-hatted, cigar-wielding bankers – precisely the image that Bolsheviks would use for capitalists in future.

20 Charskaya, *Svoi, ne boites*. See Stites, *Russian Popular Culture*, 34–36 with references; and Brooks, *When Russia Learned to Read*, 162, 314.

21 Hellman, *Poets*, 118–132.

22 Charskaya, *Svoi, ne boites*; for a sample of graphics on Austria, see Lebedev's back covers of *Voina*, 41 and 42 (January 1915). Russian soldiers mockingly called the multiethnic Austrian army "the Gypsy bazaar."

23 *Slava nam, smert vragam* (Director, Evgeny Bauer, 1914).

24 See Jahn, *Patriotic Culture*, fig. 32; Brooks, *When Russia Learned to Read*, 162, 314. *Voina* 14 (1914), contains a collection of crude ethnic jokes, fables, and anecdotes focusing on Turkish cunning, greed, and corruption. Bebutova, *Krovavyi polumesyats: strashnyi pauk* (Petrograd, 1915) is actually a sequel on the same theme begun in a pre-war novel subtitled *In the Land of the Odalisques* (1913).

25 *Belgiiskaya zhertva* (Moscow, 1914); *Voina Rossii s nemtsami: zverstva nemtsev* (Moscow, n.d.); *Voina*, 20 (1915).

26 Andreev, *Sorrows of Belgium* (*The King, the Law, and Freedom*), tr. H. Bernstein (New York, 1915); Ben Hellman, "Leonid Andreev v nachale pervoi mirovoi voiny: put ot 'Krasnogo Smekha' k pese 'Korol, Zakon, i

Svoboda',," *Studia russica helsingiensia et tartuensia*, II (Tartu, 1990), 81–101; Jahn, *Patriotic Culture*, 127–131.

27 *Liliya Belgii* (1915; rereleased in *Early Russian Cinema*, 10 vols., III, Milestone Video, 1992); Hellman, *Poets*, 63–7; S. N. Durylin, *Mariya Nikolaevna Ermolova, 1853–1928* (Moscow, 1953), 492; Souritz, *Soviet Choreographers*, 28–38.

28 B. S. Likhachëv, "Materialy k istorii kino v Rossii (1914–1916)," *Iz istorii kino*, 3 (1960), 45–57; Lincoln, *Passage through Armageddon*, 153–154. At the peak of the tragic events in Poland in 1915, a presumably serious dramatic treatment on the Vilna stage, *Polish Blood*, was a failure, though I have not been able to locate it; on the same stage, Offenbach operettas, a favorite genre of pre-war audiences, did well. See *Teatralnaya gazeta*, 9:27 (5 July 1915). For the plight of the Jews, see Frank Schuster, *Der Krieg an der "inneren Front": Russlands Deutsche und Juden in Westrussischen Kriegsgebiet, 1914–1916* (Giessen, 1997).

29 Hellman, *Poets*, 67–80.

30 Ibid., 84–118 (qu. 99). The song "To the Slavs" is in *"Geroi Kryuchkov" i drugie pesni voiny* (Moscow, 1914), vii.

31 For explorations of these lines, see Lewis Siegelbaum, *The Politics of Industrial Mobilization in Russia, 1914–17* (New York, 1983); Linda Edmondson, *Feminism in Russia 1900–17* (London, 1984), 158–176; and Stites, *The Women's Liberation Movement in Russia*, 2nd ed. (Princeton, 1991), 278–289. Bryusov in Hellman, *Poets*, 102–111.

32 Jahn, *Patriotic Culture*, 116–118 and qu. 115; Heinz-Dietrich Löwe, *Antisemitismus und reaktionäre Utopie* (Hamburg, 1978), *passim* for Krushevan.

33 Press citations are numerous; for one example, see *Bich* (Scourge), 4 (14 September 1916), 5. Ministerial grumbling in: A. N. Yakhontov, *Prologue to Revolution: Notes on the Secret Meetings of the Council of Ministers, 1915*, ed. M. Cherniavsky (Englewood Cliffs, 1967), 83, 134–136; draftees into monks: Hamm, *Kiev*, 221–222; Zem-Hussars in Lincoln, *Passage through Armageddon*, 210. Apparently readers did not tire of reading about the high life: see Bebutova's society novel, *Zhizn-kopeika* (Petrograd, 1916), describing a lavish ball.

34 *Kak russkie vzyali Berlin v 1760g.; Skobelev o nemtsakh* (Odessa, 1915). The war did, however, repeat his notorious massacres of Central Asians in 1916.

35 On Kryuchkov: *Geroicheskii podvig donskogo kazaka Kuzmy Firsovicha Kryuchkova* (Moscow, 1914) (trans. to appear in James von Geldern and Louise McReynolds, eds., *Russian Middlebrow Culture*) and *"Geroi Kryuchkov" i drugie pesni voiny. Shtabs-Kapitan P. N. Nesterov: geroi-aviator* (Moscow, 1914); Gippius, *Kak my voinam pisali* (1915) in *Poets*, 147–149; N. A. Vakhrusheva, "Soldatskie pisma i tsenzorskie otchëty kak istoricheskii istochnik (1915–1917)," *Oktyabr v Povolzhe i priurale* (Kazan, 1972), 67–89; soldiers were in fact given canned letters which they could sign and send home: Jahn, *Patriotic Culture*, 48; Alfred Meyer, "The Impact of World War I on Russian Women's Lives," in Barbara Clements *et al.*, eds., *Russia's Women: Accommodation, Resistance, Transformation* (Berkeley, 1991), 208–224; see *Voina* 16 (1914) for exaltation of the Cossack style of combat and 24 (1915) for grotesque depictions of women at war.

36 Hellman, *Poets*, 33–34, 186–190, and *passim*. One must consult this book as a whole for context and developing nuances among the Symbolists regarding the war. The theme of war as a simplifying and purifying force was taken up in popular fiction by Evdokiya Nagrodskaya in her *Evil Spirits*, in which the heroine's tangled love knot is cut in St. Isaac's Cathedral as the war breaks out: *Zlye dukhi*, 2nd ed. (Petrograd, 1916).

37 Maria Carlson, *No Religion Higher than Truth* (Princeton, 1993), 76–88.

38 Hellman, "Kogda vremya slavyanofilstvovalo: Russkie filosofy i pervaya mirovaya voina," *Studia russica helsingiensia et tartuensia*. ed. Liisa Bückling and Pekka Pesonen, I (Helsinki, 1989), 211–239. France of course had been an ally since 1894 and Britain a semi-ally since 1907.

39 Hellman, "A Houri in Paradise: Nikolaj Gumilev and the War," *Studia slavica finlandensia*, I (Helsinki, 1984), 22–37; Elaine Rusinko, "The Theme of War in the Works of Gumilëv," *Slavic and East European Journal*, 21:2 (1977), 204–213. A character in Mikhail Artsybashev's play *Voina* (Eng: *War* [New York, 1916], 43) muses over the "tragic beauty" of war, but he does so from a great distance and is ridiculed by other characters.

40 *The Story of a Life*, tr. J. Barnes (New York, 1964), 463, 274, 276 and *passim*.

41 Quotation in Chris Chulos, "Peasant Religion in Voronezh Province 1880–1917" (University of Chicago dissertation, 1993), 381. Galicia: Lincoln, *Passage through Armageddon*, 89. Russians did not have enough time to set up in Galicia the kind of elaborate German cultural-occupation system found in Ober Ost (the Baltic, Lithuania, Belarus): see Vejas Liulevicius, *Warland: Peoples, Lands, and National Identity on the Eastern Front in World War I* (Ph.D. Dissertation, University of Pennsylvania, 1994).

42 Frank Golder, *War, Revolution, and Peace in Russia* ed. Terence Emmons and Bert Patenaude (Stanford, 1992). The two Jews: oral testimony.

43 For exceptions, see Jahn, *Patriotic Culture*, 113–14, 133. The Jews of Russia did raise their own voice, however. The Moscow journal *The War and the Jews* featured Jewish war heroes, including a cartoon of a ferocious Private Katz bayonetting Germans, and news about Jewish participation in the war and its effect upon the Jewish population in Poland. See *Voina i Evrei*, 3 (1914). See also Segel and Roshwald, chapters 3 and 4, this volume.

44 Compare *Sbornik soldatskikh pesen* (Petrograd, 1915) with *Sbornik soldatskikh, kazatskikh, i matrosskikh pesen*, ed. N. K. Vessel, 2 ed. (St. Petersburg, 1886). In origin, these seem to be military equivalents of composed "folk songs." As with the Yanks in France, Russian soldiers probably adapted them to indecent lyrics. Nor could the occasional forays to the front by popular entertainers (Jahn, *Patriotic Culture*, 98) be considered trench culture.

45 For an introduction to this rich history, see: Daniel Orlovsky, in Abbott Gleason *et al.*, eds., *Bolshevik Culture* (Bloomington, 1985); Christopher Read, "The Cultural Intelligentsia," in Robert Service, ed., *Society and Politics in the Russian Revolution* (London, 1992), 86–102; V. P. Lapshin, *Khudozhestvennaya zhizn Moskvy i Petrograda v 1917 g.* (Moscow, 1983); and N. A. Nilsson, ed., *Art, Society, Revolution: Russia, 1917–1921* (Stockholm, 1979).

2 GERMAN CULTURE IN THE GREAT WAR

1 Julius Bab, *Die deutsche Kriegslyrik 1914–1918* (Stettin, 1920), 26.
2 I.e., war (*Krieg*), victory (*Sieg*), fatherland (*Vaterland*), hand of God (*Gottes Hand*), valor (*Mut*), blood (*Blut*), fury (*Wut*), battle (*Schlacht*), guard (*Wacht*), power (*Macht*).
3 Walter Kollo and Willi Bretschneider (music) and Rudolf Bernauer and Rudolf Schanzer (text), *Extrablätter! Heitere Bilder aus ernster Zeit. Textbuch der Gesänge* (Berlin, 1914), 15.
4 For example, see Walter Kollo (music) and Hermann Haller and Willi Wolff (text), *Immer feste druff! Vaterländisches Volksstück* (Berlin, 1914).
5 Max Schröder (music) and Otto Reutter (text), *Landwehrmann und Pikarde. Zeibild mit Gesang in einem Akt* (Berlin, 1915), 14.
6 Otto Reutter, "1914," act 3, 9–10; typescript in Landesarchiv Berlin. That archive houses the censors' copies of plays and songs performed on Berlin's stages up to 1918.
7 Wolfgang Poensgen, *Der deutsche Bühnen-Spielplan im Weltkriege* (Berlin, 1934), 69.
8 Cited in Jürgen Kocka, *Klassengesellschaft im Krieg. Deutsche Sozialgeschichte 1914–1918* (Göttingen, 1973), 42. For domestic conditions during the war, see also Gerald Feldman, *Army, Industry, and Labor in Germany 1914–1918* (Princeton, 1966).
9 Otto Reutter, "Berlin im Krieg," act 1, 26; typescript in Landesarchiv Berlin.
10 Otto Reutter, "Der Einbruch," typescript in Landesarchiv Berlin.
11 Otto Reutter, "Geh'n Sie blos nicht nach Berlin," act 1, 19; typescript in Landesarchiv Berlin.
12 Ibid., 15–17.
13 Report of performance in Wintergarten variety theater on 2 January 1918, in Brandenburgisches Landeshauptarchiv, Pr. Br. Rep. 30 Berlin C, Pol. Präs. Tit. 74, Th 1453, fs. 19–20.
14 Michael Esser, "Das Zittern der Bilder oder warum das Kino-Publikum Ernst Lubitsch nicht mehr sehen konnte," in Berliner Geschichtswerkstatt, ed., *August 1914. Ein Volk zieht in den Krieg* (Berlin, 1989), 256.
15 Jerzy Toeplitz, *Geschichte des Films* (Berlin, 1979), I, 138–139.
16 Toeplitz, *Geschichte des Films*, I, 137–138.
17 For Lubitsch's films during the war, see Michael Hanisch, *Auf den Spuren der Filmgeschichte. Berliner Schauplätze* (Berlin, 1991), 289–320.
18 Cited in Friedrich Terveen, "Die Anfänge der deutschen Film-Kriegsberichterstattung in den Jahren 1914–1916," in Wilfried von Bredow and Rolf Zurek, eds., *Film und Gesellschaft in Deutschland. Dokumente und Materialien* (Hamburg, 1975), 92.
19 Ibid., 100.
20 Cited in Hans Barkhausen, *Filmpropaganda für Deutschland im Ersten und Zweiten Weltkrieg* (Hildesheim, 1982), 3–4.
21 Wolfgang Mühl-Benninghaus, "Newsreel Images of the Military and War, 1914–1918," in Thomas Elsaesser, ed., *A Second Life: German Cinema's First Decades* (Amsterdam, 1996), 183.

22 In October 1917 Bufa officials wrote a frank assessment of the superiority of French and American film: see Bild- und Filmamt, "Der Propagandafilm und seine Bedingungen, Ziele und Wege," reprinted in Bredow and Zurek, *Film und Gesellschaft*, 73–87.

23 Ibid., 80.

24 Reproduced in Rainer Rother, ed., *Die letzten Tage der Menschheit. Bilder des Ersten Weltkrieges* (Berlin, 1994), 203.

25 Ludendorff, "Schreiben an das Kgl. Kriegsministerium vom 4. Juli 1917," in Bredow and Zurek, *Film und Gesellschaft*, 102.

26 Ibid., 103–104.

27 The relative status decline of the *Bildungsbürgertum*, and the attempts of that class to recoup its losses through pro-war rhetoric, are discussed in Thomas Rohkrämer, "August 1914 – Kriegsmentalität und ihre Voraussetzungen," in Wolfgang Michalka, ed., *Der erste Weltkrieg. Wirkung, Wahrnehmung, Analyse* (Munich, 1994), 759–777; and Helmut Fries, "Deutsche Schriftsteller im Ersten Weltkrieg," ibid., 825–848. See also Reinhard Rürup, "Der 'Geist von 1914' in Deutschland. Kriegsbegeisterung und Ideologisierung des Krieges im Ersten Weltkrieg," in Bernd Hüppauf, ed., *Ansichten vom Krieg. Vergleichende Studien zum Ersten Weltkrieg in Literatur und Gesellschaft* (Königstein, 1984), 1–30.

28 For a summary of scholarship on the "sack of Louvain," see Mark Derez, "The Flames of Louvain: The War Experience of an Academic Community," in Hugh Cecil and Peter Liddle, eds., *Facing Armageddon: The First World War Experienced* (London, 1996), 617–629.

29 "Lettre ouverte à Gerhart Hauptmann," in Roman Rolland, *L'Esprit libre* (Paris, 1971), 57–59.

30 "Antwort an Herrn Romain Rolland," in Gerhart Hauptmann, *Sämtliche Werke* (Frankfurt am Main, 1974), 848.

31 Cited in "Pro Aris," in Rolland, *L'Esprit libre*, 65.

32 Ibid., 67.

33 Thomas Mann, "Gedanken im Kriege," *Die neue Rundschau*, 25 (1914), 1471, 1473, 1475, 1479, 1482.

34 Rolland, "Pro Aris," 64.

35 Mann, "Gedanken im Kriege," 1483.

36 Thomas Mann, "Brief an die Zeitung 'Svenska Dagbladet,' Stockholm," *Die neue Rundschau*, 26 (1915), 830.

37 Ibid., 834.

38 Gordon Craig, *Germany 1866–1945* (New York, 1978), 361–362.

39 "O Freunde, nicht diese Töne!" in Hermann Hesse, *Politik des Gewissens. Die politischen Schriften 1914–1932* (Frankfurt am Main: 1977), I, 39.

40 Heinrich Mann, "Zola," *Die weißen Blätter*, 2 (1915), 1348–1349.

41 "Tagebücher," in Georg Heym, *Dichtungen und Schriften* (Hamburg, 1960), III, 139.

42 "Eine Sehnsucht aus der Zeit," in Alfred Walter Heymel, *Gesammelte Gedichte 1895–1914* (Leipzig, 1914), 9.

43 Wilhelm Klemm, "Schlacht an der Marne," *Die Aktion*, 4 (1914), 834.

44 "Seeschlacht," in Reinhard Goering, *Prosa, Dramen, Verse* (Munich, 1961), 295.

45 Ibid., 318.
46 See reproduction in Rother, *Die letzten Tage der Menschheit*, 454.
47 See Peter Paret, *The Berlin Secession: Modernism and its Enemies in Imperial Germany* (Cambridge, 1980), 235–247; and Claudia Büttner, "'Kriegszeit-Künstlerflugblätter.' Ein Beitrag Berliner Künstler zum Krieg," in Berliner Geschichtswerkstatt, *August 1914*, 194–202.
48 Cited in Rother, *Die letzten Tage der Menschheit*, 105.
49 Richard Cork, *A Bitter Truth: Avant-Garde Art and the Great War* (New Haven, 1994), 173–175.
50 Ibid., 94–95.
51 Mathias Eberle, *Der Weltkrieg und die Künstler der Weimarer Republik* (Stuttgart, 1989), 31–62.
52 Cork, *A Bitter Truth*, 26–28, 110–112.
53 Cited in Rother, *Die letzten Tage der Menschheit*, 98.
54 For Grosz's acitivities in the war, see Roland März, "Metropolis – Krawall der Irren. Der apokalyptische Grosz der Kriegsjahre 1914 bis 1918," in Peter-Klaus Schuster, ed., *George Grosz. Berlin – New York* (Berlin, 1994), 122–131; and Helen Adkins, "Die Zeit der Kohlrübe in Deutschland," ibid., 133–139. The relationship between the experience of war and images of violence against women is discussed in Maria Tatar, *Lustmord: Sexual Murder in Weimar Germany* (Princeton, 1995).
55 Richard Huelsenbeck, "Dadaistisches Manifest," in Karl Riha and Hannes Bergius, eds., *Dada Berlin. Texte, Manifeste, Aktionen* (Stuttgart, 1977), 22–25.
56 Huelsenbeck, "Erste Dadarede in Deutschland," ibid., 17.
57 Barkhausen, *Filmpropaganda für Deutschland*, 109–111; and Jeanpaul Goergen, "'Filmisch sei der Strich, klar, einfach.' Georg Grosz und der Film," in Schuster, *George Grosz*, 211–214.

3 CULTURE IN POLAND DURING WORLD WAR I

1 For a good general history of Poland in English covering the period of World War I, see Norman Davies, *God's Playground: A History of Poland. Vol. II, 1795 to the Present* (New York: Columbia University Press, 1982). For biographies of Piłsudski in English, see Wacław Jędrzejewicz, *Piłsudski: A Life for Poland* (New York: Hipocrene Books, 1982) and Andrzej Garlicki, *Józef Piłsudski, 1867–1935*, tr. and ed. John Coutouvidis (Hants: Scolar Press, 1995). Jędrzejewicz's book is more popular and admiring; the one by Garlicki is an abridged translation of a serious scholarly work by a leading Polish specialist on Piłsudski.
2 For a good new introduction to Dmowski's life and career, see Krzysztof Kawalec, *Roman Dmowski* (Warsaw: Editions Spotkania, 1996).
3 On the differences in political outlook between Dmowski and Piłsudski, the general reader would do well to read the section "The Duel: Dmowski versus Piłsudski," in Norman Davies, *Heart of Europe: A Short History of Poland* (New York: Oxford University Press, 1986), 129–148.
4 For a more specialized study of the origins of Piłsudski's legions, see Andrzej Garlicki, *Geneza legionów: Zarys dziejów Komisji Tymczasowej Skonfederowanych Stronnictw Niepodległościowych* (Warsaw: Książka i Wiedza, 1964).

5 *Poezja polska 1914–1939: Antologia*, ed. Ryszard Matuszewski and Seweryn Pollak (Warsaw: Czytelnik, 1962), 48–49.

6 This and the following stanzas allude to the lukewarm reception accorded Piłsudski's Riflemen when they first crossed into Congress Poland in mid-August 1914 expecting to make a show of independent military action against the Russians and to recruit volunteers. What Piłsudski did not count on was the fear of the Germans among the local Polish population and their fear as well that if the Russians prevailed in their campaign against the Germans they would take reprisals against Poles who had openly supported Piłsudski's army.

7 Krzysztof A. Jeżewski, ed., *W blasku legendy: Kronika poetycka życia Józefa Piłsudskiego* (Paris: Editions Spotkania, 1988), 57–59.

8 *Pieśń o Józefie Piłsudskim* (Wilno, 1916; n.p.), 1. A note informs the reader that the paraphrase arose in March 1915.

9 The closing words of the poem, "from sea to sea," refer to the Baltic and Black Seas.

10 The Kalisz bombardment is discussed in Jerzy Holzer and Jan Molenda, *Polska w pierwszej wojnie światowej*, 3rd. ed. (Warsaw: Wiedza Powszechna, 1973), 72–73.

11 For the full text, in translation, of Grand Duke Nikolai Nikolaevich's "Manifesto to the Polish Nation," see Davies, *God's Playground*, 382–383. Grunwald refers to the 1410 battle between Germans and Slavs.

12 Krzysztof Dunin-Wąsowicz, *Warszawa w czasie pierwszej wojny światowej* (Warsaw: Państwowy Instytut Wydawniczy, 1974), 43–44. For the text of the proclamation of 5 November 1916, see Paul Roth, *Die politische Entwicklung in Kongresspolen während der deutschen Okkupation* (Leipzig: Verlag K. F. Koehler, 1916), 41–42.

13 Dunin-Wąsowicz, *Warszawa*, 55.

14 *Muchy* (2 December 1915), 2.

15 *Muchy* (23 December 1915), 4.

16 *Muchy* (2 December 1915), 4.

17 *Muchy* (2 December 1915), 6.

18 For a good account of Warsaw theatrical life during World War I, see Ludwik Sempoliński, *Wielcy artyści małych scen* (Warsaw: Czytelnik, 1977), 104–139.

19 *Muchy* (2 December 1915), 4.

20 *Muchy* (2 December 1915), 5.

21 This pun, and the two that follow, are reproduced in Dunin-Wąsowicz, *Warszawa*, 189.

22 Kazimierz Krukowski, *Mała antologia kabaretu* (Warsaw: Wydawnictwa Radia i Telewizji, 1982), 145.

23 On the early history of cabaret in Poland, see Harold B. Segel, *Turn-of-the-Century Cabaret: Paris, Barcelona, Berlin, Munich, Vienna, Cracow, Moscow, St. Petersburg, Zurich* (New York: Columbia University Press, 1987), 221–253. For a Polish survey of cabaret, with texts, see Ryszard Marek Groński, *Taki był kabaret* (Warsaw: Wydawnicwto Polskiego Towarzystwa Wydawców Książek, 1994). There is also good material on cabarets and other small theaters in Ludwik Sempoliński, *Wielcy artyści małych scen* (Warsaw:

Czytelnik, 1977). For an account in English on the interwar Warsaw cabaret, see Ron Nowicki, *Warsaw: The Cabaret Years* (San Francisco: Mercury House, 1992).

24 For a good general survey of Warsaw theaters from 1748 to 1975, see Barbara Król-Kaczorowska, *Teatry Warszawy: Budynki i sale w latach 1748–1975* (Warsaw: Państwowy Instytut Wydawniczy, 1986). On Warsaw theatrical life specifically in the period 1918–1939, see Edward Krasiński, *Warszawskie sceny 1918–1939* (Warsaw: Państwowy Instytut Wydawniczy, 1976).

25 For the complete text in Polish, see Groński, *Taki był kabaret* 108–110. "Lev" refers to Tolstoy.

26 "Halban," *Szopka Warszawska* (Warsaw: 1916, n.p.), 4, 10, 16.

27 *Żydzi podczas wojny* (n.p., n.d.; photocopy available at Harvard Deposit Library), 21.

28 For the best history of the early Polish film, see Władysław Banaszkiewicz and Witold Witczak, *Historia filmu polskiego I: 1895–1929* (Warsaw: Wydawnicwta Artystyczne i Filmowe, 1989).

29 Groński, *Taki był kabaret*, 84.

30 Leopold Matrschak, *Byłem przy tym . . . wspomnienia 1914–39* (Warsaw: Czytelnik, 1973), 120–121.

4 JEWISH CULTURAL IDENTITY IN EASTERN AND CENTRAL EUROPE DURING THE GREAT WAR

1 I would like to thank Steven Beller, David Goldfrank, Steven Marks, Mordecai Roshwald, Richard Stites, and Jeff Veidlinger for their helpful suggestions and observations regarding this chapter. I bear sole responsibility for whatever inaccuracies or flaws it may contain.

2 The term Congress Poland referred to the role of the 1814–15 Congress of Vienna in its creation as a Russian-ruled kingdom.

3 For comprehensive treatments of these topics, see John Doyle Klier, *Imperial Russia's Jewish Question, 1855–1881* (Cambridge: Cambridge University Press, 1995); Hans Rogger, *Jewish Policies and Right-Wing Politics in Imperial Russia* (London: Macmillan, 1986).

4 Shaul Stampfer, "Gender Differentiation and Education of the Jewish Woman in Nineteenth-Century Eastern Europe," in Antony Polonsky, ed., *From Shtetl to Socialism: Studies from Polin* (London and Washington: Littman Library, 1993).

5 Klier, *Imperial Russia's Jewish Question, 1855–1881*, 148–149; Theodore R. Weeks, *Nation and State in Late Imperial Russia: Nationalism and Russification on the Western Frontier, 1863–1914* (Dekalb, IL: Northern Illinois University Press, 1996), 59–64, 165–171, and *passim*.

6 S. An-sky (Shlomo-Zanvill Rappoport), *Der yidisher khurbn fun Poilen, Galitsye un Bukovina fun tag-buch 1914–1917* (The Jewish Catastrophe in Poland, Galicia, and Bukovina from the 1914–17 Diary) in *Gezamelte Shriftn* (Collected Writings), IV–VI (Warsaw, Vilna, New York: An-sky Publishing Company, 1927–28), IV, p. 11; Steven J. Zipperstein, "The Politics of Relief: The Transformation of Russian Jewish Communal Life

during the First World War," in Jonathan Frankel, ed., *Jews and the Eastern European Crisis, 1914–21* (Oxford: Oxford University Press, 1988); David G. Roskies, *Against the Apocalypse: Responses to Catastrophe in Modern Jewish Culture* (Cambridge, MA: Harvard University Press, 1984), 92. Ironically, the massive refugee crisis that the government's own policies had created led the regime to abolish the Pale of Settlement in August 1915. Most Jews were still banned from residing in St. Petersburg, Moscow, and a handful of other districts (Rogger, *Jewish Policies and Right-Wing Politics*, 100–105).

7 David Roskies, *Against the Apocalypse*, 83. See also David Aberbach, "Hebrew Literature and Jewish Nationalism in the Tsarist Empire, 1881–1917," *Nations and Nationalism*, 3: 1 (1997), 33.

8 The fact that the destructions of the First and Second Temples (in 586 BC and 70 AD, respectively) are supposed to have occurred on the same day of the year can itself be seen as a collapsing of two symbolically identical yet temporally separated events into a single moment that transcends history (Yosef Hayim Yerushalmi, *Zakhor: Jewish History and Jewish Memory* [Seattle: University of Washington Press, 1982], 40–41).

9 Roskies, *Against the Apocalypse*, ch. 2; Yerushalmi, *Zakhor*, 107, n. 1.

10 As quoted in Roskies, *Against the Apocalypse*, 83.

11 Ibid., ch. 4; Aberbach, "Hebrew Literature and Jewish Nationalism," 33–34; David Aberbach, *Bialik* (New York: Grove Press, 1988), 60–62, 125, n. 5.

12 An-sky, *Khurbn, Gezamelte Shriftn*, IV, 85–87.

13 See Book of Esther 7.

14 The association of Haman with latter-day anti-Semitic oppressors was so common that during the reading of the Scroll of Esther on Purim 1917 in a synagogue in Russian-occupied Bukovina (an Austro-Hungarian province that is today partitioned between Ukraine and Romania), the children were restrained from their customary drowning out of Haman's name for fear that the authorities would interpret this as a veiled insult to the tsar! (An-sky, *Khurbn, Gezamelte Shriftn*, VI, 140–141).

15 An-sky, *Khurbn, Gezamelte Shriftn*, V, 79–80.

16 An-sky, *Khurbn, Gezamelte Shriftn*, IV, 5–14, 29–38. Mendel Beilis was the accused in the last anti-Semitic blood libel that came to trial in Russia, in September 1913. He was acquitted (Rogger, *Jewish Policies and Right-Wing Politics*, ch. 3).

17 See Maxim Gorky, Leonid Andreyev, and Fyodor Sologub, eds., *The Shield*, English-language ed. (New York: Knopf, 1917); Richard Stites, chapter 2 in the present volume. See also Ruth Apter-Gabriel, ed., *Tradition and Revolution: The Jewish Renaissance in Russian Avant-Garde Art, 1912–1928* (Jerusalem: The Israel Museum, 1988), 50.

18 Egmont Zechlin, *Die deutsche Politik und die Juden im Ersten Weltkrieg* (Göttingen: Vandenhoeck & Ruprecht, 1969), 241.

19 An-sky, *Khurbn, Gezamelte Shriftn*, IV, 14. Roskies points out that this represented "a grotesque reversal of [the first] Passover," when the Israelites had marked their doorposts so as to avert God's curse on the firstborn of Egypt (Roskies, *Against the Apocalypse*, 115).

20 An-sky, *Khurbn, Gezamelte Shriftn*, IV, 39–41.
21 Mark Slobin, ed. and trans., *Old Jewish Folk Music: The Collections and Writings of Moshe Beregovski* (Philadelphia: University of Pennsylvania Press, 1982), 267. See also the other songs transcribed on pp. 267–270.
22 The credo is also recited in full during daily prayers.
23 An-sky, *Khurbn, Gezamelte Shriftn*, IV, 41–44. On the other hand, the *Israelitisches Gemeindeblatt* – a Jewish newspaper published in Cologne, Germany – cheerily asserted that the demonstration by each country's Jews of how committed they were to their particular nation's war effort would shatter once and for all the anti-Semitic myth of an international Jewish conspiracy. See press review in *Ha-Tsefirah* (Warsaw), 3 January 1916.
24 An-sky, *Khurbn, Gezamelte Shriftn*, IV, 21–24.
25 Emanuel S. Goldsmith, *Architects of Yiddishism at the Beginning of the Twentieth Century: A Study in Jewish Cultural History* (Cranbury, NJ: Associated University Presses, 1976), ch. 5 and 234–235.
26 Roskies, *Against the Apocalypse*, 138.
27 Ibid., 137; An-sky, *Khurbn, passim*.
28 An-sky, *Khurbn, Gezamelte Shriftn*, VI, 58–63. The Talmudic line is: "The Tables were broken, yet the Letters flew up" (*Babylonian Talmud*, Tractate *Pesachim*, 87b). My thanks to Mordecai Roshwald for this reference. I believe David Roskies is mistaken in identifying the image with the story about Rabbi Hanina's martyrdom, although this would be an equally ironic allusion (Roskies, *Against the Apocalypse*, 54).
29 Abel Pann, *In the Name of the Tsar*, a collection of wartime drawings found in deteriorating condition and with no publication information at the YIVO Institute for Jewish Research, New York. See also the selections published in the Viennese art magazine *Faun*, 22 (1925). When, in early 1917, the French authorities prevented Pann from publishing these drawings for fear of antagonizing their Russian ally, he left France for New York, subsequently settling in Palestine (Abel Pann, *Autobiographie: Odyssée d'un peintre israélien né en Russie tsariste et français d'adoption* [Paris: Cerf, 1996], 119–120).
30 Vejas Gabrielius Liulevicius, "War Land: Peoples, Lands, and National Identity on the Eastern Front in World War I" (Ph.D. diss., University of Pennsylvania, 1994), ch. 1; Wiktor Sukiennicki, *East Central Europe during World War I: From Foreign Domination to National Independence*, vol. I (Boulder, CO: East European Monographs, 1984), ch. 14 and 333–335. In the course of 1917–1918, German armies were to capture even more extensive stretches of Russian imperial territory.
31 Sammy Gronemann, *Hawdoloh und Zapfenstreich* (Havdalah [Jewish ceremony marking end of Sabbath] and [Military] Tattoo) (Berlin: Jüdischer Verlag, 1925), insert after p. 24. See also Zosa Szajkowski, "The German Appeal to the Jews of Poland, August 1914," *The Jewish Quarterly Review*, new ser., 59 (1969), 311–320. *Kol Mevaser* was named after the first major Yiddish newspaper, which had appeared in Russia in 1862 (Nahma Sandrow, *Vagabond Stars: A World History of Yiddish Theater* [New York: Harper and Row, 1977], 34).

32 A collection of these photographs is located in the Visual Documentation Center of *Beit Hatefutsoth* (The Museum of the Jewish Diaspora, referred to hereafter as Diaspora Museum), Tel Aviv, Israel. See also An-sky, *Khurbn, Gezamelte Shriftn*, IV, 50.

    Concern with public opinion in the United States also played a role in the German government's diplomatic intervention with the Ottoman government, which helped avert the complete wartime eradication of the *Yishuv*, the Jewish settlement in Palestine. See Isaiah Friedman, *Germany, Turkey, and Zionism, 1897–1918* (Oxford: Oxford University Press, 1977), part III.

33 Saul Friedländer, "Die politischen Veränderungen der Kriegszeit und ihre Auswirkungen auf die Judenfrage," Werner Jochmann, "Die Ausbreitung des Antisemitismus," and Eva G. Reichmann, "Der Bewusstseinswandel der deutschen Juden," in Werner Mosse, ed., *Deutsches Judentum in Krieg und Revolution, 1916–1923* (Tübingen: J. C. B. Mohr, 1971). See also Peter Jelavich, chapter 2 in the present volume.

34 Zechlin, *Die deutsche politik und die Juden*, ch. 13.

35 One joke that made the rounds during this period suggested that the Polish word for Germans – *Niemcy* – was nothing other than the Yiddish phrase "*Nem tsu*" – take away! (Zosa Szajkowski, "East European Jewish Workers in Germany during World War I" [Jerusalem: 1975], reprint of article from Salo Wittmayer Barron Jubilee Volume, 9–10).

36 Jürgen Matthäus, "Prelude to the Holocaust? Germany and Eastern European Jews during World War I," lecture delivered at the United States Holocaust Museum in Washington, DC, 11 June 1996; Liulevicius, "War Land," ch. 2.

37 Gronemann, *Hawdoloh und Zapfenstreich*, 184–188; Arnold Zweig, *Das Ostjüdische Antlitz* (1920; 2nd ed., Berlin: Welt-Verlag, 1922), 104–114.

38 Roskies, *Against the Apocalypse*, 116–121; Susan A. Slotnick, "Oyzer Varshavski's *Shmuglares* [sic]: A Study in Form and Meaning," in Marvin I. Herzog *et al.*, eds., *The Field of Yiddish: Studies in Language, Folklore, and Literature*, 4th collection (Philadelphia: Institute for the Study of Human Issues, 1979); Oyzer Varshavski, *Shmuglars* (1920; Warsaw and New York: Weissenberg Ferlag, 1921). To be sure, organized prostitution and smuggling had been quite widespread in the Pale even before the war.

39 Hirsh Abramovich, *Farshvundene geshtalten (Zikhroynes un Silueten)* (Disappeared Figures [Memories and Silhouettes]) (Buenos Aires: Tsentral Ferband fun Poylishe Yiden in Argentine, 1958), 297–299. My thanks to Dina Abramowicz of the YIVO institute for bringing this useful source to my attention.

40 Matthäus, "Prelude to the Holocaust?"

41 Diaspora Museum photograph collection.

42 Matthäus, "Prelude to the Holocaust?"; Pam Maclean, "Control and Cleanliness: German–Jewish Relations in Occupied Eastern Europe during the First World War," *War and Society*, 6: 2 (1988), 47–69; Steven E. Aschheim, *Brothers and Strangers: The East European Jew in German and German Jewish Consciousness, 1800–1923* (Madison: University of Wisconsin Press, 1982), 143–150.

43 Maclean, "Control and Cleanliness"; Aschheim, *Brothers and Strangers*, 148; Abramovich, *Farshvundene geshtalten*, 301–302. An exception to this rule arises in the event that the person's death falls on a Friday, in which case the funeral is deferred until after the Sabbath.

44 See YIVO Photo Archive, catalogue number F2710 – frame 42695.

45 It must be pointed out that among Jews of East European background there were some who internalized many of the negative German-Jewish stereotypes about *Ostjuden*. The Galician-born, German-language author Karl Emil Franzos is a notable example. See Miriam Roshwald, *Ghetto, Shtetl, or Polis? The Jewish Community in the Writings of Karl Emil Franzos, Sholom Aleichem, and Shmuel Yosef Agnon* (San Bernardino: Borgo Press, 1997).

46 Aschheim, *Brothers and Strangers*, 156.

47 Ibid., 160–163. Such efforts, modeled on the activities of the French Alliance Israélite Universelle, had actually begun a decade before the war (ibid., 37–38).

48 Ibid., 157–160; Zosa Szajkowski, "The Struggle for Yiddish during World War I: The Attitude of German Jewry," *Leo Baeck Institute Year Book IX* (London, 1964), 131–158; Zosa Szajkowski, "The Komitee für den Osten and Zionism," in Raphael Patai, ed., *Herzl Year Book*, VII (New York, 1971), 199–240.

49 The Polish Agudat Israel lives on today as a non-Zionist political party in the State of Israel.

50 Among other things, this decision reflected the German government's concern not to offend the nationalist sensibilities of the Poles on the occasion of their ostensible achievement of national self-determination under Austro-German auspices.

51 Aschheim, *Brothers and Strangers*, 165–168; Zechlin, *Die Deutsche Politik und die Juden*, chs. 9–11; Gershon C. Bacon, "The Poznanski Affair of 1921: Kehillah Politics and the Internal Political Realignment of Polish Jewry," in Frankel, ed., *Jews and the European Crisis*; Robert Moses Shapiro, "Aspects of Jewish Self-Government in Łódz, 1914–1939," in Polonsky, ed., *From Shtetl to Socialism*. Well into the interwar period, Galician-based Hasidic movements remained more wedded to traditional Orthodox apoliticism, and hence reluctant to join Agudat Israel, than did those in Congress Poland (William O. McCagg Jr., *A History of Habsburg Jews, 1670–1918* [Bloomington and Indianapolis: Indiana University Press, 1992], 205).

52 Gronemann, *Hawdoloh und Zapfenstreich*, 45–53; Aschheim, *Brothers and Strangers*, chs. 5–6 and 163–165; Jack Wertheimer, *Unwelcome Strangers: East European Jews in Imperial Germany* (New York and Oxford: Oxford University Press, 1987), 151–153. Buber himself was the product of a mixed Central and Eastern European upbringing, having been born in Vienna but raised in Galicia, later returning to Vienna and then on to Leipzig, Zurich, and Berlin for his higher education (Maurice Friedman, *Encounter on the Narrow Ridge: A Life of Martin Buber* [New York: Paragon House, 1991], ch. 1).

53 Ibid., Friedman, *Encounter*, 136.

54 Gronemann, *Hawdoloh und Zapfenstreich*, 45–55, 63–77, 245–247, and *passim*; Arnold Zweig (with fifty-two drawings by Hermann Struck), *Das Ostjüdische Antlitz* (1920; 2nd ed., Berlin: Welt-Verlag, 1922), 13–59 and *passim*; Aschheim, *Brothers and Strangers*, ch. 8.

55 My thanks to Peter Pfeiffer for providing background information on Dehmel.

56 Zweig's and Struck's portraits of East European Jewry can be interpreted as mirroring their own idealized notions of Jewish authenticity. See Wilhelm von Sternburg, *Arnold Zweig* (Frankfurt am Main: Anton Hain, 1990), 93–105; Leslie Morris, "Reading the Face of the Other: Arnold Zweig's *Das Ostjüdische Antlitz*," in Sara Friedrichsmeyer, Sara Lennox, and Susanne Zantop, eds., *The Imperialist Imagination: German Colonialism and its Legacy* (Ann Arbor: University of Michigan Press, 1998). On literary representations of *batei midrash* as emblematic of both positive and negative stereotypes about East European Jewish life, see Miriam Roshwald, *Ghetto, Shtetl or Polis?*, 40–41, 43–45, 133. On the Sabbath (discussed below) see ibid., 160–165.

57 Avigdor Ha-Meiri, *Be-gehinom shel matah: reshimot katsin 'ivri be-shvi rusiyah* (In the Hell Below: the Notes of a Hebrew Officer in Russian Captivity) (Tel-Aviv: Dvir, 1989), 94, originally published in 1932, based on a draft completed in Odessa in 1920. Another notable Jewish POW in Russia was Hans Kohn, a native of Prague who organized Zionist educational activities and discussion groups that at one point drew close to 400 participants among his fellow Jewish captives in Siberian prison camps. Most of the books used in what one historian has dubbed Kohn's "Zionist university" arrived in care packages sent by his family. Kohn returned to active involvement in the Zionist movement after the war, and later became a pioneering figure in the study of nationalism and a prominent member of the History faculty at the City University of New York. See Michael Berkowitz, *Western Jewry and the Zionist Project, 1914–1933* (Cambridge: Cambridge University Press, 1997), 16–17; Hagit Lavsky, *Before Catastrophe: The Distinctive Path of German Zionism* (Jerusalem: The Magnes Press, and Detroit: Wayne State University Press, 1996), 141, 147.

58 Aschheim, *Brothers and Strangers*, 191–192; Shulamit Volkov, "The Dynamics of Dissimilation: *Ostjuden* and German Jews," in Jehuda Reinharz and Walter Schatzberg, eds., *The Jewish Response to German Culture: From the Enlightenment to the Second World War* (Hanover, NH: University Press of New England, 1985), 210–211; Robert Alter, *Necessary Angels: Tradition and Modernity in Kafka, Benjamin and Scholem* (Cambridge, MA: Harvard University Press, 1991), 30–31; Gershom Scholem, *From Berlin to Jerusalem: Memories of my Youth*, English trans. (New York: Schocken Books, 1980), ch. 5.

59 A similar school for young Jewish refugees was established by Zionists in Prague (Ritchie Robertson, *Kafka: Judaism, Politics, and Literature* [Oxford: Oxford University Press, 1985], 156).

60 Aschheim, *Brothers and Strangers*, 193–203; Lavsky, *Before Catastrophe*, 35–39; Scholem, *From Berlin to Jerusalem*, 76–80. Aschheim points out

that, in practice, even the Volksheim essentially functioned as a one-way street in which German Jews sought to teach East European Jews how to rid themselves of the cultural and psychological baggage of the ghetto. On Arlosoroff's wartime conversion from German nationalism to socialist Zionism, see Shlomo Avineri, *Arolosoroff* (New York: Grove Weidenfeld, 1989), 6–9.

61 Conversely, the horror of the war led some Jewish internationalists to rethink their attitude to Jewish national identity. Eduard Bernstein, the leading Revisionist ideologue of the German Social Democratic Party (SPD), penned an essay in 1917 in which he expressed guarded sympathy for certain aspects of Zionism and rejected the assimilationist ideal, arguing instead that it was the special duty of the Jews *as Jews* (and as citizens of their respective countries) to mediate among the nations in the interests of world peace. See Eduard Bernstein, *Von den Aufgaben der Juden im Weltkriege* (Berlin: Erich Reiss Verlag, 1917); Robert S. Wistrich, "Eduard Bernsteins Einstellung zur Judenfrage," in Ludger Heid and Arnold Paucker, eds., *Juden und deutsche Arbeiterbewegung bis 1933: Soziale Utopien und religiös-kulturelle Traditionen* (Tübingen: J. C. B. Mohr, 1992).

62 Aschheim, *Brothers and Strangers*, 173–178.

63 Robertson, *Kafka*, 143–152, 157; Friedman, *Encounter on the Narrow Ridge*, 86–94; Laurence J. Silberstein, *Martin Buber's Social and Religious Thought: Alienation and the Quest for Meaning* (New York: New York University Press, 1989), 113–115.

64 Alter, *Necessary Angels*, 12–13, ch. 3.

65 Evelyn Torton Beck, *Kafka and the Yiddish Theater* (Madison: The University of Wisconsin Press, 1971), ch. 2; Ronald Hayman, *Kafka: A Biography* (New York: Oxford University Press, 1982), chs. 9, 17 and pp. 191–193; Alter, *Necessary Angels*, chs. 3–4; Robertson, *Kafka*, chs. 3–5. See also Steven Beller, chapter 5 in the present volume.

66 Gronemann, *Hawdoloh und Zapfenstreich*, 142–144.

67 Ezra Mendelsohn, *Zionism in Poland: The Formative Years, 1915–1926* (New Haven: Yale University Press, 1981), ch. 1; Zechlin, *Die Deutsche Politik und die Juden*, 176–178; *Der Moment* (Yiddish-language daily), 13 July 1917 and various other articles on Palestine relief, summer 1917. On the establishment of the Folkspartei (initially known as the Folks komitet), which was supported by the KfdO, see also Szajkowski, "The Struggle for Yiddish," 147.

68 Mendelsohn, *Zionism in Poland*, 65.

69 Ibid., ch. 1.

70 Ha-Shomer Ha-Tsair is to be distinguished from the Poalei Tsion (Workers of Zion) party, a much more rigidly doctrinaire Marxist Zionist organization founded before the war, which assailed the General Zionist party as an irredeemably bourgeois organization (ibid.).

71 Ibid.

72 Ibid. For an analysis of the generational divide on the broader European stage, see Robert Wohl's, *The Generation of 1914* (Cambridge, MA: Harvard University Press, 1979). Unlike many of the cases Wohl examines, the predominant political inclination of the Jewish generation of 1914 was not

toward neo-conservatism or fascism, although elements of neo-romantic idealism clearly did creep in.

73 *Ha-Tsefirah*, 2 January 1916 and other issues from the same month.

74 Ibid., 3 January 1916. See also issue of 12 January 1916. It should be noted that *Ha-Tsefirah*'s editors criticized the tone of all German Jewish articles about Eastern European Jews, including those written by German Zionists, as drenched in arrogance: "The long and short of all the articles ... is – 'these Hottentots are strange creatures. ...'" (ibid., 19 January 1916). Warsaw's Folkist-oriented Yiddish daily, *Der Moment*, also criticized the German Jewish press for the condescending tone with which it held forth about the *Ostjuden* (*Der Moment*, 7 January 1916).

75 See articles in *Der Moment*, 4 January 1916, 23 July 1917, and *passim*.

76 *Ha-Mitspeh*, 19 and 26 September 1917.

77 A small minority of Jewish girls did attend *cheder* with boys. Stampfer, "Gender Differentiation and Education of the Jewish Woman," 187–189.

78 Zechlin, *Die deutsche Politik und die Juden*, ch. 12; Liulevicius, "War Land," ch. 4. The Ober Ost's nationalities policy ultimately backfired (ibid., ch. 6).

79 Mendelsohn, *Zionism in Poland*, 77; Szajkowski, "The Struggle for Yiddish", 140; Abramovich, footnote on p. 292 in *Farshvundene geshtalten*; Lucjan Dobroszycki and Barbara Kirshenblatt-Gimblett, *Image Before My Eyes: A Photographic History of Jewish Life in Poland, 1864–1939* (New York: Schocken, 1978), 203. The German Jewish Orthodox establishment also took a hand in the creation of modern religious educational institutions in Poland and Lithuania (Gronemann, *Hawdoloh und Zapfenstreich*, 210–214). It should also be noted, however, that Jews were much more inclined than people of other nationalities to send their children to German-language schools established by the occupation authorities (Liulevicius, "War Land," 158).

80 Abramovich, "Di Vilner Gezelshaft 'Hilf durch Arbet'" and "A yidishe landwirtshaft-shule in Poilen" in *Farshvundene geshtalten*, 327–339, 340–356; Gronemann, *Hawdoloh und Zapfenstreich*, 84–85; "Aus dem Arbeitsleben des Rabbiner Dr. Sali Levi" (pamphlet published in memory of Rabbi Sali Levi by the board of directors of the Jewish community of Mainz, 21 April 1951), 4–6, YIVO. Photographs of Jewish stands at the Vilna craft fair can be found in the Diaspora Museum's collection of German wartime photographs.

81 This tendency sometimes produced comical results. Sammy Gronemann, who served as Yiddish translator for the Ober Ost administration's press section, was responsible for the compilation of the *Sieben-Sprachenwörterbuch* (Seven-Language Dictionary) designed to provide local-language equivalents for every imaginable German bureaucratic term. Given that many of the translators had an imperfect command of the languages for which they were held responsible (Gronemann himself claims to have relied on a local Jewish bathhouse attendant to render German military proclamations into Yiddish for him!), and since many of the bombastic German bureaucratic compound words were in any case untranslatable if not unintelligible, his colleagues and he simply concocted plausible-sounding equivalents for their respective languages. The result was a linguistic parody of German

bureaucratic militarism whose official editor was identified on the title page as none other than the *Oberbefehlshaber Ost* (Eastern commander-in-chief). See Gronemann, *Hawdoloh und Zapfenstreich*, 120–124. In his discussion of the cultural imperialism that informed the *Sieben-Sprachenwörterbuch*, Liulevicius seems unaware of the official publication's self-parodying subtext (Liulevicius, "War Land," 142–145).

82 Szajkowsky, "The Struggle for Yiddish"; Gronemann, *Hawdoloh und Zapfenstreich*, 34–35.

83 One of the funniest examples of how German bureaucratism could be subverted in minor ways by the local population is cited by Gronemann. He recalls that the Ober Ost authorities' attempt to oblige *melamdim* (*cheder* teachers) to attend certification classes taught by German Jewish instructors in Kovno failed miserably when the first class turned out to be composed of petty merchants and traders from small towns who had presented themselves as *melamdim* so as to obtain travel permits to the big city (Gronemann, *Hawdoloh und Zapfenstreich*, 169–173).

84 *Ha-Tsefirah*, 19 January 1916; Gronemann, *Hawdoloh und Zapfenstreich*, 189–195. Unfortunately, Gronemann fails to mention the title of the novel selected by the Bialystok Cultural Union.

85 On the wartime film industry in Poland, see Harold Segel, chapter 3 in the present volume.

86 Gronemann, *Hawdoloh und Zapfenstreich*, 204–205.

87 J. Hoberman, *Bridge of Light: Yiddish Film between Two Worlds* (New York: The Museum of Modern Art and Schocken Books, 1991), 23, n. 6 and 42–44. In the memoir of his Russian captivity, Avigdor Ha-Meiri tells the story of a chaste young Jewish woman whose use of a yellow ticket to gain a residence permit leads to her painful humiliation when her best friend's father turns out to be the doctor responsible for the periodic renewal of registered prostitutes' health certificates (Ha-Meiri, *Be-gehinom*, ch. 32).

88 Goldfadn also ended up in New York toward the end of his life.

89 Sandrow, *Vagabond Stars*, chs. 3, 5–6 and p. 214.

90 Gronemann referred to this brand of theatrical entertainment as "Schmiertheater" – farcical theatre (Gronemann, *Hawdoloh und Zapfenstreich*, 195–198).

91 Sandrow, *Vagabond Stars*, chs. 5, 7. Kaminska's standard productions, in which she appeared with her daughter Ida, were schmaltzy old favorites like Gordin's *Chasye di yesoyme* (Chasye the Orphan Girl) and Zalmen Libin's *Dos dorfs meidel* (The Village Girl) or comedies such as *Tsvilingshvester* (The Twin Sister). (Theatrical playbills from 1917, YIVO, Catalogue No. 178642A/4922.)

92 Sandrow, *Vagabond Stars*, ch. 8; Gronemann, *Hawdoloh und Zapfenstreich*, 195–198; Luba Kadison and Joseph Buloff, with Irving Genn, *On Stage, Off Stage: Memories of a Lifetime in the Yiddish Theatre* (Cambridge, MA: Harvard University Press, 1992), 6–10; Liulevicius, "War Land," 185–186.

93 As quoted in Gronemann, *Hawdoloh und Zapfenstreich*, 201–202.

94 This is a paraphrasing of Nahma Sandrow's comments in *Vagabond Stars*, 221.

95 Ibid., chs. 7–8; Kadison and Buloff, *On Stage, Off Stage*, 6–10 and *passim*.

96 Seth L. Wolitz, "The Jewish National Art Renaissance in Russia" and John E. Bowlt, "From the Pale of Settlement to the Reconstruction of the World," in Apter-Gabriel, ed., *Tradition and Revolution*.

97 Wolitz, "The Jewish National Art Renaissance," Chimen Abramsky, "Yiddish Book Illustrations in Russia: 1916–1923," Ruth Apter-Gabriel, "El Lissitzky's Jewish Works," and Nicoletta Misler, "The Future in Search of its Past: Nation, Ethnos, Tradition and the Avant-Garde in Russian Jewish Art Criticism," in *Tradition and Revolution*. See also El Lissitzky, "Memoirs Concerning the Mohilev Synagogue" (first published in Yiddish in Berlin, 1923), in *Tradition and Revolution*, 233–234.

98 Jeff Veidlinger, "Moscow's Yiddish Stage" (Ph.D. diss., Georgetown University, 1998), ch. 1; Bowlt, "From the Pale of Settlement," 47.

99 Hoberman, *Bridge of Light*, 42, 46.

100 Wolitz, "The Jewish National Art Renaissance," 34–36. The quotation of the Kultur Lige's motto is on 34–35.

101 As quoted in ibid., 36. See also Roskies, *Against the Apocalypse*, 281.

102 Wolitz, "The Jewish National Art Renaissance" and Bowlt, "From the Pale of Settlement"; Veidlinger, "Moscow's Yiddish Stage," ch. 1.

103 Roskies, *Against the Apocalypse*, 122.

104 An excellent, impressionistic overview of the diversity and vitality of Jewish culture in interwar Poland is to be found in the YIVO – produced historical-documentary film, *Image Before My Eyes* and the accompanying book, cited earlier. My thanks to Naomi Hordes for introducing me to this source.

105 An-sky, *Khurbn, Gezamelte Shriftn*, VI, 104–113.

5 THE TRAGIC CARNIVAL: AUSTRIAN CULTURE IN THE FIRST WORLD WAR

1 *Der Merker*, 1 October 1918, no. 19, 669.

2 The "Republic of German-Austria" (*Deutschösterreich*) was later renamed "Austria" after the victorious allies vetoed the original name as a too obvious encouragement of union with Germany.

3 Elke Calaitzizs, "Das Burgtheaterpublikum von Wilbrandt bis zum Dreierkollegium," in Margret Dietrich, ed., *Das Burgtheater und sein Publikum* (Vienna: Österr. Akademie der Wissenschaften, 1976), 470–471; Franz Hadamowsky, *Wien, Theatergeschichte: Von den Anfängen bis zum Ende des ersten Weltkrieges* (Vienna: Jugend und Volk, 1988), 413.

4 Calaitzizs, "Burgtheaterpublikum," 473–474; Hadamowsky, *Wien, Theatergeschichte*, 413; Renate Wagner, *Arthur Schnitzler: Eine Biographie* (Vienna: Molden, 1981), 295; W. E. Yates, *Theatre in Vienna: A Critical History 1776–1995* (Cambridge, 1996), 192.

5 Margret Dietrich, "Burgtheaterpublikum und Öffentlichkeit in der ersten Republik," in Margret Dietrich, ed., *Das Burgtheater und sein Publikum* (Vienna: Österr. Akademie der Wissenschaften, 1976), 492–495. Andrian's rationale is quoted at length from a memorandum to Rudolf Lothar.

6 Dietrich, "Burgtheaterpublikum und Öffentlichkeit," 492.

7 Albert Berger, "Lyrische Zurüstung der 'Österreich-Idee'," in Klaus Amann and Hubert Lengauer, eds., *Österreich und der große Krieg, 1914–1918* (Vienna: Brandstätter, 1989), 145–150; Robert A. Kann, "Trends in Austro-German Literature during World War I: War Hysteria and Patriotism," in Kann *et al.*, *Habsburg Empire in World War I*, 167–171.

8 Emmerich Kalman, *Gold gab ich für Eisen* (Regie u. Soufflierbuch) (Vienna: Karczag, 1914), 9.

9 Jeroen Bastiaan van Heerde, *Staat und Kunst: Staatliche Kunstförderung 1895–1918* (Vienna: Böhlau, 1993), 311–313.

10 Heinz Geretsegger and Max Peintner, *Otto Wagner 1841–1918: The Expanding City: The Beginning of Modern Architecture* (New York: Rizzoli, 1979), 23–24.

11 Van Heerde, *Staat und Kunst*, 309–310.

12 Karl Hans Strobl, *Die Weltgeschichte und das Igelhaus: Vom Nachmittag des Lebens* (Budweis: Moldavia, 1944), 62–63.

13 Van Heerde, *Staat und Kunst*, 312–313.

14 Ibid., 308–310.

15 Hadamovsky, *Wien, Theatergeschichte*, 748; Hans Pemmer and Nini Lackner, *Der Prater* (Vienna: Jugend und Volk, 1974), 167; Bertrand M. Buchmann, *Der Prater: Die Geschichte des Unteren Werd* (Vienna: Zsolnay, 1979), 79–80.

16 Walter Fritz, *Kino in Österreich 1896–1930* (Vienna: Öst. Bundesverlag, 1981), 67–71.

17 Mark Cornwall, "News, Rumour, and the Control of Information in Austria-Hungary, 1914–1918," *History*, 27: 249 (February 1992), 52–54.

18 Peter Broucek, "Das Kriegspressequartier und die literarischen Gruppen im Kriegsarchiv 1914–1918," in Amann, *Österreich und der Grosse Krieg*, 136–137; Donald A. Prater, *European of Yesterday; A Biography of Stefan Zweig* (Oxford, 1972), 78.

19 Mark Cornwall, "Morale and Patriotism in the Austro-Hungarian Army, 1914–1918," in John Horne, ed., *State, Society and Mobilization in Europe during the First World War* (Cambridge, 1997), 183–191; Richard G. Plaschka, 'Contradicting Ideologies: The Pressure of Ideological Conflicts in the Austro-Hungarian Army of World War One,' in R. A. Kann, B. Király, and P. S. Fichtner, eds., *The Habsburg Empire in World War One* (New York: East European Quarterly, 1977), 108–115.

20 For what small efforts there were on the domestic front, see Cornwall, "Morale and patriotism," 179–180.

21 Frank Field, *The Last Days of Mankind: Karl Kraus and his Vienna* (London: Macmillan, 1967), 82; Cornwall, "Morale and patriotism," 184–185.

22 Arthur Schnitzler, *Tagebuch 1913–1916* (Vienna: Öst. Akademie der Wissenschaften, 1983), 139.

23 Plaschka, "Contradicting Ideologies," 108.

24 Hugo Wolff, "Buchbesprechung aus dem Felde," in *Der Merker*, 15 April 1917, no. 8, 316.

25 Cornwall, "News, Rumour," 50ff.; Cornwall, "Morale and patriotism," 181–182.

26 Plaschka, "Contradicting Ideologies," 112.

27 Ibid., 115; Cornwall, "Morale and Patriotism," 190–191.

28 Cornwall, "News, Rumour," 63; Ludwig Windischgraetz, *Helden und Halunken: Selbsterlebte Weltgeschichte 1899–1964* (Vienna: Frick, 1965), 134–135.

29 Edward Timms, *Karl Kraus: Apocalyptic Satirist: Culture and Catastrophe in Habsburg Vienna* (London: Yale, 1986), 352–354.

30 Cornwall, "News, Rumour," 54–57.

31 Ibid., 59–63.

32 Timms, *Kraus*, 354–356.

33 Hadamowsky, *Wien, Theatergeschichte*, 777–785.

34 Carmen Ottner, "Hans Gregor: Direktor der Wiener Hofoper in schwerer Zeit (1911–1918)," in Carmen Ottner, ed., *Oper in Wien 1900–1925* (Vienna: Doblinger, 1991), 115; Calaitzizs, "Burgtheaterpublikum," 470.

35 Hadamowsky, *Wien, Theatergeschichte*, 644.

36 Gerhard Eberstaller, *Ronacher: Ein Theater in seiner Zeit* (Vienna: Jugend und Volk, 1993), 89.

37 Fritz, *Kino in Österreich*, 64–67.

38 Calaitzizs, "Burgtheaterpublikum," 471.

39 Ottner, "Hans Gregor," 107, 115; Egon Seefehlner, "Die Direktoren und ihre Ensembles," in Andrea Seebohm, ed., *Die Wiener Oper: 350 Jahre Glanz und Tradition* (Vienna: Ueberreuter, 1986), 92; a list for 1917–1918 season in *Der Merker*, 15 August 1918, no. 15/16, 517, shows Verdi's operas enjoying 34 performances at the Court Opera, Wagner's 36, Mozart's 21, Richard Strauss's 19, Massenet's 19, Meyerbeer's 11. This list also shows that even the *Volksoper*, with a clearly more Austro-Germanocentric mission, while giving Wagner works 60 performances, still played Verdi 39 times, Offenbach 20, Mascagni 18, Leoncavallo 17, and Bizet 12.

40 Ottner, "Hans Gregor," 115–116; Calaitzizs, "Burgtheaterpublikum," 474.

41 Murray G. Hall, "Das Buch als 'Bombengeschäft'," in Amann, *Österreich und der grosse Krieg*, 139–140.

42 Wagner, *Schnitzler*, 302–303.

43 Fritz, *Kino in Österreich*, 64, 68–69.

44 Ibid., 62–64.

45 Paul Stauber, "Wiener Theater-Rundschau," in *Der Merker*, 15 April 1917, no. 8, 309.

46 Paul Stauber, "Protest gegen ein neues Operettentheater in Wien," in *Der Merker*, 15 January 1918, 52–53; Hadamowsky, *Wien, Theatergeschichte*, 787.

47 Yates, *Theatre in Vienna*, 197.

48 Ronald W. Clark, *Freud: The Man and the Cause* (London: Cape, 1980), 386–387.

49 Kann, "Trends in Austro-German Literature," 173–175.

50 Herbert Exenberger, "Alfons Petzold im Ersten Weltkrieg," in Amann, *Österreich und der Grosse Krieg*, 170–172; Donald Prater, *A Ringing Glass: The Life of Rainer Maria Rilke* (Oxford, 1986), 252–253.

51 Clark, *Freud*, p. 368.

52 Donald A. Prater, *European of Yesterday: A Biography of Stefan Zweig* (Oxford, 1972), 72.

53 Schnitzler, *Tagebuch 1913–1916*, 127–141.

54 Ray Monk, *Ludwig Wittgenstein: The Duty of Genius* (New York: Free Press, 1990), 111–112; Frank Whitford, *Oskar Kokoschka: A Life* (New York: Atheneum, 1986), 97–100.

55 Heinz Lunzer, *Hofmannsthals politische Tätigkeit in den Jahren 1914–1917* (Frankfurt am Main: Lang, 1981), 26–35.

56 Kann, "Trends in Austro-German Literature," 177.

57 Wilfried Berghahn, *Robert Musil* (Reinbek: Rororo, 1963), 68–70.

58 H. H. Stuckenschmidt, *Arnold Schoenberg: His Life, World and Work* (London: Calder, 1977), 193, 239–244.

59 Prater, *Ringing Glass*, 273–275; Ralph Freedman, *Life of a Poet: Rainer Maria Rilke* (New York: Farrar, Strauss and Giroux, 1996), 380–382, 405–408; Franz Karl Ginzkey, *Zeit und Menschen meiner Jugend* (Vienna: Wiener Verlagsgesellschaft, 1942), 343–350.

60 Frank Whitford, *Egon Schiele* (London: Thames and Hudson, 1981), 142, 160–178.

61 Schnitzler, *Tagebuch*, 140–143, 177–178, 225.

62 Whitford, *Kokoschka*, 99–119.

63 Liselotte Popelka, *Albin Egger-Lienz, 1868–1926* (Vienna: Heeresgeschichtliches Museum, 1976), 3–23; Heinrich Hammer and Franz Kollreder, *Albin Egger-Lienz: Ein Bildwerk* (Innsbruck: Tyrolia, 1963), 106–115.

64 Steven Beller, *Francis Joseph* (London: Longman, 1996), 222–225.

65 Whitford, *Schiele*, 178; Whitford, *Kokoschka*, 115.

66 Peter Stephan Jungk, *Franz Werfel: A Life in Prague, Vienna and Hollywood* (New York: Grove Weidenfeld, 1990), 58–62.

67 Stefan Zweig, *Die Welt von Gestern: Erinnerungen eines Europäers* (Frankfurt am Main: Fischer, 1982), 293–297.

68 Prater, *European of Yesterday*, 75–101.

69 *Der Merker*, 15 October 1918, no. 20, 697.

70 Leoš Janáček, *Jenufa*, text by Gabriele Preiss, trans. Max Brod (New York: Pullman, 1924); Norbert Tschulik, *Musiktheater in Österreich: Die Oper im zwanzigsten Jahrhundert* (Vienna: Bundesverlag, 1984), 60.

71 Richard Strauss, *Salome*, text by Oscar Wilde, trans. Hedwig Lachmann (Berlin: Fürstner, 1905).

72 Ernst Bartolo, *Die Wiener Oper: Die aufregenden Jahre seit 1625* (Vienna: Karolinger, 1992), 71.

73 Sigurd Paul Scheichl, "Journalisten leisten Kriegsdienst: Die Neue Freie Presse im September 1915," in Amann, *Österreich und der Große Krieg*, 104–108.

74 Schnitzler, *Tagebuch*, 159.

75 Viktor Suchy, "Die 'österreichische Idee' als konservative Staatsidee bei Hugo von Hofmannsthal, Richard von Schaukal und Anton Wildgans," in Friedbert Aspetsberger, ed., *Staat und Gesellschaft in der modernen österreichischen Literatur* (Vienna: Öst. Bundesverlag, 1977), 21–27; Lunzer, *Hofmannsthals politische Tätigkeit, passim*.

76 Karl Wagner, "Sinn-Soldaten: Rosegger und der *Heimgarten* im Ersten Weltkrieg," in Amann, *Österreich und der Große Krieg*, 121–125.

77 Bernhard Doppler, " 'Ich habe diesen Krieg immer sozusagen als meinen Krieg angesehen.' Der katholische Kulturkritiker Richard von Kralik (1852–1934)," in Amann, *Österreich und der Große Krieg*, 95–101.

78 Van Heerde, *Staat und Kunst*, 314; Johann Sonnleitner, "Eherne Sonette: Richard von Schaukal und der Erste Weltkrieg," in *Österreich und der Große Krieg*, 152–156.

79 Kann, "Trends in Austro-German Literature," 163; Irene Nierhaus, "Das Zwiegesicht: Facetten der Kunst und Politik der Vereinigung bildender Künstler – Wiener Secession 1914–1945," in *Wiener Secession*, 72.

80 Hans Müller, *Könige* (Stuttgart: Cotta, 1916); Calaitzizs, "Burgtheaterpublikum," 471; Wagner, *Schnitzler*, 294.

81 Johann Holzner, "Jagdszenen aus der Alpen- und Donau-Anarchie: Bemerkungen zur Entwicklung des Volkstücks von Anzengruber bis Scönherr," in Amann, *Österreich und der Große Krieg*, 51; Calaitzizs, "Burgtheaterpublikum," 473.

82 Johannes Sachslehner, "Todesmaschine und literarische Heroik: Zur Mobilmachung des Helden im historischen Roman," and Klaus Zelewitz, "Deutschböhmische Dichter und der Erste Weltkrieg," both in Amann, *Österreich und der Große Krieg*, 159–162, 185–191 resp.

83 Ilona Sármány-Parsons, *Gustav Klimt* (New York: Crown, 1987), 82; Frank Whitford, *Klimt* (London: Thames and Hudson, 1990), 191–204.

84 Schnitzler, *Tagebuch*, 140.

85 Wagner, *Schnitzler*, 278–307; Timms, *Kraus*, 300–301.

86 Patrick Bridgwater, "Georg Trakl and the Poetry of the First World War," in Walter Methlagl and William E. Yuill, eds., *Londoner Trakl-Symposion* (Salzburg: Otto Müller, 1981), 101, 110; Monk, *Wittgenstein*, 119.

87 Monk, *Wittgenstein*, 111–147; Allan Janik and Stephen Toulmin, *Wittgenstein's Vienna* (New York: Touchstone, 1973).

88 Stuckenschmidt, *Schoenberg*, 237–254.

89 Alexander L. Ringer, *Arnold Schoenberg: The Composer as Jew* (Oxford, 1990), 37–9, 74–5; Stuckenschmidt, *Schoenberg*, 242–243.

90 Clark, *Freud*, 376–377.

91 Paul Michael Lützeler, *Hermann Broch: A Biography* (London: Quartet, 1987), 35–43; Hermann Broch, *The Sleepwalkers* (London: Quartet, 1986).

92 Ritchie Robertson, *Kafka: Judaism, Politics and Literature* (Oxford, 1985), 131–132, 156–164.

93 Ibid., 189.

94 Ibid., 134–137, 184–217. See Aviel Roshwald, chapter 4 in this collection, p. 112.

95 Rudolf G. Ardelt, *Friedrich Adler: Probleme einer Persönlichkeitsentwicklung um die Jahrhundertwende* (Vienna: Öst. Bundesverlag, 1984).

96 Jungk, *Werfel*, 40–62.

97 Timms, *Kraus*, 297–299.

98 Zweig, *Welt von Gestern*, 293–297.

99 Stefan Zweig, *Jeremias: Eine dramatische Dichtung* (Leipzig: Insel, 1920), 26–27. The following assumes this is an unchanged edition of the play.

100 Ibid., 32–39.

101 Ibid., 41, 83, 123, 126.

102 Ibid., 120, 144.
103 Ibid., 115.
104 Ibid., 51–60.
105 Ibid., 37, 39, 138.
106 Ibid., 70–71.
107 Ibid., 216.
108 Ibid., 186–215.
109 Karl Kraus, *Die letzten Tage der Menschheit* (Frankfurt am Main: Suhrkamp, 1986), 353–354.
110 On the play, see Timms, *Kraus*, 267–376; Field, *Last Days of Mankind*, 75–129; Harry Zohn, *Karl Kraus* (New York: Ungar, 1971), 68–85.
111 Technically, *Die letzten Tage der Menschheit* is not a product of wartime, but of the post-war period. It only reached its final form in May 1922. Nevertheless, it very much took shape during the war, and much of the material in it was taken over directly from articles in Kraus's *Fackel* published during the conflict. Timms, *Kraus*, 369; Field, *Last Days of Mankind*, 84–118.
112 For instance, Kraus, *Die letzten Tage der Menschheit*, 336, 347–349, 645–648, 700–703.
113 Ibid., 505–508; Timms, *Kraus*, 329–332.
114 Timms, *Kraus*, 315–323; Kraus, *Die letzten Tage der Menschheit*, 660–665, 744–746.
115 Kraus, *Die letzten Tage der Menschheit*, 750–754; Field, *Last Days of Mankind*, 104.
116 Timms, *Kraus*, 334–373; cf. Robertson, *Kafka*, 141.
117 Kraus's "Kultur" was not the same as Thomas Mann's irrational force; rather Kraus defined it as the insistence on people being treated as human beings instead of as consumers: Timms, *Kraus*, 308–315; cf. Kraus, *Die letzten Tage der Menschheit*, 191–204, esp. 203.
118 Field, *Last Days of Mankind*, 110; Kraus, *Die letzten Tage der Menschheit*, 744.
119 Kraus, *Die letzten Tage der Menschheit*, 353–354; Field, *Last Days of Mankind*, 95.
120 Kraus, *Die letzten Tage der Menschheit*, 195–196, 353–355, 504.
121 In Karl Kraus, *Worte in Versen*, Kraus, *Werke*, vol. VII (Munich: Kösel, 1959), 109–114.
122 Julius Bittner, *Das höllisch Gold: ein deutsches Singspiel* (Vienna: Universal, 1916); Tschulik, *Musiktheater*, 71–73.
123 Ibid., 19.
124 Wolfgang Häusler, "Stereotypen des Hasses: Zur Geschichte antisemitischer Ideologien und Bewegungen in Österreich bis 1918," in Amann, *Österreich und der Große Krieg*, 29; Helmut Gruber, *Red Vienna: Experiment in Working-Class Culture 1919–1934* (Oxford, 1991), 26–27.
125 Timms, *Kraus*, 338–341, 365.
126 Fritz, *Kino in Österreich*, 75–77; cf. Kraus, *Die letzten Tage der Menschheit*, 766.
127 Gerald Stieg, "*Die letzten Tage der Menschheit*: Eine negative Operette?" in Amann, *Österreich und der Grosse Krieg*, 182.

128 Ibid., 180, 184; Kraus, *Die letzten Tage der Menschheit*, 675.

129 Stieg, "Eine negative Operette?" 180–181; Field, *Last Days of Mankind*, 88.

130 Otto Brusatti and Wilhelm Deutschmann, eds., *FleZiWiCsa & Co.: Die Wiener Operette* (Vienna: Museen der Stadt Wien, 1984), 49.

131 Paul Stauber, "Wiener Theater-Rundschau," *Der Merker*, 15 April 1917, no. 8, 309.

132 Paul Stauber, "Protest gegen ein neues Operettentheater in Wien," *Der Merker*, 15 January 1918, no. 2, 52–54.

133 For an account of the elite disdain for operetta, see Moritz Csáky, *Ideologie der Operette und Wiener Moderne Ein kulturhistorischer Essay zur österreichischen Identität* (Vienna: Böhlau, 1996), 15–24.

134 Stieg, "Eine negative Operette?" 182.

135 Martin Lichtfuss, *Operette in Ausverkauf* (Vienna: Böhlau, 1989), 19–21, 28, 121; Brusatti *et al.*, *FleZiWiCsá*, 9; Thorsten Stegemann, "*Wenn man das Leben durchs Champagnerglas betrachtet*": *Textbücher der Wiener Operette zwischen Provokation und Reaktion* (Frankfurt am Main: Lang, 1995), 224–225.

136 Ibid., 71–72.

137 Oskar Straus (libretto by Leopold Jacobson and Robert Bodanzky), *Nachtfalter* (Vienna: Karczag, 1917), 88.

138 Emmerich Kálmán (libretto by Leo Stein and Bela Jenbach), *Die Csardasfürstin* (New York: Kazuko Hillyer, 1984).

139 Oskar Nedbal (libretto by Leo Stein and Julius Wilhelm), *Die Winzerbraut* (Vienna: Doblinger, 1916) (Director's book).

140 Edmund Eysler (libretto by A. M. Willner and Robert Bodanzky), *Wenn zwei sich lieben!* (Vienna: Karczag, 1915) (Director's book).

141 Franz Lehár (libretto by A. M. Willner and Heinz Reichert), *Wo die Lerche singt . . .* (Vienna: Karczag, 1918).

142 Cf. Bruno Granichstädten, *Walzerliebe* (Vienna: Karczag, 1918), 18, where a point is made of the abundance of food and provisions in Budapest.

143 Kálmán, *Die Csardasfürstin*, 2, 13. My translation.

144 Volker Klotz, "Cancan contra Stechschritt: Antimilitarismus mit Rückfällen in der Operette," in Amann, *Österreich und der Große Krieg*, 53–54. Klotz is mistaken in thinking that Lehár was not involved in writing "patriotic" operettas, as he contributed his name and at least one composition, "Kriegslied," to *Komm' deutscher Bruder!* See Edmund Eysler and Franz Lehár, *Komm' deutscher Bruder!* (Text by August Niedhart and Karl Lindau) (Vienna: Karczag, 1914) (Songbook), 17.

145 Kálmán, *Gold gab ich für Eisen* (textbook), 27; Leo Ascher, *Botschafterin Leni* (Vienna: Robitschek, 1915), 90; Oscar Straus, *Liebeszauber* (Vienna: Doblinger, 1916), 134.

146 Bruno Granichstädten, *Auf Befehl der Kaiserin! Ein Operetten-Idyll aus alten gemütlichen Zeiten* (Leipzig, Vienna: Karczag, 1915), title in Austria *Auf Befehl der Herzogin!*, see 1, 4; Leo Fall, *Fürstenliebe* (Vienna: Eibenschütz & Herté, 1916), esp. 16, 24.

147 Ibid., 25, 41–42, 68, 76, 104, 127.

148 Kálmán, *Gold gab ich für Eisen*, 1.

149 Ibid., 60.

150 Ed. Henry Grunwald, *Ein Walzer muss es sein: Alfred Grünwald und die Wiener Operette* (Vienna: Überreuter, 1991), 52.

151 Leo Fall, *Die Rose von Stambul* (Vienna: Karzag, 1916), esp. 9–16, 28–33, 54, 101–104.

152 Ibid., 56, 86, 90–5.

153 Josef Mayerhöfer, *Operette in Wien* (Vienna: Öst. Theatermuseum, 1979), 23, Brusatti, *FleZiWiCsa*, 52.

154 Leo Ascher, *Bruder Leichtsinn* (Vienna: Karczag, 1918), 19, 36, 46, 62.

155 Ibid., 55.

156 Ibid., 73.

157 Ibid., 65.

158 Ibid., 57.

159 Cf. Oscar Straus, *Eine Ballnacht* (Vienna: Weinberger, 1917) (Director's book), 38.

160 Gruber, *Red Vienna*, 9, 85–87, 98–102, 114–135; Stuckenschmidt, *Schoenberg*, 252.

161 The concept comes from Allan Janik.

162 Kraus, *Die letzten Tage der Menschheit*, 659.

6 AMBIVALENT PATRIOTS: CZECH CULTURE IN THE GREAT WAR

1 L. L. Farrar, Jr., "The Short-War Illusion," in Holger H. Herwig, *The Outbreak of World War I* (Lexington, MA: D.C. Heath, 1991), 24–30. Many Czechs were so convinced of the imminent victory of the Central Powers in the early stages of the war, that they refused to believe the stories of returning soldiers about the true state of affairs. František Pražák, *Půl století: Paměti* (A half-century: memoirs) (Prague: Vydavatelstvo Družstevní práce, 1946), 219.

2 In April 1915, the 28th regiment surrendered to the Russians, leaving only 150 soldiers, of an original 2,000, on the side of the Dual Monarchy. Shortly thereafter, 1,600 soldiers from the 36th infantry of Mlada Boleslav surrendered to the Russians. Both of these regiments were dissolved in dishonor. Otto Urban, *Česká společnost 1848–1914* (Czech Society) (Prague: Svoboda, 1982), 588. Information on popular anti-war sentiment in the early stages of the war is in *ibid.*, 585–587; Karel Pichlík, Bohumír Klípa and Jitka Zabloudilová, *Českoslovenští legionáři: 1914–1920* (Czech legionaries: 1914–1920) (Prague: Mladá fronta, 1996), 17–20; and Louis H. Rees, *The Czechs during World War I: The Path to Independence* (Boulder, CO: East European Monographs, 1992), 12–14.

3 The Bohemian Diet had been closed because of nationalist disorders since 1913, and the government closed the diets for Moravia and Silesia, along with the imperial parliament in Vienna, after war was declared.

4 "Pražská kronika" (Prague chronicle), *Pražská lidová revue: časopis věnovaný vzdělání a kulturním potřebám lidu*, 10 (1915), 178–179.

5 Charles L. Hoover to Frederick C. Penfield, 17 January 1916, quoted in Arthur J. May, *The Passing of the Hapsburg Monarchy 1914–1918*, 2 vols. (Philadelphia: University of Pennsylvania Press, 1966), I, 364–365.

6 Miloslav Novotný, "Doslov" (Introduction), in Miloslav Novotný, ed., *Naše umění v odboji* (Prague: Evropský literární klub, 1938), 232.

7 *Moderní revue* resumed publication after a six-month suspension, ibid., 232–233. Among the new cultural journals founded during the war were *Kmen: týdenní úvahy a poznámky o umění a životě* (The tribe: weekly essays and notes on art and life) edited by the Czech writer, F. X. Šalda, and *Lípa: Týdenník pro poesii, umění, život duchovní a sociální* (Linden: a weekly for poetry, art, and spiritual and social life) founded by the writer Růžena Svobodová. Both were launched in 1915. *Novina: Týdenník literaturní a kulturní* (New Books: a literary and cultural weekly), edited by the Realist politician, Jan Herben, appeared in October 1915 but was suspended by the censors in January 1916.

8 See, "Vzpomínky na činnost ve Svazu osvětovém" (Reminiscences of the activity of the Cultural Union), in Alois Žipek, ed., *Domov za války (svědectví účastníků)* (The home front during the war (testimony of participants)), 5 vols. (Prague: Pokrok, 1929–1931), V, 401–405. See also, Jan Havlasa, "Hrst vzpomínek" (A handful of memories), *Domov za války*, V, 405–409.

9 Otokar Fischer, "Mezi válkou a uměním" (Between war and art), *Umění v odboji*, 89.

10 Arne Novák, *Czech Literature*, tr. Peter Kussi, ed. William Harkins (Ann Arbor, MI: Michigan Slavic Publications, 1976), 315. See also, Novotný, "Doslov," 233. Karel Čapek contended that the Czechs never produced a wartime literature, but rather remained silent on this issue. Karel Čapek, "Česká literatura za války" (Czech literature during the war), in *O umění a kultuře II* (Karel Čapek spisy XVIII) (orig. pub. *La République tchécoslovaque*, January 1919) (Prague: Československý spisovatel, 1985), 9–10.

11 Novák, *Literature*, 315; and Jan V. Novák and Arne Novák, *Přehledné dějiny literatury české od nějstarších dob až po naše dny* (A systematic history of Czech literature from the earliest time to the present), 4th ed. (Olomouc: R. Promberger, 1936–1939), 1271–1272.

12 Fischer, "Mezi válkou," 91.

13 Viktor Dyk, "Pozdrav na jiný břeh" (A greeting to the other shore), in *Umění v odboji*, 46. See also, Robert B. Pynsent, *Questions of Identity: Czech and Slovak Ideas of Nationality and Personality* (Budapest, London, New York: Central European University Press, 1994), 103.

14 For Dyk's political evolution, see František Kautmann, *Naděje a úskalí českého nacionalismu: Viktor Dyk v českém politickém životě* (The hopes and obstacles of Czech nationalism: Viktor Dyk in Czech political life) (Prague: Česká expedice, 1992).

15 Viktor Dyk, *Vzpomínky a komentáře 1893–1918* (Reminiscences and commentaries 1893–1918), 2 vols. (Prague: Ladislav Kuncíř, 1927), II, 84.

16 The entire poem is reproduced in *Umění v odboji*, 105–106.

17 Books were relatively inexpensive, at least in the early years of the war, and were often the main form of entertainment for the educated population of provincial towns. Božena Trávníčková, "Domov za války" (The home front during the war), in *Domov za války*, IV, 27.

18 On the *Zlatokvět* series, see *Pražská lidová revue*, 9 (1916), 192. The Topič venture is announced in ibid., 125.

19 Diary entry, 4 January 1915, in Jan Herben, *Lístky z válečného deníku 1914 až 1918* (Pages from a wartime diary 1914 to 1918) (Prague: Réva, 1933), 50.

20 Jaroslav Hašek, *The Good Soldier Švejk and his Fortunes in the World War*, tr. Cecil Parrott (London/New York: Penguin, 1973), 166.

21 Jan Hajšman, comp., *Veselá mysl z fronty a zázemí: Humor českého lidu za války* (The comic spirit at the front and in the hinterland: the humor of the Czech people during the war) (Prague: Orbis, 1935), 8–9.

22 Novák, *Literature*, 315; and Novák and Novák, *Dějiny*, 1274–1275.

23 Some of Hašek's work for the Legions is reproduced in *Umění v odboji*, 205, 207, 209, and 210.

24 Jitka Zabloudilová, "Film a fotografie v československém vojsku v Rusku, 1914–1920" (Film and photography in the Czechoslovak army in Russia, 1914–1920), *Illuminace: časopis pro teorii, historii a estetiku filmu*, 2 (1995), 111–114.

25 Czech volunteers in France formed a small unit, of about 250, within the French Foreign Legion. That unit was disbanded after suffering heavy losses in the battles of 1915. In 1917, the French government permitted the formation of a Czech army in France. Like their co-nationals in Russia, Czechs in Italian POW camps carried out cultural activities and later joined the Czech army corps that was formed in Italy in 1918. Ibid., 111; and Josef Kopta, "Umění a kniha v zahraničním odboji" (Art and literature in the foreign resistance), in *Umění v odboji*, 228–230.

26 Alfred French, *The Poets of Prague: Czech Poetry Between the Wars* (London: Oxford University Press, 1969), 6; and Novák and Novák, *Dějiny*, 1309, 1333.

27 William E. Harkins, *Karel Čapek* (New York and London: Columbia University Press, 1962), 51–55.

28 Bruce Garver, "Czech Cubism and Fin-de-Siècle Prague," *Austrian History Yearbook*, 19–20:1 (1983–1984), 97. Kupka served in the Czech unit formed within the French Foreign Legion, but Gutfreund, who had joined as well, became disillusioned and ended up in a French jail after complaining about conditions. Alexander von Vegesack, ed., *Czech Cubism: Architecture, Furniture, and Decorative Arts 1910–1925* (London: Lawrence King Publishing, 1992), 84.

29 The one significant exhibit of Cubist art held during the war took place in 1918, Vegesack, ed., *Czech Cubism*, 83 and 330. Contemporary articles on art tended to ignore the war. An example is Vlastislav Hofman, "Rozhovor o novém umění, čili nazírání na věci" (A discourse on modern art, or an observation on the subject), *Lípa*, 1 (1917), 389–392, 411–414, 422–424.

30 Pražák, *Století*, 219; see also, Novák and Novák, *Dějiny*, 1329.

31 The three companies were in Plžen, Brno, and Kladno, the last founded only in 1915. František Černy and Ljuba Klosová, eds., *Dějiny českého divadla/III: Činohra 1848–1918* (A history of Czech theater/III: The play 1848–1918) (Prague: Academia, 1977), 414, 425, 439–440, 451.

32 An account of a 1918 tour of the Italian front is in the biography of Eduard Vojan, the leading Czech actor of the day. František Kožík, *Fanfáry pro krále: Eduard Vojan a jeho doba* (Fanfares for the king: Eduard Vojan and his time) (Prague: Melantrich, 1983), 411.

33 Completed in 1834, *Fidlovačka* had music by František Škroup and a libretto by Josef Kajetan Tyl. While it was only performed once in Tyl's lifetime, during the war it played seventeen times in the Vinohrady Theater, and was put on eighteen times by an amateur troupe from the Bohemian city of Hradec Kralové. Ibid., 408; and Černý and Klosová, eds., *Dějiny divadla*, 439 and 451.

34 Novák, *Literature*, 324. A similar assessment was expressed during the war in "Naše divadla za války" (Our theaters during the war), *Pražská lidová revue*, 10 (1915), 207–208.

35 Černý and Klosová, eds., *Dějiny divadla*, 324 and 390–391.

36 Quoted in Luděk Pacák, *Opereta: Dějiny pražských operetních divadel* (Operetta: a history of the operetta theaters in Prague) (Prague: Josef Dolejší, 1946), 146. An overview of operetta performances in two Prague theaters between 1910 and 1923 shows no drop-off in performances during the war years. Most of these operettas were of Austrian German or Hungarian origin, but some came from outside the Monarchy, including works by Offenbach and by Gilbert and Sullivan. Ibid., 164–167, see also, 186–187, and 210.

37 Stanislav Langer, *Aréna na Smíchově: stručná historie* (The Arena Theater in Smíchov: a short history) (Prague: Manuscript in the Library of the Theatrical Institute, 1959), 11. Langer's use of German military terms conveys an amusingly contemptuous tone.

38 A description of puppet performances in a front-line military hospital is in Jan Širůček, "U polní nemocnice č. 805 roku 1918" (At field hospital no. 805 in 1918), in *Domov za války*, V, 373–382.

39 The Kopecký brothers, renowned puppeteers, carried on their craft in Italian POW camps and later in the Czech armed force formed from these camps, Černý and Klosová, eds., *Dějiny divadla*, 542.

40 A study of Švejk's songs, with an explanation of their origins, is Václav Pleta, ed., *Písničky Josefa Švejka* (The songs of Josefa Švejka) (Prague-Bratislava: Supraphon, 1968).

41 Josef Waltner, "O pražských zábavních podnicích minulých dob" (About Prague's entertainment enterprises of an earlier time), *Přehled rozhlasu*, 2 (1933), 7–8.

42 One writer has argued that Czech cabaret was a generational revolt of young intellectuals against primitive beer hall humor. Josef Kotek, "U zdrojů českého kabaretního humoru" (At the sources of Czech cabaret humor), in Jaromír Kazda and Josef Kotek, eds., *Smích červené sedmy: za zlaté doby českého kabaretu, 1910–1922* (The laughter of the Red Seven: from the golden age of Czech cabaret, 1910–1922) (Prague, Československý spisovatel, 1981), 11.

43 Černý and Klosová, eds., *Dějiny divadla*, 494. Lucerna changed its leadership and style several times during the war. In 1915, it became purely German for a while, with cabaret acts from Vienna. Waltner, "O podnicích," 7; and Ján L. Kalina, *Svet kabaretu* (The world of cabaret) (Bratislava: Obzor, 1966), 367.

44 Bass's humor was based on current events and newspaper stories and is collected in Eduard Bass, *Letáky: satiry, verše, písničky* (Leaflets: satire, verses, songs) (Prague: Českloslovenský spisovatel, 1955). See also, Kalina, *Svet*, 70.

45 "Brave Huber, Who Fought Like a Bull," in Kazda and Kotek, eds., *Smích červené sedmy*, 101–103. Cabaret music, including that of the Red Seven, is discussed in Josef Kotek, *Dějiny české populární hudby a zpěvu (1) 19. a 20. století (do roku 1918)* (The history of Czech popular music and song (1) 19th and 20th centuries (to 1918)) (Prague: Academia, 1994), 191–196.

46 Černý and Klosová, eds., *Dějiny divadla*, 496; and Kalina, *Svet*, 369. Roger Shattuck's review of recent biographies of Marcel Duchamp, entitled "Confidence Man," in *The New York Review of Books* (27 March 1997) discusses the use of *mystification* by the Dadaists.

47 This is partly a reflection of the changing nature of the industry. Films had originally been presented by traveling companies, that purchased them to show in halls or beer gardens. The advent of distributorships in the pre-war period made permanent movie houses feasible. Luboš Bartošek, *Náš film: Kapitoly z dějin (1896–1945)* (Our cinema: chapters from its history (1896–1945)) (Prague: Mladá fronta, 1985), 19; and Jiří Havelka, *Kronika našeho filmu 1898–1965* (A chronicle of our cinema, 1989–1965) (Prague: Filmový ústav, 1967), 99.

48 Zdeněk Šťábla, *Data a fakta z dějin čs. kinematografie 1896–1945* (Dates and facts from the history of the Czechoslovak film industry 1896–1945) (Prague: Československý filmový ústav-interní tisk, 1988), 256, n. 2.

49 In 1913, Czech film studios made thirteen films, most of them short. The total fell to four in 1914, two in 1915, and only one in 1916, rising again to four in 1917 and reaching twenty in 1918. Havelka, *Kronika*, 39 and 43. The most successful of these films were "Zlaté srdečko" (Heart of gold) and "Pražští adamité" (Prague Adamites), produced in 1916 and 1917, respectively. The first was a film version of a popular play, featuring actors from a local theater, the second was a more cinematic enterprise. Both were genre stories set in Prague with no references to the war. Ibid., 241–242, and 302; Bartošek, *Film*, 51–54.

50 Zdeněk Šťábla, "Vývoj filmového obchodu za Rakousko-Uherska a Československé republiky (1906–1939)" (The development of the film industry in Austria-Hungary and in the Czechoslovak Republic (1906–1939)), *Filmový sborník historický*, 3 (1992), 5–12.

51 The most famous Italian film at this time was *Cabiria*, a sweeping costume epic set at the time of the Punic Wars that introduced many innovations into filmmaking, such as the use of a movable camera. Begun in the pre-war period, its political references were directed against Britain and France, Italy's colonial rivals in the Mediterranean. Jerzy Toeplitz, *Dejiny filmu: I. díl 1895–1918* (A history of cinema: Part 1: 1895–1918), tr. from the Polish by Richard Vyhlídal (Prague: Panorama, 1989), 78–79. See also, Šťábla, "Vývoj," 12.

52 Šťábla, *Data a fakta*, 246 and 269.

53 Ibid., 248. German films, on the other hand, were popular among the Germans in the Czech lands, who identified with their co-nationals across the border. This attitude gave rise to a wartime joke: disturbed about the unrest in his Czech provinces, Emperor Francis Joseph summoned the Bohemian governor, Count Thun, for an audience. Seeking the source of the discontent, Francis Joseph asked the governor, "Are there Russophiles in my Bohemian crownlands?" Thun replied, "That's the Czechs." Francis

Joseph continued, "Are there Prussophiles there?" Thun replied, "That's the Germans." Exasperated, Francis Joseph asked, "So where are the Austrians?" Thun replied, "Just the two of us, Your Majesty!" Hajšman, *Veselá mysl*, 19.

54 Among the few examples of Czech-language propaganda were two books intended for schoolchildren, both published in Moravia, more Catholic and loyalist than neighboring Bohemia: Ant. Hlinecký, *Za císaře a vlast: Sbírka loyálních básní a písní* (For the emperor and fatherland: a collection of loyalist poems and songs), 3 vols. (Žamberk: privately pub., 1916–1917); and Frant. Střížovský, *Modlitby vlastenecké 1915* (Patriotic prayers) (Olomouc: Matice cyrilmedějské, 1915). In addition, newspapers carried heroic accounts from the front under the heading, "The Golden Book of the Austro-Hungarian Army." See, Vincenc Červinka, "Persekuce válečná, hlavně tisková" (Wartime persecution, mainly of the press), *Domov za války*, III, 21–22.

55 The 1915 Hus celebrations are described in Alois Žipek, "Husův rok" (The year of Hus), *Domov za války*, II, 7–11.

56 Jaroslav Kvapil, "Projev českých spisovatelů roku 1917" (The declaration of Czech writers in 1917), *Domov za války*, IV, 7–16, and 178–183.

57 This event is described in Jan Grmela and Antonín Buriánek, "Národní přísaha 13. dubna 1918" (The national oath of April 13, 1918), *Domov za války*, V, 161–169.

58 A description of this event, including many reproduced speeches, is "Jubilejní slavnosti Národního divadla (1868–1918)" (The anniversary celebrations of the National Theater (1868–1918)), *Domov za války*, V, 267–277. See also, Miloš Jirko, "Jaroslav Kvapil vypravuje o divadlu v odboji" (Jaroslav Kvapil talks about the theater in the resistance), *Domov za války*, V, 312–316; and Kožík, *Fanfáry*, 416–418.

59 Jirko, "Kvapil," 315.

60 On this effort, see Garver, "Czech Cubism," 104; and John Willett, "Is There a Central European Culture?" *Cross Currents*, 10 (1991), 5–6.

61 Jarka M. Burian, "High Points of Theatre in the First Czechoslovak Republic," *Modern Drama*, 27:1 (March 1984), 99.

7 CULTURE IN HUNGARY DURING WORLD WAR I

1 For two definitions see *Webster's New Encyclopedic Dictionary* (New York, 1993) 24, and *The New Shorter Oxford Dictionary on Historical Principles*, ed. Leslie Brown (Oxford, 1993), I, 568.

2 For this observation I am indebted to the marvelous volume by John Lukács, *Budapest 1900: A Historical Portrait of a City and Its Culture* (New York, 1988), 77.

3 This is the reason for my caution in ascribing the term "modern" to urban culture alone in Hungary. Urban culture – or rather the culture of the capital city, Budapest, that most historians think of when discussing urban culture in Hungary – has contained many contemporary elements, but the term "modernity" is so vague and amorphous that its use for urban culture would be unwarranted.

4 Péter Hanák described the atmosphere this way: "Part of the educated middle class of the end of the century withdrew [from public life] because the powers-in-being had become impersonal, inhuman; public life was filled with weeds, society and its culture became mass-oriented, the crisis of politics, morals and the arts became overwhelming, and they felt themselves neurotic, tired and unnecessary," "Századvégi képeslap" (Postcard from the End of the Century), *História* (Budapest) 18:5–6 (1996), 3.

5 Several surveys of popular culture have been published in Hungary during the last half century. Some of the most comprehensive of the surveys are Elemér Cakó, *A magyarság néprajza* (Folklore of the Hungarians), 4 vols. (Budapest, 1933–1937); *Magyar néprajzi lexikon* (Encyclopedia of Hungarian Folklore), 5 vols. (Budapest, 1977–1982); Iván Balassa and Gyula Ortutay, eds., *Magyar néprajz* (Hungarian Folklore) (Budapest, 1979).

6 Tekla Dömötör was a folklorist, a pioneer of research in this field. The quote was taken from her *Néprajz mindenkinek. Régi és mai népszokások* (Folklore for Everyone. Ancient and Contemporary Folk Customs) (Budapest, 1986), 5.

7 The massive publication, edited by Attila Paládi-Kovács, *Magyar néprajz* (Hungarian Folklore), 3 vols. (Budapest, 1990), III, D. Tekla, M. Hoppál, G. Barna, eds., entitled *Népszokás, néphit, népi vallásosság* (Folklore, Popular Customs, Popular Beliefs, Popular Religiosity), contains a tremendous amount of information about popular culture. The first four volumes of this ambitious work had been published when the Hungarian Academy of Sciences sold its publishing firm to a Netherlands-based company. Since then, the publication of such works – originally subsidized by the government – has been suspended. The information listed above is based on vol. III, 9–19 of this work. All subsequent references to it are from vol. III.

8 See Julia Bellér, "Születés, keresztelő Szentsimonban (Birth and Baptism in Szentsimon) (Ózd, 1972); Bálint Bellosics, "A gyermek a magyar néphagyományban" (The Child in Hungarian Folk-traditions) (Baja, 1903); Bea Vidacs, "Komaság és kölcsönösség Szentpéterszegen" (Sponsorship and Mutuality in Szentpéterszeg), *Ethnográfia* (Budapest), 96 (1985), 509–529; Zsigmond Szendrey and Ákos Szendrey, "Születés és gyermekkor" (Birth and Childhood), in Cakó, *A magyarság néprajza*, IV, 155–169.

9 See Zsuzsa Széman, "A lakodalom hagyományőrző szerepe és társadalmi funkciója Felsőtárkányon (The Role of Marriage Customs in Preserving Traditions and their Social Functions in Felsőtárkány), *Ethnográfia*, 94 (1983), 285–296; Ibolya Szathmári, "Lakodalmi szokások Hajdúszováton" (Wedding Customs in Hajdúszovát), *A Déri Múzeum évkönyve* (Yearbook of the Museum at Dér) (1974), 567–618; Mihály Sárkány, "A lakodalom funkciójának megváltozása falun" (Changes in the Function of Wedding Ceremonies in the Villages), *Ethnográfia*, 94 (1983), 279–285; Mária Molnár, "A párválasztás és házasság néprajzi vizsgálatához" (Concerning the Examination of Folk-Customs of the Selection of Partners in Marriage), *Néprajzi Közlemények 1–2* (Budapest, 1965), 387–416.

10 Zoltán Kodály, "Zoborvidéki népszokások" (Folk-customs in the Region of Zobor) *Ethnográfia*, 20 (1909), 29–36, 116–121, and 245–247; András Krupa, "Születési és házassági szokások" (Customs Surrounding Births and

Marriage), in József Szabadfalvi and Gyula Viga, eds., *Néprajzi tanulmányok a Zemplén hegyvidékről. A miskolci Herman Ottó Múzeum Néprajzi Kiadványai* (Folklore-studies from the Mountainous Region of Zemplén. Published by the Otto Herman Museum on Folklore) (Miskolc, 1984), 257–311.

11 See Éva Pócs, "A falu hiedelemvilágának összetevői" (Components of the Belief-structure of the Village), in Ágnes Szemerkényi, ed., *Nógrádsipek. Tanulmányok egy észak-magyarországi falu mai folklórjáról* (Studies of the Contemporary Folklore of a North-Hungarian Village) (Budapest, 1980), 269–358, 574–670. See also Géza Róheim, *Magyar néphit és népszokások* (Hungarian Popular Beliefs and Popular Customs) (Szeged, 1925).

12 Sándor Bálint, *Karácsony, húsvét pünkösd. A nagyünnepek hazai és középeurópai hagyományvilágából* (Christmas, Easter, Epiphany. The Customs of High Holy Days in Hungary and Central Europe), 2nd. ed. (Budapest, 1976); Bálint, *Jeles napok* (Significant Days), 213–313.

13 It is interesting to note that most Hungarian historians have a rather low opinion of cultural life in the rural towns. Typical is the comment by Péter Hanák, one of the best known historians of modern Hungary, who stated: "Most of our towns were not yet modern urban centers, but they were huge villages, spread over great expanses of land, especially in the Great Plain, Kecskemét, Nagykőrös, etc.; or they were centers of agricultural trades, or administrative centers filled with the spirit of the gentry, such as Zalaegerszeg, Kaposvár, Szekszárd, Nyíregyháza. Peter Hanák, *Magyarország a Monarchiában. Tanulmányok* (Hungary in the Monarchy. Studies) (Budapest, 1975), 343.

14 Researchers in Hungary have not yet focused on the culture of rural towns. Although the Populist writers of the 1930s had done pioneering work on the life of the peasantry, much of this work produced advocacy literature. A conference held in 1986, in the north Hungarian city of Salgótarján produced a volume detailing some of the current research. See for instance, Péter Pifkó, "Családi kapcsolatok szerepe Esztergom kultúrális életében a XIX. század végén" (The Role of Family Relations in the Cultural Life of Esztergom at the End of the Nineteenth Century) in A. László Varga, ed., *Rendi társadalom – polgári társadalom. Társadalomtörténeti módszerek és forrástipusok* (Society of Estates – Society of Citizens. Methods of Social History and its Types of Sources) (Salgótarján, 1986), 77–81. The description was from 77–80.

15 See Judit Tóvári, "Polgárosodás és helyi politika 1872–1917 között" (Embourgeoisement and Local Politics between 1872 and 1917), in Varga, *Rendi társadalom*, 277–285.

16 Ágnes Losonczy, *Életmód időben és térben* (Dimensions of Time and Space in the Way of Life) (Budapest, 1978), 169.

17 Six towns in the "storm corner" possessed secondary schools at the turn of the century. By 1914, twelve such schools existed. See Ferenc Szabó, "Polgári értékrend és paraszti hagyomány" (Bourgeois Values and Peasant Traditions), *Historia*, 18, (1996/5–6), 40. This was part of a lecture delivered by the author at a conference in the *Európa Intézet* in Budapest in 1991. According to his research, literacy rates were high; in the county of Békés, 78.2 percent of people over six years of age knew how to read and write; in

Csanád county, the rate was 65.5 percent, and in Csongrád it reached 78.5 percent.

18 This was the case of the "Felvidéki Közművelődési Egyesület" (General Educational Association of Upper (Northern) Hungary (today Slovakia)), which agreed to finance the distribution of Slovak-language pamphlets and books in the elementary schools. See Sándor Bősze, "Az egyesületek mint forrástipusok és ezek kutatása – különös tekintettel a dualizmuskori Somogyra" (Associations as Source-Types, and their Research – with Special Attention to Somogy (county) during the Age of Dualism), in Varga, *Rendi társadalom*, 37–40.

19 János Hajdu, "Felsőbb oktatásügy és tömegnevelés" (Higher Education and Mass Education) in Domanovszky, *Magyar művelődéstörténet*, V. 349.

20 It is worth pointing out that of the three higher educational institutions established in the twentieth century, two were in areas where Magyars (ethnic Hungarians) were not predominant. Although this was later derided by Czechoslovak and Romanian propagandists according to whom these institutions were intended to spread Hungarian culture – which may have indeed been part of the intentions of the Hungarian government – the new universities were bound to increase the intellectual level of these regions.

21 See Lukács, *Budapest*, 71.

22 See Hanák, *Magyarország*, 345. The literature on modern Budapest is enormous.

23 For the gentry, see Iván Berend, *Válságos évek* (Budapest, 1982), 34–52.

24 István Nemeskürty, *Word and Image. History of the Hungarian Cinema* (Budapest, 1968), 9.

25 Lajos Körmeny-Ékes, *A mozi* (The Movie) (Budapest, 1915), 102–104. Quoted in Nemeskürty, *Word and Image*, 13.

26 For further details about the development of the Hungarian cinema see Nemeskürty, *Word and Image*.

27 Lukács, *Budapest*, 82.

28 The reports of Ferenc Molnár, famed author and playwright, who served as war correspondent in Serbia and Russia, were typical of the genre. His stories were published in various newspapers and were collected in two volumes after the war, entitled *Egy haditudósító emlékei* (Memoirs of a War Correspondent) (Budapest, 1926). The tone of the reports was moderate; his nationalism was sensible, and he described the war not as a heroic enterprise, but a harrowing experience in which honor and loyalty were more important than foolish pride. Molnár, a Jew, eventually left Hungary in the 1930s, and became a successful playwright with the Broadway production of his play, *Liliomfi* (English stage title *Carousel*).

29 See the excellent book by Gabor Vermes, *Tisza István* (Budapest, 1994).

30 See Iván T. Berend *et al.*, eds., *A szociológia első magyar műhelye. A Huszadik Század köre* (The First Hungarian Workshop of Sociology. The Circle of Huszadik Század) (Budapest, 1973), 7–8. The *Nyugat* periodical mentioned in the quotation was a literary journal established in 1908, and it gathered a new generation of young writers, poets, and social critics around itself. They were immediately embroiled in controversies with the older writers. See my earlier study, "Young Hungary. The *Nyugat* Periodical, 1908–1914"

in Stanely Winters and Joseph Held., eds., *Intellectual History in the Habsburg Empire from Maria Theresa to World War I* (Boulder, CO, 1975), 75–92.

31 A very perceptive work by Zoltán Horváth, *A magyar századforduló. A második reform-nemzedék története* (The New Century in Hungary. The History of the Second Reform Generation) (Budapest, 1961), provides a very thorough description of the struggles of the generation of 1900 for the fundamental reform of Hungarian culture and society. Horváth very aptly noted that these struggles failed, partly because of the outbreak of the First World War, and partly because Hungarian society as a whole was not receptive to new ideas which this generation introduced. For a more general but equally penetrating analysis, see Berend, *Válságos évek*, 53–102.

32 The best example for this was Ervin Szabó, a serious thinker who openly professed to be a Marxist. However, when he described his ideas about "proletarian culture," he proved to be quite moderate and sensible. He said:

> It is possible for someone to be basically a Socialist or Anarchist, Catholic or feudalist by conviction – and a great artist; but anyone whose creations can be labeled as social democratic or People's Party or standing on the platform of the Constitutional Party, is not an artist . . . No one can, therefore, speak of proletarian poetry, or proletarian art. Nor can one speak of proletarian science, proletarian humanism, proletarian sociology, or proletarian technology. Similarly, there is no bourgeois poetry, feudal science, or Catholic mathematics . . . But proletarian poetry? What could it be?

In "Proletárköltészet (Várnai Zseni verseskönyve alkalmából)" (Proletarian Poetry. On the Occasion of the Poems of Zseni Várnai), *Nyugat*, 8:1 (1914), 644.

33 This was the basis of Oszkár Jászi's negotiations with the emerging successor states and Romania in 1918, when he became minister of nationalities in the revolutionary government of Count Mihály Károlyi.

34 For the latest studies on Hungarian populism in English, see Miklós Lackó, "Populism in Hungary: Yesterday and Today", György Csepeli, "In the Captivity of Narratives: The Political Socialization of Populist Writers in Hungary, and the Origin of National Narratives in Eastern Europe," and Péter Hanák, "The Anti-Capitalist Ideology of the Populists," in Joseph Held, ed., *Populism in Eastern Europe: Nationalism, Racism, and Society* (New York, 1996), 107–128, 129–144, and 145–162 respectively.

35 Following the failed general strike, there was disillusionment with the Social Democratic Party among the workers. This was reflected in the erosion of the membership of the trade union movement, dominated by the Social Democrats. At the end of 1912, there were 130,000 organized workers; at the end of 1913, there were a little over 107,000, and by June 1914, there remained only 96,000. See Horváth, *Magyar századforduló*, 529. This provided a field-day for contemporary conservatives who crowed over the liberals' failure. Ferenc Herczeg, a leading conservative writer-journalist, wrote: "Radicalism, considered only recently to be so dangerous, whose leaders were constantly offering themselves to the workers and to every enemy of Hungary, had become bankrupt," in *Magyar figyelő*, 5:10 (1914), 2–3.

36 Macartney, together with Hungarian historians, describes the gentry as part of the conservative bourgeois stratum. He was correct; many, but not all, of the gentry were descendants of the nobility who lost their rural holdings and

moved to Budapest and other cities and towns. They sought and obtained positions in the state and local bureaucracies. That they brought their traditional outlook with them and succeeded in preserving it appeared "uncanny" to Macartney. He stated that the gentry, instead of collecting their income from the peasants, now acquired it from state institutions.

37 The liberal bourgeoisie was not a unified social stratum. There were many of foreign descent, especially assimilated Germans and Czechs, and a considerable number of Jews. But the Jewish segment itself consisted of several layers, among them the financiers, most of whom had long since been assimilated and spoke mostly Hungarian (though sometimes Yiddish) and many newcomers who immigrated from Russian Poland. Many Jews arrived in Hungary during the late nineteenth century, escaping from the pogroms in the Russian Empire. In 1840, their number was 290,000; by 1900 their numbers had grown to 830,000. Of these, 167,000 lived in Budapest, constituting 23.4 percent of the entire population of the city. The capitalist development of Hungary was almost entirely their work. Their occupational distribution, according to the statistics of 1910, showed that 12.5 percent of self-employed industrialists, 21.8 percent of salaried industrial employees, 54 percent of self-employed traders and 62.1 of their employees, 85 percent of persons in banking and finance, and 42 percent of their employees, were Jewish. Jewish landowners possessed 19.9 percent of arable-land properties of over 1,000 hold (one hold = 2.4 acres) and a large percentage of leased estates. A correspondingly large number of Jews could be found in journalism, in medicine, and other free professions. See Macartney, *The Habsburg Empire* (London, 1968), 710. The history of anti-Semitism generated by the success of some Jewish citizens has not yet been fully explored. Péter Hanák's work, *Zsidókérdés, asszimiláció, antiszemitizmus. Tanulmányok a zsidókérdésről a huszadik századi Magyarországon* (The Jewish Question, Assimilation, Anti-Semitism. Studies about the Jewish Problem in Twentieth-century Hungary) (Budapest, 1984), began to explore this issue but his studies have not yet been followed up by others. See also the study by William O. McCagg, *Jewish Nobles and Geniuses in Modern Hungary* (Boulder, CO, 1972).

38 See Margit Prahács, "Zene és zenekultúra" (Music and Musical Culture), in Domanovszky, *Magyar művelődéstörténet*, V, 659–660.

39 See the brilliant, short summary of pre-World War I culture by Péter Hanák, "Századvégi képeslap. Lázadások a közép-európai kultúrában" (Postcard from the End of the Century. Revolts in the Culture of Central-Eastern Europe), *Historia*, 18:5–6 (1996), 5.

40 See László Moholy Nagy, "Vita az új tartalom és az új forma problémájáról" (Debates about the Problem of the New Content and Form) in Karl Polányi, *The Great Transformation. The Political and Economic Origin of our Time* (Boston, 1964), 20.

41 Berend, *Válságos évek*, 96.

42 See Miklós Szabó, "Politikai Gondolkodás és kultúra Magyarországon a Dualizmus utolsó negyedszázadában" (Political Thinking and Culture in Hungary during the Last Quarter-Century of Dualism) in Péter Hanák and Ferenc Mucsi, eds., *Magyarország története 1890–1918* (History of Hungary), 7:2 (Budapest, 1978), 954.

43 Endre Ady's last volume of poetry was entitled, almost frighteningly, *A halottak élén* (At the Head of the Dead) (Budapest, 1918). It painted a gloomy picture of contemporaneous Hungarian life.

44 Ady's first two collections of poems were entitled *Új versek* (New Poems) (published in 1906), and *Vér és arany* (Blood and Gold) (1907). These established him as the *enfant terrible* of his generation. However, similarly to Bartók, he was not always understood, and his heavy symbolism was rejected outright by the public.

45 Endre Ady, "A föltámadott Jókai" (Jókai Resurrected), *Nyugat* (16 May 1916).

46 In an issue of *Nyugat*, 10:1 (1917) an entire page was left blank, but the title of the intended article, "A Monarchia háborús céljai" (The War Aims of the Monarchy) was prominently displayed. Other than this, no evidence of censorship exists, in spite of several of the journal's previous articles criticizing the government's internal policies.

47 For samples of the many articles in question, see the following: Ignotus, "Az orosz háború" (The Russian war), *Nyugat*, 7:2 (1914), 453–456; Zoltán Ambrus, "Háborús jegyzetek (Szent egoizmus)" (Notes on the War [Holy Egotism]), ibid., 8:1 (1915), 583–585; Andor Nagy, "Tábori posta. Przemisli emlékek" (Mail from the Front. Memories of Przemyśl), ibid., 8:1 (1915), 379–381; Gyula Halász, "Utolsó napjaim orosz földön" (My Last Days on Russian Land), ibid., 8:1 (1915), 187–205; László Boros, "A világháború Grey hattyúdaláig" (The World War up to the Swan-song of Grey), ibid., 10:2 (1917), 617–630, and many others.

48 This was especially true of Zoltán Ambrus, several of whose articles used the expression described above. See, for instance, "Írók a háborúról" (Writers about the War), *Nyugat*, 8:1 (1915), 116–121.

49 Zoltán Ambrus, "A háború magasztalói" (The Warmongers), *Nyugat*, 8:1 (1915), 229–231.

50 Józsi Jenő Tersánszky, "Levél Ignotushoz" (Letter to Ignotus), *Nyugat*, 8:1 (1915), 264.

51 Ignotus, "A német válság" (The German Crisis), *Nyugat*, 10:2 (1917), 603–606.

52 Aladár Schöpflin, "A szavak háborúja" (War of Words), *Nyugat*, 7:2 (1914), 362–365.

53 Gyula Havas, "Szomory Dezső, Harry Russel-Dorsan a francia hadszintérről" (Dezső Szomory, H R-D from the French Front), *Nyugat* 11:1 (1918), 933–936.

54 Miklós Fekete, "Gazdasági figyelő" (Economic Observer), *Nyugat*, 10:1 (1917), 311–314; Ervin Szabó, "Köztisztviselők és munkások" (Public Servants and Workers), ibid., 10:2, 731–735; Ernő Éber, "A magyar mezőgazdaság átalakítása" (The Transformation of Hungarian Agriculture), ibid., 10:2 (1917), 727–730; Lajos Fülep, "Magyar épitészet" (Hungarian Architecture), ibid., 10:1 (1917), 683–694; by the same author, "Európai művészet és magyar művészet" (European Art and Hungarian Art), ibid., 11:1 (1918), 484–499, etc.

55 Aladár Schöpflin, "A Halottak élén. Ady Endre háborús költészetéhez" (At the Head of the Dead. About the Wartime Poetry of Endre Ady), *Nyugat*, 11:2 (1918), 825–828.

56 Aladár Schöpflin, "A forradalom és a magyar lateiner osztály" (The Revolution and the Hungarian Lateiner Class), *Nyugat*, 11:2 (1918), 697–701.

8 CULTURE IN THE SOUTH SLAVIC LANDS, 1914–1918

1 During this period Macedonia, called Southern Serbia by the Belgrade authorities, was not recognized as a separate cultural entity. Although the Macedonian national awakening began in the late nineteenth century, I have not been able to discover any noteworthy events relating to Macedonian culture during the war years. From late 1915, of course, the Macedonian capital, Skoplje, was occupied by Bulgarian forces, and any cultural activity was of a Bulgarian, rather than a specifically Macedonian character.

2 According to an article in *Tedenske slike* (Ljubljana), 26 July 1916, in the 1915–1916 season the Croatian National Theater took in some 400,000 crowns through ticket sales. These monies were supplemented by a subsidy of 232,000 crowns of which the emperor gave 40,000, the Croatian government 142,000, and the city of Zagreb 50,000.

3 *Repertoar Hrvatskih Kazališta: 1840–1860–1980*, 2 vols. (Zagreb: Globus, 1990) gives full performance information for all Croatian theaters in this period. It is worth noting that, although contemporary art from enemy countries was generally banned during the war, French and Russian operatic and theatrical works by dead authors appear to have presented no problem.

4 Aristophanes' play, which debuted in 411 BC as Athens was on the verge of ruin in the Peloponnesian War, is the oldest surviving piece of anti-war literature. It tells the story of Lysistrata, the leader of the Athenian women, who persuades the women of Athens to withhold their sexual favors from their husbands until the men make peace. Unable to stand this punishment, the men give in, and the play concludes with peace and marital concord.

5 As reported in "Naši klerikalci i literatura," *Savremenik*, 10:5–6 (May–June 1915), 234.

6 Ibid., 234.

7 *Savremenik* printed a long article by the composer on the subject in 12:3 (May 1917) 119–124. The opera was performed fifteen times between its premiere and the end of the 1918–1919 season. Another large and glowing review appeared in *Jutarnji list* (27 April 1917), 2. Miloš Obilić (Kobilić?) was a Serbian nobleman. Apparently, he killed the Turkish Sultan Murad at the disastrous Battle of Kosovo (15 June 1389), and was subsequently killed by the Turks. Prince Marko (Kraljević Marko) became a Turkish vassal in the period just after the defeat at Kosovo. He is, nevertheless, the most popular Serbian epic hero, beloved for his unique combination of cunning and strength with all-too-human frailties. For a good translation of the epic song on which Konjović's opera was based, see *Marko the Prince*, tr. Anne Pennington and Peter Levi (Duckworth: London, 1984), 33–36.

8 For details, see Milan Marjanović, "Genij Jugoslovenstva Ivan Meštrović i njegov hram," *Jugoslovenska biblioteka*, 1 (New York, 1915).

9 Kosta Strajnić, "Umetnost Meštrovića," *Savremenik*, 10:3–4 (March–April 1915), 115–116.

10 The story appeared in the December 1918 issue of the journal, after the author's death in battle.

11 *Hrvatska prosvjeta* (January–February 1916), 16.

12 *Savremenik*, 12:5 (August 1917), 189–201. I will discuss this story in detail below.

13 Unsigned feuilleton, *Savremenik*, 12:7 (October 1917), 318. The Slovenian journal, *Ljubljanski zvon* (The Ljubljana Bell), was even more overt in its espousal of Vojnović as first and foremost a Yugoslav writer. An unsigned article in the journal called him "the greatest Yugoslav dramatist," and ended as follows: Slovenians join in the sincere feelings of Serbs and Croats to congratulate this great herald of Yugoslavism," *Ljubljanski zvon*, 37:11 (November 1917), 615.

14 In fact, *Ženski svijet* was the second such South Slavic publication. The first, *Slovenka*, was published in Trieste between 1897 and 1899 and edited by Marica Bartol.

15 "Zadaci vremena." *Književni jug*, 1:1 (1 January 1918), 3–4. Njegoš and Prešeren were the greatest Serbian and Slovenian romantic poets respectively, Kranjčević was a major Yugoslav-oriented Croatian lyric poet of the late nineteenth century, and Župančič was the major Slovenian lyric poet of the first half of the twentieth century.

16 Preradović (1818–1872) followed a rather unusual career path for a future Yugoslav national poet. The son of a military officer, he himself joined the Austrian army, rising eventually to the rank of general. Most of his education was in German, as was his first poetry, and he claimed almost to have completely forgotten his native language. During the early 1840s, however, Preradović became interested in the literary situation of his native land, and began to write Croatian-language "Illyrian" poetry, that was immediately acclaimed by the burgeoning Croatian cultural establishment.

17 All of this was reported in the 20 March 1918 number of *Tedenske slike* (Ljubljana). Major Croatian periodicals all produced special issues devoted to Preradović, including the entire 15 March 1918 number of *Književni jug* (1:6).

18 "Podnevna simfonija" (Noon Symphony), which came out in the final 1916 number of *Savremenik*, was reviewed by Julije Benešić who said that the work was "not only a good poem in and of itself, and it is not only one of our own Croatian poems in its feelings and thoughts, but it is ours – and this is crucial – in its music." Quoted in Enes Čengić, *Krleža* (Zagreb: Mladost, 1982), 125.

19 According to a review of 1917 by Iljko Gorenčević, "Miroslav Krleža is an innovator in Croatian literature. He is a fighter and he is going on a road that no one in our country has followed. Like the majority of Serbian poets, he is a student of Europe. The newest Europe. Perhaps there he learned to value the artistic-theoretical bases of new art: genius, the free expression of the creative personality, individual artistic form that corresponds perfectly to the artistic subject" ibid., 127.

20 Originally published as a free-standing work, the "Rhapsody" would eventually be included as the final section of his *Hrvatski bog Mars* (The Croatian God of War, 1933), a series of stories set during World War I.

21 The Union (founded 1906), Apollo (1912), Edison, Metropol, Helios, and Cyril and Methodius. See Sretan Jovanović, "Kinematografija u Zagrebu," *Filmska kultura*, 18:95–96 (1974), 119–153.

22 Advertisement in *Jutarnji list* (28 August 1917).

23 For purposes of comparison, a kilo of grade A meat cost 11 crowns, a kilo of flour 4 crowns, a kilo of bread, 0.5 crowns.

24 In the period from 1896 to 1914 on the territory of Croatia sixty-three documentaries were shot by foreign firms (mostly travel and landscape pictures) and seven by Croatian ones. No feature films were produced. During the war, twenty-two documentaries were shot by foreign firms and seven by Croatian as well as seven Croatian feature films. The first Croatian film production company was privately registered by Julije Bergman in 1917. A second company was formed after the first went bankrupt by this same Bergman with Hamilkar Bošković. In 1917 they produced *Matija Gubec* (Peasant Uprising) directed by Aca Binički. For information on all seven Croatian wartime feature films, as well as some surviving stills, see Dejan Kosanović, "Filmovi snimljeni na teritoriji Hrvatske do 1918, godine," *Filmska kultura*, 24:123 (1980), 107–122 and Petar Volk, *Istorija Jugoslovenskog filma* (Belgrade: Institut za film, 1986).

25 See reviews devoted to its production and screening in *Jutarnji list* (Zagreb), 2:8 (1917), 26:8 (1917), and 29:8 (1917).

26 Oktavijan Miletić, "Povodom 'Brcka u Zagrebu' (Uspomene)", *Filmska kultura*, 24:126 (1980), 113–116. The writer worked as an assistant on this film as a very young man.

27 Ibid.

28 *Jutarnji list* (11 December 1917). The film was evidently fairly long, as advertisements for it indicate that it was screened at $1\frac{1}{2}$ hour intervals.

29 See *Slovenski narod* (10 January 1918), 3.

30 I was not able to find records of any specific order banning a journal, but I suspect that the disappearance of *Glas juga* (Voice of the South) 1:2 (May 1914), was no accident. The journal, edited by V. M. Zalar, was typical for pro-Yugoslav publications of this period. In the program statement that appears in the first pages by A. Jenko, we read: "we will present in this regard all the material necessary for the creation of a strong national culture, built on new foundations of national individuality, independence, and optimism . . . the creation of a Yugoslav nation is for us the logical conclusion to a long historical process, which leads unavoidably to the unification of groups related by blood, and which share common interests, in particular a common struggle for existence and for the preservation of their individuality," *Glas juga*, 1:1 (March 1914), 3.

31 All the statistical information in the paragraphs that follow was culled from Dragan Matič, "Kulturni utrip Ljubljane v sezonah 1913/14–1917/18" (The Cultural Pulse of Ljubljana in the Seasons 1913/14–1917/18) (Master's thesis, Ljubljana, 1994).

32 For information on the latter, see *Slovenski narod* (22 August 1915).

33 *Ljubljanski zvon*, 35:5 (May 1915), 193–195.

34 Review of "Vojaške narodne pesmi za šolo in dom" (Military Songs for School and Home), ed. Anton Kosi (Ljubljana: Katoliška bukvarna, 1915). Reviewed in *Ljubljanski zvon*, 35:10 (October 1915), 480.

35 *Ljubljanski zvon*, 36:8 (August 1916), 379.

36 See, for example, the obituary of Dr. Jan. Ev. Krek, *Ljubljanski zvon*, 37:11 (November 1917), 611.

37 *Ljubljanski zvon*, 37:10 (October 1917), 556.
38 Ivan Cankar, *Izbrano delo* (Ljubljana: Mladinska knjiga, 1967), VII, 225.
39 *Tedenske slike* (19 July 1916), 433.
40 No. 1 (12 August 1914), 13.
41 The Serbian government frequently contributed financially to these publications, and sometimes even appointed their editors. For an exhaustive description of government-sponsored cultural and propaganda efforts, see Ljubinka Trgovčević, *Naučnici Srbije i stvaranje jugoslovenske države, 1914–1920* (Belgrade: Narodna knjiga, 1986), especially 65–73 and 128–145.
42 The latter was published under the imprimatur of the Serbian Ministry of Education and Religious Affairs on Corfu in early 1918.
43 Vladislav Petković-Dis, *Pesme* (Novi Sad: Matica Srpska, 1959), 197.
44 These poems were published as a collection entitled *Lirika Itake* (Ithaca Lyrics) in 1919.
45 Andrić's family was Roman Catholic, and, as a citizen of the Habsburg Empire, his early literary and cultural orientation was to Zagreb. Later in life, however, Andrić self-identified either as a Yugoslav or as a Serb writer.
46 Ivo Andrić, *Ex Ponto, Sabrana dela Ive Andrića* (Sarajevo: Svetlost, 1984), XI, 14.
47 Both are reproduced in Vanja Kraut, *Ljubomir Ivanović* (Belgrade: Galerija SANU, 1976), plates 6 and 7.
48 Reproduced in Katerina Ambrozić, *Nadežda Petrović* (Belgrade: Srpska književna zadruga, 1978), 412. It is now in the Museum of Modern Art, Belgrade.
49 Dimitrije Djordjevic, "The Yugoslav Phenomenon," *The Columbia History of Eastern Europe in the Twentieth Century*, ed. Joseph Held (New York: Columbia University Press, 1992), 315.
50 Ibid., 310–311.
51 For the best treatment of the political problems of post World War I Yugoslavia, see Ivo Banac, *The National Question in Yugoslavia: Origins, History, Politics* (Ithaca: Cornell University Press, 1984). For a detailed discussion of the cultural problems, see Andrew Wachtel, *Making a Nation, Breaking a Nation: Literature and Cultural Politics in Yugoslavia* (Stanford: Stanford University Press, 1998).

9 BETWEEN APOLOGY AND DENIAL: BULGARIAN
   CULTURE DURING WORLD WAR I

1 I. Berend, *The Crisis Zone of Europe* (Cambridge, 1986), 72.
2 C. Derijan, "Voina i iskustvo," *Vazhod*, 1 (1920), 17.
3 Oral history interview of the author with Dr. Khristo Grancharov in Peshtera, Summer 1983.
4 R. Koneva, *Goliamata sreshta na balgarskija narod* (Sofia, 1995), 188.
5 K. Tosheva, "Balgarskia frontovi teatar," manuscript, p. 4. I am grateful to the author for letting me use her valuable work.
6 Ibid., 23.
7 Ibid., 26.
8 Ibid., 31–33.

9 *Otechestvo*, 3 (1918), 18.

10 *Mir*, 4822 (16 March 1916).

11 G. Markov, *Goliamata voina i balgarskiat kliuch za evropieskiat pogreb 1914–1916* (Sofia, 1995), 218.

12 *Otechestvo*, 2 (1917), 28.

13 A. Grozev, *Nachalato: Iz istoriata na balgarskoto kino 1895–1956* (Sofia, 1985), 34.

14 *Statisticheski godichnik na Bulgarskoto tsarstvo* (Sofia, 1924), 62.

15 Zh. Chankov, *Gramotnost na naselenieto v Bulgaria* (Sofia, 1926), 25.

16 E. Kelbetcheva, "Voina i tvorchestvo," *Godishnik na Sofiiskiia Universitet "Sv. Kliment Ohridski,"* 5:80–81 (1987–1988), 101–174.

17 D. Babev, "Poezia i voina," *Vestnik na vestnitsite*, 2 (1917), 48.

18 I. Vazov, *Pesni za Makedonia* (Sofia, 1916); *Novi ekove* (Sofia, 1916); *Ne shte zagine* (Sofia, 1919).

19 K. Hristov, *Na Nozh* (Sofia, 1912).

20 K. Hristov, *Sabrani sachinenija*, I (Sofia), 660.

21 K. Todorov, "Voinata i poeziata," *Sila*, 1 (1919), 8.

22 TsDIA (Tsentralen Darzhaven Arhiv), f. 798, op. 4, a.e. 2, 54.

23 Koneva, *Goliamata*, 62–65. An interesting fact is that in 1918, the first Bulgarian woman assistant in mathematics was appointed at the University of Sofia. During the war the first Medical Faculty was inaugurated with an incoming class of 100 students, 15 of whom were women.

24 Ibid., 71–74.

25 Ibid., 73.

26 Ibid., 74.

27 P. Penchev, *Istoria na balgarskia dramatichen teatar* (Sofia, 1975), 248.

28 *Muzikalna misal*, 1 (1917), 17.

29 Koneva, *Goliamata*, 84.

30 Ibid., 96.

31 A. Bozhkov, *Balgarska istoricheska zhivopis* (Sofia, 1978), II, 240.

32 Ibid., 241.

33 S. Skitnik, "Iskustvoto ni prez voinata," *Zlatorog*, 1 (1920), 68–82.

34 Ts. Minkov, "Poetite malchat," *Sila*, 21 (1919), 7.

35 A. Balabanov, "Voina i pesen," *Democraticheski kalendar*, 1 (1914).

36 K. Galabov, "Misli varhu poesiata ni prez voinata," *Priaporets*, 283 (1918), 24–35; Galabor, "Nashata poesia prez voinata," *Voenni izvestia*, 60 (1918), 38–49.

37 Skitnik, "Iskustvoto," 82.

38 L. Stoyanov, "Epilog na edin spor," *Hiperion*, 6–7 (1923), 355–365.

39 S. Igov, *Kratka istoria na Bulgarskata literatura* (Sofia, 1996), 375–423.

40 R. Likova, *Portreti na Bulgarski simvolisti* (Sofia, 1987), 98–119.

41 Ibid., 30–31.

42 V. Balabanova, "Teodor Trayanov," *Literaturni anketi* (Sofia, 1980), 156–157.

43 This term refers to traditional folk songs devoted to Bulgarian guerrillas who fought the Turks.

44 V. Pundev, "'Karvavi petna' ot V. Musakov," *Zlatorog*, 1 (1920), 95.

45 G. Raichev, "Manichak sviat: Besumie," *Izbrani sachinenia*, V (Sofia, 1957).

46 E. Konstantinova, *G. Raichev – zhiznen i tvorcheski pat* (Sofia, 1982), 85.

47 Ibid., 96.

48 T. Genov, *Vava kazarmata i na fronta s D. Debelianov* (Sofia, 1957), 24.

49 Geo Milev, *Hristo Yasenov, Sergey Rumiantsev v spomenite na savremennitsite si* (Sofia, 1965), 53.

50 BIA (Bulgarski Istoricheski Arhiv), f. 26, a.e. 32, 48.

51 Milev, *Stihotvorenia, Poemi, Kritika* (Sofia, 1980), 181.

52 Ibid., 206.

53 D. Dimitrov, "Kam vaprosa za ideino-esteticheskite vazgledi na Vladimir Dimitrov-Maistora do kraja na Papvata svetovna voina," *Iz istoriata na Bulgarskoto izobrazitelno izkustvo* (Sofia, 1984), II, 136, 144.

54 Y. Yovkov, *Letopis 1912–1918*, 165.

55 Y. Yovkov, "Posledna radost," *Zlatorog*, 2 (1920), 273.

56 Ibid.

57 V. Vassilev, "Marshat na pobedata i na smartta," *Zlatorog*, 1 (1920), 45–61.

10 ROMANIA: WAR, OCCUPATION, LIBERATION

1 Research for this chapter was supported in part by a grant from the International Research and Exchanges Board (IREX), with funds provided by the National Endowment for the Humanities and the United States Department of State under the Title VIII program. None of these organizations is responsible for the views expressed.

2 Although George Enescu later became internationally known as one of the century's avant-garde composers under the French version of his name, Georges Enesco, in this chapter I will refer to him in the same form his contemporaries mentioned him during the war.

3 See Paul Fussel, *The Great War and Modern Memory* (New York: Oxford University Press, 1975); Modris Eksteins, *Rites of Spring: The Great War and the Birth of the Modern Age* (Boston: Houghton Mifflin, 1989); and Jay Winter, *The Great War and the Shaping of the Twentieth Century* (New York: Penguin Studio, 1996).

4 A classic treatment of the war is Constantin Kirițescu, *Istoria războiului pentru întregirea României, 1916–1919* (Bucharest: Editura Științifică și Enciclopedică, 1989). For an attempt to provide a popular narrative of life on the home front see Constantin Rădulescu-Zoner, *Bucureștii în anii primului război mondial (1914–1918)* (Bucharest: Ed. Albatros, 1993).

5 Barbu Brezianu, "Gruparea 'Arta Română'," *Studii și Cercetări de Istoria Artei. Seria Arta Plastică*, 11:1 (1964), 144–151.

6 Nicolae Manolescu, *Sadoveanu sau utopia cărții* (Bucharest: Editura Eminescu, 1976), 133.

7 Ioan Massoff and Radu Tănase, *Tănase* (Bucharest: Editura Meridiane, 1969), 84.

8 *Adevărul*, 24:9858 (22 August 1914), 1.

9 *Adevărul*, 24:9812 (7 July 1914), 3.

10 Emil Nicolau, "Cronica teatrală," *Universul*, 32:117 (3 May 1914), 2. After this particular performance of a Zaharia Bârsan play, the audiences sang

"Deşteaptă-te Române" (Awake Romanians!), the most famous song of the 1848 Revolution, which carried strong irredentist overtones.

11 Mircea Dem. Rădulescu, "Treziţi-vă latini!," *Flacăra*, 4:3–4 (8 November 1914), 1. The Romanian text follows: "Treziţi-vă victorioşi soldaţi, / Mândria, forţa, vechea noastră fală, / Să tremure masivele'n Carpaţi / De năvălirea voastră triumfală."

12 Ibid. Basarab was the first voivod of the Wallachian voivodate, a symbol of military heroism in Romanian nationalist historiography. The Romanian version follows: "Voi tremuraţi ca cei mişei şi slabi / In faţa oceanului ce vine? / Unde sânteţi nepoţi de Basarabi / Să ne spălaţi tot neamul de ruşine!"

13 Mefisto, "Regelui Ferdinand," *Flacăra*, 4:5–6 (22 November 1914), 27. The Romanian follows: "Ca bun Român? . . . O, iartă Maiestate, / Să nu urez o astfel de durere / Acestui neam ce-aşteaptă în tăcere, / Privind la Tron, o rază de dreptate."

14 "Rolul teatrului în mişcarea războinică," *Teatrul*, 1:5–6 (November–December 1914), 4.

15 Alex. Coriolan, "Războiul," *Viaţa Nouă*, 11:4 (11 June 1916), 130–132.

16 My analysis includes *Viaţa Românească, Rampa, Teatrul, Convorbiri Literare* and *Flacăra*.

17 Alexis Nour, "Germania beligerantă," *Viaţa Românească*, 10:7–9 (July–September 1915), 158.

18 Alexis Nour, "Din enigma anilor 1914–15," *Viaţa Românească*, 10:1–3 (January–March 1915), 142.

19 Octav Botez, "Asupra imperialismului german," *Viaţa Românească*, 11:1–3 (January–March 1915), 213.

20 *Flacăra*, 4:14 (17 January 1915), 91.

21 *Flacăra*, 4:1–2 (25 October 1914), 7.

22 Eugen Lovinescu. "Revizuiri morale. Barbu Delavrancea, factor al conştiinţei naţionale," *Flacăra*, 5:12 (2 January 1916), 138 and "Revizuiri morale," *Flacăra*, 5:15 (23 January 1916), 169–170.

23 Thespis, "La d. G. Enescu," *Rampa*, 1:5 (6 September 1915), 2.

24 See positive review of *Ultima oră* in *Adevărul*, 34:9815 (10 July 1914), 4.

25 See *Adevărul*, 34:9840 (4 August 1914), 1: *Adevărul*, 34:9841 (5 August 1914), 1; and *Veselia*, 36:13 (26 March 1915), 1.

26 *Veselia*, 36:14 (2 April 1915), 1.

27 Elena Văcărescu, "Taina sângelui," *Adevărul* 24:9864 (28 August 1914), 1.

28 George Ranetti, "Cronica teatrală," *Teatrul*, 1:3 (September 1914), 17–18. The Romanian version follows: "Că publicul vrea veselie / Vrea operetă . . . ca la Parc . . . / O clipă să uităm măcelul . . . / Şi să ne-nchipuim războiul / Că-i doar un simplu vis urât!"

29 Iaşi, Craiova, Bîrlad, Constanţa and Galaţi were also regular stops for movies that toured through the country.

30 *Universul*, 36:121 (5 May 1914), 1.

31 *Universul*, 36:117 (1 May 1914). Iulian was a very popular comedian, who appeared mostly in reviews, operettas, and light comedies.

32 Eugen Lovinescu, "Literatura războiului," in *In Cumpăna Vremei. Note de Război* (Bucharest: Editura Librăriei Socec, 1919), 28–29.

33 Constantin Mille, "Presa," *Adevărul*, 26:10662 (7 November 1916), 1.
34 Rădulescu-Zoner, *Bucureştii* . . . , 170.
35 For the 1917–1918 repertoire of the Romanian theaters see *Scena*, 1:1–3 (30 September 1917), 4. They included some German plays, along with a play by Ibsen and one by Molière. However, most of the repertoire was composed of Romanian plays.
36 Ibid.
37 Letter to the minister of culture, dated 24 March 1918. Fond Ministerul Instrucţiunii, dos. 255/1918, p. 82. Arhivele Statului, Direcţia Generală, Bucharest.
38 Paul I. Prodan, "Grădinile de vară," in *Teatrul Românesc în Războiu* (Bucharest: Tiparul Românesc, 1921), 99–100 [1918].
39 Oral interview with Zoanel Gheorghiu, recorded in Bucharest, June 1996. Author has the tape.
40 Massoff and Tănase, *Tănase*, 84–95.
41 *Teatrul de Mâine*, 1:2 (1 May 1918), 15, and 1:14 (1 March 1919), 101.
42 "Versurile d-lui Iorga," *Chemarea*, 1:9 (18 December 1917), 142.
43 Nicolae Iorga, "Printr'o expoziţie de pictură," *Neamul Românesc*, 13:33 (3 February 1918), 1.
44 For reproductions of works by these three artists see *Grafica Militantă Românească* (Exhibition catalogue) (Bucharest: Editura Minerva, 1963). Nicolae Tonitza is well known for his still lifes and intimate portraits. One of his lesser known drawings is included in this catalogue. It is a dramatic, stark depiction of a group of prisoners whose faces are obscured and who are dragging themselves about in rags, depersonalized to the point of looking ghostly.
45 Liviu Rebreanu, letter to Corneliu Moldovan dated 2 April 1918, in I. Moldovan, ed., *Corneliu Modovan în Corespondenţă* (Bucharest: Editura Minerva, 1982), 274–275.
46 Massoff and Tănase, *Tănase*, 93–94.
47 See Savia Bratu, *Mihail Sadoveanu* (Bucharest: Editura pentru literatură, 1963), 336 and "Prefaţă," in Vasile Voiculescu, *Antologie* (Bucharest: Editura Eminescu, 1981), 73.

11　OCCUPATION, PROPAGANDA, AND THE IDEA OF BELGIUM

1 Jean Massart, *Belgians Under the German Eagle* (London, 1916), 360.
2 Quoted in Modris Eksteins, *Rites of Spring: the Great War and the Birth of the Modern Age* (London, New York, 1989), 209.
3 More details concerning the points raised in this paragraph are presented in my *De Groote Oorlog: Het Koninkrijk België tijdens de Eerste Wereldoorlog* (Amsterdam, 1997), chs. 2, 3 and 5.
4 See Michel Dumoulin, "La propagande belge dans les pays neutres au début de la première guerre mondiale," *Revue Belge d'histoire militaire*, 22 (1977), 246–259; Michel Dumoulin, ed., *Jules Destrée, Souvenirs des temps de guerre* (Louvain, 1980); and Suzanne Tassier, *La Belgique et l'entrée en guerre des Etats-Unis* (Brussels, 1951).

5 The neutrality and the atrocity questions were analyzed in, respectively, the
   sociologist Emile Waxweiler's *La Belgique neutre et loyale* (Paris, Lausanne,
   1915), and the sociologist Fernand Van Langenhove's *Comment naît un
   cycle de légendes: francs-tireurs et atrocités en Belgique* (Paris, Lausanne, 1916).
   The latter is an insightful piece of social psychological research on the war
   paranoia that befell the German infantry invading Belgium. The soundness
   of its conclusions (and of its methods) has since been corroborated: Lothar
   Wieland, *Belgien 1914. Die Frage des belgischen 'Franktireurkrieges' und die
   deutsche öffentliche Meinung von 1914 bis 1936* (Frankfurt am Main, Bern,
   New York, 1984) and Alan Kramer, "Les 'atrocités allemandes': mythologie
   populaire, propagande et manipulations dans l'armée allemande," in Jean-
   Jacques Becker *et al.*, eds., *Guerre et cultures 1914–1918* (Paris, 1994), 147–
   164.
6 Archives Générales du Royaume/Algemeen Rijksarchief, Brussels (hereafter
   AGR), *Bureau Documentaire Belge, 1915–1920*, Internal report of 25 October 1918 by Fernand Passelecq (director), Nr. 1, Document 2, 7.
7 *King Albert's Book: A Tribute to the Belgian People from Representative Men
   and Women Throughout the World* (London, 1914), 70.
8 *Berliner Tageblatt* (2 November 1914) quoted in Waxweiler, *La Belgique
   neutre*, 105.
9 Thus did several commentators argue, for instance, that the country lacked
   "geographical" reasons for independent existence. See Konrad Kretschmer,
   "Die territoriale Entwicklung der Belgischen Staates," *Der Belfried (Eine
   Monatsschrift für Geschichte und Gegenwart der Belgischen Lande)*, vol. I (1917),
   162–168, especially 163; and Josef Langhammer, *Belgiens Vergangenheit und
   Zukunft* (Warnsdorf, 1916), especially 48.
10 Henri Pirenne, *La nation belge et l'Allemagne: quelques réflexions historiques*
   (Ghent, 1920), 7.
11 On this emphasis on the "pre-eminence of life force," see Eksteins, *Rites of
   Spring*, 159.
12 In general, see de Schaepdrijver, *De Groote Oorlog*, chs. 4 (on the first half
   of the occupation) and 7 (on the second half). An indispensable work –
   originally published in 1928, and still unsurpassed – is Henri Pirenne, *La
   Belgique et la guerre mondiale*, reprinted in Pirenne, *Histoire de Belgique des
   origines à nos jours* (Brussels, 1975), V.
13 Now that it was invaded, however, plans towards permanent German rule
   over Belgium began to sprout manifold: Frank Wende, *Die belgische Frage in
   der deutschen Politik des Ersten Weltkrieges* (Hamburg, 1969), 24–29, 42–45.
14 The stalemated Western front cut through Western Flanders, leaving a
   small corner of the country unoccupied.
15 Strictly speaking, the governor-general's authority began only at some
   distance east of the front line; the roughly 75-mile swath behind the front –
   some one-third of occupied Belgium – called the *Etappengebiet*, was a front-
   hinterland zone under very heavy military control, where the Fourth Army
   ruled.
16 Brand Whitlock, *Belgium: A Personal Narrative* (New York, 1919), I, 533.
17 The literature on Belgian relief is vast. A few titles: Liane Ranieri, *Emile
   Francqui ou l'intelligence créatrice (1863–1935)* (Paris, Gembloux, 1985);

Peter Scholliers and Frank Daelemans, "Standards of Living and Standards of Health in Wartime Belgium," in Richard Wall and Jay Winter, eds., *The Upheaval of War: Family, Work, and Welfare in Europe, 1914–1918* (Cambridge, 1988), 139–158; Albert Henry, *L'Oeuvre du Comité National de Secours et d'Alimentation pendant la guerre* (Brussels, 1920); and vol. I (*The Relief of Belgium and of Northern France, 1914–1930*) in Hoover's autobiography, *An American Epic* (Chicago, 1959). An insightful and irreverent look behind the scenes is offered in *The Letters and Journal of Brand Whitlock*, Allan Nevins, ed. (New York, London, 1936).

18 Pirenne, *La Belgique*, 347.

19 Petrus Van Nuffel, *De Duitschers in Aalst* (Aalst 1921), 212 (the observation pertains to the fall of 1917).

20 The 13 October 1914 decree stated that all printing and distribution of texts, pictures, and sheet music would henceforth be subject to censorship by the Imperial German Government-General. Those found guilty of printing or distributing materials without permission from the censors' office were to be punished according to military law. The printed matter in question was to be seized and all printing instruments destroyed. (It should be noted that the notion of "distribution" was not confined to reproduction, but pertained to any form of "publication," e.g., placing the objectionable material on public view in cafés, libraries, railway stations and so on.) Equally subject to censorship were theatre productions, concerts, poetry readings, moving-picture shows, or slide shows: all of these had to be approved by the censors' office beforehand (meaning that any item on the program that seemed to carry anything resembling "patriotic" overtones, had to be dropped from the program – even pieces of music without text were censored for traces of the national anthem). Those found guilty of staging any of the above without permission were equally to be punished according to military law, and all materials (film reels, slides, stage sets, etc.) were to be confiscated. The 13 October decree was followed by a 4 November 1914 order by the governor-general, reminding the Belgian population that all newspapers and other news media not expressly *authorized* by the military government were expressly *banned*. See Charles H. Huberich and Alexander Nicol-Speyer, eds., *Deutsche Gesetzgebung für die Okkupierten Gebiete Belgiens* (The Hague, 1915–1918), I, 21–22, Ludwig von Köhler, *Die Staatsverwaltung der besetzten Gebiete*, I: *Belgien* (Stuttgart, 1927), 25–27, and Jacques Pirenne and Maurice Vauthier, *La législation et l'administration allemandes en Belgique* (Paris, n.d.), 138–140.

21 Quotation from a patriotic song titled "A bas l'Allemagne" (Down with Germany), which appeared in the Brussels paper *La Vérité* (n.d., c. October 1915) 8–9. On Raemaekers, who had fled to the Netherlands and whose work was published in London, Amsterdam, Paris, and Rome, and also smuggled into occupied Belgium (where it appeared in the clandestine papers *La Cravache* and *Patrie!*, among others), see the catalogs *L'oeuvre de Louis Raemaekers pendant la guerre* (n.p., n.d.) and the 8-volume *Raemaekers cartoons* (London, 1916). On the clandestine press generally, see Jean Massart, *La presse clandestine dans la Belgique occupée* (Paris, Nancy, 1917), which offers an interesting (though necessarily incomplete) overview. On *La Libre*

Belgique, see, among other accounts, Albert Van De Kerckhove, *L'histoire merveilleuse de la Libre Belgique* (Paris, Brussels, 1919), edited with a preface by Brand Whitlock – who took care not to repeat his private observation that the whole paper had been "but a useless piece of bravado" (*Journal,* 170). The *Libre* went underground a second time during World War II, and still exists as the most important francophone Catholic paper in Belgium.

22 A complaint in *La Vérité* (n.d., c. June 1916), 13.

23 Karel Van De Woestijne, *Verzameld journalistiek werk,* Ada Deprez, ed. (Ghent, 1992), IX, 84 (24 April 1916).

24 The text of Maeterlinck's lecture appeared in *Le Figaro* of 2 December 1914, and was subsequently published as a brochure under the title *Pour la Belgique: discours prononcé par M. Maurice Maeterlinck à la Scala de Milan* (Paris, 1915), quotation on first page. In the event, Maeterlinck's lecture did not take place at La Scala, but at the rather more modest Teatro dei Filodrammatici: see Dumoulin's excellent edition of Destrée's *Souvenirs,* 122. Destrée, a socialist representative, art critic, and exponent of the budding Walloon Movement, spent the war years mainly in Italy, drumming up support for Belgium – among other things by writing the puppet-play *Il drammatico matrimonio della principessa Belgia e del cavaliere Onore* (Rome, 1916).

25 "Allemagne! Allemagne! / O faiseuse de crépuscule!" in the poem *L'Allemagne, exterminatrice de races* (Germany, Exterminator of Races): Emile Verhaeren, *Les ailes rouges de la guerre: poèmes,* 20th ed. (Paris, 1917), 195–201, quotation 198.

26 On Waxweiler's war work, see note 5; he was also a confidant of King Albert I, and until shortly before his death had been on a mission probing possibilities for a peace accord. See Marie-Rose Thielemans, *Albert I: carnets et correspondance de guerre 1914–1918* (Paris, Louvain-la-Neuve, 1991), 51–62, also Firtz Fischer, *Griff nach der Weltmacht. Die Kriegszielpolitik des kaiserlichen Deutschland 1914–1918* (Düsseldorf, 1961), 262–274. On Waxweiler, see E. De Bie, *La sociologie d'Emile Waxweiler* (Brussels, 1974).

27 Dumoulin, *Destrée,* 132. See also Kufferath's pamphlets *Pro Patria! Causerie sur la Belgique* (Geneva, 1914) and *Il n'est pas vrai . . . A propos des déportations en Belgique* (Geneva, 1917).

28 On the wartime Brussels art market, see the notes on "Art in Brussels" in Van De Woestijne, *Journalistiek werk,* VIII and IX, especially VIII, 64–71 (April 1915), 163–169 (June 1915), 655 (1 March 1916), 673–675 (March 1916), and IX, 386–389 (October 1918).

29 Whitlock, *Belgium,* II, 61.

30 Service Historique de l'Armée de Terre, Château de Vincennes, France (hereafter Vincennes), Archives de la Guerre Série N, box 17 N 268 (Mission Militaire Française auprès de l'Armée Belge), file 5 (Belgique Envahie), anonymous report, Brussels, 8 August 1917, p. 2.

31 In a very few cases, books were antedated in order to bypass censorship. An example is given in Cynthia Skenazi, ed., *Marie Gevers, Correspondance 1917–1974* (Brussels, 1986), 20, also 131 note 5.

32 Stijn Streuvels, *In oorlogstijd (het uitgegeven en het onuitgegeven dagboek 1914–1918),* Luc Schepens, ed. (Bruges, Nijmegen, 1979), 448. See also Fernand

Van Langenhove, *Comment naît un cycle*..., 106–108, and Lode Wils, *Flamenpolitik en aktivisme* (Louvain, 1974), 15–19. The Tyl Uylenspiegel theme (after the sixteenth-century folk hero, immortalized as the emblem of mischievous resistance to foreign oppression in Charles De Coster, *La légende et les aventures héroïques, joyeuses et glorieuses d'Uylenspiegel et de Lamme Goedzak au pays de Flandre et ailleurs*, 1867) became a staple of Belgian patriotic rhetoric.

33 Interview in *La Belgique*, 5 September 1917. The interview was to cost Eekhoud dearly: because of it – and because he had permitted work of his to be published in German translation during the war – the Brussels city authorities dismissed him from his teaching position in December 1918. This punishment proves the extent to which wartime publishing decisions were tied to notions of national duty and honor, certainly in the post-Armistice climate of slightly paranoid hyperpatriotism (a climate which subsequently abated: in 1920, Eekhoud was offically rehabilitated).

34 In contrast to Goethe's, Gilkin's *Egmont* is heavy on *couleur locale* – banquet and carnival scenes, snippets of popular wisdom, opulent Flemish maidens, etc. His eponymous hero is endowed with sundry putatively national qualities – *bon-vivant* gregariousness, religious tolerance, firmness of principle – and is given more to reflections on the national consequences of his choices and fate than is Goethe's essentially individualist Count Egmont. See Paul Gorceix, "Une réplique à Goethe: *Egmont* d'Iwan Gilkin (1858–1924)," in Hans-Joachim Lope, ed., *L'écrivain belge devant l'histoire* (Frankfurt am Main, 1993), 51–66, quotation on 51.

35 See the wartime chronicle by Louis Gille, Alphonse Ooms, and Paul Delandsheere, *Cinquante mois d'occupation allemande*, 4 vols. (Brussels, 1919), I, 291 (15 March 1915); Wils, *Flamenpolitik*, 15; Whitlock, *Belgium*, I, 529–532; Van De Woestijne, *Journalistiek werk*, VIII, 353 (9 October 1915), IX, 113–116 (13 May 1916).

36 A. Vander Plasse, "Toneel- en concertleven in oorlogstijd," *West-Vlaanderen*, 13 (1964), 247–251; Roland Schacht, "Brüsseler Theaterspiel während des Krieges", *Der Grenzboten*, 4 October 1916, 13–18; J. Sales, *Théâtre de la Monnaie 1856–1970* (Nivelles, 1971); André Capiteyn, "Niet alleen ellende: het cultuur- en ontspanningsleven", in André Capiteyn, ed., *Gent en de eerste wereldoorlog. Het stadsleven in de jaren 1914–1918* (Ghent, 1991), 89–92; and Van De Woestijne, *Journalistiek werk*, VII (6 December 1914), 617–619, VIII, 61–62 (April 1915), 71–78 (April 1915), 101–102 (May 1915), 394–395 (7 November 1915), IX, 151–152 (25 May 1916).

37 Examples of this and other forms of "unpatriotic" behavior punished by local relief committees are given in Georges Rency, *La vie matérielle de la Belgique durant la Guerre Mondiale* (Part I in the series *La Belgique et la Guerre*), 2nd ed. (Brussels, 1924), 206–214.

38 Auguste Vierset, *Mes souvenirs sur l'occupation allemande en Belgique* (Paris, 1932), 220–221 (dance-halls). On cinemas, see Emile Béco, *La croisade entreprise contre les mauvais cinémas pendant la guerre* (Turnhout, 1919). Local relief officials would suspend families' assistance if their children were found in cinemas. Yet, as Béco (who was the Brabant provincial governor) estimated, by the middle of the occupation, 200,000 children went to the

movies weekly in Brussels (a city of 800,000 inhabitants) alone. See also Van De Woestijne, *Journalistiek werk* VIII, 472–473 (26 September 1914), VIII, 230–234 (22 July 1915), IX, 151 (25 May 1916), and *La Libre Belgique*, No. 44, September 1915, 4; see also Capiteyn, "Niet alleen ellende."

39 Pirenne, *Guerre*, 289; see especially Guido Convents, "Cinema and German Politics in Occupied Belgium," in Karel Dibbets and Bert Hogenkamp, eds., *Film and the First World War* (Amsterdam, 1995), 171–178.

40 As voiced in his 132-page poem about wartime Antwerp, *Bezette stad* (Occupied City), written in Berlin in the fall of 1920. Paul Van Ostaijen, *Verzameld werk: Poëzie*, Gerrit Borgers, ed. (Antwerp, The Hague, Amsterdam, 1952), II, 7 (see also 247).

41 On local brass bands in wartime, see, among others, F. Bertrand, *La presse francophone dans les tranchées* (Brussels, 1971), 53. On pigeons, see, among others, Whitlock, *Belgium*, I, 279–280, II, 53–54. On national symbols, see, among others, Van De Woestijne, *Journalistiek werk*, VII, 585 (11 November 1914), VIII, 14 (15 February 1915), 186 (26 June 1915, the date of the decree banning national emblems); see also Pirenne and Vauthier, *La législation*, 140–141.

42 Vincennes (see note 30).

43 On pastimes under occupation generally, see Rency, *La vie matérielle*, 79–84; on sports, Bertrand, *La presse francophone*, 67, and Van De Woestijne, *Journalistiek werk*, VIII, 359–362 (11 October 1915); on reading and popular education, Pirenne, *La Belgique*, 278, Bertrand, *La presse francophone*, 67–68, Lode Wils, *Honderd jaar Vlaamse beweging*, II: *Geschiedenis van het Davidsfonds 1914–1936* (2nd. ed., Leuven, 1985), 33, and Van De Woestijne, *Journalistiek werk*, VIII, 295–299 (7 September 1915), and 430–433 (28 November 1915) on the heightened demand for Pascal's *Pensées* among the formerly so frivolous Brussels middle classes.

44 Mercier became the figurehead of Belgian patriotism, used in this guise for Belgian charity propaganda abroad. See Ilse Meseberg-Haubold, *Die Widerstand Kardinal Merciers gegen die deutsche besetzung Belgiens 1914–1918: ein Beitrag zur politischen Rolle des Katholizismus im ersten Weltkrieg* (Frankfurt am Main, 1982). See also Bertrand, *Presse francophone*, 49–50, 66, Gille et al., *Cinquante mois*, I, 453 (15 October 1915), Van De Woestijne, *Journalistiek werk*, VIII, 225 (21 July 1915), and Van Nuffel, *De Duitschers*, Streuvels, *In oorlogstijd*, and Whitlock, *Belgium, passim*.

45 On different cultural initiatives by the relief organization, see the post-war *Rapport général sur le fonctionnement du Comité de Secours et d'Alimentation*, vol. III: *Départements secours et oeuvres créés ou subsidiés par lui*, 2 vols. (Brussels, 1920), also Pirenne and Vauthier, *La législation*, 137, and Whitlock, *Belgium, passim*. The observation was made by Van de Woestijne, *Journalistiek werk*, VIII, 600 (6 February 1916); see also IX, 239–244 (30 August 1916). The connection between the culture of war, the desire for a return to "normality," and the enforcing of gender roles has been brilliantly explored for post-war France in Marie-Louise Roberts, *Civilization without Sexes: Reconstructing Gender in Postwar France 1917–1927* (Chicago, 1994).

46 Jacques Marx, "Résurrection et les courants modernistes," in Jean Weisgerber, ed., *Les avant-gardes littéraires en Belgique. Au confluent des arts*

et des langues (Brussels, 1991), 213–232; Frederik Leen *et al.*, *Avant-garde in België 1917–1929* (Brussels, 1992), 21–23, 190–191; Robert Hoozee, ed., *Moderne Kunst in België 1900–1945* (Antwerp, 1992), 109; Klaus H. Kiefer, "Carl Einstein and the Revolutionary Soldiers' Councils in Brussels," and Ulrich Weisstein, "Der letzte Zivilist? Carl Sternheim at La Hulpe," both in Rainer Rumold en O.K. Werckmeister, eds., *The Ideological Crisis of Expressionism: the Literary and Artistic German War Colony in Belgium 1914–1918* (Columbia, SC, 1990), 97–114, 115–132; and Henri Plard, "Bruxelles occupée (1915–1917) vue par deux écrivains allemands: Gottfried Benn et Otto Flake," *Académie Royale de Belgique: Bulletin de la Classe des Lettres et des Sciences Morales et Politiques*, 5th ser. 74 (1988), 123–142, especially 127–128. On the Occupation Government's fueling of "Friedenssehnsucht," see Meseberg-Haubold, *Mercier*, 325 note 130, and Winfried Dolderer, *Deutscher Imperialismus und belgischer Nationalitätenkonflikt. Die Rezeption der Flamenfrage in der deutschen Öffentlichkeit und deutsch-flämische Kontakte 1890–1920* (Melsungen, 1989), 192–210 and *passim*.

47 Leen, *Avant-garde*, 93–126; Hoozee, *Moderne kunst*, 95–111; Paul Hadermann, "De modernistische doorbraak," in Mathieu Rutten and Jean Weisgerber, eds., *Van "Arm Vlaanderen" tot "de voorstad groeit": de opbloei van de Vlaamse literatuur van Teirlinck-Stijns tot Louis-Paul Boon* (Antwerp, 1988), 271–364, especially 275–278, 293–306; Gerrit Borgers, *Paul Van Ostaijen, een documentatie*, 2 vols. (The Hague, 1971), and Francis Bulhof, ed., *Nijhoff, Van Ostaijen, "De Stijl". Modernism in the Netherlands and Begium in the First Quarter of the 20th century* (The Hague, 1976).

48 Gille *et al.*, *Cinquante mois*, I, 61 (18 September 1914) and II, 280 (20 August 1916).

49 His August 1915 project of rebuilding the Belgian cities that had been ruined during the invasion, for instance, was met with a storm of protest from the clandestine press, which shuddered at the idea of "banal" and "rectilinear" German architecture being introduced in Belgium: "Down with that horrible 'practical' stuff, the mass-produced houses, the concrete squares . . . the corrugated roofs and all of the other horrors!" *La Vérité*, no. 5 (September 1915), 12–13; see also *La Libre Belgique*, no. 51 (November 1915), 4.

50 See, for instance, AGR, *Documents Klein, Gesichtspunkte für die Politik in Belgien,* unsigned memorandum [probably Von der Lancken], n.d. [Spring 1917], 2–3.

51 Otto Flake, *Das Logbuch* (Gütersloh 1970), 195. On Flake's (and Gottfried Benn's) experiences in Brussels, see the insightful article by Plard, "Bruxelles occupée."

52 Flake, *Logbuch*, 185.

53 For additional details concerning the points raised in this paragraph, see de Schaepdrijver, *De Groote Oorlog*, chs. 5 and 8.

54 The Flemish Movement – the general term for a collection of caucuses, learned societies, and Leagues of various kinds – strove to end the *de facto* domination of French in Belgium (which endured in spite of the Linguistic Equality Law of 1898, and the fact that 54 percent of Belgians spoke Flemish). Having emerged as a romantic-philological preservationist drive,

around the *fin-de-siècle* it developed a more emancipatory emphasis on intellectual and social uplift. At the time of war's outbreak, *flamingants* (as militants of the Flemish Movement were called) were demanding the establishment of a purely Dutch-speaking university in lieu of the existing one at Ghent, where courses were taught mainly in French. See Aristide Zolberg, "The Making of Flemings and Walloons: Belgium, 1830–1914," *Journal of Interdisciplinary History*, 5 (1974), 179–235; T. Hermans *et al.*, *The Flemish Movement: A Documentary History 1780–1990* (London, 1992); Carl Strikwerda, *A House Divided: Catholics, Socialists and Flemish Nationalists in Nineteenth-Century Belgium* (Lanham, MD, 1997), and ch. 1 in de Schaepdrijver, *De Groote Oorlog*.

55 On *Flamenpolitik* and its Flemish followers, the most important works are Lode Wils, *Flamenpolitik en aktivisme* (Leuven, 1974), especially; Lode Wils, *Honderd jaar Vlaamse beweging*, II; Wende, *Die belgische Frage*; and certainly Dolderer, *Imperialismus*. See also Hendrik Elias, *Vijfentwintig jaar Vlaamse beweging 1914/1939* (Antwerp, 1969), I: *De eerste wereldoorlog en zijn onmiddellijke nasleep*; Reginald De Schryver, ed., *De Vlaamse Beweging tijdens de Eerste Wereldoorlog* (Leuven, 1974); a lively account in Maurits Basse, *De Vlaamsche Beweging van 1905 tot 1930*, 2 vols. (Ghent, 1933), and the amply researched Daniel Vanacker, *Het aktivistisch avontuur* (Ghent, 1991). Documents are presented in Rudiger (pseud. of Armand Wullus), *Flamenpolitik* (Brussels, 1921) and in the collections *Les Archives du Conseil de Flandre* (Brussels, 1928) and *Aperçu historique de l'activisme* (Brussels, 1929).

56 See his Dresden speech of 4 March 1915: Karl Lamprecht, *Deutsche Zukunft – Belgien. Aus den nachgelassenen Schriften* (Gotha, 1916), 52 and *passim*. See also Roger Chickering, *Karl Lamprecht: a German Academic Life* (Atlantic Highlands, NJ, 1993), especially 439 and 444, n. 61, and Dolderer, *Imperialismus*, 47–50, 53, 70–71.

57 Vanacker, *Aktivistisch avontuur*, 32; Dolderer, *Imperialismus*, 47–48.

58 For the main protest manifestos and open letters clandestinely distributed in occupied Belgium, see the collections *Hoe Vlamingen Duitsche Vlaamschgezindheid schatten* (How the Flemings appreciate German *flamingantism*) and *Wat de Belgen in bezet België over de bestuurlijke scheiding denken* (What the Belgians in occupied Belgium think of the administrative separation), both published by the Belgian Documentary Bureau in Le Havre in 1918 in the original Dutch version and in a French translation. Anti-*Flamenpolitik flamingants* eventually created their own underground papers: *De Vlaamsche Leeuw* (The Lion of Flanders) in Brussels (1916–1918) and *De Vlaamsche Wachter* (The Flemish Guardian) in Antwerp (1917–1918).

59 Van De Woestijne, *Journalistiek werk*, 8:26 (23 February 1915).

60 René De Clercq, "Havere tegen Vlaanderen," *Dietsche Stemmen* (December 1915), 56. De Clercq's activist poems would later be collected under the title *De Noodhoorn* (The Tocsin) (Utrecht, 1916); a cheap edition was printed (with the then-staggering run of 32,600 copies) under the significant title *Vaderlandsche Liederen* (Patriotic Songs), to be distributed at activist propagandist meetings. Koen Hulpiau, "Dichter René De Clercq als

flamingant – Voor Vlaanderen en Groot-Nederland," *Wetenschappelijke Tijdingen*, 42 (1983), 237–247, 238.

61 Which was indignantly decried abroad: see the widely distributed pamphlet by the Danish academic Christoph Nyrop, *The Imprisonment of the Ghent Professors Paul Fredericq and Henri Pirenne: A Question of Right and Might* (Lausanne, 1917).

62 Zentrales Staatsarchiv Potsdam, Germany (hereafter Potsdam), *Nachlass Beyerle*, 90 Be 8, no. 1, 82 (Kisky to Beyerle, 26 July 1916).

63 Ibid., 85 (Kisky to Beyerle, 18 August 1916).

64 E.g. Heinrich Gelzer, "Wallonische Art im Spiegel Wallonischer Sprichwörter", *Der Belfried*, 3 (July 1918), 21–27. *Der Belfried*, a wartime political-literary monthly specializing in "Belgian" themes, especially Flemish ones, published several accounts of the Walloon Movement in that same year.

65 See J. Vandereuse, *La chanson wallonne et la guerre de 1914–1918* (n.p., n.d.) It should be noted that local wartime chronicles suggest a comparable role for Flemish dialect culture. On Walloon activism, see L. Hoton, *Y eut-il un activisme wallon durant la guerre?* (Liège, 1936); Pirenne, *La Belgique*, 319–328. Walloon-activist manifestos include Franz Foulon, *La question wallonne* (Brussels, 1917) and Paul Ruscart, *Propos d'un Wallon sur la question flamande* (Namur, 1918). For Ruscart's interviews, see *La Belgique*, 20 August 1917 (with René De Clercq); *La Belgique*, 26 August 1917 (with Pieter Tack), and *La Belgique*, 5 September 1917 (with Richard De Cneudt).

66 *Aperçu historique*, 28.

67 Potsdam, *Nachlass Mumm*, 90 Mu 3, no. 90, 180, Bogaerts to Mumm, 28 February 1918, underlined in letter.

68 By May 1918, the Central Propaganda Bureau possessed services or at least correspondents in 411 Flemish cities, towns, and villages. From January 1918 onwards, it received a monthly subsidy of 150,000 francs; by September 1918, that sum had risen to 185,000. (By contrast, the 1918 budget of the modestly staffed Belgian Documentation Bureau at Le Havre amounted to 161,000 francs for the entire year.)

69 Announcements in the activist dailies *Nieuwe Gentsche Courant* and *Gazet van Brussel*, 30 May 1918.

70 Review in *Het Vlaamsche Nieuws*, 10 July 1918.

71 On activist literary magazines, see Robert Roemans, *Bibliographie van de moderne Vlaamsche Literatuur*, part I: *De Vlaamsche Tijdschriften* (Kortrijk, 1930), 729–822, and Hadermann, "De modernistische doorbraak," 275–292. On Pansaers, see Leen, *Avant-garde*, 191. On Rubiner, Wolfgang Paulsen, *Expressionismus und Aktivismus, eine typologische Untersuchung* (Bern, 1935), 55; the quotations from Van Ostaijen in Hadermann, "De modernistische doorbraak," 304, 360.

72 Leo Van Puyvelde (a leading *flamingant* and art historian), in an essay written in December 1917: "De Vlaamsche Beweging en de Oorlog," *De Gids*, 82: 1 (1918), 316–339, 323. For a comparable, earlier essay in the same Dutch magazine, see his "Het Keerpunt der Vlaamsche Beweging," *De Gids*, 80: 4 (1916), 1–12. Both articles were published in French translation as *Le mouvement flamand et la guerre* (Amsterdam, 1918) and *L'orientation nouvelle du mouvement flamand* (Amsterdam, 1917), respectively.

73 In "De Droom aller Vlamingen" (The Dream of all Flemings), originally published in the *Young-Flemish De Vlaamsche Post*, 8 December 1915; reprint in Marc Somers, ed., *Timmermans en het activisme* (Lier, 1992), 39–41, 41.

74 See especially Convents, "Cinema." The reluctance of the Council's Central Propaganda Bureau *vis-à-vis* moving-picture plans shows in its correspondence (see AGR, *Raad van Vlaanderen*, Boxes D 62/1 and D 62/2).

75 AGR, *Raad van Vlaanderen*, Box D 67/1, Prenau to Faingnaert, 24 September 1917, 1.

76 AGR, *Raad van Vlaanderen*, Box 62/1, Moens to Faingnaert, 31 August 1918, 3.

77 Which seem to have wearied the public somewhat. One representative in rural Limburg complained that Brussels was sending them one lyrical orator after another, whereas effective mass propaganda called for more "cool, businesslike" platform speakers, who were in exceedingly short supply (AGR, *Raad van Vlaanderen*, Box 62/1, Werbruggen to Faingnaert, 12 September 1918, 1).

78 For a sharp contemporary analysis of this language fetishism, see Van Puyvelde, "De Vlaamsche Beweging," and "Het Keerpunt der Vlaamsche Beweging."

79 AGR, *Raad van Vlaanderen*, Box D 67/1, invitation to a propaganda workshop in Sint-Niklaas, 8 June 1918. The book in question was Richard De Cneudt's 276-page *De vervlaamsching van het lager onderwijs in Groot Brussel* (The Flemishization of Primary Education in Greater Brussels) (Brussels, 1918). The poet De Cneudt, a *Young-Flemish* former grade-school teacher (now a member of the Council of Flanders *and* a top-ranking official at the Flemishized Ministry of Arts and Sciences) was regularly hailed in the activist press as an orator of great lyrical power and as a Flemish fighter who "has dared to attack the dragon of *fransquillonism* in its filthy lair" (*Het Vlaamsche Nieuws*, 4 August 1917, 1).

80 L. Goudtveldt, *Catechismus met uitleg ten gebruike van ons volk* (Ghent, 1917), 23 (italics in text). This was a cheap edition, distributed massively in occupied Flanders and also sent to Belgian POW camps in Germany.

81 AGR, *Fonds-Van Der Essen*, Folder 10, file "Van Der Meulen", supplement to *Het Vlaamsche Nieuws*, date unavailable [probably late September 1917], 2.

82 Vanacker, *Aktivistisch avontuur*, 325.

83 Quoted in *De Vlaamsche Leeuw*, 16 (August 1917), 3. De Clercq's Belgian patriotic verses were collected in *De Zware Kroon* (The Heavy Crown) (Bussum, 1915).

84 René De Clercq in *Gazet van Brussel*, 30 March 1918. (After his return from the Netherlands in the summer of 1917 – a return engineered by the *Politische Abteilung* – De Clercq had been given the editorship of this activist daily: Hulpiau, "Dichter René De Clercq," 239 and 241.)

85 AGR, *Raad van Vlaanderen*, Box 62/2, Jacobs to De Schaepdryver, 15 September 1918.

86 *Aperçu Historique*, preface, II; see also Elias, *Vijfentwintig jaar*, I, 98–99.

87 Quoted in Wils, *Honderd jaar*, II, 57.

88 Robert Graves, *Goodbye to All That* (London, 1960), 153.

89 An excellent analysis in Sally Marks, *Innocent Abroad: Belgium at the Paris Peace Conference of 1919* (Chapel Hill, 1981).

90 See especially the monumental, multivolume *Rapports et documents d'enquête* edited by the Belgian *Commission d'enquête sur les violations des règles du droit des gens, des lois et des coutumes de la guerre* (Brussels, Liège, 1921–1923).

91 On post-war Belgium, see de Schaepdrijver, *De Groote Oorlog*, ch. 9.

92 Heinrich Waentig, *Belgien* (Halle, 1919), 7.

12   CULTURAL LIFE IN FRANCE, 1914–1918

1 The term *poilu* (literally, "hairy one") was the commonly used slang term for the French infantryman, roughly equivalent to the British "Tommy" or American "doughboy."

2 A. Besançon, M. Ferro, and A. Kriegel, "L'expérience de la Grande Guerre," *Annales*, 2 (1965), 331–334.

3 Quoted in Marc Ferro, *La Grande Guerre 1914–1918* (Paris, 1970; 2nd ed., 1990), 215–222.

4 Ibid.

5 As quoted in Philippe Soulez, ed., *Les philosophes et la guerre de 14* (Paris: Presses Universitaires de Vincennes, 1988), 21.

6 See Christophe Prochasson, *Les intellectuels, le socialisme et la guerre: 1900– 1938* (Paris, 1993), 151–152.

7 Quoted in ibid., 94.

8 Pascal Ory and J. F. Sirinelli, *Les intellectuels en France, de l'affaire Dreyfus à nos jours* (Paris, 1986), 70.

9 Kenneth Silver, *Esprit de Corps: The Art of the Parisian Avant-Garde and the First World War, 1914–1925* (Princeton: Princeton University Press, 1989), ch. 2; Richard Cork, *A Bitter Truth: Avant-Garde Art and the Great War* (New Haven and London: Yale University Press, 1994), chs. 2 and 5. On *imagerie d'Epinal*, see also Jay Winter, *Sites of Memory, Sites of Mourning: The Great War in European Cultural History* (Cambridge: Cambridge University Press, 1995), 127–132.

10 I discovered these images in 1964, and they appear in the film, *La Grande Guerre* (The Great War), produced by Pathé.

11 See Stéphane Audoin-Rouzeau and A. Becker, "Violence et consentement, la culture de guerre du premier conflit mondial," in J. P. Rioux and J. P. Sirinelli, *Pour une histoire culturelle* (Paris: Le Seuil, 1997), 251–271.

12 Ibid.

13 Hubert Bourgin, *L'École Normale et la politique, de Jaurès à Léon Blum* (Paris, 1970), 411–426.

14 See Prochasson, *Les intellectuels, le socialisme et la guerre*, 115–116.

15 "I am not one of those Frenchmen who regards Germany as barbarous," were Rolland's famous words in this essay, first published in *Le journal de Genève* (Geneva) on 2 September 1914, and subsequently in book form in France in June 1915.

16 See Pascal and Sirinelli, *Les intellectuels en France*, 66–68.

17 For a comprehensive history of French internationalism during the war, see Annie Kriegel, *Aux origines du communisme français*, 2 vols. (Paris: Mouton,

1964). On worker culture and socialist culture, see Marc Ferro and Sheila Fitzpatarick, eds., *Culture et Révolution* (Paris: EHESS, 1989), esp. the essay by J. Sherrer on pp. 11–25 of that volume. On reactions to the 1917 revolution, see Marc Ferro, *L'Occident et la Révolution Soviétique: l'histoire et ses mythes* (Brussels: Complexe, 1991).

18 Pascal and Sirinelli, *Les intellectuels en France*, 62.

19 Paul Gerbod, "Les publications philosophiques françaises et la grande guerre," in Soulez, *Les Philosophes*, 33–47.

20 Laurent Mannoni, "Éclair," *1875*, 12 (1982), 9–53.

21 See Winter, *Sites of Memory*, 15–22, 133–138.

22 *Boche* was the French derogatory term for Germans, equivalent to "Hun" in wartime Anglo-American slang.

23 André Mare, *Carnets de Guerre*, Laurent Graffin, ed. (Paris, 1996).

24 Norton Cru, *Témoins* (Nancy, 1993; 1st ed., 1929).

25 J. Meyer, J. Ducasse, G. Perreux, *Vie et mort des Français* (Paris, 1959).

26 Jacques Péricard, *Verdun*, 4 vols. (Paris, 1938).

27 Rémy Cazals, "La culture de L. Barthas, tonnelier," in P. Valery, ed., *Pratiques et cultures politiques dans la France contemporaine* (University of Montpellier III, 1995), 425–437. See also the paper by P. Barral delivered at the Colloque de Carcassonne, 24–27 April 1996.

28 During the war, *La Madelon* and *La Marseillaise* took the place of the socialist anthem, the *Internationale* (though the latter reappeared in 1917). See Marc Ferro, *L'Internationale, histoire d'un chant* (Paris: Noesis, 1996), 110. At the front, singing was a common form of entertainment and relaxation, with popular folk melodies being sung to alternative – often cynical or humorous – lyrics expressive of soldiers' feelings. Upon returning home after the armistice, soldiers found that accordion music – soon followed by jazz – had replaced the old familiar folk songs. See Ribouillot Calude, *La musique au fusil avec les poilus dans la grande guerre* (Paris: Editions du Rouergue, 1996), 288.

13   THE IMPACT OF WORLD WAR I ON ITALIAN POLITICAL CULTURE

1 See Vera Zamagni, *The Economic History of Italy 1860–1990* (Oxford, 1993), 78–83. Most industry was concentrated in the "industrial triangle" bounded by Turin, Milan, and Genoa.

2 For good discussions, see Adrian Lyttelton, *The Seizure of Power* (Princeton, 1987), 1–41; Lyttelton, "Landlords, Peasants and the Limits of Liberalism," in John Davis, ed., *Gramsci and Italy's Passive Revolution* (London, 1979), 104–135; and Richard Bellamy, *Liberalism and Modern Society* (University Park, Pa., 1992), 105–156.

3 On the early Italian state and its Piedmontese origins, see Alberto Caracciolo, *Stato e società civile* (Turin, 1960), 14.

4 See Piero Melograni, *Storia politica della grande guerra 1915–18*, 2 vols. (Bari, 1977), I, 6, who estimates that in 1914 PSI membership was only 1,300 in Milan, 950 in Turin, and 530 in Rome.

5 The most original analysis of this point remains Antonio Gramsci, *Quaderni del carcere*, 4 vols. (Turin, 1975), especially III, 2035–46.

6 Martin Clark notes that "in Basilicata [at the tip of the boot] the rural population almost doubled between 1871 and 1911." See his *Modern Italy 1871–1982* (London, 1984), 162.

7 Zamagni, *Economic History of Italy*, 203.

8 For an analysis of this unevenness, see David Forgacs, *Italian Culture in the Industrial Era 1880–1980* (Manchester, 1990), 21–29.

9 Ibid., 35.

10 See John Rosselli, *The Opera Industry in Italy from Cimarosa to Verdi: The Role of the Impresario* (Cambridge, 1984) and William Weaver, *The Golden Century of Italian Opera from Rossini to Puccini* (London, 1980).

11 John Rosselli, *Music and Musicians in Nineteenth-century Italy* (London, 1991), 142.

12 See Andrea Camilleri, *I teatri stabili in Italia (1898–1918)* (Bologna, 1959).

13 See Gramsci's discussion in David Forgacs and Geoffrey Nowell-Smith, eds., *Antonio Gramsci: Selections from Cultural Writings* (Cambridge, MA, 1985), 54–65.

14 For the early history of the Italian film, see Gian Piero Brunetta, *Storia del cinema italiano 1895–1945* (Rome, 1979), and Carlo Lizzani, *Il cinema italiano 1895–1979* (Rome, 1979).

15 Brunetta, *Storia del cinema italiano*, 58–59.

16 Lizzani, *Il cinema italiano*, 32.

17 There were some revolutionary socialists on the interventionist side (Gramsci, for example) and some of the most fervent interventionists were of the so-called "democratic" type whose political views were left-of-center. By the end of the war, however, as will be argued below, left-interventionism was too weak to affect the fundamentally nationalist and right-wing character of interventionist (and, by then, ex-combatant) politics.

18 On the myth of the "second Italy," see my *Avant-garde Florence* (Cambridge, MA, 1993), 86–87, 146, 205, 233, and 282 n 148.

19 On the peasant role in the war, see Arrigo Serpieri, *La guerra e le classi rurali italiane* (Bari and New Haven, 1930). According to his calculations, of the total of 5.75 million men who served in the Italian armed forces during the war, about 2.6 million were peasants.

20 Estimates of the number of Italian volunteers vary widely. At one extreme, Prezzolini put the number at 200,000; at the other extreme (probably much closer to the truth), Melograni has them at 8,171. Yet everyone agrees that the typical volunteer was an urban interventionist, almost never a peasant. See Giuseppe Prezzolini, *Tutta la guerra* (Milan, 1968), 61; and Melograni, *Storia politica della grande guerra*, I, 25.

21 For historical perspective on the Italian army, see John Whittam, *The Politics of the Italian Army 1861–1918* (London, 1977); and John Gooch, *Army, State, and Society in Italy, 1870–1915* (Basingstoke, 1989).

22 Melograni, *Storia politica della grande guerra*, I, 168.

23 Ibid., 44.

24 For examples of Cadorna's icy approach to written communications with his subordinates, see Prezzolini, *Tutta la guerra*, 127–136, and Attilio

Frescura, *Diario di un imboscato* (Milan, 1981), 294–95 (where the subject is decimation).

25 For a vivid, eyewitness account of one such (attempted) decimation, see Emilio Lussu, *Un anno sull'Altipiano* (Turin, 1976), 194–201.

26 See Melograni, *Storia politica della grande guerra*, I, 165–166.

27 Ibid., I, 227.

28 Besides the many accounts by intellectuals (to be considered further on), we have a number of war accounts by peasants themselves that conform to this picture. For a particularly well-written and moving one by a peasant with a third-grade education, see Giuseppe Capacci, *Diario di guerra di un contadino toscano* (Florence, 1982). See also Sandro Fontana and Maurizio Pieretti, eds., *La Grande Guerra* (Milan, 1980), 69–446; and Leo Spitzer, *Lettere di prigionieri di guerra italiani 1915–1918* (Turin, 1976), especially 123–152, 193–224.

29 Antonietta Giacomelli, *Diario di una samaritana*, in Prezzolini, *Tutta la guerra*, 385–386.

30 One acute observer of common soldiers, Curzio Malaparte, dated the "explosion of iniquitous resentment against whoever did not know the mud, lice and blood of the front lines" precisely from the first Christmas leave of December 1915, the moment at which "infantrymen learned to hate the so-called 'paese.'" See his *La rivolta dei santi maledetti*, in *L'Europa vivente e altri saggi politici (1921–1931)* (Florence, 1961), 65–66.

31 This is suggested in Frescura, *Diario di un imboscato*, 17, which explains why the vantage-point of his own "diary of an *imboscato*" is from the front lines. On the concept of the *imboscato*, see also Melograni, *Storia politica della grande guerra*, I, 110–120. For a working-class perspective, see Gramsci, *Quaderni del carcere*, I, 616–618.

32 A Turin metalworker in 1915 received 7.6 lire per day; see Melograni, *Storia politica della grande guerra*, I, 116. However, the percentage of teenage workers increased steadily during the war (in one Sicilian munitions plant it reached 44 percent in 1917), and their wages rarely exceeded 5 lire per day even in the north. See Bruna Bianchi, *Crescere in tempo di guerra: Il lavoro e la protesta dei ragazzi in Italia, 1915–1918* (Venice, 1995), 79, 84.

33 For examples of this spiritual identification of interventionist intellectuals with peasant soldiers, and from quite diverse political positions, see Ardengo Soffici, *I diari della grande guerra* (Florence, 1986); Piero Jahier, *Con me e con gli alpini* (Florence, 1953), especially 177–183; and Lussu, *Un anno sull'Altipiano*.

34 For this story, see Giovanni Sabbatucci, *I combattenti nel primo dopoguerra* (Bari and Rome, 1974). It should be noted, however, that early fascism was relatively weak in the south where peasants tended to remain apolitical despite being disgruntled.

35 War literature here refers both to diaries and other first-hand accounts as well as more literary re-enactments in novels and stories when these are based on first-hand experience. It should be noted that while much of this material was written and published just after, or even during, the war, much of it was issued later, especially in the early depression years when the war seems to have provoked a certain nostalgia in Italy.

36 On Fiume, see Michael Ledeen, *The First Duce* (Baltimore, 1977).

37 On D'Annunzio's fascination with flight, see Robert Wohl, *A Passion for Wings* (New Haven, 1994), 114–122, 287.

38 Gabriele D'Annunzio, *Notturno* (Milan, 1983), 130.

39 Ardengo Soffici, *I diari della Grande Guerra* (Florence, 1986); see also my *Avant-garde Florence*, 209–212. Despite the vividness with which Soffici wrote about the war landscape and the troops, he did few paintings based on subject-matter from the war.

40 Paolo Monelli, *Le scarpe al sole: Cronaca di gaie e di tristi avventure di alpini di muli e di vino* (Milan, 1965).

41 Ibid., xi, 48–49.

42 For Rosai, see his *Il libro di un teppista* (Florence, 1930) and my *Avant-garde Florence*, 212–214.

43 F. T. Marinetti, *L'alcova d'acciaio: Romanzo vissuto* (Milan, 1985); see also his *Taccuini*, ed. Alberto Bertoni (Bologna, 1987).

44 Piero Jahier, "Ritratto del soldato Somacal Luigi," in *Con me e con gli alpini* (Florence, 1953), 177–183.

45 Mario Puccini, *Il soldato Cola* (Milan, 1978).

46 Ibid., 61, 83.

47 Carlo Emilio Gadda, *Diario di guerra e di prigionia* (Turin, 1965), and *Il castello di Udine* (Turin, 1961).

48 Giovanni Comisso, *Giorni di guerra* (Milan, 1987), 229.

49 Serra, who died on 19 July 1915, wrote an intensely depressing "Diario di trincea," now in his *Scritti letterari, morali e politici*, ed. Mario Isnenghi (Turin, 1974), 551–563.

50 On 27 October 1917, Cadorna telegraphed Rome: "Army falls not from external but internal enemy." See Melograni, *Storia politica della grande guerra*, II, 434–435.

51 Ibid., II, 404–423.

52 Prezzolini, *Tutta la guerra*, 9–10.

53 The *Servizio P.* was linked to another institutionalized effort of foreign propaganda developed late in 1917 and led by the nationalist Romeo Gallenga Stuart, with whom many intellectuals also worked; see Luciano Tosi, "Romeo A. Gallenga Stuart e la propaganda di guerra al estero (1917–1918)," *Storia contemporanea*, 2 (1971), 519–543.

54 Lombardo Radice offers a cogent summary of the new cultural policy of 1918 in *Nuovi saggi di propaganda pedagogica* (Turin, 1922), 27–35.

55 On the trench journals, see Mario Isnenghi, *Giornali di trincea (1915–1918)* (Turin, 1977).

56 "Amici in casa: Il pignolo," *L'Astico* 1 (14 February 1918), signed "barba Piero" (Piero the Beard).

57 Lyttelton, *The Seizure of Power*, 28–29.

58 A good account of war censorship is Mario Isnenghi, *Le guerre degli italiani* (Milan, 1989), 137–151.

59 Dramatic evidence of this policy of self-censorship can be found in *L'Illustrazione Italiana*, which functioned as the *Life* or *Look* magazine of the era in Italy. Devoting about 75 percent of each weekly issue during the war to photos of the war, it typically confined itself to file photos of captured

towns, troops marching or relaxing in trenches, or enemy soldiers surrendering. It almost never showed troops firing (exceptions were made only for English and French troops in the war's northern theater) or being hit; a few photos of wounded Italian troops came only late in the war and pictures of corpses were confined to the German and Austrian enemy and labeled as such.

60 Ibid., 143. See also Angelo Schwarz, "Le fotografie e la Grande Guerra representata," in Diego Leoni and Camillo Zadra, eds., *La Grande Guerra: Esperienza, memoria, immagini* (Bologna: Il Mulino, 1986), 745–764.

61 As if to capitalize on misfortune, the Treves publishing house put out a cookbook in 1917 called *Cucina buona in cattivi tempi* (Good Cooking for Bad Times) by C. Giuseppe Monte. See the ad for it in *L'Illustrazione Italiana* (29 April 1917), 346.

62 For a careful and detailed analysis of the increase in retail prices from August 1914 until February 1916, see "Il vertiginoso aumento dei prezzi dal principio della guerra europea, agosto 1914, a tutto il febbraio 1916," *L'Illustrazione Italiana* (16 April 1916), 354–355.

63 See Antonio Gibelli, "L'esperienza di guerra: Fonti medico-psichiatriche e antropologiche," in Leoni and Zadra, *La Grande Guerra*, 49–72.

64 See Alice Kelikian, "From Liberalism to Corporatism: The Province of Brescia during the First World War," in Davis, *Gramsci and Italy's Passive Revolution*, 213.

65 A similar story can be told for youth, whose employment and crime rates both increased substantially during the war; see Bianchi, *Crescere in tempo di guerra*.

66 See Cordelia, *Le donne che lavorano* (Milan, 1916) and the review of it in *L'Illustrazione Italiana* (18 June 1916), 538.

67 Melograni, *Storia politica della grande guerra*, II, 335. See also "Le donne italiane per la guerra," *L'Illustrazione Italiana* (20 May 1917), 416–425.

68 See Anna Bravo, "Donne contadine e Prima Guerra Mondiale," *Società e storia*, 10 (1980), 843–862.

69 See Claudia Salaris, "Le donne futuriste nel periodo tra guerra e dopoguerra," in Leoni and Zadra, *La Grande Guerra*, 298.

70 For such an argument, see Michela De Giorgio, "Dalla 'Donna Nuova' alla donna della 'nuova' Italia," in Leoni and Zadra, *La Grande Guerra*, 307–329.

71 Giuseppe Prezzolini, *La cultura italiana* (Florence, 1923), 346.

72 See Emilio Gentile, *Il culto del littorio: La sacralizzazione della politica nell'Italia fascista* (Rome, 1993).

14 POPULAR CULTURE IN WARTIME BRITAIN

1 José Harris, *Private Lives, Public Spirit: a Social History of Britain, 1870–1914* (Oxford: Oxford University Press, 1993). See also D. Owen, *English Philanthropy, 1660–1960* (Cambridge, MA: Harvard University Press, 1965); F. K. Prochaska, *The Voluntary Impulse: Philanthropy in Modern Britain* (London: Faber, 1988); and Prochaska, *Women and Philanthropy in Nineteenth-century England* (Oxford: Clarendon Press, 1980).

2 A. T. Peacock and J. Wiseman, *The Growth of Public Expenditure* (Cambridge: Cambridge University Press, 1967).

3 Charles Carrington, *Soldier from the Wars Returning* (London: Constable, 1965), among many others.

4 For his poem, "Blighters," see Siegfried Sassoon, *Collected Poems* (London: Faber and Faber, 1947); on the theme of the estrangement of soldiers and civilians, see Eric J. Leed, *No Man's Land. Combat & Identity in World War I* (Cambridge: Cambridge University Press, 1979).

5 John Fuller, *Troop Morale and Popular Culture among British and Dominion Forces in the First World War* (Oxford: Oxford University Press, 1990); and Susan Grayzel, "Women, Culture, and Modern War: Gender and Identity in Britain and France, 1914–1918," unpublished manuscript derived from her Berkeley Ph.D. dissertation (1993) of the same title.

6 Fuller, *Troop Morale, passim.*

7 To judge by the language of the trench newspapers analyzed by Fuller, the word or notion "defeat" was not in the vocabulary of soldiers. Indeed, official documents show the same blithe ignorance of the possibility of defeat. The exception is among naval personnel in 1917 during the height of the U-boat campaign. They worried about food supplies being cut off, but at no other time in the war do Cabinet papers or other state documents use the word "defeat." In the Second World War, the word (and the reality) recurred regularly.

8 This discussion relies on the splendid study of Peter Martland, *A Business History of the Gramophone Company 1890–1918* (Ph.D. diss., Cambridge University, 1992).

9 Martland, *Gramophone*, 434.

10 I am grateful to Peter Martland for this information. He also tells me that the title of the review is the source of the name "Bing" Crosby, another link between wartime popular culture and the later entertainment industry.

11 As cited in Fuller, *Troop Morale*, 87.

12 See Jean-Louis Robert's remarks in Jay Winter and Jean-Louis Robert, *Capital Cities at War: Paris, London, Berlin: 1914–1919* (Cambridge: Cambridge University Press, 1997), ch. 4.

13 Martland, *Gramophone*, 433.

14 Milan Voyković, *The Culture of Thriller Fiction in Britain, 1898–1945: Authors, Publishers and the First World War* (Ph.D. diss., University of New South Wales, 1996). See also Michael Birch, "The Popular Fiction Industry: Market, Formula, Ideology," *Journal of Popular Culture*, 21 (1987); J. G. Cawalti, *Adventure, Mystery, and Romance. Formula Stories as Art and Popular Culture* (Chicago: University of Chicago Press, 1976); Michael Denning, *Cover Stories. Narrative and Ideology in the British Spy Thriller* (London: Routledge & Kegan Paul, 1987); and Jerry Palmer, *Thrillers. Genesis and Structure of a Popular Genre* (London: Edward Arnold, 1978).

15 Rosa Maria Bracco, *Merchants of Hope* (Leamington Spa: Berg, 1992). On the spurious high/low divide, see John Carey, *The Intellectuals and the Masses: Pride and Prejudice among the Literary Intelligentsia, 1880–1939* (London: Faber & Faber, 1992).

16 Voyković, *Thriller*, 28–38. See also John Attenborough, *A Living Memory. Hodder and Stoughton, Publishers, 1868–1975* (London: Hodder & Stoughton, 1975).

17 Voyković, *Thriller*, 65–67.

18 Ibid., 38. See also, John Feather, *A History of British Publishing* (London: Routledge & Kegan Paul, 1991), David Glover, "Looking for Edgar Wallace: The Author as Consumer," *History Workshop Journal*, 37 (1994), and Ernest Mandel, *Delightful Murder. A Social History of the Crime Story* (London: Pluto Press, 1984).

19 This discussion rests on Tony Mason, *Association Football and English Society 1863–1915* (Brighton: Harvester Press, 1980), ch. 9. The literature on rugby, cricket, and other sports is vast, and requires separate treatment. For references, see Wray Vamplew, *Pay Up and Play the Game: Professional Sport in Britain, 1875–1914* (Cambridge: Cambridge University Press, 1988).

20 Martin Middlebrook, *The First Day on the Somme* (London: Fontana, 1975), 124, 254.

21 Fuller, *Troop Morale*, 137.

22 Ibid., 139.

23 Gordon Irving, *Great Scot. The Life Story of Sir Harry Lauder, Legendary Laird of the Music Hall* (London: Leslie Frewin, 1968), 88–94. For analysis of music hall and other theatrical entertainments, see Dagmar Kift, *The Victorian Music Hall: Culture, Class and Conflict*, tr. Roy Kift (Cambridge: Cambridge University Press, 1996), Eileen Yeo and Stephen Yeo, eds., *Popular Culture and Class Conflict 1590–1914: Explorations in the History of Labour and Leisure* (Brighton: Harvester, 1981), G. Rowell, *The Victorian Theatre* (Oxford: Oxford University Press, 1967), and Michael R. Booth, *Victorian Spectacular Theatre 1850–1910* (London: Routledge & Kegan Paul, 1981).

24 Ramona Curry, "How Early German Film Stars Helped Sell the War(es)," in Karel Dibbets and Bert Hogenkamp, eds., *Film and the First World War* (Amsterdam: Amsterdam University Press, 1994), 141–142.

25 I am grateful to Nick Hiley for his advice on this point. He discusses the film in episode 4 of the 1996 PBS/BBC television series "The Great War and the Shaping of the Twentieth Century."

26 Kevin Brownlow, *The War, the West and the Wilderness* (New York: Knopf, 1979), 40–41.

27 Brownlow, *The War*, 41.

28 *Kinematograph Weekly*, 20 April 1917, 61, as cited in Brownlow, *The War*, 41.

29 Denis Gillford, *Chaplin* (New York: Doubleday, 1974), 91. On Pickford, see L. M. Debauche, "Mary Pickford's Public on the Home Front," in Dibbets and Hogenkamp, eds., *Film*, 149–159.

30 Charles T. Maland, *Chaplin and American Culture. The Evolution of an Image* (Princeton: Princeton University Press, 1989), 38.

31 Charles Chaplin, *My Autobiography* (New York: Simon & Schuster, 1964), 215.

32 J. M. Winter, *The Great War and the British People* (London: Macmillan, 1985), ch. 7.

33 Jim Obelkevitch, *Religion and Rural Society: Lindsey, 1825–1875* (Oxford: Clarendon Press, 1976); Hugh McLeod, *Religion and Society in England, 1850–1914* (Basingstoke: Macmillan, 1976); McLeod, *Religion and the Working Class in Nineteenth-century Britain* (London: Macmillan, 1984).

34 B. Mathews, ed., *Christ and the World at War* (London: James Clarke & Co., 1917), 42.

35 Jay Winter, *Sites of Memory, Sites of Mourning. The Place of the Great War in European Cultural History* (Cambridge: Cambridge University Press, 1995), ch. 3.

36 Catherine Moriarty, "Christian Iconography and First World War Memorials," *Imperial War Museum Review*, 6 (1991), 63–75.

37 J. M. Winter, "The University of Oxford and the First World War," in B. Harrison, ed., *The History of the University of Oxford in the Twentieth Century* (Oxford: Oxford University Press, 1992).

38 Paul Fussell, *The Great War and Modern Memory* (Oxford: Oxford University Press, 1975).

39 A brilliant corrective is Samuel Hynes, *A War Imagined. The Great War and English Culture* (London: Bodley Head, 1991).

40 For a full elaboration of this argument, see Winter, *Sites of Memory*.

41 Leslie Hannah, *The Rise of the Corporate Economy* (London: Methuen, 1983).

42 Nick Hiley, "The British Film Auditorium," in Dibbets and Hogenkamp, eds., *Film*, 189.

43 On the European side of this phenomenon, see Paul Monaco, *Cinema and Society: France and Germany during the Twenties* (New York: Elsevier, 1976).

44 J. M. Winter, "British National Identity and the First World War," in S. J. D. Green and R. C. Whiting, eds., *The Boundaries of the State in Modern Britain* (Cambridge: Cambridge University Press, 1995), 261–277.

CONCLUSION

1 Jacques Barzun, *Race: A Study in Modern Superstition* (London, 1938), 239–240.

2 Vejas Gabrielius Liulevicius, "War Land: Peoples, Lands, and National Identity on the Eastern Front in World War I" (Ph.D. diss., University of Pennsylvania, 1994), 188–196. See also in this volume, Evelina Kelbetcheva on Bulgaria, chapter 9 and Maria Bucur on Romania, chapter 10.

3 On French trench journalism, see Stéphane Audoin-Rouzeau, *Men at War 1914–1918: National Sentiment and Trench Journalism in France during the First World War* (Oxford: Berg, 1992).

4 Richard Bessel, "The Front Generation and the Politics of Weimar Germany," in Mark Roseman, ed., *Generations in Conflict: Youth Revolt and Generation Formation in Germany, 1770–1968* (Cambridge: Cambridge University Press, 1995), 121–136.

5 Michael Klimenko, *Ehrenburg: An Attempt at a Literary Portrait* (New York, 1990), 25.

6 See in this volume Marc Ferro, chapter 12, Peter Jelavich, chapter 2, and Sophie de Schaepdrijver, chapter 11.

7 Steven G. Marks, "The Russian Century: Russia's Global Legacy from the 1890s to the Present" (manuscript), chs. 3–4.

8 See Aviel Roshwald, chapter 4 in this volume.

9 See Sophie de Schaepdrijver, chapter 11 in this volume.

10 Modris Eksteins, *Rites of Spring: The Great War and the Birth of the Modern Age* (New York: Doubleday, 1989), 307.

11 See Walter Adamson, chapter 13, Peter Jelavich, chapter 2, Evelina Kelbetcheva, chapter 9, and Richard Stites, chapter 1 in this volume.

12 See J. G. Fuller, *Troop Morale and Popular Culture in the British and Dominion Armies, 1914–1918* (Oxford: Oxford University Press, 1990) and Audoin-Rouzeau, *Men at War 1914–1918.*

13 Kenneth Silver, *Esprit de Corps: The Art of the Parisian Avant-Garde and the First World War, 1914–1925* (Princeton: Princeton University Press, 1989), ch. 2; Richard Cork, *A Bitter Truth: Avant-Garde Art and the Great War* (New Haven and London: Yale University Press, 1994), chs. 2 and 5; Jay Winter, *Sites of Memory, Sites of Mourning: The Great War in European Cultural History* (Cambridge: Cambridge University Press, 1995), 127–132.

14 Cork, *A Bitter Truth*, 60, 111, 230–234.

15 Ibid., 168–169.

16 Sophie de Schaepdrijver does point out, however, that the Flemish "activists'" mass-oriented propaganda was overwhelmingly neo-romantic in tone.

17 See, for instance, some of the developments in theater, variety show, and cabaret in Romania, Poland, Germany, Austria, the Czech lands, and among the Jews, as discussed in this book. Steven Beller argues that even Austrian operetta, though an avowedly non-modernist art form, lent itself to the expression of a progressive social and political critique in a number of instances.

18 Russel Nye, *The Unembarrassed Muse: The Popular Arts in America* (New York, 1971).

19 To be sure, British press coverage of the war was shockingly misleading by any standard of journalistic objectivity.

20 See Joseph Darracott, ed., *The First World War in Posters* (Mineola, NY: Dover Publications, 1974), 6, 10, 42, 43, 56, 70; Audoin-Rouzeau, *Men at War 1914–1918*, ch. 5.

21 Walter L. Adamson, chapter 13, Mark Ferro, chapter 12, Richard Stites, chapter 1, and Evelina Kelbetcheva, chapter 9 in this volume.

22 Jay Winter and Jean-Louis Robert, *Capital Cities at War: Paris, London, Berlin, 1914–1919* (Cambridge: Cambridge University Press, 1997), especially chs. 1 and 4.

23 Robert Graves, *Good-Bye to All That* (London, 1929).

Index